W9-ALN-487

Issues for Debate in American Public Policy

SEVENTH EDITION

CQ PRESS

A Division of Congressional Quarterly Inc. Washington, D.C.

SELECTIONS FROM THE **CQ RESEARCHER**

CQ Press
1255 22nd Street, NW, Suite 400
Washington, DC 20037

Phone: 202-729-1900; toll-free, 1-866-4CQ-PRESS (1-866-427-7737)

Web: www.cqpress.com

Cover designer: Kimberly Glyder
Cover photo: Photodisc Green/Getty Images
Title page photo: Scott Ferrell, Congressional Quarterly Inc.

∞ The paper used in this publication exceeds the requirements of the American National Standard for Information Sciences—Permanence of Paper for Printed Library Materials, ANSI Z39.48-1992.

Printed and bound in the United States of America

10 09 08 07 06   1 2 3 4 5

A CQ Press College Division Publication

Director	Brenda Carter
Acquisitions editor	Charisse Kiino
Marketing manager	Christopher O'Brien
Production editor	Belinda Josey
Composition	Olu Davis
Managing editor	Stephen Pazdan
Electronic production manager	Paul Pressau
Print and design manager	Margot Ziperman
Sales manager	James Headley

ISSN: 1543-3889
ISBN: 1-933116-86-2

Contents

CONTENTS

HOMELAND SECURITY AND FOREIGN POLICY

Annotated Contents

The 16 *CQ Researcher* reports reprinted in this book have been reproduced essentially as they appeared when first published. In the few cases in which important new developments have since occurred, updates are provided in the overviews highlighting the principal issues examined.

EDUCATION

Evaluating Head Start

Since its founding in 1965, the federal preschool program has offered poor children and their parents comprehensive services ranging from health care to parenting education. Preliminary data from the first nationwide appraisal of the program show that Head Start youngsters do better on some intellectual, behavioral and health measures than similar children not enrolled in Head Start. But some critics say the program should dispense with health care and parental education, in order to focus on pre-academic skills. To improve Head Start's performance, the Bush administration proposed turning it over to the states, but Congress refused; instead Congress wants to require half of all Head Start teachers to obtain BA degrees or higher by 2011. Meanwhile, states are launching their own preschool programs, raising new questions about whether Head Start — now serving some 900,000 youngsters — should be under federal or state control.

No Child Left Behind

More than four years have passed since President Bush signed the No Child Left Behind act. The controversial legislation mandates "highly qualified" teachers in every classroom and holds schools that accept federal funds accountable for raising the achievement of all students, particularly those with disabilities, those from low-income families and racial and ethnic minorities and those with limited English proficiency. Supporters call the law an evolutionary change in education policy while critics call it a revolutionary federal incursion into states' historic domain that makes too many unfunded demands. Eight school districts and the nation's largest teachers' union have sued the Department of Education over the law's funding provisions, and legislators in several states have introduced bills seeking exemptions from the law. Supporters, meanwhile, worry that No Child Left Behind is not being enforced stringently enough and is in danger of being diluted.

HEALTH CARE

Drug Safety

The sudden withdrawal of the blockbuster arthritis drug Vioxx and warnings about similar medications — including heightened suicide risks from antidepressants — have focused unprecedented negative attention on the Food and Drug Administration (FDA). Two congressional committees, the Government Accountability Office and the Institute of Medicine have begun looking at the agency's performance, and several lawmakers are proposing overhauling the way the FDA operates. Critics say the agency suffers from deep-seated flaws, including conflicts of interest, an inattention to safety issues and a lack of enforcement authority. An FDA medical reviewer testified recently that the agency's close relationship with the drug industry and its tendency to rush drugs to market have left the country "virtually defenseless." But the FDA and drug-industry officials say the United States still enjoys the safest drug system in the world and that proposed reforms, including creation of a new safety oversight board, will create transparency and provide a safety backup system.

Avian Flu Threat

As deaths from bird flu continue to mount in Asia — and now threaten Europe — concern about a worldwide epidemic has prompted calls to action at the highest levels of government. In December 2005, in response to President Bush's emergency request, Congress approved $3.8 billion to develop new vaccines and stockpile anti-flu medications. Some critics say it's too little too late. If a pandemic hit tomorrow, the nation would have drugs to treat only very few people, no approved vaccine and a public health system that is woefully unprepared for a pandemic. With each new case of human infection, the danger increases that bird flu could easily pass among humans, health authorities warn. But some scientists doubt the virus will mutate into one that is easily transmitted from human to human. So far, most victims had close contact with poultry. But even skeptics agree that a flu pandemic is inevitable at some point, and that the nation needs to shore up its response.

SOCIAL POLICY

Upward Mobility

Wealth has become more concentrated in the United States, with the top 1 percent of households now commanding a bigger share of the nation's prosperity than at any time since the 1920s. Average middle-class family incomes, meanwhile, have been mostly stagnant for more than 30 years. As the gap between the rich and everyone else grows wider, some sociologists and economists worry that the "Horatio Alger" dream of economic success through hard work and merit is dead and that getting ahead now depends mostly on your family's affluence, education and social connections. Others say living standards are rising for nearly everyone, newcomers still can find their fortunes here and middle-class Americans live better than their parents did. President Bush, meanwhile, is encouraging wealth creation, but critics say his "ownership society" proposals pose greater economic risks and won't help spread the nation's good fortune to all.

Birth-Control Debate

Most sexually active American women use birth control, but a vocal minority in this country — mostly conservative Christians — has long argued that easy access to contraception increases the rates of abortion, teen pregnancy and divorce. Debates over access to birth control have heated up recently as a handful of pharmacists have begun refusing to fill prescriptions for birth control on ethical grounds, and the Bush administration has blocked measures easing access to emergency contraceptives — pills that prevent pregnancy when taken after intercourse. Meanwhile, in state legislatures, women's groups are pushing for laws requiring health insurance plans to cover birth control and hospitals to dispense emergency contraception to sexual assault victims. However, pharmacists and Catholic hospitals that morally object to birth control are also pressing state lawmakers to expand "conscience clause" exemptions that allow health providers to refuse to provide some legally required services if they have moral or religious objections.

Minimum Wage

The federal minimum wage — $5.15 an hour — has not changed since 1997. Since then, minimum-wage earners have lost 17 percent of their purchasing power to inflation. Supporters of increasing the rate say it would lift many Americans out of poverty, but business groups say an increase would hurt the working poor because it would cause companies to lay off low-wage workers. In any case, they say, many minimum-wage earners are middle-class teens earning pocket money, not poor adults. Attempts in Congress to raise the minimum wage failed in 2005, but perennial sponsor Sen. Edward M. Kennedy, D-Mass., says he will try again in 2006. Seventeen states and Washington, D.C., now have higher minimum wages than the federal level, and 130 cities and counties have so-called living-wage laws requiring public contractors to pay significantly higher wages. Nevada and Florida recently passed minimum-wage ballot initiatives, and more state battles are looming.

ENVIRONMENT

Domestic Energy Development

Hurricanes Katrina and Rita damaged oil and gas facilities throughout the Gulf of Mexico region, exacerbating the nation's energy problems. Since 1999, world oil prices have doubled and the U.S. cost of natural gas has tripled. In response, the Bush administration is pressing for increased domestic oil and gas production, and Congress is considering expanding energy development in areas currently off-limits, such as the Arctic National Wildlife Refuge and offshore oil fields. The administration already has relaxed limits on energy exploration on public lands and supports building new refineries and gas-delivery systems. Opponents say such actions could cause serious environmental damage and that states should have more control over energy development decisions. Environmentalists say relying more on conservation and renewable fuels would foster greater energy security.

Climate Change

Scientists generally agree that the globe has warmed over the past 40 years, due largely to human activities that raise carbon-dioxide levels in the atmosphere. The Kyoto Protocol mandating limits on carbon emissions took effect in 2005, eight years after it was written. But the United States — the world's biggest carbon emitter — has not ratified the treaty. Debate over global warming has shifted from whether human activities are causing climate change to whether the possible changes will be severe enough to justify the hefty expense of developing cleaner energy technologies. Economists and even some energy companies have recently proposed taxing carbon as an incentive to consumers and industry to shift to low-carbon fuels. Some multi-state coalitions also hope to issue tradable emissions permits to industry. Congress has begun to show some interest, but the Bush administration still argues strongly against any mandates to cut carbon-fuel use.

CIVIL LIBERTIES, CIVIL RIGHTS AND JUSTICE

Death Penalty Controversies

Critics and opponents of the death penalty are warning that capital trials and sentencing hearings are so riddled with flaws that they risk resulting in the execution of innocent persons. Supporters of capital punishment discount the warnings, emphasizing that opponents cannot cite a single person in modern times who was executed and later proven to have been innocent. The debate over erroneous convictions has increased in recent years because DNA testing now allows inmates to prove their innocence years after their convictions. The Supreme Court opened its term in October 2005 with two closely watched cases pending on rules allowing state inmates to use newly discovered evidence to challenge their convictions in federal courts, based on "actual innocence," as well as constitutional violations. Meanwhile, death penalty critics want states to follow Illinois' example and impose moratoriums on executions.

Identity Theft

Assembling a new identity used to be the specialty of spies and master criminals. Now, ordinary crooks are acquiring consumers' personal information — Social Security numbers, addresses, mothers' maiden names and other data — and opening new accounts in other peoples' names. Nearly 10 million consumers are affected annually by lost or stolen data at a cost to the economy of $53 billion. Moreover, victims spend almost 300 million hours a year trying to clear their names and reestablish good credit ratings. Congress and state legislatures are looking at ways to stop identity theft, but financial and data-collection companies argue any solutions that slow down the business of buying and selling personal data would hurt the economy. Meanwhile, in the biggest in a series of recent security breaches, Citigroup announced in June 2005 that computer tapes containing personal data on 3.9 million consumers were missing.

BUSINESS AND THE ECONOMY

Pension Crisis

Many private pension plans won't be able to pay the benefits they have promised; they are underfunded by an estimated $450 billion. Even the federal agency that insures them is in the red by $23 billion — and its shortfall could hit $142 billion in 20 years. The biggest pension failures have involved companies in struggling industries such as auto, steel and airlines — but even healthy corporations such as IBM, Verizon and Hewlett-Packard have recently frozen their pension plans. Congress is crafting legislation to make the nation's private pension system more stable, but many observers worry that tightening funding rules could lead more companies to drop their pension programs. It seems certain that more of the responsibility of saving for retirement will fall to individuals — and Americans are notoriously bad savers. As the first wave of baby boomers

turns 60, many experts warn that they and coming generations won't be able to retire as comfortably as their parents.

Rebuilding New Orleans

Five months after Hurricane Katrina flooded most of New Orleans, some 80 percent of the "Crescent City" remained unrepaired. Damage is estimated at $35 billion. Most schools and businesses were still closed, and two-thirds of the 460,000 residents have moved out. How many will return remains troublingly uncertain. Questions about who will help the city's poorer residents — many of them African American — hang over the city, along with concern about how much of New Orleans' storied popular culture will survive. Meanwhile, as a new hurricane season approaches, efforts to repair and strengthen the protective system of levees, canals and pumps lag behind schedule.

HOMELAND SECURITY AND FOREIGN POLICY

Disaster Preparedness

The flawed response to Hurricane Katrina by local, state and federal officials has experts worried that the nation is unprepared for another major disaster. Nearly every emergency-response system broke down in the days immediately following the monster storm — the costliest disaster in American history. Some disaster experts say the government's preoccupation with terrorism — including the deployment of thousands of National Guard and reserve troops in Iraq — has jeopardized domestic emergency-response capabilities. President Bush proposes putting active-duty troops in charge when states and local communities are overwhelmed by a disaster — whether manmade or natural — but many state officials don't want to give up control. Both Congress and the White House are investigating post-Katrina emergency operations to avoid similar mistakes next time. Meanwhile, disaster officials say Katrina showed the need for individual citizens to be prepared to serve as first-responders for their own families.

Illegal Immigration

More than 10 million illegal immigrants live in the United States, and 1,400 more arrive every day. Once concentrated in a few big states like Texas and California, they are rapidly moving into non-traditional areas such as the Midwest and South. Willing to work for low wages, the migrants are creating a backlash among some residents of the new states, which have seen a nearly tenfold increase in illegal immigration since 1990. While illegal immigrants only make up about 5 percent of the U.S. workforce, critics of the nation's immigration policies say illegal immigrants take Americans' jobs, threaten national security and even change the nation's culture by refusing to assimilate. But immigrants' advocates say illegal migrants fill the jobs Americans refuse to take and generally boost the economy. Proposals for increased immigration controls and a guest-worker program have divided Congress evenly as massive demonstrations in cities across the country have polarized the issue among the public.

War in Iraq

The U.S.-led invasion of Iraq in March 2003 was supposed to be quick and easy — a repeat of the 1991 Persian Gulf War that chased Iraq out of Kuwait. Operation Iraqi Freedom quickly ousted dictator Saddam Hussein from power, but three years later U.S., Iraqi and coalition troops are still fighting an increasingly violent insurgency. Many Americans — members of the public as well as lawmakers — are questioning how long U.S. troops should stay in Iraq and whether the war is making the United States safer from terrorism. Over 2,000 American soldiers and at least 10 times that many Iraqi civilians have died in Iraq since the invasion in 2003. Public support for the war is at an all-time low. Critics say the U.S. presence in Iraq is turning it into a magnet for terrorists determined to kill Americans and that it's time to get out. Supporters say leaving now could mean civil war in Iraq and more turmoil in the oil-rich Middle East.

Preface

I s the United States prepared for a pandemic? Does reliance on imported oil and gas threaten U.S. security? Should illegal immigrants in the United States be allowed to acquire legal status? These questions — and many more — are at the heart of American public policy. How can instructors best engage students with these crucial issues? We feel that students need objective, yet provocative examinations of these issues to understand how they affect citizens today and will for years to come. This annual collection aims to promote in-depth discussion, facilitate further research and help readers formulate their own positions on crucial issues. Get your students talking both inside and outside the classroom about *Issues for Debate in American Public Policy.*

This seventh edition includes sixteen up-to-date reports by *CQ Researcher*, an award-winning weekly policy brief that brings complicated issues down to earth. Each report chronicles and analyzes executive, legislative and judicial activities at all levels of government. This collection is divided into seven diverse policy areas: education; health care; social policy; the environment; civil liberties, civil rights and justice; business and the economy; and homeland security and foreign policy — to cover a range of issues found in most American government and public policy courses.

CQ RESEARCHER

CQ Researcher was founded in 1923 as *Editorial Research Reports* and was sold primarily to newspapers as a research tool. The magazine was renamed and redesigned in 1991 as *CQ Researcher.* Today, students are its primary audience. While still used by hundreds of journalists and newspapers, many of which reprint portions of the reports, the *Researcher*'s main subscribers are now high school, college and public libraries. In 2002, *Researcher* won the American Bar Association's coveted Silver Gavel Award for magazine excellence for a series of nine reports on civil liberties and other legal issues.

Researcher staff writers — all highly experienced journalists — sometimes compare the experience of writing a *Researcher* report to drafting a college term paper. Indeed, there are many similarities. Each report is as long as many term papers — about 11,000 words — and is written by one person without any significant outside help. One of the key differences is that writers interview leading experts, scholars and government officials for each issue.

Like students, staff writers begin the creative process by choosing a topic. Working with the *Researcher*'s editors, the writer identifies a controversial subject that has important public policy implications. After a topic is selected, the writer embarks on one to two weeks of intense research. Newspaper and magazine articles are clipped or downloaded, books are ordered and information is gathered from a wide variety of sources, including interest groups, universities and the government. Once the writers are well informed, they develop a detailed outline and begin the interview process. Each report requires a minimum of ten to fifteen interviews with academics, officials, lobbyists and people working in the field. Only after all interviews are completed does the writing begin.

CHAPTER FORMAT

Each issue of *CQ Researcher*, and therefore each selection in this book, is structured in the same way. Each begins with an overview, which briefly summarizes the areas that will be explored in greater detail in the rest of the chapter. The next section, "Issues," is the core of each chapter. It chronicles important and current debates on the topic under discussion and is structured around a number of key questions, such as "Is the Iraq war making America safer from terrorism?" and "Should employers fund their workers' retirements?" These questions are usually the subject of much debate among practitioners and scholars in the field. Hence, the answers presented

are never conclusive but detail the range of opinion on the topic.

Next, the "Background" section provides a history of the issue being examined. This retrospective covers important legislative measures, executive actions and court decisions that illustrate how current policy has evolved. Then the "Current Situation" section examines contemporary policy issues, legislation under consideration and legal action being taken. Each selection concludes with an "Outlook" section, which addresses possible regulation, court rulings and initiatives from Capitol Hill and the White House over the next five to ten years.

Each report contains features that augment the main text: two to three sidebars that examine issues related to the topic at hand, a pro versus con debate between two experts, a chronology of key dates and events and an annotated bibliography detailing major sources used by the writer.

ACKNOWLEDGMENTS

We wish to thank many people for helping to make this collection a reality. Thomas J. Colin, managing editor of *CQ Researcher*, gave us his enthusiastic support and cooperation as we developed this seventh edition. He and his talented staff of editors and writers have amassed a first-class library of *Researcher* reports, and we are fortunate to have access to that rich cache. We also thankfully acknowledge the advice and feedback from current readers and are gratified by their satisfaction with the book.

Some readers may be learning about *CQ Researcher* for the first time. We expect that many readers will want regular access to this excellent weekly research tool. For subscription information or a no-obligation free trial of *Researcher*, please contact CQ Press at www.cqpress.com or toll-free at 1-866-4CQ-PRESS (1-866-427-7737).

We hope that you will be pleased by the seventh edition of *Issues for Debate in American Public Policy*. We welcome your feedback and suggestions for future editions. Please direct comments to Charisse Kiino, Chief Acquisitions Editor, College Division, CQ Press, 1255 22nd Street, N.W., Suite 400, Washington, D.C. 20037, or *ckiino@cqpress.com*.

—The Editors of CQ Press

Contributors

Thomas J. Colin, managing editor of *CQ Researcher*, has been a magazine and newspaper journalist for more than 30 years. Before joining Congressional Quarterly in 1991, he was a reporter and editor at the *Miami Herald* and *National Geographic* and editor in chief of *Historic Preservation*. He holds a bachelor's degree in English from the College of William and Mary and in journalism from the University of Missouri.

Marcia Clemmitt is a veteran social-policy reporter who joined *CQ Researcher* after serving as editor in chief of *Medicine and Health*, a Washington-based industry newsletter, and as staff writer for *The Scientist*. She also has been a high school math and physics teacher. She holds a bachelor's degree in arts and sciences from St. Johns College, Annapolis, and a master's degree in English from Georgetown University.

Marc Ferris is a freelance writer based in Hastings, New York, whose work has appeared in *The New York Times*, *Newsday* and several national magazines.

Sarah Glazer specializes in health, education and social-policy issues. Her articles have appeared in *The New York Times*, *The Washington Post*, *Glamour*, *The Public Interest* and *Gender and Work*, a book of essays. Glazer covered energy legislation for the Environmental and Energy Study Conference and reported for United Press International. She holds a bachelor's degree in American history from the University of Chicago.

Alan Greenblatt is a staff writer for Congressional Quarterly's *Governing* magazine, and previously covered elections and military and agricultural policy for *CQ Weekly*. Recipient of the National Press Club's Sandy Hume Memorial Award for political reporting, he holds a bachelor's degree from San Francisco State University and a master's degree in English literature from the University of Virginia.

Kenneth Jost, associate editor of *CQ Researcher*, graduated from Harvard College and Georgetown University Law Center, where he is an adjunct professor. He is the author of *The Supreme Court Yearbook* and editor of *The Supreme Court A to Z* (both published by CQ Press). He was a member of *CQ Researcher* team that won the 2002 American Bar Association Silver Gavel Award.

Peter Katel is a veteran journalist who previously served as Latin America bureau chief for *Time* magazine in Mexico City, and as a Miami-based correspondent for *Newsweek* and the *Miami Herald*'s *El Nuevo Herald*. He also worked as a reporter in New Mexico for 11 years and wrote for several non-governmental organizations, including International Social Service and The World Bank. His honors include the Interamerican Press Association's Bartolome Mitre Award. He is a graduate of the University of New Mexico with a degree in university studies.

Barbara Mantel is a freelance writer in New York City whose work has appeared in *The New York Times*, *Journal of Child and Adolescent Pyschopharmacology* and

Mamm Magazine. She is a former correspondent and senior producer for National Public Radio and has received such journalistic honors as the National Press Club's Best Consumer Journalism Award and Lincoln University's Unity Award. She holds a bachelor's degree in history and economics from the University of Virginia and a master's degree in economics from Northwestern University.

Patrick Marshall is a freelance writer based in Bainbridge Island, Washington, who writes about public policy and technology issues. His recent *CQ Researcher* reports include "Policing the Borders" and "Marijuana Laws."

Pamela M. Prah is a veteran reporter who covers elections at Stateline.org. She previously was a staff writer for *CQ Researcher* and has also written for *Kiplinger's Washington Letter* and the Bureau of National Affairs. She holds a master's degree in government from Johns Hopkins University and a journalism degree from Ohio University.

Jennifer Weeks is a freelance writer in Watertown, Mass., who specializes in energy and environmental issues. She has written for *The Washington Post*, the *Boston Globe Magazine*, *Environment*, *On Earth* and other publications, and spent 15 years as a congressional staffer, lobbyist and public policy analyst. She holds a bachelor's degree from Williams College and master's degrees from the University of North Carolina and Harvard University.

1

Evaluating Head Start

Marcia Clemmitt

Nathan Miller, 5, triumphantly finishes a lesson with a teacher's aide at a Head Start center in Shreveport, La. A new national study shows that Head Start children make small, but significant, gains on several education and behavior measures, compared with non-Head Start children. But critics say they still start kindergarten far behind middle-class kids. Congress will consider legislation this fall requiring half of all Head Start teachers to obtain B.A. degrees by 2011.

From *CQ Researcher*,
August 26, 2005.

The trip from Worland, Wyo., to the nearest university takes five-and-a-half hours by car, says Elaine Laird, director of 10 Head Start programs in the area.

But if Congress approves pending Head Start legislation this fall, many teachers from Laird's programs will have to make the journey on a regular basis. Designed to improve school outcomes, the legislation would require roughly half of all the teachers in Head Start's 1,800 local programs nationwide to obtain bachelor of arts (B.A.) degrees by 2011.

Laird agrees that continuing teacher education is vital. But for her teachers — spread over a 25,000-square-mile expanse of northern Wyoming — getting to campus for classes would mean an 11-hour roundtrip.

Head Start is the federally funded preschool program for low-income children that was established in 1965 as part of President Lyndon B. Johnson's War on Poverty. Now celebrating its 40th anniversary this year, it serves some 900,000 children at 20,000 local centers.

When Congress in 1998 required half the nation's Head Start teachers to have associate of arts (A.A.) degrees by 2003, Laird's staff enthusiastically complied. "Some of our teachers had been with us 25 years and went back to school in their late 50s" to get the A.A., she says. Today, "even our cooks have the degree."

But while associate degrees could be earned at the local community college, the closest place to get a four-year degree is the University of Wyoming, in distant Laramie.

Laird's dilemma reflects the challenge facing both Head Start and the growing number of state-funded preschools: As the No

Two-Thirds of Teachers Have Degrees

The percentage of Head Start teachers with degrees in early-childhood education (ECE) has doubled since 1997, with 36 percent holding bachelor's degrees. Congress is considering legislation requiring half of Head Start teachers to obtain bachelor's degrees.

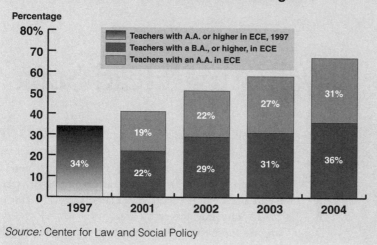

Head Start Teachers with ECE Degrees

Teachers with A.A. or higher in ECE, 1997
Teachers with a B.A., or higher, in ECE
Teachers with an A.A. in ECE

Source: Center for Law and Social Policy

and children's language scores . . . and other important measures of success." [1]

Wade Horn, assistant secretary of Health and Human Services for children and families, who oversees Head Start, points out the program was established in an era when language and math drills for preschoolers were out of educational fashion. Instead, more creative social- and emotion-centered teaching was popular.

"I'm just old enough to remember the days when, if Head Start program reviewers found a set of alphabet letters up on the wall, teachers were told to take it down," Horn remembers.

The administration has not specifically endorsed Congress' proposal to beef up pre-academics, Horn points out. While "degrees are not unimportant," he says, the data don't firmly demonstrate that having degreed teachers will improve educational outcomes, so requiring them "may be just giving ourselves some self-comfort" without improving results.

In any case, supporters of the existing program say that focusing more on academic skills is difficult because the law requires Head Start to target low-income families — the very people who can benefit most from extra health and nutrition services, which are designed to improve children's overall mental, emotional and physical well-being. Such services — along with work on developing social and emotional skills — are vital in helping the lowest-income children, says Sarah Greene, president of the National Head Start Association (NHSA). The group represents about 90 percent of the nation's 1,800 Head Start programs.

Moreover, Head Start also offers parenting education and involves parents in staffing and directing Head Start centers, giving them some control over their own lives and families. For example, 54 percent of Laird's staff members are program parents, she says. Some Head Start advocates fear that focusing more on academics or allowing states to integrate the program into newly launched state preschool programs — as the Bush administration

Child Left Behind law and international economic competition put pressure on U.S. schools to turn out more accomplished graduates, preschools are being asked to put greater emphasis on pre-academic skills.

Critics, including Bush administration officials, say Head Start has been so intent on providing comprehensive services — including health care, parenting classes and nutrition — to children and their families that it has neglected basic school-related skills, such as recognizing letters. While children in the very worst circumstances do need the extra services, the critics say, others do not. Moreover, more Head Start teachers with B.A. degrees would boost the program's pre-academic focus, some members of Congress say.

"Compelling evidence suggests that teachers with bachelor's degrees in early-childhood development or education are much more likely to provide children with the literacy skills and vocabularies needed to do well in school," wrote Joan Fitzgerald, director of the law, policy and society program at Northeastern University, in Boston. "Voluminous research" dating back to the 1970s shows "a positive correlation between teacher education

has proposed — would dilute comprehensive services such as parental involvement and health care.

Critics of Head Start say that, unlike the early 1960s when Head Start was created, other state and federal programs now offer a wide range of health care, housing assistance and substance-abuse treatment, so Head Start does not need to offer the same level of services.

But Greene says "desperate poverty" still afflicts many neighborhoods served by Head Start, and that Head Start teaches parents how to access social services. To prepare poor children to learn, Head Start must continue to remedy their home circumstances, she says, whether it's by guiding a parent losing welfare payments into job training or helping a family find $300 to pay a medical bill.

While the Bush administration is not specifically pushing college degrees for teachers, it is promoting greater school readiness and holding Head Start accountable for achieving that goal, Horn says, primarily by getting good information on which teaching strategies work.

For years, critics have complained that there are virtually no rigorous, nationwide data demonstrating that Head Start improves children's outcomes. Most of the data showing that preschool has positive effects come from analysis of smaller, more expensive, experimental preschool programs. To find out what Head Start itself accomplishes, Congress in 1998 mandated a multiyear, national study in which Head Start students would be compared to a control group of similar children not enrolled in the program.

Scheduled for completion next year, the Head Start Impact Study released its first preliminary results this spring, showing that Head Start children make small, but significant, gains on a variety of measures, including pre-reading skills and behavior problems, compared with non-Head Start children. [2]

The study shows "how the average child in Head Start compares to the same child whose parents wanted to get him or her into Head Start but there wasn't room," explains Greg Duncan, an economist and professor at Northwestern University's School of Education and Public Policy. His own research analyzes the out-

Head Start at a Glance

More than 900,000 children, mostly 4-year-olds, participate in Head Start, the federally funded preschool program for disadvantaged children. Hispanic participants now slightly outnumber blacks; in 1992, only 23 percent were Hispanic, and 37 percent were black.

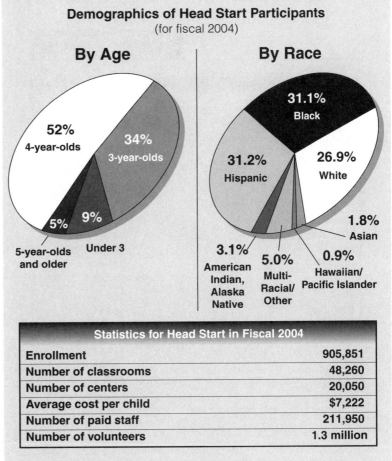

Demographics of Head Start Participants
(for fiscal 2004)

By Age

52% 4-year-olds
34% 3-year-olds
5% 5-year-olds and older
9% Under 3

By Race

31.1% Black
26.9% White
31.2% Hispanic
1.8% Asian
3.1% American Indian, Alaska Native
5.0% Multi-Racial/Other
0.9% Hawaiian/Pacific Islander

Statistics for Head Start in Fiscal 2004	
Enrollment	905,851
Number of classrooms	48,260
Number of centers	20,050
Average cost per child	$7,222
Number of paid staff	211,950
Number of volunteers	1.3 million

Source: Head Start Fact Sheet, Administration for Children and Families, Department of Health and Human Services, 2005

Preschool Expenditures Vary Widely

The amount states spend on state-run preschool varies dramatically, ranging from $936 per child in Maryland to $8,739 in New Jersey. Eleven states have no preschool programs outside of Head Start.

Selected State Pre-K Programs, by Spending
(2002-2003) *

	Amount spent per child in state pre-K
New Jersey	$8,739
Head Start	$7,089
Minnesota	$6,672
Oregon	$6,525
Connecticut	$5,601
Delaware	$5,287
Massachusetts	$4,104
Louisiana	$3,922
Georgia	$3,824
Nevada	$3,686
Hawaii	$3,478
New York	$3,347
West Virginia	$3,309
Virginia	$3,090
Iowa	$2,925
Texas	$2,746
Kentucky	$2,484
Oklahoma	$2,368
New Mexico	$1,765
Kansas	$1,721
South Carolina	$1,303
Vermont	$1,197
Maryland	$936

* The most up-to-date data available

Source: National Institute for Early Education Research, "The State of Preschool: 2004 State Preschool Yearbook," 2004

FPG Child Development Institute at the University of North Carolina-Chapel Hill, says classrooms that foster high achievement have certain known characteristics.

But the "answer is going to be much more complex" than many have hoped, says Early, who is part of a team that has studied 11 states' preschool programs. For example, "you won't know who a good teacher is based on a set of certificates" or degrees earned. Instead, it will take one-on-one training and expert observation in the classroom. [3]

As America seeks to improve school achievement for all its students, interest in Head Start and state preschools will continue to grow, says Early.

But even if the interest is sustained, it's not clear that taxpayers will ante up money to pay for preschool education, says Greene. Numerous states have scaled back their preschool plans over the past few years in the face of budget deficits. And federal funding also has slowed. While Congress has boosted Head Start funding over the past four years, the increases have dropped from $337 million in fiscal 2002 to $69 million last year.

Head Start's fiscal 2005 appropriation is $6.84 billion. Last year's funding increase was so small that it didn't keep up with rising expenses and thus actually amounted to an enrollment cut, according to Greene. Centers cut available slots by about 9,000 in the last school year, she says. This year, Congress is mulling an increase in the $37-million to $55-million range, which she estimates would lead to elimination of between 15,000 and 18,000 slots.

comes of many kinds of social interventions aimed at changing the lives of the disadvantaged. And "an unfortunately large number" of programs "have no impact," he says. "So, though it may not seem like much, the Head Start study is showing improvements."

With data accumulating on what preschool could achieve, Head Start and state preschool programs now are trying to pinpoint just what creates positive impacts and to replicate those conditions. Diane Early, a researcher at the

As lawmakers and educators debate the effectiveness and role preschool should play in a changing education system, here are some of the questions they are considering:

Is Head Start failing children?

Over the years, Head Start has had plenty of supporters, both Democratic and Republican. However, some conservatives have long grumbled that Head Start has not lived up to its promise to raise the IQs of low-income children to the same level as middle-class children by the time they reach kindergarten.

"Too many children in Head Start are being left behind," said Rep. John A. Boehner, R-Ohio, chairman of the House Education Committee. "Head Start's graduates beginning in kindergarten are more than 25 percentage points below in average skills like recognizing letters, numbers, shapes and colors." [4]

Moreover, Brookings Institution Senior Fellow Ron Haskins, who helped craft the Bush administration's plan to overhaul Head Start, says state-run preschool programs as well as the federal Head Start program fail to properly prepare poor children for kindergarten. "Billions of dollars in federal and state spending on preschool education is failing the nation's poor children," he maintains. "Test scores show that [children in government-run preschool programs] are far behind their more advantaged peers when they enter school." (*See "At Issue," p. 17.*)

As for Head Start, Haskins contends that studies show that the academic skills and knowledge of Head Start children "improve only slightly during the Head Start year. They still start school performing far below other students." [5]

Thus, Haskins says, Head Start fails to achieve its original goal of bringing kids to the starting line as equals — a goal Haskins calls "not theoretically impossible."

Head Start proponents, however, say that while it may be possible — in theory — for a one- to two-year program to make up for a lifetime of intellectual deprivation, it will take a lot more money and time.

For one thing, preschools that demonstrate the biggest and longest-lasting improvements have spent from two to five times as much per child as Head Start spends, says Northwestern's Duncan. But even with less spending, Head Starters achieve more than their non-Head Start peers, he adds, citing the new Impact study, which he says showed a "big gap" between the achievement obtained by Head Starters and their non-Head-Start peers.

Besides money, time and training are crucial, says Bowman of the Chicago Public Schools. "We have a pretty good knowledge of what middle-class kids know and what low-income kids need to learn," she says. "But how do you do it in a half-day program with untrained people?" *

Nicholas Zill, director of child and family studies at Westat, a research firm in Rockville, Md., and a lead investigator on the Impact study, says Head Start is "basically a good program." But, he adds, "it could be doing more," based on the advances in children's skills achieved by small, experimental programs, as shown by earlier studies. "The older studies reported bigger changes, so we have concrete evidence that it could be done better." (*See sidebar, p. 6.*)

However, in the end, "We can make a significant difference, but we're not going to totally erase the family background," he says, adding that preschool has traditionally been oversold for political reasons, and that the goal of achieving complete parity is "overly optimistic."

Those earlier studies examined increases in IQ levels of children enrolled in more intensive and expensive preschool programs. Most found that, while scores rose initially, they dropped again after several years, points out Isabel Sawhill, head of the Brookings Institution's economic-studies program.

Sawhill says that those who say preschool produces no long-term benefits are looking at IQ gains only. "There is more to it than that," she says, adding that studies show Head Start children can stay on task and follow directions better than their non-Head Start peers, skills that the studies indicate "have durability."

In fact, recent analysis suggests that early childhood interventions like Head Start "have the best chance of all [known] interventions" of increasing the skills and abilities that make people contributing members of society, according to Duncan. "Completed schooling is a strong predictor of successful adult outcomes" such as longevity, career attainment, crime avoidance and successful parenting, he wrote. And graduates of experimental, publicly funded preschool programs for poor children have "higher rates of high-school graduation and lower rates of juvenile delinquency." [6]

Adults who attended Head Start are significantly less likely to report being booked or charged with a crime than their siblings who attended another preschool, according to economist Eliana Garces of the University of California-Los Angeles.

---

* Head Start programs vary from a few hours a day to all day.

Nationwide Studies Finally Evaluating Programs

A growing body of research is shedding new light on such questions as what can preschools accomplish and how can all preschool classrooms be made good as the best.

Until recently, solid data on the long-term effectiveness of preschool education came only from studies of a handful of small, highly intensive, experimental preschool programs serving disadvantaged children. The studies tracked long-term outcomes for both those who attended preschools and a control group of similar children who did not attend preschool. The data showed clearly that intensive early educational interventions helped.

For example, the Carolina Abecedarian Project randomly assigned 111 low-income children to receive either intensive, high-quality child care and preschool or no intervention at all, from infancy through age 5, and then tracked the children until age 21. The preschool group had significantly higher test scores on mental ability and reading and math achievement than the non-preschool group. About 35 percent of the preschool attendees had graduated from or were attending a four-year college, compared to only 14 percent of the non-preschool group. And the preschool group waited to have children until age 19, on average, while the non-preschool group had their first child at an average age of 17. [1]

Similarly strong long-term gains were found in studies of other intensive programs, including the Chicago Public Schools' Child-Parent Center program and the Perry Preschool program in Ypsilanti, Mich.

But Head Start had not been studied comprehensively, largely because it was not considered appropriate for a government program to deny preschool to the disadvantaged children who would be in a control group.

Now two large, recent studies have begun to fill that void. First, the federal government in 1997 launched the national Family and Child Experiences Survey (FACES) to periodically gather information on child outcomes and program quality for a randomly selected national sample of Head Start programs.

The 2000 FACES results found that the average Head Start child entered the program knowing four letters of the alphabet and graduated knowing about nine letters. The average reading-ready middle-class child knows about 10 letters at the same age. Head Start children also turned out to be more cooperative and less hyperactive than non-Head Start children after only a year in the program. [2]

The second major study of Head Start — the Head Start Impact Study — is following about 5,000 children through first grade. They were randomly assigned to either Head Start or child care. The study, which began in 2002 and continues through 2006, this year produced the first experimental data on Head Start. It showed that Head Start children make much smaller — but still significant — gains

But these long-term positive outcomes are more likely for white children who attend Head Start than for African-Americans, Garces pointed out. Among white children, "participation in Head Start is associated with a significantly increased probability of completing high school and attending college, and we find some evidence of elevated earnings in one's early 20s," she wrote in 2001. Because the initial gains in test scores are the same for whites and African-Americans, the fact that the black children's gains "fade out" over time probably has "less to do with the Head Start program and more to do with the child's experiences after finishing." [7]

Other economists note that Head Start children usually end up in the lowest-quality elementary schools, and some research suggests that Head Start's positive impact continues only in the better elementary schools. Teachers in poor neighborhoods often are so occupied with helping children with extremely low skills, Duncan observes, that they don't have time to help higher-achieving children — such as Head Start graduates — continue making gains.

Should Head Start focus more on pre-academic skills?

In addition to the comprehensive services provided outside of the classroom, Head Start has broad goals inside. It must teach social, emotional and behavioral skills as well as the skills needed to learn reading and mathematics.

But some critics, including the Bush administration, say Head Start does not teach enough pre-academic skills, such as recognizing the look of printed words or learning the alphabet. This contention is hotly debated, however.

on a variety of measures than the children in the intensive experimental preschools examined in the earlier studies. [3]

Head Start supporters point out that the earlier studies examined intensive, experimental programs that at most involved a few hundred children and spent between two and five times more per child than Head Start. By contrast, Head Start is a huge, nationwide network of 1,800 local programs operating 20,000 centers with quality that varies from state to state.

Initial data from the Impact study show, for example, that Head Start kids scored a little better than control-group children on pre-reading, pre-writing and vocabulary skills. Parents of Head Start children reported that problem behavior was less frequent and less severe than was reported by the non-Head-Start parents. Head Start parents also reported sharing more educational activities with their children than non-participants, and more Head Start children received dental care.

Perhaps equally as important as finding out what preschool achieves, however, is learning what constitutes an effective preschool program.

In addition to the FACES survey, the U.S. Department of Education is funding a multi-state study of pre-kindergarten by researchers from the University of North Carolina (UNC) at Chapel Hill, the University of California at Los Angeles (UCLA) and the University of Virginia. The researchers observed public preschools in 11 states, about 15 percent of which were Head Start centers.

"While sufficient resources can make a good, small program, we still don't know how" to translate good, small-scale results to a statewide — let alone nationwide — scale, says UNC researcher Diane Early. For one thing, she continues, "We have this naive notion, 'She's a nice person and a good mom, so she can do it.' "

But using "good mom" skills to teach pre-reading, pre-math and pre-science to 16 children is difficult, Early says. She and her colleagues also are studying how difficult it is to get kids talking during routine activities like snack time or even during story time. Interactive conversation builds children's language, thinking and social skills, she notes, but the study has found that preschool children spend about 73 percent of their time not interacting with a teacher and about 44 percent of their time not participating in learning or active play.

"Of course, eating and hand washing are critical activities, said Sharon Richie of UCLA. "We just wish that . . . routine times were opportunities for conversations . . . or time for singing or playing number games." [4]

[1] FPG Child Development Institute, University of North Carolina-Chapel Hill, "The Carolina Abecedarian Project," www.fpg.unc.edu/~abc/summary.cfm.

[2] Department of Health and Human Services, "Head Start FACES 2000: A Whole-Child Perspective on Program Performance," Fourth Progress Report, Child Outcomes Research and Evaluation, May 2003.

[3] U.S. Department of Health and Human Services, "Head Start Impact Study First Year Findings," June 2005; www.acf.hhs.gov.

[4] Quoted in "Pre-K Education in the States," Early Developments, National Center for Early Development and Learning, FPG Child Development Institute, spring 2005; www.fpg.unc.edu/~ncedl/pages/ED9.cfm, p. 25.

"There is good reason for increasing attention" on academic skills, wrote Deborah Stipek, dean of the Stanford University School of Education. "Studies show low-income children entering kindergarten to be on average a year to a year-and-a-half behind middle-class children in language and other cognitive skills. This is a gigantic gap when you consider that we are talking about 5- to 6-year-olds." [8]

Poor children often miss out on even the most basic literacy-related experiences at home, say conservative critics. "Head Start should be able to . . . make up for some of the environment that children in poor homes don't have," said Krista Kafer, an education-policy analyst at the conservative Heritage Foundation. "Letters, numbers, reading to children and having them follow along — these are things regularly taught in middle- and upper-class homes but routinely deprived in underprivileged homes." [9]

Some child-development experts worry, however, that increased emphasis on skills like recognizing letters could create a "drill and kill" atmosphere — pushing children to learn facts by rote at too early an age, killing their enthusiasm for learning.

"Middle-class children do not achieve their academic advantage by repeatedly writing the letters of the alphabet and counting to 10," Stipek contends. "Moreover, studies have shown that highly didactic instructional approaches can undermine young children's motivation to learn. Surely, we want children to desire to read as much as we want them to be able to identify the letters." [10]

If direct instruction — highly scripted, mainly teacher-directed rote learning — were to dominate Head

Start, little might be gained, Stipek continued. Direct instruction "has its place, even in preschools," but many important pre-academic skills cannot be taught effectively through direct instruction, she added.

Critics of increasing the academic approach say pressure to change Head Start's curriculum is caused by the 2002 No Child Left Behind Act (NCLB), in which the Bush administration has emphasized testing as a way to improve school achievement. [11]

Stipek points out that such proposals threaten individual Head Start programs with an accountability "stick": "Make progress toward your goals or lose funding." That requirement, she says, will give "considerable influence over the curriculum and instructional practices" to whatever test is used to assess children's skills.

"If the assessment requires children to count to 10, I can guarantee that children will spend time counting to 10 and not much time learning what '10' means" through hands-on activities like collecting 10 objects in a bag, for example, Stipek wrote.

In 2003, the administration launched the National Reporting System (NRS) to assess Head Start children. Given the test's narrow focus, many Head Start teachers are concerned about how it will be used to judge centers' performance.

"We have reason to be very concerned," says Stipek, adding that the most recent version of the test, which is still under development, "assesses recognition and knowledge completely decontextualized from meaningful activities." [12]

Devising a test that does not focus on out-of-context material is difficult, said Barbara Bowman, the Chicago Public Schools' chief officer for early-childhood education and a professor at Erikson Institute, a graduate school and education-research center. "What we can ask children that is easily coded on a test tends to be the most superficial knowledge that they have," she said. "There is a great concern that, in order to devise a test that is economically feasible, we have to stick with content that is unimportant." [13]

Early-childhood education experts also worry that those pushing for more emphasis on academics will offer curricula that are not age-appropriate. Many elementary schools are being asked to teach third-grade curriculum in second grade, rather than teaching second-graders skills that will help them do third-grade work later, says Bowman, and preschool educators fear that may happen

to them. "There is a rich history of push-down academics in public schools," she says.

Nevertheless, focusing on pre-academics doesn't have to mean eliminating more context-rich teaching, Bowman insists: "I don't see why we can't have both."

A preschool that focuses on literacy skills like recognizing letters won't necessarily scrimp on context skills, says Zill. Teachers can use the same teaching methods employed by an educated middle-class mother when they take a child to the grocery store or the zoo, he says. "Yes, there are higher-order skills being taught. But a lot of it also is just, 'Name this. . . . What's that letter?' " These naming skills could be taught by rote, but instead "it's being done in a more humane way."

While skills like letter recognition make a difference in the early grades, in third-grade and beyond — where the ability to understand what one reads becomes paramount — broader general knowledge and a richer vocabulary make a bigger difference, says Zill.

By increasing emphasis on comprehension-related skills, like vocabulary, Head Start centers "could do better than average," he says. For example, teachers could receive lists of target words, interesting books that feature those words and a coordinated plan of activities for helping children recognize the words when they hear them and begin to use them in speech. Such activities would include repeatedly reading the books with the target vocabulary then asking the children questions that must be answered with the target words.

Federal Head Start administrators could help "if you had more of a sense of national goals" for pre-academics and told local centers, "We have these goals, and here are some ways you can meet them," Zill suggests.

Meanwhile, others argue that Head Start's comprehensive services would have to be scaled back to make room for more pre-academic learning.

Douglas Besharov, a scholar analyzing child and family policy at the conservative American Enterprise Institute (AEI), says that while the "most disorganized families" may need such services, local programs should be free to decide which families do — and don't — get such services. Then, some of the resources devoted to comprehensive services could be used beefing up school readiness.

"In a day when there is Medicaid and the [State Children's Health Insurance Program], why do we celebrate [Head Start's] provision of medical care?" he asks.

However, the NHSA's Greene says Head Start's services do not overlap those provided by Medicaid or any other program. For example, only about half of Head Start children receive Medicaid, and Head Start does not provide their care, she says. In addition, Head Start provides other health services, she argues, such as partnering with civic organizations to get glasses for children whose parents work in industries that do not provide health coverage.

Should affordable preschool be available to all children?

The perennial debate over how to improve Head Start is taking place today against a new backdrop — a movement among the states to open public preschools to more children. As mothers join the work force and states struggle to improve education, more attention is being paid to whether preschool should be made available to all children, either free or subsidized on a sliding scale based on family income.

Many state officials hope that establishing preschools will help states reach NCLB goals of improving the academic performance of all students, says UNC's Early. Under the 2002 law, states risk losing some federal funding if they fail to raise test scores for all children, including the very poor, such as those who graduate from Head Start. [14]

States are also interested in preschools because as knowledge and technology advance, students must learn more and more, so increasingly elementary schools expect children to arrive ready to tackle demanding academics. "In Connecticut . . . what we're asking from first-graders and second-graders now is much different from what we were asking from them 10 years ago," said elementary-school principal Gary Gemini. [15]

State preschools also can fill a serious gap for low-income working parents, says NHSA's Greene. "Working families tell us that when they get off TANF [Temporary Aid to Needy Families] and get a job, they can't afford child care," she says. Under the 1996 welfare-reform law, families are only eligible for the federal cash welfare program for a limited time before they must take jobs. [16]

As interest in preschools grows, so do questions about where the money will come from to pay for them. For example, a special lottery funds Georgia's program — one of the nation's largest. But now neighboring Tennessee and South Carolina are starting their own lotteries, and "there's concern in Georgia that its lottery will be less of a cash cow," David Kirp, professor of public policy at the University of California, Berkeley, wrote recently. [17]

Meanwhile, Florida voters in 2002 approved a constitutional amendment guaranteeing all children access to high-quality education, beginning at age 4. Last May, however, state legislators allocated only $2,500 per eligible child — about a third of the average amount Head Start spends per child. [18]

As states struggle to pay for preschools, however, some prominent economists are urging the states to make them a priority. Investing in people pays economic dividends, and the most efficient investments, by far, are those made in young children, according to Nobel Prize-winning University of Chicago economist James Heckman. Every time children learn a skill — intellectual, emotional or social — it becomes both easier and more likely they will pick up additional skills that build on the first, Heckman argues. "Skill begets skill, and younger persons have a longer horizon over which to recoup the fruits of their investments." [19]

In fact, two economists from the Federal Reserve Bank of Minneapolis argue that state and local governments that try to build their economies by competing to attract companies and jobs would be far better served if they invested in preschool education instead. "The conventional view of economic development typically includes company headquarters, office towers . . . and professional sports stadiums," wrote Senior Vice President Art Rolnick and Regional Economic Analyst Rob Grunewald. Instead, they contend, "any proposed economic development list should have early-childhood development at the top. The return on investment . . . is extraordinary, resulting in better-working public schools, more educated workers and less crime." [20]

Skeptics, however, say that it would be smarter to invest more in older children and leave young children to be cared for at home. States should cease their flirtation with expanding preschools, argues Darcy Olsen, president of the conservative Goldwater Institute, in Phoenix, because upper grades needs the resources more.

American elementary-school students "are 'A' students on the international curve," she wrote, but that advantage does not last. "By eighth grade . . . test performance is mediocre. By 12th grade U.S. students are 'D' students on the international scale." [21]

C H R O N O L O G Y

1800s–1820s *Social reformers in Europe and the United States begin opening "infant schools" for children up to age 5 to ease the effects of industrial poverty and to provide child care for poor working mothers.*

1823 American educator and chemist John Griscom opens the first American infant school, in New York City.

1830s–1870s *U.S. infant school trend dies out, in part because a "cult of domesticity" encourages mothers to care for their own children.*

1880s–1920s *Social reformers raise new alarms about the dangers of urban poverty for young children and establish free kindergartens and day nurseries.*

1909 President Theodore Roosevelt urges Congress to establish a federal office to promote children's well-being.

1912 President William Howard Taft creates the Children's Bureau, the first federal agency dedicated to children's welfare.

1930s–1980s *Interest in early-childhood education increases. Head Start is launched during the Lyndon Johnson administration.*

1962 The Early Training Project in Murfreesboro, Tenn., enrolls 65 low-income African-American children considered at risk for mental retardation. The participants' IQ scores rise by five to 10 points, and officials view the program as a possible model for a federal preschool initiative.

1965 As part of the War on Poverty, President Lyndon B. Johnson launches Head Start.

1968 Head Start funds the development of "Sesame Street," a new educational television program.

1969 The "Westinghouse Report" concludes that children whose IQ scores are raised by Head Start lose those gains within a few years.

1971 Congress passes — but President Richard M. Nixon vetoes — the Comprehensive Child Development Act, a Democratic proposal that would have made Head Start the foundation of a national network of child-care centers for all children.

1972 Congress orders that at least 10 percent of Head Start's national enrollment consist of disabled children. . . . Head Start launches an initiative to train and certify Head Start staff and volunteers in early-childhood education.

1975 As Americans debate the effectiveness of Head Start, the program issues its first Program Performance Standards for all local programs to meet.

1977 Bilingual and migrant Head Start programs are established.

1990s–2000s *State interest grows in publicly funding preschool, to both improve educational outcomes and assist a growing cadre of working mothers with child care.*

1992 Georgia launches a lottery-financed pilot preschool program for lower-income children.

1995 Early Head Start program is created to provide services to pregnant women and children up to age 3. . . . Georgia expands eligibility for its state-funded preschool to all 4-year-olds.

1997 New York authorizes universal preschool for 4-year-olds.

1998 Oklahoma authorizes universal preschool for 4-year-olds.

2002 President Bush proposes — but Head Start supporters in Congress quash — a plan to let some states to take control of Head Start.

2005 Head Start Impact Study releases the first nationwide experimental data showing that Head Start children do better on some measures of progress than a comparable group of children not enrolled. . . . Congress proposes requiring that half of Head Start teachers have B.A. degrees by 2011.

Furthermore, while Head Start was created "to remedy some of the social inequalities visited upon low-income children," wrote Olsen, a "significant body of research shows that formal early education can be detrimental to mainstream children. By attempting to teach the wrong things at the wrong time, early instruction can permanently damage . . . self-esteem, reduce a child's natural eagerness to learn and block a child's natural gifts and talents." [22]

Pennsylvania state Rep. Sam Rohrer, R-Berks County, also has doubts about the value of public preschooling. The programs are expensive, he said, and inappropriately compete with the role of parents. "Government has to really resist that tendency to fill a void that only a parent can fill," Rohrer said. [23]

BACKGROUND

Early Roots

The federal Head Start program for low-income preschoolers celebrates its 40th anniversary this year. But the idea of preschool education for poor children has been around for nearly 200 years. In the early 19th century, British and French "infant" schools — what we now consider preschools — were established to improve the health and upbringing of poor children and to allow poor mothers to work.

In the early years of the Industrial Age, factories drew thousands of people to Europe's cities. Manchester, England, for example, saw its population swell from 25,000 in 1770 to almost 250,000 by 1820. Men, women and children as young as 6 or 7 worked for 13 or 14 hours a day in factories, poor neighborhoods grew rife with crime and disease mushroomed.

Born into that harsh environment, Britain's first infant schools were developed by reformers influenced by British philosopher John Locke, a key Age of Enlightenment thinker. Locke theorized that the mind of a young child was a *tabula rasa*, a blank slate on which early experiences write heavily, with good or bad results for later life. [24]

And too often, thought Manchester-born factory owner and social reformer Robert Owen, the results were disastrous. Distressed by the "wretchedness" in the lives of "that immense mass of population which is now allowed to be so formed as to fill the world with crimes," he banned factory employment for children under age 10. He also established schools for his workers' children — including an infant school opened in 1816 for children as young as 2 — in New Lanark, Scotland, where he owned spinning mills. Owen sought to replace potentially damaging influences in children's poverty-blighted neighborhoods with a clean, kind, interesting environment that would help "form them into rational beings . . . useful and effective members of the state." [25]

With American cities also burgeoning in the early 19th century — and becoming crime ridden — Owen's idea of educational intervention early in poor children's lives soon traveled across the Atlantic.

In 1823, American educator John Griscom established one of the earliest American infant schools in New York City. [26] In the 1820s and '30s, other schools were formed, mostly in large East Coast cities, but also in some smaller towns, such as Franklin, Tenn.

Philadelphia had the largest network of infant schools, supported by three charitable groups. And in New York state, Gov. DeWitt Clinton encouraged private charities to establish the schools "as a means of allowing poor mothers to earn a living while ensuring that their young children received proper moral and character training," wrote Maris Vinovskis, a University of Michigan history professor. [27]

While British advocates of infant schools were most worried about rising crime, supporters in the United States mainly wanted to reduce poverty and welfare costs, according to Vinovskis. "Most American reformers . . . did not see urban problems in this country as severe or as threatening as in Great Britain," he wrote. "However, they feared that unless immediate, corrective steps were undertaken, the quality of life in American cities would rapidly deteriorate."

Child-welfare advocates hoped that early intervention in poor children's lives would improve their prospects as citizens, workers and parents. The Infant School of the City of Boston boasted of its potential: "A ray of millennial light has shone on us, and reveals a way in which poverty, with all its attendant evils — moral, physical and intellectual — may be banished from the world." [28]

Infants in School

The spread of preschools for the poor spurred interest — and even envy — among some middle-class parents, who worried that their children might be at a disadvantage

Giving Parents a Head Start, Too

In 1974, Head Start workers in Fond du Lac, Wis., urged Margarita de Christianson to enroll her 3-year-old son. "Soon," wrote de Christianson, "they were encouraging me to learn how to drive, to learn English and to volunteer in Head Start classrooms. I did, and it has been the most rewarding and productive thing in my life." [1]

Head Start changes parents' lives as well as the lives of their children, not only teaching parenting skills but also how to get a job or go to college, according to the National Head Start Association (NHSA). Since its inception in 1965, Head Start has been required to offer services to program parents and encourage them to become involved in Head Start as volunteers, paid workers and members of local councils that set policy for Head Start programs. Nationwide, 29 percent of Head Start staff are parents of current or former Head Start children. [2]

Giving parents the right to make decisions about their local Head Start "has been one of the greatest strengths of the program," says NHSA President Sarah Greene.

But as Congress looks for ways to improve Head Start, many in the anti-poverty community worry that changes could end the program's long tradition of empowering parents. Under current standards, local Head Starts jointly govern their programs with a policy council, at least 51 percent of whose members must be parents of current students.

But if some states eventually are allowed to weave Head Start into their own preschool systems, as the Bush administration has proposed, including parents on policy councils would surely end within a few years, Greene argues. According to studies, she says, when programs are turned over to state control, "In five years, you can't recognize them."

Opponents of the changes also see potential threats to parental involvement in the Senate version of legislation being considered by Congress. The bill would expand oversight of Head Start's governing board "in a way that could diminish the Parent Policy Councils," according to Results, an international anti-poverty advocacy group with U.S. headquarters in Washington, D.C. "While increased accountability is a plus, the bill should not take away from accountability measures that empower parents and are already in place," the organization argues. [3]

Gayle Cunningham, Head Start director for Jefferson County (Birmingham), Ala., told the House Subcommittee on Education Reform in April that encouraging parental involvement is vital, because children's learning largely takes place at home.

"Not only has my child grown and matured from the program, but so have I," wrote Melissa L. Johnson, a local parent. "I had him when I was 16, so I thought the teachers would teach him. They have done a great deal, but they showed me that the learning has to start from the home." [4]

Head Start staff members are required to try to make at least two home visits to each family per year and to schedule at least two parent-teacher conferences. They also must help families obtain additional services such as mental-health assistance, literacy education for parents, employment training and emergency assistance to obtain housing, transportation and other necessities.

Staff are also required to develop "family partnership agreements" that lay out parents' goals — including timetables — for improving their own and their children's lives. In 2002, 81 percent of families had partnership agreements, according to the Center for Law and Social Policy (CLASP), an advocacy group for low-income people. [5]

The extraordinary efforts are needed, Head Start supporters say, because the lowest-income families face additional stresses not experienced by other families — such as low levels of parental education, domestic violence and men-

---

because of the early schooling the poor children were getting, according to Vinovskis.

"We have been told that it is now in contemplation, to open a school for . . . infants besides the poor," noted an 1829 *Ladies Magazine* article. "If such a course be not adopted, at the age for entering primary schools those poor children will assuredly be the richest scholars. . . . Why should a plan which promises so many advantages . . . be confined to children of the indigent?" [29]

Some reformers pushed to make infant schools part of public-education systems, and middle-class families began enrolling their children. But enthusiasm for preschool faded after a couple of decades. The strict academic training in some public schools didn't mesh with the gentler instruction that prevailed in preschool classrooms. Public schools also worried that adding preschools would drain their finances.

tal-health problems — that can cause learning or behavior difficulties for children.

For example, in a national study of Early Head Start — a program for pregnant mothers and children up to age 3 — 48 percent of women who were pregnant or caring for infants reported suffering from depression, and a third of mothers with 3-year-olds said they were depressed. [6] Low-income mothers with mental-health disorders are 25 percent less likely to work, according to the Annie E. Casey Foundation, which collects information on child poverty. "Besides jeopardizing economic stability, parental depression can put children at heightened risk of developing behavioral problems, school difficulties and physical health problems," said the Kids Count Data Book Online. [7]

Moreover, Head Start's outreach is more effective than many other social programs, says Greene. Parents report that "when they go to other social agencies, workers don't treat them respectfully," she says, while Head Start has a history and tradition of treating families with respect.

The required home visits also help Head Start staff better understand families' needs and problems, she says, and some parents writing on the NHSA Web site agree.

"Head Start basically raised me," wrote Patty Cooper, a parent in Beaverton, Ore. When her oldest child entered Head

Parents Receive Wide-Ranging Help

Nearly one-third of Head Start families received parenting training and more than a quarter received health education.

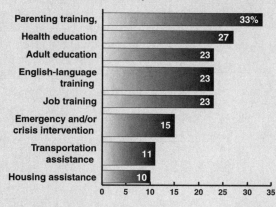

Services Received by Head Start Parents

- Parenting training, 33%
- Health education 27
- Adult education 23
- English-language training 23
- Job training 23
- Emergency and/or crisis intervention 15
- Transportation assistance 11
- Housing assistance 10

Source: Center for Law and Social Policy; data are for 2002

Start in 1977, Cooper says that as a recently separated mother of three she "had no family support and Head Start became my family." Among the skills she learned from the program was advocating for her children.

When Cooper's son was diagnosed with bone cancer, she writes, "thanks to what I had learned from Head Start and . . . the boost in self-esteem Head Start gave me, I was able to talk with doctors and ask questions and advocate for my son. I was also supported by the program during this difficult time." [8]

[1] National Head Start Association, www.igotaheadstart.org.

[2] See Rachel Schumacher, "Family Support and Parent Involvement in Head Start: What Do Head Start Program Performance Standards Require?" Center for Law and Social Policy, May 22, 2003; www.clasp.org.

[3] Results, "Background on 2005 Head Start Reauthorization"; www.results.org/website/article.asp?id+618.

[4] Cunningham read Johnson's e-mail message as part of her testimony before the House Subcommittee on Education Reform, April 14, 2005.

[5] Schumacher, *op. cit.*

[6] Department of Health and Human Services, Administration for Children and Families, "Research to Practice: Depression in the Lives of Early Head Start Families," January 2003; www.acf.dhs.gov.

[7] Annie E. Casey Foundation, "2005 Kids Count Data Book Online"; www.aecf.org/kidscount/sld/essay/essay6.jsp.

[8] National Head Start Association, *op. cit.*

Finally, a popular, new trend that emphasized the virtues of stay-at-home motherhood raised questions about whether young children should ever be cared for outside the home. In the 1830s and '40s, middle-class parents began withdrawing their children from preschools, delivering the final blow to the short-lived U.S infant-school movement. [30]

Nevertheless, reformers continued seeking ways to intervene early in the lives of disadvantaged children to counteract the effects of poverty. For example, in the late 19th century many U.S. cities adopted another European notion — free kindergarten, supported by public or private funds.

Many middle-class families enrolled their children for educational enrichment. But kindergartens' strongest supporters were social activists who saw them as a vital service for the many immigrant children living in increasingly crowded cities, according to RAND analysts. "It was

The 900,000 children who participate in the nation's 1,800 Head Start programs reflect its changing demographics. In 1992, about 23 percent were Hispanic and 37 percent were black. Today, 31.2 percent of participants are Hispanic, slightly outnumbering blacks, and 27 percent are white.

hoped that kindergarten would compensate for economic disadvantage in early childhood experiences, promote cultural assimilation and provide safe child care for working mothers in urban industrial slums," they wrote. [31]

War on Poverty

In the 20th century, new ideas about child development revived interest in early-childhood education. Studies suggested that social programs might help improve the lives of poor or disabled children.

In the 1920s, for example, Yale University psychologist Arnold Gesell laid out a timetable showing ages at which a "normal" child should develop specific abilities. In the 1940s, the theories of psychologists J. McVicker Hunt of Brown University and the University of Chicago's Benjamin Bloom became influential. Hunt argued that children's intellectual capabilities were diminished by deprived environments during early childhood. Bloom theorized that 50 percent of a person's intellectual development occurs by age 4. [32]

But it wasn't until the 1960s that Americans' interest in child development translated into a major, early intervention for the disadvantaged. In 1964, Congress and President Johnson launched the War on Poverty, a massive federal effort to improve the lives of poor people. Initially, there was no preschool component.

Instead, the initiative — run by the new Office of Economic Opportunity (OEO) — focused on poor adults. It included programs such as the Job Corps, which offered young adults employment training, and the Community Action Program (CAP), which some activists saw as the core of the effort. CAP grants to cities and towns were intended to help local groups of poor people organize programs to fight poverty.

Through CAP, "we intend to strike at poverty at its source — in the streets of our cities and on the farms of our countryside," Johnson wrote in a March 1964 message to Congress." [33]

In his first year as OEO director, R. Sargent Shriver had $300 million in CAP grants to distribute but no takers for about half the money, wrote Yale University psychologist Edward Zigler, one of Head Start's early architects. Mayors were leery of opening CAP agencies after a New York City program on which CAP was modeled was accused of undermining the authority of city government, mishandling funds and harboring communists. [34]

In search of a use for his unspent dollars, Shriver took a new look at U.S. poverty statistics. When he discovered that almost half the country's 30 million poor people were children, mostly under age 12, the idea for Head Start was born. "It was clear that it was foolish to talk about a 'total war against poverty' . . . if you were doing nothing about children," said Shriver. [35]

The program was modeled on several experimental preschools influenced by psychologists like Hunt and Bloom. A President's Panel on Mental Retardation in 1962 had stated that preschools in disadvantaged areas could reduce mental retardation by 50 percent, and early analyses of some programs supported the idea that preschool could raise IQ scores.

By the time Head Start opened in summer 1965 as an eight-week program serving more than 500,000 children ages 3-5, it had gained additional responsibilities. These included providing health care and — in the CAP spirit of empowering the poor — enlisting parents to serve on policy-setting committees. Unlike other public education in the United States — which is funded and run by states — Head Start programs are locally run, funded by direct federal grants.

After the eight-week summer program ended, Congress expanded it. By 1969, some Head Start centers were operating year round, and by 1972 most had expanded beyond the summer-only format. Special efforts were made to establish Head Start in the nation's 300 poorest counties. [36]

Head Start quickly became popular with lawmakers and the public. But controversy also began early.

Some pediatricians and psychologists who shaped the program believed that its most solid achievements would come from improving children's physical health and their emotional and social functioning. "I . . . did not share the then-popular vision that an early-intervention program could permanently raise children's IQs," wrote Zigler. "I thought that instead of trying to improve children's intellectual capacities, we would be better off trying to improve their motivation to use whatever intelligence they had." [37]

But to much of the public, as well as to the press and many lawmakers, raising IQ scores was Head Start's most compelling promise.

Studies over the next 40 years would show repeatedly that IQ scores do rise significantly when children attend the program. For instance, Leon Eisenberg, a professor of child psychiatry at Johns Hopkins University, evaluated the Head Start program in Baltimore and found "a measurable increase in the intelligence quotient . . . of between 8 1/2 and 10 points, on the average," Shriver told the U.S. House Committee on Education and Labor in 1966. "We have yet . . . to receive the first report claiming that Head Start failed to produce measurable gains." [38]

In 1969, however, the Westinghouse Learning Corp. and Ohio University concluded that, while Head Start temporarily raised IQ scores, gains were lost as children moved through elementary school. [39]

Higher Salaries May Lure Teachers Away

The average kindergarten teacher earns $43,530 compared with only $25,963 for a Head Start teacher with a bachelor's degree in early-childhood education (ECE). Critics of proposed legislation that would require more Head Start teachers to obtain bachelor's degrees warn that they may abandon Head Start for higher salaries as kindergarten teachers once they get their degrees.

Average Teacher Salary by Level of Education

Head Start Salaries	
Child Development Associate	$19,904
A.A. in ECE	$21,907
B.A. in ECE	$25,963
Graduate Degree in ECE	$32,629
Kindergarten Salaries	$43,530

Sources: Bureau of Labor Statistics, "2003 Head Start Program Information Report"

Universal Preschool

While critics may doubt Head Start's achievements, in the past 40 years a growing number of middle-class and upper-income American families have paid to send their children to private preschools. As mothers began joining the work force during the late 1970s and '80s, preschool became a near necessity as well as a source of academic and social enrichment.

By the 1990s, states began jumping on the preschool bandwagon. Worried about lagging student achievement and spurred by new research on the importance of early brain development, states plowed funds into preschool, raising new questions about how Head Start should operate in the 21st century.

In 1992, Georgia launched one of the earliest programs, financed primarily with lottery proceeds. At first, the state targeted low-income children but later expanded eligibility to all 4-year-olds. In 1997, New York established universal pre-kindergarten, which lawmakers hoped would be available to all 4-year-olds by 2002. Oklahoma, which had sponsored a small program since 1980, passed legislation in 1998 expanding eligibility to all 4-year-olds. [40]

Other states have initiated programs in response to court rulings. For example, in *Sheff v. O'Neil*, the Connecticut Supreme Court found in 1996 that low-income children tended to be isolated in lower-quality school districts and that the state should remedy the educational harm children suffered as a result. In response, Connecticut in 1997 authorized grants for low-income districts and schools to make preschool education universally available in their areas. [41]

By the 2002-2003 school year, 738,000 children around the country were attending state-funded preschools, up from 693,000 the previous year, according to Rutgers University's National Institute for Early Education Research. But recent budget deficits have caused most states to expand preschool eligibility more slowly than they had initially planned. [42] For example, New York legislators have not fully funded their program, which in 2004 reached only about a quarter of 4-year-olds. [43]

Then in January 2002, President Bush signed into law the federal No Child Left Behind Act, which holds states accountable for improving academic achievement of all children in the third grade and higher. The law gave states an added reason to focus on preschool: If test scores did not rise for all students — including those who attend Head Start — states would lose some federal funding.

CURRENT SITUATION

Reform Plan

When the White House asked Congress to revamp the Head Start program in 2003, it set off alarm bells among program supporters.

The administration proposed training Head Start's 50,000 teachers in improving children's literacy skills. In addition each child's progress on specific learning goals would have to be assessed three times a year and some states given control over their Head Start programs. States would receive additional federal child-care money if they established preschool learning guidelines that meshed with their kindergarten-through-12th-grade academic-achievement goals and developed a plan for coordinating at least four early-childhood programs, which could include Head Start.

"Efforts to improve early-childhood learning will not work unless they involve states and school districts, which shoulder the primary responsibility for providing public education," the White House said. [44]

But many advocates saw the plan as a way for the federal government to shift funding responsibility to states, "a budget-cutting exercise in disguise," says Sawhill of Brookings.

"Far from 'improving' Head Start," said the NHSA, the administration's plan within five years would "dead end" the program because it would rely "on budget-deficit-crippled states that currently are slashing funds for early-childhood development and education." [45]

"Alignment of standards" would be a good thing if state preschools also had to adopt Head Start's comprehensive performance goals, says NHSA President Greene. But allowing states to adopt narrower, academic-only standards to govern Head Start would ill serve the program's clients, she adds, who come from "the very most vulnerable populations."

Besides, by law and in practice, says Greene, Head Start and state programs already coordinate their efforts, including initiatives to ease children's transition to public school. So, "When people say, 'We need more coordination,'" she says, "I think they want to take over."

Distrust of the Bush overhaul plan was exacerbated by longstanding tensions between the Head Start community and some Republican policymakers. While both Republicans and Democrats have supported Head Start over the years, some advocates have feared since the Reagan administration that admitting any flaws meant the program would be zeroed out of the budget, says the AEI's Besharov. So advocates tend to "circle the wagons" to resist modifications — particularly Republican-sponsored proposals — in fear of losing the program altogether, he says.

Worsening the conflict in recent years was the troubled tenure of Windy M. Hill, who served as associate commissioner of the Head Start Bureau in Washington, beginning in 2002. Hill first alarmed Head Starters in 2003 when she questioned an NHSA request asking centers to encourage staff and parents to share their views of the Bush proposal with members of Congress. The NHSA request "appears to encourage . . . programs to use . . . funds and/or staff in a manner that is in direct violation of the laws," Hill wrote. [46] NHSA sued, charging that the somewhat vaguely worded warning was a stealth attack on freedom of speech, and Hill backed down.

Other disputes followed, until NHSA called for Hill's resignation in April 2004, pointing to evidence that she had mismanaged funds at the Texas Head Start program she ran before coming to Washington. She resigned in May 2005.

Should states have more control over Head Start?

YES

Ron Haskins
Senior Fellow, Brookings Institution

Written for *CQ Researcher*, August 2005

Billions of dollars are being spent on preschool education for the nation's poor children, and the effort is failing. Test scores from a representative sample of these children show that they are far behind their more advantaged peers when they enter school. Worse, national data on children who attended Head Start show that their academic skills and knowledge improve only slightly during the Head Start year. They still start school performing far below other students.

In response, the Bush administration and House Republicans have proposed allowing states to exert more control over Head Start to coordinate it with state preschool programs. House Democrats and other Head Start allies charged that Republicans were trying to destroy Head Start to save money. Republicans responded by proposing to allow only a few states to conduct demonstrations of coordinated funding. This proposal too was greeted with hostility, prompting Republicans to drop it. The status quo will be maintained, although Congress appears poised to require some long-term changes in Head Start teacher qualifications.

Four things are needed to improve the school readiness of poor children. First, Congress should clearly express its concern that poor and minority children are far behind and that Head Start is doing too little to eliminate the gap. Second, Congress should adopt a modified version of the Republican proposal by allowing a few states to experiment with improving preschool programs. To do so, states should be given the authority to coordinate Head Start funding with state funding of preschool education. But to be selected for this new authority, states should also be required to present a plan for how they will improve all preschool education in the state. The improvement plan could include better teacher training, better preschool curriculum, more parent involvement, more than one year of preschool attendance or other reforms. Third, Congress should provide selected states with additional funding to implement their reforms. Fourth, Congress should pay for third-party evaluations of these state experiments.

With no serious changes in Head Start in prospect, and with splintered funding for preschool programs continuing, millions of poor and minority children will still be ill-prepared for the rigors of schooling. States that are now leading the charge in preschool education should be given the opportunity to coordinate all state and federal resources, to obtain new resources and to experiment with new ways to achieve President Lyndon B. Johnson's original vision of poor and minority children entering school ready to compete.

NO

Danielle Ewen
Senior Policy Analyst, Center for Law and Social Policy

Written for *CQ Researcher*, Aug. 23, 2005

The question of state control over Head Start has been discussed during the debate over the program's reauthorization, but a better question is: "How can Congress raise the quality of Head Start?"

The answer lies in improving teacher education standards; oversight and accountability at the federal level; support for collaboration and coordination by states, federal agencies and Head Start grantees; and increased resources to help local programs serve more children and make investments in quality. State control does nothing to ensure improved quality or availability, risks the diminution of existing services and standards and misses an opportunity to use research and data to improve programs.

Head Start works. The national Head Start Impact Study shows that "children in Head Start are making gains in pre-reading, pre-writing, vocabulary and parent reports of children's literacy skills." Nearly a million children and their families have access to comprehensive services including health care, dental care, family literacy and other supports. Babies and toddlers are receiving high-quality services. Head Start programs join in state pre-kindergarten programs, form collaborative agreements with states, participate in joint outreach, training and mentoring activities and partner with schools to transition children from preschool to kindergarten.

But Head Start can — and should — do better. Every eligible child should have access to the program. Children in Head Start should have teachers with bachelor's degrees and training in early-childhood education. Ongoing appropriate assessment should be used to ensure that programs are of the highest quality. More programs should provide full-day and year-round services. Early Head Start should reach more eligible children. Head Start programs can benefit from state pre-kindergarten and other programs in their communities.

A change in governance would not assure these outcomes. State control risks the loss of comprehensive services and less targeting of scarce federal resources to the children most at risk. Most state pre-K programs have fewer resources per child, do not include comprehensive services, have lower standards and serve a smaller percentage of the eligible population than Head Start.

Collaboration and strategic state-level planning among Head Start, education and child-care programs, and additional funding for these activities can help achieve these outcomes.

The best solution for every child in Head Start is not a restructuring of governance but rather a stronger commitment of resources and improvements in quality.

President Bush visits a Head Start program in Landover, Md. The Bush administration has proposed turning Head Start over to the states, but critics say the plan would undermine the program's steady funding and comprehensive services for poor children, such as parental involvement and health care.

Tests and Distrust

In 2003, amid the turmoil stirred up by Hill, the Bush administration launched the National Reporting System (NRS) to periodically assess the progress of Head Start children and local programs. Early versions of the test focus on pre-academic skills such as letter recognition, but later versions will assess progress on Head Start's comprehensive list of goals.

Virtually everyone agrees that Head Start should be accountable for meeting program goals. But advocates complain that local programs have been given far too little information about how test results will be used or what will happen to centers that don't perform well. Many also argue that the current tests are seriously flawed.

Since preschoolers can't write, individuals must question each child, which "takes an immense amount of time," especially since Hispanic children must be tested twice — in both English and Spanish — says Judy Battista, education manager of Holyoke-Chicopee-Springfield Head Start Inc., in Springfield, Mass. Nationwide, Hispanic children represent 31 percent of Head Start enrollment.

Moreover, the tests provided so far are "not developmentally appropriate," Battista says, because, for example, they ask questions about pictures with too many small details that can distract small children.

The Government Accountability Office (GAO), a nonpartisan government agency that advises Congress, concluded in May 2005 that the tests have potential but need significant improvement. For example, said the GAO, it has not been shown that the NRS measures what it is intended to measure or will produce reliable results over time. The government also hasn't explained "what level of progress is expected, how it will use NRS scores to target training and technical assistance or how it will hold grantees accountable for achieving results," according to the agency. [47]

However, Assistant Secretary Horn replies that the NRS is a work in progress and a crucial first step toward understanding exactly what aspects of Head Start are working and what may need to be changed. Without exact measurements of progress — which NRS will provide — it's impossible to target resources appropriately, he says.

For example, before NRS, Horn says, "If I said, 'We need to educate people on better ways to teach vocabulary,' I would need to bring in all 1,800" Head Start programs for training. With NRS, "for the first time, I can bring in [only] those who need that technical assistance the most."

Horn says he does not understand why Head Start advocates "are so fearful of the NRS," and why NHSA "intentionally misunderstands" it. "It seems to me that NHSA should be as interested as we are in improving outcomes for kids. And I'm not sure they are."

For the administration, the NRS represents concrete progress toward its goal of holding Head Start programs accountable. After two years of trying, however, the Republican majority in Congress was unable to enact the White House's other key proposal — turning some control of Head Start over to the states.

After heavy lobbying against the Bush proposal by Head Start advocates, the House watered it down, allowing just eight states to integrate Head Start into their preschool systems as pilot projects. But Democrats and some moderate Republicans still were leery, arguing that states' mostly fledgling preschool programs are underfunded, do not meet the same performance goals Head Start has established and do not offer the comprehensive services very low-income children may need.

"The bottom line is I don't know why we're doing this," said Rep. Christopher Shays, R-Conn. "I feel we're trying to fix something that's not broken." [48]

After House supporters added language requiring states to match at least 50 percent of the Head Start funding they received and "generally meet or exceed" Head Start's performance standards in their state preschool, the House passed its plan for a pilot study by a one-vote margin in July 2003. Rep. John Sullivan, R-Okla., who was recovering from a car accident, was pushed into the House chamber in a wheelchair to cast the deciding vote at 1 a.m. on July 25. [49]

But after the House squeaker, the bill wasn't even considered in the Senate, where even some prominent Republicans opposed it. For example, Sen. Lamar Alexander, R-Tenn. — a former Tennessee governor and U.S. secretary of Education — said he was "not persuaded" the House bill was the best way to improve Head Start. [50]

This spring backers of the plan gave up, and the House and Senate education committees unanimously approved bills taking a different approach to beefing up Head Start's pre-academic focus — requiring more teachers to earn bachelor's degrees over the next several years.

Many people in and out of Head Start agree that increasing the number of teachers with degrees in early education is probably a good idea. "Both formal education levels and recent, specialized training in child development have been found . . . to be associated with high-quality [teacher-child] interactions and children's development," according to a joint National Research Council/Institute of Medicine expert panel. [51]

Later this fall, Congress expects to enact the degree requirement. However, many worry that there won't be enough money for the ambitious initiative. Annual funding increases for domestic programs like Head Start have been slowed over the past few years to help pay for tax

cuts, the war in Iraq and other priorities. The funding slowdown is expected to continue.

Meanwhile, raising the educational requirements will increase costs, not only to help pay for schooling but also to increase teacher pay, says the Center for Law and Social Policy (CLASP), an advocacy group that supports Head Start. CLASP estimates that an additional $2.7 billion to $3.4 billion will be needed over the next six years to fully fund the requirements, depending on whether the House or Senate version is enacted.

If significant extra funding doesn't back the plan, Head Start risks becoming a "revolving door" for teachers, because once they are college graduates they will be able to earn much more teaching in public schools — nearly twice as much in some states — as they earn in Head Start, says NHSA's Greene.

Offering higher salaries right away to teachers who earn degrees also is imperative, says Wyoming Head Start Director Laird. In the past, her program helped pay for three teachers to obtain bachelor's degrees, then lost them to the public schools, with their higher pay and better benefits, she says.

And rural Head Start programs, like Laird's, worry about the special difficulties they will face if the Senate bill passes, rather than the House version. Senators would require half the teachers in each local Head Start program to have bachelor's degrees by 2011, while the House version would require only that half the teachers nationwide earn degrees by then.

Like most Head Start directors, Laird favors more teachers being college-trained. But she says programs in ultra-rural areas such as northern Wyoming, Montana and South Dakota will need extra time and more money to get the job done.

And the teachers will need extra help with their college tuition costs if they must take days off from work — unpaid — and rent hotel rooms overnight to attend classes, says Laird. Centers also must hire substitute teachers to cover for those away on campus, but substitutes are hard to find in sparsely populated areas.

Members of Congress from both parties agree that funding the requirement remains a major concern and pledge to seek solutions, such as increasing Head Start's budget or enacting individual loan-relief and grant programs to help students pursuing degrees in early education.

OUTLOOK

Universal Preschool?

Most people don't yet realize it, but preschool is the next big trend in American education, according to UNC's Early. Many states already teach a large number of 4-year-olds, and "in 15 years I wouldn't be at all surprised that the majority of 3- and 4-year-olds are in pre-kindergarten," Early says.

Preschool enrollments have been steadily rising for years. Besides the approximately 900,000 children in Head Start, in the 2002-2003 school year 738,000 3- and 4-year-olds — or about 10 percent of U.S. children in that age group — attended state-funded preschools, up from 693,000 in 2001-2002, according to the National Institute for Early Education Research, at Rutgers University. [52]

When private preschools are counted, it's clear that school for the under-5 set is an established and growing U.S. institution, according to Stanford's Stipek. In 1965, when Head Start began, only 5 percent of American 3-year-olds and 16 percent of 4-year-olds went to preschool. By 2002, 42 percent of 3-year-olds and 67 percent of 4-year-olds attended some kind of preschool. [53]

"School success is 20 times more important now than" in the 1960s when Head Start opened, says Bowman, of the Chicago Public Schools. "Technology has moved to the forefront, and the technological revolution is altering society as dramatically as did the Industrial Revolution of the prior age," she wrote. "Today, the mantra of business and government is that children who are not adequately educated cannot participate in the new economy and will become a drain on the society. This means that we must educate poor children as well as rich children." [54]

But states' growing interest in preschool could change things for Head Start, Bowman says. School systems already have trouble with coordination. For example, kindergartens and first grades in the same school building may use different base vocabulary lists. And coordination questions only grow worse when states manage one set of preschools, with local centers, and the federal government directs the Head Start schools.

Moreover, the expansion of state preschool programs eventually will raise questions about why "we only segregate poor children" into Head Start, Bowman says.

One scenario she could envision down the line: States take over education for all 3- and 4-year-olds, while Head Start becomes a program for children up to age 3.

While Congress and Head Start's vocal advocacy community have pushed the issue off the legislative table for now, the question of how best to coordinate Head Start and growing state preschool systems will return, Steven Barnett, director of the National Institute for Early Education Research, told the House Education Reform Subcommittee in April.

"As an economist who has studied the returns to high-quality preschool education for over 20 years, I find that America pays a high price because public programs for young children have low standards and too little funding," Barnett said. Because there is both "potential for better services through cooperation and integration" and "potential for confusion," it is now "essential to enable states [and] Head Start . . . to jointly develop and test new approaches."

But, while states may be interested in preschool, "their funding commitment has been unstable," says NHSA's Greene. During the state budget crises in the early 2000s, preschool was one of the first things most states cut, she says. Head Starts that already were integrated into state systems, "had state money and degreed teachers, and then they couldn't afford it any more."

If states eventually gain control of Head Start, "in five years you won't be able to recognize it any more," Greene predicts.

Meanwhile, reform proponents see a gloomy future, the Brookings Institution's Haskins warns: "With no serious changes in Head Start likely and with splintered funding for preschool programs continuing, millions of poor and minority children will still be ill-prepared for the rigors of schooling."

NOTES

1. Joan Fitzgerald and Daphne Hunt, "Raising the Bar," *The American Prospect Online*, Nov. 1, 2004.

2. U.S. Department of Health and Human Services, "Head Start Impact Study First Year Findings," June 2005; www.acf.hhs.gov.

3. For reports on the studies, see www.fpg.unc.edu.

4. Quoted in Jennifer Niesslein, "Spanking Head Start," *The Nation*, Oct. 20, 2003, p. 8. For example,

see results of the Department of the Health and Human Services' Head Start Family and Child Experiences Survey (FACES) at www.acf.hhs.gov/ programs/opre/hs/faces/.

5. For example, see results of the Department of Health and Human Services' Head Start Family and Child Experiences Survey (FACES) at www.acf.hhs.gov/ programs/opre/hs/faces/.

6. Greg J. Duncan and Katherine Magnuson, "Individual and Parent-based Intervention Strategies for Promoting Human Capital and Positive Behavior," www.north-western.edu/ipr/publications/papers/2004/duncan/17 jacobsconference.pdf.

7. Eliana Garces, *et al.*, "Longer Term Effects of Head Start," ideas.repec.org/a/aea/aecrev/v92y2002i4p999-1012.html.

8. Deborah Stipek, "Head Start: Can't We Have Our Cake and Eat It Too?" *Education Week*, May 5, 2004, p. 52.

9. Quoted in Jessica Reaves and Katherine Bonamici, "A New Proposal: Head Start for All" Time, July 12, 2001, www.time.com/time/education/printout/ 0,8 816,167401,00.html.

10. Stipek, *op. cit.*

11. For background see Barbara Mantel, "No Child Left Behind," *CQ Researcher*, May 27, 2005, pp. 469-492 and Kenneth Jost, "Testing in Schools," *CQ Researcher*, April 20, 2001, pp. 321-344.

12. *Ibid.*

13. Quoted in "Early Childhood Assessment: Problems and Possibilities," The Albert Shanker Institute National Press Club Forum, Oct. 6, 2004.

14. For background, see Barbara Mantel, "No Child Left Behind," *CQ Researcher*, May 27, 2005, pp. 470-491.

15. Quoted in Angela Pascopelia, "Overhauling an Early Education Program," Curriculum Administrator, August 2001, p. 34.

16. "Welfare, Work and the States," *CQ Researcher*, Dec. 6, 1996.

17. David Kirp, "All My Children," *The New York Times*, July 31, 2005, p. 4A.

18. Christopher Conte, "The Politics of Preschool," *Governing*, June 2005, p. 35.

19. Quoted in Dana E. Friedman, "The New Economics of Preschool," Early Childhood Funders' Collaborative, October 2004, www.earlychildhoodfinance.org/hand-outs/FriedmanArticle.doc.

20. Art Rolnick and Rob Grunewald, "Early Childhood Development: Economic Development With a High Public Return," Fedgazette, Federal Reserve Bank of Minneapolis, March 2003, minneapolis-fed.org/pubs/fedgaz/03-03/earlychild.cfm.

21. Darcy Olsen, "Assessing Proposals for Preschool and Kindergarten," *Goldwater Institute Policy Report*, Feb. 8, 2005.

22. *Ibid.*

23. Quoted in Jane Carroll Andrade, "Kindergarten May Be Too Late," *State Legislatures*, June 2002, p. 24.

24. Lynn A. Karoly, *et al.*, *Investing in Our Children: What We Know and Don't Know About the Costs and Benefits of Early Childhood Interventions*, RAND Corporation, 1998, p. 11. www.rand.org/publica-tions/MR/MR898/.

25. Quoted in Peter Gordon, "Robert Owen," Prospects: The Quarterly Review of Education, UNESCO International Bureau of Education, 1999, pp. 279-96.

26. Quoted in Maris A. Vinovskis, "Early Childhood Education: Then and Now," *Daedalus*, 1993, p. 151.

27. *Ibid.*

28. Quoted in Vinovskis, *ibid.*

29. Quoted in Vinovskis, *ibid.*

30. *Ibid.*

31. Karoly, *op. cit.*, p. 12.

32. *Ibid.*, p. 15..

33. Lyndon B. Johnson, Special Message to Congress, March 16, 1964, www.fordham.edu/halsall/mod/ 1964johnson-warpoverty.html.

34. Susan Muenchow and Edward Zigler, *Head Start: The Inside Story of America's Most Successful Educational Experiment* (1992), p. 3.

35. Quoted in Muenchow, *op. cit.*, p. 4.

36. Vinovskis, *op. cit.*

37. Muenchow, *op. cit.*

38. Quoted in Vinovskis, *op. cit.*

39. Karoly, *op. cit.*, p. 42.

40. Scott Scrivner and Barbara Wolfe, "Universal Preschool: Much to Gain But Who Will Pay?" Institute for Research on Poverty, July 2003, www.fcd-us.org/uploadDocs/UWisc%20wolfe.pdf.

41. *Ibid.*

42. For background, see William Triplett, "State Budget Crises," *CQ Researcher*, Oct. 3, 2003, pp. 821-844.

43. Steven Barnett, *et al.*, "The State of Preschool: 2004 State Preschool Yearbook," National Institute for Early Education Research, 2004.

44. "Good Start, Grow Smart: The Bush Administration's Early Childhood Initiative," www.whitehouse.gov/infocus/earlychildhood/earlychildhood.html.

45. www.saveheadstart.org/032603release.html.

46. www.saveheadstart.org/Bush_Administration_letter_to_HS_officials.pdf.

47. "Head Start: Further Development Could Allow Results of New Test to Be Used for Decision Making," Government Accountability Office, May 2005.

48. Quoted in Barbara Miner, "Head Start or Head Backwards?" *Rethinking Schools*, Fall 2003, www.rethinkingschools.org.

49. William Swindell and Kate Schuler, "Scaled-Back Head Start Bill a Squeaker Win for GOP," *CQ Weekly*, July 26, 2003, p. 1895.

50. William Swindell and Kate Schuler, "Just Enough GOP Moderates Swayed to Pass Head Start Bill," *CQ Today*, July 25, 2003.

51. J.P. Shonkoff and D.A. Phillips, eds., *From Neurons to Neighborhoods: The Science of Early Childhood Development* (2000).

52. Barnett, *op. cit.*

53. Deborah Stipek, "Early Childhood Education at a Crossroads," *Harvard Education Letter*, July/August 2005, www.edletter.org/current/crossroads.shtml.

54. Barbara Bowman, "Teaching Young Children Well: Implications for 21st Century Educational Policies," *Perspectives on Urban Education*, www.urbanedjournal.org/archive/Issue%201/FeatureArticles/article0001.pdf.

BIBLIOGRAPHY

Books

Ceglowski, Deborah, *Inside a Head Start Center: Developing Policies from Practice*, Teachers College Press, 1998.
An associate professor of child development at the University of North Carolina at Charlotte describes her experiences working in a Head Start center in rural Minnesota and the conclusions she drew about the federal program's policies and administration.

Tobin, Joseph, David Wu and Dana Davidson, *Preschool in Three Cultures: Japan, China, and the United States*, Yale University Press, 1991.
An Arizona State University education professor examines the different behavior and learning goals that three very different cultures emphasize in preschool education.

Vinovskis, Maris A., *The Birth of Head Start: Preschool Education Policies in the Kennedy and Johnson Administrations*, University of Chicago Press, 2005.
A history professor at the University of Michigan outlines political and policy debates about nationalized early-childhood education that surrounded the founding of Head Start.

Zigler, Edward, and Sally J. Styfco, eds., *The Head Start Debates*, Paul H. Brookes Publishing Co., Inc., 2004.
Fifty-three education, medicine and social-work researchers with a variety of political perspectives discuss Head Start's goals, effectiveness and potential.

Zigler, Edward, and Susan Muenchow, *Head Start: The Inside Story of America's Most Successful Education Experiment*, Basic Books, 1994.
A Yale University psychologist (Zigler) who was a founder and early federal administrator of the Head Start programs recounts the program's history through the 1980s.

Articles

Kirp, David, "All My Children," *The New York Times*, July 31, 2005, Sec. 4A, p. 20.
The author, a professor of public policy at the University of California at Berkeley, describes current American

attitudes toward universal preschool and how they are playing out in practice.

Vinovskis, Maris A., "Early Childhood Education: Then and Now," *Daedalus*, Winter 1993, p. 151.
A University of Michigan history professor describes early-childhood education in 19th- and 20th-century Europe and America.

Reports

Barnett, W. Steven, *et al.*, "The State of Preschool: 2004 State Preschool Yearbook," National Institute for Early Education Research, 2004.
An economist and education economics professor at Rutgers University assembles state-by-state information on the political history, educational philosophy, administrative structures, enrollment statistics and funding sources for the nation's publicly funded preschool programs.

Bowman, Barbara T., *et al.*, eds., "Eager to Learn: Educating Our Preschoolers," National Academies Press, 2000.
A panel of researchers and educators explains how children's early experiences affect their later learning ability and examines the results achieved by competing theories of preschool education.

Karoly, Lynn A., *et al.*, "Assessing Costs and Benefits of Early Childhood Intervention Programs: Overview and Application to the Starting Early Starting Smart Program," RAND, 2001.
Researchers from a public-policy research group analyze the history, costs and benefits of early-childhood interventions against poverty and disability as they relate to early-childhood initiatives proposed by the Bush administration.

Lynch, Robert G., "Exceptional Returns: Economic, Fiscal, and Social Benefits of Investment in Early Childhood Development," Economic Policy Institute, 2004.
An associate professor of economics at Washington College in St. Louis analyzes the potential of early-childhood interventions to cut the monetary and social costs of poverty.

Olsen, Darcy, "Assessing Proposals for Preschool and Kindergarten: Essential Information for Parents, Taxpayers, and Policymakers," Goldwater Institute, February 2005.
The president of a conservative think tank presents evidence and analysis disputing the idea that universal preschool would be of value in the United States.

Shonkoff, Jack P., and Deborah A. Phillips, eds., "From Neurons to Neighborhoods: The Science of Early Childhood Development," National Academies Press, 2000.
A panel of researchers examines the light that brain science sheds on children's development and early learning.

Snow, Catherine E., *et al.*, eds., "Preventing Reading Difficulties in Young Children," National Academies Press, 1998.
A panel of scholars examines the biological, social and cultural factors that put children at risk for being poor readers and describes strategies to combat those factors for preschool children.

For More Information

Administration for Children and Families, 370 L'Enfant Promenade, S.W., Washington, DC 20201; www.acf.hhs.gov. The federal agency that oversees Head Start and other family-assistance programs.

Center for Law and Social Policy, 1015 15th St., N.W., Suite 400, Washington, DC 20005; (202) 906-8000; www.clasp.org. Liberal-leaning nonprofit organization that advocactes for low-income families and children.

Children's Defense Fund, 25 E St., N.W., Washington, DC 20001; (202) 628-8787; www.childrensdefense.org. National advocacy group that supports and provides information on programs for children, especially those living in poverty.

Fight Crime: Invest in Kids, 1212 New York Ave., N.W., Suite 300, Washington, DC 20005; (202) 776-0027; www.fightcrime.org. National advocacy organization of law-enforcement officials and others that support publicly funded preschool education.

FPG Child Development Institute, University of North Carolina, CD#8180, Chapel Hill, NC 27599-8180; (919) 966-4250; www.fpg.unc.edu. Provides scientific and policy research on early-childhood development and preschool education.

Goldwater Institute, 500 East Coronado Road, Phoenix, AZ 85004; (602) 462-5000; www.goldwaterinstitute.org. Provides research on education topics.

Institute for Research on Poverty, University of Wisconsin-Madison, 1180 Observatory Dr., 3412 Social Science Building, Madison, WI 53706-1393; (608) 262-6358; www.irp.wisc.edu. Federally funded interdisciplinary academic center that conducts research into the causes and consequences of poverty.

John Locke Foundation, 200 West Morgan St., Raleigh, NC 27601; (919) 828-3876; www.johnlocke.org. Provides analysis of education initiatives and policy, especially state-funded preschool, from a conservative viewpoint.

National Association for the Education of Young Children, 1313 L St. N.W., Suite 500, Washington, DC 20005; (202) 232-8777; www.naeyc.org. Provides research on developmentally appropriate education for children.

National Head Start Association, 1651 Prince St., Alexandria, VA 22314; (703) 739-0875; www.nhsa.org. Represents most Head Start programs.

National Institute for Early Education Research, 120 Albany St., Suite 500, New Brunswick, NJ 08901; (732) 932-4350; http://nieer.org. Research group — based at Rutgers University — specializing in early-childhood education.

Pre-K Now, 1025 F St., N.W., Suite 900, Washington, DC 20004; (202) 862-9871; www.preknow.org. Advocacy organization that provides information about universally available preschool for the United States.

Yale Child Study Center, 230 South Frontage Rd., New Haven, CT, 06520; (203) 785-2513; http://info.med.yale.edu/chldstdy/. A Yale University School of Medicine Program that provides research on child development.

2

No Child Left Behind

Barbara Mantel

President Bush visits with students in St. Louis, Mo., on Jan. 5, 2004, the second anniversary of the No Child Left Behind Act. Bush has called the sweeping overhaul of federal education policy the start of "a new era, a new time in public education." But today the bipartisan legislation is under heavy criticism from Republicans and Democrats alike. Besides seeking exemptions from parts of the law, legislators are pressing Congress for more money to implement the act.

From *CQ Researcher*,
May 27, 2005.

Politics indeed makes for strange bedfellows: There was President Bush standing on a Boston stage flanked by four jubilant legislators, two Republicans and two Democrats, including liberal lion Sen. Edward M. Kennedy of Massachusetts. The occasion was the signing on Jan. 8, 2002, of the No Child Left Behind Act — a sweeping, bipartisan overhaul of federal education policy.

Cheering crowds greeted Bush and the four lawmakers that day as they touted the new law on a whirlwind, 12-hour tour of three states, with the president calling the legislation the start of "a new era, a new time in public education."

Kennedy, who played a key role in negotiating the bill's passage, told Bush: "What a difference it has made this year with your leadership." [1]

The law is actually the most recent reauthorization of the Elementary and Secondary Education Act (ESEA), which since 1965 has tried to raise the academic performance of all students.

"This legislation holds out great promise for education," said education researcher G. Gage Kingsbury, director of research at the Northwest Evaluation Association, in Lake Oswego, Ore. "But it also has strong requirements and includes a host of provisions that have never been tried on this scale before." [2]

No Child Left Behind (NCLB) increases the reach of the federal government into the management of local schools and raises the stakes for schools, districts and states. It increases funding for schools serving poor students, mandates "highly qualified" teachers in every classroom and holds schools that accept federal funds accountable for raising the achievement of all students. Schools that

Few States Make the Grade on Teacher Quality

Only three states — Connecticut, Louisiana and South Carolina — received a grade of A for their efforts to improve teacher quality, according to a 2005 assessment by *Education Week*. In every state except New Mexico, more than 50 percent of secondary teachers majored in the core academic subject they teach. But only eight states had more than 75 percent of secondary school teachers who majored in their core subject.

Rating State Efforts to Improve Teacher Quality

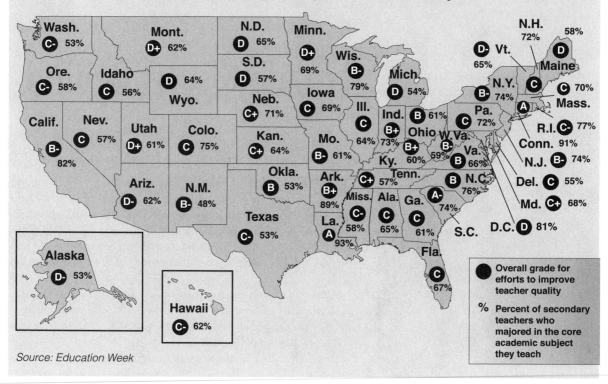

Source: Education Week

don't meet state benchmarks two years in a row are labeled "in need of improvement" and suffer sanctions.

Most significantly, NCLB sets a deadline: By 2014 all students must be grade-level proficient in reading and math — as evidenced by their scores on annual tests in grades 3-8, and once in high school. (*See sidebar, p. 27.*)

But more than three years after its passage, the bipartisan accord that produced the bill appears badly frayed. Kennedy now says No Child Left Behind "has been underfunded, mismanaged and poorly implemented and is becoming the most spectacular broken promise of this Republican administration and Congress. America's children deserve better." [3]

In the states, politicians from both parties are equally unhappy, including GOP legislators from some "red states" that overwhelmingly supported Bush in last year's presidential election. "I wish they'd take the stinking money and go back to Washington," said state Rep. Steven Mascaro, R-Utah. [4]

"We have to fight back," Gov. John Baldacci, D-Maine, said. "We have to tell them we're not going to take it any more." [5]

It hasn't been just talk. In early May, Utah's Republican governor signed legislation giving precedence to the state's education policies when they conflict with NCLB, and in the past year and a half more than 30

The ABCs of NCLB

Here are the basic provisions of the No Child Left Behind Act, which spells out its standards and requirements in more than 1,000 pages of regulations:

Standards and Testing — As in the previous version of the law, each state must adopt challenging standards for what its students should know and be able to do. Academic standards must contain coherent and rigorous content and encourage the teaching of advanced skills. States must also develop tests aligned to the standards and establish cutoff scores that classify student achievement as basic, proficient or advanced. What has changed is the amount of testing states must do. Beginning in September 2005, states must test children annually in grades 3-8 and once in high school. Previously, schoolchildren had to be tested only four times in grades K-12.

Public Reporting — For the first time, states must publicly report their test results, with student scores broken down into four subgroups: economically disadvantaged students; major racial and ethnic groups; students with disabilities and students with limited English proficiency. States must report each school's progress in raising student performance and the difference in teacher qualifications in high-poverty versus low-poverty schools.

Accountability — All students must reach proficiency in reading and math by 2014. States must establish annual benchmarks for their schools, with special emphasis on closing achievement gaps between different groups of students. Since 1994 states had been required to make "adequate yearly progress" (AYP) in raising achievement, but there was no firm timetable or deadline for students reaching proficiency. Now if a school does not make AYP, the state and district must develop a two-year plan to help the school improve.

Sanctions — If a school receiving Title I funds — designed to improve the performance of low-income students — does not make AYP in raising student performance for two years in a row, the state must designate it a school "in need of improvement." [1] Most states are applying this rule to all schools in a Title I district, even those that do not take Title I money. Students in these schools must be given the option of transferring out, and if a school fails to achieve its AYP for three consecutive years, it must pay for tutoring, after-school programs and summer school for those low-income students who remain. After four years, the state must restructure the school.

Teachers — For the first time, teachers must be "highly qualified," meaning they have a college degree and are licensed or certified by the state. Newly hired middle-school teachers must have a major or pass a test demonstrating their knowledge in the subjects they teach. Veteran teachers can do the same or demonstrate their competency through an alternative system developed by each state.

[1] About 55 percent of the schools in the nation's 100 largest districts were eligible for Title I funds in the 2001/2002 school year; http://nces.ed.gov/pubs2003/100_largest/table_05_1.asp.

states have introduced bills that would release them from some of the law's requirements.

Besides seeking exemptions from parts of the law, legislators are pressing Congress for more money to implement the act. Much of the controversy stems from the fact that Congress has appropriated $27 billion less than it authorized for the law's implementation.

But the act's supporters say enough money is being provided, pointing out that federal funding for public education has increased by more than 30 percent since the NCLB was enacted. "The education reforms contained in the No Child Left Behind Act are coupled with historic increases in K-12 funding," according to the Web site of Sen. Judd Gregg, R-N.H., who made the whirlwind trip with Bush and Kennedy three years ago. [6]

Nevertheless, in April the National Education Association, the nation's largest teachers' union, sued the Department of Education on the grounds that the act is not properly funded. In addition, Connecticut also is threatening to sue, estimating that NCLB will cost the state an extra $41.6 million dollars in the next few years. The atmosphere has gotten so disagreeable at times that Secretary of Education Margaret Spellings angrily called Connecticut officials "un-American."

Part of the states' resentment stems from the fact that Congress provides only 8 percent of total funding for public education — $501.3 billion in the last school year — but since the 1960s has passed laws giving the Department of Education increasing powers over the nation's 96,000 schools. [7] The NCLB is the most far reaching yet.

Supporters of the act say it represents an evolutionary change, while critics say it is a revolutionary incursion of the federal government into the historic domain of the states.

"I don't know any educator or parent who doesn't think our schools should be accountable," said state Rep. Margaret Dayton, R-Orem. "The question is: To whom should they be accountable? Under No Child Left Behind our local schools are accountable to Washington, D.C., and here in Utah, we think our schools should be accountable to the parents and the communities where they are." [8]

Even supporters acknowledge that NCLB's provisions have been overwhelming for states without the administrative staff to implement the law.

In 2004, No Child Left Behind became "a significant force affecting the operations and decisions of states, school districts and schools," according to the Center on Education Policy, an independent advocate for public education. [9] For example, the law has compelled states and school districts to step up efforts to test students in more grades and put "highly qualified" teachers in every classroom. In addition, for the first time entire school districts have been labeled "in need of improvement."

However, as the law's requirements take hold, the debate about its fairness and efficacy has been escalating. Besides the debate over funding, critics argue that the law is too rigid and that too many schools — even good schools — are being told they need to improve. This has sparked widespread opposition to President's Bush's proposal to extend the law's annual testing requirements to high school students. (*See "At Issue," p. 41.*)

On the other side of the debate, many of NCLB's staunchest defenders worry that the Department of Education has become too flexible in implementing the law, citing a recent relaxation of requirements for testing disabled students and department approval of what some see as lax state plans to ensure that veteran teachers are "highly qualified."

And voices from all sides call for more guidance and technical support to localities from the Department of Education.

As the public discussion grows louder leading up to the law's reauthorization fight in 2007, coalitions have begun to form. The American Association of School Administrators, the Children's Defense Fund, the Learning Disabilities Association of America, the National Education Association and several other groups joined together last fall to call for significant revisions in the law. Proponents — including the Citizens' Commission on Civil Rights, the National Alliance of Black School Educators, Just for Kids, the Education Trust and the Business Roundtable — formed their own coalition, called the Achievement Alliance, to vigorously defend the law.

Here are some of the questions parents, educators, children's advocates, lawmakers, and researchers are asking:

Has No Child Left Behind raised student achievement?

The goal of the NCLB law is to ensure that by 2014 all children are at grade-level proficiency in reading and math. The law requires states to measure student achievement by testing children in grades 3-8 every year, and once in high school.

But each state determines its own academic standards, the courses taught, the standardized tests used and the cutoff scores that define a student as proficient. Thus, the rigor varies between the states, making it impossible to compare one state to another. Colorado may have reported 87 percent of its fourth-graders proficient in reading in 2003 and Massachusetts 56 percent, but no one knows what that says about the relative achievement of their students. [10]

It is possible, however, to look at student achievement within a state and ask, for example, how this year's fourth-graders compare to last year's.

With a growing number of states administering annual tests, researchers have conducted some preliminary studies. They all show that student achievement, for the most part, is improving.

The Center on Education Policy surveyed states and a sampling of school districts and reported that 73 percent of states and 72 percent of districts said student achievement is improving. In addition, states and districts were more likely to say that achievement gaps between white and black students, white and Hispanic students, and English-language learners and other students were narrowing rather than widening or staying the same. [11]

Similarly, the Council of the Great City Schools, a coalition of 65 of the nation's largest urban school systems, reported that while math and reading scores in

Thousands of Schools Missed Progress Targets

Eleven thousand public schools — or nearly 12 percent of the nation's 96,000 public schools — failed in 2004 for the second year in a row to meet "adequate yearly progress" (AYP) targets set by the No Child Left Behind law. Such schools are labeled "in need of improvement" and must offer all students the right to transfer; after missing AYP for three consecutive years, they must offer low-income students supplemental services, like after-school tutoring. After four years, the state must restructure the school.

Number of Public Schools Needing Improvement
(based on failure to meet "adequate yearly progress" targets)

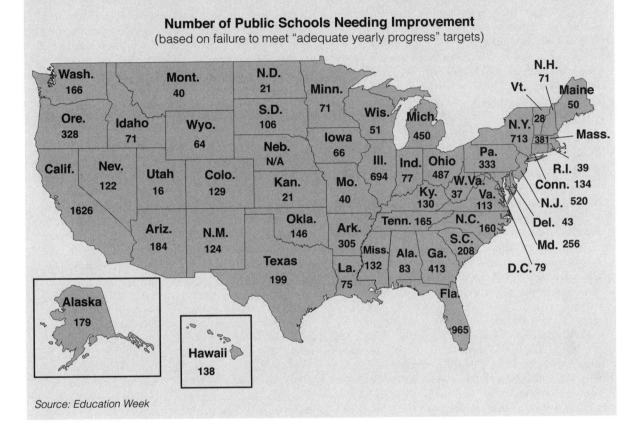

Source: Education Week

urban schools remain lower than national averages, they are rising and achievement gaps are narrowing. [12]

The Education Trust, a nonprofit advocate of school reform, also analyzed proficiency rates since No Child Left Behind took effect. It found that in most states it studied, achievement scores of elementary school students had risen, and achievement gaps had narrowed. But when the Trust looked at middle and high schools, the results were more mixed. While the majority of states in the study reported an increase in the percentage of proficient students, there was much less success in narrowing achievement gaps. [13]

Delaware is a case in point. The state has made some of the largest strides in raising achievement and narrowing gaps among elementary students. For instance, the gap in Delaware between the percentage of reading-proficient white and Hispanic fifth-graders narrowed from 31 points in 2001 to less than five points in 2004, and for African-American students, the gap narrowed from 22 points to 16. [14] But in middle schools, achievement gaps have actually widened.

"It is a little harder to get a reform groundswell in middle schools and high schools," says Delaware's Secretary of Education Valerie Woodruff. "In math, for

Is Testing Crowding Out Art and Recess?

Testing required by the No Child Left Behind Act is taking a toll on education, says George Wood, an Ohio high school principal and director of The Forum for Education and Democracy. "School people are no fools," Wood wrote in the 2004 book *Many Children Left Behind*. "Tell them what they will be measured on, and they will try to measure up."

"Test preparation crowds out much else that parents have taken for granted in their schools," Wood said. Recess for elementary school students, nap time for kindergarteners and music and art for middle school students are some of the things being eliminated from the school day, he contends, along with reductions in class time for social studies and creative writing.

Diane Rentner, project coordinator at the Center on Education Policy, says the cutbacks haven't been too bad so far. "It's not huge, it's not a revolution yet," she says. In a March 2005 survey of school districts, the center found "a slight movement toward cutting down on other subjects to focus on reading and math," Rentner says.

More than two-thirds of districts reported that instructional time on subjects other than math and reading had been reduced minimally or not at all. However, 27 percent of the districts reported that social studies class time had been reduced somewhat or to a great extent, and close to 25 percent said instruction time in science, art and music had been reduced.

While the center's findings don't support a revolutionary shift in class time, Rentner still calls the trend worrisome and expects that as state proficiency benchmarks rise, there may be additional pressure on schools to focus more time on reading and math. "It would be sad if there were no arts in the schools, and students didn't learn civic education," she says.

Rentner also points out another potentially troubling survey result: The poorer the school district, the more likely it was to require schools to allot a specific amount of time to math and reading. "You could jump to the next conclusion that low-income kids are receiving a less rich curriculum," Rentner says. While that might be necessary in the short term to bring kids closer to proficiency in math and reading, Rentner hopes that it doesn't have to continue.

It is this impact on low-income and minority schools that most concerns Wood. An opponent of NCLB, Wood calls for a moratorium on high-stakes testing until more research shows it to have some link to student success after leaving high school.

But Daria Hall, a policy analyst at the Education Trust, which generally supports the goals and methods of No Child Left Behind while criticizing the government's implementation of the law, says that's the wrong response. "We don't deny that focusing so much on math and reading means that other subjects might not receive the attention they deserve," says Hall. But that doesn't have to happen, she says, citing schools, many in poor districts, that have integrated math and reading instruction into their other subjects.

"So, for example, there is no need to give short shrift to social studies," she claims. "We can teach the content of social studies while at the same time covering state standards on reading." The same can be done, she says, with math and science.

But it's not something that one teacher or even one school can do alone, Hall adds. "There needs to be research from the U.S. Department of Education on how to effectively integrate standards across the curriculum," she says. "It needs to really be a systemic effort."

example, we don't have enough well qualified teachers at the middle school level."

The fundamental question is how much of the documented improvement is a result of No Child Left Behind. Daria Hall, a policy analyst at the Education Trust, says it is a significant amount. Educators "are using the standards to develop a challenging curriculum for all students," she says. "They are using assessment results to inform their instruction in the classroom."

NCLB, Hall says, gives administrators leverage to make needed changes.

Diane Rentner, project coordinator at the Center on Education Policy, is hearing something different. The center did not specifically ask state and district officials if they thought the law was responsible for achievement gains. But Rentner says district officials later said they "were almost offended that No Child Left Behind would be viewed as this great catalyst of change because they felt like they had been working for years to improve student achievement."

"Our math curriculum has been completely reviewed from K-12 and in the majority of cases exceeds state standards," says Margo Sorrick, an assistant superintendent in Wheaton, Ill. For instance, the district now requires three years rather two years of math for high school graduation. "These changes have nothing to do with No Child Left Behind," says Sorrick.

But the law does shine a new light on those reforms. Now that states must report their progress in raising student achievement, the press routinely covers the release of so-called state report cards. Stiffening graduation requirements, revising the curriculum and replacing staff at the worst schools have taken on more urgency, Rentner says. "We jokingly say the news media have become the enforcer of the law," she adds.

But trying to figure out the law's exact impact is still all but impossible. Besides the difficulty of teasing out the roles of pre- and post-NCLB reforms, there are gaps in the data. Most states started testing students only six or seven years ago, and many changed their tests, making before-and-after comparisons unreliable.

Several experts also warn that initial gains in achievement scores may be deceptive. Brian Stecher, a senior social scientist at the Rand Corporation, a nonprofit research organization, says that on new, high-stakes tests teachers often feel pressure to coach students in test-taking skills and to teach the material emphasized on the test. "That can allow you to get initially a relatively big gain in scores," Stecher says, "and then the increase tapers off."

That's of particular concern to states because the pace of recent improvement is not fast enough to ensure 100 percent student proficiency by 2014. "Progress needs to be accelerated," Hall says bluntly.

Are too many schools being labeled "in need of improvement?"

Holding states accountable for student achievement is central to No Child Left Behind. The law gives states a firm goal and a firm deadline, and to reach it each state must come up with annual benchmarks. In Wisconsin, for instance, 67.5 percent of a school's students must be proficient in reading this school year, 87 percent six years later and finally 100 percent in 2014. [15]

But it's not enough for a school to look at its students as a single, undifferentiated block. NCLB requires schools to divide students into subgroups — ethnic, racial, low-income, disabled and English-language learner — and each must meet the proficiency benchmarks as well.

Schools also must test at least 95 percent of students in a subgroup, meet state-determined attendance requirements and improve high school graduation rates.

Schools that meet all of these targets are deemed to have made "adequate yearly progress" (AYP). But if a school misses just one target it doesn't make AYP, and the district and state must create a two-year intervention plan. Options include reducing class size, providing extra help for disadvantaged students and increasing professional development for teachers. Local and state officials decide on the details, and the federal government provides extra funding.

Sanctions prescribed by the law, however, kick in when a school doesn't make AYP for two consecutive years. Such schools, if they take Title I funds, are labeled "in need of improvement" and must offer all students the right to transfer; after missing AYP for three consecutive years, they must offer low-income students supplemental services, like after-school tutoring. After four years, the state must restructure the school.

This system of accountability is among the most contentious elements of NCLB. While praising the overall goals of the law, the National Conference of State Legislatures called the system rigid and overly prescriptive. Too many schools, it said, are being labeled "in need of improvement," and the law, therefore, "spreads resources too thinly, over too many schools, and reduces the chances that schools that truly are in need can be helped." [16]

Last year, 11,008 public schools — nearly 12 percent of the nation's total — were identified as needing improvement. [17] Critics of the law see that number rising dramatically. "Essentially, all schools will fail to meet the unrealistic goal of 100 percent proficient or above," wrote testing expert Robert Linn, "and No Child Left Behind will have turned into No School Succeeding." [18]

But Keri Briggs, senior adviser to Acting Deputy Secretary of Education Raymond Simon, strongly disagrees. "We have identified schools that have beat expectations; there are several in many states," says Briggs. "We know it's possible."

Critics, however, say the accountability system has several flaws, such as not recognizing progress made by schools that start with large numbers of low-performing students. A school that significantly raises the percentage of students reading at proficiency, for example, would still not make AYP if that percentage remains below the state benchmark. Such schools "should be given credit," says Scott Young, a senior policy specialist at the National Conference of State Legislatures.

But the law does provide a so-called safe harbor alternative for these schools: If a subgroup of students falls short of the benchmark, the school can still make AYP if the number below the proficiency level is decreased by 10 percent from the year before. But according to Linn, that's something even the best schools would have difficulty accomplishing. "Only a tiny fraction of schools meet AYP through the safe-harbor provision because it is so extreme," Linn wrote. [19]

After protests from both Republican and Democratic governors, Secretary Spellings announced in April she would appoint a panel to consider allowing states to use a "growth model" to reward schools whose students make significant progress but that still miss AYP. Such a model would follow individual students as they move from grade to grade. By contrast, the current system compares the current fourth-grade class, for example, with last year's fourth-graders.

Kingsbury, at the Northwest Evaluation Association, likes the growth-model idea but says goals and timetables are needed. Otherwise, Kingsbury explains, "there is no guarantee students will end up at a high level of proficiency when they graduate."

Another frequent complaint is that the accountability system is too blunt an instrument. "The problem," says Patricia Sullivan, director of the Center on Education Policy, "is the lack of distinction between the school that misses by a little and the school that misses by a lot." The school that misses the benchmark for one subgroup for two consecutive years is identified as needing improvement just like the school that misses the benchmark for several subgroups. Both face the same sanction: All students would have the option to transfer.

Since urban schools tend to be more diverse and have more subgroups, it is harder for them to make AYP. But the Education Trust's Hall says those who complain care more about the adults working in urban schools than the kids. "Is it fair to expect less of schools that are educating diverse student bodies?" Hall asks. "Is it fair to those students? Absolutely not."

The Department of Education has signaled its willingness to compromise, to a degree. Many districts have complained that requiring all students with disabilities to be grade-level proficient by 2014 is unfair and unrealistic. The law does allow 1 percent of all students — those with significant cognitive disabilities — to take alternative assessments. Secretary Spellings recently declared that another 2 percent — those with persistent academic disabilities — could take alternative tests, geared toward their abilities and not necessarily at grade level. States would have to apply to the Department of Education in order to use this option.

The reaction from educators was muted. Betty J. Sternberg, Connecticut's education commissioner, said, "The percentages are fine. They help us. The problem may be in the details of what they are requiring us to do to have access to the flexibility." [20]

But advocates for disabled students worry that the department is backpedaling. Suzanne Fornaro, board president of the Learning Disability Association of America, is particularly concerned about students with learning disabilities: "If the changes result in lowering expectations, they might result in decreasing a student's access to the general curriculum and high-quality instruction."

Is No Child Left Behind improving the quality of teaching?

Teaching quality may be the single most important in-school factor in how well students learn. While it's difficult to know precisely what makes effective teachers, there are some common yardsticks, including mastery of their subject area. Yet government surveys show that, "One out of four secondary classes (24 percent) in core academic subjects are assigned to a teacher lacking even a college minor in the subject being taught." (*See map, p. 26.*) That figure rises to 29 percent in high-minority schools and 34 percent in high-poverty schools. [21]

No one blames teachers. It's rarely by choice that teachers are assigned to a subject out of their field. But NCLB requires a "highly qualified" teacher in every classroom by the end of the 2005/2006 school year. Highly qualified teachers must have a bachelor's degree, be licensed or certified by the state and demonstrate that they know each subject they teach. New teachers can qualify by either passing a state test or having completed a college major in their subject area. Veteran teachers have a third option: an alternative evaluation created by each state, known by the acronym HOUSSE (high objective uniform state standard of evaluation).

Most states are likely to claim success by the deadline. Many say they are already close. But whether teaching actually will have changed is less certain. In "Quality Counts 2005," a report by *Education Week*, researchers graded states on their efforts to improve teacher quality, looking at the amount of out-of-field teaching allowed, the quality of the state certification process and the amount and quality of professional development. (*See map, p. 26.*) Only three states got As, 14 got Bs and the rest received Cs and Ds. [22]

No Child Left Behind's ability to alter the picture may be limited, critics say. They point to the problems rural and urban schools are having recruiting and retaining skilled teachers and to many states' less-than-rigorous HOUSSE plans.

"I love my job. I know how kids learn," says Jon Runnalls, Montana's "Teacher of the Year" in 2003, "and for someone to come and say that now I'm not highly qualified, that's a slap in the face." Runnalls has taught middle school science for 31 years, but his college degree is in elementary education with an emphasis in science. According to NCLB, he'd have to go back to school, take a state test or pass the state's alternative evaluation. But Montana doesn't have a test, and its HOUSSE plan has not yet been approved by the Department of Education. It's really not a plan at all; it simply says that a veteran certified teacher is, by default, highly qualified.

Not surprisingly, Montana reports 98.8 percent of its classes are taught by highly qualified teachers.

Ten other states, like Montana, don't evaluate veteran teachers, arguing that the state certification process is a rigorous enough hurdle. But even many of the states that do have more elaborate HOUSSE plans have faced criticism.

Most states use a system in which veteran teachers accumulate points until they have enough to be considered highly qualified. "The most prevalent problem is that states offer too many options that veteran teachers can use to prove they are highly qualified — options that often have nothing to do with content knowledge," says Kate Walsh, president of the National Council on Teacher Quality. While states give points for university-level coursework, states also give them for sponsoring a school club, mentoring a new teacher and belonging to a national teacher organization. Teachers also get points for experience.

But according to Walsh, "The purpose of HOUSSE is to ensure that teachers know their content, not to count the number of years in the classroom." [23]

Even with the flexibility offered by the HOUSSE option, some schools in rural and urban areas are struggling to meet the law's requirements, although the Department of Education has given rural districts a three-year extension. After studying a rural district in Alabama that offered a $5,000 signing bonus to new teachers, researchers from the Southeast Center for Teaching Quality noted: "Central office staff told us that to ensure the bonus worked, they could only require recipients work two years. Most teachers take the bonus, serve their two years and leave." Urban districts the researchers studied struggled to find experienced teachers prepared to work with few resources and students with diverse learning and emotional needs. [24]

As a result, rural and urban schools are more likely to assign teachers to instruct in multiple subjects, often outside their field. These schools are also more reliant on teachers who have entered the profession through some alternative route, usually with little or no classroom experience. No Child Left Behind says such teachers are highly qualified if enrolled in an intensive induction and mentoring program and receiving high-quality professional development.

But Tom Blamford, an associate director at the National Education Association, says the quality of these programs is often poor. "We know what it takes to change classroom practice," Blamford says. "It has to do with knowledge, coaching, feedback and more knowledge, and it's a cyclical process. It's very rare that professional development meets those standards." Usually, he says, it's someone standing in front of a group of teachers lecturing them.

What rural and urban schools need to do, according to Scott Emerick, a policy associate at the Southeast Center for Teaching Quality, is use federal funds more effectively to improve working conditions, design better professional-development programs and devise sophisticated financial incentives to attract and retain teachers. But Emerick says they often don't know how, and the federal government is not providing enough guidance.

"These districts need on-the-ground assistance beyond accessing a federal Web site that tells you what other people are doing," he says.

C H R O N O L O G Y

1950s-1960s *A legal challenge and federal legislation initiate an era of education reform.*

1954 In *Brown v. Board of Education*, the Supreme Court decides "separate educational facilities are inherently unequal."

1958 Congress passes National Defense Education Act in response to the Soviet launch of *Sputnik*.

1965 President Lyndon B. Johnson signs Elementary and Secondary Education Act (ESEA) providing funds to school districts to help disadvantaged students.

1966 Congress amends ESEA to add Title VI, establishing grants for the education of handicapped children.

1966 Sociologist James S. Coleman's "Equality of Educational Opportunity" report concludes that disadvantaged black children learn better in well-integrated classrooms, helping to launch an era of busing students to achieve racial balance in public schools.

1968 Congress amends ESEA to add Title VII, called the Bilingual Education Act.

1970s-1980s *Studies criticize student achievement, and the standards movement gains momentum.*

1975 Coleman issues a new report concluding busing had failed, largely because it had prompted "white flight."

1980 U.S. Department of Education is established, ending education role of Department of Health, Education, and Welfare.

1983 National Commission on Excellence's "A Nation at Risk" report warns of a rising tide of mediocrity in education and recommends a common core curriculum nationwide.

1989 President George H.W. Bush convenes nation's governors in Charlottesville, Va., for first National Education Summit, which establishes six broad objectives to be reached by 2000.

1989 National Council of Teachers of Mathematics publishes *Curriculum and Evaluation Standards for School Mathematics.*

1990s-2000s *Congress requires more standards, testing and accountability from the states.*

1994 President Bill Clinton signs the Goals 2000: Educate America Act, which adopts the goals of the first National Education Summit. The act creates the National Education Standards and Improvement Council with the authority to approve or reject states' academic standards. The council, however, becomes ineffective after Republicans take control of Congress during midterm elections and object to the increasing federal role in education. . . . Clinton later signs Improving America's Schools Act of 1994, requiring significantly more testing and accountability than the original ESEA.

Jan. 8, 2002 President George W. Bush signs No Child Left Behind Act, increasing funding to states while also increasing federal mandates and sanctions to an unprecedented degree. States must increase student testing, place "highly qualified" teachers in every classroom and meet state-determined annual targets for student proficiency in reading and math. By 2014, all students must be 100 percent proficient. Title I schools not meeting annual targets must offer transfers to students and provide supplemental services, like tutoring.

April 7, 2005 Secretary of Education Margaret Spellings announces her willingness to provide some flexibility to states in meeting the requirements of No Child Left Behind.

April 19, 2005 Republican-dominated Utah legislature passes a bill giving priority to state educational goals when those conflict with No Child Left Behind and ordering officials to spend as little state money as possible to comply with the federal law.

April 20, 2005 The nation's largest teachers' union and eight school districts in Michigan, Texas and Vermont sue the Department of Education, accusing the government of violating a No Child Left Behind Act provision that states cannot be forced to spend their own money to meet the law's requirements.

Are Schools' Graduation Rates Accurate?

The No Child Left Behind Act holds schools accountable not just for student achievement but also for graduation rates. High schools must raise their graduation rates if they are to make adequate yearly progress. Increasing the percentage of graduates is a worthy goal, but it serves another purpose as well. The requirement is designed to prevent schools from improving achievement scores by encouraging their lowest-performing students to leave.

The system depends, of course, on accurate reporting. But researchers say that high school graduation rates reported by most states are just not believable.

The problem: States don't really know how many kids are dropping out of school.

States "consistently underestimate the number of dropouts, thereby overstating the graduation rates, sometimes by very large amounts," says Jay P. Greene, a senior fellow at the Manhattan Institute for Policy Research. In a recent report, Greene called some states' rates "so improbably high they would be laughable if the issue were not so serious." [1]

Although a few school districts have been accused of falsifying dropout data, researchers don't believe deception is at the root of the problem. Rather, they say the cause is more benign: Most schools don't know what happens to students who leave. Did a student transfer to another school? Move to another state? Or really drop out? Trying to answer those questions may be a secretary or clerk who often has other responsibilities as well.

"You basically have to do detective work," says Christopher Swanson, a senior research associate at The Urban Institute's Education Policy Center. "That takes time, effort and resources that may not be available to the school." Swanson says schools don't have an incentive to distinguish dropouts from transfers if it means that the graduation rates they report will be lower as a result.

Even states with sophisticated systems to track individual students over time — and there are a handful — can still report inflated graduation numbers. Texas, which reported an 84.2 percent graduation rate for its Class of 2003, counts as graduates students who have left school and either received or are working toward a General Educational Development certificate (GED). [2] No Child Left Behind prohibits the practice.

Both Swanson and Greene have developed methods for estimating how many students are actually graduating that do not rely on dropout data. Instead, they use two pieces of basic information they say are less subject to manipulation: the number of students enrolled in high school and the number of graduates. Their formulas differ, but both researchers come up with similar graduation rates that are far lower than those published by the states.

For example, South Carolina reported a high school graduation rate of 77.5 percent for the class of 2002; [3] Greene calculated the rate as 53 percent. [4] California reported a 2002 graduation rate of 87 percent; Greene put it at 67 percent. Indiana reported a graduation rate of 91 percent; Greene says it was 72 percent.

To fix the problem, Greene would like to see all states assign each student a unique identifying number for tracking their school careers, with reasonable definitions of who is a dropout and who is a graduate and an auditing program to ensure the quality of the data.

"Starbucks knows exactly what sells," Greene says. "Wal-Mart knows what inventory it has in every store. Schools have no idea."

Some states are developing such systems, but doing so will be time consuming and costly. In the meantime, some critics of the current reporting methods want the Department of Education to require states to estimate graduation rates using methods similar to Greene's or Swanson's. "The department's role does not end with the collection of data," the Education Trust says. "It must ensure that state calculations are accurate, complete and accessible to the public." [5]

However, federal education officials believe the responsibility lies elsewhere. While the Department of Education will provide technical assistance to states as they create more sophisticated systems for tracking students, it believes that the quality of the data is the states' responsibility. "Anytime there is a problem in the states, parties are always prone to point the finger," says Deputy Assistant Secretary for Policy Darla Marburger. "And folks point the finger at the U.S. Department of Education. But it is not really a problem in our house."

---

[1] Jay P. Greene, "Public High School Graduation and College Readiness Rates: 1991-2002," Education Working Paper No. 8, Manhattan Institute for Policy Research, p. 2, February 2005.

[2] www.tea.state.tx.us/peims/standards/wedspre/index.html?r032.

[3] Education Trust, "Telling the Whole Truth (or Not) About High School Graduation," December 2003, p. 4.

[4] Greene, *op. cit.*, Table 1.

[5] Education Trust, *op. cit.*

AP Photo/Daily Herald/Matt Smith

Gov. Jon Huntsman, R-Utah, prepares to sign a state measure on May 2, 2005, defying the No Child Left Behind Act, aided by a Provo elementary school student. In the past year and a half, more than 30 states have introduced bills that would release them from some of the law's requirements.

Is No Child Left Behind adequately funded?

The funding question is so contentious it has divided former congressional supporters of the law and prompted both Republican and Democratic state lawmakers to introduce bills exempting their states from portions of the law.

The issue also has generated nearly two-dozen studies from think tanks, lobbying groups, school districts and states. Their conclusions about the adequacy of funding range from modest surpluses to shortfalls of millions, and in a few cases, even billions of dollars.

Beneath the competing claims are radically different estimates of the costs of implementing the law. Researchers can't even agree on what costs should be included, let alone their size. Adding to the problem, said a study, "is the evolving nature of the regulations, guidance and other advisories issued by the U.S. Department of Education." [25]

After reviewing the studies, the National Conference of State Legislatures concluded a shortfall is more likely and released a report in February calling for change. "We would ask Congress to do one of two things," says senior policy specialist Young. "Either increase funding to levels that would allow states to meet the goals of the law or

provide states waivers from having to meet requirements where there is insufficient funding."

In response, the Education Department embraced the studies projecting plenty of funds. "The perpetual cry for more money . . . simply does not comport with the facts: Since taking office, President Bush has increased education funding by . . . 33 percent," said a department press release.

To understand the debate, it is helpful to break down the costs of implementing the law into two categories: complying with the letter of the law versus bringing students to grade-level proficiency by 2014, which several states claim may be much more costly.

To comply with the letter of the law, states must establish academic standards, create assessments, monitor schools' progress, help schools needing improvement, pay for students to transfer and receive tutoring and place a highly qualified teacher in every classroom. Connecticut recently called its estimate of these costs "sobering." The state said that through fiscal 2008 it would have to spend $41.6 million of its own money to comply with the law. [26] Minnesota said its cost would be $42 million. [27]

Other states go even further. They say doing what's explicitly called for in the law will not be enough to bring 100 percent of students to proficiency in reading and math by 2014. In order to reach that goal, several states say they'll have to do much more. "It might involve after-school services and making sure children are well nourished," Young says. "Early-childhood education is a big one, essential to preventing the achievement gap from occurring."

Ohio commissioned a study that adopted an expanded notion of costs and included summer school, an extended school day and intensive in-school student intervention. The study calculated the annual cost of fully implementing NCLB at $1.5 billion; the additional federal funding that Ohio receives through the law, however, is only $44 million. [28]

The authors of the Ohio study acknowledged, "the task of assigning costs to the requirements of No Child Left Behind presents a formidable challenge." [29] Their assumptions, and the assumptions of other state studies, have come under attack.

A report in *Education Next*, a journal devoted to education reform, last spring accused the state studies of gross exaggeration. The authors, including the chairman of the Massachusetts Board of Education, contended that while there may be a shortage of money to evaluate schools and help those that need intervention, the gap can be filled by giving states more flexibility to shift existing federal money around. And it concludes, "No one — neither critics nor supporters of NCLB — really has any idea what it would cost to bring all students to proficiency by 2014, or even if it can be done at all." [30]

Accountability Works, a nonprofit research and consulting firm, goes a step further, concluding there is "little solid evidence that NCLB is insufficiently funded." In fact, the firm concluded some states might even have surpluses.

Echoing *Education Next*, Accountability Works said the reports claiming NCLB provides insufficient funding contain significant flaws. "Often, expenditures that are not required by NCLB are included in the calculations," the report said. "In other cases, such studies included expenditures that were required by prior federal law." [31]

Given the huge range of estimates and the fact that some of the repercussions of the law are just beginning to be felt, it may take years for the true costs of implementation to become clear.

But one thing is clear: State education departments are often overwhelmed. Many don't have the staff or the expertise to effectively carry out No Child Left Behind's requirements: creating data systems to monitor each school's adequate yearly progress; putting teams together to help schools in need of improvement and, as more fail, to restructure schools; and evaluating outside suppliers of tutoring services. Many states have never had to do these things, on this scale, before, and the alarm has been sounded not only by the states but also by private researchers and even the Government Accountability Office.

The Department of Education's Briggs says the federal government is helping. "We have held conferences where we have tried to bring states together to learn together."

But many states say the problem is rooted in past state budget cuts and resulting staff reductions. The extra money provided by NCLB is being used to create assessment tests or reduce class size, with little left over to hire administrative staff. That's the case in Idaho, says Allison Westfall, public information officer at the state Department of Education. "We have a very small Title I staff — we're down to five people now — who are often on the road visiting schools," she says. "So we've had to bring in people from other departments, and we're stretched really thin." And there are no plans to hire.

"This lack of capacity — not a lack of will — on the part of most states is the single, most important impediment to achieving the gains of No Child Left Behind," said Marc Tucker, president of the National Center on Education and the Economy, a research group. On average, state education departments have lost 50 percent of their employees in the past 10 years, he says, calling it "the hidden issue." [32]

BACKGROUND

Federal Reforms

On April 11, 1965, President Lyndon B. Johnson returned to the Texas school he had attended as a child to sign the nation's first comprehensive education law, the Elementary and Secondary Education Act. "As president of the United States," he declared, "I believe deeply no law I have signed or will ever sign means more to the future of America." [33]

The primary assumption in ESEA — enacted as part of Johnson's War on Poverty — was that higher-quality education would move poor students out of poverty.

With ESEA, the federal government began to address the causes of the achievement gap. In the process, the federal role in education policy — until then a strictly local affair handled by the nation's 15,000 independent school districts — expanded dramatically. ESEA's signature program, Title I, initially allocated more than $1 billion a year to school districts with high concentrations of low-income students. To administer the program, federal and state education bureaucracies grew, as did the federal and state roles in local school districts.

During the next decade, minority achievement improved marginally, but dissatisfaction with public education grew faster, as did resentment over federal infringement on local education affairs. In 1981, President Ronald Reagan took office vowing to abolish the U.S. Department of Education.

The next year, Reagan and Secretary of Education Terrell Bell appointed the National Commission on Excellence in Education to report on the quality of public education. Eighteen months later, the commission's explosive report, "A Nation at Risk," declared, "the educational foundations of our society are presently being eroded by a rising tide of mediocrity that threatens our very future as a Nation and a people." [34]

"These Are the Very Weakest Programs Offered"

Arthur E. Levine, president of Teachers College, Columbia University, led a four-year assessment of the 1,200 university programs that prepare most of the nation's school principals and administrators. Released in March 2005 by Levine's Education Schools Project, the study, "Educating School Leaders," says most university-based preparation programs for administrators range in quality from "inadequate to appalling." Levine recently discussed the report with writer Barbara Mantel.

CQ: Does No Child Left Behind make the issue of how we train school leaders more urgent?

AL: No Child Left Behind demands assessment; it demands effective curricula that will move students to achievement of standards and requires that all students achieve those standards. Principals and superintendents have to lead that transformation of the schools, which requires a very different set of skills and knowledge from their predecessors.

CQ: What is your overall characterization of university-based programs that train school administrators?

AL: The quality is very weak. These are the very weakest programs offered by America's education schools. While a relatively small proportion could be described as strong, the majority vary in quality from inadequate to appalling.

CQ: Do most principals and superintendents come through these programs?

AL: I can't give you numbers on superintendents. For principals, it is 89 percent.

CQ: In what areas do these programs fall short?

AL: First of all, the curriculum for the master's degree is irrelevant to the job of being a principal, appearing to be a random grab bag of survey courses, like Research Methods, Historical and Philosophical Foundations of Education and Educational Psychology.

CQ: Your report also talks about admission standards.

AL: The standardized test scores for students in leadership programs are among the lowest of all students at graduate schools of education, and they're among the lowest in all academe. But the larger problem is that the overwhelming majority of students in these programs are in them primarily for a bump in salaries. All 50 states give salary increases for educators who take master's degrees or graduate credits. So people want quickie programs and easy degrees. There is a race to the bottom among programs as they compete for students by dumbing down the curriculum, reducing the length of the program, cutting the number of credits required to graduate and lowering expectations of student performance.

CQ: Your report also says the degrees offered don't make sense.

AL: Generally the master's degree is considered prepa-

The report focused on how poorly American students compared with students from other countries; the steady decline in science scores; a drop in SAT scores; the functional illiteracy of too many minority students; and complaints from business and military leaders about the poor quality of U.S. high school graduates.

To overcome the problems, the report called for rigorous and measurable academic standards, establishment of a minimum core curriculum, lengthening of the time spent learning that curriculum and better teacher preparation.

"A Nation at Risk" marked the beginning of a movement for national standards and testing. Over the next decade, seven groups received federal financing to develop standards for what students should know, including the National Council of Teachers of Mathematics, the National History Standards Project and the National Standards in Foreign Language. [35]

In September 1989, President George H.W. Bush — the self-described "education president" — convened an education summit in Charlottesville, Va. Ignoring traditional Republican reluctance to actively involve Washington in education policy, Bush teamed with the president of the National Governors' Association — Democratic Gov. Bill Clinton, who had been active in education reform in his home state of Arkansas.

"The movement gained momentum with the 1989 education summit," wrote Andrew Rudalevige, an associate professor of political science at Dickinson College, in Carlyle, Pa. [36] Bush and the governors set broad performance goals for American schools to reach by the year 2000. It was hoped that all children would attend preschool, that 90 percent of all high school students would graduate, that all students would be proficient in core subjects, that U.S. students would be first in the

ration for principalship and the doctorate for a superintendency. Why does anybody need a doctorate to be a superintendent? A doctorate is a research degree. What does that have to do with running a school system?

CQ: What are some of your key recommendations?

AL: States and school boards should eliminate salary increases based on taking degrees. Or they can give people raises based on master's degrees but require that the field be germane to their work. If you're a math teacher, I can understand giving an increase in salary for taking a degree in mathematics or advanced teaching skills. Number two: close down failing programs. States can clean this up if they want to. They are in charge of the authorization of university programs and the licensure of school administrators. But I would like to see universities try first before the states step in.

CQ: How much time would you give the universities to do this?

Arthur E. Levine, president, Teachers College, Columbia University

AL: I would give universities two years to clean up their house, and then the state has an obligation to step in if they fail to do that.

CQ: What other recommendations do you have for universities?

AL: Eliminate the current master's degree and put in its place something I've been calling a master's of educational administration, which would be a two-year degree combining education and management courses, theory and practical experience. The doctor of education degree (EdD) would be eliminated. It has no integrity and no value. The PhD in education leadership should be reserved for the very tiny group of people who wish to be scholars and researchers in the field.

CQ: And your last recommendation?

AL: There is a tendency of universities to use these programs as cash cows. They encourage these programs to produce as much revenue as possible by reducing admission standards, using adjuncts and lowering academic standards for graduation in order to get enough cash to distribute to other areas. Universities need to stop doing that.

---

world in science and math, that every adult would be literate and every school free of drugs and violence.

In 1994, President Clinton signed the Goals 2000: Educate America Act, which adopted the summit's ambitious agenda and provided federal funds to help states develop standards. The real sea change came later that year, Rudalevige wrote, when reauthorization of ESEA "signaled a nationwide commitment to standards-based reform." [37] The law required states to develop content and performance standards, tests aligned with those standards and a system to measure a school's "adequate yearly progress" in bringing all students to academic proficiency. But there was no deadline, and it took several years for the Education Department to develop the accompanying regulations and guidelines. By 1997, only 17 states were fully complying with the law, according to Krista Kafer, senior education policy analyst at the Heritage Foundation. [38]

In January 2001 former Texas Gov. George W. Bush became president, having made education a centerpiece of his campaign. Three days after his inauguration, he proposed what became the blueprint for No Child Left Behind. Its standards-and-testing strategy wasn't new, but accountability provisions were. They significantly raised the stakes for states, local districts and schools.

The proposal called for annual testing in grades 3-8, school and state report cards showing student performance by ethnic and economic subgroups, a highly qualified teacher in every classroom and sanctions for schools not showing progress in bringing students to proficiency.

Congress finally passed NCLB after nearly a year of intense debate and political horse-trading, which included the elimination of private school vouchers, increases in funding and addition of a provision requiring that all students reach proficiency in math and reading in 12 years.

"The political compromises written into No Child Left Behind make the regulatory process crucial," said Rudalevige. [39] That's because the law grants the secretary of Education the power to grant waivers and interpret the rules and, until the bill is reauthorized, determine the flexibility states will have to meet their goals.

Achievement Gaps

Most educators say the best thing about No Child Left Behind is its focus on minorities and low-income students.

"When you say to a school that you expect every subgroup of kids to meet standards," says Delaware Education Secretary Woodruff, "that really makes schools pay closer attention to all kids." It is now possible, for instance, to track how minority and low-income students perform on state tests at each school and to calculate the achievement gaps between them and their peers. The fundamental goal of No Child Left Behind is to close these gaps while raising the achievement of all students, which has been the goal of education reforms for decades.

But to get a sense of how students have been performing historically, researchers must look to national data, because state testing is too new.

To get that information, the U.S. Department of Education has been measuring American students' achievement levels since 1969 through its National Assessment of Educational Progress (NAEP). NAEP periodically administers what it calls a "trend assessment" to a nationally representative sample of students at ages 9, 13 and 17 and breaks down the results for white, black and Hispanic students.

The data show that black and Hispanic students have made long-term gains, thus narrowing the achievement gap. From 1971 to 1999 for example, the last year for which data is available, the difference between the average reading scores of 13-year-old white and black students shrank from 39 points to 29 points. In math, the gap plummeted 14 points — from 46 points to 32 points. [40]

However, most of the reductions in the achievement gap occurred during the 1970s and 1980s, as minorities made notable gains while white students' average achievement increased slightly or not at all. Then, in the 1990s, the gap stopped shrinking; in fact, in many cases it grew. Black and Hispanic students continued making modest gains in math and Hispanic students in reading, but those improvements no longer exceeded those of whites. [41]

"When achievement goes up for all groups," the Center on Education Policy noted, "African-American and Hispanic students must improve at a faster rate than others for the gap to close." [42]

While still smaller than decades ago, the achievement gap remains quite large. For instance, the 32-point difference in math scores for black 13-year-olds and their white peers in 1999 is the equivalent of roughly three grade levels. [43]

"What, then, are the most probable explanations for the achievement gap?" asked the Center on Education Policy in a report examining minority achievement. "A complex combination of school, community and home factors appear to underlie or contribute to the gap," it answered. [44]

CURRENT SITUATION

States Push Back

Mounting state resistance to NCLB — including its level of funding and strict achievement timetables — has led to a mini-revolution in the states.

In 2004, legislatures in 31 states introduced bills challenging aspects of the law. [45] This year, so far, 21 states have either introduced or reintroduced legislation, and the numbers are likely to grow if more states decide to test Education Secretary Spellings' promise to take a "common sense" approach to enforcing the law. [46]

In Colorado, Republican state Sen. Mark Hillman proposed allowing school districts to opt out of No Child Left Behind if they forgo Title I funds; he suggested a tax increase to replace the lost federal funds. In Idaho, two Republican state senators introduced legislation demanding that predominantly rural states be exempt from the law. In Maine, Democratic state Sen. Michael Brennan sponsored a bill directing the state's attorney general to sue the federal government if federal funding is insufficient to implement No Child Left Behind.

Despite the blizzard of proposals, only three states actually passed legislation. The Republican-dominated Utah legislature passed a bill on April 19 — and the governor signed it on May 2 — allowing schools to ignore NCLB provisions that conflict with state education laws or require extra state money to implement. Spellings has warned that Utah could lose $76 million of the $107 million it receives in federal education funding.

"I don't like to be threatened," an angry state Rep. Mascaro told *The New York Times*. [47]

Should annual testing be extended to high school?

YES Bob Wise
President, Alliance for Excellent Education

Written for *CQ Researcher*, May 5, 2005

Achieving the national goal of building a better educated, more competitive work force for the 21st century requires effective tools. With two-thirds of high school students either dropping out or graduating unprepared for college, the majority of our nation's young people need more support than they are currently getting from their secondary schools and teachers. An increased number of required tests at the high school level could help to leverage the academic assistance many students require, if those tests are designed and implemented appropriately.

Last fall, President Bush set off a major debate when he proposed extending the reading and math tests required by the No Child Left Behind Act for third- through eighth-graders and in one year of high school to students in grades nine, ten and eleven. "We need to be sure that high school students are learning every year," he said.

At the Alliance for Excellent Education, we believe all children deserve an excellent education that prepares them for the economic and social challenges that follow high school. And we agree with the president that our schools must be held accountable for providing that high-quality education. Testing students during their high school years has the potential to provide needed data about their progress — as a whole, and by gender, race and ethnicity — and could allow us to better measure the effectiveness of the schools supposed to be preparing all of our young people to become productive members of American society.

But tests should help schools understand and address the needs of their students. If we are going to hold schools accountable for their students' ability to perform at high academic levels, we must also give them the resources necessary to provide the additional, targeted instruction that many teens need to become proficient in reading, writing, math and other subjects.

To be taken seriously by students, tests need to be relevant. High school tests should be aligned to the expectations of colleges and employers and provide both educators and students with a gauge to measure progress toward a successful transition to postsecondary education, technical training or rewarding jobs.

Finally, the federal government should fully cover the cost of designing and administering the exams, thus ensuring that states can adequately and effectively implement the tests they are required to give.

Tests alone won't make a difference. But as a part of a toolkit designed to improve the nation's graduation and college-readiness rates, they are worthy of our consideration.

NO Paul Houston
Executive Director, American Association of School Administrators

Written for *CQ Researcher*, April 27, 2005

High school reform should not focus on a test but rather on what is being learned. I recently visited the Olathe, Kan., school district to learn more about a series of programs called 21st Century Schools, which have been implemented in all the high schools. These are "vocational" schools. In other words, they are focused on the future work life of students, and the programs are very rigorous and produce great results. But more important, the programs are meaningful, engaging and hands on, using the students' motivation to create a vehicle for excellence.

As I walked through Olathe Northwest High School, I saw students and teachers engaged in hard work. In one classroom, they were constructing a "battlebot," a robot that is used in gaming to battle other robots — with the last one running being the winner. The students were looking forward to taking their creation to a national competition later this year. While this sounds fun (some may say "frivolous"), what is really happening is that students are experiencing deep learning about metallurgy, structures, engines, insulation and a hundred other things I didn't understand. They were excited and knowledgeable about what they were doing — and about how much fun they were having with the learning process.

There were about a dozen students who stayed after the bell to talk with me, and every one of them plans to attend college and study engineering. There is no shortage of engineering candidates in Olathe. I asked them why they liked what they were doing, and the answer was simple. One told me he got to use what he was learning in class. "Telling me that calculus is good for me isn't very meaningful," he said. "Now I see how I can use it."

I would suggest to those who want to reform high schools that the place to start is in places like Olathe, where the school district has figured out that the best way to get students to learn more is to give them engaging, imaginative work that creates meaning for them. And we must give schools adequate resources to provide state-of-the-art opportunities for students to receive hands-on learning.

Those who are interested in reform should focus on getting schools the resources they need to do the job and then challenging them to make schools interesting and engaging places. Reform will not be achieved by mandating more testing. Education has always been about the whole child, and unless we take that into consideration, the current effort to reform high schools will be just as unsuccessful as the others that preceded it.

Raul Gonzales, legislative director at the National Council of La Raza, which advocates for Hispanic-Americans, agrees that money is tight in states still suffering from a four-year-long budget crisis. [48] "States are trying to implement this law on the cheap," Gonzales says, "because there isn't really enough money."

For example, under the law states are allowed to test English-language learners for up to three years in their native language, but most states don't have reading tests in native languages. "We're not accurately measuring what kids can do because we're using the wrong tests," he says.

Perry Zirkel, a professor of education and law at Lehigh University, in Bethlehem, Pa., says the states' resistance to the law is still mostly "sparks, not fire." He points out that New Mexico, Virginia and Utah are the only states to pass legislation.

"Despite all the talk," Zirkel says, "I don't think there has been sufficient momentum to convince the majority of the public that No Child Left Behind is, on a net basis, a bad law."

Moreover, a coalition of Hispanic, African-American and other educators have voiced concerns that the Utah legislature's effort to sidestep provisions of the federal law might allow minority students to fall through the cracks. [49]

Teachers' Union Sues

One day after the Utah legislature made its move, the NEA and eight school districts in Michigan, Texas and Vermont sued the Department of Education, contending it is violating an NCLB provision that says states cannot be forced to use their own money to implement the law:

"Nothing in this Act shall be construed to authorize an officer or employee of the Federal Government to mandate, direct, or control a State, local education agency, or school's curriculum, program of instruction, or allocation of State or local resources, or mandate a State or any subdivision thereof to spend any funds or incur any costs not paid for under this Act."

"We don't disagree when the Department of Education says federal funding has increased," explains NEA spokesman Dan Kaufman. "We just don't believe that the funding has been enough for the types of really strict, comprehensive things that it requires states to do." The teachers' union would like to see Congress appropriate the full amount it authorized when passing the bill. So far, it is $27 billion short.

"We . . . look forward to the day when the NEA will join us in helping children who need our help the most

in classrooms, instead of spending its time and members' money in courtrooms," the Department of Education said in response. [50]

The lawsuit was filed in the U.S. District Court for the Eastern District of Michigan, which has jurisdiction over one of the school districts joining the suit. The suit asks the court to declare that states and school districts do not have to spend their own funds to comply with NCLB and that failure to comply for that reason will not result in a cutoff of federal education funds.

Some legal experts say that, regardless of its merits, the lawsuit could be dismissed on procedural grounds. First of all, the teachers' union may not have the legal standing to bring suit because it doesn't have a direct stake in the outcome, even though its members do. The experts also say the court could rule that the lawsuit is premature, and that NCLB does not specify that there is a right to sue.

Moreover, several legal experts said, courts typically don't want to take on messy political debates. Just deciding the facts and determining the costs of No Child Left Behind would be extremely complex.

"The courts' view is that if you have problems with this law, then go lobby Congress to change it," Lehigh's Zirkel says. In fact, the lawsuit may actually be an indirect way to lobby Congress, he adds, and it may be more effective because it's more public.

War of Words

Zirkel says Connecticut's threat to sue may also be an indirect attempt at lobbying Congress. In early April, Connecticut Attorney General Richard Blumenthal announced he would sue the Department of Education on grounds that the federal government's approach to the law is "illegal and unconstitutional." [51] Connecticut's argument is essentially the same as the teachers' union's, but the state — which has a direct stake in the outcome — has better legal standing, Zirkel says. Blumenthal has estimated the annual testing required by the law would create an additional financial burden for the state, which now tests students every other year.

While a few school districts have sued the government over the law, Connecticut would be the first state to do so, but as of May 25, Blumenthal had yet to act.

Meanwhile, the state's dispute with the Education Department has become very public. "We've got better things to spend our money on," Connecticut Education

Commissioner Sternberg said in explaining her opposition to annual testing. "We won't learn anything new about our schools by giving these extra tests." [52]

But Secretary Spellings clearly will not compromise on annual testing, consistently calling it one of the "bright lines" of NCLB. She and Sternberg have been having a war of words, with Spellings calling the law's opponents "un-American" and Sternberg demanding an apology.

Spellings also has accused Connecticut of tolerating one of the nation's largest achievement gaps between white and black students. Sternberg has said the huge gap was due to the extraordinary performance of white students in Connecticut's affluent suburbs.

The two finally met in mid-April, but the meeting was inconclusive.

OUTLOOK

Reform Unlikely?

If the NEA's lawsuit and Connecticut's threat to sue are indirect ways of lobbying Congress, their timing may be off.

Jeffrey Henig, a professor of political science and education at Columbia University's Teachers College, says some constituents in prosperous suburban school districts are beginning to grumble as well-regarded schools fail to make "adequate yearly progress" because one or two subgroups of students miss proficiency targets.

"But I don't think it has really gelled into clear, focused pressure on Congress to reform the law," Henig says, adding that the situation could change if more schools fall into that category.

But lawmakers are extremely reluctant to revisit the law before it comes up for reauthorization in 2007, Henig says. Moderate Democrats are committed to the law's focus on raising achievement levels for minority, low-income and disabled students, he says, and they fear that any reworking could result in easing the pressure on states to shrink the achievement gap. And a core group of Republicans is committed to the law's tough accountability provisions. Both groups, Henig says, would prefer "to hold to the legislation and to placate any dissatisfied groups through the regulatory process."

The Department of Education has already amended the law's regulations, guidelines and enforcement. For instance, in 2003 and 2004 it allowed English-language learners to be tested in native languages for their first three years, gave rural districts more time to place highly qualified teachers in classrooms and allowed some flexibility on testing participation rates.

In April, Spellings — then in her new job as secretary for just three months — told states they could apply to test a greater portion of disabled students using alternative assessments. In addition, Spellings said she would grant states flexibility in other areas if they could show they were making real progress in closing achievement gaps and meeting proficiency targets.

But Young of the National Conference of State Legislatures says states are trying to decipher what she means. "There is no indication of what that flexibility would include," he says, "and there is no indication of how states would be judged by these indicators."

So far, Spellings is holding firm on annual testing, but she did grant North Dakota a waiver temporarily allowing new elementary school teachers to be rated highly qualified without taking a state test.

"The Department of Education is really feeling the heat and is trying to compromise," says educational consultant Scott Joftus, former policy director at the Alliance for Excellent Education.

The department also has allowed some states to lower the cutoff point for proficiency on their student assessment tests and to use averaging and other statistical methods to make it easier for schools to make adequate yearly progress. Young calls it gaming the system and expects it to continue unless Congress reforms No Child Left Behind.

In 2007, when the law comes up for reauthorization, Congress could negotiate changes, but the process could take years. Last time, it took two-and-a-half extra years.

NOTES

1. Dana Milbank, "With Fanfare, Bush Signs Education Bill," *The Washington Post*, Jan. 9, 2002.

2. Northwest Evaluation Association, "The Impact of the No Child Left Behind Act on Student Achievement and Growth: 2005 Edition," April 2005, p. 2.

3. http://kennedy.senate.gov/index_high.html.

4. Sam Dillon, "Utah Vote Rejects Parts of U.S. Education Law," *The New York Times*, April 20, 2005.

5. "Governor worried about costs of Bush education reform law," The Associated Press State & Local Wire, April 26, 2005.

6. http://gregg.senate.gov/forms/myths.pdf.

7. www.ed.gov/nclb/overview/intro/guide/guide_pg11.html#spending.

8. National Public Radio, "Talk of the Nation," May 3, 2005.

9. Center on Education Policy, "From the Capital to the Classroom: Year 3 of the No Child Left Behind Act," March 2005, p. v.

10. *Ibid.*, p. 4.

11. *Ibid.*, p. 1.

12. Council of the Great City Schools, "Beating the Odds: A City-By-City Analysis of Student Performance and Achievement Gaps on State Assessments," March 2004, pp. iv-vi.

13. The Education Trust, "Stalled in Secondary: A Look at Student Achievement Since the No Child Left Behind Act," January 2005, p. 1.

14. University of Delaware Education Research and Development Center, "Awareness To Action Revisited: Tracking the Achievement Gap in Delaware Schools, State of Delaware Report," March 2005, p. 2.

15. www.dpi.state.wi.us/dpi/esea/pdf/wiaw.pdf.

16. National Conference of State Legislatures, "Task Force on No Child Left Behind: Final Report," February 2005, p. vii.

17. http://edcounts.edweek.org.

18. Center for the Study of Evaluation, "Test-based Educational Accountability in the Era of No Child Left Behind," April 2005, p. 19.

19. *Ibid.*, p. 14.

20. Susan Saulny, "U.S. Provides Rules to States for Testing Special Pupils," *The New York Times*, May 11, 2005, p. A17.

21. The data are from 2000, the most recent available. See The Education Trust, "All Talk, No Action: Putting an End to Out-of-Field Teaching," August 2002, p. 4.

22. Education Week Research Center, "Quality Counts 2005," January 2005, p. 92. www.edweek.org/rc/index.html.

23. National Council on Teacher Quality, "Searching the Attic," December 2004, p. 12.

24. Southeast Center for Teaching Quality, "Unfulfilled Promise: Ensuring High Quality Teachers for Our Nation's Students," August 2004, pp. 8-9.

25. Augenblick, Palaich and Associates, Inc. "Costing Out No Child Left Behind: A Nationwide Survey of Costing Efforts," April 2004, p. 1.

26. Connecticut State Department of Education, "Cost of Implementing the Federal No Child Left Behind Act in Connecticut," March 2, 2005, p. iii.

27. Center on Education Policy, *op. cit.*

28. Ohio Department of Education, "Projected Costs of Implementing The Federal 'No Child Left Behind Act' in Ohio," December 2003, p. vi.

29. *Ibid.*

30. James Peyser and Robert Castrell, "Exploring the Costs of Accountability," *Education Next*, spring 2004, p. 24.

31. Accountability Works, "NCLB Under a Microscope," January 2004, p. 2.

32. Joetta L. Sack, "State Agencies Juggle NCLB Work, Staffing Woes," *Education Week*, May 11, 2005, p. 25.

33. www.lbjlib.utexas.edu/johnson/archives.hom/speeches.hom/650411.asp.

34. www.ed.gov/pubs/NatAtRisk/risk.html.

35. For background, see Kathy Koch, "National Education Standards," *CQ Researcher*, May 14, 1999, pp. 401-424, and Charles S. Clark, "Education Standards," *CQ Researcher*, March 11, 1994, pp. 217-240.

36. www.educationnext.org/20034/62.html.

37. *Ibid.*

38. Heritage Foundation, "No Child Left Behind: Where Do We Go From Here?" 2004, p. 2.

39. www.educationnext.org/20034/62.html.

40. National Center for Education Statistics, "Trends in Academic Progress: Three Decades of Student Performance," 2000, p. 39.

41. *Ibid.*, p. 33.

42. Center on Education Policy, "It takes more than testing: Closing the Achievement Gap," 2001, p. 2.

43. *Ibid.*, p. 1.

44. *Ibid.*, p. 3.

45. National Conference of State Legislatures, "No Child Left Behind Quick Facts: 2005," April 2005.

46. www.nea.org/lawsuit/stateres.html.

47. Dillon, *op. cit.*

48. For background, see William Triplett, "State Budget Crisis," *CQ Researcher*, Oct. 3, 2003, pp. 821-844.

49. Dillon, *op. cit.*

50. U.S. Department of Education, "Statement by Press Secretary on NEA's Action Regarding NCLB," April 20, 2005, p. B1.

51. Sam Dillon, "Connecticut to Sue U.S. Over Cost of School Testing Law, *The New York Times*, April 6, 2005.

52. Michael Dobbs, "Conn. Stands in Defiance on Enforcing 'No Child'," *The Washington Post*, May 8, 2005, p. A10.

BIBLIOGRAPHY

Books

Meier, Deborah, and George Wood, eds., *Many Children Left Behind: How the No Child Left Behind Act Is Damaging Our Children and Our Schools*, Beacon Press, 2004.
Meier, the founder of several New York City public schools, and Wood, a high school principal and the founder of The Forum for Education and Democracy, and other authors argue that the law is harming the ability of schools to serve poor and minority children.

Peterson, Paul E., and Martin R. West, eds., *No Child Left Behind: The Politics and Practice of School Accountability*, Brookings Institution Press, 2003.
Peterson, director of the Program on Education Policy and Governance at Harvard, and West, a research fellow in the program, have collected essays that examine the forces that gave shape to the law and its likely consequences.

Rakoczy, Kenneth Leo, *No Child Left Behind: No Parent Left in the Dark*, Edu-Smart.com Publishing, 2003.
A veteran public school teacher offers this guide to parents for becoming involved in their children's education and making the most out of parent-teacher conferences in light of the new law.

Wright, Peter W. D., Pamela Darr Wright and Suzanne Whitney Heath, *Wrightslaw: No Child Left Behind*, Harbor House Law Press, 2003.
The authors, who run a Web site about educational law and advocacy, explain the No Child Left Behind Act for parents and teachers.

Articles

Dillon, Sam, "New Secretary Showing Flexibility on 'No Child' Law," *The New York Times*, Feb. 14, 2005, p. A18.
Education Secretary Margaret Spellings has shown a willingness to work with state and local officials on No Child Left Behind, saying school districts need not always allow students in low-performing schools to transfer to better ones if it caused overcrowding.

Friel, Brian, "A Test for Tutoring," *The National Journal*, April 16, 2005.
Friel examines the controversy surrounding some of the outside tutoring firms providing supplemental services to students under provisions of No Child Left Behind.

Hendrie, Caroline, "NCLB Cases Face Hurdles in the Courts," *Education Week*, May 4, 2005.
Hendrie describes the hurdles facing the National Education Association's lawsuit against the Department of Education.

Ripley, Amanda, and Sonja Steptoe, "Inside the Revolt Over Bush's School Rules," *Time*, May 9, 2005.
The authors examine efforts by states to seek release from aspects of No Child Left Behind and the teachers' union's lawsuit against the federal government.

Tucker, Marc S., and Thomas Toch, "Hire Ed: the secret to making Bush's school reform law work? More bureaucrats," *Washington Monthly*, March 1, 2004.
The authors discuss staffing shortages at state departments of education that are slowing implementation of No Child Left Behind.

Reports and Studies

Center on Education Policy, *From the Capital to the Classroom: Year 3 of the No Child Left Behind Act*, March 2005.
The center examines the implementation of No Child Left Behind at the federal, state and local levels and points out positive and negative signs for the future.

Citizens' Commission on Civil Rights, *Choosing Better Schools: A Report on Student Transfers Under the No Child Left Behind Act,* **May 2004.**
The commission describes the early efforts to implement the school-choice provision of No Child Left Behind, calling compliance minimal.

National Conference of State Legislatures, *Task Force on No Child Left Behind: Final Report,* **February 2005.**
The panel questions the constitutionality of No Child Left Behind and calls it rigid, overly prescriptive and in need of serious revision.

Northwest Evaluation Association, *The Impact of No Child Left Behind Act on Student Achievement and Growth: 2005 Edition,* **April 2005.**
The association reports the percentage of proficient students is rising on state tests but also notes the disparity between the achievement growth of white and minority students.

Southeast Center for Teaching Quality, *Unfulfilled Promise: Ensuring High Quality Teachers for Our Nation's Students,* **August 2004.**
The center finds that rural and urban schools don't have the skills and training to recruit and retain highly qualified teachers and offers recommendations for change.

For More Information

Achieve, Inc., 1775 I St., N.W., Suite 410, Washington, DC 20006; (202) 419-1540; www.achieve.org. A bipartisan, nonprofit organization created by the nation's governors and business leaders that helps states improve academic performance.

Alliance for Excellent Education, 1201 Connecticut Ave., N.W., Suite 901, Washington, DC 20036; (202) 828-0828; www.all4ed.org. Works to assure that at-risk middle and high school students graduate prepared for college and success in life.

The Center for Teaching Quality Inc., 976 Martin Luther King Jr. Blvd., Suite 250, Chapel Hill, NC 27514; (919) 951-0200; www.teachingquality.org. A regional association dedicated to assuring all children have access to high-quality education.

Center on Education Policy, 1001 Connecticut Ave., N.W., Suite 522, Washington, DC 20036; (202) 822-8065; www.cep-dc.org. Helps Americans understand the role of public education in a democracy and the need to improve academic quality.

Council of the Great City Schools, 1301 Pennsylvania Ave., N.W., Suite 702, Washington, DC 20004; (202) 393-2427; www.cgcs.org. A coalition of 65 of the nation's largest urban public school systems advocating improved K-12 education.

Editorial Projects in Education Inc., 6935 Arlington Rd., Suite 100, Bethesda, MD 20814-5233; (301) 280-3100; www.edweek.org. A nonprofit organization that publishes *Education Week, Teacher Magazine,* edweek.org and *Agent K-12.*

Education Commission of the States, 700 Broadway, Suite 1200, Denver, CO 80203-3460; (303) 299-3600; www.ecs.org. Studies current and emerging education issues.

The Education Trust, 1250 H St., N.W., Suite 700, Washington, DC 20005; (202) 293-1217; www2.edtrust.org/edtrust. An independent nonprofit organization working to improve the academic achievement of all students.

National Conference of State Legislatures, 7700 East First Pl., Denver, CO 80230; (303) 364-7700; www.ncsl.org. A bipartisan organization serving the states and territories.

Northwest Evaluation Association, 5885 Southwest Meadows Rd., Suite 200, Lake Oswego, OR 97035; (503) 624-1951; www.nwea.org. A national nonprofit organization dedicated to helping all children learn.

U.S. Department of Education, No Child Left Behind Web site, www.ed.gov/nclb/landing.jhtml?src=pb. Describes the provisions of the No Child Left Behind law.

Wrightslaw, www.wrightslaw.com. Provides information about effective advocacy for children with disabilities, including "Wrightslaw: No Child Left Behind."

3

Drug Safety

Marc Ferris

Susan Halvorsen's husband, Jim Gjebic, died of a heart attack at age 34 in 2001 after taking Vioxx. Merck & Co. withdrew the popular drug in September 2004, four years after learning Vioxx may double the risk of heart attacks. Halvorsen and other Michigan residents want to sue Merck, but a new state law — similar to one the administration is advocating nationwide — shields drugmakers if the FDA had approved the drug.

From *CQ Researcher*, March 11, 2005.

L ate last year, like many other doctors and pharmacists, University of Pittsburgh internist Anthony Fiorillo fielded a deluge of inquiries from worried patients. They were alarmed by the sudden withdrawal of the blockbuster arthritis drug Vioxx and warnings that similar medications might also be dangerous.

" 'They are experimenting on us,' " he remembers his patients complaining. [1]

Fears that patients are being used as guinea pigs for undertested drugs have rippled throughout the 20th century. But in recent years, the reputation of the nation's drug-safety system has been especially tarnished after several prescription drugs approved by the U.S. Food and Drug Administration (FDA) were later found to have dangerous side effects for some users, triggering voluntary manufacturer recalls.

"The increase in attention we've seen over the past few months beats all previous episodes," Steven Galson, acting director of the FDA's Center for Drug Evaluation and Research (CDER), says after recent revelations that long-term users of Vioxx, Celebrex and Bextra may be at higher risk of heart attacks and strokes.

Opinion over drug safety is polarized. Sidney Wolfe, longtime director of Public Citizen's Health Research Group and coauthor of *Worst Pills, Best Pills: A Consumer's Guide to Avoiding Drug-Induced Death or Illness*, has been one of the FDA's most vocal critics since the 1970s.

But Sam Kazman, general counsel at the Competitive Enterprise Institute, says drug safety is a non-issue. He warns that further delays in approving new treatments would be like deciding to inspect and approve a rope before throwing it to a drowning man, who dies during the process.

Drug Withdrawals Increased After New Law

The 1992 Prescription Drug User Fee Act (PDUFA) speeded up drug approvals, as designed, but since its enactment a slightly higher percentage of drugs has been withdrawn from the market for safety reasons, according to a government study. Some scientists, consumer groups and government watchdogs see a link between fast-tracking approvals under PDUFA and the recent drug-safety lapses.

Rate of Safety-Related Drug Withdrawals Pre- and Post-PDUFA (1985-2000)

1985-1992	(six of 193 FDA-approved drugs were withdrawn)	**3.10%**
1993-2000	(nine of 259 FDA-approved drugs were withdrawn)	**3.47%**

Source: General Accounting Office, based on FDA data, "Effect of User Fees on Drug Approval Times, Withdrawals and Other Agency Activities," September 2002

As one of the nation's oldest and largest regulatory bodies, the FDA oversees the $235 billion prescription-drug trade and the sale of over-the-counter medications, medical devices, cosmetics, cell phones and, along with the Department of Agriculture, the country's food supply. Yet critics say the agency suffers from deep-seated flaws, including conflicts of interest, an inattention to safety issues and a lack of enforcement authority. Two congressional committees, the Government Accountability Office (GAO) and the Institute of Medicine (IOM) have begun investigations or evaluations of the agency's performance, several high-profile drug-safety-related lawsuits are bringing additional scrutiny to the beleaguered agency and lawmakers are proposing ways to overhaul the way the FDA operates.

"The credibility of the FDA is on the line," said former FDA chief David Kessler. [2]

Partly in response to the recent criticisms, the Bush administration on Feb. 14 nominated Acting FDA Commissioner Lester M. Crawford as the new head of the agency — a position that has been vacant for nearly a year. The next day, Michael O. Leavitt, secretary of Health and Human Services (HHS) appeared with Crawford at FDA headquarters to announce "a new culture of openness and enhanced independence."

Toward that end, the administration has announced it will appoint a new Drug Safety Oversight Board made up of medical experts from the FDA, other HHS agencies and government departments, which would consult with outside medical experts and representatives of patient and consumer groups.

Moreover, Janet Woodcock, acting deputy commissioner for operations at the FDA, told the Senate Health, Education, Labor and Pensions Committee on March 3, 2005, that the drug-safety system is "the strongest it's ever been," despite the recent revelations about Vioxx and heightened suicide risks from antidepressants used by children.

Woodcock's testimony echoed the March 1 remarks of Sandra L. Kweder, deputy director of the FDA's Office of New Drugs, who said the agency is making progress in communicating the risks of drugs and that a major overhaul of its authority is unnecessary.

But critics question whether the board can improve the performance of an agency that has been chronically understaffed and underfunded.

Some scientists, consumer organizations and government watchdogs say the recent safety lapses began after Congress passed the 1992 Prescription Drug User Fee Act (PDUFA), which was designed to speed up drug approvals. Since the law was passed, the time it has taken to approve new drugs has been cut in half, according to a GAO study. The report also concluded that a "higher percentage of drugs has been withdrawn from the market for safety-related reasons since PDUFA's enactment." [3]

The law required drugmakers to pay hefty fees to the FDA with every new drug application to defray the cost of expanding the agency's drug-review staff. Critics say the so-called "user fees" — which amounted to $274 million in 2004 — make the agency too beholden to the industry. Moreover, the critics say, while the law boosted the number of drug approvals, it did not provide additional funds for monitoring safety problems that might arise after "fast-tracked" drugs were released onto the market.

Moreover, in 1997 the agency had removed restrictions on direct-to-consumer drug advertising, which critics charge routinely omits information about side effects and inflates consumer expectations — as well as health-care costs. [4] However, as medications for life-threatening diseases and unwanted lifestyle conditions became ubiquitous — turning "erectile dysfunction" into a household term — manufacturers were pulling high-profile drugs off the market for safety problems, including the diet drug Fen-Phen, Propulsid (for heartburn), Posicor (for cardiovascular problems) and the anti-cholesterol drug Baycol.

And, of course, in 2003 millions of older American woman were shocked to learn that heavily promoted hormone-replacement therapy (HRT) — touted as a protection against breast cancer and heart disease — actually increased the risk of developing those conditions. [5]

Then last spring, media reports revealed that the FDA and drugmakers had known about links between antidepressants and suicidal tendencies in children and teenagers since the 1980s, but that agency officials had stifled the findings. [6]

The crisis of confidence in the FDA reached a crescendo on Sept. 30, 2004, when Merck voluntarily withdrew Vioxx from the market after a company-sponsored study in 2000 suggested it increased the risk of heart attacks and strokes. Since Merck was selling about $2.5 billion worth of Vioxx a year at the time, the incident attracted widespread media and congressional scrutiny. The Securities and Exchange Commission is probing whether Merck misled stockholders, and the Justice Department has launched a criminal investigation.

In the aftermath, both FDA critics and defenders battled over the data and its interpretation. Eric Topol, vice chairman of the Cleveland Clinic's Lerner Research Institute, for instance, argued that both the agency and Merck knew — or should have known — about the danger but dawdled in notifying the public. Citing his own 2001 study, Topol called the entire Vioxx drug class

Twenty Percent of New Drugs Get OK

After animal testing, three phases of human testing are required for all new drug applications before the FDA approves a drug. On average, about 20 drugs will be approved for marketing for every 100 new drug applications submitted to the FDA. In rare instances, the testing phases can be bypassed in the case of a drug designed to treat a serious or life-threatening illness for which no therapy exists or existing therapies are far less beneficial.

	Number of Patients	Length	Purpose	Percent of Drugs Successfully Tested
Phase 1	20-100	Several months	Mainly safety	70 percent
Phase 2	Up to several hundred	Several months to 2 years	Some short-term safety but mainly effectiveness	33 percent
Phase 3	Several hundred to several thousand	1-4 years	Safety, dosage, effectiveness	25-30 percent

Source: FDA, Center for Drug Evaluation and Research

(known as Cox-2 inhibitors) a house of cards "destined for potential collapse." [7]

But Kweder told a congressional hearing in late 2004 the agency had been monitoring cardiovascular issues with Vioxx since they were discovered by Merck's own research in 2000. After nearly two years of negotiations with the company, she said, the FDA had finally gotten the company to rewrite the medication's label in 2002, recommending that high-dose use be limited to five days. [8]

Similarly, in mid-October 2004, after a long-running controversy, the FDA required antidepressant labels to indicate a potential for elevated suicide risk in children and teens.

To stanch the bad publicity, Acting Commissioner Crawford announced that the agency would commission the IOM to review FDA safety procedures for all drugs. Crawford also pledged to conduct a series of drug-safety workshops for doctors and health professionals, publish risk-management guidelines for drug manufacturers and appoint a permanent director of the Office of Drug Safety, a key position vacant since October 2003.

But the scandal would not go away. On Nov. 18, explosive hearings before the Senate Finance Committee generated more negative publicity. The Vioxx debacle

David Graham, associate director for science at the FDA's Office of Drug Safety, told a congressional committee in November 2004 that his superiors stopped him from publishing a study concluding that Vioxx had caused from 88,000 to 139,000 heart attacks.

was perhaps "the single greatest drug-safety catastrophe in the history of this country," said David Graham, associate director for science at the Office of Drug Safety. The problem could have been avoided, he said, but the Office of New Drugs is often "extremely resistant to full and open disclosure of safety information." [9]

The FDA "as currently configured," Graham insisted, "is incapable of protecting America against another Vioxx." Moreover, he added, five other medications approved by the agency warranted re-evaluation: Accutane (acne), Meridia (weight loss), Crestor (cholesterol), Bextra (pain) and Serevent (asthma).

The FDA's Kweder responded that the agency had "worked actively and vigorously with Merck" to inform public-health professionals about heart risks associated with Vioxx and was pursuing "further definitive investigations to better define and quantify this risk." She later

acknowledged that there had been "lapses" in the agency's actions in the Vioxx case. [10]

Raymond V. Gilmartin, Merck's chief executive, told the hearing that the firm believed wholeheartedly in Vioxx and had followed rigorous scientific procedures every step of the way regarding the drug.

"Over the past six years, we have promptly disclosed results of numerous Merck-sponsored studies to the FDA, physicians, the scientific community and the media," Gilmartin said.

He added: "My wife was taking Vioxx, using Vioxx, up until the day we withdrew it from the market."

With the spotlight focused on drug safety, the agency moved against other drugs that Graham had questioned, including Accutane, which can cause birth defects and miscarriages in some users, along with depression and suicide. The FDA announced on Nov. 23, 2004, that pharmacists must acquire proof that a patient is not pregnant before dispensing the drug, among other precautions. [11]

In December, concerns about three other Vioxx-type drugs created a new crisis. During a trial studying Celebrex, the National Cancer Institute identified an elevated risk of heart disease and promptly ended the study. The FDA asked Pfizer, maker of Celebrex and Bextra, to voluntarily suspend its promotion of the drugs pending a safety review and recommended that doctors "consider alternative therapies." [12]

Days later, the National Institutes of Health (NIH) halted a study on Alzheimer's patients taking Naproxen — the Bayer pain reliever sold over the counter as Aleve — for longer than the 10-day manufacturers' recommendation after it appeared the drug might increase cardiovascular incidents.

The pharmaceutical companies then began trying to clarify consumers' confusion over the cascading series of revelations. Bayer produced a television ad stating that Naproxen is safe if used as directed. Pfizer CEO Hank McKinnell also defended his company's products, pointing to contradictory findings and claiming that several recent studies were issuing doses that exceeded the amount and duration indicated on the label. "Celebrex, when used as recommended — which does not mean 800 milligrams a day continuously for three years — is safe and effective," he said. [13]

But when AstraZeneca — days after Graham's testimony — placed full-page newspaper and television ads defending Crestor, an emboldened FDA sent the company a warning letter calling the ads "false and misleading." [14]

However, Alan Goldhammer, vice president for regulatory affairs at the Pharmaceutical Research and Manufacturers of America (PhRMA), says the current drug-safety debate is needlessly negative. "If you put it into the proper perspective, there are more than 10,000 pharmaceutical products on the market, and in the vast majority of cases they are safely and effectively treating patients," he says.

Galson agrees. "You have to keep the benefits of the drug in mind when you're looking at safety," he says. "It makes no good public-health sense to separate the two functions."

The controversy has taken its toll on FDA scientists and staff, many of whom could be making much more money in the private sector. "There are a lot of professional critics who have never worked at the FDA and are not required to put themselves in our place," says Galson. "This is a watershed moment in the agency's history, and it is important for us to adequately deal with it."

As the controversy continues, here are some of the issues being debated:

Is drug testing adequate?

Critics say that FDA regulators rush to review applications for new medicines but are slow to address safety problems that come to light after a drug has entered the marketplace. FDA proponents, however, say the understaffed agency lacks strong regulatory authority over the industry and is under enormous pressure to make new medications available to those who need them while balancing the potential benefits of drugs against their risks.

"If you only look at risk, we wouldn't have any drugs," Deputy Commissioner Woodcock said on March 3. "You have to have the benefits side in front of you."

Many observers trace the FDA's current problems to the 1980s, when AIDS activists demanded that the agency speed up approval of new, potentially life-saving drugs. Congress responded in 1992 by passing the Prescription Drug User Fee Act (PDUFA), which imposed substantial drug-review application, or user fees, on pharmaceutical companies to help beef up the agency's drug-review staff and enable "fast-track" drug reviews.

At the same time, the law required the agency to assess most new drugs within a year. Critics and some former agency officials say that shifted the agency's priorities from safety evaluation to rapid drug approvals.

"The FDA became preoccupied with rapid drug reviews, and less attention was paid to safety," said former FDA chief Kessler, now dean of the School of Medicine at the University of California, San Francisco. [15]

Today, the drug-review process typically takes 13 to 14 months, compared to an average of 33 months in 1992. The expedited process is largely attributed to the fact that the Office of New Drugs now employs more than 1,000 people. By comparison, the Office of Drug Safety has only 110 employees to oversee post-market problems with drugs — a fact some critics say clearly shows the law shifted the agency's priorities. [16]

But PhRMA's Goldhammer says patient care has improved dramatically under PDUFA. "We've come a long way in the last 12 years," he said, "and the beneficiaries are the millions of patients who now receive life-sustaining medicines more quickly."

The law has also had a positive effect on drug safety, according to Woodcock. "It really improves the pre-market program," she said. "It [provides] a lot more science, a lot more ability to do scrutiny, [more] people to do work-ups of drugs." [17]

Most consumers assume that if the FDA has approved a medication it is safe and has undergone several years of clinical trials. In fact, drug companies only conduct short-term trials — usually about a year — before drugs are released to the general public. Thus, long-term negative effects — such as cancer or heart damage — are only discovered after a drug has been in public circulation over several months or years.

"We deliberately allow [medications] on the market knowing that some side effects won't be detected for months or years down the line," said Brian Strom, professor of public health and preventive medicine at the University of Pennsylvania School of Medicine. [18]

PhRMA's Goldhammer insists that pre-market testing represents the "gold standard of drug reviews," and that companies spend extraordinary time and money during clinical development. "But we need to do a better job of communicating all the activities that go into risk assessment and risk management," he adds.

For instance, he says, new drug applications can be accompanied by upwards of 100,000 pages of data. New compounds are always tested on animals first, and then companies test the drugs on up to 5,600 human volunteers during three separate phases of clinical trials. (*See box, p. 49.*)

FDA Panelists Had Ties to Drug Firms

Ten of the 32 members of the FDA panel that voted against banning three controversial drugs were paid consultants to the drugmakers. Nine of the 10 voted to allow marketing of the drugs to continue. If those with drug-company ties had not voted, two of the three drugs would have received approval recommendations.

Should marketing of the following drugs be allowed to continue?

	Yes	No
Bextra (Pfizer)		
Total vote	17	13
Panelists with financial ties	9	1
Panelists with no known ties*	8	12
Vioxx (Merck)		
Total vote	17	15
With financial ties	9	1
No financial ties	8	14
Celebrex (Pfizer)		
Total vote	31	1

* Two panelists abstained.

Sources: FDA; Center for Science in the Public Interest

Within the FDA itself, says the CDER's Galson, half of the agency's resources are spent on pre-market safety evaluation of new drugs; most of the remaining resources are spend reviewing what the companies report about their own safety studies.

After a drug company presents the results of its clinical trials, an FDA expert advisory panel sometimes holds public meetings to provide scientific guidance on controversial or highly technical issues. It then votes on whether the proposed drug's benefits outweigh the risks — votes that are rarely overturned by agency officials.

Throughout the approval process, Galson says, the agency strives to balance the benefit of giving the public access to new pharmaceuticals with the need for safety. "These are important societal questions — access versus safety," he says. "This is one of the thorniest regulatory decisions around, and I think we have it just about right."

Kenneth Kaitin, director of the Tufts University Center for the Study of Drug Development, says the FDA is open to improvements in pre-market testing, citing the agency's Critical Path initiative to improve the delivery of innovative drugs and medical products to patients, adopted in March 2004.

"Better markers have been detected by clinicians in animal research to determine which drugs may have safety problems later on," Kaitin says, "and tests for liver enzymes can detect potential drug problems."

However, Harvard Medical School Professor Jerry Avorn, author of *Powerful Medicines*, says companies sometimes cherry-pick candidates for pre-market testing pools — which range from several hundred to a few thousand participants — potentially skewing the results. He recommends that drug-test pools include a more representative sample of the patients who will be taking the drug in question once it hits the market.

Some critics also say drug companies routinely suppress damaging evidence revealed during clinical trials. To remedy the perceived problem, Sens. Charles Grassley, R-Iowa, and Christopher Dodd, D-Conn., introduced the Fair Access to Clinical Trials Act, which would create a clinical trial database. It would consist of a registry and results databank that would require reporting of research outcomes, demographic information on subjects, funding sources for the trial and significant adverse effects.

Despite extensive pre-market testing of drugs, most experts say a drug's true dangers are not usually known until it is released to the general population. "Pre-market trials can't replace the experience you gain when a drug is on the market," Kaitin says. But critics say the nation's post-market surveillance system is broken and that FDA has no authority to mandate post-market testing. (*See sidebar, p. 58.*)

"The real question is, 'Are we doing enough once these drugs are out there [in the marketplace] in the way of post-marketing surveillance?' " asks Strom of the University of Pennsylvania. "And the answer to that has to be 'no.' " [19]

With the agency approving so many more drugs each year and with the companies heavily promoting those drugs, critics like Strom say the Office of Drug Safety's resources and authority to track post-market problems should be significantly improved.

Often the key to a drug's safety is not the tests the drug companies conduct before a drug is approved but the tests they avoid after it's been approved, critics say. For example, in 2002 — three years after Vioxx was approved for the market — Merck abruptly canceled a trial planned to study the connection between Vioxx and heart disease.

"It raises the issue of who knew what and when," says Sharon Levine, associate executive director of Kaiser Permanente's Northern California region.

When the agency has a problem with an approved drug, it cannot order a company to revise its label for the drug but can only negotiate with the manufacturer. In the Vioxx case, for instance, label-wording negotiations went on for nearly two years after Merck research revealed the increased cardiovascular risks associated with the drug — even as the company was aggressively marketing the drug to the public.

Off-label use of drugs is another complication, says Susan Winckler, vice president for policy and communication at the American Pharmacists Association. The FDA does not have authority to restrict drugs from being used to treat conditions for which the agency has not explicitly approved the drug's use. Yet such off-label use of Fen-Phen caused cardiovascular problems and 123 deaths before it was finally withdrawn in 1997.

Often, post-market problems aren't discovered until a company is testing a drug's effectiveness to treat a disorder different from the one for which it was originally approved. The post-market trials that tainted Celebrex and Vioxx, for example, were investigating whether they were effective in preventing cancer; the problems with Naproxen were discovered when Bayer was examining its effect on Alzheimer's disease.

However, post-market surveillance is among the agency's biggest challenges. The current system, called MedWatch, relies on voluntary compliance by drug companies and doctors, who submit data on drug reactions to the FDA. The system may catch only 10 percent of drug reactions, says Avorn, and it is difficult to pin-

Sandra L. Kweder, deputy director of the FDA's Office of New Drugs, tells Congress in September 2004 the agency is making progress in communicating the risks of drugs and that a major overhaul of its authority is not necessary. Secretary of Health and Human Services Michael O. Leavitt announced on Feb. 15, 2005, that the FDA will establish a new independent Drug Safety Oversight Board to monitor FDA-approved medicines.

Getty Images/Matthew Cavanaugh (Kweder); Department of Health and Human Services (Leavitt)

point whether the drug caused the reaction or some other factor was involved.

Some agency officials say post-marketing surveillance is the new frontier in ensuring drug safety. "We're looking at . . . using large databases like Medicare to look at outcomes from the use of drugs and at who got a specific drug and following adverse effects more comprehensively than we currently do," Galson says.

Is the FDA too close to the drug industry?

Some observers say the application fees created by the Prescription Drug User Fee Act (PDUFA) made FDA regulators financially dependent on the industry they were regulating.

"At the very least, it created an appearance of a conflict of interest," said Arthur Levin, who heads the Center for Medical Consumers, an advocacy group in New York City. [20]

According to Public Citizen, because of the fees the FDA "has come to see the drug companies more as 'clients' than as a regulated industry. This may have made it harder for the agency to deny approval for new drugs that pose a threat to the public's health." [21]

The FDA's Graham said the law also skews the way the agency views drug-safety studies. "You don't get rewards for doing the work that gets a drug taken off the market," he said. [22] "The Office of New Drugs drives the bus and calls the shots and makes the policy. But they cannot remain objective and impartial."

For instance, Graham says his superiors initially forbade him from publishing his study concluding that Vioxx probably caused from 88,000 to 139,000 heart attacks and pressured him to change his conclusions. [23] Then, to his surprise, he says the agency in September approved Vioxx for use in children with rheumatoid arthritis, and some supervisors dismissed his research premise regarding Vioxx' toxicity — eight days before Merck voluntarily withdrew the drug from the market.

The assumption by top agency officials, according to former FDA statistical reviewer Michael Elashoff, is that a drug would be approved, especially for products made by so-called Big PhRMA firms. "It's called the drug-approval process," he pointed out. "It's not called the drug-review process." [24]

After Elashoff told an FDA advisory panel that the flu drug Relenza was harmful and worthless, it refused to recommend approval of the drug. Elashoff says his superiors promptly barred him from making future presentations to advisory panels and approved the drug despite the panel's conclusion. The drug is still on the market. [25]

Nearly one in five FDA medical reviewers surveyed by HHS in 2002 said they felt pressured to switch their recommendation over a suspect drug during the review process. The survey of some 400 FDA scientists, released in December 2004, said that about two-thirds of those surveyed are less than fully confident in the agency's monitoring of the safety of prescription drugs now being sold. [26]

However, researchers at the University of Michigan and Harvard found no evidence that products produced by Big PhRMA firms received preferential treatment from the FDA after PDUFA's passage. Their study also debunked the idea that PDUFA alone was responsible for the accelerated approval times. The hiring of new reviewers, no matter the funding source, served as the determining factor. [27]

The FDA's Galson categorically rejects the contention that the agency gives the industry preferential treatment. "Complaints from drug companies fill my in-box," he says. "The companies would be very surprised by the assertion that we are connected. We're agnostic as to the source of our funding. Our people are public servants who are not paid well compared to private industry but do a great job."

Former FDA Commissioner Kessler agrees. "Just because you pay an application fee when you apply to college doesn't mean you get in," he said. "I do not believe we lowered our standards one bit." [28]

Tufts' Kaitin points out that the recall rate of drugs approved by the FDA, 3.5 percent, has "changed little" in the last 30 years, indicating that PDUFA has not resulted in unsafe drugs being approved.

However, Public Citizen claims "an unprecedented number" of drugs have been approved and then withdrawn for safety reasons since passage of PDUFA. The group says five drugs approved during the eight-year period immediately preceding passage of the law were later withdrawn for safety reasons, compared to nine drugs approved since the law's passage. [29]

The pharmaceutical industry, which has more Washington lobbyists than there are members of Congress, is unquestionably powerful. In the last decade, PhRMA-affiliated companies have spent $558 million to advance their legislative agenda through lobbying, political contributions and campaign donations, says Mary Boyle, a spokeswoman for Common Cause, a citizen's advocacy organization.

Critics claim the industry's tentacles reach deep into the halls of the FDA's antiquated headquarters in Rockville, Md. In October 2004, for instance, Sen. Grassley, chairman of the Senate Finance Committee, said he had uncovered evidence of collusion between Merck executives and FDA officers who had promised to tip off company officials if the agency found any potentially damaging information about Vioxx.

"We've seen evidence over the last year that the agency has become too cozy with drug companies," Grassley said recently. "In some cases the FDA has disregarded important concerns and warnings from its own best scientists." [30]

"I refuse to accept any discussion that the FDA is biased toward industry," said Goldhammer of PhRMA.

Meanwhile, questions arose in late February 2005 about whether the public could trust FDA advisory panels to make decisions free of commercial bias after press investigations revealed that several members of the advisory panel reviewing the safety of all of the Cox-2 drugs had ties to the drugs' manufacturers. [31]

The New York Times revealed that 10 of the 32 FDA scientific advisory board members who recommended that Vioxx, Celebrex and Bexta should continue to be marketed had consulted recently for the drugmakers. [32]

Concerns about government scientists accepting drug money were raised last year after a congressional committee charged that 100 NIH scientists had secretly accepted hundreds of thousands of dollars in consulting fees — some as high as $1 million — from drug companies. An NIH investigation subsequently cleared most of the scientists, but not before the agency instituted strict, new conflict-of-interest rules.

Will creation of the Drug Safety Oversight Board protect public health?

When HHS Secretary Leavitt announced plans to create a new safety board, he said it was needed to restore public confidence in the nation's prescription-drug supply. The public wants "more oversight and openness," he said. "They want to know what we know, what we do with the information and why we do it."

Leavitt said the board will be charged with disseminating via the Internet and fliers information about risks discovered about a drug after it is released to the market. In the past, FDA Acting Commissioner Crawford said, the agency traditionally has not been as forthcoming as it perhaps should have been about such post-market risk discoveries. The agency's reticence, he said, was primarily motivated by a desire to avoid unduly alarming the public, especially when drug trials revealed conflicting results. [33]

Medical experts have suggested establishing an independent drug-safety oversight board repeatedly over the past 30 years. In the 1970s, a distinguished panel reviewing FDA procedures recommended just such an independent office — with full regulatory authority. In 1998, *The New England Journal of Medicine* echoed the call for an independent board. [34]

Reformers usually suggested the board be modeled on the National Transportation Safety Board — a highly regarded independent agency that investigates air and other transportaion accidents. Because the NTSB is independent from the Federal Aviation Administration, which oversees — and some say is too friendly with — the airline industry, its findings are generally considered highly credible.

In December 2004, outgoing HHS Secretary Tommy G. Thompson revived the call for an independent advisory board.

However, no sooner had Leavitt made his announcement than critics complained that the board envisioned by the administration would be only advisory and would lack authority to quickly recall unsafe drugs. Others doubted the board could be independent.

Consumers Union said the panel could not be truly independent if — as Leavitt indicated — it is to be composed entirely of FDA, HHS and other government staff while outside medical experts, patient and consumer groups serve only as consultants. "We need an independent drug safety office with scientific staff that can quickly identify unreasonable health risks and quickly notify the public of those concerns," said Janell Mayo Duncan, the group's legislative and regulatory counsel.

Moreover, the board will not be able to do anything to stem the flood of direct-to-consumer drug advertising that permeates the airwaves, nor will it boost the FDA's enforcement authority, said Bruce M. Psaty, a professor of medicine, epidemiology and health services at the University of Washington. "It's hardly an adequate solution," he said. [35]

Some members of Congress concur and are proposing legislation that would create a board with more clout. Sen. Dodd called the proposed board "a step in the right direction, but it doesn't go nearly far enough. Consumer confidence in the FDA has been shaken to the core, and it will take more than cosmetic reforms to fix structural problems within the agency." [36]

Critics say that while the board will better be able to disseminate information to the public, it will not do much to ensure greater drug safety because the FDA still will not have the authority to demand that companies conduct clinical trials after a drug is approved.

Neither will the board be able to force companies to report all the results of their clinical trials — both positive and negative.

But others say an independent oversight board isn't needed at all. "This is an overreaction by the FDA to a highly politicized environment," Tufts' Kaitin said. "What's wrong with the NTSB analogy is that the risk tolerance for plane crashes is zero, but for drugs, it's not so simple."

Kazman at the Competitive Enterprise Institute also takes issue with the NTSB comparison. He says a permanent agency modeled on the transportation safety board is a bad idea because it would spend inordinate resources going after the so-called "last 10 percent" of potential hazards and would be compelled to find safety problems to justify its existence.

Some critics of the FDA say an independent board is needed because the Office of Drug Safety occupies sec-

CHRONOLOGY

1900-1930s *Muckraking journalists uncover abuses, prompting key laws regulating drug firms.*

1902 Biologics Control Act ensures the safety of serums and vaccines.

1906 Pure Food and Drug Act bars interstate commerce in mislabeled or adulterated foods and drugs.

1927 Food and Drug Administration (FDA) is established.

1938 Landmark Food, Drug and Cosmetic Act requires manufacturers to prove the safety of their products before approval.

1950s-1970s *Congress requires new safeguards against unsafe drugs.*

1958 Food Additives Amendments require manufacturers to demonstrate the safety of additives; Delaney Clause bars cancer-causing food additives.

1959 Sen. Estes Kefauver, D-Tenn., begins investigating drug companies; FDA medical reviewers air safety concerns.

1962 Thalidomide, an anti-nausea drug for pregnant women, causes birth defects in Europe. Drug's distribution in U.S. is blocked by a skeptical FDA reviewer. . . . Congress requires drugmakers to prove the efficacy as well as the safety of drugs.

1974 FDA medical reviewers tell Senate committee that agency officials are too cozy with drug-industry officials and that safety issues are addressed.

1976 Congress passes Medical Device Amendments.

1980s-1990s *Drug industry is charged high fees in an attempt to speed the drug-approval process. Fears rise that dangerous compounds have slipped through the FDA safety net.*

1985 FDA approves an AIDS blood test to protect patients from infected donors.

1990 Congress passes Nutrition Labeling and Education Act. Safe Medical Devices Act requires hospitals to report dangerous devices.

1992 Prescription Drug User Fee Act (PDUFA) creates a fee system to accompany new drug applications. In return, the drug companies receive fast-tracking of promising new drugs.

1994 President Bill Clinton signs Dietary Supplement Health and Education Act, authorizing FDA to issue good-manufacturing practice regulations.

1997 Congress renews PDUFA. . . . Five drugs that are approved are later voluntarily withdrawn; "black box" warnings are later issued for two other drugs.

2000-Present

2001 The drug Baycol is pulled after problems with liver damage emerge.

Spring 2004 Concerns emerge about antidepressants and possible links to suicide.

September 2004 Merck pulls Vioxx off market after tests suggest an elevated heart-disease risk. FDA issues warnings about two other drugs in Vioxx's class.

October 2004 After years of debate, FDA requires antidepressant labels to indicate a potential for elevated suicide risk in children and teens.

Nov. 18, 2004 David Graham, associate director for science at the Office of Drug Safety, tells the Senate Finance Committee the Vioxx debacle was perhaps "the single, greatest drug-safety catastrophe in the history of this country" and that the Office of New Drugs is often "extremely resistant to full and open disclosure of safety information."

December 2004 National Cancer Institute abruptly ends trial of Celebrex after identifying an elevated risk of heart disease. FDA asks Pfizer to suspend promotion of Celebrex and Bextra pending a safety review.

February 2005 Michael O. Leavitt, secretary of the Department of Health and Human Services, appoints Acting FDA Commissioner Lester M. Crawford as the new head of the agency, filling a yearlong vacancy . . . . The administration announces it will appoint a new, independent Drug Safety Oversight Board.

ond-class status within the agency and that higher-ups overturn underlings' decisions. With a budget of $25 million for 2005 and a staff of 110, the Office of Drug Safety has about one-tenth the employees of the Office of New Drugs — which has a $111 million budget to evaluate and fast-track new drug applications.

Moreover, critics say Drug Safety Office recommendations lack binding authority, and all discussions over regulatory actions must be negotiated with personnel in the Office of New Drugs, who are reluctant to admit that medicines they approved turn out to be hazardous once they have entered the marketplace.

"The Office of New Drugs proved to be extremely resistant to full and open disclosure of safety information," Graham told Congress, "especially when it called into question an existing regulatory position. In these situations, the new-drug reviewing division that approved the drug in the first place and that regards it as its own child, typically proves to be the single, greatest obstacle to effectively dealing with serious drug-safety issues."

But FDA's Galson disputes Graham's portrayal. "There is no pressure for anyone to change conclusions," he says. "In a hierarchical scientific organization, we want different people to look at the science, but there is a real risk in separating the assessment of safety from the efficacy of drugs."

PhRMA's Goldhammer agrees. "It's a misconception that the Office of Drug Safety is linked to the Office of New Drugs," he says. "We have the best safety record in the world."

"The expertise in the agency on the safety and efficacy of drugs resides in the Office of New Drugs," Galson says, "but we are working to exchange the communication between working groups and bring other voices to the table about how we manage safety issues that are not unduly influenced by the new-drug staff."

BACKGROUND

Deep Roots

The FDA's roots go back to the Agriculture Department's Division of Chemistry, founded in 1862 to police the freewheeling food and patent-medicine industries. Before refrigeration, many food makers used questionable preservatives. And nostrums often contained downright harmful concoctions. Some were merely water and flavoring; others contained cocaine, morphine and alcohol. Even children's elixirs like Mrs. Winslow's Soothing Syrup included opium. Whatever the ingredients, the healing powers they claimed invariably were outlandish.

Powerful then as now, the industry was one of the first to advertise nationally and kept newspapers from reporting on drug issues by threatening to withdraw their ads if negative articles were published.

In the early 1900s, however, the American Medical Association (AMA), the trade association for doctors, began hearing reports that the additive *acetanilide*, used to relieve pain, caused heart attacks, and muckraking magazines like *Ladies' Home Journal* and *Collier's* seized on the issue of drug safety.

The exposés they published helped pass the 1906 Food and Drug Act, which created the nation's first regulatory agency by expanding the Division of Chemistry's powers. The act required truth in advertising but only required concoctions to list their ingredients if they included alcohol, opium, cocaine, morphine, chloroform, marijuana or *acetanilide*. Fliers, brochures, newspaper ads and posters were exempted.

Because the agency was required to wait until damage occurred before going to court, the losses tended to outweigh the gains. In its first case, the agency won a conviction after Cuforhedake Brane-Fude, sold as a brain tonic and headache cure, killed 22 people. A jury agreed that the label's claims of being "harmless" constituted fraud, but the $700 fine barely dented drugmaker Robert Parker's bank account or tarnished his reputation. [37]

In 1912, the Supreme Court ruled in favor of the makers of Dr. Johnson's Mild Combination Treatment for Cancer, deciding that the agency had the jurisdiction to police the label's ingredients, not its curative claims.

A name change to the Food and Drug Administration in 1927 spurred the agency's professionalization, but anyone still could concoct a purported cure-all in the kitchen sink, put it in a fancy bottle and be in business, knowing that the FDA had no power to test it or pull it from the market.

New Deal reformers in the 1930s began tackling the law's loopholes by preparing new legislation, backed by concerned consumer groups. In 1933 the book *100,000,000 Guinea Pigs* exposed false claims made by medicine manufacturers and went through 27 printings.

When the industry retaliated, using scare tactics to mobilize merchants and patients, the FDA mounted a traveling "Chamber of Horrors" exhibit depicting dan-

Improving Post-Marketing Surveillance

Concerns about the FDA's ability to monitor drug dangers that come to light after drugs have been approved for the market have spurred calls for different approaches to post-marketing surveillance in the United States.

In fact, a recent survey of FDA scientists by the Department of Health and Human Services showed far more concern about the government's drug-safety monitoring after medicines hit the marketplace than about the quality of safety assessments conducted before FDA approval. Two-thirds of the respondents had doubts about the FDA's post-market surveillance capabilities, but the same percentage was mostly or completely confident in pre-approval safety assessments. [1]

The government's existing post-market surveillance system, called MedWatch, was instituted in 1993. It relies on doctors and drug companies to voluntarily report suspected cases of drug reactions. But reports trickle in — with only about 10 percent of adverse reactions being reported — and tracking lacks rigor.

"MedWatch is a bust," says Kenneth Kaitin, director of Tufts University's Center for the Study of Drug Development.

The FDA announced in February 2005 that it would institute systemic drug-safety reforms, including creation of an independent Drug Safety Oversight Board, which would disseminate information — via an Internet Web site and fliers — about drug-safety concerns that arise after drugs have been on the market. However, critics complain the board will not have the authority to quickly recall a drug that is found to be dangerous or require additional clinical trials.

Meanwhile, many medical facilities and HMOs have instituted their own innovative initiatives to improve data collection on potential drug interactions and side effects. In addition, several hospitals have beefed up their in-house pharmacology departments to add drug investigators and devise comparisons of drugs based on efficacy and cost.

For instance, Brigham & Women's Hospital in Boston, the teaching facility of Harvard Medical School, added its Department of Pharmacoepidemiology and Pharmacoeconomics in 1998 to research the benefits, risks and costs of prescription drugs and disseminate its findings in user-friendly formats.

At Wishard Memorial Hospital in Indianapolis, prescriptions are made over a computerized Entry Order System, which provides interactive information regarding the patient's medical history and other medications he or she is taking. After a drug is administered, doctors and pharmacists look for signals, such as a liver abnormality, that may indicate a drug reaction, says Clement McDonald, director of the hospital's Regenstreif Institute. The system, developed internally in 1986, sends doctors rules and reminders that pop up when they type their prescriptions, though the hospital had to tinker with the alerts.

"Too many, and it gets to be like spam, so we had to work on the balance," McDonald says. The key to the system's success is to have doctors and pharmacists looking at prescription patterns together, McDonald says.

gerous medicines and cosmetics. Examples included Lash Lure mascara, which caused blindness or death in 1 percent of users, and Mountain Valley Mineral Water — actually Atlanta tap water — sold as a cure for cardiac problems, diabetes and rheumatism.

The drugmakers seemed to have the reform bill squelched when disaster occurred. In 1937 a Tennessee company that put its new antibacterial medication into liquid form used a poisonous additive — FDA drug-safety officer Graham recently referred to it as anti-freeze — and 107 people died, mostly children. Once alerted, FDA agents scoured the country and retrieved all but six of the 240 gallons in the batch that had been distributed.

Tough, New Law

After the tragedy, Congress quickly passed the 1938 Food, Drug and Cosmetic Act, which required manufacturers to prove their products were safe before marketing. They hired scientists and outfitted laboratories, improving drug safety and revolutionizing the industry, whose mantra became "Patent, Produce, Promote." Miracle medicines like penicillin, insulin and sulfa drugs led boosters to tout the potential of pharmaceuticals to one day eliminate disease.

Rapid changes in science and business overwhelmed the FDA, which relied on drug companies for data and rarely pressed when problems occurred. Parke-Davis officials, for example, knew its antibiotic chloram-

The hospital also participates in a data-sharing arrangement with five other Indianapolis hospitals and exercises extreme caution over new drugs. "We don't use new drugs unless there's nothing else like them on Earth," says McDonald. "Otherwise, we wait four or five years."

At Intermountain Health Care Hospital in Salt Lake City, pharmacists receive alerts about possible symptoms of drug reactions, then visit patients' bedsides looking for signs of adverse events.

Independent programs, some initiated by the federal government, are synthesizing and translating scientific data into digestible, comparative studies of various classes of drugs. Beginning in 1997, the federal Agency for Healthcare Research and Quality has awarded a series of five-year contracts to 12 public and private institutions in the United States and Canada to establish evidence-based practice centers. One of the most active, the Oregon Health & Science University in Portland, established a Drug Effectiveness Review Project and has issued several reports and updates.

Institutions of all sizes — from the 200-doctor Everett Clinic in Washington state to the giant Kaiser Permanente HMO in California — have adopted in-house initiatives to improve drug safety. Both Kaiser and Everett, for example, bar drug-company representatives from visiting doctors unless specifically invited and ban free samples. They also provide doctors with expert pharmacological "counter-detailing," or price and efficacy comparisons designed to counter the promotional claims made by drug companies and their sales representatives.

"We've been counter-detailing the Cox-2s for years," said Jennifer Wilson Norton, director of pharmacy services at the Everett Clinic. "The [cardiovascular] problems weren't news to us or to our providers."

In January, Kaiser Permanente pharmacies stopped stocking Bextra, the first time the HMO has ever banned an FDA-approved drug.

Other countries have developed effective post-market surveillance techniques. [2] For example, more than 20 "pharmaco-vigilance centers" in France have evolved into vast repositories of information about medications. In case of an adverse event, the centers work with doctors to determine if it is tied to a drug or another factor. All information is passed to the country's central drug regulators. The system unearthed a problem with the anti-psychotic drug olanzapine (marketed as Zyprexa in the United States) that was significant enough to warrant a label change.

In England, black triangles are required on the labels of newly approved drugs to signal the need for vigilance by doctors. In addition, the Drug Safety Research unit of Britain's Medicines and Health Care Products Regulatory Agency sends so-called "Green Cards" to doctors seeking information about certain drugs. The compliance rate is better than half.

Pharmacists in England also report adverse reactions to drugs, and computers record long-term side effects. In January 2005, England's health minister announced that regulators would begin collecting and publishing online patient reports of adverse drug side effects.

---

[1] Department of Health and Human Services.

[2] Anna Wilde Mathew, "Second Opinion: As Drug Safety Worries Grow, Looking Overseas for Solutions; French Vigilance Centers Spot Problems, and U.K. Traces Issues with 'Green Cards;' A High-Tech Prescription Pad," *The Wall Street Journal*, Dec. 31, 2004, p. A1.

phenicol caused aplastic anemia, a debilitating blood disease, in a small number of users but covered it up. Once the FDA realized the danger, it restricted the company's advertisements and notified physicians, though few heeded the warnings. Despite 100 deaths, innumerable lawsuits and reams of studies, the FDA dallied, calling on the National Research Council three times in a decade to weigh in on the issue. The drug is still on the market.

During this era, the FDA had a powerful ally in the AMA. In 1949, the AMA's journal published an editorial entitled "Too Many Drugs?" and AMA representatives inspected drug laboratories, shutting down those it deemed unsafe. Harvard Medical School Professor Dale Friend wrote "it is impossible for the practicing physician to have information to select drugs wisely." Of the 8,000 medications available, "there are many agents that are unwanted, useless, undesirable, of limited value, or actually harmful." That skepticism began to fade in the 1950s as doctors became willing prescribers of powerful new drugs touted as miracle cures.

John Lear, science editor of *Saturday Review* magazine, reported in 1959 that doctors felt overwhelmed by the onrush of new products. As the only agency able to serve as an impartial source of information about drug

Merck & Co President Raymond V. Gilmartin announces a voluntary worldwide withdrawal of the painkiller Vioxx, on Sept. 30, 2004; a 2000 study showed increased risks of heart attack and stroke for long-term users. The Securities and Exchange Commission and Justice Department are investigating possible wrongdoing by Merck.

Still, Kefauver's efforts stalled until the infamous drug thalidomide, designed to treat morning sickness and other symptoms of pregnancy, cast the agency in a heroic light. Richardson-Merrill, a U.S. drug firm, had licensed thalidomide from a German company, which had suppressed tests revealing the drug's connection with nerve poisoning and birth defects.

Luckily, Richardson-Merrill's application to distribute thalidomide in the United States crossed the desk of drug reviewer Frances Oldham Kelsey in 1960. She found the evidence weak and asked for more data, but the company portrayed the request as another example of a faceless bureaucrat impeding the march of progress. Meanwhile, trial packets of the drug had been sent to doctors around the country without keeping records, as then permitted under FDA regulations.

Then, news from Europe began arriving about deformed babies born to women who had taken the drug while pregnant. FDA inspectors tracked down the experimental shipments and removed most of them, but tragically, 17 babies were born in the United States with severe deformities — typically flipper-like arms and legs. Kelsey went from goat to savior overnight. "Heroine of the FDA Keeps Bad Drug Off Market," trumpeted *The Washington Post.*

Sen. Hubert H. Humphrey, D-Minn., said the more the committee learned, the more "shocked and disappointed" it became to find that "drugs have been approved that the FDA says should never have been approved."

The tragedy made the reform bill — known as the Kefauver-Harris Amendments — inevitable in 1962. The new law put health and empirical evidence first, business second. Every new drug would not only have to be proven safe but also effective, as demonstrated by "adequate and well-controlled investigations." Drug companies were required to acquire patient consent, notify the FDA before experiments began and keep complete records. However, limited funds accompanied the new requirements: in 1965, for example, only 14 reviewers tackled 2,500 drug applications.

The FDA commissioned the National Academy of Sciences to conduct a comprehensive Drug Efficacy Study to examine all the drugs then on the market. It determined 7 percent to be ineffective and 50 percent to be effective to some degree, delivering a blow to the industry's prestige and prompting pharmaceutical firms to withdraw some 300 drugs.

safety, he wrote, the FDA abdicated its position as respected umpire when it accepted company-written packaging inserts without question and when agency scientists took money from drug companies. For example, Henry Welch, chief of the FDA's antibiotics division, received $287,000 from 1953 to 1960. [38]

The man who would change the FDA, Sen. Estes Kefauver, D-Tenn., began investigating the drug industry in 1959 after he became aware of its huge profits. His Health Committee probe soon expanded to include safety issues.

Barbara Moulton, an FDA medical officer, told Kefauver's committee that drug company officials had more sway with her supervisors than agency medical officers, who she said routinely ignored her concerns about drug safety.

Over the next two decades, the FDA clarified the term "safe and effective." As the agency attempted to create scientific standards for drugs, the Nixon administration sought to replace what it called whistleblowers and obstructionists at FDA with political appointees.

At subcommittee hearings chaired by Sen. Edward M. Kennedy, D-Mass., FDA drug reviewers testified that drug companies refused to cooperate with the agency's scientific reforms and that its leadership, in an effort to avoid confrontation, often overruled them when they tried to deny a drug application. [39]

Industry Pressure

Despite the pleas of legislators and drug-safety crusaders to put science first, industry pressure built on the agency to accelerate approval times.

In the 1970s, the agency adopted internal reforms, including opening meetings to the public and forming 66 advisory committees by 1974. FDA Commissioner Jere Goyan, appointed by President Jimmy Carter, pressed to close the information gap between prescription medications and over-the-counter treatments by pushing through new labeling requirements in 1980.

Carter's successor, Ronald Reagan, openly hostile to government intervention in the private sphere, signed Executive Order 12291, which declared the president had "the power to control all regulations" attempted by federal agencies. The act designated the White House Office of Management and Budget (OMB) as the clearinghouse to which every agency would have to apply if it wanted to implement regulations, "and it was from OMB that orders emanated to dismantle regulations already in place."

OMB also tried to overturn the labeling changes and neutralize the FDA's authority, even though agency researchers had discovered that manufacturer-sponsored trials manipulated data to favor positive outcomes for proposed drugs.

In 1988, AIDS activists staged an all-day protest at the agency's headquarters in Rockville, Md., demanding access to experimental drugs. The next year, a bribery scandal led to the conviction of FDA officials for taking money from generic-drug companies to speed up drug reviews.

The agency's budgetary restraints led to an infusion of industry money when Congress passed PDUFA in 1992. Meanwhile, Commissioner Kessler caused a firestorm

when he announced his agency's intention to regulate tobacco. That triggered an attempt by Rep. Newt Gingrich, R-Ga., and others to permanently dissolve the agency and let companies oversee safety. Taken aback, several high-level drug-industry officials distanced themselves from the proposal, recognizing that FDA approval conferred cachet on their products.

The review of new drug applications accelerated, but the so-called "nightmare year" of 1997 foreshadowed problems. Five drugs approved that year were withdrawn, two were required to use highly restrictive labels — known as black box warnings; one of the two, Meridia, is still available.

From 1997 to 2000, 11 drugs were taken off the market, an unprecedented number for a three-year period. Meanwhile, Baycol, made by Bayer, marked the sixth entry into the crowded market for cholesterol-reducing drugs known as statins. All statins can trigger rhabdomyolysis, an incapacitating muscle disease, though some are more dangerous than others. The FDA required Baycol drug packages to carry black box alerts and sent out "Dear Doctor" letters, but prescriptions barely waned. After 31 deaths, Bayer pulled the drug in August 2001.

Reflecting on the FDA's first century, author Philip Hilts noted that regulation, though despised by free-market advocates, is a vital part of American society. "The lesson we can see throughout the past century of conflict is not that business will sometimes exploit citizens for profit, or that government agencies will sometimes make mistakes," he wrote, "but that regulation and commerce are part of the same equation of progress." [40]

CURRENT SITUATION

Courts as Backup?

Some current and former drug-safety officials say that since the FDA cannot possibly detect all instances of unsafe drugs, other regulatory agencies and the civil courts serve as a necessary backup system to protect consumers.

"It's unreasonable and unrealistic to think that the FDA can catch 100 percent of the problems," says former FDA attorney Ted Parr, who worked in the office of the FDA's chief counsel in the 1990s.

Indeed, investigators at the Securities and Exchange Commission and the Justice Department are investigating

New Role for Over-the-Counter Drugs?

Earlier this year, amid the scandal over Cox-2 painkillers, the FDA considered allowing mild doses of the prescription cholesterol-lowering drug Mevacor to be sold on drug store shelves. It would have been the first time remedies once only available by prescription to treat chronic conditions would have been sold over the counter (OTC) — along with aspirins and decongestants.

In 2000, the agency had rejected OTC sales of low doses of Mevacor and Pravachol, both members of the statin drug class — the world's largest-selling, with 2004 sales of $15.5 billion. Statins scrub fatty deposits from artery walls, but they are not for everyone. Mevacor is targeted at men over 45 and women over 55 with high levels of "bad" cholesterol and at least one risk factor for heart disease, such as smoking or high blood pressure. Studies have estimated that statins are taken by fewer than half the people who could benefit from them.

The makers of the two drugs said their increased availability would lead to a drop in cholesterol levels and fewer heart attacks. The low doses ostensibly would decrease the risk of side effects, such as liver damage. Pregnant women are advised to avoid the drug, which can also interact with other medications.

At a joint meeting of FDA advisory panels in January 2005, the drugmakers argued that although there are no symptoms for high cholesterol and only a blood test can reliably establish the medicine's appropriateness and efficacy for a particular patient, customers nonetheless could make informed choices about using what the company intended to market as Mevacor Daily.

Zocor, another statin, is available in England behind-the-counter but without a prescription. Consumers must answer a questionnaire before buying it.

Some panel members were concerned that patients would use Mevacor Daily as an excuse to skip doctor visits, avoid exercise and ignore sensible diets. They also wanted drug labels to indicate Mevacor's liver risk, which company representatives opposed.

Panelists also disagreed with the findings from an unusual study by the drugmakers, in which 14 mock storefronts were set up around the country to test their theory that consumers would self-select the correct drugs. Of the 3,316 people who entered the "pharmacies," 1,061 bought Mevacor. Researchers then tracked purchasers for six months.

At the hearing, the companies reported that 84 percent of the study's participants made appropriate initial-use decisions, including those who didn't buy it. One-third of users reported lower cholesterol.

Panel members, however, noted that some participants took the medication even though they didn't know their cholesterol levels. In a study of label comprehension, only 1 percent of participants who made the self-diagnosis that they could use the drug were considered appropriate candidates. The rest, they found, had their medical condition or other criteria wrong and required consultation with a doctor to take the medication correctly. Moreover, said one panel member, long-term compliance was "terrible." [1]

Ultimately, the panel voted 20 to 3 against approving Mevacor for OTC sales, due to concerns about patients' inability to accurately select or comply with long-term treatment. But members encouraged the company to continue its quest and expressed interest in exploring an alternative.

Meanwhile, at least one statin may be available over the counter in the near future: Bristol-Myers Squibb is expected to submit an application for OTC sales of Pravachol by the end of 2005.

[1] "Mevacor Daily Long-Term Consumer Compliance is One Concern For Cmte. Members," FDAAdvisoryCommittee.com.

whether Merck criminally deceived stockholders and hid damaging information about Vioxx or misled doctors and the public. "Doctors are not getting the straight scoop from drug companies," Parr says. "Doctors don't really know that other doctors are sometimes paid to hawk the products."

But perhaps the biggest impact of the Vioxx scandal will be felt in the civil courts, where patients claiming to have been harmed by the drug have filed more than 800 civil lawsuits against Merck. The suits could cost the company more than $10 billion. [41]

The liability system "is our only real defense against corporate negligence," writes Robert B. Reich, secretary of Labor in the Clinton administration and now a professor at Brandeis University. "The FDA is no longer able to do its job effectively," and "an important factor

Is the FDA protecting the public from harmful drugs?

YES

Sandra Kweder, M.D.
Deputy Director, Office of New Drugs, Center for Drug Evaluation and Research, U.S. Food and Drug Administration

From testimony before the Senate Finance Committee, Nov 18, 2004

It is well recognized that FDA's drug review is a gold standard. Indeed, we believe that FDA maintains the highest worldwide standards for drug approval. FDA grants approval to drugs after a sponsor demonstrates that they are safe and effective.

Experience has shown that the full magnitude of some potential risks does not always emerge during the mandatory clinical trials conducted before approval to evaluate these products for safety and effectiveness. Occasionally, serious adverse effects are identified after approval, either in post-marketing clinical trials or through spontaneous reporting of adverse events. That is why Congress has supported and FDA has created a strong post-market drug-safety program designed to assess adverse events. . . . The most recent actions concerning the drug Vioxx illustrate the vital importance of the ongoing assessment of the safety of a product once it is in widespread use.

All approved drugs pose some level of risk. . . . We cannot anticipate all possible effects of a drug during the clinical trials that precede approval. An adverse drug reaction can range from a minor, unpleasant response to a response that is sometimes life threatening or deadly. Such adverse drug reactions may be expected — because clinical-trial results indicate such possibilities — or unexpected — because the reaction was not evident in clinical trials. It may also result from errors in drug prescribing, dispensing or use. . . .

FDA worked actively and vigorously with Merck to inform public-health professionals of what was known regarding [cardiovascular] risk with Vioxx, and to pursue further definitive investigations to better define and quantify this risk. FDA also reviewed and remained current on new epidemiologic studies that appeared in the literature. Indeed, the recent study findings disclosed by Merck, leading to its decision to voluntarily withdraw Vioxx from the marketplace, resulted from FDA's vigilance in requiring these long-term outcome trials to address our concerns.

Detecting, assessing, managing and communicating the risks and benefits of prescription and over-the-counter drugs is a highly complex and demanding task. FDA is determined to meet this challenge by employing cutting-edge science, transparent policy and sound decisions based on the advice of the best experts in and out of the agency. . . . Medicines that receive FDA approval are among the safest in the world, and the measures we are taking are designed to strengthen this quality, as well as consumer confidence. . . .

NO

David Graham, M.D.
Associate director for science, Office of Drug Safety, U.S. Food and Drug Administration

From testimony before the Senate Finance Committee, Nov 18, 2004

The problem . . . is immense in scope. Vioxx is a terrible tragedy and a profound regulatory failure. I would argue that the FDA, as currently configured, is incapable of protecting America against another Vioxx. We are virtually defenseless.

It is important that this committee and the American people understand that what has happened with Vioxx is really a symptom of something far more dangerous to the safety of the American people. Simply put, the FDA and its Center for Drug Evaluation and Research (CDER) are broken. . . .

The organizational structure within CDER is entirely geared towards the review and approval of new drugs. When a CDER new-drug-reviewing division approves a new drug, it is also saying the drug is "safe and effective." When a serious safety issue arises post-marketing, their immediate reaction is almost always one of denial, rejection and heat. They approved the drug so there can't possibly be anything wrong with it. The same group that approved the drug is also responsible for taking regulatory action against post-marketing. This is an inherent conflict of interest.

At the same time, the Office of Drug Safety [ODS] has no regulatory power and must first convince the new-drug-reviewing division [the Office of New Drugs] that a problem exists before anything beneficial to the public can be done. Often, the new-drug reviewing division is the single, greatest obstacle to effectively protecting the public against drug-safety risks. A close second, in my opinion, is the ODS management that sees its mission as pleasing the Office of New Drugs.

The corporate culture within CDER is also a barrier to effectively protecting the American people from unnecessary harm due to prescription and [over-the-counter] drugs. The culture is dominated by a worldview that believes only randomized clinical trials provide useful and actionable information and that post-marketing safety is an afterthought. This culture also views the pharmaceutical industry it is supposed to regulate as its client, overvalues the benefits of the drugs it approves and seriously undervalues, disregards and disrespects drug safety.

Finally, the scientific standards CDER applies to drug safety guarantee that unsafe and deadly drugs will remain on the U.S. market. . . .

in convincing Merck to remove Vioxx from the market was the mounting threat of lawsuits." [42]

However, the Bush administration — as part of its proposal to overhaul the tort system — wants to cap damage claims in civil cases involving adverse drug reactions to $250,000 per victim if a drug was FDA-approved. Michigan has already instituted such a cap and has "effectively killed" liability suits, says Parr, who now represents plaintiffs in drug cases.

"I was at a meeting of about 300 lawyers litigating over Vioxx, and the speaker asked if anyone from Michigan was present. Not a hand went up," Parr says.

"It's not 'reform' when you're taking away people's rights," says Carlton Carl, a spokesman for the Association of Trial Lawyers of America. "This is just payback to the insurance, drug and health-care industries, which supported the president's campaign."

But the Competitive Enterprise Institute's Kazman says tort reform could lower the prices of prescription drugs, which have liability-insurance costs built into their prices.

Moreover, Kazman says, if the FDA becomes overly safety conscious, "it will increase the pressure to slow down drug approvals, which is a disaster that dwarfs other problems, because people will suffer. That's something that isn't often addressed."

Just as the Enron scandal sparked accounting reform, the recent drug dust-up should lead to demands that "CEOs of pharmaceutical manufacturers certify the accuracy of the safety data their epidemiologists submit," Harvard's Avorn writes. "Things must be pretty bad if we need tort lawyers to save the day." [43]

Reform Proposals

Congress has taken an especially keen interest in prescription drugs ever since it agreed in 2004 to begin paying for some elderly patients' medications through the federal Medicare program. [44] Prescription drugs also represent the fastest-rising segment of the nation's health-care tab, a cost that is expected to grow as the population ages.

In addition, consumers and some members of Congress have begun calling for greater government oversight of drugs already on the market following the Vioxx brouhaha and other recent revelations. And, as manufacturers become increasingly aggressive in marketing prescription medications, the likelihood grows that undesirable side effects and other problems will occur

because more people will be using the new drugs, critics say, making it all the more important that regulators be able to act quickly if threats are identified.

HHS Secretary Leavitt says he supports the idea of increasing post-market surveillance. "We need to ratchet up our monitoring of drugs after approval," he told the Senate Finance Committee on Feb. 16, 2005. "And we have the technology tools to do it. We have the capacity to capture millions of data points. And we have been, up to this point, more passive than we must be in the future." [45]

But, while Leavitt said the new safety oversight board would go a long way toward improving post-marketing oversight, consumer advocates and many lawmakers said the plans don't go far enough. Besides demanding an oversight board with more independence and authority, they want the FDA to make its internal deliberations more public and require drugmakers to post the results of all clinical trials, including those unfavorable to the company.

Sens. Grassley and Dodd plan to recommend establishing a public database detailing the results of all clinical drug trials, their sponsors and their methods. Currently, such information is not made public, and — in some cases — even if the FDA learns of safety issues concerning a drug, it is forbidden from revealing the negative results because they are considered trade secrets.

"The companies only have to give whatever information they need to support their drug application," Grassley says. "I want to . . . get evidence to the people who want to go back and check up on what the FDA is doing."

Grassley also wants the FDA's Office of Drug Safety — which monitors adverse side effects that emerge after drugs have been approved for the market — to be made independent from the Office of New Drugs, which approves the drugs for sale in the first place.

"It [is] necessary that the drug-safety office within the FDA be made a truly independent entity from the office of new drugs," he said, adding that his proposal will "clearly establish this independence and provide the office the authority needed to do its job." [46]

Sen. Dodd is preparing a bill that would establish an independent Office of Patient Protection within the FDA that could withdraw dangerous drugs from the market, end consumer advertising for risky drugs, order a company to change a drug's label and restrict uses of a drug. It would also have the power to mandate post-market safety studies of a drug, including contracting with large database-holders to conduct studies.

Dodd says his proposal would cost about $100 million, but Grassley says with budgets tight this year some of the proposed changes may not be affordable. The Bush administration's proposed $6.5 million increase in the Office of Drug Safety's budget represents a 24 percent boost and will allow the agency to hire 25 additional employees. But Dodd says the added funding is inadequate and that the agency's reorganization plan does not address "structural problems within the agency."

Sen. Kennedy wants FDA's resources to monitor drugs "dramatically increased" and says the FDA must be given authority "to require drug companies to initiate and complete appropriate safety studies." Some consumer advocates point out that the government spends $29 billion to fund basic drug research at the National Institutes of Health — research that helps drug companies develop new drugs — but only spends $1.8 billion on the entire FDA budget. [47]

Harvard's Avorn agrees that drug-safety resources need to be enhanced. "If the health-care system can spend $5 billion on Cox-2s," he says, "we should be able to find a couple of hundred million for safety."

After the hearings in February and March on FDA reform, Kennedy and Sen. Michael B. Enzi, R-Mont., chairman of the Senate Health, Education, Labor and Pensions Committee, began preparing proposals to beef up both the agency's budget and its post-marketing surveillance program.

In the meantime, Avorn says, the agency could be more aggressive with its existing powers. Besides requesting voluntary post-market tests, tinkering with labels, sending letters to doctors and regulating advertising, the agency rarely invokes its most powerful weapon — the ability to influence public opinion.

"If the FDA called a press conference and said that they had found worrisome signals with Vioxx and that Merck declined to move forward with a trial, and therefore the agency is issuing a public-health advisory, you would have that trial started in 24 hours," Avorn says. "There's an awful lot you can do with a bully pulpit, and I'd like to see them use it more."

In addition, former FDA counsel Parr points out, the FDA is extremely timid about using its authority to declare a drug an imminent health hazard and pull it off the market. In fact, no drug has been recalled in recent memory, he says, only a medical device — the silicone breast implant.

"The last item they banned was breast implants," Parr says. "Almost everyone agrees that was a disaster, so they're not going to do that again any time soon."

At least one former FDA official appears to agree. Scott Gottlieb, a former senior policy adviser, told the Senate Health Committee on March 1, 2005, that the agency does not need more authority but needs to exercise its existing powers more astutely.

Part of the problem is cultural, says Winckler at the American Pharmacists Association. "We as a society are extraordinarily casual with medications," she says. "Change would have to occur from the FDA on down to patients."

OUTLOOK

Access to Information

Experts say drug safety hinges in part on access to adequate information for HMOs, hospitals, doctors, pharmacists and patients. "Before they walk out of the office, patients need to have a thorough discussion with their physician about the medication they have just been prescribed," PhRMA's Goldhammer says. "Pharmacists have an important role, too."

Thus, one of the major tasks of the administration's proposed Drug Safety Oversight Board would be to establish a new Drug Watch Web Page on the Internet, which would provide the public with emerging information about safety issues that may alter the risk/benefit analysis of a drug. One-page information sheets also would be provided for all drugs, offering basic information and safety updates in a consumer-friendly format. Health-care providers will receive more detailed material.

"Prescription-drug consumers have been left in the dark, with no readily accessible source of objective, accurate prescription-drug information, written in non-technical language, even though the FDA first proposed the mandatory distribution of such information in 1979," says Larry D. Sasich, a pharmacist and research analyst at Public Citizen's Health Research Group.

It is too early to tell if the recent negative publicity about drug safety will spur true change in the flow of accurate drug information, or whether it will merely result in more studies, hearings and a reshuffling of the bureaucratic deck. If Congress doesn't act during the next two years, it will have to revisit the drug-approval process in 2007, the year PDUFA comes up for reauthorization.

"This is a real reform effort," the FDA's Galson said about the agency's new oversight board plan. "We've been working on this proposal for months. We are changing our management and how we look at drug-safety problems and how we communicate with the public about emerging risks. Before, we had an onerous, deliberative process that took a long time to get information to the public."

But to Sen. Grassley, the changes are "like having the fox guard the chicken coop." "The culture within the FDA is no different than the culture at a whole lot of different organizations and agencies that are worried about their PR," he says. "They never want to admit a mistake."

Meanwhile, Senate Health Committee Chairman Enzi advocates a go-slow approach to changing the FDA's monitoring authority, warning that trying to develop a system that aims "for an impossible standard of zero risk" is not in the public's best interest. [48]

NOTES

1. Ali Mohamadi, "Doctors Ponder FDA Drug Controversy: What Should Doctors and Their Patients Do About Possible Drug Risks?" ABC News Original Report, Nov. 22, 2004. www.abcnews.go.com/Health/story?id=26707&page=2.

2. Quoted in Judith Graham and Frank James, "Flaws in drug agency put consumer at risk; Critics of FDA cite conflicts of interest, lack of enforcement authority," *Chicago Tribune*, Feb. 20, 2005, p. 1.

3. General Accounting Office and Food and Drug Administration, "Effect of User Fees on Drug Approval Times, Withdrawals, and Other Agency Activities," September 2002.

4. For background, see David Hatch, "Drug Company Ethics," *CQ Researcher*, June 6, 2003, pp. 521-544.

5. For background, see David Masci, "Women's Health," *CQ Researcher*, Nov. 7, 2003, pp. 941-964.

6. CBS Evening News, "FDA Mum on Suicidal Effects?" March 30, 2004. www.cbsnews.com/stories/2004/03/30/eveningnews/printable609491.shtml.

7. Eric J. Topol, "Arthritis Medicines and Cardiovascular Events — House of Coxibs," *Journal of the American Medical Association*, Jan. 19, 2005, Vol. 293, p. 366.

8. Statement of Sandra Kweder, M.D., deputy director, Office of New Drugs, Center for Drug Evaluation and Research, U.S. Food and Drug Administration, before Senate Finance Committee, Nov. 18, 2004.

9. Graham and James, *op. cit.*

10. See Gardiner Harris, "F.D.A. Official Admits 'Lapses' on Vioxx," *The New York Times*, March 2, 2005, p. A12.

11. For information on Accutane restrictions, see http://www.fda.gov/bbs/topics/ANSWERS/2004/ANS01328.html.

12. "FDA Statement on Celebrex DTC Promotion," FDA news release, Dec. 20, 2004.

13. Ron Insana, "Pfizer Leader Steps Up to the Plate for Celebrex," *USA Today*, Jan. 4, 2005, p. B4.

14. Gardiner Harris, "Federal Drug Agency Calls Ads for Crestor 'False and Misleading," *The New York Times*, Dec. 23, 2004, p. A16.

15. Quoted in Graham and James, *op. cit.*

16. *Ibid.*

17. *Ibid.*

18. *Ibid.*

19. *Ibid.*

20. Graham and James, *op. cit.*

21. Public Citizen, www.citizen.org/congress/reform/drugsafety/articles.cfm?ID=7442.

22. www.forbes.com/sciencesandmedicine/2004/12/13/cx_mh_1213faceoftheyear.html.

23. In January, Graham received agency clearance to publish his results in a British medical journal.

24. "Dangerous Prescription," Frontline, interview with Michael Elashoff; www.pbs.org/wgbh/pages/frontline/shows/prescription/interviews/elashoff.html.

25. *Ibid.*

26. The Associated Press, "Oversight Is Lacking, FDA Scientists Say," *The New York Times*, Dec. 17, 2004.

27. Daniel Carpenter *et al.*, "Approval Times for New Drugs: Does The Source of Funding for FDA Staff

Matter?" *Health Affairs*, Web Exclusive, Dec. 17, 2003.

28. Graham and James, *op. cit.*

29. Public Citizen, *op. cit.*

30. "Grassley Questions Merck About Communication With the FDA on Vioxx," press release, Senate Finance Committee, Oct. 15, 2004.

31. Mary Agnes Carey, "Lawmakers Say New Drug Safety Board Lacks Teeth," *CQ Today*, Feb. 15, 2005.

32. Gardiner Harris and Alex Berenson, "10 Voters on Panel Backing Pain Pills Had Industry Ties," *The New York Times*, Feb. 25, 2005, p. A1.

33. Gardiner Harris, "F.D.A. to Create Advisory Panel to Warn Patients About Drugs," *The New York Times*, Feb. 16, 2005, p. A1.

34. Alastair Wood, *et al.*, "Making Medicines Safer — The Need for an Independent Drug Safety Board," *The New England Journal of Medicine*, Vol. 339: No. 25, Dec. 17, 1998, pp. 1851-1854.

35. Quoted in Graham and James, *op. cit.*

36. *Ibid.*

37. Unless otherwise noted, information in this section is from Philip Hilts, *Protecting America's Health: The FDA, Business, and One Hundred Years of Regulation* (2003), pp. 58-59.

38. *Ibid*, pp. 138-139.

39. The joint hearings were held by the Labor and Public Welfare Health Subcommittee and the Committee on the Judiciary Administrative Practice Subcommittee in August 1974.

40. Hilts, *op. cit.*

41. Harris, *op. cit.*

42. Robert B. Reich, "A Suitable Remedy: When the FDA is Weak," *The Washington Post*, Jan. 9, 2005, p. B5.

43. Jerry Avorn, M.D., *Powerful Medicines: The Benefits, Risks, and Costs of Prescription Drugs* (2004), p. 371.

44. For background, see Adriel Bettelheim, "Medicare Reform," *CQ Researcher*, Aug. 22, 2003, pp. 673-696.

45. Rebecca Adams, "Cries Grow to Increase FDA's Drug Oversight," *CQ Weekly*, Feb. 21, 2005, p. 438.

46. Carey, *op. cit.*

47. Adams, *op. cit.*

48. Kate Schuler, "FDA Says Drugs Are Safe, Need No Extra Monitoring," *CQ Today*, March 3, 2005.

BIBLIOGRAPHY

Books

Angell, Marcia, *The Truth About the Drug Companies*, Random House, 2004.
A Harvard Medical School lecturer and former editor of *The New England Journal of Medicine* takes a hard-hitting look at drug company practices, with an emphasis on the dark side.

Avorn, Jerry, *Powerful Medicines: The Benefits, Risks, and Costs of Prescription Drugs*, Alfred A. Knopf, 2004.
A Harvard Medical School professor provides a thorough overview of the current debate over drug safety and costs.

Hilts, Philip J., *Protecting America's Health: The FDA, Business, and One Hundred Years of Regulation*, Alfred A. Knopf, 2003.
This popular history by a *New York Times* reporter focuses on the FDA's drug-safety efforts.

Wolfe, Sidney M., Larry D. Sasich and Rose-Ellen Hope, *Worst Pills, Best Pills: A Consumer's Guide to Avoiding Drug-Induced Death*, Pocket Books, 2005.
The 900-plus page book provides easy-to-understand information on 538 prescription drugs.

Articles

Barry, Patricia, "The Insiders," *AARP Bulletin Online*, November 2004.
A sales representative, a lobbyist for Pfizer and Merck and a Pfizer executive reveal the tricks of their trade.

Fontanarosa, Phil B., *et al.*, "Postmarketing Surveillance — Lack of Vigilance, Lack of Trust," *Journal of the American Medical Association*, Dec. 1, 2004, Vol. 292, No. 21, pp. 2647-2650.
The editorial outlines the perceived inadequacies of the post-marketing surveillance system, with a focus on MedWatch.

Harris, Gardiner, and Robert Pear, "After Lengthy Wait, Acting Head of F. D. A. Is Picked to Be Leader," *The New York Times*, Feb. 15, 2005, p. A1.
Acting FDA Commissioner Lester M. Crawford is nominated to fill the post of commissioner, vacant since March 2004.

Harris, Gardiner, "F. D. A. to Create Advisory Panel to Warn Patients About Drug Safety," *The New York Times*, Feb. 16, 2005, p. A1.
HHS Secretary Michael O. Leavitt announces the creation of a new, independent Drug Safety Oversight Board.

Herper, Matthew, "Face of the Year: David Graham," Forbes.com, Dec. 13, 2004.
An interview with the FDA whistleblower details his deeply held Christian beliefs and professional background.

Insana, Ron, "Pfizer Leader Steps Up to the Plate for Celebrex," *USA Today*, Jan. 4, 2005, p. B4.
Pfizer CEO Hank McKinnell outlines the company's take on the Cox-2 controversy.

Lamb, Gregory M., "Drug Tests: Too Speedy — or Safe Enough?" *The Christian Science Monitor*, Jan. 6, 2005, p. 14.
Government regulators were once cautious, but now they seem to be seeking to approve medicines as quickly as possible.

Meier, Barry, "Merck Canceled an Early Study of Vioxx," *The New York Times*, Feb. 8, 2005, p. D1.
Despite denials it had conducted clinical trials of Vioxx, documents reveal the drugmaker pulled the plug on tests in 2002.

Reich, Robert B., "A Suitable Remedy: When the FDA is Weak," *The Washington Post*, Jan. 9, 2005, p. B5.
The former Labor secretary defends the tort system as the only way to get drug companies to police themselves.

Schultz, William B., "How to Improve Drug Safety," *The Washington Post*, Dec. 2, 2004, p. A35.
The president of Amnesty International offers suggestions about improving the FDA's drug-monitoring capabilities.

Wechsler, Jill, "Drug Safety and Access Top Policy Concerns for 2005," *Pharmaceutical Technology*, January 2005, pp. 28-36.
A round-up of drug issues focuses on Medicare modernization and FDA oversight of drug safety.

Willman, David, "NIH Seeks 'Higher Standard': Banning Staff Deals With Drug Firms Will Help Set an Ethical Example, the Agency Director Says," *Los Angeles Times*, Feb. 2, 2005.
Willman details efforts to institute ethics reform at the agency.

Reports and Studies

"Drug Safety: Most Drugs Withdrawn in Recent Years Had Greater Health Risks for Women," General Accounting Office, Jan. 19, 2001.
Most of the drugs recalled for safety reasons had a disproportionate effect on women.

Carpenter, Daniel, *et al.*, "Approval Times for New Drugs: Does The Source of Funding for FDA Staff Matter?" *Health Affairs*, Web Exclusive, Dec. 17, 2003.
A University of Michigan/Harvard study finds that FDA approval times have been cut by hiring more reviewers.

For More Information

Consumers Union, 1666 Connecticut Ave., N.W., Suite 310, Washington, DC 20009-1039; (202) 462-6262; www.consumersunion.org. The nonprofit group offers analyses of prescription drugs at www.bestbuydrugs.org.

Henry J. Kaiser Family Foundation, 1330 G St., N.W., Washington, DC 20005; (202) 347-5270; www.kff.org. Offers information on major health-care issues; not affiliated with Kaiser Permanente or Kaiser Industries.

National Library of Medicine, 8600 Rockville Pike, Bethesda, MD 20894; 1-888-FIND-NLM (346-3656); www.nlm.nih.gov. The nation's largest medical library.

Pharmaceutical Research and Manufacturers of America, 1100 15th St., N.W., Washington, DC 20005; (202) 835-3400, www.phrma.org. PhRMA is the drug-industry's trade and advocacy group.

Public Citizen Health Research Group, 1600 20th St., N.W., Washington, DC 20009; (202) 588-1000; www.citizen.org. Headed by Sidney Wolfe, the nonprofit advocacy group aggressively monitors drug and medical issues. The group's drug-safety information Web site for consumers is at www.worstpills.org.

U.S. Food and Drug Administration, 5600 Fishers Lane, Rockville, MD 20857-0001; 1-888-INFO-FDA (463-6332); www.fda.gov. The FDA monitors the safety of drugs, cosmetics and medical devices.

4

Avian Flu Threat

Sarah Glazer

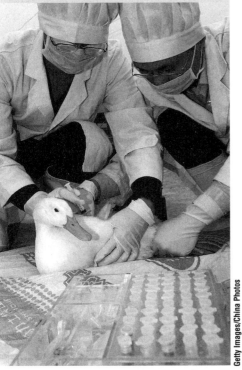

Health workers take blood samples from a duck in Sichuan Province, China, on Nov. 11, 2005, to see if it is infected with bird flu. Since 1997, the disease has infected millions of poultry in Asia and Europe. So far, about 75 of the more than 145 people known to be infected by the disease have died.

From *CQ Researcher,*
January 13, 2006.

Chickens started dying mysteriously in Srisomboon, in northern Thailand, in August 2004. Like most children in the sleepy village, 11-year-old Sakuntula had daily contact with the birds. When she developed a stomachache and fever, the nurse at a nearby clinic dismissed her symptoms as a bad cold.

Five days later, Sakuntula began coughing up blood and was rushed to the district hospital. Her mother, Pranee Thongchan, was summoned from her job at a garment factory near Bangkok and found her daughter gasping for breath. The child died that night. Two weeks later, Pranee, 26, died, suffering from muscle aches and exhaustion, which were blamed on grief. * Viral pneumonia was listed as the official cause of death, however. [1]

Then, on Sept. 28, 2004, the World Health Organization (WHO) announced that the mother's death represented the first person-to-person transmission of the avian flu strain known as H5N1.

Researchers received the news with understandable concern. If H5N1 becomes easily transmissible from human to human, a worldwide epidemic — or pandemic — could occur, causing widespread infection and death from a virus to which most humans are believed to have little natural immunity.

The WHO has reassuringly called the Thongchans' daughter-to-mother transmission a "viral dead-end," because the virus does not appear to have mutated into a form that is easily passed from human to human. [2]

---

* Symptoms of avian flu in humans have ranged from no symptoms to typical flu-like symptoms (fever, cough, sore throat and muscle aches) to eye infections, pneumonia, severe respiratory diseases and other life-threatening complications.

Migratory Birds May Spread Virus

Migratory birds may be spreading avian flu as it moves westward from Asia to Europe. Researchers say migratory-bird densities were at their peak when most of the outbreaks in Southeast Asia occurred in 2003-2004. The pattern of H5N1 outbreaks worldwide, however, does not track the migratory flyways of wild birds in all countries.

Flight Patterns of Migratory Birds

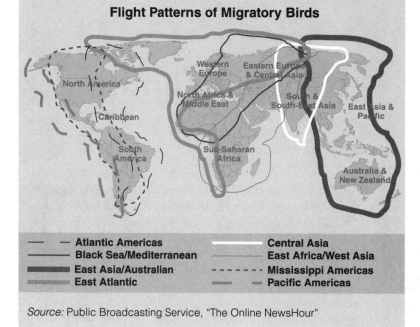

—— Atlantic Americas	—— Central Asia
—— Black Sea/Mediterranean	—— East Africa/West Asia
—— East Asia/Australian	- - - - Mississippi Americas
—— East Atlantic	—— Pacific Americas

Source: Public Broadcasting Service, "The Online NewsHour"

Ankara, a major metropolitan city that is relatively well off and where humans and animals do not customarily share the same living quarters. By Jan. 9, at least 10 of 81 Turkish provinces reported having found sick birds, compared to only three provinces a few days earlier. [3]

Currently, there is no government-approved vaccine for human avian flu, although there is one for the version that attacks poultry. If a pandemic flu were to hit the United States tomorrow, it could take up to a year after the virus strain was identified to manufacture a targeted vaccine, but domestic-manufacturing capacity would only be able to produce enough doses to cover barely a tenth of the nation's population. *

Currently, the only treatment for the disease is thought to be Tamiflu and Relenza, antiviral medications known to work against seasonal flu. But no one knows for sure how effective they would be against a new pandemic flu strain.

Since 1997, H5N1 outbreaks have infected millions of poultry and more than 140 humans around the world as it has spread from flocks in Southeast Asia to Central Asia and Europe. ** More than 75 people have died, about half of those said to be infected. The high 50-percent mortality rate worries experts. However, many think it is probably overstated because milder cases probably are not being reported. And some infected people who may have developed antibodies won't show any

Today, the H5N1 virus is "like a key that doesn't quite fit the lock" of human-to-human contagion, explains Michael T. Osterholm, a professor at the University of Minnesota's School of Public Health. "But if you jiggle the key enough times, occasionally it will open the door. The virus is moving closer to the key that would really open the door. That's when you get sustained human-to-human transmission."

And each new human case gives the virus an opportunity to mutate into a fully transmissible strain among people, according to the WHO. International health officials were particularly alarmed by this month's deaths of three children in Turkey, the first victims of the disease reported outside of East Asia. Within a week, more Turks had contracted the disease, apparently after handling infected birds. About 50 others were hospitalized with suspected cases of the bird flu — 20 of them near

---

* To create sufficient capacity to cover the entire population, most experts agree the nation needs to convert to new cell-based technology, which has more flexibility to expand the number of doses than current egg-based technology. It would take 2-5 years to get government approval for the new method and to build plants using the new technology.

** Infected birds shed large quantities of the virus in their feces, creating abundant opportunities for exposure. Exposure is considered most likely during slaughter, defeathering, butchering and preparation of poultry for cooking.

symptoms. By contrast, a worldwide flu outbreak in 1918 — the most lethal in recent history — killed only 2.5 percent of its victims, but that amounted to 40 million to 100 million worldwide — including about 675,000 Americans. [4]

But some experts think the avian flu will never mutate into a humanly transmissible virus. Michael Fumento, a senior fellow at the conservative Hudson Institute, maintains that H5N1 was first discovered in Scottish chickens in 1959. "It's therefore been mutating and making contact with humans for 47 years. If it hasn't become transmissible between humans in all that time, it almost certainly won't," he writes. (*See "At Issue," p. 87.*)

Because no one knows whether or when an avian flu pandemic might occur, the U.S. government is in a quandary over how aggressively to act. Some experts believe a global disaster threatens. "The situation right now in Asia is ripe for a perfect storm," says Osterholm. "You've got the virus circulating, you've got it moving closer to human pathogens and you've got a world ill-prepared."

Modern transportation permits a single person to spread disease to several continents within days, as the rapid spread of SARS demonstrated in 2003, when an infected doctor traveling out of China managed to spread the disease to Vietnam, Singapore and Canada within a month. [5] (Although SARS never became the worldwide epidemic that was predicted, before it was effectively contained it had spread to 30 countries, infected 8,000 people and killed 800.)

If a new avian flu pandemic develops, Osterholm paints a bleak picture of nations closing their borders and disrupting global economic trade in self-protection. And since the United States imports 80 percent of the raw materials used to produce crucial pharmaceuticals, he says, medicine would be scarce.

Efforts to contain the disease in Asia — including China's efforts to vaccinate every one of its 14 billion poultry — won't work, some experts say, because some vaccines are likely to be fake or overly diluted. [6] In a

At Least 78 Deaths Reported

The number of humans infected with avian flu doubled between 2004 and 2005, but the outbreak remained in Asia. On Jan. 10, 2006, Turkish health officials reported 15 patients confirmed with the disease and more hospitalized with symptoms suggesting the avian flu — more cases than the World Health Organization's totals (below). Three children in Turkey had died from the infection as of Jan. 10.

Confirmed Avian Flu Cases and Deaths

	2003 cases/ deaths	2004 cases/ deaths	2005 cases/ deaths	2006 cases/ deaths	Total
Cambodia	0/0	0/0	4/4	0/0	4/4
China	0/0	0/0	7/5	1/0	8/5
Indonesia	0/0	0/0	16/11	0/0	16/11
Thailand	0/0	17/12	5/2	0/0	22/14
Turkey	0/0	0/0	0/0	4/2	4/2
Vietnam	3/3	29/20	61/19	0/0	93/42
Total	**3/3**	**46/32**	**93/41**	**5/2**	**147/78**

Source: World Health Organization

phone interview from Hong Kong, virologist Robert Webster of St. Jude Children's Research Hospital in Memphis, Tenn., and one of the world's leading authorities on bird flu, said "crap vaccines" already are being used in China. There are no international standards for agricultural vaccines, he notes.

Administering a weak vaccine causes a "bloody disaster," he explains, because only the symptoms, not the virus itself, tend to disappear. "The chicken doesn't die; instead, if it's infected it goes on pooping out virus for days and days and spreads the virus and increases the rate of evolution" of the virus, he says.

H5N1 has also been found in migratory birds, which may explain its spread to Europe, and in ducks, which do not show symptoms but may play an increased role in transmitting H5N1 to both poultry and humans. [7]

The situation looks dire to some advocates. The National Institutes of Health (NIH) is testing an experimental vaccine against a Vietnamese strain of H5N1 that infects humans, and the government has ordered more doses of it to be made. But it will be two to five years before the United States could build enough capacity to vaccinate everyone in the country.

A pigeon is vaccinated in Beijing in an effort to curb the spread of bird flu. China plans to vaccinate every one of its 14 billion birds. There is no approved vaccine yet for the human version of the disease.

Meanwhile, the government has begun stockpiling Tamiflu, but has only ordered enough to treat 5 percent of the population. (While Relenza is considered as effective as the Tamiflu capsule, it must be inhaled using a special inhaler, making it a less desirable medicine for mass distribution and stockpiling.)

"You can't prevent it if you don't have the vaccine; you can't treat it if you don't have the medication," says Kim Elliott, deputy director of the Trust for America's Health, a public-health advocacy group. [8]

That leaves isolating infected people as the only strategy for preventing spread of the disease. The Centers for Disease Control and Prevention (CDC) has proposed new regulations giving it authority to stop sick travelers from getting off international flights. But, unlike SARS, people with the flu are contagious for about a day before they have symptoms.

"When people push me, I say if society comes apart you have to be prepared to exist for three months with what you have in your house," says Webster. "It won't work, but what else have we got?"

"To have effective quarantine, you have to tell everyone to stay home [because we won't know] who's sick. That's just not possible," says Elliott.

In November 2005, President Bush proposed $7.1 billion in emergency funding to prepare for a flu pandemic, mainly to produce and stockpile vaccines and

antiviral drugs and to improve reporting of bird flu cases at home and abroad. In December, Congress approved half that amount — $3.8 billion for 2006 — enough to "jump start" the plan this year, according to the Trust for America's Health. [9] The legislation also created sweeping protection from lawsuits for pandemic-vaccine manufacturers, which consumer groups blasted as an "unprecedented giveaway" to drug companies. [10]

But some critics say even the president's full request was too little too late. "That's less than the cost of an aircraft carrier," observes Tara O'Toole, director of the Center for Biosecurity at the University of Pittsburgh Medical School. "If we don't deal with this, we are facing a potential destabilizing and existential threat. You have to have countermeasures. That will require spending real money — money that you measure in [national] defense terms."

Other experts agree with Fumento and doubt this strain of flu will jump from birds to humans. Some believe it could evolve into something no more lethal than typical seasonal flu. "I'm just not persuaded this is a clear-cut case of avian virus waiting to cause the next pandemic," says Peter Palese, a leading microbiologist at Mount Sinai School of Medicine in New York. Like most scientists, Palese expects a flu pandemic of some kind eventually to occur as successive generations lose immunity to older viruses, but he says it could be 20 years from now and bear little relation to H5N1.

Of the 20th century's three flu pandemics, only the 1918 outbreak was extremely lethal. The 1957 and 1968 outbreaks caused about 75,000 and 34,000 U.S. deaths, respectively. Today, a mild pandemic on that scale would cause about 100,000 deaths in the United States — about three times the estimated 36,000 deaths that occur annually from seasonal flu, the Congressional Budget Office (CBO) projects.

Based on the historical frequency of pandemics over the past 300 years, in which mild pandemics have predominated, the chances of a severe pandemic occurring in the future are very small — only 0.3 percent, according to the CBO. [11]

A 1918-scale flu, nonetheless, would infect about 90 million people in the United States and cause 2 million U.S. deaths, according to the CBO.

If a pandemic were to hit tomorrow, most agree our medical system would be woefully unprepared. "If this is anything like 1918, hospitals will be overwhelmed; if hospital workers are home sick with the flu, how you increase capacity becomes almost insoluble," says O'Toole, noting that most hospitals already run at close to 100 percent capacity. "If you ask them to double or triple their capacity, they collapse," she says.

Yet if the president were to start an even more ambitious pandemic-preparedness effort today — such as building new hospitals — the effort would be both costly and possibly unnecessary, as President Gerald Ford discovered with "swine flu." In 1976, the new strain of flu was projected to kill 1 million people, and Ford pushed for a mass-vaccination campaign. But only a few deaths occurred from the swine flu, and the government had to spend millions to compensate hundreds hurt or killed by the vaccine.

President Bush seemed to take note of this inevitable uncertainty when he unveiled his pandemic flu plan on Nov. 1. "While avian flu has not yet acquired the ability to spread easily from human to human, there is still cause for vigilance," he said. "Our country has been given fair warning of this danger to our homeland — and time to prepare. It's my responsibility as president to take measures now to protect the American people from the possibility that human-to-human transmission may occur." [12]

So why is Bush so concerned about preparing for a pandemic? "I have one word for you — [Hurricane] Katrina," says Michael Fumento, a senior fellow at the conservative Hudson Institute, who believes the current bird flu strain will never become a human pandemic.

Yet if a pandemic does arrive soon — whether from this bird flu or another virus — many experts say it could be a disaster, given the nation's beleaguered public health system, inadequate vaccine-production capacity and insufficient stores of antiviral medicine.

Here are some of the questions being debated in Congress, the scientific community and international organizations:

Is the United States prepared for a pandemic?

Top federal health officials have candidly admitted that if a pandemic arrived tomorrow the United States would not be prepared. [13] However, they contend that President Bush's proposal to spend billions on preparation, together with the detailed action plan released by the Department of Health and Human Services (HHS) in November, are steps in the right direction. About 95 percent of the president's proposal would go toward pro-

ducing and stockpiling vaccines, antiviral drugs and other medical supplies and improving systems for detecting and reporting flu cases here and abroad. [14]

Critics charge that the administration's failure to stockpile antiviral medication earlier or to encourage the development of pre-pandemic vaccines has put the U.S. far behind European countries, which are competing with us for scarce anti-flu medications.

Under the HHS plan, $4.7 billion would be spent to help private companies create production capacity for pandemic influenza vaccine and to build a stockpile. The ultimate goal is to have the capacity to produce enough vaccine for the entire U.S. population — almost 300 million people — within six months of an outbreak.

But current U.S. production capacity falls far short of that goal. The major flu vaccine manufacturer located in the United States is sanofi pasteur, the vaccine-producing arm of the French pharmaceuticals group Sanofi Aventis, which can produce only about 60 million doses each winter. According to most experts, 600 million doses — two shots for every American — would be needed to protect against a pandemic. "You do the math; it's frightening," says Elliott.

Moreover, there is no federally approved vaccine in the United States to protect against the bird flu strains circulating in Asia. The federal government has tested an experimental H5N1 vaccine in healthy people and is stockpiling the active ingredient needed for the vaccine, known as an antigen, in bulk form. The vaccine requires 12 times as much antigen per dose as seasonal flu vaccine and is expected to require two shots. Based on this formula, some experts say the government will only have enough H5N1 antigen to protect 4 million people by February 2006. [15]

The administration is hoping to stretch that supply with two methods shown in ongoing studies to enhance the immune response — diluting the vaccine with additives known as adjuvants and administering it into the skin rather than the muscle. However, it's unclear how far the supply can be stretched using these methods, according to Bruce Gellin, director of the National Vaccine Program Office, which authored the HHS plan. [16]

It is also unclear whether the H5N1 vaccine being tested by NIH will work against whatever virus appears on our shores. Virologist Webster doubts that it will prevent people from getting sick, though it may prevent deaths. "The viruses that are circulating out here are no

How Dangerous Is the Virus?

The lethal 1918 "Spanish flu" virus was probably descended from an avian virus and shares some genetic features with today's H5N1 bird flu, but its exact origin remains mysterious, according to molecular pathologist Jeffery K. Taubenberger. He and his research team at the Armed Forces Institute of Pathology recently reconstructed the deadly virus from frozen tissue samples. [1]

Their genetic analysis, published in October 2005, suggested that all eight genes of the 1918 flu came directly from a bird virus and moved into humans after gradually mutating. Federal health officials said at the time that H5N1 flu has already acquired some of the genetic-sequence changes that apparently allowed the 1918 virus to become easily transmissible among humans. [2]

Of the more than 140 people infected with H5N1, most had contact with infected poultry. The potential similarities between the catastrophic 1918 flu and the H5N1 flu — which has caused at least 75 deaths so far — have put the global public health community on edge. [3]

If, as Taubenberger suggests, the 1918 flu was a completely novel virus to which humans had never been exposed — and therefore had developed no immunity — that might help explain why so many people became sick and died. By contrast, the milder pandemics of 1957 and 1968 are believed to have been the combined product of a human flu and an avian virus that exchanged genes after either a human or a pig caught both viruses.

However, this explanation for the greater lethality of the 1918 flu is not universally accepted. It's also possible that the 1918 virus or versions of it had circulated in humans or other animals before it became pandemic, skeptics argue. Because no genetic information exists about any pre-1918 human viruses, no one can know for sure whether the 1918 virus was unique in makeup or whether it may have infected humans at some earlier point.

One of the skeptics, Mount Sinai School of Medicine microbiologist Peter Palese, says, "I don't think we can say [the 1918 flu] was an avian virus that jumped into humans." It's "equally likely" that the 1918 flu was a product of both human and avian viruses, like the 1957 and 1968 pandemics, he says.

Palese is one of several scientists who are not convinced that H5N1 will become a human virus, citing research dating from 1992 indicating that many Chinese already have antibodies to it. "The H5 virus has had ample opportunity to jump from avian populations into humans," he says.

What about mounting reports of humans contracting bird flu since 2003, half of whom have died? Palese thinks the widespread perception from media reports that there has been a jump in cases and a high fatality rate is erroneous. Many bird flu cases probably are not being reported, he says, because they are either mild or asymptomatic (in the case of people with antibodies). So the fatality rate is probably much lower than the apparent 50 percent rate, he says.

Many other scientists also suspect that cases of bird flu are being underreported, especially in China. For example, by the end of 2005, Vietnam had announced more than 90 cases of bird flu, while China — vastly larger than Vietnam — had reported only seven. [4] Some experts, like Palese, suspect that the numbers infected in China are actually in the hundreds. [5]

longer closely related to the vaccine strain," he said in December, speaking by phone from Hong Kong.

In any case, it will probably be another two to five years before the United States can develop a vaccine and manufacturers can build enough production capacity to vaccinate everyone for a pandemic. (*See sidebar, p. 82.*)

Antiviral medications — such as Tamiflu, which helps people recover from the flu and acts as a preventive — are the second pillar of the administration's pandemic strategy. Under the plan, $1 billion would go toward purchasing enough antiviral drugs for a quarter of the U.S. population — the proportion recommended by the WHO.

However, as of December 2005, the administration had stockpiled only 4.3 million courses of Tamiflu, according to Gellin, far short of the 75 million needed. "There's no question more than 4 million Americans would become sick. We're woefully under-stockpiled there," says Elliott.

In response, Gellin cites computer simulations suggesting a pandemic could be stopped in its tracks by using Tamiflu to treat the small number of people initially

Nevertheless, the U.S. government is planning for a worst-case scenario with a 2.5 percent death rate, as experienced in 1918. Since influenza viruses also tend to lose lethality over time, some scientists argue that any increase in transmissibility will produce a massive drop in virulence, because killing the host (i.e. humans) impedes a virus' evolution into a more lethal strain. [6]

No one can predict whether the virus will become humanly transmissible, or how virulent it will be, including Robert G. Webster, the scientist at St. Jude Children's Research Hospital in Memphis, Tenn., who has been warning of its potential dangers for years. When asked how serious it might be, all he can do is "hand wave" a guess. "My hand-waving would be if it does go human-to-human, the first wave will be a catastrophe for the world — for two, three, four months," he suggests. "The second wave will be less pathogenic and the third wave will go back to being somewhat benign." This is similar to the pattern observed in ducks, Webster says.

This month, however, Taubenberger and epidemiologist David M. Morens of the National Institutes of Health played down the similarities between the 1918 flu and H5N1. They noted that while the 1918 virus is "avianlike," researchers have been unable to trace the 1918 virus to any particular bird and that there is no historical data indicating that a precursor virus attacked domestic poultry in large numbers, as H5N1 has. No highly pathogenic avian virus has ever been known to cause a human pandemic, they noted. And despite Taubenberger's genetic-sequencing work, the biological basis for converting a virus into a humanly transmissible form — the prerequisite for a human pandemic — remains "unknown," they said. [7]

"The 1918 virus acquired this trait, but we do not know how, and we currently have no way of knowing whether H5N1 viruses are now in a parallel process of acquiring human-to-human transmissibility," they wrote. "Despite an explosion of data on the 1918 virus during the past decade, we are not much closer to understanding pandemic emergence in 2006 than we were in understanding the risk of H1N1 'swine flu' emergence in 1976," which turned out to be a false alarm. [8]

On the reassuring side, if H5N1 were to become a pandemic flu, the availability of modern antibiotics, which did not exist in 1918, would combat secondary bacterial infections, which caused many of the deaths in 1918.

But other unprecedented aspects of the virus worry scientists. The infection now has been found in tigers and domestic cats and in migratory birds, previously considered safe from such viruses. "We have to accept the fact that we're watching the evolution of this virus," says Webster. "Will it ever go human-to-human? Let's hope not. But we'd better be prepared for it."

[1] J. K. Taubenberger, et al., "Characterization of the 1918 influenza virus polymerase genes," Nature, Oct. 6, 2005, pp. 889-893.

[2] "Bird Flu and the 1918 Pandemic," editorial, The New York Times, Oct. 8, 2005, p. A14.

[3] Congressional Research Service, "Pandemic Influenza: Domestic Preparedness Efforts," Nov. 10, 2005, p. 6.

[4] WHO, "Confirmed number of human cases," Dec. 19, 2005, www.who.int.

[5] See Elisabeth Rosenthal, "Experts Doubt Bird Flu Tallies from China and Elsewhere," The New York Times, Dec. 2, 2005, p. A8.

[6] Dennis Normile, "Pandemic Skeptics Warn Against Crying Wolf," Science, Nov. 18, 2005, pp. 1112-1113.

[7] Jeffery K. Taubenberger and David M. Morens, "1918 Influenza," Emerging Infectious Diseases, January 2006; www.cdc.gov/ncidod/EID/vol12no01/05-0979.htm.

[8] Ibid.

infected and by giving it as a preventive to those in the surrounding area. "Three million treatment courses in one model has been shown to be the amount that's needed," he says, adding that the government hopes soon to have enough to treat twice that number of people. However, some experts doubt the government would be able to act fast enough to contain a pandemic this way. (Tamiflu must be taken within 48 hours of becoming ill.)

The United States has ordered 12 million treatment courses of Tamiflu from Roche, the Swiss pharmaceutical giant that developed the drug, but critics say the administration was so slow in placing its order that it is far down on the two-year waiting list behind other countries. And its order would only cover 5 percent of the population. Gellin responds that while the order won't be complete until sometime in 2007, the government will continue to get partial shipments in the intervening months. *

However, as governments were racing to buy Tamiflu, doubts suddenly emerged in late December

* Under pressure from the global community, Roche agreed last fall that it would license partner companies to produce Tamiflu.

2005 about its efficacy, at current doses, after the prestigious *New England Journal of Medicine* reported that half of eight bird flu patients in Vietnam who were treated with Tamiflu had died — including two who developed resistance to the drug. [17]

Under the HHS plan, state and local governments would be largely responsible for distributing vaccines, anti-viral drugs and other medical supplies. But critics say state and local health departments, crippled by years of budget cuts and often sorely understaffed, will be hard-pressed to shoulder the burden. Many said the plan provided too little money for planning and none for implementation. Other critics say many states can't afford the 75 percent share the government is expecting them to kick in to buy 31 million courses of Tamiflu.

"I don't know where the states are going to come up with the money," says Elliott, who calculates the states' share of the cost at $510 million. "Look at Louisiana and Mississippi [post-Katrina]," she says. "They don't have it. It should not matter where you live or what your state's fiscal health is as to whether you get treated during a pandemic."

The administration argues that some $15 billion appropriated since 2001 to counter bioterrorism have helped states build up the same kind of public health capacities that would be needed in a flu pandemic. "Since 9/11 there's been a substantial investment to enhance that infrastructure," says Gellin. "A lot of those investments are helping precisely for the kind of threats we're facing now." Moreover, he says, pandemic planning should be a "shared responsibility" with the states.

But state officials say bioterrorism funds don't make up for cuts in their most crucial resource — people. "The tragedy is the hole was so big that the billions for public health preparedness are not enough when you cut school health programs. When something bad happens, that's where you get your nurses from," says Georges C. Benjamin, executive director of the American Public Health Association. "If the resources aren't there, you end up with a big bottle of Tamiflu and no one to manage it."

In a pandemic, up to 5-10 million Americans would need hospitalization — far exceeding the nation's 900,000 staffed hospitals beds. And the flood of patients would overwhelm the need for crucial equipment, such as the nation's 100,000 ventilators, according to the CBO. [18]

The administration's plan contains a long list of recommendations for how hospitals should handle the over-flow patients during a pandemic. But "there's no way hospitals could implement even a fraction of what's recommended without federal funds," which are absent from the administration's plan, says the Center for Biosecurity's O'Toole.

Some experts say the administration should put more emphasis on quarantine. "If our states and federal government are only focused on vaccines, and there's no plan for the interim to slow the spread of disease, then it will spread like wildfire," says David Heyman, director of the homeland security program at the Center for Strategic and International Studies and author of a study proposing quarantine guidelines. State officials have been calling him for advice, he said, because they've received so little guidance from the federal government. [19]

But many experts say a quarantine to control pandemic flu won't work. Unlike SARS, people infected with flu can be contagious before they show any symptoms, and some carriers may never show symptoms at all.

However, skeptics like Fumento, at the Hudson Institute, say H5N1 is unlikely to mutate into a human form. And if the next pandemic is not an avian flu, then all the government vaccine efforts aimed at producing an H5N1 vaccine "will be completely useless."

As for the administration's plan in general, "A lot of this is going to be wasted," Fumento says. "It's true of any government crash program. That's how you get $500 toilet seats."

Will liability protection encourage more companies to manufacture vaccines?

"In the past three decades, the number of vaccine manufacturers in America has plummeted, as the industry has been flooded with lawsuits," President Bush declared in his Nov. 1 pandemic speech. The fact that only one major company now manufactures flu vaccine on U.S. soil, Bush said, leaves "our nation vulnerable in the event of a pandemic." [20]

He urged Congress to shield drug makers from lawsuits in order to encourage more of them to manufacture vaccine. A provision providing sweeping protection from liability was approved by Congress in December (*see p. 88*).

The number of manufacturers producing vaccine for the U.S. market has declined precipitously — from 26 companies in 1967 to five today — for all types of vaccines. Only three companies produce flu vaccine for the U.S. market — sanofi pasteur, in Swiftwater, Pa.,

Chiron, which manufactures its vaccines in England, and MedImmune, based in Gaithersburg, Md.

While thousands of lawsuits claiming vaccine-related injuries to children have flooded the courts in recent years, there have been very few lawsuits — only 10 in the last 20 years — over flu vaccines, according to a recent study in the *Journal of the American Medical Association* (*JAMA*). While two resulted in awards — of $1.9 million and $13.5 million — the rest were settled for much smaller amounts or were dismissed on summary judgment. [21]

Some experts argue that market factors have been more important in discouraging drug makers than liability fears, including the uncertain seasonal demand and the low profitability. Profit margins are much lower for vaccines, which patients receive only once a year, than for drugs for chronic conditions like high blood pressure, which are often taken daily. Indeed, when Wyeth Pharmaceuticals stopped making flu vaccine in 2002, its reasons were "not specifically related to liability," says Wyeth Vice President Peter Paradiso. "We were unable to sell 8-10 million doses out of 20 million in 2002," he says. "It became clear there wasn't a demand for our product."

Nevertheless, insurers' perception of litigation threats has made it difficult for manufacturers to obtain insurance, and a similar perception among manufacturers may have been as important as the reality, the *JAMA* study's authors suggest.

"The economics have not always been favorable, and liability has been a factor in determining the profitability of participating in vaccine manufacturing," says sanofi pasteur spokesman Len Lavenda. "For example, today there are thousands of lawsuits pending against manufacturers of thimerosol" — a mercury additive in childhood vaccines.

But Howard Shlevin, president and CEO of Solvay Pharmaceuticals, in Marietta, Ga., said his company decided in 1998 to build a U.S. flu vaccine plant utilizing the newest cell-based technology, before there was any talk of liability protection. "From Solvay's perspective, if someone wants to give me a free ride, that's nice, but that's not what I'm looking for," he said. The company has, however, applied for a federal grant to help build the new plant, he said.

In any case, most agree that drug companies will need some protection from litigation when it comes to producing a vaccine specifically for a flu pandemic. In a pandemic, there probably won't be enough time to test it extensively for side effects. In addition, notes Lavenda,

"When we're talking about a new vaccine combined with a particularly virulent disease and immunizing perhaps 300 million individuals, we have the ingredients for liability exposure far in excess of that normally associated with immunization programs. That's why congressional liability protection is essential for companies supplying pandemic vaccines."

But consumer groups and public health workers' unions maintain that the threat of lawsuits prevents shoddy practices and that the government should not abolish citizens' ability to sue in court unless it also compensates those hurt by the vaccines.

Members of an expert panel convened by the Institute of Medicine (IOM) in 2003 say there are better ways than liability protection to encourage drug companies to produce vaccines. To provide greater supply and price certainty, they recommended the government guarantee an advance purchase of vaccines at a negotiated price. To encourage universal vaccination, they proposed the government require health insurers to cover vaccination and provide government vouchers to people without health insurance. [22]

"Make it worth the manufacturer's while to produce the vaccine. The way other nations do it is by guaranteeing the supply and purchase," says panel member Sara Rosenbaum, chairwoman of the Department of Health Policy at George Washington University. "Until we're ready to do this, I really don't think that an incentive that's speculative at best and meaningless at worst will contribute much to the problem," she said of a sweeping liability approach. The U.S. government already contracts with manufacturers to purchase certain childhood vaccines, which it provides free to children without health insurance under the Vaccines for Children program launched in 1994. [23] Since then, the market for those vaccines has been "robust," according to Rosenbaum. *

Duke University Professor of economics Frank Sloan, who chaired the IOM committee, attributes drug-makers' antipathy to vaccines to low profits, uncertainty about sales and high regulatory costs. "Just taking tort rights away is unjust," he says. "The government regulation of drug companies should be the first guard against contam-

---

* The government also limited the liability of childhood vaccine manufacturers in 1986, when it required families of children injured by routine childhood vaccines to first seek relief through the federal Vaccine Injury Compensation Program before seeking redress in the courts. Seasonal flu vaccines were added to the program in 2004, but vaccines for use in pandemics were not covered.

CHRONOLOGY

1900s-1970s *"Spanish flu" pandemic kills millions; vaccines and antibiotics become available later.*

1918 "Spanish flu" kills up to 100 million, including 675,000 in U.S.

1957 Asian flu kills 75,000 in U.S.

1968 Hong Kong flu kills 700,000 worldwide, 34,000 in U.S.

1976 President Gerald R. Ford orders mass vaccination for "swine flu." Pandemic fizzles, but vaccinations kill 32 and make hundreds sick.

1977 Russian flu, another pandemic that never materializes, infects children and young adults in U.S.

1990s *H5N1 bird flu is isolated in humans; new antiviral medications enter market.*

1997 H5N1 is first isolated in humans; infects 18 in Hong Kong; six die. Hong Kong slaughters all chickens.

1999 New antiviral drugs, Relenza and Tamiflu, licensed in U.S., Europe.

Early 2000s *Terrorist attacks in U.S. raise concern about possible bioterrorism; bird flu reappears in Asia.*

December 2002 President Bush orders smallpox vaccinations for health workers and military; few sign up.

February 2003 Two people contract H5N1 virus in Hong Kong; one dies.

Mid-2003 First wave of H5N1 infection begins with outbreaks in animals in Asia.

December 2003 Bush administration compensates those injured by smallpox vaccine. South Korea reports first avian flu outbreak in chickens.

2004 *Avian flu spreads through Southeast Asia, killing 32 people in Thailand, Vietnam.*

January 2004 Bird flu appears in poultry in Vietnam, Japan, Thailand; fatalities reported in Vietnam.

Summer 2004 Second wave of H5N1 infection strikes poultry in China, Indonesia, Thailand, Vietnam. Eight more fatalities occur in Thailand, Vietnam.

November 2004 World Health Organization (WHO) warns of possible pandemic.

December 2004 Third wave of infection occurs among poultry in Indonesia, Thailand and Vietnam; new human case reported in Vietnam.

2005 *Congress approves crash plan to develop and manufacture vaccine and handle a pandemic, as bird flu spreads to more than 20 countries. . . . Cumulative worldwide totals reach more than 140 cases and 75 deaths.*

January 2005 First account of human-to-human transmission of avian flu published by *New England Journal of Medicine.*

March 2005 Bird flu has spread to 20 countries and killed 50 million chickens.

July 2005 Research on dead migratory birds suggests virus is carried along winter migration routes of geese. . . . Russia becomes first European country with virus outbreak in poultry.

October 2005 Virus confirmed in poultry in Turkey, Romania, Croatia.

November 2005 President Bush requests $7.1 billion to boost vaccine capacity, buy drugs.

December 2005 Congress approves $3.8 billion for flu plan, enacts liability protection for vaccine manufacturers. . . . Two cases of resistance to Tamiflu reported in Vietnam.

2006 *First human victims of H5N1 infection reported outside Asia.*

Jan. 5, 2006 Three children die from H5N1 in Turkey. . . . U.S farmers begin testing chickens for flu. . . . WHO reports 144 infected to date, including 76 fatalities.

ination" of vaccines like that discovered at Chiron's British plant in 2004. "But suppose it failed? Then you should have tort as a backup." [24]

Should the U.S. government do more to combat avian flu overseas?

Like other wealthy governments, the Bush administration has made its first priority stockpiling enough vaccine to inoculate everyone in the country and enough antiviral medication for those who get the flu. But that approach concentrates most of the world's medical supplies in rich countries. The poorer countries of Asia, like steerage passengers on the doomed *Titanic*, will be left without any lifeboats.

Fewer than 10 countries have domestic vaccine companies working on a pandemic vaccine. Based on present trends, the majority of developing countries would have no access to a vaccine during the first wave of a pandemic and possibly its entire duration, according to the World Health Organization (WHO). Some 23 countries have ordered antiviral drugs for national stockpiles, but the principal manufacturer, Swiss drugmaker Roche, will not be able to fill all orders for at least another year, according to the WHO. [25]

One solution to this bottleneck would be for the government to suspend Roche's Tamiflu patent so other companies could produce it. In October, Sen. Charles E. Schumer, D-N.Y., threatened legislation to this effect unless Roche issued licenses to other companies. [26]

Bowing to international criticism, Roche agreed to license its product to 12 new partners out of 200 interested companies globally to help a number of countries meet their stockpile needs.

For its part, the WHO has recommended that wealthy countries contribute to an international stockpile of antiviral medications and cooperatively develop a "world vaccine." But so far, there's been more talk of coordination than action, according to David Nabarro, the new United Nations official in charge of avian flu. [27]

One computer model suggests that a big flu outbreak in rural Thailand could be contained within a month by giving antiviral medications to the first group of people infected and to uninfected people in the surrounding area. "Several million courses sent to Thailand would be more effective than hoarding [doses] for 300 million people" in the United States, said the model's creator, Emory University Professor of biostatistics Ira Longini. [28]

However, most Asian countries where avian flu has become endemic don't have big stockpiles of the drugs. Cambodia has only 150 doses of Tamiflu, enough for one dose per province, according to CBS' "60 Minutes." [29]

The limited supplies raise a major ethical as well as practical dilemma: Should the United States be prepared to hand over its stockpile of a few million antivirals to a country like Cambodia if the disease emerges there first — if only to protect itself?

A blunt "no," answers Osterholm, because he considers Longini's predictions of stopping the disease "a fairy tale."

For the strategy to work, the first human clusters of virus would have to be rapidly detected, reported and diagnosed. But in far-flung rural villages, local clinic staff usually do not recognize an unusual virus, and lengthy waits are common to get diagnoses from far-off laboratories. "I see no reasonable way to stop the virus in Asia," the University of Minnesota's Osterholm says.

He also doubts it will be possible to keep people from leaving a cordoned-off area. "People are going to flee," he says. Moreover, he asks, what government would be willing to announce that it's the first site of a deadly contagious virus when that news will instantly ostracize them economically?

Conventional wisdom dictates that Tamiflu must be taken within 48 hours of getting sick to be effective, but some recent research suggests that it must be taken within hours of infection, Osterholm says, a near-impossibility in a backward, rural area. And handing out Tamiflu willy-nilly raises the threat that resistance will develop. "Trying to use Tamiflu wisely now is like trying to land a 747 on an aircraft carrier," he maintains.

The WHO acknowledges many of these difficulties in its report recommending shipping Tamiflu from an international stockpile to the first region where the virus takes hold. "While pursuit of this option . . . has no guarantee of success, it nonetheless needs to be undertaken, as it represents one of the few preventive options," the WHO report says. Even if this doesn't stop the virus dead in its tracks, a delay would at least give other countries time to get prepared, it argues. [30]

Once a pandemic hits, nations with vaccine manufacturers are sure to nationalize those industries, preventing any domestically produced vaccine from leaving their borders, warns the Center for Biosecurity's O'Toole, unless some international cooperation forestalls them.

New Technique Could Speed Up Vaccine Production

If a flu pandemic were to break out tomorrow, it would take up to a year to develop a vaccine against the virus, by which time it could have circled the globe, creating death and economic havoc worldwide.

Why does it take so long to develop a vaccine? For every dose of flu vaccine, a manufacturer must infect a chicken egg with the particular influenza virus that is causing the new flu epidemic. Using a laborious process that hasn't been updated since the 1950s, a manufacturer aiming to make 20 million doses of a new vaccine must first order 20 million chicken eggs many months before the flu even hits.

"You have to plan in advance for egg deliveries, but there's no assurance you will get them," says Harold Shlevin, CEO of Solvay Pharmaceuticals in Marietta, Ga. "Just the logistics of getting 20 million eggs that you hope will grow properly, isolating and processing them [takes] closer to 9-12 months." Further complicating matters, for a virus that attacks birds as well as humans — such as the H5N1 avian flu now circulating in Asia — the virus could kill the eggs. So manufacturers today face the prospect of "no chickens, no eggs, no vaccine," says Shlevin.

His company has developed a new way to produce flu vaccine that relies on a line of cells harvested from a cocker spaniel's kidney in 1958 and kept alive ever since. President Bush has proposed a $2.8 billion crash program to accelerate development of vaccines using this approach — called cell-based technology — in order to produce enough flu vaccine for every American within six months after a pandemic hits. But it could be another two-to-five years before the United States has such a capacity — the estimated time manufacturers need to obtain government approval and build plants using the new technology.

Under Shlevin's process, rather than ordering millions of eggs, a manufacturer would only need to go to the freezer, pull out a vial of cells, inoculate them with the virus and place them in a large tank, called a bioreactor, to grow.

"If you want to make more simultaneously, you just need another bioreactor," says Shlevin, who likens it to a tank in which beer is brewed. Once the flu strain is isolated, the process could take as little as 90 days, Shlevin estimates.

Solvay is building a plant in Holland to produce a cell-based flu vaccine and has approval to sell it there. Close behind is Chiron, which is conducting clinical trials with cell-based flu vaccine in Europe and expects to apply for approval to sell the vaccine there in 2007.

Normally, it would take another three-to-four years to get the vaccine approved in the U.S. and possibly longer before new plants could be built here, according to Shlevin. However, representatives from both companies say the Food and Drug Administration (FDA) has been discussing expediting their procedure.

The FDA's vaccine advisory committee was asked if it could speed up some of its approval procedures without endangering safety. Panel member David Markovitz, a professor of infectious diseases at the University of Michigan, said he was favorably disposed after Nov. 16 presentations by Chiron and Solvay. Although the meeting was non-binding, Markovitz said, "The fact that the committee was very much in favor would suggest that it's likely to be licensed soon as technology for making flu vaccines."

Markovitz explains that while the vaccine would probably be safe, the residual dog cells could produce cancer in a vaccine recipient, because the cells are "immortalized" — managed so that they "just keep growing," and often some cells are abnormal. But, he adds, "The odds of that in most of these lines seem quite low."

Meanwhile, other vaccine technologies are being tested. The National Institutes of Health (NIH), for instance, is testing a vaccine against one strain of H5N1 in healthy people

"There's nothing in the president's speech or the [HHS] plan that indicates the United States is going to try to lead a coalition of the world's vaccine manufacturers to maximize the global vaccine supply or has any intention of giving our vaccine away to countries that might be at the center of the storm," she notes. "The blowback from the United States acting as fortress America and having made no attempt to help less developed countries will harm America's standing in the world for a generation."

O'Toole knows it will be hard to persuade government leaders to share scarce vaccine. Her organization recently held a role-playing exercise to find out what would happen if bioterrorists attacked nations with smallpox. Former Secretary of State Madeleine K. Albright played the role of a U.S. president, and former prime ministers played other countries' leaders.

and next will test it in the elderly. Like seasonal flu vaccines, it uses a killed, or inactivated, virus. However, during a pandemic an individual influenza strain can undergo changes, a process known as "drift," so a virus stockpiled now might not be effective against a future pandemic strain. For example, the H5N1 strains now circulating in Asia are different from strains that caused the flu in Hong Kong in 1997.

A newer-generation vaccine can be made from a live flu virus that has been weakened, or attenuated, so it cannot cause disease. The NIH is developing a live attenuated vaccine for H5N1 with MedImmune Vaccines Inc., which produces FluMist, a nasal spray made from a live attenuated vaccine currently available in the United States.

Live attenuated vaccines appear to create broader protective immunity against strains that have changed over time than vaccines made from killed viruses, according to Ruth Karron, an influenza vaccine expert at the Johns Hopkins Bloomberg School of Public Health. The school will begin testing MedImmune's new, live attenuated vaccine this spring. "We have evidence that this is true for some of the human influenza viruses that circulate each year," she said. For instance, for unknown reasons, FluMist "seems to work better against drifted strains than inactivated influenza vaccine." [1]

Live attenuated vaccine is currently made using egg-based technology but could be made with cell-based techniques once they are available.

Purdue University researcher Suresh Metal examines a cell infected with a bird flu gene. U.S. researchers are trying to develop a vaccine in tissue cultures rather than chicken eggs, thus allowing faster production.

AFP Photo/Jeff Haynes

Meanwhile, the idea of a single vaccine to protect against all types of flu has always been the "holy grail" for flu vaccine researchers, but no one knows whether it can be achieved. In the event of a pandemic, a universal vaccine would dramatically reduce the turn-around time needed now to develop a vaccine tailored to a specific strain, according to NIH researcher Gary Nabel, who is exploring this possibility. [2]

Finally, researchers are also in the early stages of investigating a DNA-based vaccine, which would inject the DNA from a flu virus into people instead of the killed virus itself, causing a person's cells to make the virus proteins. Theoretically this could speed up production of a vaccine, because the DNA vaccine could be grown in fast-growing bacteria in a matter of weeks. DNA vaccines work well in mice, but "there's no good evidence they induce enough protective immunity in humans," according to Mount Sinai School of Medicine microbiologist Peter Palese. Given the data available now on DNA vaccines, he says, "I would seriously question whether it's really protective against a pandemic strain."

---

[1] John Hopkins Bloomberg School of Public Health, "Preparing for a Pandemic — Bloomberg School Tests Potential Avian Flu Vaccine," Oct. 19, 2005.

[2] Richard Harris, "Pandemic Flu Spurs Race for New Vaccine Methods," National Public Radio, Dec. 6, 2005, at www.npr.org.

"We saw that national leaders become very ungenerous when their own stocks of vaccine are limited," O'Toole reports. In one scenario, Albright was prepared to share vaccine with Turkey. But when an American city was also attacked, Albright refused to send vaccine, saying, "'We paid for this,'" says O'Toole. "All the other countries did the same thing."

BACKGROUND

"Spanish Flu"

Worldwide influenza epidemics — called pandemics — were first documented about 300 years ago, and since then an estimated 10-13 pandemics have occurred. The 20th century saw three flu pandemics: Two were mild, but the 1918-1919 "Spanish flu" epidemic infected an estimated 25-30 percent of the world's population. About 675,000 Americans died from the flu in 1918 — nearly half of all U.S. deaths that year. Worldwide, from 40 million up to 100 million people died. [31]

The 1918 flu was unusual in its high rate of mortality and the large percentage of deaths among young adults between ages 15 and 35, often within hours after the first symptoms appeared. Young people have the strongest immune systems of any age group, and, paradoxically, their immune system response to the foreign virus was so powerful that it killed them, explains author and chronicler of the 1918 epidemic John M. Barry. Many young adults suffered from acute respiratory distress syndrome, in which disease-fighting cells overreact, filling the lungs with fluid and debris, and ultimately suffocating the victim.

In 1997, pathologists noticed something similar in the first six people who died from H5N1 in Hong Kong. Many of the victims' organs were under attack from a "renegade" immune system, Barry writes. Indeed, the deaths reported so far from H5N1 have largely occurred in children and young, healthy adults — a similarity that worries some scientists. [32]

The two milder 20th-century pandemics — in 1957 and 1968 — probably were caused by the exchange of genes between human and avian flu viruses, known as reassortment, which occurred after either a human or a pig caught both viruses.

The second principal mechanism by which flu becomes easily contagious among humans is called adaptive mutation, a more gradual process in which the virus' ability to bind to human cells increases during subsequent infections of humans. Some scientists have suggested that the 1918 flu falls into the latter category.

The 1957 Asian flu outbreak, so-called because it was first identified in Asia, spread to the United States during the summer, killing about 70,000 people. Health officials responded quickly, and limited vaccine supplies were available by August. The 1968 Hong Kong flu killed 33,800 people in the United States, making it the mildest pandemic of the 20th century. A normal seasonal flu outbreak kills about 36,000 Americans each year.

The '57 and '68 pandemics were mild partly because the viruses were less virulent and partly because of advances in medicine. Global detection had improved, allowing public health officials to quickly isolate the viruses, and manufacturers were able to provide vaccines

for the two strains. Antibiotics were also widely available to treat secondary bacterial infections, in contrast to 1918, and there were fewer cases of viral pneumonia.

Recent Flu Scares

Several 20th-century flu scares failed to live up to their billing. The 1976 "swine flu" scare began when an 18-year-old soldier at Fort Dix in New Jersey succumbed to a novel virus thought to be related to the Spanish flu virus. After health officials predicted a 1918-scale epidemic, President Ford initiated a program to inoculate every American.

But the pandemic never arrived. Moreover, the vaccination program was stopped after hundreds of people suffered from a rare neurological disorder — Guillain-Barre syndrome — later linked to the vaccine, which killed 32. Congress provided liability protection for the manufacturers and $90 million in compensation for those claiming injuries. [33]

Ever since, the swine flu incident has stood as a cautionary tale to public officials fearful of crying wolf. "In this case, the consequences of being wrong about an epidemic were so devastating in people's minds that it wasn't possible to focus properly on the issue of likelihood," Harvey V. Fineberg, now president of the Institute of Medicine, concluded later. "Nobody could really estimate the likelihood then or now. . . . And at a higher level [The White House] the two — likelihood and consequence — got meshed." [34] In 1977, the so-called Russian flu involved a virus strain that had been in circulation before 1957. The virus primarily sickened children and young adults, who lacked prior immunity to it.

H5N1 Emerges

The current concern about the H5N1 virus dates from 1997, when outbreaks of the highly pathogenic virus occurred in chickens and humans in Hong Kong. Six people died — out of 18 who became sick after handling infected poultry. To prevent further outbreak, Hong Kong's chicken population was slaughtered in three days. Researchers later found that the virus had originated among Chinese geese and found its way into Hong Kong's poultry markets before infecting the first humans. [35]

After several quiet years, the virus reappeared in 2003 — among birds in several Chinese mainland provinces. Alarm bells again sounded that February, when H5N1 infected two people in Hong Kong, killing one. In December, the virus killed two tigers and two leopards in a Thai zoo that had been fed fresh chicken carcasses; it was the first report of influenza causing disease and death in big cats. In January 2004, Vietnam and Thailand reported their first cases of human infection with H5N1. [36]

A second wave of infections began in summer 2004, with reports of infected poultry in China, Indonesia, Thailand and Vietnam. Research showed that H5N1 had become progressively more lethal for mammals and could kill wild waterfowl, long considered a disease-free natural reservoir. More human cases — eight fatal — were reported in Thailand and Vietnam.

In September 2004, researchers found that domestic cats experimentally infected with H5N1 could spread infection to other cats, previously considered resistant to all influenza A viruses — the broad category that includes H5N1. The following month, H5N1 was confirmed in two eagles illegally imported to Brussels, Belgium, from Thailand, and research confirmed that ducks were excreting large quantities of the virus without showing any signs of illness. [37]

The WHO warned in November 2004 that the H5N1 bird flu virus might spark a deadly pandemic. [38] And in 2005 the Institute of Medicine reported H5N1 apparently had accumulated mutations making it both increasingly infectious and deadly in mammals. [39]

Poultry outbreaks in Indonesia, Thailand and Vietnam in December 2004 marked the beginning of a third wave of worldwide infection, according to the WHO. The first — and so far only — human-to-human transmission of avian flu occurred in Thailand in September 2004, according to an early 2005 report in *The New England Journal of Medicine.* [40] Cambodia then reported its first human cases, all fatal, as did Indonesia.

Last April, wild birds began dying at Quinghai Lake in Central China, where hundreds of thousands of migratory birds congregate. More than 6,000 birds died in the ensuing weeks. In July, researchers found transmission of the virus among migratory geese and suggested it may be carried along winter migratory routes. [41] (*See map, p. 72.*)

On July 23, 2005, Russia became the first European country to report an outbreak of the virus — in poultry in Western Siberia — followed by Kazahkstan the next month. By October, the virus was confirmed among poultry in Turkey, Romania and Croatia.

Then in August the British medical journal *Lancet* reported Relenza was at least as effective as Tamiflu, but with fewer side effects and no evidence of resistance. By

How to Avoid Risk

- Poultry and eggs should be fully cooked — no "pink" parts and no runny yolks. Normal temperatures used for cooking poultry (158 degrees F. in all parts of the food) will kill the virus.

- If handling raw poultry in the kitchen, wash hands and disinfect cooking surfaces with hot water and soap. Raw poultry juices should never mix with food eaten raw.

- If you have no contact with birds, the risk is "almost non-existent," according to the World Health Organization.

Source: World Health Organization

contrast, it reported resistance levels in up to 18 percent of those taking Tamiflu. The researchers recommended stockpiling both drugs. [42]

Fear of Vaccine

After the attacks on the World Trade Center and the Pentagon on Sept. 11, 2001, U.S. officials increasingly worried that terrorists might attack with a biological weapon, such as anthrax or smallpox. [43] In December 2002, President Bush announced that all frontline health-care workers and military personnel should be vaccinated against smallpox, saying countries like Iraq were harboring secret reserves of smallpox and could use it as a biological weapon. However, many health workers and some hospitals refused to go along with the program, saying the vaccine was not safe. [44]

In response, Congress passed legislation in early 2003 to compensate people injured as a result of receiving the smallpox vaccine. But the compensation program was not launched until the end of that year, which critics said came too late to convince most health-care personnel, and the program fell far short of its goal. [45] Only about

40,000 individuals out of the 500,000 to several million health workers targeted have been vaccinated to date. [46] Labor unions and consumers have cited this failure in arguing that any successful mass-vaccination program for flu must include compensation for injuries.

CURRENT SITUATION

Global Efforts

The most dramatic effort to stem the H5N1 virus is taking place in China, where the government is trying to vaccinate an estimated 14 billion domestic chickens and ducks against the virus. In theory, the virus could be stopped this way.

In 2004, when H5N1 was rampant in Asia, Hong Kong did not have a single case in poultry or humans because it "used good vaccines and monitored to see that every chicken imported into Hong Kong was vaccinated with H5N1 vaccine," according to Memphis virologist Webster. But Hong Kong is a small, wealthy city surrounded by water, making it relatively easy to stop every poultry delivery.

By contrast, China is an enormous country, where people — especially in far-flung rural areas — live in close proximity to their poultry and where the prevalence of fake vaccines worries scientists. Government vaccinators have also been seen inoculating birds without wearing gloves and discarding used needles on the ground — raising the potential of further spreading the disease. [47]

When it comes to detecting the virus, the world's early warning system is "weak," the WHO reported last year. Since the countries most affected by avian flu cannot afford to compensate farmers adequately for killing their infected poultry, farmers have little incentive to report outbreaks in the rural areas where most human cases have occurred, WHO concluded. Farmers have suffered more than $10 billion in economic losses already, the organization estimates. [48]

The deadly consequences of failing to report bird flu outbreaks were illustrated in early January 2006, when human cases of bird flu began to multiply in rural eastern Turkey. International health officials said they believed the disease had existed among poultry for months, but because there were no earlier reports of bird flu in the area, humans had no way of knowing they were at risk in handling poultry. [49]

The United States is helping to prevent the spread of H5N1 by funding detection, reporting and education programs. [50] The U.S. Agency for International Development is spending $13.7 million to control and prevent avian flu in Asia, and the Centers for Disease Control and Prevention is spending $6 million on international detection and reporting. But a November 2005 report prepared by the U.N. Food and Agriculture Organization suggested that the amounts committed by member nations so far have been insufficient to control avian flu in animals. [51]

Moreover, the WHO's efforts to get developed countries to cooperate in providing vaccines to developing countries and building an international stockpile of antiviral medications, have had only limited success. [52]

Worldwide, current manufacturers could only produce enough H5N1 bird flu vaccine to inoculate about 1.5 percent of the world's population, which the University of Minnesota's Osterholm says would be "like trying to fill Lake Superior with a garden hose." [53] The scientific journal *Nature* says WHO's fledgling international effort to establish a coalition to fight the spread of the disease is "shaky and far from united or sure in its purpose" and "grossly underfunded." [54]

The discovery in 2004 of the two infected eagles smuggled into Belgium from Thailand in airline carry-on baggage highlighted the severely under-policed illegal trade in exotic animals — second in size only to the drug trade — as another possible vector for spread of the disease. Robert A. Cook, vice president and chief veterinarian at the Wildlife Conservation Society, calls U.S. laws governing the import of illegal animals "dangerously lax." [55]

Increasingly, new human diseases — such as AIDS and SARS — have originated in wild animals, according to Cook. "You take these animals out of the wild, and they [bring] with them a whole new range of diseases we haven't seen before," he says.

Washington imposed some new import restrictions after monkey pox, which causes fevers and ulcers, infected 71 Midwesterners in 2003. The outbreak was triggered when imported African rodents infected prairie dogs at a pet shop. But it is still legal in the United States to import most exotic species.

Domestic Efforts

On Nov. 1, recalling that the 1918 flu infected one-third of Americans, President Bush unveiled his pandemic

Is there a serious risk of a human pandemic of avian flu?

YES
Michael T. Osterholm
Director, Center for Infectious Disease Research and Policy, University of Minnesota

From testimony before House Committee on International Relations, Dec. 7, 2005

We must never forget that influenza pandemics are like earthquakes, hurricanes and tsunamis; they occur. The most recent came in 1957-58 and 1968-69, and although tens of thousands of Americans died in each one, these were considered mild compared to others. According to a recent analysis, [the 1918-19 pandemic] killed 50-100 million people globally. Today, with a population of 6.5 billion — more than three times that of 1918 — even a mild pandemic could kill many millions.

A number of recent events and factors have heightened our concern that a specific near-term pandemic may be imminent. Some important preparatory efforts are under way, but much more needs to be done throughout the world.

Based on our past experiences with outbreaks such as SARS, if an influenza pandemic began today, borders will close, the global economy will shut down, pharmaceutical supplies — including important childhood vaccines — will be in extreme short supply, health-care systems will be overwhelmed and panic will reign. Access to pandemic influenza vaccines and effective antiviral drug treatments will be limited for the entire world for years to come because of our lack of modern vaccines and a grossly inadequate worldwide production capability.

An influenza pandemic will be like a 12-to-18-month global blizzard that will ultimately change the world as we know it today. Foreign trade and travel will be reduced or even ended in an attempt to stop the virus from entering new countries — even though such efforts will probably fail, given the infectiousness of influenza and the volume of illegal crossings that occur at most borders.

One part of pandemic preparedness planning that must receive immediate attention is the implementation of a concept that I have called "critical product continuity" (CPC) — the determination of those products and services that must be available during a pandemic in order to minimize potentially catastrophic collateral health and security consequences — and the subsequent comprehensive actions that must be taken by both governments and the private sector to ensure their availability.

While I have chosen to highlight the issue of critical product continuity and the pharmaceutical industry, there are many other product areas that must be considered as we plan for getting through the next 12-to-18-month pandemic.

NO
Michael Fumento
Senior Fellow, Hudson Institute

Written for *CQ Researcher*, Jan. 4, 2006

It is only a matter of time before an avian flu virus — most likely H5N1 — acquires the ability to be transmitted from human to human, sparking the outbreak of human pandemic influenza." So declared Dr. Lee Jong-wook, director-general of the World Health Organization.

Terrifying statement. False statement.

It is the best-kept secret of the pandemic panic purveyors that H5N1 hasn't just been around since its Hong Kong appearance in 1997 but actually was discovered in Scottish chickens in 1959. It's therefore been mutating and making contact with humans for 47 years. If it hasn't become transmissible between humans in all that time, it almost certainly won't.

Despite what you've been told, H5N1 isn't even slowly mutating in the direction of becoming pandemic. There are no evolutionary pressures upon it to either become more efficiently transmitted from bird to man or man to man. Rather, as one mutation draws the virus closer to human transmissibility, another is as likely to draw it farther away.

Certainly an avian flu pandemic won't let media hysteria dictate its appearance and therefore be upon us before effective vaccines become widely available in a couple of years. If "a matter of time" means several years from now, we'll be quite prepared, thank you.

But aren't we "overdue" for a pandemic, with H5N1 the likeliest cause? Google "avian flu," "pandemic," and "overdue," and you'll get more than 35,000 hits. Anthony Fauci, director of the National Institute of Allergies and Infectious Diseases, insists we're "overdue," explaining that there were three pandemics in the 20th century, the last one 38 years ago.

Yet the time between the second and third pandemics was only 11 years. There's no cycle. As risk-communication expert Peter Sandman of Rutgers University says, the "overdue pandemic" is mere superstition.

None of which should discourage such sensible measures as mass poultry vaccinations, killing infected flocks and teaching Asian farmers to have as little contact with their birds and bird droppings as possible. These steps can reduce or even eliminate the few human cases now occurring and cut the chance of pandemic from nearly zero to zero.

But there is no gain in spreading an epidemic of hysteria. The false fears we sow today we shall reap in the future as public complacency when a monster is truly at the door.

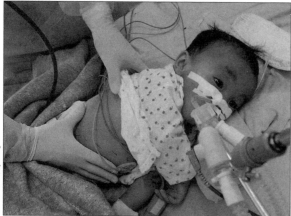

A Vietnamese infant receives avian flu treatment in Hanoi. Health experts say antiviral medications like Tamiflu could lessen the severity of the disease. However, some bird flu patients in Vietnam who took Tamiflu died.

plan to the nation. "If history is our guide, there is reason to be concerned," he said. [56]

But in December, when Congress approved only $3.8 billion for pandemic spending — about half the president's $7.1 billion request — lawmakers said the money was enough to get the program started in 2006. [57] Public health advocates hope Congress will appropriate the rest of Bush's request next year.

Of the total, $3 billion is earmarked to prepare for a pandemic, including the purchase of vaccines and antiviral drugs, $350 million for state and local preparedness — more than Bush had requested — and $267 million for overseas detection and reporting of flu cases. The legislation also allows HHS to negotiate contracts with vendors through which states could order antiviral drugs and be reimbursed by the federal government. The legislation would permit the use of federal funds to construct or renovate private facilities for the production of vaccines.

Critics immediately complained that the plan did not specify what localities should do once their hospitals are filled to capacity. European nations are far ahead of the United States in planning so-called surge capacity, according to Elliott, of the Trust for America's Health. "Every single hotel in Great Britain knows whether or not they're going to be a surge hospital," she says.

The plan says health workers should get top priority for vaccinations and allows states to decide who should

be in subsequent priority groups. George E. Hardy, Jr., executive director of the Association of State and Territorial Health Officials, says states would like more consistency on who is at the top of the list.

"Whether you live in Alabama or Montana, the priority groups should be the same," he says.

Liability

In December, Congress approved sweeping provisions shielding manufacturers of pandemic vaccines from liability lawsuits. [58] President Bush and GOP lawmakers had argued that the liability protection was necessary to encourage drug makers to get into the vaccine business.

Tacked onto the Defense appropriations bill in the middle of the night, the liability language was immediately attacked as a "backroom deal" by consumer groups complaining that the provision was never subjected to a separate floor vote or discussion.

Senate Majority Leader Bill Frist, R-Tenn., described the measure as "targeted liability protection." Lawsuits could only be brought if the federal government sues on behalf of a patient's wrongful death or serious injury. But the suits can only be brought for "willful misconduct," and negligence or recklessness are not defined as willful misconduct.

"There's no reason to immunize a company against recklessness," says Amy Widman, a lawyer for the Center for Justice and Democracy, arguing that a threat of lawsuits checks corporate irresponsibility.

The center was part of a coalition of five consumer groups that complained to senators that under this narrow definition drug companies would only be held responsible if "the company had actual knowledge the product would kill someone."

The legislation would exempt companies from liability for "countermeasures" — drugs, vaccines or medical devices — designed to protect Americans in public "emergencies," to be defined by the HHS secretary. Consumer advocates said the legislation could cover everything from cholesterol drugs to Tylenol. Widman calls it "a giveaway to drug companies" seeking to incorporate "a lot of things they've been trying to get for many, many years."

"The Republican leadership in Congress cut a backroom deal to give a massive Christmas bonus to the drug companies," Sen. Edward M. Kennedy, D-Mass., said in a statement after the House vote. [59]

But Frist said he was "proud" of the provisions that had been incorporated into the defense appropriations bill. "The bill strikes a reasonable balance where those who are harmed will be fairly compensated and life-saving products will be available in ample supply to protect and treat as many Americans as possible," he said. [60]

The new law directs HHS to sets up a compensation fund to reimburse anyone injured by a vaccine or other medication covered by the legislation. Consumer and labor groups, however, pointed out that no money was appropriated for the fund, which would be inoperable until funded.

Without funding for compensation, said Barbara Coufal, legislative affairs specialist for the American Federation of State, County and Municipal Employees (AFSCME), "We're worried [that] it may never be realized."

Quarantines

In the event of a pandemic, say many public health experts, it may be nearly impossible to isolate the infected from the well, since people infected with the flu are contagious for at least a day before they show symptoms. The more likely scenario would be a wholesale shutdown of public places like schools, workplaces, shopping malls and theatres.

In November, the CDC proposed new quarantine rules that include influenza as one of the illnesses subject to a quarantine ordered by the president. The new rules would also require airlines to keep copies of passenger manifests for 60 days, which could be made available to the CDC within 12 hours if ill passengers arrive on international or domestic flights. [61] But experts say preventing sick or exposed persons from getting off airplanes is unlikely to prevent avian flu from entering the country.

"What if I fly from Thailand to Europe to Canada and drive to Seattle? Are they going to flag me and stop me?" asks the University of Minnesota's Osterholm. "I don't think we're going to stop it."

On Nov. 1, New York City's health department offered free flu vaccines to anyone who showed up at a downtown clinic in an experiment aimed at simulating what might happen during a major outbreak. Many people waited more than three hours, prompting some to wonder whether the city could handle a real emergency. [62]

"Most state and local public health agencies lack the people, money and political clout to manage an epi-demic," according to the Center for Biosecurity at the University of Pittsburgh. [63]

Governors have put most of their health dollars into mandatory programs like Medicaid, according to Elliott rather than public health departments where spending is discretionary. "We have an aging work force and not a lot of new blood coming in because it's not a lucrative profession," she says. There are not enough workers now to handle regular vaccinations and health needs, she points out.

On the other hand, since 9/11, every state has developed a federally funded plan for responding to a bioterrorist attack. "We're much better prepared than we were a year ago," says Hardy of the Association of State and Territorial Health Officials. However, federal funds for state and local bioterrorism preparedness programs were cut 14 percent in the fiscal 2006 appropriations bill, which the Trust for America called "ill-advised" in view of their pandemic responsibilities.

"The first thing we learned in Hurricane Katrina is you put public health leaders in charge of a health crisis, not first responders" like police, says Elliott, of the Trust for America's Health. "Otherwise we have situations like triaging folks in an airport and putting masses of people in a convention center with no water or sanitary facilities. Public health officials would never have done that."

Late-Breaking News

Multiplying human cases of bird flu appeared in early January 2006 in Turkey, putting health officials in Europe on "high alert." An unusual cluster of human cases (15 confirmed as of Jan. 10), including some 50 other people hospitalized for possible H5N1, raised the possibility that the virus might have mutated to become more contagious to humans. But as of Jan. 11, WHO scientists had detected no changes in the H5N1 virus samples from Turkey that might make it more transmissible to humans. [64]

American chicken farmers apparently are taking the disease more seriously, given the announcement that nearly all flocks would be tested for avian flu starting Jan. 16. [65] With the fall bird migration ended, some experts declared that North America had dodged the bird flu — at least for the 2005-2006 winter flu season. But international health officials warned that Europe might still be vulnerable from the spring 2006 migration. [66]

OUTLOOK

Economic Disaster?

Many experts hope a pandemic doesn't arrive for another five years or so, which would give the United States time to increase manufacturing capacity for vaccines. The administration is pinning its hopes on the new cell-based vaccines that would take less lead time than today's old-fashioned technology.

Meanwhile, NIH researchers are working on developing a universal vaccine that would prevent all flu strains — considered the holy grail of vaccine researchers.

Many agree that new, more effective antiviral medications need to be developed, especially if resistance develops in whatever flu strain hits our shores. But others say it's most important to rebuild the U.S. public health system, so there will be enough workers to vaccinate and treat the sick.

The gloomiest forecast is painted by the University of Minnesota's Osterholm, who foresees a collapse in our increasingly global economy if a pandemic forces nations to shut down their borders. For instance, most masks, gloves and syringes are manufactured offshore, as are the raw materials for antibiotics. As a result, modern medicine's advantages won't really be available, he predicts.

"When a pandemic flu hits, we'll go back to 1918 medicine; we're going to care for people in large gyms and stadiums; we will have a major shortage of intravenous equipment; we'll have a shortage of antibiotics and health-care workers, and no masks are being stockpiled. So you tell me how that's different from 1918. If you don't call that a perfect storm, I don't know what is."

But some economists say the U.S. economy is so resilient that even a severe pandemic — like that in 1918 — would not produce an economic disaster. A mild pandemic like that in 1968 would "probably not cause a recession and might not be distinguishable from the normal variation in economic activity," according to a recent CBO report. [67]

There are so many gaps in the scientific knowledge about viruses that "there is no scientific basis to predict anything," according to Masato Tashiro, director of the WHO's Collaborative Center for Influenza Surveillance and Research at Japan's National Institute of Infectious Diseases in Tokyo. [68]

Although some scientists are skeptical that H5N1 bird flu will cause the next pandemic, and others believe it will be mild, virtually everyone agrees there will be another flu pandemic eventually, and that the country should start preparing now.

NOTES

1. This description is from Mike Davis, *The Monster at Our Door* (2005), pp. 4-8.

2. *Ibid.*, p. 7.

3. Elisabeth Rosenthal, "Bird Flu Reports Multiply in Turkey, Faster Than Expected," *The New York Times*, Jan. 9, 2006, p. A4.

4. Institute of Medicine, *The Threat of Pandemic Influenza: Are We Ready? A Workshop Summary* (2005), p. 8.

5. For background, see Mary H. Cooper, "Fighting SARS," *CQ Researcher*, June 20, 2003, pp. 569-592.

6. That is the number needed in order to kill all poultry in China over a year's time.

7. Institute of Medicine, *op. cit.*, p. 19.

8. http://healthyamericans.org.

9. Trust for America's Health, press release, "TFAH commends U.S. House of Representatives for Passing Down Payment," Dec. 19, 2005.

10. "Don't Support a Defense Spending Bill that Has Backroom Special Interest Protections," Dec. 20, 2005, letter to senators from U.S. PIRG and other interest groups at www.uspirg.org.

11. Congressional Budget Office (CBO), "A Potential Influenza Pandemic: Possible Macroeconomic Effects and Policy Issues," Dec. 8, 2005, p. 6.

12. White House, "President Outlines Pandemic Influenza Preparations and Response," Nov. 1, 2005, at www.whitehouse.gov/news/releases/2005/11/2005110 1-1.html.

13. See for example, comments by Anthony Fauci on CBS' "60 Minutes:" "Right now . . . if we had an explosion of H5N1 we would not be prepared for that;" "Chasing the Flu," Dec.4, 2005, at www.cbsnews.com/stories/2005/12/02/60minutes/main1094515.shtml.

14. The president's proposal and HHS plan can be found at www.pandemicflu.gov.

15. Congressional Budget Office, *op. cit.*, p. 22.

16. Sanofi pasteur announced Dec. 15 study results showing it could produce an H5N1 vaccine requiring only four times as much antigen using adjuvants. See "Sanofi says H5N1 vaccine with adjuvant may go further," Dec. 15, 2005, at www.cidrap.umn.edu.

17. Andrew Jack, "Deaths cast doubt over use of Tamiflu," *Financial Times*, Dec. 22, 2005, p. 6.

18. CBO, *op. cit.*, p. 29.

19. David Heyman, "Model Operational Guidelines for Disease Exposure Control," Nov. 2, 2005, at www.csis.org/index.php?option=com_csis_pubs&task=view&id=2504.

20. White House press release, "President Outlines Pandemic Influenza Preparations and Response," Nov. 1, 2005.

21. Michelle M. Mello and Troyen A. Brennan, "Legal Concerns and the Influenza Vaccine Shortage," *JAMA*, Oct. 12, 2005, pp. 1817-1820.

22. Institute of Medicine, *Financing Vaccines in the 21st Century: Assuring Access and Availability* (2003), at www.nap.edu.

23. www.cdc.gov/nip/vfc/Parent/parent_home.htm#1.

24. In October 2004, British government regulators withdrew the license from Liverpool, England, flu vaccine manufacturer Chiron after 4 million doses were found to be contaminated. On Oct. 5, 2004, Chiron announced that it could not provide its expected production of 46-48 million doses of flu vaccine — about half the expected U.S. influenza vaccine supply — setting off a major shortage of flu vaccine in the winter flu season of 2004.

25. World Health Organization (WHO), *Responding to the Avian Influenza Pandemic Threat: Recommended Strategic Actions* (2005), p. 2. Also see Ira M. Longini, Jr., *et al.*, "Containing Pandemic Influenza at the Source," *Science*, Aug. 12, 2005, pp. 1083-1087.

26. See press releases from Sen. Schumer "As Avian Flu Closes in on U.S. Schumer Calls for Immediate Action: Demands Suspension of Tamiflu Patent So Vaccine Can be Mass-Produced," Oct. 16, 2005, and "Schumer Praises Roche Agreements with 2 Major U.S. Generic Drug Companies," Dec. 8, 2005.

27. See Council on Foreign Relations, Conference on the Global Threat of Pandemic Influenza, Session 2: Containment and Control, Nov. 16, 2005 at www.cfr.org/publication/9244/council_on_foreign_relations_conference_on_the_global_threat_of_pandemic_influenza_session_2.html. David Nabarro is U.N. System Coordinator for Avian and Human Influenza.

28. Quoted in Michael Fumento, "Fuss and Feathers: Pandemic Panic Over the Avian Flu," *The Weekly Standard*, Nov. 21, 2005.

29 "60 Minutes," *op. cit.*

30. WHO, *op. cit.*, p. 12.

31. CBO, *op. cit.*, p. 6. It is unclear why the outbreak was called the "Spanish flu," since it did not originate in Spain or hit that country particularly hard. Some theorize that the term arose because of heavy coverage by Spanish newspapers.

32. John M. Barry, *The Great Influenza* (2004), p. 250.

33. Laurie Garrett, "The Next Pandemic?" *Foreign Affairs*, July/August 2005, pp. 3-23.

34. Quoted in *ibid.*, p. 10.

35. *Ibid.*; also see Institute of Medicine (2005), p. 13.

36. WHO, "H5N1 Avian Influenza: Timeline," Oct. 28, 2005.

37. *Ibid.*

38. "Avian Flu Timeline," *Nature* Web site at www.nature.com/nature/focus/avianflu/timeline.html.

39. Institute of Medicine (2005), p. 12.

40. K. Ungchusak, *et al.*, "Probable Person-to-person Transmission of Avian Influenza A (H5N1)," *The New England Journal of Medicine*, Jan. 27, 2005, pp. 333-40.

41. WHO, *ibid.*

42. Nature Web site, *op. cit.*

43. For background, see David Masci, "Smallpox Threat," *CQ Researcher*, Feb. 7, 2003, pp. 105-128.

44. Jeffrey Gettleman, "Threats and Responses: Biological Defenses," *The New York Times*, Dec. 19, 2002, p. A19.

45. The program hoped to vaccinate 500,000 people, but by October 2003 only 37,901 had been vaccinated. A hundred people suffered injuries. See

CIDRAP News, "Study shows few serious problems among smallpox vaccinees," Dec. 14, 2005, at www.cidrap.umn.edu.

46. CBO, *op. cit.*, p. 27.

47. Howard W. French, "Bird by Bird China Tackles Vast Flu Task," *The New York Times*, Dec. 2, 2005, p. A1.

48. WHO, "Responding to the Avian Influenza Pandemic Threat," *op. cit.*

49. Elisabeth Rosenthal, "Bird Flu Reports Multiply in Turkey, Faster Than Expected," *New York Times*, Jan. 9, 2006, p. A4.

50. In September, Bush announced an International Partnership on Avian and Pandemic Influenza, a global network that requires participating countries that face an outbreak to provide samples to the WHO. As of Nov. 1, 88 countries had joined the effort.

51. *Ibid.*

52. Congressional Research Service, Pandemic Influenza: Domestic Preparedness Efforts, Nov. 10, 2005, p. 17.

53. Based on current doses of H5N1 vaccine, Osterholm calculates that capacity exists for about 100 million of the world's population of about 6.5 billion.

54. "On a Wing and a Prayer," *Nature*, May 26, 2005, pp. 385-386, www.nature.com/nature.

55. William B. Karesh and Robert Cook, "The Human-Animal Link," *Foreign Affairs*, July/August 2005, pp. 38-50.

56. White House, "President Outlines Pandemic Influenza Preparations and Response," Nov. 1, 2005.

57. "House Approves Pandemic Funding Far Below Bush Request," CIDRAP News at www.cidrap.umn.edu/cidrap/content/influenza/panflu/news/dec1905funding.html.

58. Sheryl Gay Stolberg, "Legal Shield for Vaccine Makers is Inserted into Military Bill," *The New York Times*, Dec. 20, 2005, p. A26.

59. *Ibid.*

60. Sen. Bill Frist press release, "Frist Hails Passage of FY06 Defense Appropriations Conference Report," Dec. 21, 2005.

61. Lawrence K. Altman, "C.D.C. Proposes New Rules in Effort to Prevent Disease Outbreak," *The New York Times*, Nov. 23, 2005, p. A22.

62. Shadi Rahimi, "Just a Drill, But Flu Shots were Real, And Popular," *The New York Times*, Nov. 2, 2005, p. A1.

63. Center for Biosecurity, "National Strategy for Pandemic Influenza," Nov. 7, 2005.

64. See Rosenthal, *op. cit.*, Jan. 9, 2006; Reuters, "Turkey Struggles with Bird Flu as Children Fall Ill," *The New York Times*, Jan. 7, 2006, and Elisabeth Rosenthal, "New Bird Flu Cases in Turkey Put Europe on 'High Alert,' " *The New York Times*, Jan. 7, 2006, p. A3.

65. Donald G. McNeil Jr., "U.S. Farmers to Begin Testing Chickens for Flu," *The New York Times*, Jan. 6, 2006, p. A19.

66. See "If the Avian Flu Hasn't Hit, Here's Why. Maybe," *The New York Times*, Jan. 1, 2006, "News of the Week in Review," p. 10, and U.N. Food and Agriculture Organization, "Wild Birds and Avian Influenza," at www.fao.org/ag/againfo/subjects/en/health/diseases-cards/avian_HPAIrisk.html.

67. CBO, *op. cit.*, pp. 1-2.

68. Dennis Normile, "Pandemic Skeptics Warn Against Crying Wolf," *Science*, Nov. 18, 2005, p. 1113.

BIBLIOGRAPHY

Books

Barry, John M., *The Great Influenza: The Epic Story of the Deadliest Plague in History*, Penguin Books, 2004.
This history of the deadly 1918 influenza pandemic cites similarities with the H5N1 bird flu now in Asia. Barry is distinguished visiting scholar at the Center for Bioenvironmental Research of Tulane and Xavier universities.

Davis, Mike, *The Monster at Our Door: The Global Threat of Avian Flu*, The New Press, 2005.
Science writer Davis expresses outrage at poor countries' lack of access to vaccines and antiviral medicines and recommends governments take over their manufacture if the free market can't distribute them cheaply.

Garrett, Laurie, *The Coming Plague: Newly Emerging Diseases in a World Out of Balance*, Penguin Books, 1994.

In a wide-ranging look at modern diseases that some have compared to Rachel Carson's celebrated *Silent Spring*, a Pulitzer Prize-winning journalist warns that infectious microbes pose increasing danger as humans disrupt the Earth's ecology.

Articles

Fumento, Michael, "Fuss and Feathers: Pandemic Panic over the Avian Flu," *The Weekly Standard*, Nov. 21, 2005; www.weeklystandard.com.
A senior fellow at the conservative Hudson Institute downplays the risk of bird flu and charges that politicians, public health officials and the press are crossing the line between informing the public and starting a panic.

Garrett, Laurie, "The Next Pandemic?" *Foreign Affairs*, July/August 2005, pp. 3-23.
Journalist Garrett, now a senior fellow at the Council on Foreign Relations, describes the recent history of H5N1 and why it might create the next pandemic.

Karesh, William B., and Robert A. Cook, "The Human-Animal Link," *Foreign Affairs*, July/August 2005, pp. 38-50.
Two veterinarians explain why diseases like bird flu that originate in animals are a growing threat to humans.

Normile, Dennis, "Pandemic Skeptics Warn Against Crying Wolf," *Science*, Nov. 18, 2005, pp. 1112-1113.
Some scientists doubt that H5N1 bird flu will become the next human pandemic and worry the "current hype" could undermine efforts to prepare for the next genuine pandemic.

Orent, Wendy, "Chicken Little," *The New Republic*, Sept. 12, 2005; www.tnr.com.
Those warning of a new H5N1 epidemic are being alarmists, the author says.

Osterholm, Michael T., "Preparing for the Next Pandemic," *Foreign Affairs*, July/August 2004, pp. 24-37.
A professor of public health at the University of Minnesota discusses why the world is unprepared for a pandemic and what steps should be taken.

Taubenberger, Jeffery K., and David M. Morens, "1918 Influenza: The Mother of All Pandemics," *Emerging Infectious Diseases*, January 2006; www.cdc.gov/ncidod/EID/vol12no01/05-0979.htm.
Taubenberger, the scientist who sequenced the genes of the 1918 flu, and epidemiologist Morens downplay earlier reported similarities between the 1918 virus and H5N1 virus.

Reports and Studies

Congressional Budget Office, *A Potential Influenza Pandemic: Possible Macroeconomic Effects and Policy Issues*, Dec. 8, 2005; www.cbo.gov.
A severe flu pandemic would cause a recession, the CBO concludes in this up-to-date summary of policy debates over avian flu.

Congressional Research Service, *Pandemic Influenza: Domestic Preparedness Effort*, Nov. 10, 2005; www.fas.org/sgp/crs/homesec/RL33145.pdf.
The CRS provides a good overview of efforts by domestic and international agencies to prepare for a pandemic as well as proposed legislative approaches.

Institute of Medicine, *Financing Vaccines in the 21st Century: Assuring Access and Availability*, 2003; www.nap.edu.
A panel of experts recommended that the government mandate health-insurance coverage of vaccination in order to encourage drug companies to get into the vaccine market.

Institute of Medicine, *The Threat of Pandemic Influenza: Are We Ready?*, 2005; www.nap.edu.
This report, which grew out of a 2004 workshop at the Institute of Medicine, contains papers by contributors as well as recommendations on how to prepare for a pandemic.

World Health Organization, *Responding to the Avian Influenza Pandemic Threat: Recommended Strategic Actions*, 2005; www.who.int/csr/resources/publications/influenza/WHO_CDS_CSR_GIP_05_8-EN.pdf.
After assessing the global threat of H5N1 flu virus, this report recommends that nations contribute to a worldwide stockpile of antiviral medications, among other steps.

For More Information

American Public Health Association, 800 I St., N.W., Washington, DC 20001-3710; (202) 777-APHA; www.apha.org. Represents public health professionals worldwide.

Association of State and Territorial Health Officials, 1275 K St., N.W., Suite 800, Washington, DC 20005-4006; (202) 371-9090; www.astho.org. Represents chief health officials.

Center for Biosecurity, University of Pittsburgh Medical Center, The Pier IV Building, 621 E. Pratt St., Suite 210, Baltimore, MD 21202; (443) 573-3304; www.upmc-biosecurity.org. An independent organization concerned with epidemics caused by natural and terrorist agents.

Center for Infectious Disease Research & Policy, University of Minnesota, Academic Health Center, 420 Delaware St., S.E., MMC 263, Minneapolis, MN 55455; (612) 626-6770; www.cidrap.umn.edu. Carries daily breaking news on avian flu on its Web site.

Center for Justice and Democracy, 90 Broad St., Suite 401, New York, NY 10004; (212) 267-2801; http://centerjd.org. A consumer group active on liability issues involving vaccine manufacturers.

pandemicflu.gov. The official U.S. government Web site on pandemic flu and avian flu is managed by the Department of Health and Human Services, with links to the White House and other federal agencies.

Pharmaceutical Research and Manufacturers of America, 1100 15th St., N.W., Washington, DC 20005; (202) 835-3400. www.phrma.org. Represents the country's leading pharmaceutical research and biotechnology companies.

Trust for America's Health, 1707 H St., N.W., 7th Floor, Washington, DC 20006; (202) 223-9870; http://healthy americans.org. A nonprofit public health advocacy group.

U.S. Centers for Disease Control and Prevention, 1600 Clifton Rd., Atlanta, GA 30333; (404) 639-3534; www.cdc.gov. The chief federal health agency dealing with avian flu.

5

Upward Mobility

Alan Greenblatt

Union construction jobs were once a ticket to the middle class. But as union membership has declined, good-paying construction work increasingly is going to immigrants willing to accept less pay and fewer benefits.

J ack Haugsland has gone farther than he ever could have dreamed while growing up next door to his father's service station in Madison, Wis. "We had gasoline fumes 24/7," he recalls. Haugsland twice dropped out of college to come home and help with his four siblings. Between stints at college and in the Army, Haugsland drove a Greyhound bus for more than 10 years.

It wasn't a terribly promising start, but after he became a union representative, he was offered the chance to work as a manager himself. He soon began climbing the corporate ladder, bouncing around the country and even running a Greyhound operation in Saudi Arabia. For the past decade, Haugsland, 65, has been Greyhound's chief operating officer — the No. 2 official at one of the nation's largest transportation companies.

"You sometimes have to recognize opportunities and have the initiative to take advantage of those opportunities," Haugsland says. "A lot of time that takes a lot of extra effort and work."

Haugsland's story is just one more retelling of the American dream: dizzying success by dint of hard work. Stephen Girard and John Jacob Astor became America's two richest men during the early 19th century after arriving as immigrants without any special connections. [1] In our own time, real-life Horatio Alger stories continue to be written. * Ray Noorda, the son of a janitor, loaded rail cars as a young man but eventually became the top officer at Novell Corp., accumulating a $500 million fortune. [2] In his 2004 book

---

* The heartwarming stories of American author Horatio Alger Jr. (1834-1899) promoted the "American dream" — that any poor but deserving boy, armed only with industriousness and ingenuity, can become successful.

From *CQ Researcher,*
April 29, 2005.

Poor Lost Most Income During Recession

Income loss was unbalanced during the recession and jobless recovery from 2000 to 2003, with the greatest losses at the bottom and middle of the income scales than at the top. The largest declines occurred among the 20 percent of American families with the lowest incomes.

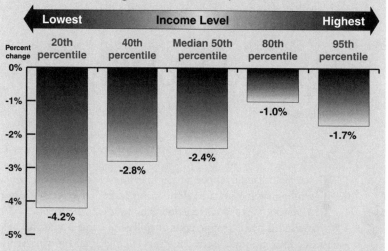

Change in real income, 2000-2002

Source: Lawrence Mishel, *et al., The State of Working America, 2004-2005,* Economic Policy Institute, based on Census Bureau data

The Working Poor, journalist David K. Shipler recounts how his grandfather got an 8-cent-an-hour job on the Jersey City docks and rose to become president of Bethlehem Steel's steamship lines. [3]

But now Shipler, along with many economists and sociologists, worries there aren't enough new names being added to the list because of growing income inequality. The richest 20 percent of Americans are watching their incomes rise at much faster rates than the rest of the population. For most people, that makes the ladder to success much steeper and harder — or at least no easier — to climb.

"A growing body of evidence suggests that the meritocratic ideal is in trouble in America," according to *The Economist,* a British news magazine. "Income inequality is growing to levels not seen since the Gilded Age, around the 1880s. But social mobility is not increasing at anything like the same pace." [4]

In 2000 the average income of the top 1 percent of American households was 189 times that of the bottom 20 percent, compared to 1979 when the top was earning 133 times as much. By 2001, *The Economist* reports, the top 1 percent of American households earned 20 percent of the income and held 33.4 percent of all net worth — their biggest slice since the 1920s. [5] Meanwhile, the middle class' share of total income was the lowest it had been for a half-century. [6] The disparity in wealth (tangible assets such as stocks, bonds and property) is even greater than the disparity in income.

"Everyone agrees that income inequality has gone up," says Katharine Bradbury, a senior economist at the Federal Reserve Bank of Boston. "[But] a lot of people argue that we don't have to worry about this because there's a lot of mobility — that the gap doesn't matter as much if people who are poor don't stay that way long."

Sociologists generally measure social mobility by comparing how many individuals move from one income group to another. For example, someone in the lowest 40 percent of income in 1990 might have reached the top 20 percent today.

However, Bradbury's research shows that people no longer are moving up as much as before. During the 1990s, 40 percent of families stayed within the same income bracket that they started the decade in, compared with 37 percent in the 1980s and 36 percent in the 1970s. "Basically, people were somewhat more stuck in the '90s than they were in the '70s," she says.

Several other studies reach similar conclusions, although it is notoriously difficult to gauge the success of groups of individuals and families across long periods. Most sets of numbers don't show a great deal of change in the number of people moving up in income class today compared with 20 years ago, but there does seem to be a slight downward tilt.

Still, even if people aren't moving up in rank, their living standards are improving over time. "By global or historical standards, much of what Americans consider poverty is luxury," Shipler notes. "Most impoverished people in the world would be dazzled by the apartments, telephones, television sets, running water, clothing and other amenities that surround the poor in America." [7]

Some conservatives, such as W. Michael Cox, chief economist at the Federal Reserve Bank of Dallas, maintain that rising living standards mean that even if some Americans are not as well off as others, everyone is doing better than they once were. Cox points to improvements in medicine, technology and the availability of cheaper consumer goods — thanks largely to trade globalization — in arguing that today's poor are better off than even the upper middle class was 35 years ago.

The poor also receive the lion's share of benefits from social programs funded by upper-income taxpayers, Cox points out. According to the Heritage Foundation, the top fifth of U.S. households pay 82.5 percent of total federal income taxes and two-thirds of federal taxes overall. The bottom 20 percent pay only 1.1 percent. [8]

Still, Shipler maintains that today's working poor lack the financial cushion enjoyed by those with higher incomes and are just one failed car engine or bout of bad health away from losing their homes or their livelihoods.

Moreover, other observers say, the 1996 welfare reform law, which ended uncapped cash entitlements and imposed work requirements on recipients, hasn't lifted people out of poverty because it did not provide sufficient support services such as child care. [9]

"We've turned the welfare poor into the working poor, but we haven't helped their kids go to better preschools or reduced dropouts," says Timothy M. Smeeding, director of the Center for Policy Research at Syracuse University's Maxwell School. "We're not increasing mobility in any real sense."

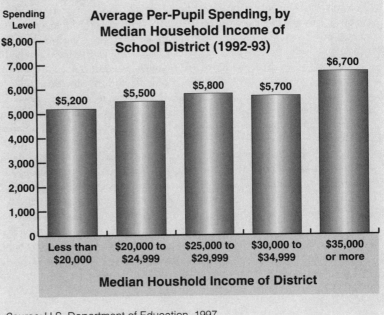

Wealthy Districts Get Most School Funding

Spending on education is typically higher in wealthier than in poorer districts, largely because most funds for public schools are raised through local property taxes. Thus per-pupil spending in 1992-93 in districts with median household incomes above $35,000 was 27 percent higher than spending in districts with median incomes below $20,000.

Average Per-Pupil Spending, by Median Household Income of School District (1992-93)

Spending Level

Less than $20,000	$20,000 to $24,999	$25,000 to $29,999	$30,000 to $34,999	$35,000 or more
$5,200	$5,500	$5,800	$5,700	$6,700

Median Houshold Income of District

Source: U.S. Department of Education, 1997

Meanwhile, middle-class Americans also feel their jobs are more tenuous, thanks to new technology, the "downsizing" trend of the late 1980s and the globalization of the work force. During the 1980s and '90s, U.S. companies eliminated a large number of middle- management jobs, creating more streamlined operations but fewer chances for advancement. [10] Today, many good-paying manufacturing jobs are being sent overseas, as are many of the high-tech jobs that were supposed to replace them.

"The pressure is going to be on the middle class, to a significant extent," says Richard Freeman, a Harvard University economist and director of the labor studies program at the National Bureau of Economic Research. "Any job that has a lot of digitalization is at risk in this country. How are you going to get a wage increase if you're competing with [lower-wage workers] overseas?"

Will Bush's "Ownership Society" Help the Poor?

As the centerpiece of his domestic agenda, President Bush wants to create an "ownership society" by increasing Americans' investment and wealth. To do that, he proposes cuts or outright elimination of federal taxes on income, savings, stock earnings and dividends, health expenses and inheritance. Most controversially, Bush wants to let workers shift part of their Social Security payments into "personal accounts" holding investments in stocks and bonds.

"We will widen the ownership of homes and businesses, retirement savings and health insurance," Bush said during his inaugural address in January. "By making every citizen an agent of his or her own destiny, we will give our fellow Americans greater freedom from want and fear and make our society more prosperous and just and equal."

Glenn Yago, director of capital studies at the Milken Institute, an economic think tank in Santa Monica, Calif., sees Bush's agenda as part of a presidential continuum, noting that Thomas Jefferson and Abraham Lincoln also were great promoters of ownership, encouraging the settling of the interior through land grants. "For the longest time in the U.S., proprietorship was key to being a part of the polity," Yago says. "The ownership-society debate is really not just about income distribution, it's about asset distribution as well."

Bush's program would give individuals more power to make their own economic decisions. While it's hard to find anyone opposed to that idea in theory, many critics worry that millions of individuals won't be able to rise to all its possible challenges.

"You're moving from a situation where you're pooling risk to a situation where you're putting more of the risk on individuals," says Frank Levy, an economist at the Massachusetts Institute of Technology. Levy argues that, given the other macroeconomic challenges ahead, such as increased competition from China and India and continuing changes in technology, the workplace is becoming more uncertain. Given the uncertainty and accompanying risk, he says it's unreasonable to ask America's workers to adapt and accept responsibility for their own retirements.

Levy and others argue that Bush's goals are unrealistic because many Americans have trouble meeting their current bills, let alone putting enough aside for the future. Two years ago, Bush proposed two new types of savings accounts that would have allowed people to shelter more of their income from taxes, with a limit of $7,500 per person — more than double current limits on Individual Retirement Accounts (IRAs). But fewer than 10 percent of Americans put away the maximum amounts allowed by current IRA and 401(k) plans. [1]

However, Cox and other economists across the political spectrum maintain that education still is a readily attainable tool for any American seeking to get ahead in today's economy. And that fact alone, he says, makes upward mobility easier to attain than it once was.

"A hundred years ago, with the Industrial Age capitalists, to break into the top you had to have money from other generations," Cox says. "But there's a democracy of consumption in education. Anybody who goes to school and listens to the teacher is going to get ahead in this country."

Today's college-educated workers receive a larger wage premium over their high-school-graduate peers than their predecessors enjoyed 25 years ago. Frank Levy, an economist at MIT, says during the 1970s college graduates at age 30 could expect to make about 17 percent more than their peers who only finished high

school. But as the industrial Midwest turned into the Rust Belt during the 1980s and many well-paid union jobs disappeared, Levy says, the wage premium for college graduates spiked to about 45 percent and has remained nearly constant since. [11]

"Some form of higher education is now a prerequisite for middle-class success," Levy says.

The percentage of Americans who have graduated from college is higher than ever, but it's hardly universal: In 2003, only 27 percent of Americans 25 or older had college degrees, according to the Census Bureau. [12]

What about the remaining three-quarters of American adults? They may be out of luck, if you believe the more pessimistic observers. "There's basically no career ladder for people with modest levels of education," says Ruy Teixeira, a fellow at the Center for American Progress and the Century Foundation. "The best they

According to David Wright, a sociologist at Wichita State University, the top 1 percent of Americans owned 51.4 percent of all stocks, and the next 9 percent owned 37 percent. The bottom 90 percent only had 11 percent of the shares between them. Most Americans not only don't control sizable portfolios but aren't good savers either. Savings rates have been in decline for a quarter-century. Americans save less than the citizens of any other industrialized country — less than 1 percent of after-tax income in 2004. [2]

Because it protects assets, Bush's plan does have the potential of widening an already deep gap in wealth — savings, real estate and stock holdings — between top earners and people lower on the income scale.

"If you did it in a way that would let low-income people build up a stake, that would be great," says Matthew Miller, a senior fellow at the liberal Center for American Progress and former Clinton administration budget official. But he notes that the Bush plan lacks incentives that would help poor people sock money away — such as the cash payments the British government will soon set aside for all its young subjects. "The way the president has laid it out, it's basically rewarding people who already own everything," Miller says.

Perhaps sensing the greater burden Bush's proposed Social Security changes could place upon them, only about a third of Americans tell pollsters they support the idea. Support for the package seems to go up according to the size of one's income. [3]

Bush and his supporters argue that the ownership society platform has the potential to transform Americans'

economic habits, encouraging them to think like investors so that they would not only put more money away but also understand, as Bush said in a campaign ad last year, that "if you own something you have a vital stake in the future."

Richard A. Epstein, director of the law and economics program at the University of Chicago, says the ownership society has the potential to "shake things up," much as Prime Minister Margaret Thatcher did in the England of the 1980s by encouraging wider investment in stocks and housing and overhauling the state pension system.

"It's your account — you can control how it's invested," says Harvey Rosen, chair of the president's Council of Economic Advisers. "This in itself is getting people adjusted to taking control of their financial lives."

But millions of Americans may not be able to take full advantage of the ownership society package. "Too many Americans do not have the skill set they need to become successful, self-reliant citizens in the free-market economy," says Robert Duvall, president of the National Council on Economic Education. "How can you talk about managing their retirement plans, when our studies show that 40 percent of Americans don't know what an annuity is?"

[1] John Cassidy, "Tax Code," *The New Yorker*, Sept. 6, 2004, p. 70.

[2] Drake Bennett, "Spendthrift Nation," *The Boston Globe*, Jan. 30, 2005, p. K1.

[3] See Jonathan Weisman, "Bush Social Security Plan Proves Tough Sell Among Working Poor," *The Washington Post*, April 18, 2005, p. A1.

can hope for is to land one of these low-level blue-collar jobs, and there are fewer of them."

Making matters worse for blue-collar workers, real wages for high school graduates and dropouts alike have fallen since the 1970s. The fastest-growing job categories either require a college degree, such as teaching and nursing, or offer limited opportunity for advancement, such as customer service representatives. [13] "The whole thrust of the information age has been to reward education and widen the income gap between the educated and the uneducated," writes *New York Times* columnist David Brooks. [14]

The dark side of a meritocracy is that not everyone is good at the things that are rewarded with good pay. "The transition to an information economy has put a premium on people who are comfortable manipulating symbols and language, no question, and that has driven

some income inequality," says Joseph Bast, president of the Heartland Institute, a research center in Chicago.

But the American entrepreneurial spirit is alive and well, Bast argues, and many people without highly specialized skills are moving up the managerial ranks in a handful of growing fields, such as health care. Real buying power and household income are still on the rise, he says, citing various Federal Reserve Bank studies that consider benefits and other factors that are not generally included in surveys of inflation-adjusted incomes.

And even the more pessimistic Teixeira says most people are still getting ahead, even if they can't hope to catch up with the wealthiest Joneses. "People perceive less security than they used to, even though, on average, they're living better than their parents," he says.

Many Americans believe they can beat the odds posed by growing inequality. They look upon the high

President Bush says his "ownership society" program would help people to invest and manage their own money, but critics say the wealthy would mainly benefit. Treasury Secretary John Snow is at left.

incomes, large houses and fancy playthings of the wealthy not with resentment but with hope that eventually they'll share in such bounty. "All I can think of is, like, wow, I'd like to have this stuff some day," said Lori, a 24-year-old who has $8,000 in credit card debt, about the houses she cleans for a living in Maine. "It motivates me, and I don't feel the slightest resentment because, you know, it's my goal to get where they are." [15]

As people debate the state of economic equity in this country, here are some of the specific questions they're asking:

Has social mobility declined?

Given the disproportionate growth in income enjoyed by top wage earners, as well as the upper class' greater share of the nation's wealth (savings, stocks, bonds, real estate and other investments), no one doubts that income disparities between the rich and everybody else have grown in recent years. But there's plenty of argument about how much that matters.

If those at the bottom and middle are still able to move up, income disparity is a temporary condition that is not too troubling. But if people don't have ready advancement opportunities, income inequality could lead to permanent class stratification — something no one wants in a democratic society.

Finding out whether people are still getting ahead, however, is tricky because it is difficult to track individuals across 20 or more years of their working life to find out whether they've advanced from where they started out. It's even harder to get a sense of how far children advance as adults relative to their parents.

"Social mobility is one of the hardest questions to get firm, empirical evidence on," says Jeff Madrick, director of policy research at the Schwartz Center for Economic Policy Analysis at the New School for Social Research and editor of *Challenge* magazine.

Cox, at the Federal Reserve Bank of Dallas, says survey information compiled by the University of Michigan shows that there is still plenty of economic mobility in the United States. "Only 5.1 percent of the people who were at the bottom [income level] in 1975 were still there in 1991," Cox says.

More anecdotally, he points out that the ranks of the super-rich are no longer closed off to all but the children of the wealthy. Citing statistics from *Forbes* magazine's annual roundup of the 400 richest Americans, Cox notes that in 1984, 146 of the richest 400 Americans attained their positions through inheritance, but by 2003 it had declined to 63.

"One hundred years ago, we had much less mobility between the income classes," he says.

But researchers at the Economic Policy Institute (EPI), a liberal think tank, say family income mobility slowed somewhat between the 1970s and '90s. The share of the population moving from the bottom fifth of the economic ladder to the top two-fifths declined, while the share of families in the top fifth grew. [16]

The change in both these sets of numbers may be slight, says Jared Bernstein, co-director of research at EPI, but they are heading in the wrong direction. "You're starting out further from others, and you're no more likely — in fact, less likely — to jump across that space," he says.

Christopher Jencks, a professor of social policy at Harvard University's Kennedy School of Government, says an individual's chances of bridging the income gap haven't changed much in recent decades. It may be hard to move up, but it's not any harder than it was a generation ago, he says.

"It's not a story about how we used to be a more fluid, open society and now it's closed down," Jencks says.

Nothing proves that, says Cox, more than the continuing success of long-term immigrants. The poverty rate among immigrants who arrived before 1970 is lower than for the United States overall, Cox says, even though he admits that the poverty rate among recent immigrants — those who arrived after 1990 — is higher than among the population as a whole.

Jencks concedes that because the income gap has gotten wider the stakes for people wanting to move up the ladder have become greater. For some, the fact that the mountain has grown higher means it is now harder to climb. "The difference between the top and the bottom is getting wider," says Smeeding, a professor of economics and public administration at Syracuse, "and wider inequality at one point in time means movement up and down the income-distribution [ladder] is harder because you have to move further."

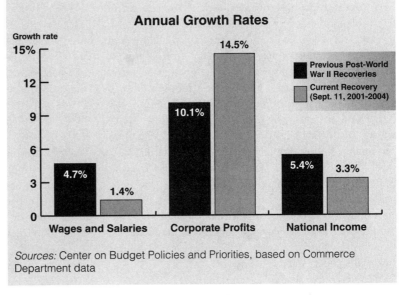

Recent Gains Lag Far Behind Previous Increases

Worker salaries during the recent economic recovery grew at a slower rate than other post-World War II recoveries, but corporate profits during the recent recovery outpaced previous recoveries.

Annual Growth Rates

Sources: Center on Budget Policies and Priorities, based on Commerce Department data

However, Smeeding says income differences are "just a small part" of the advantages enjoyed by the upper crust and, particularly, their children. Other advantages include wealth accumulation — because upper-income individuals can save more — and the ability to help children pay for first homes and college educations.

John Karl Scholz, an economist at the University of Wisconsin, has done research that suggests children whose parents were able to pay for higher education tend to perform better once they're out in the job market. "Certain kids have a leg up relative to other kids by virtue of what families they're in," Scholz says. "That could be anything from being read to as a kid to the quality of the neighborhood they grow up in."

Both Cox and Madrick agree that education is the key to moving up because of the specialized skills demanded by today's economy. But while Cox says anyone who pays attention in school can get ahead, Madrick is less optimistic. Education, he suggests, is fast becoming an inherited advantage. "It's an aristocracy of sorts, because access to education is through money, mostly because of the need to live in the right neighborhoods" in order to have access to good schools, Madrick says.

"My guess is that probably social mobility has decreased," he says. "If we know there is a greater inequality, a greater distance between the high and the low, and you haven't improved the ability to move from the low to the high or the middle to the high, something in America has gotten worse."

Is the middle class getting squeezed?

The journalist Barbara Ehrenreich once argued that children born into the middle class have less of a guarantee of maintaining their class status than either the rich or poor. "If you are born into the upper class you can expect to remain there for life," she writes. "Sadly, too, most of those born into the lower classes can expect to remain where they started out." Only membership in the middle class, she suggests, is not a matter of birth or background, but effort. [17]

Many economists say the middle class is hollowing out as the rich pull farther away from the poor, and the ranks in the middle thin out. After a long period of income stagnation between the 1970s and the late-1990s, middle-class lifestyles and comfort were propped up in many cases only because more women entered the workforce, creating two-income families.

Still, household debt is rising, as are the costs of real estate, health care and college tuition — each of which is growing faster than inflation. And many employers are cutting benefits for middle-tier workers, including health insurance subsidies and pensions.

As a result, millions of middle-class Americans feel their jobs and comfortable incomes are at risk due to globalization, economic and technological change and the decline of labor unions. Less than 8 percent of private sector workers are unionized today, compared to nearly 20 percent 25 years ago. The loss of a spouse's job can lead to major debt or, sometimes, loss of a home.

"It's not just the lower end — absolutely not — that's facing this feeling that they can't move up," says Beth Shulman, a former union official and author of the 2003 book *The Betrayal of Work.* "Even people making $60,000 can't afford many colleges."

Meanwhile, most states have cut their higher-education budgets sharply in recent years, leading to double-digit tuition hikes and leaving many parents and students wondering whether they can afford the upward-bound ticket of a college degree.

While it is true that college tuitions have been increasing faster than the historical norm, the College Board points out that after inflation, grant aid and education tax benefits are factored in, the average cost of attending a four-year college has actually dropped over the last decade. [18]

"There's no question that lots of middle class people feel squeezed," says Jencks, the social policy professor at Harvard, "but a lot of the reason they're squeezed is that they're kind of committed to a higher standard of living than they can afford, not that they couldn't get by on what they've got."

Jencks says income tends to fluctuate more than it did 30 years ago, another reason people adopt lifestyles that often must be underwritten by borrowing. "The message from the corporate employer community is, don't count on as much stability as you would have had 30 years ago," Jencks says, "yet a lot of people are ignoring that and saving less than they used to, not more than they used to."

Likewise, the Heartland Institute's Bast also doesn't see any real squeeze on the middle class. "People's expectations have gone off the board," but high hopes that don't pan out don't equal deprivation, he says.

The question of whether middle- class workers have more money than they used to depends on what mea-sures you look at, he says. Average after-inflation income went down 8 percent between 1970 and 1998, but Bast argues that if benefits are taken into account as well, the picture looks brighter. "Household income increased dramatically — by 85 percent," he says.

Both Bast and Jencks believe the consumer price index has overstated inflation over the years. "If you measure real purchasing power . . . there's more that people can afford," Jencks says. "If you look at how they're doing compared to the middle class of the past, by most measures they're better off."

Should the government do more to close the income gap?

The idea that government has an important role to play in helping struggling citizens catch up with their wealthier neighbors has been a central tenet of modern liberalism. Not surprisingly, administration critics say that notion has gone out of vogue with conservatives dominating Washington politically.

Instead, the Bush administration is pursuing an "ownership society" agenda that would move government farther away from the business of making economic decisions for individuals. (*See sidebar, p. 98.*) Bush also has proposed cutting programs that specifically help the poor, including Medicaid, housing assistance and community development block grants. Unveiling his fiscal 2006 budget in February, the president said that "the poor and disadvantaged" need to ask whether "programs achieve a certain result. We get tired of asking that question, so finally [we] take resources and direct them to programs that are working."

Even on the left, many Democrats have grown skeptical about the idea of using the government to try to level the economic playing field. Former President Bill Clinton and about half the congressional Democrats supported the 1996 welfare reform law, which ended the entitlement to cash assistance.

"Part of the background of the struggles in the Democratic Party, between Clinton-era people and people to their left, is do they want to go back to the redistributive paradigm," says John Samples, director of the libertarian Cato Institute's Center for Representative Government.

Samples is skeptical that the government can play much of a role in the economic advancement of individuals. "The Constitution does not include a right to an equal, or closer to equal, income or distribution of wealth in the way that it includes a right to freedom of speech," he says.

Setting aside the question of whether government has a role in affecting economic outcomes, Samples and others doubt that the government can smooth out the financial differences between the rich and poor. "Despite massive amounts of money flowing through government in the name of reducing income inequality, this inequality has remained effectively unchanged," says Dwight Lee, co-director of the Center for Economic Education at the University of Georgia.

Government subsidies inevitably are structured to reward those with the strongest political connections, Lee says. "Most money that is transferred is not from the rich to the poor; it is from the politically unorganized to the politically organized," he says. "Can we expect those who have failed in market competition to succeed in political competition? The only reasonable answer is, 'Not very well.' "

However, the federal earned-income tax credit (EITC) program — created in 1975 and expanded several times since — gets kudos for helping the poor. "The earned-income tax credit is one of those rare anti-poverty programs that appeals both to liberals and conservatives, invoking the virtue of both government help and self-help," writes journalist Shipler. [19]

The credit is available to working people who earn less than $35,000 (depending on their marital status and number of children). Last year, 21 million Americans collected more than $36 billion through the program. [20] As a result of the credit, the lowest 40 percent of wage earners have a negative individual income tax burden, according to the Urban-Brookings Tax Policy Center — so they get back more than they put in.

Public education also enjoys nearly universal support. Both conservatives and liberals maintain that the best way government can help citizens is to provide quality public schools and access to higher education. Bush has increased federal spending on education by 40 percent since taking office in 2001, although he has proposed a slight cut this year.

Every state constitution except South Carolina's promises citizens will be provided with an education, and courts have ruled that these supersede other concerns, such as tax limitation laws. [21] Numerous states face billion-dollar lawsuits contending that they don't provide

"adequate" public education. [22] Per-pupil spending tends to be higher in wealthier school districts because many districts still rely on property taxes to finance education.

Matthew Miller, a senior fellow with the Center for American Progress, recently published a book, *The Two Percent Solution*, in which he argues that the government could provide far better education and health care through innovative ideas, such as greatly increasing salaries for excellent teachers at inner-city schools, which would cost a total of 2 percent of GDP. "We've lost what ought to be central to our democracy — equality and access to a decent life," Miller says.

Academics have also suggested government-sponsored interventions to lift up all economic boats. Yale law professors Bruce Ackerman and Anne Alstott, for example, in their 1999 book *The Stakeholder Society* called for the government to provide all 18-year-olds with $80,000 for education or other purposes. The idea was to help all young Americans start out their adult lives on a strong financial footing, regardless of their parents' level of wealth. A much-scaled down version of the idea is being tried out in Britain.

Lee and Samples, however, say the government has neither the mandate nor the money to engage in such large-scale social experiments.

In response, Madrick, of the Schwartz Center for Economic Policy Analysis, says the government was once much more ambitious in creating programs to promote the general good, such as universal public education and the GI Bill. The government should return to that model, he argues, to respond to current needs.

"We're the richest society in the history of mankind," Madrick says. "In my view, the government has been widely irresponsible about many issues. We've had the rise of the two-worker family, and yet we still have no serious pre-kindergarten education in America or high-quality day care." (Disagreement over funding for child care has kept the federal welfare law, scheduled to be reauthorized in 2002, from being updated.)

Even Madrick and other liberals, such as Harvard economist Freeman, say the government doesn't have any business trying to rectify individuals' poor economic outcomes once it has provided a good education.

"The government should step aside and let us all compete fairly in the market, with some modest social insurance for those who fare poorly," Freeman says.

CHRONOLOGY

1960s-1970s *The long postwar boom gives way to rising oil prices, inflation and stagnant family incomes.*

1962 Michael Harrington's *The Other America* exposes poverty during a time of affluence, influences President Lyndon B. Johnson's "war on poverty" programs.

1965 Congress passes numerous "Great Society" programs, including Medicare, Medicaid, Head Start and the Higher Education Act.

1968 Number of U.S. millionaires passes the 100,000 mark.

1975 Congress approves the earned-income tax credit (EITC), in part to offset the burden of Social Security taxes and to provide an incentive to work.

1979 U.S. manufacturing employment peaks at 21.4 million workers.

1980s-1990s *The country's longest period of uninterrupted growth creates new wealth but is slow to raise average family incomes.*

1981 President Ronald Reagan convinces Congress to pass the largest tax cuts in U.S. history.

1982 Unemployment rates enter double digits for the first time since the Great Depression.

1986 Labor economists Barry Bluestone and Bennett Harrison contend that three-fifths of the net new jobs created in the economic expansion pay low wages.

1987 On Oct. 19 — "Black Monday" — the Dow Jones Industrial Average loses 23 percent of its value.

1992 Democrat Bill Clinton is elected president after promising to create "good jobs with good wages."

1996 Congress passes a welfare reform law that puts time limits on cash benefits to the chronically unemployed, ending a 60-year entitlement for cash assistance. . . . Advisory Commission to Study the Consumer Price Index finds the index had overstated the U.S. inflation rate for 20 years, exaggerating declines in real family income.

1997 Federal minimum wage is raised to $5.15 an hour; it has not been raised since.

1999 Dow closes above 10,000 mark for the first time. . . . Concerns about EITC abuses prompt IRS to audit tax returns of low-income workers at a higher rate than the returns of the wealthy.

2000s *President Bush begins to shift the federal government's focus away from social-assistance programs and toward creating tax incentives to encourage wealth accumulation.*

2001 Congress passes $1.35 billion tax cut, the first of a series during President Bush's first administration. . . . The longest period of uninterrupted economic expansion ends as the country falls into recession.

2003 Bush proposes creating two new types of savings accounts that would allow individuals to shelter $7,500 a year from taxes, more than twice the amount allowed in current Individual Retirement Accounts (IRAs). . . . Number of Americans without health insurance grows for third-straight year, but net coverage falls only for families with incomes under $75,000.

2004 Homeownership rate hits 69 percent of U.S. households, an all-time high. . . . Federal appeals court upholds the "living wage" law in Berkeley, Calif., rejecting the first major challenge to civic ordinances requiring contractors to pay above-poverty wages.

Feb. 2, 2005 Bush's State of the Union address outlines his planned Social Security overhaul, including allowing workers to put up to 4 percent of their income into private investment accounts.

March 17, 2005 Senate rejects proposal to cut Medicaid by $14 billion.

April 13, 2005 House votes for the fourth time in four years to permanently repeal inheritance taxes.

April 20, 2005 Bush signs law making it harder for debtors to file for bankrupty to escape repayment.

But many on the left believe government policy is heading entirely in the wrong direction: The federal tax system is being made less progressive just as the marketplace is producing greater inequalities.

Robert M. Solow, a Nobel Prize-winning economist, said in reviewing one of Madrick's books: "At a time when impersonal economic forces seem to be pushing by themselves in the direction of widening inequality, for public policy to be doing the same thing is not a technical mistake but a moral disaster." [23]

BACKGROUND

The Expanding Republic

Social mobility," writes author Joseph Epstein, "has been one of the preponderant themes in American life." [24] The idea that America is a land of opportunity is more than a cliché: The nation's economic opportunities have extended to millions of native poor and penniless immigrants alike.

Yet America, which once attracted primarily European immigrants seeking escape from the limitations of rigid class structures at home, now has the largest gaps between rich and poor in the industrialized world. The periods of greatest economic growth in this country have generally been periods when wealth becomes more concentrated in fewer hands.

Throughout U.S. history, such periods of growing income inequality have typically triggered political challenges, with the citizenry electing candidates promising a more egalitarian distribution of wealth. "Two kinds of power seem always in competition in our democracy," wrote Supreme Court Justice Robert H. Jackson during the 1940s. "There is political power, which is the power of voters, and there is the economic power of property, which is the power of its owners. Conflicts between the two bring much grist for the mill." [25]

During the first half of the 19th century, wealth became more concentrated, but tremendous New World prosperity created endless opportunity for all (except African-American slaves) and attracted great waves of immigrants. Europe in 1848 was the scene of revolutions and workers' barricades, but in the United States average people were too busy thriving to engage in such protests.

In the 1850s farm input and property values doubled. Congress' decision to give away public land to settlers —

via the Homestead Act of 1862 — led to rapid settlement of the interior and helped turn a struggling ex-colony into a major nation. [26]

The Civil War, although devastating to the South, led to a surge in national income and Northern manufacturing. Annual capital investment in manufacturing jumped from $1 billion in 1860 to $10 billion by 1900. [27] During the late 1880s, a period Mark Twain dubbed the "Gilded Age," enormous fortunes were made by men like J.P. Morgan, John D. Rockefeller, Andrew Carnegie and Jay Gould — all of whom had avoided military service by paying substitutes to take their places and took full advantage of the economic opportunities presented by the war and its aftermath.

Political power swayed between the major parties from the 1870s until 1896, with agrarian third-party candidates running in several presidential elections and several Western states electing populist governors. Discontent over wealth concentration fueled the populism. In 1890, the top 1 percent of families held more than 50 percent of the nation's wealth — up from 29 percent in 1860. [28] Farm income in the 1890s was lower than it had been before the Civil War.

But the economy still grew fast enough to draw millions of newcomers — more than 20 million immigrants arrived on these shores between 1870 and 1910. [29] "The apparent rich-poor dichotomy concealed a huge engine of upward mobility," writes the British historian Paul Johnson. "The ability of America, led by New York, to transform immigrant millions — most of whom arrived penniless and frightened — into self-confident citizens, wealth creators and social and cultural assets, was the essential strength of the expanding republic." [30]

During this period, one of the biggest media stars was Horatio Alger Jr., who wrote hundreds of novels that are remembered as quintessential rags-to-riches stories of rural youths who overcame hardships to become successful in the big city. In reality, though, many of the stories were about young men who struggled until they came into their proper inheritances.

Depression to Compression

Although the government had taken a largely laissez-faire approach to business regulation during the Gilded Age, at the start of the 20th century social unrest — including violent strikes — led to more regulation. President Theodore Roosevelt, who railed against "malefactors of

America's Blue-Collar Military

When Charles Moskos graduated from Princeton University in 1956, about half of his class of 900 students — its ranks including a future *New York Times* columnist, governor of Delaware and president of Harvard — were drafted for the armed services. Out of Princeton's 1,100-member Class of 2004, however, only nine students have enlisted.

Moskos, a military sociologist at Northwestern University, argues that the military no longer serves as an institution in which all social and economic classes can mix. "That's how the military used to perform," he says, "moving people up the ladder of society and having privileged young people rub shoulders on an equal basis with less privileged youth."

No one denies that today's men and women in uniform are disproportionately members of racial minorities and from working-class backgrounds. "We look at where our soldiers come from and it's Middle America," says Leonard Wong, a professor of military strategy at the U.S. Army War College. "We get the fabric of America, but we don't get the fringes."

But the fact that the children of the wealthy tend not to serve is not necessarily new, says Robert L. Goldrich, a specialist in national defense at the Congressional Research Service. "There have been very few periods in American history when people from elite, Eastern universities served in very large proportions in the armed forces," he says.

David R. Segal, director of the University of Maryland's Center for Research on Military Organization, notes that in colonial times wealthy members of society — such as plantation owners and whale ship captains — were exempted from service in the militias. And during the Civil War, rich Americans could buy their sons out of conscription for $300 (about $6,000 in today's money). [1]

Even at the start of World War II, men from Harvard and Harlem did not serve together (the military wasn't desegregated until 1948), and the elites were shifted toward safer berths. "It wasn't until the end of the war, when they ran out of infantry, that they canceled a bunch of these elite programs," says James T. Quinlivan, a senior analyst with the RAND Corporation, a think tank in Santa Monica, Calif.

During the unpopular Vietnam War, many wealthy and well-educated Americans stopped feeling any obligation to serve. "For the first time, it was chic and righteous in influential power circles not to go to war," writes Myra MacPherson, a historian of the 1960s generation. "Avoiding Vietnam was more of a badge of honor than going." [2]

In 1973, President Richard M. Nixon abolished the draft. By the end of the '70s, the idea of military service had reached its nadir among the nation's privileged classes. "There was one year in the late 1970s when the Army had something like six college graduates join the enlisted ranks in the entire year," Quinlivan says.

---

great wealth," created a Commerce Department to monitor corporate behavior and helped promote the 16th Amendment, ratified in 1913, which paved the way for graduated income taxes. By 1915, many states had passed laws to limit the length of workdays and to require companies to contribute to state insurance plans to compensate workers injured on the job. Some had passed minimum wage laws, and most had passed child labor laws.

But progressive policies did little to dilute the concentration of wealth, which continued to increase during the 1920s as presidents Warren G. Harding and Calvin Coolidge adopted pro-business platforms. Congress, meanwhile, repealed taxes on excess profits and gifts.

Nevertheless, homeownership and participation in the stock market spread widely, even though average wage levels were stagnant. The young automobile industry accounted for 4 million jobs by 1929, about one-tenth of the work force. [31] Cars "gave farmers and industrial workers a mobility never enjoyed before outside the affluent class," according to historian Johnson. [32] Meanwhile, union membership began to fall, with one organizer complaining, "As long as men have enough money to buy a secondhand Ford and tires and gasoline, they'll be out on the road and paying no attention to union meetings." [33]

All that changed with the stock market crash of 1929 and the Great Depression that followed. Union mem-

While social classes may no longer mix easily in the military, it is still a place where millions of Americans can get a leg up the economic ladder. Lower-income recruits profit from the extensive training and college benefits provided by the services, which spend more than $200 million a year underwriting tuition for programs ranging from vocational/technical training through graduate school. [3]

Gen. Richard Myers, chairman of the joint chiefs, poses with enlisted troops in Baghdad last Dec. 14. The military helps lower-income Americans move up the economic ladder.

Moreover, in the all-volunteer military, personnel are serving longer, and officers typically are well educated — often holding advanced degrees earned while in uniform.

"If you look at current generals and admirals, most of them do not come from a military background . . . [nor] from the economic upper elite," says Theodore Stroup, former deputy chief of staff of the Army for personnel. "They're from blue-collar, working-class folks and got their college degrees through ROTC, military schools and Officer Candidate School."

But Moskos, Segal and others worry that today's citizenry doesn't feel the same commitment to foreign wars that it might if the children of congressmen and presidents still donned a uniform.

That's one reason public opinion has steadily soured on the war in Iraq, Moskos says. "The country only accepts casualties over the long term when we [also] have the privileged youth serving," he says. In part to answer such concerns, Rep. Charles Rangel, D-NY, has called for reinstating the draft, but President Bush insisted during the 2004 campaign that there would be no draft.

"A citizen who sees and acknowledges the deepening chasm separating those who serve from those whom they serve," writes Josiah Bunting III, president of the Harry Frank Guggenheim Foundation, "can only deplore a civic culture that removes the burdens of military service from those it has blessed most abundantly." [4]

---

[1] Pete Hamill, "The Fellowship of the Ring," *The New York Times*, March 25, 2005, Section 7, p. 5.

[2] Myra MacPherson, *Long Time Passing: Vietnam & the Haunted Generation* (1984), p. 34.

[3] Michael R. Thirtle, *Educational Benefits and Officer-Commissioning Opportunities Available to U.S. Military Servicemembers* (2001), p. 51.

[4] Josiah Bunting III, "Class Warfare," *The American Scholar*, winter 2005, p. 18.

---

bership rose sharply during the 1930s, encouraged by the Wagner Act of 1935 (which allowed for collective bargaining). President Franklin D. Roosevelt's New Deal created Social Security and a federal welfare entitlement, as well as numerous new financial regulatory agencies. Roosevelt himself saw parallels between his efforts and the 19th-century battles against what he called "an unjust concentration of wealth and economic power."

World War II, however, put wealth expansion on the fast track. It created countless jobs for engineers, technicians and skilled workers, and farmers profited from higher prices. Manufacturing wages shot up 89 percent from 1939 to 1945. [34] The rich, meanwhile, paid hefty wartime taxes, and the top 1 percent saw their share of

the nation's wealth drop from 17.2 percent in 1929 to 9.6 percent in 1946. [35]

The shift in wages was, perhaps, even more startling. In 1939 the middle three-fifths of wage earners were receiving only 47.8 percent of total wages, while the top fifth were earning 48.7 percent. But by 1949, workers in the middle were making 55.3 percent of all wages, compared with just 40.1 percent for the top fifth. [36]

Some economists refer to this mid-century period of rising income equality as "the great compression." The United States dominated world trade following the war, and Middle Americans benefited from the fast-growing economy as well as a wider availability of consumer goods. They were further helped by changes in govern-

Wealthy Benefit Most From Tax Cuts

Income-tax cuts in 2003 saved a two-parent household earning $75,000 about $2,000, or 2.6 percent of the total family income, while a family earning $1 million gained almost $40,000, or almost 4 percent of its total income.

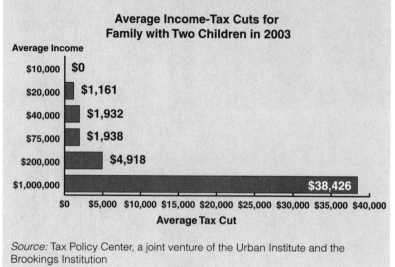

Average Income-Tax Cuts for Family with Two Children in 2003

Average Income

Average Income	Average Tax Cut
$10,000	$0
$20,000	$1,161
$40,000	$1,932
$75,000	$1,938
$200,000	$4,918
$1,000,000	$38,426

Average Tax Cut

Source: Tax Policy Center, a joint venture of the Urban Institute and the Brookings Institution

ment policy, including the increase in the dependent tax exemption in 1944 and that year's GI Bill, which paid for the college careers of millions of veterans.

Between 1952 and 1960, real family income rose 30 percent and jumped another 30 percent from 1960 to 1968. [37] Millions of Americans moved to the suburbs, where they bought homes and left behind the income disparities that had been natural to city life. Sociologists began to look at suburbs as the "true melting pot" — homogenous and nearly classless. "Disparities in income between suburban communities might be large, but such disparities within a particular community were usually small," writes historian Richard Polenberg. [38]

Road to Stagflation

Of course, not everyone shared in the prosperity. African-Americans had long been blocked from many jobs and were still victims of legal discrimination. [39] In 1964, President Lyndon B. Johnson declared an "unconditional war on poverty," saying that "we have the opportunity to move not only towards the rich society and the powerful society, but upward to the Great Society." [40] After his landslide re-election that year, Johnson pushed through a slew of civil rights laws and social programs, including Medicare, Medicaid, fair housing, the first major commitment of federal funds to mass transit, Head Start and the Higher Education Act.

Johnson's goal was to create new educational opportunities for the disadvantaged and reduce poverty among the elderly. But the Great Society came at a price. Combined with his prosecution of the Vietnam War, Johnson inaugurated a period of permanent deficits. His ideas also brought about resistance from Americans skeptical about such a dominant federal role in the welfare of individuals. The result was a voter backlash in the elections of 1966 and 1968. "Most American voters . . . had long since moved away from the politics of economic distribution," writes commentator Michael Barone. [41]

Distrust of government programs grew as poverty rates remained high and middle-class buying power was eroded by inflation. The Consumer Price Index (CPI) tripled between 1966 and 1982, as oil prices shot up. By the late 1970s the U.S. share of world manufacturing and trade was half what it had been in the immediate postwar period. By comparing the income, earnings and educational status of sons with their fathers at similar ages, sociologists found that most children were not exceeding the education and income levels their parents had achieved, according to the Department of Commerce's *Social Indicators, 1976.* [42] For the middle class, the bottom came in 1982, when unemployment rates reached double-digit rates for the first time since the Great Depression, and median family income dropped to mid-1970s levels.

Elected in 1980, President Ronald Reagan pursued a combination of tight monetary policy to fight inflation and loose fiscal policy — pursuing the largest tax cuts in the nation's history and heavy spending on defense and entitlements. "What I want to see above all is that this remains a country where someone can always get rich," he said. [43]

Following a recession early in Reagan's first term, the stock market began a record bull run, more than tripling in value between 1982 and 1992, creating perhaps the most rapid rise in income disparity ever seen. The richest 1 percent held 39 percent of the nation's wealth in 1989, compared with 22 percent in 1979. [44]

Reagan also triggered an anti-union movement among employers by breaking the air traffic controllers' union. Despite the disparities, however, many average Americans shared in the good times during the 1980s. Consumption increased dramatically; the number of shopping centers shot up by two-thirds. [45]

"It was an increasingly prosperous country, with almost universally and visibly rising living standards," writes Johnson. "Even those officially defined as 'poor' were manifestly living better." [46] The poor of the early 1990s were living as well as the middle class had in the early 1970s, says Federal Reserve Bank economist Cox. [47]

Inside the Bubble

As world trade began to open up in the late 1980s, American industry found it had to downsize and streamline in order to compete with lower-cost companies overseas. The layoffs fell disproportionately hard on white-collar and middle-income workers. Arkansas Gov. Bill Clinton, whose unofficial presidential campaign slogan in 1992 was "It's the economy, stupid," won the presidency by complaining that "the rich got the gold mine and the middle class got the shaft."

Nevertheless, Clinton's most ambitious attempt at social engineering — his plan to provide universal healthcare coverage — foundered of its own weight in 1994, leading to another Republican backlash in the midterm congressional elections that year. Clinton expanded some programs to aid the poor — notably the earned-income tax credit — but signed a 1996 law that ended the cash entitlement guaranteed under the old welfare program.

Clinton's fiscal austerity, which helped bring the federal budget into surplus by the end of his presidency in 2001, led to lower interest rates. Cheap money, along with the technology boom, lifted the stock market to record levels and created the longest period of uninterrupted growth in the nation's history (surpassing even Reagan's record).

But the mostly service-related jobs created by the largely non-union "new economy" were not as lucrative as the old economy's heavily unionized manufacturing

New York City residents wait for free coal in 1931 during the Great Depression. President Franklin D. Roosevelt's New Deal programs — including Social Security — addressed what he called "an unjust concentration of wealth and economic power."

Getty Images/General Photographic Agency

jobs had been. By 1995, the bottom 40 percent of Americans had a lower net worth, adjusted for inflation, than they'd had in 1973. In fact, during the 1990s, the concentration of wealth in the United States surpassed that of Europe, according to New York University economist Edward N. Wolff.

However, by the late 1990s, fueled by a demand for labor in an overheated economy, real wages earned by lower- and middle-income workers began to rise rapidly for the first time in decades. Amidst the boom, *Forbes* magazine declared on a 1999 cover, "Everyone ought to be rich."

But not everyone was. *The New York Times* reported in September 1999 that "the gap between rich and poor has grown into an economic chasm so wide that this year the richest 2.7 million Americans, the richest 1 percent, will have as many after-tax dollars as the bottom 100 million" — more than double the 1977 ratio. [48] Microsoft

Chairman Bill Gates alone owned as much as 40 percent of the U.S. population. [49]

The stock market peaked in April 2000 and then began the deepest one-year decline in its history.

CURRENT SITUATION

"Ownership" and Tax Cuts

President Bush cut taxes during each of his first four years in office. During his second term he would like to overhaul the federal tax system to make it flatter and fairer — perhaps even replacing the personal income tax with a national consumption or sales tax. More tax cuts are likely this year but Bush's plans to overhaul the tax system are on hold, at least for 2005, as he pursues other aspects of his "ownership society" package. (*See sidebar, p. 98.*) He has not yet released details of his plans to restructure Social Security but favors releasing at least a portion of each person's Social Security account for private investment.

"It makes sense to have people being able to own and manage their own money — a part of their own money in the Social Security system," he told an audience in Parkersburg, W.Va., on April 5, during a tour to promote his plan. "The American dream is built on the independence and dignity [deriving] from ownership."

Despite making it his top domestic priority, Bush has yet to convince most Americans that turning their old-age pensions into individual investment accounts is a good idea. Many critics of the ownership society proposals say they would only shelter the assets of the well-to-do without helping lower-income Americans save or invest more.

"If his plans are implemented, a lot of people are going to end up a lot poorer in their old age than they otherwise would have been," writes financial columnist James Surowiecki. "A lot of people will end up a lot richer, too. The result would be Social Security without the security part." [50]

Bush clearly believes in getting the government out of the way of individuals determining their own economic fortunes. During his first term, Bush and the Republican-led Congress were generous in funding domestic programs, despite the heavy tax-cutting. They increased federal spending on education by 40 percent and created an expensive, new prescription drug program through Medicare, set to take effect in 2006. But in his fiscal 2006 budget, Bush recommended slashing some social spending, such as Medicaid, adult education, housing assistance and community development block grants.

Although the government programs Bush wants to cut are designed to help poor or low-income individuals, he doubts their effectiveness. But his proposed changes in economic policy represent more than skepticism that a few social programs aren't delivering the best bang for the buck. Bush's proposals run counter to government policy for the past 70 years, challenging the social insurance programs that have provided health care, housing and income assistance to those who did not succeed in the free-market system.

Some critics of Bush's plan, of course, are fighting to protect funding for programs that date back to the New Deal or Great Society eras. During its budget deliberations in March the Senate blocked the president's proposed cuts to Medicaid and community development block grants.

But the general mood in Washington favors cutting both programs and taxes rather than expanding the government's role in personal financial matters. In April, the House voted, for the fourth time in four years, to permanently repeal the estate tax. Inheritance taxes were cut during the 2001 round of tax cutting and are set to be eliminated by 2010. The House rejected a Democratic amendment that would have preserved taxes on the three-tenths of 1 percent of estates worth more than $3.5 million for individuals or $7 million for couples.

Valuing Education

The 2001 recession hit state budgets hard because of the way their tax systems are set up, and their revenues have been slow to recover. There has been little desire to raise state taxes, so most states have been cutting spending to fill billion-dollar shortfalls. Most of the cuts have been in aid to cities and counties and to higher education.

As a result, many public universities have raised tuition by double-digit percentages in each of the last two years, even as many schools have stepped up their financial aid programs. [51] The big trend is toward merit-based scholarships. In an Arizona program inaugurated last year, for instance, high school students who exceed state graduation requirements in reading, writing and math are now eligible for a "high honors" tuition-waiver scholarship. Fourteen states now offer merit-based schol-

Are there two Americas?

YES

Sen. John Edwards, D-N.C.

From remarks in Des Moines, Iowa, during the presidential campaign, Dec. 29, 2003

Today, under George W. Bush, there are two Americas, not one: One America that does the work, another America that reaps the reward. One America that pays the taxes, another America that gets the tax breaks. One America that will do anything to leave its children a better life, another America that never has to do a thing because its children are already set for life. One America — middle-class America — whose needs Washington has long forgotten, another America — narrow-interest America — whose every wish is Washington's command. One America that is struggling to get by, another America that can buy anything it wants, even a Congress and a president.

Dividing us into two Americas — one privileged, the other burdened — has been his agenda all along. Just look at what he wants to do to our tax code. From the beginning, this president has had one solitary goal: to shift the tax burden away from the wealth of the most fortunate and onto the work of the middle class. He wants to cut the capital gains tax, eliminate the dividends tax and the estate tax and create new tax shelters for millionaires' stocks that are bigger than most people's salaries.

The president has a new name for this: He calls it the ownership society. After four years, we know what George Bush means by an ownership society: an America where those who own the most get the most, while those who work hardest own less and owe more. By the time he's done, the only people who pay taxes in America will be the millions of middle-class and poor Americans who do all the work.

Middle-class families have gone from being able to save for retirement or buy a house to now teetering on the edge of bankruptcy. These aren't poor Americans; they're the working middle class. And they are terrified that if something goes wrong — a lost job or a health-care disaster — they're just one bad break away from falling off the cliff. For these families, the American dream of building something better is being replaced by the hope of just getting by.

If the current trend continues, one out of seven middle-class families with children will go bankrupt by the end of the decade. It means the middle class — the foundation of our country — is sinking.

We cannot go on as two nations, one favored, the other forgotten. It is wrong to reward those who don't have to work at the expense of those who do.

NO

Robert Rector
Senior research fellow
Rea S. Hederman Jr.
Senior Policy Analyst, The Heritage Foundation

From "Two Americas: One Rich, One Poor? Understanding Income Inequality in America," Aug. 24, 2004

Class warfare has always been a mainstay of liberal politics. For example, vice presidential candidate John Edwards had declared, "There are two Americas . . . one privileged, the other burdened."

The income-distribution figures from the Census Bureau serve as the foundation for most class-warfare rhetoric. The Census figures, however, are incomplete and therefore misleading. In the first place, they ignore taxes and most of the social safety net. Each year, higher-income working families pay heavy taxes to support safety-net benefits for the less affluent. These benefits absorb over 8 percent of total personal income and represent a mammoth transfer of resources from those who work a lot to those who work less or not at all — a shift that is not reflected in conventional Census income-inequality figures.

When taxes and benefits are counted, the gap between the affluent and the poor shrinks noticeably. Is the distribution of income becoming less equal over time? According to conventional Census numbers, the income share of the top 5 percent of households rose from 15.8 percent of total income in 1980 to 21.7 percent in 2002. But all of that increase occurred in the 1980s and mid-1990s. For the past five years, the distribution of income has been static.

The top fifth of U.S. households, with incomes above $84,000, remain perennial targets of class-warfare enmity, but these families perform a third of all labor in the economy, contain the best educated and most productive workers and provide a disproportionate share of the investment needed to create jobs and spur economic growth.

Nearly all are married-couple families, many with two or more incomes. Far from shirking the tax burden, they pay 82.5 percent of total federal income taxes. . . .

In one sense, John Edwards is correct: There is one America that works a lot and pays a lot in taxes and another that works less and pays little, but the reality is the opposite of what he suggests. It is the higher-income families who work a lot and pay nearly all the taxes. Raising taxes even higher on hard-working families would be unfair and, by reducing future investments, would reduce economic growth, harming all Americans in the long run.

Factory worker Arbie Keels, 48, lost his job at a now-defunct mobile home factory in Lumberton, N.C. Communities across the country have seen manufacturing jobs outsourced to workers overseas — triggering unemployment, bankruptcy and crime.

arships, which eat up 25 percent of state aid money — up from 10 percent a decade ago. [52]

Tuition increases and the move toward merit — rather than need-based — scholarships have made it that much tougher for students from low-income families to attend college. A 2003 study found that only 3 percent of freshmen at the 146 most selective universities came from families in the bottom 25 percent of U.S. households, ranked by income. "There is even less socioeconomic diversity than racial or ethnic diversity at the most selective colleges," said Anthony P. Carnevale, vice president of the Educational Testing Service and a coauthor of the study. [53]

To address that problem, several top universities — including Harvard, Yale, Rice, Princeton and the University of North Carolina — recently announced generous aid packages to low-income students. Harvard, for instance, said families earning less than $40,000 would pay nothing toward their children's educations. [54]

States have been reluctant to cut K-12 funds, and many, in fact, are under court order to step up their school funding as a result of "equity" lawsuits claiming that states provide sub-par educations in low-income districts, violating state constitutional guarantees of an "adequate" education. [55] New York state, for example, is under court order to increase its spending by $1.4 billion in New York City alone. [56] States also complain that Bush has not fully funded the 2002 No Child Left

Behind law, which imposes annual testing requirements from grade 3 through 8. [57]

Bush favors extending the law's requirements into high school, but state lawmakers are wary of that idea. The National Governors' Association in February hosted a summit on high school reform in Washington, D.C. Several states are considering overhauling their high schools to better educate an American work force that can compete in today's global marketplace.

"If we keep the system as it is, millions of children will never get a chance to fulfill their promise because of their ZIP code, their skin color or their parents' income," Microsoft's Gates told the governors' summit. "That is offensive to our values, and it's an insult to who we are."

Health and Labor

States also have cut back on Medicaid, the state and federally subsidized health insurance program for low-income Americans. Many states expanded Medicaid eligibility during the 1990s economic boom, but since 2001 all states have cut Medicaid, either by reducing the amount paid to physicians or putting new limits on eligibility. Gov. Phil Bredesen, D-Tenn., for example, is trying to cut 323,000 individuals from his state's overburdened Medicaid system. Missouri is cutting 90,000 people from its rolls. Oregon has cut 62,000 from its state health plan over the last two years, with another 14,000 scheduled to be dropped by July 1. [58]

Cutbacks in health coverage at both the state and federal level are worrisome for millions of Americans, some 40 million of whom lack insurance. A series of RAND Corporation studies indicates that poverty contributes to high rates of obesity, injury, asthma and premature death. [59] British epidemiologist Michael Marmot argues in *The Status Syndrome* that both poverty and income inequality harm health.

"A lot of factors are in play in life expectancy, but it is notable that all but three of the 26 countries [with longer life expectancy than] the United States have more equal income distributions," he writes. [60]

Most Americans receive health coverage through their employers, but soaring premium costs are driving many employers to cut back — especially on coverage for workers with low-wage jobs. According to former union official Shulman, 80 percent of American workers who earn salaries above $40,000 have health insurance, compared with less than half of those earning under $20,000.

Despite declining enrollment, organized labor has racked up some victories in recent years. More than 120 cities, including Los Angeles and New York, have enacted "living wage" ordinances requiring contractors and other companies that receive certain benefits from the city to offer salaries above the poverty level. [61] Berkeley's law, passed in 2000 and upheld by a federal appeals court last year, required covered employers to pay at least $9.75 an hour (the amount rises with inflation) and offer health coverage. [62] In addition, 14 states and the District of Columbia require employers to pay minimum hourly wages higher than the federal level, which has not been raised since 1997.

But corporate America is doing quite well at the dawn of the 21st century, both in the marketplace and in Washington. After-tax profits last year were at their highest levels in 75 years. Over the past three years, corporate profits increased by 60 percent, while wages rose by just 10 percent. [63] (*See graph, p. 101.*)

The Republican-controlled Congress this year has approved several measures long sought by the business sector, including protection from class-action lawsuits and a new law, signed by Bush on April 20, to make it harder for people to forgo debt repayments by declaring bankruptcy.

Since 1898, federal bankruptcy law has allowed individuals who went broke to make a fresh start by wiping out their debts. Under the new law, individuals earning more than their state median income will remain liable for debt repayment for up to five years. The Senate refused to exempt veterans or those whose debts were caused by medical problems or identity theft. But Congress retained an exemption for wealthy individuals after the Senate refused to limit "asset protection trusts," which allow citizens to shelter portfolios of any size from creditors and federal bankruptcy proceedings. [64]

Bush said the bill would make it easier for all Americans, especially the poor, to receive access to credit. The law's critics say credit card companies made it too easy for individuals to get into debt in the first place.

"These common sense reforms will make the system stronger and better so that more Americans — especially lower-income Americans — have greater access to credit," Bush said. "Bankruptcy should always be a last resort in our legal system," Bush added. "If someone does not pay his or her debts, the rest of society ends up paying them."

"Last night, [the GOP] repealed the estate tax, a gift to the wealthiest individuals in our society," Rep. John Conyers Jr., D-Mich., complained during House floor debate on the bankruptcy bill. "Today they pushed through the special-interest bankruptcy bill, punishing the very poorest members of our society."

OUTLOOK

Land of Opportunity?

Some critics say the bankruptcy bill, which has few provisions that affect corporations, could make individual entrepreneurs warier about starting businesses or taking other financial risks. Starting a business has always entailed a risk. But the potential rewards for making a big score have always been one of the major drivers of the American economy.

"The hope of earning large profits, not just average profits, inspires countless acts of risk-taking and experimentation that otherwise would not occur," says the Heartland Institute's Bast.

Several recent books — such as psychologist John D. Gartner's *The Hypomanic Edge: The Link Between (A Little) Craziness And (A Lot of) Success In America* — contend that the United States has always attracted and produced immigrants and others possessing a certain kind of exuberance. Hypomania, a condition in which a person thrives on risk and other excitement, may be an essential part of the American character, he maintains.

"These people have a boldness and a self-confidence that sets them apart from the average citizen," said Manhattan therapist Alden Cass. "Hypomania is great for business." [65]

Americans desire not just average comfort but great wealth, despite their longstanding belief in a classless society. They don't mind social hierarchies, as long as they, or their children, have a chance at reaching the head of the pack.

In researching his book *The Working Poor* journalist Shipler asked employers who could afford to offer their lowest-paid workers more money why they didn't do that. They told him "that if they raised their manual laborers' pay, they would have to do the same for their foremen, accountants and executives to maintain a substantial difference between salaries. In other words, the national ethic decries the disparity on one hand (such as complaining that some CEOs get 500 times their workers' lowest wage) while embracing the difference as virtuous. It is somehow morally wrong not to pay an accountant more than a secretary." [66]

As Shipler himself notes, Americans seek equality of opportunity, not of outcomes. Most people embrace the concept of a salary ladder, in hopes that they'll be able to climb to the top themselves.

But not everyone is able to take those steps. Most politicians believe now that education holds the key to prosperity, and many actions are being taken to improve public education. Still, nearly three-quarters of Americans don't acquire the college degrees that could potentially help them earn about 50 percent more than their high-school-graduate peers.

Some economists also worry that President Bush's ownership society agenda will exacerbate disparities, rewarding the already-wealthy and shifting more of the tax burden onto labor. "Unless we make a policy reversal . . . we're very likely to have a wealth distribution characteristic of Third World countries — a kind of have and have-not society that's absolutely at odds with American values," warns Anne Alstott, a Yale law professor.

Others worry that cuts in social insurance programs that pool risk, such as Medicaid and Social Security, will leave millions more vulnerable just as the economy is shifting due to global and technological pressures.

"Ownership programs are a complement, and they can't replace the [social welfare] programs," says Edward M. Gramlich, a member of the Federal Reserve Board. "Some will use them well, but others won't. As a humane society, it's great to talk about ladders, but I want to preserve nets, too."

Clearly, however, while some popular programs such as Social Security may be preserved in their present form, there almost certainly will not be any new large-scale government programs to match the efforts of the New Deal or Great Society. "We're seeing a great deal of middle-class unease, but there's not a sense that the public wants governmental intervention," says Bernstein of the Economic Policy Institute.

That's a relief to many people. Few Americans believe the government, rather than the free market, has made this the richest country in history. No one wants to see income and wealth disparities grow much larger. But preserving opportunities for striking it rich, rather than trying to level the economic playing field through confiscatory taxes or other means, should remain a central goal for society, say conservatives such as Cox of the Federal Reserve Bank of Dallas.

"America is still a land of opportunity," Cox says. "The Horatio Alger story still applies."

NOTES

1. Kevin Phillips, *Wealth and Democracy* (2002), p. xii.

2. George Anders, "A Fight Over $20 Million With the 'Grandfather From Hell,' " *The Wall Street Journal*, March 9, 2005, p. C1.

3. David K. Shipler, *The Working Poor* (2004), p. 91.

4. "Ever Higher Society, Ever Harder to Ascend," *The Economist*, Jan. 1, 2005, "Special Report."

5. *Ibid.*

6. Griff Witte, "As Income Gap Widens, Uncertainty Spreads," *The Washington Post*, Sept. 20, 2004, p. A1.

7. Shipler, *op. cit.*, p. 8.

8. Robert Rector and Rea S. Hederman, Jr., "Two Americas: One Rich, One Poor? Understanding Income Inequality in the United States," The Heritage Foundation, Aug. 24, 2004, www.heritage.org/research/taxes/bg1791.cfm.

9. For background, see Sarah Glazer, "Welfare Reform," *CQ Researcher*, Aug. 3, 2001, pp. 601-632.

10. For background, see Kenneth Jost, "Downward Mobility," *CQ Researcher*, July 23, 1993, pp. 625-648.

11. See Louis Uchitelle, "College Degree Still Pays Off, But It's Leveling Off," *The New York Times*, Jan. 13, 2005, p. C1.

12. Nicole Stoops, "Educational Attainment in the United States: 2003," U.S. Census Bureau, June 2004, p. 1.

13. Les Christie, "Where the Hot Jobs Will Be," CNN/*Money*, Feb. 4, 2005, http://money.cnn.com /2005/02/03/pf/hotjobs/.

14. David Brooks, *Bobos in Paradise* (2000), p. 37.

15. Quoted in Barbara Ehrenreich, *Nickel and Dimed* (2001), p. 118.

16. Lawrence Mishel, Jared Bernstein and Sylvia Allegretto, *The State of Working America 2004/2005* (2005), p. 75.

17. Barbara Ehrenreich, *Fear of Falling: The Inner Life of the Middle Class* (1989), p. 75.

18. The College Board, press release, Oct. 10, 2004, www.collegeboard.com/press/article/0,,38993,00.html.

19. Shipler, *op. cit.*, p. 14.

20. "Earned Income Tax Credit (EITC) Can Lower Federal Tax Liabilities — Ask How!" Internal Revenue Service, www.irs.gov/individuals/article/0,,id=96406,00.html.

21. Alan Greenblatt, "Courting a Supermajority," *Governing*, October 2003, p. 61.

22. Dennis Farney, "Insufficient Funds," *Governing*, December 2004, p. 26.

23. Robert M. Solow, "Mysteries of Growth," *The New York Review of Books*, July 3, 2003.

24. Joseph Epstein, *Snobbery: The American Version* (2002), p. 67.

25. Quoted in Paul Kalra, *The American Class System* (1995), p. 73.

26. See Paul Johnson, *A History of the American People* (1997), p. 294. The Homestead Act, which became law on Jan. 1, 1863, allowed anyone to apply for 160 acres of free public land. After five years the settler would own the land if he had built a house on it, dug a well, plowed at least 10 acres, fenced a specified amount and lived on the land.

27. Phillips, *op. cit.*, p. 34.

28. *Ibid.*, p. 46.

29. Allan Nevins and Henry Steele Commager, *A Pocket History of the United States* (1967), p. 281.

30. Johnson, *op. cit.*, p. 579.

31. Phillips, *op. cit.*, p. 58.

32. Johnson, *op. cit.*, p. 718.

33. Quoted in *ibid.*, p. 724.

34. Phillips, *op. cit.*, p. 75.

35. *Ibid.*, p. 71.

36. *Ibid.*, p. 76.

37. *Ibid.*, p. 78.

38. Richard Polenberg, *One Nation Divisible* (1980), p. 141.

39. For background, see Alan Greenblatt, "Race in America," *CQ Researcher*, July 11, 2003, pp. 593-624.

40. Quoted in Johnson, *op. cit.*, p. 873.

41. Michael Barone, *Our Country* (1990), p. 419.

42. Cited in Polenberg, *op. cit.*, p. 263.

43. Quoted in Haynes Johnson, "Riches; There's More to America Than Just a Horatio Alger Dream," *The Washington Post*, July 3, 1983, p. A3.

44. Phillips, *op. cit.*, p. xiii.

45. Matthew Dallek, "Reagan and His Times," *The Washington Post*, April 17, 2005, p. T13.

46. Johnson, *op. cit.*, p. 924.

47. See W. Michael Cox and Richard Alm, *Myths of Rich and Poor* (1999), p. 15.

48. David Cay Johnston, "Gap Between Rich and Poor Found Substantially Wider," *The New York Times*, Sept. 5, 1999, p. A16.

49. Thomas Frank, *One Market Under God* (2000), p. 12.

50. James Surowieki, "The Risk Society," *The New Yorker*, Nov. 15, 2004, p. 40.

51. For background, see Tom Price, "Rising College Costs," *CQ Researcher*, Dec. 5, 2003, pp. 1013-1044.

52. Frank Greve, "Merit-Based College Scholarships on the Rise," *Contra Costa Times*, Feb. 27, 2005, p. 4.

53. Quoted in David G. Savage, "Ranks of Poor Are Thin at Top Colleges," *Los Angeles Times*, April 6, 2003, p. A34.

54. Greg Winter, "Yale Cuts Expenses for Needy in a Move to Beat Competitors," *The New York Times*, March 4, 2005, p. B5.

55. For background, see Kathy Koch, "Reforming School Funding," *CQ Researcher*, Dec. 10, 1999, pp. 1041-1064.

56. Al Baker, "In Budget Push, Albany Avoids Schools Issue," *The New York Times*, March 19, 2005, p. B1.

57. For background, see Kenneth Jost, "Testing in Schools," *CQ Researcher*, April 20, 2001, pp. 321-344.

58. For background, see Rebecca Adams, "Medicaid Reform," *CQ Researcher*, July 16, 2004, pp. 589-612.

59. "Does Neighborhood Deterioration Lead to Poor Health?," RAND Corporation, RB-9074, 2005, www.rand.org/publications/RB/RB9074.

60. Michael Marmot, "Life at the Top," *The New York Times*, Feb. 27, 2005, p. 13.

61. For background, see Jane Tanner, "Living Wage Movement," *CQ Researcher*, Sept. 27, 2002, pp. 769-792.

62. Henry Weinstein, "Berkeley's Living Wage Ordinance Is Upheld in Federal Appeals Court," *Los Angeles Times*, June 17, 2004, p. B6.

63. "Breaking Records," *The Economist*, Feb. 10, 2005, p. 12.

64. David Broder, "A Bankrupt 'Reform,'" *The Washington Post*, March 13, 2005, p. B7.

65. Quoted in Annie Murphy Paul, "The Hypomanic American," *The Boston Globe*, Feb. 27, 2005, p. D1.

66. Shipler, *op. cit.*, p. 89.

BIBLIOGRAPHY

Books

Bowles, Samuel, *et al.*, *Unequal Chances: Family Background and Economic Success*, Princeton University Press, 2005.
Studies by social scientists examine whether economic outcomes are largely determined by family backgrounds.

Cox, W. Michael, and Richard Alm, *Myths of Rich & Poor: Why We're Better Off Than We Think*, Basic Books, 1999.
An economist and a business reporter contend "upward mobility is possible for most Americans."

Mishel, Lawrence, *et al.*, *The State of Working America 2004/2005*, Cornell University Press, 2005.
Scholars at the liberal Economic Policy Institute conclude the wages of middle-class Americans are not rising.

Phillips, Kevin, *Wealth and Democracy: A Political History of the American Rich*, Broadway Books, 2002.
A former Republican consultant argues that periods of great prosperity lead to inequalities in wealth and so are typically followed by political backlashes.

Shipler, David K., *The Working Poor: Invisible in America*, Knopf, 2004.
A veteran journalist shows how the working poor struggle to retain decent housing and health care.

Articles

Bernstein, Aaron, "Waking Up From the American Dream," *Business Week*, Dec. 1, 2003, p. 54.
Dead-end jobs and the cost of a college education have kept mobility from returning to its pre-1970s levels.

Brooks, David, "The Sticky Ladder," *The New York Times*, Jan. 25, 2005, p. A19.
A columnist concludes that education and meritocracy are becoming inherited advantages as highly educated parents help their children re-create their experiences.

Easterbrook, Gregg, "America the O.K.," *The New Republic*, Jan. 4, 1999, p. 26.
A veteran journalist concludes that life in America is getting better.

Epstein, Richard A., "It's a Win-Win Situation, Even if Some Win More Than Others," *Los Angeles Times*, June 27, 2005, p. M5.
A University of Chicago economics professor says life expectancy and other measures of progress are trending up.

"Meritocracy in America: Ever Higher Society, Ever Harder to Ascend," *The Economist*, Jan. 1, 2005, "Special Report."
The British newsmagazine summarizes research that indicates average citizens are having more difficulty moving up.

Sawhill, Isabel V., "Still the Land of Opportunity?" *The Public Interest*, Spring 1999, www.brookings.edu/views/articles/sawhill/1999spring.htm.
A Brookings Institution fellow argues that families and schools should be the focus of efforts to aid the disadvantaged.

Witte, Griff, "As Income Gap Widens, Uncertainty Spreads," *The Washington Post*, Sept. 20, 2004, p. A1.
The middle class is undergoing changes due to global competition and rapid advances in technology.

Reports and Studies

Alesina, Alberto, *et al.*, "Inequality and Unhappiness: Are Europeans and Americans Different?" *National Bureau of Economic Research Working Paper 8198*, April 2001.

Survey data find that Americans, except for rich leftists, are not unhappy about income inequality.

Gottschalk, Peter, and Sheldon Danziger, "Inequality of Wage Rates, Earnings and Family Income in the United States, 1975-2002," *Population Studies Center Research Report No. 04-568,* **Sept. 30, 2004, www.psc. isr.umich.edu/pubs/pdf/rr04-568.pdf.**
Two economists conclude that inequality in wage rates and family income accelerated during the early 1980s, increased more slowly through the early 1990s and then stayed at a high level into the early 2000s.

Neckerman, Kathryn M., ed., *Social Inequality,* **Russell Sage Foundation, 2004.**
A massive compendium of studies by economists and social scientists examines the effects of income inequality on health, schools, political participation and other aspects of American life.

Piketty, Thomas, and Emmanuel Saez, "Income Inequality in the United States, 1913-1998," *The Quarterly Journal of Economics,* **February 2003, p. 1.**
Two French economists find that top earners have taken a rising share of national income since the 1980s.

Rector, Robert, and Rea S. Hederman, Jr., "Two Americas: One Rich, One Poor? Understanding Income Inequality in the United States," The Heritage Foundation, Aug. 24, 2004, www.heritage.org/ research/taxes/bg1791.cfm.
Two Heritage Foundation analysts find that standard measures of income inequality leave out factors such as government benefits received by the poor.

For More Information

Bureau of Labor Statistics, 2 Massachusetts Ave., N.E., Washington, DC 20212-0001; (202) 691-5200; www.bls.gov. The federal government's principal compiler of data on labor economics.

Economic Policy Institute, 1333 H St., N.W., Suite 300 East Tower, Washington, DC 20005; (202) 775-8810; www.epinet.org. A liberal think tank that focuses on research about low- and middle-income workers.

Federal Reserve Bank of Dallas, 2200 N. Pearl St., Dallas, TX 75201; (214) 922-6000; www.dallasfed.org. Like other regional offices of the Fed, the bank's economists track the nation's monetary policy, banking operations and economic conditions.

Heartland Institute, 19 South LaSalle St., Suite 903, Chicago, IL 60603; (312) 377-4000; www.heartland.org. A Chicago-based think tank that promotes conservative policies in education, health, environment and regulation.

The Heritage Foundation, 214 Massachusetts Ave., N.E., Washington, DC 20002-4999; (202) 546-4400; www.heritage.org. A think tank that promotes conservative, free-market policies and limited government.

Maxwell School Center for Policy Research, 426 Eggers Hall, Syracuse University, Syracuse, NY 13244-1020; (315) 443-3114; www.cpr.maxwell.syr.edu. Offers an interdisciplinary program that studies urban and regional issues, social welfare, education finance and income-security policy.

Michigan Program on Poverty and Social Welfare Policy, University of Michigan, 1015 E. Huron St., Ford School Annex, Ann Arbor, MI 48104-1689; (734) 615-5389; www.fordschool.umich.edu/research/poverty. A joint program of the University of Michigan schools of public policy, social work and law that researches poverty and social-welfare policy.

Milken Institute, 1250 Fourth St., Santa Monica, CA 90401; (310) 570-4600; www.milkeninstitute.org. An economic think tank that promotes innovative ideas for increasing prosperity.

Russell Sage Foundation, 112 East 64th St., New York, NY 10021; (212) 750-6000; www.russellsage.org. Provides funding for and performs social science research. With the Carnegie Corporation, the foundation is sponsoring several working groups examining social inequality.

Urban Institute, 2100 M St., N.W., Washington, DC 20037, (202) 833-7200; www.urban.org. A think tank that studies economic and social-policy trends and the effectiveness of government policies in such areas as taxation and housing.

6

Birth-Control Debate

Marcia Clemmitt

Julie Makimaa, who was conceived during a rape, holds up a photo of her with her mother during her testimony before the Virginia Senate Education and Health Committee on Feb. 26, 2004. The Holland, Mich., woman supported an unsuccessful bill to prevent pharmacies at state universities from dispensing morning-after birth-control pills. Religious conservatives say the pills prevent implantation of a fertilized egg and thus cause abortions, which some scientists dispute.

From *CQ Researcher*, June 24, 2005.

N eil Noesen was filling in as a back-up pharmacist at the Menomonie, Wis., Kmart when college student Amanda Phiede came in to refill her prescription for birth-control pills. Noesen is a devout Catholic who believes that birth-control pills can cause what he regards as early-stage abortions. Noesen — the lone pharmacist on duty that day — refused to fill Phiede's prescription.

"I explained to her that I couldn't give it to her with a good conscience," Noesen said. "I did not direct her to another pharmacy." [1]

Phiede went to a nearby Wal-Mart, but when the pharmacist there asked Noesen to transfer her prescription, he refused. Two days later, the Kmart pharmacy manager — who had been out of town — finally filled Phiede's prescription. By then, she had missed a pill and had to take two pills to catch up, increasing her risk of unintended pregnancy. The incident occurred in 2002.

A state administrative board eventually charged Noesen with unprofessional conduct for refusing to transfer the prescription, which is considered the patient's property. In April 2005 the state pharmacy board ordered Noesen to attend ethics classes and pay about $20,000 to cover costs of the disciplinary proceedings. He was allowed to retain his pharmacy license as long as he informs all future employers in writing that he won't dispense birth-control pills and describes steps he will take to ensure that patients get their prescriptions some other way. [2]

Noesen has remained firm in refusing to have any part in dispensing birth control pills. Using the pills is "evil," under God's moral code, he told the disciplinary hearing last October. He would not transfer a contraceptive prescription because "it would be a sin

State Birth-Control Laws Vary

Fourteen states exempt pharmacists or individual health providers from dispensing contraceptive services to which they object. Six states allow pharmacists to dispense emergency contraception without a prescription.

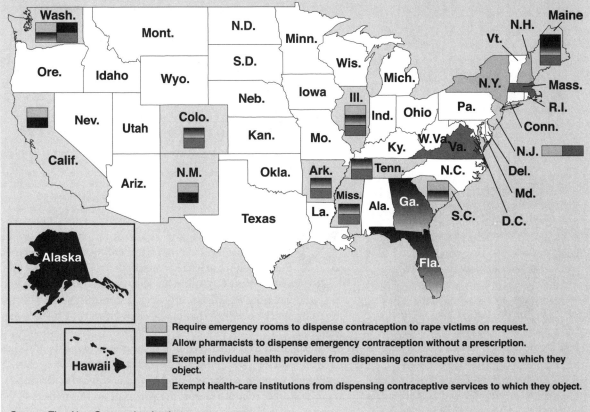

Legend:
- Require emergency rooms to dispense contraception to rape victims on request.
- Allow pharmacists to dispense emergency contraception without a prescription.
- Exempt individual health providers from dispensing contraceptive services to which they object.
- Exempt health-care institutions from dispensing contraceptive services to which they object.

Source: The Alan Guttmacher Institute

to induce another to sin"[3] and would make him "part of a bucket brigade, just another step in facilitating the end result."[4]

Over the past several years, only a handful of pharmacists have refused to dispense contraception, and even fewer have tried to prevent a patient from obtaining pills elsewhere. Nevertheless, the incidents demonstrate that birth control has become a new front in America's culture wars. While recent battles have focused on abortion, debate over birth control has intensified — pitting the religious beliefs of a minority of Americans against the desire of the overwhelming majority to retain easy access to contraception.

According to a December 2004 report by the federal Centers for Disease Control and Prevention (CDC),

contraceptive use in the United States "is virtually universal," with more than 98 percent of sexually active women of reproductive age having used "at least one contraceptive method" at some point.[5]

Moreover, most doctors — including 87.5 percent of Catholic physicians — dispense birth control. Likewise, most health-care providers and pharmacists generally support greater access, says Don Downing, a University of Washington professor of pharmacy.[6] But many hospitals — especially those affiliated with the Roman Catholic Church, which make up a growing percentage of the hospitals in America — refuse to dispense contraceptives or emergency birth control, even to women who have been raped. The church opposes both birth control and abortion.

Emergency birth control consists of a large dose of regular birth-control pills that, when taken within five days after unprotected sex can prevent a pregnancy. Some religious conservatives and pro-life advocates object to it — as well as to regular birth-control pills and intrauterine devices — because they may interfere with a fertilized egg's implantation in the uterine wall. Opponents of such birth-control methods believe life begins when the egg is fertilized and that such pills and devices, in essence, cause the fertilized egg to be aborted. (*See sidebar, p. 124.*)

But emergency contraception is not the only birth-control method stirring controversy. Some doctors, pharmacists and hospitals will not dispense or prescribe any birth control on the grounds that artificial contraception itself is wrong. Others object only to giving birth-control pills to single women who plan to use them for contraceptive purposes rather than for health reasons, such as regulating menstrual periods.

Health-care workers and hospitals that refuse on moral grounds to provide certain contraception services argue strongly that their constitutional right to religious freedom should protect them from employer sanctions, even if they refuse to refer patients elsewhere for birth control. "It [is] unethical to force practitioners to participate in specific actions involving what they believe would be a cooperation with abortions," Noesen told the Wisconsin legislature in 2003, when it was considering a conscience clause. [7]

Opponents of certain types of birth control and advocates for easy access to contraception are facing off in state legislatures across the country, as lawmakers debate a variety of bills governing contraceptives. Some states are considering mandating that hospitals and pharmacies dispense contraception — including emergency contraception — while other states are allowing health-care workers and hospitals to exercise their "conscience

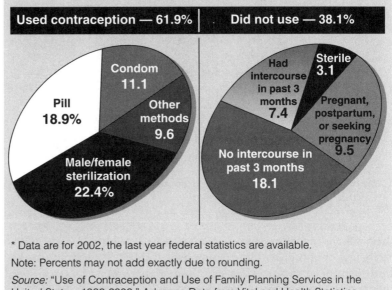

"Pill" Is Most Popular Contraceptive

Birth-control pills are the most popular non-surgical form of birth control in the United States. Overall, 62 percent of American women ages 15-44 use contraception. Among non-users, 7.4 percent had unprotected sex in the past three months. *

U.S. Contraceptive Use by Women, 2002

Used contraception — 61.9% | Did not use — 38.1%

Condom 11.1
Pill 18.9%
Other methods 9.6
Male/female sterilization 22.4%

Had intercourse in past 3 months 7.4
Sterile 3.1
Pregnant, postpartum, or seeking pregnancy 9.5
No intercourse in past 3 months 18.1

* Data are for 2002, the last year federal statistics are available.

Note: Percents may not add exactly due to rounding.

Source: "Use of Contraception and Use of Family Planning Services in the United States: 1982-2002," Advance Data from Vital and Health Statistics, Centers for Disease Control and Prevention, Dec. 10, 2004

rights" not to dispense medications they see as facilitating abortions. Some states are trying to do both.

At least seven states — Alaska, California, Hawaii, New Hampshire, New Mexico, Washington and Maine — have allowed pharmacists to dispense emergency contraception (without having received a prescription from a doctor), as long as they collaborate with a local physician and follow a predetermined protocol. "Growing numbers of people are interested in dispensing [emergency contraception]," says Downing, who developed programs to enable pharmacists to dispense emergency birth control.

Meanwhile, the U.S. Food and Drug Administration (FDA) has been asked to allow over-the-counter sales of emergency contraceptives, called Plan B. In May 2004, the agency overruled its own scientific advisory panel, which had voted 23-4 in favor of Plan B. The agency said it agreed with the minority on the panel who argued

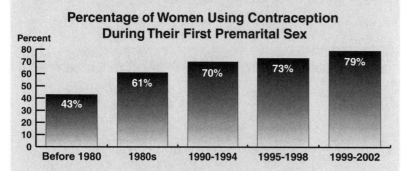

Birth-Control Use Rose for First Premarital Sex

The percentage of women using contraception during their first premarital intercourse rose from less than half the women before 1980 to more than three-quarters during the period 1999-2002.

Percentage of Women Using Contraception During Their First Premarital Sex

Source: "Use of Contraception and Use of Family Planning Services in the United States: 1982-2002," Advance Data from Vital and Health Statistics, Centers for Disease Control and Prevention, Dec. 10, 2004; data are through 2002, the last year for which federal data are available

According to James Trussell, director of the Princeton University Office of Population Research, nearly half of unintended pregnancies (47 percent) occur among the small group of women who have unprotected sex. A 43 percent increase in that population recently reported by the CDC could create up to an 18 percent increase in unintended pregnancies, he says. [8]

And more unintended pregnancies could lead to an increase in the number of abortions as well as "marital discord, domestic violence and children at high risk for developmental problems," Hogue points out.

But anti-contraception advocates argue that the same kinds of problems are triggered when birth control fails, as it often does. The result frequently is "abortion . . . single motherhood — often attended by poverty . . . or an unsuitable marriage that ends in divorce," says Janet Smith, chair of life ethics at Detroit's Sacred Heart Major Seminary and a well-known speaker on Catholic sexual ethics.

Critics of the administration's birth-control policies say the FDA's refusal to allow Plan B — only the second time in 50 years the agency rejected an advisory panel's advice — was influenced more by the religious views of minority panel members than by science.

David Hager, an obstetrician-gynecologist and one of three panel members appointed by President Bush, led the opposition to Plan B on the grounds that it may sometimes prevent implantation of a fertilized egg. He told FDA officials there was not enough evidence to show that non-prescription sales of Plan B would be safe for girls under 15. [9]

Hager stirred up a political hornet's nest when it was revealed that he had told an audience at Asbury College, in Wilmore, Ky., that although he had "argued from a scientific perspective," God had taken that information and used it to influence the decision. "Once again, what Satan meant for evil, God turned into good," Hager said. [10]

But the advisory panel's majority and many other analysts say Hager's assertion there is insufficient data on

there was not enough evidence that girls under 15 could safely take the product. The decision, which shocked birth-control advocates, was a significant victory for those opposed to emergency birth control on religious grounds.

Birth-control advocates point out that when pharmacists or hospitals refuse to dispense contraception — emergency or otherwise — it typically disadvantages those lacking easy transportation to another pharmacy or facility, most often the poor and women living in rural areas without alternative pharmacists or hospitals nearby.

Moreover, repeated federal cutbacks in family planning funds since 1998 also have disproportionately affected the poor, potentially leading to a jump in unintended pregnancies, says Carol Hogue, professor of maternal and child health at Emory University's Rollins School of Public Health. The cuts may already be reducing the use of birth control, she says, citing the CDC study, which showed that the number of adult women having unprotected sex during the previous three months rose from 5.2 percent in 1995 to 7.4 percent in 2002 — the same level as in 1982. (*See graph, p. 123.*) Low-income women rely heavily on subsidized birth control, and with government support waning, "it shouldn't be surprising that people aren't availing themselves of it as much," Hogue says.

the safety of Plan B for young girls is not based on science at all. Trussell, a panelist who voted for over-the-counter sales, says the panel reviewed numerous studies showing that adolescents can understand Plan B's package instructions "as well as anybody else."

However, aside from questions about Plan B's appropriateness for young teens, the FDA also has dragged its heels in making Plan B available without a prescription for women over 16. A year ago, Barr Laboratories applied to sell Plan B over-the-counter to women 16 and older while requiring a prescription for girls under age 16. But the FDA let a January 2005 deadline to act on that application pass without taking action. Soon after that, Democratic Sens. Hillary Rodham Clinton (N.Y.) and Patty Murray (Wash.) announced they would hold up the confirmation of FDA Acting Commissioner Lester Crawford as commissioner until the FDA acts on Barr's new application.

In March Crawford told the Senate Health, Education, Labor and Pensions Committee that the decision has been slowed because "it's a very complex kind of application never received before by the agency."

Meanwhile, the American Medical Association voted on June 20 to support legislative initiatives around the country requiring pharmacies to fill legally valid prescriptions.

If a pharmacist or pharmacy has objections, they should provide an "immediate referral to an appropriate alternative dispensing pharmacy without interference," said a resolution by the AMA's policymaking House of Delegates.

"Our position is on behalf of the patient," said Peter Carmel, an AMA board member and neurosurgeon from New Jersey. "The AMA strongly believes patients have to have access to their medications. It's the obligation on behalf of the pharmacist . . . to tell them where to go." [11]

The AMA's policy would be similar to that of the nation's largest pharmacy chain, Walgreen Co.

As the FDA, Congress and the medical community debate the birth-control dilemma, here are some of the questions being asked:

Should pharmacists opposed to emergency contraception on religious grounds be required to fill prescriptions for it?

The question is especially complicated in the case of emergency contraception, because it is only effective if taken within about five days of the unprotected intercourse.

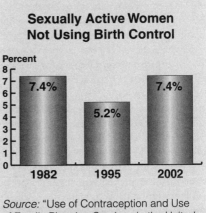

Unprotected Sex Is Up

The percentage of American women having unprotected sex has jumped in recent years, reaching 1982 levels in 2002. Critics of administration birth-control policies attribute the increase to repeated cutbacks since 1998 in federal funding for birth control for low-income women.

Sexually Active Women Not Using Birth Control

Percent

- 1982: 7.4%
- 1995: 5.2%
- 2002: 7.4%

Source: "Use of Contraception and Use of Family Planning Services in the United States: 1982-2002," advance data from "Vital and Health Statistics," Centers for Disease Control and Prevention, Dec. 10, 2004; data are through 2002, the last year for which federal data are available

Thus, refusing to fill a prescription "may place a disproportionately heavy burden on those with few options, such as a poor teenager living in a rural area that has a lone pharmacy," lawyer Julie Cantor and physician Ken Baum wrote last year in *The New England Journal of Medicine*. "A refusal to fill a prescription for a less advantaged patient may completely bar her access to medication." [12]

It's also unclear where conscientious objection would end, once permitted. The consequences could amount to "invasive" behavior, according to Cantor and Baum. "If pharmacists can reject prescriptions that conflict with their morals, someone who believes that HIV-positive people must have engaged in immoral behavior could refuse to fill those prescriptions," they point out.

Many analysts agree that pharmacists' right to follow their consciences must be balanced against patients' right

Understanding Emergency Contraception

Since ancient times, women have tried to prevent unwanted pregnancies after unprotected intercourse. As early as 1500 B.C., they were advised to try sneezing, hopping, jumping or dancing. [1] In early 20th-century America, the makers of Lysol and other household disinfectants and detergents advertised their effectiveness for "feminine hygiene." [2] Even douching with Coca Cola was rumored to interfere with conception, in the late 1960s. [3]

Since the 1970s, however, physicians have known that large hormone doses taken soon after intercourse actually can prevent pregnancy. "Oral contraceptives have been used 'off label' as emergency contraception by at least 225,000 women in the United States," according to the American Pharmacists Association. [4]

But hormonal medicines have been specifically packaged as emergency contraceptives only in recent years. In 1998, the Food and Drug Administration (FDA) approved the Preven regimen. Then, in 1999, the FDA approved Plan B, a less potent, safer and more convenient product. The same manufacturer now owns both products and removed Preven from the U.S. market last year.

Although emergency contraception has been available in the United States for seven years, confusion is rife about what it is and how it works.

For instance, in California — where some pharmacists have been allowed to dispense emergency birth control without prescription since 2002 — about three-quarters of women ages 18 to 44 polled in 2004 had heard of emergency contraception, but nearly half confused it with abortion pills. [5] Abortion pills, such as mifepristone — also known as RU-486 — were approved in Europe in the late 1980s, but opposition from religious conservatives and pro-life groups blocked their approval in the United States until 2000.

Mifepristone, which can be taken up to two months after a woman's last menstrual period, causes abortion by blocking the hormones needed to maintain a pregnancy. Methotrexate, which blocks further development of the pregnancy in the uterus, can be taken up to about six weeks after a woman's last period. To trigger contractions, the drugs are then taken in combination with misoprostol, which causes the uterus to contract and empty. [6]

On the other hand, Plan B and other emergency contraceptive pills like Preven operate like regular birth-control pills — another point of confusion. In a 2003 survey of South Dakota pharmacists, 37 percent did not know that emergency contraceptive pills — now called Plan B — work basically the same as regular hormonal birth-control pills. [7]

The mechanism by which emergency contraceptives prevent pregnancy is not completely understood, but, in general, they delay or prevent ovulation, inhibit fertilization of an egg and may sometimes alter the climate of the uterus to prevent a fertilized egg from implanting. [8] If taken after implantation, emergency contraceptives cannot abort a pregnancy. (Implantation usually begins about five days after fertilization and can take up to 18 days.)

The question of whether emergency contraception prevents implantation of a fertilized egg — known among birth-control opponents as "the post-fertilization effect" — has triggered controversies around the country. The controversy primarily involves defining the moment at which life begins: Is it when the egg is fertilized or when the fertilized egg implants itself in the uterine wall?

to have legal medications. But when it comes to achieving that balance, different people use different scales.

The issue is almost always framed as one of honoring — or not honoring — the pharmacist's conscience. But, says Rosemarie Tong, distinguished professor in health-care ethics at the University of North Carolina at Charlotte, there are always at least two consciences involved — the pharmacist's and the patient's. "Whose moral decision should be captive to the other person's in this situation?" she asks.

According to Tong, the person who risks less potential harm should yield right of conscience. In the case of emergency contraception, "the person who's going to bear the brunt of the pregnancy" risks harm that's "much greater" than the potential damage to a pharmacist who reluctantly violates his or her conscience.

Proponents of strong conscience clauses disagree. A woman seeking emergency contraception generally has plenty of other options, says physician David Stevens, executive director of the 17,000-member Christian Medical and Dental Associations. "Sign up for mail order, get a referral to another pharmacy," he suggests. But the pharmacist has only one conscience, and "conscience is the most sacred of all property."

Biomedicine has long defined the beginning of pregnancy as the time when the fertilized egg implants in the uterus. But the Catholic Church, some conservative Christians and others define it as "conception" — the moment when an egg is fertilized. These groups believe that emergency contraceptives — and even regular birth-control pills and intrauterine devices that prevent implantation — destroy life by causing early-stage abortions.

"Contraception is a misnomer in this case because [emergency contraception] commonly operates not to prevent conception but rather to ensure the death of an embryo after conception by interfering with implantation in the womb," according to U.S. Conference of Catholic Bishops testimony to the Kansas legislature in 2002. [9]

But not all Christian conservatives agree. It's difficult to argue that a non-implanted embryo constitutes a pregnancy, according to John Guillebaud, emeritus professor of family planning and reproductive health at University College, London, whose views are posted on the Web site of the Christian Medical Fellowship of the United Kingdom. [10]

While the embryo is "free in the uterine cavity, it still has 100 percent 'No Go' status," Guillebaud explained. "It is a certainty that in a few days it will be flushed through the cervix and vagina in a gush of endometrial debris and blood." For instance, the mother's body does not receive signals to begin producing pregnancy-sustaining hormones until the egg implants, he pointed out.

Moreover, up to 50 percent of embryos fail to implant naturally, he added. "Now, we know that our God is omnipotent, omniscient and omnipresent," Guillebaud continued. "How likely is it that a God, who surely has 'omni-common sense' . . . would expect us to give the status, importance and respect to this entity . . . as is rightly given after implantation — when there is a relationship with the mother and for the first time there are prospects of going to term?"

In any case, scientists may be on the verge of proving that emergency contraception has no post-fertilization effect after all. New studies on rats and monkeys — and a limited human study — have shown that emergency contraceptives do not inhibit implantation — a fact that could explain their 20 percent failure rate. [11]

[1] Catherine Lynch, M.D., "Emergency Contraception: An Update," found at www.contraceptiononline.org.

[2] Planned Parenthood, "History of Contraceptive Methods," found at www.plannedparenthood.org

[3] Lynch, *op. cit.*

[4] American Pharmacists Association, "Emergency Contraception: The Pharmacist's Role," 2000.

[5] Kaiser Family Foundation, "Emergency Contraception in California," available at www.kff.org/womenshealth/whp021804pkg.cfm.

[6] Planned Parenthood, "The Difference Between Emergency Contraceptive Pills and Medication Abortion," www.plannedparenthood.org.

[7] Kristi van Riper, et al., "Emergency Contraceptive Pills: Dispensing Practices, Knowledge and Attitudes of South Dakota Pharmacists," *Perspectives on Sexual and Reproductive Health*, March 1, 2005, p. 19.

[8] American College of Obstetricians and Gynecologists, www.acog.org.

[9] "The Protection of Conscience Project," testimony of the Secretariat for Pro-Life Activities submitted to Kansas House of Representatives by U.S. Conference of Catholic Bishops, Feb. 20, 2002, at www.consciencelaws.org.

[10] John Guillebaud, "Is Implantation the Biological Event Which Completes Conception and So Separates Conception from Induced Abortion?" Christian Medical and Dental Fellowship of Australia, www.cmdfa.org.au.

[11] "Emergency Contraception's Mode of Action Clarified," *Population Briefs*, May 2005, www.popcouncil.org.

Others argue that, given today's nationwide pharmacist shortage, druggists have more options. "What happens to the patient if a pharmacist has the right to refuse?" asks Todd Brown, an associate clinical specialist at the Northeastern University School of Pharmacy in Boston.

For pharmacists seeking so-called conscience clauses to protect them from employer retaliation if they refuse to dispense a drug, the issue hinges on whether they are going to be treated like professionals, says Noesen. Enacting a conscience clause "would simply be giving legal recognition to the professional autonomy that we already hold as pharmacists." [13]

But critics counter that professional autonomy is limited by the requirement that a pharmacist put the clients' needs first. "Professional autonomy has its limits," write Cantor and Baum. Pharmacy professionals "are expected to exercise special skill and care to place the interests of their clients above their own interest." [14]

"I don't think pharmacists should have conscience clauses," Brown says. "They're not being asked to be the patient's religious leader."

Besides, he says, student pharmacists learn early on about the various kinds of medications provided by the health system. They should decide right away whether they object to dispensing them, says Brown, and those who have moral objections should work at pharmaceutical companies, health plans, nursing homes, hospitals and elsewhere, he says, rather than working in a pharmacy serving the general public.

But those calling for broad conscience clauses say it's very difficult to predict future medical treatments. As biomedical science advances, emergency contraception represents only the "tip of the iceberg" when it comes to technologies that may be morally objectionable, Stevens says. Other morally questionable therapies include stem cells and euthanasia drugs.

The American Pharmacists Association (APhA) supports conscience clauses but thinks refusing pharmacists should refer customers to another pharmacist who will fill the prescription. When a pharmacist conscientiously objects, it is "appropriate to step away but not to step in the way," says Anne Burns, APhA's group director of pharmacy practice and research.

Individual employees' conscience objections should be discussed up front so a drug store — or an entire community — may put systems in place to protect pharmacists' conscience objections as well as patients' rights to get legal medications, Burns says. For example, "in rural areas, physicians could dispense" controversial drugs, she says.

But some health-care providers would consider that "moral complicity," Stevens says.

Similarly, Pharmacists for Life International (PFLI), which represents pharmacists who refuse to fill contraceptive prescriptions, contends that making a referral for an immoral service is "material cooperation," according to Executive Director Bo Kuhar. In fact, he writes on the group's Web site, refusing to refer a client to another pharmacist "is doing the woman and her pre-born child a favor in terms of physical and spiritual health." [15]

Should hospital emergency departments be required to offer emergency contraception to sexual assault victims?

In April 2005, Gov. Bill Owens, R-Colo., vetoed a bill that would have required hospital emergency departments to either offer rape victims emergency contraception or refer them to facilities where they could obtain it.

Bill supporters argue that offering a sexual assault victim protection against pregnancy should be a no-brainer for hospitals — an obvious and necessary policy. An estimated 5 percent of rape victims of reproductive age

become pregnant as a result of their assaults. Emergency contraception can reduce the risk of pregnancy by about 75 percent. [16]

"The psychological and mental anxiety following sexual assault is long term, and the thought that you could be pregnant plays a big part in it," says Michael Weaver, medical director of St. Luke's Hospital Sexual Assault Center in Kansas City, Mo., which has routinely offered emergency contraception to rape victims for more than 15 years.

But Owens said in his veto message to the legislature that imposing contraception referrals on Catholic hospitals "would unfairly and inappropriately infringe on the freedom of these institutions and diminish the free exercise of religion that is one of the bedrock rights Americans hold dear." [17]

Michael Rodgers, interim president of the Catholic Health Association of the United States (CHAUSA), says laws mandating emergency contraception care for rape aren't necessary, for two reasons. First, he says, most Catholic hospitals already have adopted protocols "to deal with the devastating emotional and psychological impact of rape."

In a June 2002 CHAUSA survey, 84 percent of the 410 Catholic hospitals with emergency departments that responded said their rape protocols include emergency contraception, and 96 percent said their customary practice includes "referrals to other community services," such as community rape crisis centers. [18]

"No mandated-coverage legislation is required," Rodgers says. Secondly, he says, "No laws should . . . force an individual or organization to act in ways that violate their conscience and force them to choose behavior contrary to their religious beliefs."

But critics argue that, protocols or not, many Catholic facilities don't dispense emergency contraception or offer "meaningful referrals" to obtain it quickly.

For example, another 2002 survey that polled 597 Catholic and 615 non-Catholic hospitals found that many hospitals in both groups do not routinely offer emergency birth control — with fewer Catholic facilities offering such services than other hospitals. In fact, 59 percent of Catholic hospitals surveyed said emergency contraception was unavailable under any circumstances at their facilities compared with 42 percent of non-Catholic hospitals. The study was conducted by Ibis Reproductive Health, a think tank in Cambridge, Mass., and Catholics for a Free Choice (CFFC). [19] Moreover, in hospitals where emergency contraception was unavailable, 52 percent of non-Catholic hospitals offered referrals that led to valid sources, compared to 47 percent of Catholic hospitals.

Catholic hospitals base rape treatment protocols on the church's "Ethical and Religious Directives for Catholic Health Care Services," which states that "if, after appropriate testing, there is no evidence that conception has occurred already," a victim may be treated with medications that would prevent ovulation or fertilization or incapacitate sperm. "It is not permissible, however, to initiate treatments that have as their purpose or direct effect the removal, destruction, or interference with the implantation of a fertilized ovum." [20]

Thus, says CFFC President Frances Kissling, Catholic hospitals commonly refuse emergency contraception if the hospital suspects that a woman has recently ovulated, even though having ovulated puts her at serious risk of pregnancy from a rape. "The ultimate reality is, if she needs it, you can't give it to her," Kissling says.

Kissling says the directives are "clearly, painfully constructed to leave a teeny bit of room for compassion, but not enough to get into trouble with [church] authorities." Many hospitals interpret the directives very conservatively, she says, because they fear the church will withdraw permission for the institution to call itself Catholic if its practice strays far beyond traditional Catholic opposition to all birth control.

Allowing hospitals to claim a conscience exemption from performing legal services poses a special dilemma because of the large role Catholic hospitals, in particular, play in the nation's health safety net. In 2002, about 20 percent of all U.S. hospital beds were controlled by Catholic health systems, according to the American Hospital Association, and in some rural communities the only hospital available is Catholic-affiliated.

Whenever an ethical conflict between patient and hospital can't be resolved, "the ethical solution is to refer the patient to another willing provider," says the journal *Contraception*. "But what if the patient has no access to such a provider? This is increasingly the case."

The issue is further complicated by the fact that many Catholic hospitals receive public funding, the journal says: "In spite of the significant revenues derived from the government, these quasi-religious institutions seem to be operating above the law in many states where contraceptive-equity laws have been passed." [21]

Ironically, because Catholic hospitals play a pivotal role as health-care safety nets, the government is unlikely to enforce mandatory emergency contraception, Kissling says. "We have a government that is incapable of delivering social services" and thus is "increasingly dependent" on Catholic hospitals. "The state needs them. They hold the cards."

Meanwhile, supporters of broad conscience rights for hospitals argue that birth-control advocates misunderstand the nature of the right that they themselves claim.

"Reproductive-rights activists have cleverly blurred the line in the public's mind between 'access' to a right and the right itself," writes Carol Hogan, associate director for communications and pastoral projects for the California Catholic Conference. "That tactic comes under the category of moving the privacy guarantee (upon which abortion rights rest) from a negative right, i.e., a right to be left alone, to a positive right, i.e., an entitlement to 'reproductive health services' at the time and place of one's choosing." [22]

Does easy access to birth control increase risky or promiscuous sexual behavior?

Catholics and others have long argued that increasing access to birth control — which they call a "contraceptive mentality" — fosters social problems such as higher abortion rates, sexual risk-taking by teenagers and divorce.

After effective birth control became widely available in the second half of the 20th century, sex was seen as separate from its otherwise natural consequence — pregnancy — says Smith, of Detroit's Sacred Heart Major Seminary. Viewing sex and childbearing as unrelated is "lethal for a culture," she argues. Women with easy access to birth control are likely to have sex when they are not prepared for pregnancy, she says, and are more careless in choosing sexual partners because they are not concerned about the men's suitability as fathers. Since birth control sometimes fails, she says, the result frequently is abortion, single motherhood — often attended by poverty — or an unsuitable marriage that ends in divorce.

University of Chicago physician Leon Kass, chairman of the President's Council on Bioethics, believes easy access to contraception also morally damages men. [23] Since they don't become pregnant, men have always been able to view sex as "unlinked to the future," says Kass, a non-Catholic. Pre-pill women's greater caution in

CHRONOLOGY

1800s *Many kinds of birth control are invented and improved, including condoms, diaphragms and cervical caps. But few Americans use them because of lack of information and restrictive laws.*

1870s Congress passes the Comstock Act, which outlaws the use of contraceptives — even by married couples. Many states follow suit.

1900s-1960s *Most forms of birth control see improvements, and "the pill" is invented. Americans protest restrictive laws against birth control, and Congress and the courts begin to overturn them.*

1916 Margaret Sanger opens the nation's first birth-control clinic, in Brooklyn, N.Y. Nine days later, the police close the clinic and arrest Sanger, who spends 30 days in prison. During her judicial appeals, which she loses, an appellate court gives doctors the right to offer information on contraception to protect a patient's health.

1930 Anglican Church approves the use of artificial birth control by married couples who have serious reasons to limit their family size.

1960 Hormonal birth-control pill is introduced in the United States.

1965 U.S. Supreme Court rules in *Griswold v. Connecticut* that the constitutional right to privacy guarantees married couples' right to use contraception.

1970s *Physicians discover that large doses of hormonal birth-ontrol pills can prevent pregnancy when taken after intercourse.*

1970 Congress enacts Title X, which provides subsidized birth control for poor women.

1980s-2000s *A lower-dose, safer birth-control pill is introduced; hormonal birth-control options expand to include implants and injectables; and birth-control pills are packaged to be sold as "morning after" pills. More Americans are using*

birth control, but some health-care providers refuse to provide the newer methods on moral grounds.

1990 Institute of Medicine reports that the United States has fallen far behind other countries in developing new forms of birth control.

1996 Kmart Corp. fires pharmacist Karen Brauer for falsely telling a customer that her store does not carry a progestin-only birth control "minipill," because she morally objects to dispensing the medication. Brauer goes on to found Pharmacists For Life, representing pharmacists opposed to birth-control drugs.

1998 Oregon Christian minister Randy Alcorn publishes a booklet — "Does the Birth Control Pill Cause Abortions?" — which helps persuade some doctors and pharmacists to stop prescribing and dispensing it.

1998 Food and Drug Administration (FDA) approves Preven, the first emergency contraceptive product to be sold on the U.S. market.

2001 Federal court in Seattle rules in *Erickson v. Bartell* that excluding prescription birth-control pills from health insurance that covers other prescription drugs amounts to sex discrimination.

October 2002 Abstinence-only advocate and physician Alma Golden takes over the Title X program.

December 2003 FDA expert panel recommends that Plan B emergency contraception be sold over-the-counter.

May 2004 FDA rejects the application to sell Plan B over-the-counter.

January 2005 FDA misses the deadline for ruling on an application to sell Plan B over-the-counter.

April 2005 Canada allows pharmacists to dispense emergency contraception without a prescription. . . . Gov. Rod Blagojevich, D-Ill., enacts temporary rule ordering pharmacies that stock emergency contraceptives to provide them to customers.

June 2005 American Medical Association votes to support laws that require pharmacists to fill prescriptions for contraceptives or refer patients to other pharmacies that will.

New Contraception Methods on Horizon

Key scientific discoveries — particularly the unraveling of the human genome — may soon produce completely new forms of contraception — for men as well as women.

"Recent scientific and technological advances in genomics, proteomics [the study of proteins], new materials and new drug-delivery systems, along with a new understanding of reproductive biology, offer the promise of new, safe and effective forms of contraception," an Institute of Medicine (IOM) panel concluded last year. [1]

As scientists have probed human and animal genomes over the past decade, they've turned up thousands of genes that appear to affect only reproductive tissue and gametes — sperm and egg cells — the panel said. Armed with that information, researchers have assembled catalogs of genes and proteins uniquely involved in reproduction, any one of which might serve as a target for a new birth-control drug, potentially one that would not affect other physiological processes as does today's conventional birth-control pill.

There's an "ever increasing catalog of these targets," with a discovery "almost every week," says panel Chairman Jerome Strauss, director of the University of Pennsylvania's Center for Research on Reproduction and Women's Health. For many of the targets, research has shown that the genes behave as predicted in animals, suggesting that, in principle, they should work the same way in humans, he says.

For example, an enzyme being studied at the University of North Carolina-Chapel Hill provides the considerable energy needed to move the long tails of sperm. When mice do not have this enzyme, their sperm won't move, causing infertility. [2] At the University of Pennsylvania School of Medicine, researchers have inactivated a protein specific to mice germ-line cells, producing otherwise healthy male mice with no functional sperm and healthy females with defective ovulation. [3]

But as promising as the science appears, developing new products will still be difficult, Strauss says, because of financial and liability concerns, which always pose a "bottleneck" for contraceptive development. [4] Most of the basic research occurs in university laboratories, but university-based researchers have "inadequate access to the resources and information needed" to develop drugs for the targets they've identified, the IOM explains. [5]

So drug companies must develop the drugs, but they are reluctant to tackle birth control because of liability concerns. "Healthy people will be taking these medications for a long time," so companies' legal liability could be extremely steep if a new drug turns out to be harmful, Strauss explains.

Economic issues loom large, as well, says Allan Rosenfield, dean of Columbia University's Mailman School of Public Health. Developing a new birth-control method is expensive, and most people think contraceptives should be low-cost. Because the hormonal birth-control pill "remains very profitable," he says, manufacturers are skeptical that they can price a new product low enough to sell while still recouping potentially hefty research costs.

Negative reaction from conservative groups opposed to easily accessible birth control also inhibits research, Rosenfield says. "The ideological and political issues around contraception remain big in terms of reluctance to pursue things," he says, adding that whenever research reveals a possible new contraceptive, there is always concern it will have a component that could cause an abortion.

Nevertheless, Strauss says, with so much new science available, it's time to move development forward. "Ten or 15 years ago, non-hormonal contraception for males and females was theoretical. It wouldn't have been worth the investment. Today, the science is there."

---

[1] Institute of Medicine, *New Frontiers in Contraceptive Research: A Blueprint for Action* (2004), p. 2. For background see David Masci, "Designer Humans," *CQ Researcher*, May 18, 2001, pp. 425-440.

[2] Kiyoshi Miki, *Proceedings of the National Academy of Sciences*, Nov. 23, 2004, p. 16501.

[3] Norman Hecht, *Proceedings of the National Academy of Sciences*, posted online April 14, 2005.

[4] For background, see Sarah Glazer, "Birth Control Choices," *CQ Researcher*, July 29, 1994, pp. 849-872.

[5] Institute of Medicine, *op. cit.*, p. 6.

---

choosing sex partners acted as "the crucial civilizing device," turning men into monogamous husbands, rather than "the sexually, familially and civically irresponsible creatures they are naturally always in danger of being," Kass writes. [24]

But advocates of improving access to birth control argue that sexuality plays a multifaceted role in human relationships, even when viewed through a theological lens. "God gave you your sexuality," says Marjorie Signer, communications director for the Religious

Coalition for Reproductive Choice. "In religious tradition, even the ones that impose strict control see sex as part of life, and I don't think very many say that the only purpose of sexuality is procreation."

Sexuality is "a part of the web of human relationships," and having access to and information about contraception is critical to moral decision-making, Signer says. Among other things, increasing access to contraception helps ensure that "every child enters the world wanted and loved."

Moreover, says Emory's Hogue, there is no data to support the claim that access to contraception leads to more intercourse or more abortions. "Health economists have noted for years that the demand for contraceptives is elastic" — meaning that if the cost and difficulty of obtaining birth control go up, usage goes down — while the demand for sex and abortion are "inelastic," Hogue points out. In other words, whether or not birth control is available, people will have sex at the same rates. "So with no contraception, we have more unwanted pregnancies and more abortions."

Many demographers and epidemiologists agree. In Russia, for instance, where abortion rates were particularly high and contraception was not readily available until the late 1980s, the abortion rate "declined substantially" after birth control became more accessible, according to a 2001 study by RAND Corporation researchers Julie DaVanzo and Clifford Grammich. [25]

"Rising contraceptive use eventually reduces the abortion rate in countries where abortion has been widely practiced," The Johns Hopkins Bloomberg School of Public Health reports. Data from three Central Asian republics suggest that for every 10 percent increase in contraceptive availability, abortion rates decrease between 13 percent and 20 percent, the school's Information & Knowledge for Optimal Health Project said. [26]

Studies of school-related health clinics also "consistently" demonstrate that dispensing birth control does "not hasten or increase student sexual activity," Douglas Kirby, a prominent researcher in contraceptive use, writes in the *Journal of Sex Research.* [27]

And while many analysts have long blamed the birth-control pill for triggering the "sexual revolution," some now doubt the connection. "Contrary to popular belief, the sexual revolution" did not "start in the 1960s," writes University of Florida historian Alan Petigny. Based on census data on single motherhood and premarital pregnancy,

Petigny concludes that premarital sex in the United States increased fastest between 1940 and 1960 — before the pill was introduced. [28]

The number of babies born to single mothers during that 20-year period rose from 7.1 per 1,000 women of childbearing age to 21.6 — a much steeper increase than occurred post-pill, according to Petigny. And "the apparent surge in single motherhood is all the more remarkable when one considers that the '50s was a time when couples were exchanging wedding vows at ever-earlier ages."

Petigny suggests that World War II — when many young women entered the work force and gained independence for the first time — was a greater force in liberalizing sexual behavior than access to birth control.

BACKGROUND

Crocodile Dung and Tar

Women have been searching for effective birth control for thousands of years — for reasons of health, financial well-being or just convenience.

Egyptian papyruses dating from around 1850 B.C. contain recipes for vaginal suppositories thought to prevent conception, including honey — which may have slowed down the movement of sperm — and crocodile dung. [29]

In ancient Rome, the "elite did not relish the prospect of their urbanized, civilized style of life being jeopardized by a hoard of children," writes historian Angus McLaren. "The man was primarily interested in the number of children among whom his estate would be divided; the woman was as concerned with when children were born as with how many she had. Her health depended on it." [30]

Poorer people, too, have tried to control family size. In Europe "from the 800s to the 1900s peasants allowed their families to grow only when [living] conditions improved," write historians Bonnie S. Anderson and Judith P. Zinsser. [31] "Peasant women had their own ways of avoiding conception. They believed in douches and purges, spermicides like salt, honey, oil, tar, lead, mint juice, cabbage seed."

Even the most momentous event in modern contraception — introduction of the hormone-based birth-control pill in 1960 — can be traced in part to traditional medicine. Generations of Mexican women ate a wild yam, Barbasco root, for its contraceptive properties. [32] In the 1940s, an American chemist discovered that a substance in the yam would easily transform into the female sex hormone progesterone, a discovery that accelerated development of hormonal contraceptives.

Controlling Birth Control

At the same time, social and religious leaders throughout history have tried just as avidly to stamp out contraception. "To have coitus other than to procreate children is to do injury to nature," wrote the Greek theologian Clement Alexandria in around 200 A.D. [33]

By the ninth century, "Christian theologians . . . taught that by intervening in the process of insemination and pregnancy a woman acted as a murderer." [34]

According to historian Reay Tannahill, contraception was the major sex sin in ancient times, and guidelines for priests dating from the sixth to the ninth centuries deemed it "very grave indeed, especially if it involved 'poisons creating sterility,' anal intercourse or oral intercourse." [35]

Worried about public immorality or low birth rates, governments also frequently banned contraception. In the United States in 1873, Congress passed the Comstock Act, which prohibited the sale of contraceptives as part of a broad ban on the sale of obscene materials. States then enacted similar bans, in some cases prohibiting not just the sale but also the use of birth control — even among married couples. [36]

In the early 20th century, however, opposition to birth-control bans grew. In 1936, the U.S. Supreme Court lifted the federal ban on the importation of birth control for physicians acting on behalf of patients' health. However, most of the federal and state laws banning contraception remained in force into the 1960s and '70s.

Connecticut's law was one of the strictest, authorizing the arrest of married couples for using birth control in their homes. In 1961, in a calculated move to challenge Connecticut's Comstock law, the Planned Parenthood League of Connecticut opened a clinic offering married couples birth-control instruction and medical advice. Its executive director, Estelle Griswold, was arrested and convicted of providing contraceptive information.

In June 1965 the U.S. Supreme Court overturned Griswold's conviction in a 7-2 decision. The Connecticut law "unconstitutionally intrudes upon the right of marital privacy," Justice Arthur J. Goldberg wrote in one of the opinions in the case. [37]

After the *Griswold* ruling, Americans' right to use birth control was quickly expanded. In 1970, Congress removed contraception from the list of obscenities outlawed by the Comstock Act. In a 1972 case, *Eisenstadt v. Baird*, the Supreme Court established unmarried couples' constitutional right to use birth control. In 1977, in *Carey v. Population Services International*, the court extended the right to minors.

"Conscience Clauses"

Much of the public, including some Christian groups, welcomed the new, more permissive climate. As far back as 1930, the Episcopal Church had approved contraception for the purpose of family planning within marriage. In 1954, the Evangelical Lutheran Church of America affirmed that "a married couple should plan and govern their sexual relations so that any child born to their union will be desired both for itself and in relation to the time of its birth." [38]

In the late 1960s and '70s, a steady flow of state laws and legal opinions expanding Americans' rights to receive reproductive health services alarmed the Catholic Church and other Christian conservatives, who remained staunchly opposed to birth control and abortion. [39]

Christian medical providers feared that as a price of receiving taxpayer funding they might be forced to provide reproductive services they considered immoral. Hospitals received public funds not only from the federal health insurance programs enacted in the mid-1960s — Medicare and Medicaid — but also from the 1946 Hill-Burton Act, which provided hospitals with building and expansion funds.

Sure enough, in 1972 a federal court in Montana ordered a Catholic hospital that had received government funding to allow a sterilization procedure to be performed. Then in 1973, the Supreme Court's *Roe v. Wade* decision declared that women had a constitutional right to have abortions. [40]

In response, Congress in 1973 passed the first of many federal and state "conscience clauses" for health-care providers. The Church amendment — authored by Democratic Sen. Frank Church of Idaho — remains in force today. It prohibits public officials from forcing individuals or institutions that receive public funds to perform or host sterilization or abortion procedures. [41]

By the end of 1974, more than half the states had adopted conscience clauses, and by 1978 most states had them. The early laws primarily applied only to abortion and sterilization, and many were limited to physicians or hospitals. Over the years, however, the scope of the laws has expanded, especially at the state level.

Today, at least 46 states allow some providers to refuse to provide abortion services, according to the Alan Guttmacher Institute, a think tank dedicated to protecting reproductive choices. And 12 states have expanded their conscience laws to allow certain providers to refuse to provide birth-control services. Among the states whose conscience laws cover birth control, 10 allow physicians to decline to provide contraceptive services, and four explicitly allow pharmacists to decline to dispense birth control. Ten states allow health-care institutions such as hospitals to refuse to provide contraceptive services: Virginia is the only state that only permits religious institutions to claim the exemption. [43]

Illinois has the most comprehensive conscience-protection law. It covers all health-care providers, institutions and payers and applies to all health-care services, according to Brigham Young University law Professor Lynn Wardle. Some Christian providers prefer that the Illinois statute become the nationwide model, Wardle told the U.S. House Committee on Energy and Commerce in July 2002, the last time Congress held a hearing on conscience clauses.

Other laws "are very narrow in terms of the practices, procedures or contexts in which they apply," Wardle continued. Many cover "only a small group of health-care providers, not workers in the health-care industry generally," and most "are outdated, having been written before many of the medical developments occurred that have created some of the most difficult moral dilemmas."

Birth-Control Methods Vary in Reliability

Most contraceptives use either barrier methods, which kill or block sperm or implantation, or hormonal methods, which inhibit ovulation and fertilization. Intrauterine devices can fall into either or both categories. Today's contraceptives offer varying degrees of effectiveness, as well as drawbacks. For instance, most forms are somewhat inconvenient and thus are often used incorrectly or sporadically. In addition, hormonal birth control affects other body systems besides the reproductive organs, so it may pose health risks.

Here are the types of birth control available and their effectiveness rates, or the percentage of couples who will avoid pregnancy using that method. The effectiveness depends partly on how consistently and correctly each method is used.

Barrier methods available over-the-counter:

Male condom: Thin sheath placed on the penis before intercourse. (86-97 percent effective)

Female condom: Thin sheath placed inside the vagina before intercourse. (95 percent, if used properly; typically 79 percent)

Vaginal sponge: A soft, synthetic sponge saturated with spermicide, which is moistened and placed in the vagina, over the cervix, and left in place for six to eight hours after intercourse. (76-91 percent; may be more effective for women who have not had a baby)

Spermicides: Chemical creams, jellies, foams, film or suppositories placed in the vagina to kill sperm. Spermicides are often used in combination with other methods, like condoms. (71-94 percent when used alone; higher-dose products are more effective)

Barrier methods that require a prescription:

Diaphragm: A latex cup large enough to cover the cervix. A woman coats it with spermicide and inserts it just before intercourse. It is effective for six hours after insertion and must remain in place for six hours after intercourse. (94 percent if used properly; more typically, 80 percent)

Cervical cap: A small rubber device that fits snugly around the cervix. A woman fills it with spermicide and inserts it up to eight hours before intercourse. It can remain in place for up to 48 hours. (91 percent among women who have not delivered a baby; 80 percent among those who have; typically, 60-80 percent)

Current laws offer spotty and inadequate protection in a rapidly changing system, says Stevens, of the Christian Medical and Dental Associations. Rather than forcing conscience objectors to fight "state by state battles" over emerging issues ranging from physician-assisted suicide to emergency contraception, Stevens suggests a single federal conscience law.

"No one wants our health-care system to have only ethically neutered doctors in it," he says.

Hormonal methods that require a prescription:

Birth-control pills: Modern oral contraceptives combine very low doses of estrogen and progestin, making them much safer than earlier versions. (99.9 percent when used perfectly; typically, 92 percent)

"Mini pill:" Low-dose progestin-only pills, generally recommended only for women at risk for side effects from estrogen, such as women who smoke. (90-99.5 percent)

Contraceptive patch: Adhesive patches worn on the skin that release a low dose of estrogen and progesterone through the skin. Each patch is good for one week. (99 percent; may be less effective for women over 190 pounds)

Vaginal ring: A polymer ring that releases a hormonal contraceptive. A woman inserts a ring in her vagina once during the first five days of her menstrual cycle. It remains in place for three weeks, then is removed to allow a one-week menstrual bleed. (99 percent)

Implant: Silicone rubber rods inserted under a woman's skin, usually in the upper arm, that release hormonal contraception for five years. (98-99.8 percent; effectiveness declines slightly over time)

Injectable: Synthetic hormones injected into a woman's muscle, often in the upper arm. Usually given once a month or once every three months. (99+ percent)

Others:

IUD: Flexible plastic or metal devices inserted into the uterus through the vagina by a medical professional. Some remain in place for up to 10 years. Some IUDs release contraceptive hormones and must be replaced annually. (98-99.9 percent)

Fertility awareness: Using awareness of a woman's times of fertility to schedule intercourse to avoid pregnancy. Many new methods are available to help determine fertile periods, ranging from colored beads to help women track their menstrual cycles to electronic monitors for testing urine for signs of fertility. (70-99 percent)

Withdrawal: The man pulls his penis out of the vagina before ejaculation. (70-96 percent)

Abstinence: Refraining from vaginal intercourse is 100 percent effective in preventing pregnancy but is not effective protection against sexually transmitted diseases if mutual masturbation, oral sex or anal sex is substituted for vaginal sex.

Sources: U.S. Food and Drug Administration; Haishan Fu, *et al.*, "Contraceptive Failure Rates: New Estimates From the 1996 National Survey of Family Growth," *Family Planning Perspectives*, March/April 1999, p. 56; and Richard J. Fehring, "New Low- and High-Tech Calendar Methods of Family Planning," *Journal of Midwifery and Women's Health*, 2005, www.medscape.com.

In the past decade, Congress has expanded federal conscience protections to more entities, including, for example, managed-care insurance plans, but they are limited to objections involving abortion and sterilization.

A very broad federal conscience clause was proposed in the early 1990s, however, when President Bill Clinton hoped to enact a government-subsidized expansion of health insurance coverage to all Americans. The plan included a standardized package of services that all insurance would have to cover. But Catholic organizations, which feared they would be ineligible for government funding under the national program if they excluded services like contraception, pressed for a broad conscience exemption.

As a result, the Clinton plan, which was not enacted, included "the most broad-based conscience exemption ever proposed in law," says CFFC's Kissling. The provision would have allowed a health-care institution to opt out of providing any service that it objected to morally or ethically, while continuing to receive government funding.

Who Pays?

In the late 1990s, health insurance again became the focus of birth-control disputes, as women sought coverage for contraception.

For more than three decades, the federal government's Title X program and Medicaid have helped poor women pay for birth-control services despite funding cuts in the programs and periodic threats to eliminate them. Enacted in 1970, Title X was signed into law by President Richard M. Nixon, who declared as "a national goal the provision of family-planning services . . . to all who want but cannot afford them." [43]

But while poor women are eligible for financial assistance, middle-class women in the 1990s noticed that their health insurers frequently did not pay for birth control, even though they were expanding coverage of other prescription products.

Aided by an unlikely development, advocates of insurance coverage for contraception quickly won significant victories. Just as women's groups geared up for what could have been a lengthy fight, the FDA in 1998 approved Viagra, a drug to treat male impotence. Within a year Viagra was covered by most insurance plans that offered prescription assistance. Under the banner of "contraceptive equity," women's advocates pushed for and got improved coverage of contraceptive drugs at both the federal and state levels. Since 1998, 21 states have mandated that private insurers cover contraception to the same extent that they cover other drugs or outpatient health services. By 2002, the last year for which data has been analyzed, 94 percent of insurers covered IUDs, 83 percent covered diaphragms and 97 percent covered birth-control pills. [44]

Still hotly disputed, however, is whether employers with religious affiliations should be required to cover birth control. Even tougher to answer: What constitutes a religiously affiliated employer? States have generally included only institutions like churches — which mainly employ and serve people who share the institution's religious beliefs. Social organizations run by religious groups that employ and serve a broader population have generally been excluded. Groups like Catholic Charities have fought the exclusion, arguing it violates religious freedom, but so far the states' narrower exemption has prevailed.

In April 2004, the California Supreme Court ruled 6-1 that the state's requirement that employers cover birth control does not infringe on Catholic Charities' religious liberty because the case only deals with "the relationship between a nonprofit, public benefit corporation and its employees, most of whom do not belong to the Catholic Church." [45]

Opponents of a broad religious exemption also argue that social-service groups are more taxpayer-supported than church-supported. According to Americans United For Separation of Church and State, in 2002-2003 Catholic Charities of California derived 50 percent of its funding from taxes and 8 percent from the church. [46]

CURRENT SITUATION

States Conflicted

The introduction of emergency contraception pills into the U.S. market in 1998 injected new urgency into birth-control debates. Some providers have refused to dispense the pills, even to rape victims, claiming they cause early-stage abortions. The availability of a convenient pill that could protect rape victims from pregnancy and reverse birth-control mishaps like condom failure galvanized advocates to fight for wide availability.

State legislatures, where most of the current battles over emergency birth control are taking place, are pulled in two directions on the issue — as recent debates in Illinois and Colorado show.

Early this year, the Colorado legislature approved a bill allowing health-care professionals to refuse to offer emergency contraception due to religious or moral beliefs but requiring hospital emergency departments to offer rape victims information and referrals for obtaining emergency contraception. Gov. Owens vetoed the measure in April, however, complaining that it did not offer protections to hospitals and other health-care institutions. "That is wrong," he said. "And it is unconstitutional." [47]

As a testament to lawmakers' ambivalence, when sponsors led a failed attempt to override Owens' veto, several who had voted originally for the legislation later switched sides to vote against it.

Illinois, on the other hand, has the nation's most sweeping conscience law for health-care providers as well as the most liberal law in the nation regarding emergency contraception — a law requiring all pharmacies to dispense emergency contraception. Several Illinois pharmacists are suing Democratic Gov. Rod Blagojevich over the rule, arguing that it conflicts with the state's broad conscience exemption.

If sheer numbers of supporters determined policy outcomes, laws broadening contraceptive access would be the easy winner. In a May 2005 poll, 73 percent of Americans said they believe pharmacists should be required to fill prescriptions for emergency contraception, even if they are personally opposed to it. [48]

Nevertheless, arguments based on America's constitutional tradition of religious freedom, combined with conservative Christians' new political clout, have won a hearing for expanded conscience clauses — both in Congress and in statehouses around the country.

"I believe that life begins at conception, not just when it implants in the uterus," pharmacist Susan Grosskreuz told Wisconsin legislators in 2003 as they debated a conscience law expansion that ultimately did not pass. "It goes against my conscience to dispense drugs that can terminate lives at their earliest beginnings." [49]

Should Plan B emergency contraception be available over-the-counter?

YES
Marjorie Signer
Director of Communications, Religious Coalition for Reproductive Choice

Written for *CQ Researcher*, June 2005

Improving the availability of emergency contraception should be an ethical imperative for this nation, which values informed decision-making and responsible parenthood yet has the highest rate of unintended pregnancy among both adult women and teenagers in the industrialized world.

This safe, effective method of back-up birth control — simply a high dose of the ordinary pill relied on by millions of teens and women — could spare many thousands of people the heartache of an unintended pregnancy, but only if it is used within a narrow time frame of 72 hours or less. The requirement of a physician's prescription is a significant, medically unnecessary barrier to greater use of this time-sensitive treatment.

As its name implies, emergency contraception is for use in crisis situations, such as sexual assault and contraceptive failure. The women who most need to be able to obtain emergency contraception over-the-counter are those who lack health insurance or a regular physician — young women, the working poor and those without the ability to travel or take time from work or family responsibilities for a medical appointment.

But the potentially devastating consequences of unintended pregnancy are experienced by women of all ages and economic levels, including serious health problems for themselves and their babies, such as lower birth weight; educational and economic setbacks that affect the entire family; and an increased risk of child abuse and neglect. Thus, our moral responsibility must be broadly inclusive of all women. Emergency contraception should be available as part of a national education and prevention strategy that stresses the benefits of abstinence, safe sex and family planning.

In a nation that seeks to strengthen personal responsibility, our health-care system should support women and men in making responsible decisions, not place barriers in their way. We should provide medically accurate sexuality education and improve the availability and quality of birth control. But even with adequate education and services, there will still be contraceptive failures and, tragically, sexual assault. In such cases, emergency contraception is morally responsible.

The Food and Drug Administration is acting irresponsibly in repeatedly delaying the approval of over-the-counter sales. Considering the pressing problem of unintended pregnancy, the safety of emergency contraception and the widespread support for reducing the need for abortion, the FDA should do the right thing and give women this important health-care option.

NO
Rep. Dave Weldon, M.D, R-Fla.

Written for *CQ Researcher*, June 2005

Last January, while 16-year-old Melissa Anspach lay writhing on her bedroom floor, groups like Planned Parenthood and Advocates for Youth were lobbying the Food and Drug Administration (FDA) to make emergency contraception, or Plan B, available over-the-counter (OTC) to minors. Melissa obtained Plan B without a prescription and without her parent's knowledge or consent by going to Philadelphia's Department of Public Health.

Melissa's case affirms that the FDA's decision to protect minors from careless dispensing of a powerful prescription drug was the right one. Although the powerful abortion lobby doesn't like it, the FDA sided with public health and science.

Melissa received a handful of pills without a prescription, without consultation and examination by a doctor, without any medial history, without informed consent and without the notification of her parents. The next day, she experienced a violent physiological reaction to the pills and ended up in the emergency room, much to the surprise and concern of her parents.

This is the exact circumstance with which health-care professionals and parents were concerned, and it presents a tremendous public-health risk for some of our most vulnerable populations.

As a physician, I have witnessed patients at the pharmacy relying on advertisements and hearsay instead of medical expertise. This is precisely what occurred with Melissa.

Furthermore, since teens are most vulnerable to sexually transmitted diseases, making Plan B OTC would create an enhanced perception of safety for a behavior that is potentially dangerous. OTC availability leaves physicians out of the treatment loop and could exacerbate the already epidemic levels of sexually transmitted diseases, including HIV/AIDS.

Today, teen birth and pregnancy rates are at all-time lows, mostly because of the success of abstinence education — not contraception. A new HHS report says so. OTC availability of Plan B is not a part of this success story, but it presents significant health risks that outweigh its marginal benefits — if any.

Even the most recent study of Plan B availability, conducted by advocates of the drug, show no significant impact on pregnancy among motivated, sophisticated and experienced contraceptive users. If the drug's availability had no impact — especially on pregnancies — among 'true believers' of Plan B, then I am skeptical of its benefits for the public at large.

The FDA should feel vindicated in its decision to keep Plan B's availability subject to the training and knowledge of health-care professionals. Parents should feel grateful that science and safety have taken precedence over political and social agendas. Certainly Melissa would agree with that.

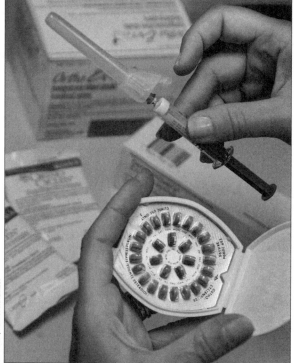

Injectable contraceptives and traditional birth-control pills are highly effective. Some pharmacists refuse to dispense the pills on moral grounds, even as states have begun passing "contraceptive equity" laws. Such legislation requires insurers who provide prescription-drug benefits to pay for contraceptives, just as they cover Viagra, a drug to treat male impotence.

Grosskreuz ended up working in a nursing-home pharmacy rather than in a retail store — as she would have preferred — because "I didn't feel I had any protection if I requested to refrain from filling prescriptions that had abortifacient potential," she told lawmakers. "Presently, pharmacists have no protection against employment discrimination if they do not want to dispense drugs which have controversial mechanisms of action." [50]

Despite all the rhetoric over limiting access to birth control, states generally have considered more pro-birth control measures recently than efforts to limit access to contraception.

For instance, at least a dozen states have considered expanding conscience clauses, but the handful that have been enacted dealt only with abortion and sterilization — not contraception. [51] Over the past two years, 10 states — Indiana, Michigan, Minnesota, Mississippi, Missouri, Ohio, Rhode Island, Vermont, Washington and Wisconsin — considered protecting pharmacists who refuse to dispense contraception on religious grounds, but the measures did not pass. [52]

So far this year, only one state is considering limiting access to emergency contraception, while four states are considering requiring parental notification and involvement when minors seek contraceptive services. [53]

On the other hand, 10 states this year have considered requiring insurance coverage for contraceptives, but only two states — West Virginia and Arkansas — actually enacted such requirements. Arkansas' law, however, excluded emergency contraception from the required coverage. Ten states also have considered requiring hospitals to provide emergency contraception or information about it to rape victims; New Jersey recently enacted its law, which exempts hospitals from providing emergency contraception to women who are already pregnant.

Three states have considered expanding family-planning services under Medicaid. Indiana has enacted an expansion, but its coverage would exclude coverage for birth control "intended to terminate a pregnancy after fertilization," a description that might apply to emergency contraception.

Plan B Stalls

In Washington, the Bush administration has taken a negative stance toward birth control on almost all fronts. In his annual budgets, the president has proposed severe funding cuts to federal family-planning programs, and executive-branch agencies have taken what some call extraordinary steps to limit government-provided information on contraception, including simple barrier methods like condoms.

For example, says California Democrat Rep. Henry Waxman, ranking minority member of the House Committee on Government Reform, scientific evidence on the effectiveness of condoms and information on how to use them "has been suppressed or distorted" on both the CDC and U.S. Agency for International Development Web sites. [54]

Some have characterized the administration's approach to contraception and condoms as a kind of "Don't ask, don't tell" approach. For example, in late 2004 experts on rape and some members of Congress complained angrily that a new Justice Department protocol on the treatment of sexual-assault victims contained no recommendation that emergency contraception be offered. Noting that pregnancy "is often an overwhelming and genuine fear" of rape victims, the 103-page document suggests simply that providers should "discuss treatment options with patients including reproductive health services."

The silence on emergency contraception, after the department had explicitly solicited input from health-care providers, was "disappointing," and "kind of negates" the intention for criminal-justice authorities to collaborate closely with health experts on the protocol, says Weaver, of St. Luke's Hospital's Sexual Assault Center in Kansas City, Mo., and an American College of Emergency Physicians (ACEP) consultant on the protocol. Protocols developed by both the ACEP and the American Medical Association stress emergency contraception for rape victims.

The FDA's foot-dragging on allowing Plan B emergency contraception to be sold without prescription further contributes to the impression that the Bush administration discourages expanded access to birth control. The nomination of Crawford as FDA administrator is still being held up by Sens. Clinton and Murray, pending agency action on Plan B.

Administration officials dispute critics' claims that the Bush administration is hostile to birth control. Budget proposals in recent years show the president "has supported continuing existing [federal] programs for contraception," says White House spokesman Trent Duffy. The president's key approach to birth control is "that it be balanced," with contraception and "abstinence supported on a level basis."

Minority Support

In 2005, congressional Democrats — who are in the minority in both the House and the Senate — have introduced several bills aimed at ensuring that pharmacies provide ready access to birth control and emergency contraception as well as measures to expand access to birth control generally.

Bills sponsored by Sens. Frank Lautenberg, N.J., and Barbara Boxer, Calif., would require pharmacies to fill all legal prescriptions "without delay" unless they are medically contraindicated. By putting the onus on pharmacies rather than pharmacists, the senators hope to get stores to work out ways to satisfy individual pharmacists' conscientious objections while allowing customers to obtain their drugs.

Senate Minority Leader Harry Reid, D-Nev., who personally opposes abortion, introduced a wide-ranging bill on contraceptive access as one of his top 10 legislative priorities. Besides requiring hospitals receiving federal funds to provide emergency contraception to rape victims on request, the measure also would expand Medicaid coverage of contraception, require group health plans to cover birth control if they cover other prescription drugs and devices and launch a federal program to inform people about emergency contraception.

Reid has long argued that improved access to birth control will limit the demand for abortions, and many Democrats hope support from their anti-abortion leader can increase the political respectability of measures to expand contraceptive access.

"Half of all pregnancies in the United States are unintended. And about half of those pregnancies are aborted," Reid said on the Senate floor March 17. "This isn't just a public-health problem. It is a public-health tragedy. But it doesn't have to be this way. Most of these unintended pregnancies — and the resulting abortions — can be prevented. One of the most important steps we can take," he continued, "is ensuring that American women have access to affordable, effective contraception."

Although many moderate GOP legislators agree with Reid on birth control, with conservative Republicans in control of the White House and in leadership positions in both houses of Congress, legislative initiatives to expand contraceptive actions most likely will not even be debated during the next two years.

OUTLOOK

Courts to Decide?

The strong public desire for contraceptive access, coupled with the growing strength of Christian conservatives in American life, promises to fuel birth-control debates into the foreseeable future, says Allan Rosenfield, an obstetrician-gynecologist and dean of Columbia University's Mailman School of Public Health. High-level political opposition to birth control "is not something that's going to go away without changing not only the administration but Congress as well, and I don't see that happening," he says.

Ultimately, the disputes will be decided by the courts, says ethicist Tong at the University of North Carolina. For instance, pharmacists in Illinois are suing the governor over the rule requiring pharmacies to dispense emergency contraception, arguing that it conflicts with Illinois' broad conscience clause.

Judicial settlements deal in the "limited language of rights" and don't necessarily deal with the full scope of these delicate issues, since they "opt out of the emotional tangles" involved, Tong says. Nevertheless, "only the courts can untangle whose conscience trumps whose," a provider's or a patient's.

Expanding access to emergency contraception for rape victims at hospitals remains a high priority for many women's groups and birth-control advocates. But with a new pope, Pope Benedict XVI, just named in April, Catholic hospitals, at least, are likely to take a very conservative stance toward reproductive health for some time, according to CFFC's Kissling.

"In every area of Catholic life, people are waiting to see if the other shoe is going to drop," she says. "Will the new pope pay attention to how health care is delivered?" Until those answers are known, "people will be very cautious. We're all in for a harder time, not an easier time."

But the CDC's recent announcement that more adult women are having unprotected sex will soon spur organizations concerned about the consequences of unintended pregnancy to launch strong efforts to increase support for family planning, says Emory University's Hogue, who opposes abortion. She is already involved in such an initiative in Georgia.

Family planning programs have been seriously neglected over the past several years, something that will take "a decade or more to turn around," she says. "But it will happen," as the public increasingly realizes the risks of unintended pregnancies — such as domestic violence and abortion.

NOTES

1. Carol Ukens, "R.Ph.'s Refusal To Transfer Lands Him in Trouble," *Drug Topics*, Feb. 23, 2004, p. 51.
2. Todd Richmond, "Board Approves Sanctions Against No-contraceptives Pharmacist," The Associated Press, April 13, 2005.
3. Anita Weier, "Rx License Is on the Line in Abortion Fight; Pharmacist Refused Pill Order Due to Faith," *The Capital Times* (Madison, Wis.), Oct. 12, 2004, p. 1A.
4. Rene Sanchez, "New Arena for Birth-control Battle," *The Star Tribune* (Minneapolis, Minn.), May 3, 2005, p. 1A.
5. Centers for Disease Control and Prevention, William Mosher, *et al.*, "Use of Contraception and Use of Family Planning Services in the United States, 1982-2002," Advance Data from Vital and Health Statistics, Dec. 10, 2004.
6. In an April 2005 survey of 1,536 U.S. physicians by HCD Research and the Muhlenberg College Institute of Public Opinion, 93 percent of physicians said they would prescribe birth control to any adult patient that requested it and for whom it was medically appropriate, http://hcdi.net.
7. The Protection of Conscience Project, Neil Noesen, testimony before the Wisconsin Assembly Labor Committee, March 5, 2003, www.consciencelaws.org.
8. "Teens Improve Contraceptive Use, But More Women at Risk for Pregnancy," *Contraceptive Technology Update*, March 1, 2005, p. 29.
9. Marc Kaufman, "Memo May Have Swayed Plan B Ruling," *The Washington Post*, May 12, 2005, p. A1.
10. *Ibid.*
11. Bruce Japsen, "Rx-filling mandate backed by AMA; Contraceptive denial prompts resolution," *Chicago Tribune*, June 21, 2005, p. C1.
12. Julie Cantor and Ken Baum, "The Limits of Conscientious Objections — Many Pharmacists Refuse to Fill Prescriptions for Emergency Contraception.," *The New England Journal of Medicine*, Nov. 4, 2004, p. 2008.
13. From www.consciencelaws.org, *op. cit.*
14. Cantor and Baum, *op. cit.*
15. Pharmacists for Life International, "Why a Conscience Clause Is a Must . . . Now!" from www.pfli.org.
16. From *The Annals of Emergency Medicine*, released online May 2005, available at www.ibisreproductivehealth.org/pub/downloads/Harrison_Availability_of_EC_A_Study.pdf.
17. Found on the Web at www.FreeColorado.com.
18. The survey is available at www.chausa.org/$memb/transform/rapesurvey.pdf.
19. *Annals of Emergency Medicine*, op. cit.

20. "Ethical and Religious Directives for Catholic Health Care Services, Directive 37," www.nccbuscc.org/bish-ops/directives.htm.

21. Pablo Rodriguez, M.D., and Wayne C. Shields, "Religion and Medicine," *Contraception*, April 2005, p. 302, Association of Reproductive Health Professionals, available at www.arhp.org/editorials/april2005.cfm.

22. Carol Hogan, "Conscience Clauses and the Challenge of Cooperation in a Pluralistic Society," California Catholic Conference, www.cacatholic.org/rfcon-science.html.

23. Leon Kass, "The End of Courtship," *Public Interest*, January 1997, www.thepublicinterest.com.

24. *Ibid.*

25. "Improvements in Contraception Are Reducing Historically High Abortion Rates in Russia," *Population Matters Policy Brief*, RAND Corporation, www.rand.org.

26. Johns Hopkins Bloomberg School of Public Health, Information & Knowledge for Optimal Health Project, report, spring 2003, www.infoforhealth.org.

27. Douglas Kirby "The Impact of Schools and School Programs Upon Adolescent Sexual Behavior," *Journal of Sex Research*, February 2002.

28. Alan Petigny, "Illegitimacy, Postwar Psychology, and the Reperiodization of the Sexual Revolution," *Journal of Social History*, fall 2004.

29. Bonnie Bullough and Vern L. Bullough, "A Brief History of Population Control and Contraception," *Free Inquiry*, spring 1994, p. 16.

30. Angus McLaren, *A History of Contraception from Antiquity to the Present Day* (1990), p. 54.

31. Bonnie S. Anderson and Judith P. Zinsser, *A History of Their Own: Women in Europe from Prehistory to the Present, Vol. I* (1988), p. 137.

32. Susan James, "Of Lemons, Yams and Crocodile Dung: A Brief History of Birth Control," *University of Toronto Medical Journal*, December 2001, p. 156.

33. Found at www.catholiclibrary.com.

34. Anderson and Zinsser, *op. cit.*

35. Reay Tannahill, *Sex in History* (1980), p. 150.

36. For background, see Sarah Glazer, "Birth Control Choices, *CQ Researcher*, July 29, 1994, pp. 649-672.

37. The case was *Griswold v. Connecticut*, 381 U.S. 479.

38. Found at Web site of the Religious Coalition for Reproductive Choice, www.rprc.org.

39. For background, see Kenneth Jost, "Abortion Debates, *CQ Researcher*, March 23, 2003, pp. 249-272.

40. For background, see Sarah Glazer, "Roe v. Wade at 25," *CQ Researcher*, Nov. 28, 1997, pp. 1033-1056.

41. Jody Feder, "Report to Congress: The History and Effect of Abortion Conscience Clause Laws," Congressional Research Service, Jan. 14, 2005.

42. "State Policies in Brief: Refusing to Provide Health Services," Alan Guttmacher Institute, www.Gutt-macher.org.

43. Found at www.plannedparenthood.org.

44. Adam Sonfield, *et al.*, "U.S. Insurance Coverage of Contraceptives and the Impact of Contraceptive Coverage Mandates, 2002," *Perspectives on Sexual and Reproductive Health*, March/April 2004.

45. Americans United for Separation of Church and State, *Church and State*, April 2004, www.au.org.

46. *Ibid.*

47. Freecolorado.com, *op. cit.*

48. HCD Research Inc., national survey of 1,200 Americans conducted with the Louis Finkelstein Institute for Social and Religious Research at The Jewish Theological Seminary, http://hcdi.net.

49. From testimony before the Wisconsin Assembly Labor Committee, The Protection of Conscience Project, March 5, 2003, www.consciencelaws.org.

50. *Ibid.*

51. Found at www.plannedparenthood.org.

52. Marilyn Gardner, "Pharmacists' Moral Beliefs vs. Women's Legal Rights," *The Christian Science Monitor*, April 26, 2004, p. 11.

53. *Ibid.*

54. "Condom Effectiveness," Politics & Science: Investigating the State of Science under the Bush Administration, House Committee on Government Reform, Democratic Minority, at http://democrats.reform.house.gov/features/politics_and_science/.

BIBLIOGRAPHY

Books

Connell, Elizabeth B., MD, *The Contraception Sourcebook*, **McGraw Hill, 2001.**
An Emory University professor emeritus provides a layperson's guide to the history, operation, advantages and disadvantages of all forms of contraception, including natural family planning.

Gordon, Linda, *The Moral Property of Women: A History of Birth Control Politics in America*, **University of Illinois Press, 2002.**
A history professor at New York University traces the history of U.S. birth control controversies, arguing that birth-control opponents generally have opposed equality for women.

Hilliard, Bryan, *U.S. Supreme Court and Medical Ethics: From Contraception to Managed Health Care*, **Continuum International Publishing Group, 2004.**
An assistant professor of philosophy at New England College examines the ethical reasoning behind the court's constitutional rulings on health care, including birth control.

Johnson, John W., *Griswold v. Connecticut: Birth Control and the Constitutional Right of Privacy*, **University Press of Kansas, 2005.**
The author, a history professor at the University of Northern Iowa, examines how the 1965 case on birth control led to judicial establishment of Americans' right to privacy.

Maguire, Daniel C., ed., *Sacred Rights: The Case for Contraception and Abortion in World Religions*, **Oxford University Press, 2003.**
Scholars assembled by a professor of moral theological ethics at Marquette University argue that the world's religious traditions — from Catholicism to Taoism — are more open to birth control than is often believed.

Riddle, John M., *Eve's Herbs: A History of Contraception and Abortion in the West*, **Harvard University Press, 1999.**
A professor of history at North Carolina State University argues that ancient and medieval women had extensive knowledge of plants that provided effective birth control and that the growing power of the Roman Catholic Church, along with consolidation of the medical profession into male-run universities, sent the knowledge underground beginning in the 13th century.

Tentler, Leslie Woodcock, *Catholics and Contraception: An American History*, **Cornell University Press, 2004.**
A professor of history at Catholic University describes how priests and ordinary Catholics struggled to cope with the changing sexual climate of the 20th century.

Tobin, Kathleen A., *The American Religious Debate Over Birth Control — 1907-1937*, **McFarland, 2001.**
A Purdue University professor of history discusses why many American religious denominations switched from an anti-contraception to a pro-contraception position.

Articles

Bollinger, Caroline, "Access Denied," *Prevention*, **www.prevention.com/article/.**
The author examines why some physicians won't prescribe the oral contraceptive pill and how birth-control advocates respond to their arguments.

Connolly, Ceci, "More Women Opting Against Birth Control, Study Finds," *The Washington Post*, **Jan. 4, 2005, Page A1.**
Fewer sexually active adult women are using birth control, a trend some population experts blame on cutbacks in government support for contraception.

Fairbank, Katie, "Moral Battle Rages in Pharmacies," *The Dallas Morning News*, **April 23, 2005.**
Fairbank examines community reaction to a small-town pharmacist who does not dispense birth-control prescriptions.

Robeznieks, Andis, "Battle of the Conscience Clause: When Practitioners Say No," *AMNews*, **April 11, 2005.**
The newspaper of the country's largest physicians' organization discusses the history of conscience laws and how physicians view conscience exemptions that include pharmacists.

Reports and Studies

Institute of Medicine, *New Frontiers in Contraceptive Research: A Blueprint for Action,* **National Academy Press, 2004.**
The report outlines steps public and private groups should take to develop safer, more effective birth control based on new scientific discoveries.

Institute of Medicine, *The Best Intentions: Unintended Pregnancy and the Well-Being of Children and Families,* **National Academy Press, 1995.**
The report recommends improving access to birth control as part of a national campaign to decrease unintended pregnancies.

For More Information

American Association of Pro Life Obstetricians and Gynecologists, 339 River Ave., Holland, MI 49423; (616) 546-2639; www.aaplog.org. Provides resources and information to support obstetrician-gynecologists who take pro-life positions.

Catholics for a Free Choice, 1436 U St., N.W., Suite 301, Washington, DC 20009-3997; (202) 986-6093; www.cath4choice.org. Provides information and advocates for safe and legal reproductive health services.

Center for Law and Religious Freedom, 8001 Braddock Rd., Suite 300, Springfield, VA 22151; (703) 642-1070; www.clsnet.org. A Christian legal society providing legal assistance and advocacy on pro-life and religious-freedom issues.

Center for Reproductive Rights, 120 Wall St., New York, NY 10005; (917) 637-3600; www.crlp.org. Provides education and legal assistance to protect reproductive freedom.

Guttmacher Institute, 1301 Connecticut Ave., N.W., Suite 700, Washington, DC 20036; (202) 296-4012; www.guttmacher.org. Provides research, policy analysis and education aimed at protecting reproductive choices.

Kaiser Family Foundation, 1330 G St., N.W., Washington, DC 20005; (202) 347-5270; www.kaisernetwork.org. Nonprofit group that publishes the free e-mail newsletter *Daily Reproductive Health Report.*

The Linacre Center for Healthcare Ethics, 38 Circus Road, St. John's Wood, London NW8 SE England; 44 (0) 20 7266 7410; www.linacre.org. Provides information on the Catholic Church's positions on bioethics, including birth control.

National Family Planning and Reproductive Health Association, 1627 K St., NW, 12th Fl, Washington, DC 20006; (202) 293-3114; www.nfprha.org. Provides information, research and training to improve the delivery of birth-control services.

Pharmacists for Life International, www.pfli.org. Provides information on making pharmacy a fully pro-life profession.

Planned Parenthood Federation of America, 1780 Massachusetts Ave., N.W., Washington, DC 20036; (202) 973-4800; www.plannedparenthood.org. Provides information about reproductive health and operates national network of health centers offering low-cost family-planning services.

Population Council, 1 Dag Hammarskjold Plaza, 9th Fl, New York, NY 10017; (212) 339-0500; www.popcouncil.org. Promotes family-planning programs around the world.

The Protection of Conscience Project, 7120 Tofino St., Powell River, British Columbia, Canada V8A 1G3; (604) 485-9765; www.consciencelaws.org. Provides information and advocates for conscience-protection legislation for health workers.

Religious Coalition for Reproductive Choice, 1025 Vermont Ave., N.W., Suite 1130, Washington, DC 20005; (202) 628-7700; www.rcrc.org. Coalition of religious groups that provides information about and advocates for reproductive rights.

7

Minimum Wage

Peter Katel

Amanda Nelson, a single mother with two children, earns minimum wage at a fast-food restaurant in Ashland, Ore., but still falls below the federal poverty line for a family of three. A recent poll found that 82 percent of Americans support raising the federal minimum wage, which has been at $5.15 since 1996.

Angela Coles has been working low-wage jobs "forever." But the 40-year-old Columbus, Ohio, woman doesn't have much to show for her efforts — not even a place to live.

She recently had to move out of her apartment after the rent jumped from $260 to more than $300. So she shuttles between a homeless shelter and the apartment shared by her two daughters. One works in a supermarket; the other was blinded by a childhood accident and receives federal disability payments.

Coles typically makes $5.50 an hour, or about $195 a week, with no benefits. Lately she has been stocking warehouse shelves. She has a car, a 1991 Nissan, thanks to a generous friend.

Coles earns more than either Ohio's $4.25-an-hour minimum wage or the $5.15 federal hourly minimum. "All I've got is my car and my clothes," says Coles, who never graduated from high school. Of her perch slightly above the minimum wage, she says, "$195 a week is nothing to survive on."

Coles is supporting a campaign to raise Ohio's minimum wage to $6.85, with annual cost-of-living increases.*

"People who work 40 hours a week should not be living in poverty. We should show that we value work," says Sarah Markey, an organizer for the Association of Community Organizations for Reform Now (ACORN), a leading support of higher minimum wages and so-called living-wage ordinances.

From *CQ Researcher,*
December 16, 2005.

* Where state and federal minimum wages differ, the higher one takes precedence. When a state minimum is lower, it covers workers exempt from the federal wage, which only applies to companies with revenues about $500,000 that take part in interstate commerce.

Most States Match Federal Minimum Wage

A majority of the states maintain state minimum wages that match the $5.15-an-hour federal minimum. Eighteen states (including Washington, D.C.) have minimums above the federal level and six below.

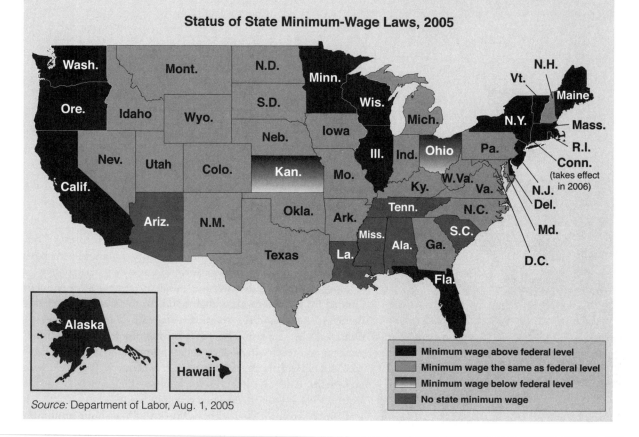

Status of State Minimum-Wage Laws, 2005

Minimum wage above federal level
Minimum wage the same as federal level
Minimum wage below federal level
No state minimum wage

Source: Department of Labor, Aug. 1, 2005

Business lobbyists acknowledge that additional labor costs often come out of employers' pockets. But they also say that raising labor costs hurts unskilled workers like Coles, who lose out to more highly skilled job seekers.

"Not only are the undereducated and those with less experience going to be hurt but also consumers, because raising prices is the only thing an employer can do to afford increasing the minimum wage," says Anthonio Fiore, labor and human resources policy director at the Ohio Chamber of Commerce in Columbus.

Such arguments prompted the Ohio legislature this year to kill a proposed increase in the state minimum wage. Unions and other backers now are trying to collect 322,899 signatures by Aug. 9, 2006, to place a constitutional amendment on next November's ballot. And in Albuquerque, N.M., following heavy lobbying by business groups, voters in October rejected a proposed city-wide minimum wage — though by only 1,479 votes. [1]

Five states, however, raised their minimum wages above the federal level in 2005, bringing to 18 the number of states (including Washington, D.C.) with hourly minimums over $5.15. [2] Meanwhile, proponents of higher minimums are gearing up for a ballot initiative drive in Arizona and considering similar efforts in Colorado and Michigan. In addition, the New Mexico legislature will take up the issue in 2006, and Gov. Edward Rendell, D-Pa., is pressing Pennsylvania's legislature as well.

Several factors have converged to produce the recent upsurge in activity. Congress last approved a minimum-wage increase 10 years ago, in 1996. Since then, inflation has reduced the minimum wage's purchasing power 17 percent, according to pro-wage-raise economists. They say the federal minimum wage now amounts to only about a third of the $18.09-per-hour national, average hourly wage — the lowest level since 1949. [3]

Moreover, 82 percent of Americans polled in January 2005 favor raising the federal minimum wage. [4] And 71 percent of Florida voters last year voted to raise the state's minimum to $6.15.

Meanwhile, affluent Americans have gotten richer while the lower economic classes are falling further behind. In 2004, for instance, the share of poor households increased from 12.5 percent to 12.7 percent of the population, even as the nation's top 5 percent in earnings saw their average income jump by 1.7 percent. [5]

"The real income of the typical household has fallen five years in a row," the liberal Economic Policy Institute concluded. At the conservative Heritage Foundation, analysts argued that the impression of income inequality is lessened when the higher taxes paid by wealthier Americans are factored into the comparison. However, they acknowledged, "The rise in poverty occurred almost exclusively among working-age adults." [6]

Perhaps as a result, proposals to raise the minimum wage are "overwhelmingly popular," says ACORN's Markey.

In Congress, however, two attempts to raise the federal minimum wage — first to $7.25 and then to $6.25 — failed this year. But sponsor Sen. Edward M. Kennedy, D-Mass., a perennial raise proponent, says a return to the issue is "inevitable" in 2006. "This doesn't go away," he said.

Lawmakers, business interests and labor unions have been fighting over raising the national minimum wage since 1938, when President Franklin D. Roosevelt won a five-year battle to enact the Fair Labor Standards Act (FLSA).

Most Minimum-Wage Workers Are Women

More than half of all minimum-wage workers in the United States are women, about three-quarters are in service occupations and more than two-thirds graduated from high school, attended college or received a college degree.

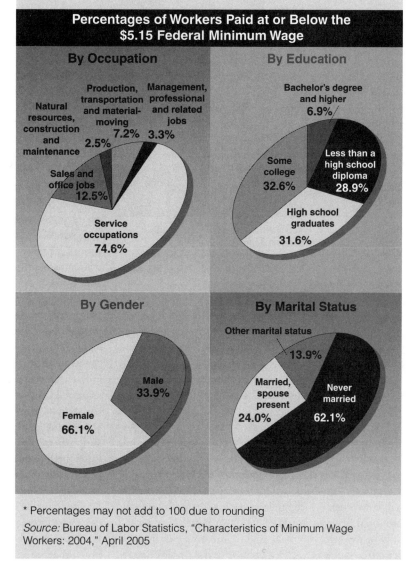

Percentages of Workers Paid at or Below the $5.15 Federal Minimum Wage

By Occupation

Natural resources, construction and maintenance 2.5%
Production, transportation and material-moving 7.2%
Management, professional and related jobs 3.3%
Sales and office jobs 12.5%
Service occupations 74.6%

By Education

Bachelor's degree and higher 6.9%
Less than a high school diploma 28.9%
Some college 32.6%
High school graduates 31.6%

By Gender

Male 33.9%
Female 66.1%

By Marital Status

Other marital status 13.9%
Married, spouse present 24.0%
Never married 62.1%

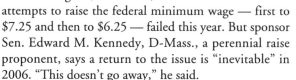

* Percentages may not add to 100 due to rounding

Source: Bureau of Labor Statistics, "Characteristics of Minimum Wage Workers: 2004," April 2005

Sen. Michael Enzi, R-Wyo., chairman of the Senate Health, Education, Labor and Pensions Committee, wants more businesses exempted from paying a higher minimum wage as well as protection for small employers from what he says would be a major hike in payroll expenses.

In the past, businesses claimed higher minimum wages would hurt the economy or significantly increase unemployment. Today, they take another tack. "I would not say this is going to drag our economy down into recession or see unemployment shoot up," says Matthew Brouillette, president of the Commonwealth Foundation, a think tank in Harrisburg, Pa., advocating low taxes and limited government, "but we're going to be harming the very people we want to help" by eliminating some entry-level jobs.

Low-wage workers represent only a small fraction of the nation's 126-million work force. Fewer than 6 percent of U.S. workers — 7.6 million people — earn less than the proposed new minimum of $7.25 an hour. Another 8.2 million workers who make slightly more would probably get immediate raises as well because of the ripple effect. [7]

The bottom line, according to two economists whose research was commissioned by the anti-wage-increase Employment Policies Institute: Raising the minimum wage to $7.25 an hour would cost employers $18.2 billion.

"Only 12.7 percent ($2.3 billion) of this cost will actually go to poor families, with only 3.7 percent going to poor African-American families," wrote Richard J. Burkauser of Cornell University and Joseph J. Sabia of the University of Georgia. "The ability of the minimum wage to target poor families is weaker and decreasing over time." [8]

Politicians and experts on both sides agree that the low-wage population is increasingly distant from the rest of the country. "Most of the people who start at minimum wage, if they pay attention to their job, are not in minimum wage very long," said Sen. Michael B. Enzi, R-Wyo., chairman of the Senate Health, Labor, Education and Pensions Committee, during an Oct. 19 floor debate over Kennedy's most recent minimum-wage-raise attempt. "If they pick up [new] skills, they get paid for those skills. That is so that they don't go somewhere else and work. But if they don't have the skills, they are lucky to get a job at all."

Two economists who studied long-term minimum-wage earners generally drew the same conclusion. "Minimum wages have virtually no effect on the careers of most workers," wrote William J. Carrington of Bethesda, Md., and Bruce C. Fallick, of the Federal Reserve Board staff. Those who remain at the minimum wage for a long time are usually "women, minorities and the less-educated." [9]

Economist Kevin Lang of Boston University concluded that raising the minimum wage would draw better-skilled job applicants into the job market, displacing workers with lesser skills. Specifically, Lang found that in states that raised their minimum wages in the late 1980s and early '90s, the percentage of workers without high school diplomas fell 2 percentage points between 1990 and 1991, while the share of workers with some postsecondary education rose by the same amount. [10] Nevertheless, Lang himself supports raising the minimum because he says the job losses are limited: "There's enough of a gain in improving poverty and reducing income inequality to offset the small, negative employment effects."

The Clinton administration, which helped push the last wage increase through Congress in 1996, shared Lang's view. The 1999 White House economic report noted that "modest increases in the minimum wage have had very little or no effect on employment." [11]

But a 2003 Bush administration report concluded there would be "significant employment losses." [12]

A leading anti-wage-raise economist makes a more nuanced argument. David Neumark of the Public Policy Institute of California, in San Francisco, concedes that low-wage workers "probably will" keep their jobs if the minimum is raised. However, he warns. "The hit, if you lose your job, is worse than the gain."

People already struggling to keep their heads above water are not impressed by the argument that a modest pay raise could be dangerous. Indeed, says Columbus warehouse worker Coles, more money would solve her most pressing everyday problems: "A higher minimum would be better."

As employers, workers and policymakers debate raising the minimum wage, here are some of the issues they are discussing:

Would raising the minimum wage reduce poverty?

No one disagrees — at least in principle — that higher salaries for low-wage workers would help reduce poverty.

Economist Nathan Newman, policy director of the newly formed Progressive Legislative Action Network, says raising the minimum wage is a direct, non-bureaucratic way to help the small portion of the work force earning minimum wage to keep their heads above water, at no cost to the taxpayers. "For that 5 to 10 percent of the population, it's the most important anti-poverty program that exists."

In practice, however, the minimum wage is no one's notion of the best, or only, way to fight poverty. For one thing, raising the minimum wouldn't, by itself, make a big dent in the poverty rate, says Jeff Chapman, an economist at the pro-wage-raise Economic Policy Institute. "A lot of people who are poor don't work and wouldn't benefit," he says. Even so, he adds, providing more income to those working at the low end of the wage scale is a worthwhile goal in itself.

But the fundamental divide over using the minimum wage as an anti-poverty tool is simply whether employers would employ fewer workers if they had to pay higher wages. Consequently, say wage-hike opponents, raising the wage floor hurts those at the bottom of the job ladder because there would be fewer low-wage jobs available.

At the most basic level, "A lot of employers find ways to work without folks," says Richard Berman, executive director of the Employment Policies Institute. "Cut one worker out of every movie theater, restaurant and small retail store and you're talking about millions of jobs."

In addition, says Fiore of the Ohio Chamber of Commerce, if employers are paying more, they will want to hire more experienced or more educated individuals in

Sen. Edward M. Kennedy, D-Mass., unsuccessfully pushed for an increase in the minimum wage to $7.25 in 2005 and says a return to the issue is "inevitable" in 2006.

order to minimize the initial investment in training. With higher wages, he says, "Employers won't look at individuals with less skills or who are less educated to fill entry-level positions."

Job training or retraining is a more effective government tool than a government-imposed wage raise, Fiore says, because it steers workers toward more stable jobs.

But liberal economists cite studies indicating that higher minimums have not resulted in fewer jobs. For instance, between 1998 and 2004, retail employment rose more than three times faster (6.1 percent) in states with minimum wages above the federal wage floor than in the states with lower minimums, according to the Fiscal Policy Institute of New York. [13]

"The argument for poverty relief is certainly persuasive by itself," says Matthew Henderson, chief New

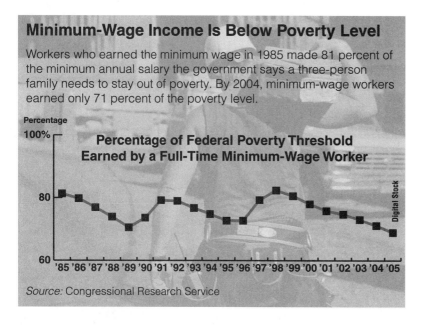

Minimum-Wage Income Is Below Poverty Level

Workers who earned the minimum wage in 1985 made 81 percent of the minimum annual salary the government says a three-person family needs to stay out of poverty. By 2004, minimum-wage workers earned only 71 percent of the poverty level.

Percentage of Federal Poverty Threshold Earned by a Full-Time Minimum-Wage Worker

Percentage

Source: Congressional Research Service

Mexico organizer for ACORN, "and now the research shows that raising the minimum is good for everyone."

But raising the minimum wage isn't designed to help everyone, argue opponents of higher minimum wages, it's supposed to benefit the working poor. And the majority of minimum-wage workers are not the poor, they say. "The average family income of a minimum-wage worker is in excess of $44,000 a year," says Berman. "That suggests that most minimum-wage workers are second and third earners in families, and those families are not in poverty."

However, economists Carrington and Fallick note that a sizable group of workers spends much of its employment career at the low-wage end of the labor market. "More than 8 percent of workers spend at least 50 percent of their first 10 post-school years working in jobs paying less than the minimum wage plus $1," they wrote in the Department of Labor's *Monthly Labor Review*. "There are particular groups whose lifetime incomes may be affected by a minimum wage." [14]

But economists commissioned by the Employment Policies Institute, which opposes the proposed $7.25 minimum, say that only 12.7 percent of the projected $18.2 billion in raises would go to poor families. [15] "It's a failed social policy to mandate anything for 85 percent of the population in order to get at 15 percent of them," says Berman.

Opponents of the increase also argue that a higher minimum traps people in low-wage work because it persuades them to quit school. "Think about three groups of workers: those who've already dropped out and may be working, those on the margin and those who stay in school no matter what," says Neumark, at the Public Policy Institute of California. "As the minimum wage goes up, employers bid up the price of slightly more skilled workers, and those students on the margin respond."

Newman, of the Progressive Legislative Action Network responds that eliminating some poverty trumps other possible negative outcomes. "If the only public policy you enact is the minimum wage, there probably are some consequences you need to deal with, but it's easier to deal with them than with the poverty you were dealing with before. To the extent you're worried about kids dropping out, promise them there will be something better for them if they graduate."

Increasing poor people's incomes has an immediate "multiplier effect," because they end up spending more in their neighborhoods, says Newman, a former union organizer. "You're talking not just about individuals, but about rebuilding communities."

Is there a better way to help low-paid workers than raising the minimum wage?

Over the past several decades, the share of the work force directly affected by the minimum wage has been shrinking. In the past decade alone, the percentage of workers earning the minimum or slightly more has shrunk from 18 percent to 12 percent. [16] Thus, say many opponents of a higher minimum, the minimum wage has become largely irrelevant to the working families who are supposed to benefit from a higher wage floor.

Still, both sides ask, how can low-wage workers keep their heads above water in a society in which the divide between them and the rest of the working population is deepening?

Many employers say the answer already exists in the form of the Earned Income Tax Credit. Using the EITC, a working couple or single person earning up to $35,548 in 2004 could get a tax credit of up to $4,300, depending on age, income and the presence of children in the household. And the EITC comes in the form of a government check, with tax obligations deducted.

In 1974, when the EITC was first being debated, it was dubbed "workfare" and pitched as an alternative to welfare payments, which many viewed as an incentive for single mothers to stay unemployed. [17] The EITC was expanded in 1993, and by 2004 low-paid workers were receiving an estimated $39.2 billion under the program, according to the Center on Budget and Policy Priorities. [18]

Berman says the "highly targeted" tax program fights poverty better than the minimum wage, which goes to young people from middle-class backgrounds as well as to poverty-stricken breadwinners. And the EITC doesn't affect business owners' decisions on whom to hire and how much to pay. "I'm usually not in favor of giving money to people," Berman says, "but I'm a huge supporter of the EITC. It's rewarding people for work. That, to me, is the right place to have the conversation" about aiding low-wage workers.

Businesses also prefer the EITC to the minimum wage because taxpayers foot the bill. Indeed, says the Economic Policy Institute's Chapman, expanding the EITC without raising the minimum wage would amount to taxpayers "subsidizing people paying substandard wages."

To be fair, Chapman argues, the EITC should be combined with a higher minimum wage, so employers would be paying their fair share and because it would produce more income for the working poor. "The way the EITC is designed, the more you earn the more EITC you get," he says. Thus, wage-raise advocates share employers' enthusiasm for the EITC — but not as a stand-alone measure. "They work in concert," he adds.

Another alternative, say employers, is to expand the EITC so that it applies to state income taxes, as 18 states (including the District of Columbia) have done. The states give low-wage taxpayers a percentage of whatever they are receiving under the federal EITC, ranging from 4 percent in Wisconsin to 32 percent in Vermont. [19]

In Pennsylvania, Brouillette of the Commonwealth Foundation says a state EITC would be preferable to a raise in the federal minimum wage. "We would be not just artificially boosting teenagers' wages but helping individuals and families that are indeed poor," he argues.

Wal-Mart employees earn an average of $9.68 per hour — well above the federal minimum wage. CEO H. Lee Scott says the nation's $5.15 minimum wage is "out of date" and that the low-cost retail giant's customers can't afford basic necessities between paychecks.

Getty Images/William Thomas Cain

But Isaac Shapiro, an associate director of the liberal Center on Budget and Policy Priorities, doubts EITC programs alone can resolve the poverty problem. "You'll never be able to get an EITC in every state that's tailored to make up for the low level of the minimum wage," he says. Nor could the federal tax program alone replace the minimum wage, he says. "It would be such a costly program that I'm not sure it would be supportable over time. And on a simple, day-to-day level, the EITC arrives only once a year, unlike a paycheck."

Additionally, EITC beneficiaries have to apply for the credit, and many don't. "The EITC remains much too complex for low-income working families," said the Center on Budget and Policy Priorities. In California's San Joaquin Valley, for example, only 36 percent of eligible Latino families applied for the EITC. [20]

Would a minimum-wage increase especially benefit single mothers?

The link between single motherhood and poverty is inescapable. In 2004, about 28 percent of households headed by single women were living below the poverty line, according to the National Poverty Center at the University of Michigan. The picture was even grimmer among minority women: Nearly 40 percent of the households headed by black and Hispanic women were living below the poverty line, compared to only 5.5 percent of married-couple households of all races and ethnicities. [21]

Many single, working mothers entered the work force after Congress overhauled the welfare system in 1996, establishing a five-year lifetime limit on the amount of time anyone can receive welfare. [22]

Economists who have studied the minimum-wage career track concluded that women are much more likely than men to have "extended stays" in jobs at or near the minimum. About 4 percent of the nation's female population spent more than 75 percent of their first nine years after high school working in jobs at the bottom of the pay scale. And women with young children are among those most likely to spend their working lives at the minimum wage or slightly above it. [23]

Thus, wage-raise advocates usually single out single mothers — and, by extension, their children — as prime beneficiaries of increases. In 1999, economists projected that increasing the minimum by $1, to $6.15 an hour, would benefit 967,000 single mothers out of a total population of 11.8 million low-wage workers. [24] By 2005, advocates said hiking the minimum wage would disproportionately benefit single mothers because they only make up 5.3 percent of the nation's work force but represent 10.4 percent of those who would get raises. [25]

"The minimum wage is not the most important means of funneling money to specific populations," says Chapman of the Economic Policy Institute. At the same time, he says, "Are those earnings important to their standard of living? The answer is, yes."

Fiore of the Ohio Chamber of Commerce argues that a modest raise in pay shouldn't be confused with the kind of workplace advancement with which a worker can break out of poverty. "A long-term solution," he says, "is education and work experience to help them sustain an increase in their wages, or a better-paying job that might have benefits."

Wage-raise advocates don't disagree, but in the meantime, they argue, single-mother households have to survive. A wage boost may not zero in on them, but they would reap the benefits of a raise, says Lang of Boston University. "They're a significant fraction of the poor that have a minimum-wage worker in the household."

To show the need for a minimum-wage hike, supporters point to what happened following single mothers' massive entry into the work force after the 1996 welfare-reform law: Their wages dropped, as the labor market responded to the swelling supply of entry-level workers. However, if the minimum wage had been "indexed" to rise automatically with annual cost-of-living increases, the wage-depressing effects of welfare reform would have been offset, wrote Aaron Bernstein of *Business Week*. [26]

Indeed, former welfare mothers who entered the work force in Oregon received, on average, a declining starting wage in the early 1990s, according to the Center on Budget and Policy Priorities. But the trend reversed itself immediately after the state increased its minimum wage in 1997. "Nearly a year after the raise took effect, the starting wage had risen 5 percent," the center found. The state's strong economic growth cannot account for that trend, the report added, because the earlier wage decline had also occurred when the economy was performing well. [27]

Still, the notion that raising the minimum can spell disaster for the most vulnerable workers applies especially keenly to single mothers, who are perhaps least equipped to cope with job loss. And even minimum-wage-raise supporters concede that some jobs could be lost if wages are boosted.

Hence, Neumark, of the Public Policy Institute of California, questions the value of minimum-wage increases "if [middle-class] teenagers get raises and poor female heads of household lose their jobs."

Lang of Boston University agrees that helping single mothers and other vulnerable workers succeed in the workplace demands highly focused programs that begin in a future worker's childhood, such as Head Start-style preparation for school. [28]

These programs almost certainly have to be financed by the national budget. "If you're asking me, what can the federal government do that is costless, I'm not sure I have a whole lot of answers for you."

BACKGROUND

New Deal

Nearly 70 years after it was enacted, the Fair Labor Standards Act (FLSA) of 1938 might seem like another piece of New Deal legislation created by President Roosevelt and eagerly accepted by a grateful nation. [29]

In fact, Roosevelt had to fight tooth and nail for five years to get the first nationwide minimum-wage law enacted. (Various states had experimented with minimum wages since Massachusetts enacted one in 1912). The last New Deal measure to get through Congress, the FLSA set a minimum wage of 25 cents an hour, rising to 40 cents by 1945 — not princely sums, even by the standards of a country emerging from the Great Depression.

Nevertheless, opponents fought the measure every step of the way. Initially, they were helped by a 1935 U.S. Supreme Court decision, *Schecter Poultry v. U.S.*, which invalidated some provisions of the National Recovery Act — the major administrative creation of the New Deal — and, by extension, the planned attempts to legislate a national minimum wage. [30] "The persons employed in slaughtering and selling in local trade are not employed in interstate commerce. Their hours and wages have no direct relation to interstate commerce," Chief Justice Charles E. Hughes wrote for the majority.

But in 1937, the court reversed course. "The exploitation of a class of workers who are in an unequal position with respect to bargaining power, and are thus relatively defenseless against the denial of a living wage, is not only detrimental to their health and well-being but casts a direct burden for their support upon the community," Hughes now wrote, upholding the constitutionality of Washington state's minimum-wage law. [31]

The court handed down that decision on March 29, 1937. Two months later Roosevelt submitted his minimum-wage proposal to Congress.

Notwithstanding the high court decision, minimum-wage opponents kept up their campaign to defeat the measure. Some of their arguments are still resounding today, such as the claim that a government-decreed wage increase would hit low-wage workers hardest. Referring to the second phase of the proposed increase, Rep. John McClellan, D-Ark., paraphrased the Bible in challenging the legislation: "What profiteth the laborer of the South, if he gain the enactment of a wage and hour law — 40 cents per hour and 40 hours per week — if he then lose the opportunity to work?" [32] Historically, wages in the South, which was not heavily unionized, have been lower than in the North.

While the New Testament imagery did not scuttle the FLSA, opponents succeeded in weakening both its wage requirement and the extent of coverage. For instance, the law exempted slightly more than a third of the country's 34 million workers, including those in agriculture, urban mass transit, retail and service establishments, as well as switchboard operators in telephone exchanges with fewer than 500 subscribers.

In addition, the FLSA did not have as sweeping an impact as supporters had hoped, primarily because state legislatures did not follow up with laws covering employees with no connection to interstate commerce. By 1945, only Connecticut, New York, Rhode Island and the territories of Puerto Rico and Hawaii (not yet a state) had passed minimum-wage laws that applied to both men and women. Eighteen states and the District of Columbia had adopted minimum wages, but only for women and minors. [33]

Postwar Recovery

At the end of World War II, President Harry S. Truman made raising the minimum wage a cornerstone of his efforts to transform a wartime manufacturing economy into a more consumer-oriented economy.

"The high prosperity which we seek in the postwar years will not be meaningful for all our people if any large proportion of our industrial wage earners receive wages as low as the minimum now sanctioned by the Fair Labor Standards Act," Truman told Congress on Sept. 6, 1945. [34]

Congress eventually raised the wage — four years later. Truman was advocating the increase at a time when wage levels were running relatively high thanks to the high-skilled, high-output standards of wartime production. Consumption was high as well, but those seeking wage increases argued that living costs had risen and wartime savings — which made the purchasing boom possible — would soon be exhausted. Opponents, however, insisted that a higher wage floor would spur inflation, slowing the peacetime conversion. [35]

Meanwhile, unions were reasserting themselves. During the war, wages had been frozen and strikes prohibited. But a wave of postwar strikes did nothing to endear Republicans and Southern Democrats — who made up the pro-business faction in Congress — to pro-labor legislation. In 1947, Congress overrode Truman's veto of the anti-union Taft-Hartley bill, which outlawed the practice of requiring workers to join unions as a condition of employment.

Two years later, Truman finally got Congress to raise the wage floor from 40 cents to 75 cents an hour, and in some cases to $1. But Congress would not extend coverage to workers whose employers were not already subject

CHRONOLOGY

1930s *President Franklin D. Roosevelt's New Deal strategy to pull the country out of the Great Depression includes creating a national minimum wage, but the plan arouses fierce opposition from the business community.*

1935 U.S. Supreme Court decision in *Schecter Poultry v. U.S.* is interpreted as barring a federal minimum wage.

1938 After Supreme Court modifies its stand on the minimum wage, Congress passes Fair Labor Standards Act, which sets the hourly minimum wage at 25 cents.

1940s-1950s *Debate intensifies over raising the minimum wage.*

1945 Democratic President Harry S. Truman proposes raising the minimum, calling it obsolete and an obstacle to rebuilding a peacetime economy.

1949 Congress raises minimum to $.75.

1955 Congress boosts the minimum to $1 following a wage-raise recommendation by President Dwight D. Eisenhower.

1960s-1970s *The minimum-wage movement flourishes during the John F. Kennedy-Lyndon B. Johnson years but then encounters opposition.*

1961 Newly inaugurated Kennedy, a Democrat, obtains congressional passage of a minimum-wage raise to $1.25 an hour.

1966 Johnson, Kennedy's Democratic successor, pushes legislation through Congress raising the minimum to $1.60 and extending coverage to 9.1 million more workers.

1972 With Republican President Richard M. Nixon in office, Congress kills an attempt to raise the minimum to $2 an hour.

1974 As the Watergate scandal saps Republican strength, Democrats boost minimum to $2.30 an hour.

1977 Congress raises minimum, to $3.35 but rejects automatic cost-of-living increases.

1980s-1990s *The political shift that elected Republican President Ronald Reagan to power contributes to the weakening of the wage-raise movement.*

1981 Reagan fires striking air-traffic controllers.

1988 Congressional Democrats propose raising the minimum to $5.15 an hour but, predicting failure, shelve the proposal.

1989 President George H.W. Bush ends a stalemate on wage increases by signing legislation raising the minimum to $4.25 an hour, with a lower, three-month "training wage" for entry-level teenagers.

1992 Economists David Card and Alan B. Krueger conclude minimum-wage raises don't cause unemployment.

1994 Baltimore enacts "living-wage" law.

1996 Clinton administration and congressional Democrats push a minimum-wage increase to $5.15 an hour through Congress.

2000s *Movements both for and against raising the minimum raise gather strength.*

2002 New Orleans voters approve a "living-wage" ordinance, which the Louisiana Supreme Court finds in violation of the state constitution.

2003 White House cites studies showing that minimum-wage hikes provoke "significant employment losses."

2004 Minimum wage of $8.50 an hour takes effect in Santa Fe, N.M.

Oct. 19, 2005 U.S. Senate rejects two proposed minimum-wage raises to $6.25 an hour, one proposed by Sen. Edward M. Kennedy, D-Mass. Earlier, on March 7, 2005, the Senate had voted down a Kennedy-proposed raise to $7.25 an hour, and a lower boost proposed by Sen. Rick Santorum, R-Pa.

to the federal minimum wage. And, to get the wage increase, supporters had to agree to shrink the number of workers covered by the law by 500,000 fewer than the original law.

New Deal Revived

In 1960, a Democratic senator from Massachusetts helped steer a minimum-wage increase through the Senate. Although the bill died in a House-Senate conference committee, partly due to a fight over how far to extend coverage, the senator held fast to the idea of raising the minimum. And when John F. Kennedy rose from the Senate to the White House in 1961, a minimum-wage increase was among his first proposals to Congress. It was part of a revived New Deal strategy of using government to help poor people improve their conditions.

On May 5, 1961, less than five months after taking office, Kennedy signed a bill launching a staged increase to $1, and then to $1.25, over four years. Equally important, the law expanded coverage to retail and service workers at companies with at least $1 million in annual gross sales — a longtime union demand.

Debate had centered on the business establishment's assertion that a raise — particularly above $1.15 an hour — would spur inflation, damage small businesses and spark unemployment. Some establishments would close, and others would substitute machine for human labor, the argument went. Pro-labor Democrats, meanwhile, argued that the economy was strong enough to handle bigger paychecks.

Kennedy's labor policies remained in force after he was assassinated on Nov. 22, 1963. His vice president, Lyndon B. Johnson, had begun his own rise to power during the New Deal, serving as Texas director of an unemployed-youth program and then using his credentials as a Roosevelt man to win a House race. As president, Johnson placed his "War on Poverty" at the top of his domestic agenda. One of his priorities was minimum-wage coverage of industries still excluded from the Fair Labor Standards Act's requirements. Johnson wanted workers at construction firms, hospitals and nursing homes, restaurants, taxi companies and food-processing companies covered by the law, and double-time pay for any hours worked beyond 48 in a week.

Johnson failed on his first attempt, in 1965, to get his proposals through Congress. But the former Senate majority leader used his legendary legislative skills to keep the issue alive. In 1966, he pushed through a bill that not only raised the $1.25 minimum to $1.60, in stages, but also extended coverage to an additional 9.1 million workers, including some farm workers. An AFL-CIO official called the legislation "the most important and best minimum-wage law that has ever been passed."

Uphill Fight

Despite Johnson's success, the unions and pro-labor Democrats who made up the wage-raise lobby didn't taste victory for another eight years. During that period Republican Richard M. Nixon was elected president in 1968 and again in 1972. That year, union allies lined up behind a bill to boost the hourly wage to $2 for non-farm workers and extend coverage to about 6 million more workers. The measure passed both chambers in different forms, but the House refused to send its version to a House-Senate conference, killing the bill. As the conflict played out, the anti-wage-raise coalition of Republicans and Southern Democrats found a new ally — McDonald's Hamburger, as the fast-food giant was then known.

Nixon and the anti-wage-raise bloc beat back another bill in 1973 that would have raised the minimum to $2.20 an hour. The bill actually passed, but its backers didn't have enough votes to override Nixon's veto.

Already, though, investigations of the political scandal known as Watergate were sapping the political strength of Nixon and his Republican comrades. In 1974 (the same year in which Nixon later resigned) wage-raise advocates reintroduced the wage-raise bill with a higher hourly rate — to $2.30 over two years. About 6 million workers, mostly domestics and government employees, would be newly covered. This time, congressional votes of 71-19 in the Senate and 245-50 in the House overwhelmed any possibility of veto.

Following Nixon's resignation and the electoral defeat of his vice president and successor, Gerald R. Ford, a Democrat once again occupied the White House. President Jimmy Carter, backed by the labor and civil-rights movements, saw boosting the minimum as a vital part of an anti-poverty strategy.

In their 1977 minimum-wage legislation, Carter and his allies had a bigger goal than simply boosting the hourly minimum. They hoped to end the periodic ritual of campaigning for minimum-wage increases. Instead, they advocated "indexing" — automatically raising the minimum every year to meet the rising cost of living.

Living-Wage Laws Face Hurdles

Since Baltimore passed a living-wage ordinance in 1994, some 130 cities have enacted similar laws to boost local wages above — often far above — the minimum wage. They range from small, liberal outposts like Santa Fe, N.M., and Burlington, Vt., to megacities like New York and Los Angeles. * [1]

But a powerful countermeasure known as state preemption is blocking city living-wage laws — and in some cases even minimum-wage laws — in a growing number of cities and counties. The conservative American Legislative Exchange Council (ALEC) is spearheading a campaign that scored its first victories in 1997, when Arizona and Louisiana passed the first so-called preemption laws barring local governments from setting their own wage requirements. Since then, nine other states have followed suit, including Georgia and Wisconsin in 2005. [2]

"State legislatures need the power to preempt local governments from enacting their own wage laws," ALEC declares. [3] The U.S. Chamber of Commerce credits the group with devising the preemption strategy, writing the template for such legislation and distributing a model bill to 3,000 state legislators. [4]

Living-wage ordinances typically require any companies with municipal contracts or subsidies to pay health benefits and a salary above the poverty line. In 2005, the federal government's poverty threshold for a family of four in the 48 contiguous states and Washington, D.C., is $19,350. [5]

Though living-wage beneficiaries make up a smaller group than minimum-wage workers, organizers see the living wage as a tool to spread prosperity to non-government workers as well. "Paying a living wage is a powerful way to stimulate demand and spur employment," a trio of labor scholars concluded two years ago. [6]

But opponents say living-wage laws cost too much for the relatively few workers who qualify. In Washington, for example, an economics columnist calculated that the city's proposed $11.75-an-hour wage requirement for city contractors would raise the pay for fewer than 2,000 workers, many of whom don't even live in the city. [7] Public-employee unions have used living-wage requirements, however, to defeat efforts to outsource their jobs to lower-paying firms both here and abroad. [8]

Despite the opposition, the living-wage movement has become a force to be reckoned with. And, given the continuing reluctance of Congress and many state legislatures to raise minimum wages, unions and other workers'-rights advocates are borrowing its strategy of working city-by-city.

Santa Fe's $8.50-an-hour living wage applies to all businesses (not just city contractors) with more than 25 employees. [9] And in Wisconsin, workers'-rights activists pushed municipal minimum-wage ordinances through city councils in Madison, Milwaukee, La Crosse and Eau Claire. [10]

Then the Republican-controlled legislature stepped in. GOP lawmakers — who had already barred Democratic Gov. Jim Doyle from raising the state minimum wage, in stages, to $6.50 an hour by executive order — moved to preempt local-government wage laws. Eventually, the two sides worked out a deal: Doyle signed the state preemption bill, and the legislature approved a statewide minimum-wage boost to $5.70 as of Jan. 1, 2006, and then to $6.50 an hour in June. [11]

---

* Other local-government entities and some private universities also have passed living-wage laws. Two of the earliest versions of such ordinances were enacted in Des Moines, Iowa, in 1988, and Gary, Ind., in 1991.

In 1977 Congress passed Carter's wage increase — to $3.35 by 1981. But indexing died, the victim of a lobbying campaign by service firms with big low-wage payrolls. Unions won a battle of their own, however, beating back an attempt to legislate a so-called "sub-minimum" for young, entry-level employees.

Ronald Reagan's electoral triumph in 1980 began a 12-year Republican revival following the Watergate debacle. The new president underscored what the Republican restoration meant for organized labor when he fired virtually all of the 11,500 federal air-traffic controllers who walked off their jobs in an illegal strike. [36]

The new era of weaker unions also saw the emergence of the new global economy. Unions' permanent campaign for higher pay, better working conditions and job protection was eroding as American wage-earners competed with Third World workers paid far below U.S. standards. [37]

In this climate, House Democrats in 1988 never even brought to the floor their bill to jack up the minimum to

But in more conservative Georgia, state preemption didn't come with a pay raise attached. In March, the legislature killed an Atlanta ordinance that gave preference in contract awards to companies paying their employees at least $10.50 an hour.

"The citizens of Georgia now can compete on an equal playing field for doing work with government agencies in their area," said state Rep. Earl Ehrhart, R-Powder Springs. "There will be no special preferences given. . . . People would rather have a job at $8 an hour than no job." [12]

The new state law "has put any sort of grassroots organizing in Atlanta at a disadvantage," acknowledges Jen Kern, director of the living-wage campaign of the Association of Community Organizations for Reform Now (ACORN). Earlier setbacks include a 2002 Louisiana Supreme Court ruling that threw out a $6.50-an-hour New Orleans minimum wage. Voters had approved the ordinance the same year, but the court said it intruded on the legislature's power. [13]

The state preemption pushback is only one reason for a slowdown in the living-wage campaign. "Most of the major cities with grassroots and labor organizing capacity already have these laws — Los Angeles, Boston, Detroit," Kern says.

Members of the Living Wage Coalition march in Atlanta's Martin Luther King Day parade in 2003.

[1] For the complete list, see, "Living Wage Successes," LivingWageResource Center, updated May, 2005, www.livingwagecampaign.org. For background, see Jane Tanner, "Living-Wage Movement," *CQ Researcher*, Sept. 27, 2002, pp. 771-790.

[2] Todd Richmond, "Minimum Wage Will Increase Wednesday," The Associated Press, *Wisconsin State Journal*, May 31, 2005, p. A1; Sonji Jacobs, "Legislature 2005: Senate votes to Kill Atlanta's Living Wage Law," *Atlanta Journal-Constitution*, March 30, 2005, p. 4B.

[3] "Talking Points: Living Wage," undated, American Legislative Exchange Council, www.alec.org/2/commerce-insurance-and-economic-developmment/talking-points/living-wage.html.

[4] Josh Ulman and John Leonard, "Living Wage: The Basics," U.S. Chamber of Commerce, Feb. 20, 2004, www.us chamber.com/issues/index/labor/livingwage.htm.

[5] Tanner, *op. cit.*, p. 771; "2005 Poverty Guidelines for the 48 Contiguous States and the District of Columbia," Department of Health and Human Services, http://aspe.hhs.gov/poverty/05fedreg.htm.

[6] Eileen Appelbaum, Annette Bernhardt and Richard J. Murnane, "Low-Wage America: An Overview," in Eileen Appelbaum *et al,, Low Wage America: How Employers Are Reshaping Opportunity in the Workplace* (2003), p. 27.

[7] Steven Pearlstein, "In Praise of Carol Schwartz," *The Washington Post*, Dec. 9, 2005, p. D1.

[8] Matt Lathrop, "Can America Survive on 'Living Wages?' " American Legislative Exchange Council, April 2001, www.alec.org/meSW Files/pdf/0103.pdf. For background, see Mary H. Cooper, "Exporting Jobs," *CQ Researcher*, Feb. 20, 2004, pp. 149-172.

[9] Martin Salazar and Mark Oswald, "Court Backs Living Wage," *Albuquerque Journal*, Nov. 30, 2005, p. A1.

[10] Richmond, *op. cit.*

[11] *Ibid*; Stacy Forster and Linda Spice, "Doyle, GOP agree on wage increase," *Milwaukee Journal-Sentinel*, May 12, 2005, p. A1.

[12] Jacobs, *op. cit.*

[13] Susan Finch and Rebecca Mowbray, "Wage Increase Rejected by Court," *Times-Picayune* (New Orleans), Sept. 5, 2002, p. A1.

$5.05 over three years, because they did not think they had the votes for passage. Their Senate colleagues failed to move a $4.55 wage bill past a Republican filibuster.

And when unions and the Democrats finally succeeded in pushing through a minimum-wage increase during the administration of Reagan's Republican successor, George H.W. Bush, the price was a major concession — creation of a sub-minimum "training wage" for teenagers — 85 percent of the new minimum for the first three months of employment for first-time workers (which expired in 1993). The minimum wage itself climbed to $4.25 over two years.

After Democrat Bill Clinton was elected president in 1992, his administration was rocked back on its heels by the loss of congressional control to the GOP in the 1994 midterm elections. The Republican sweep occurred as the U.S. economy was being transformed by globalization and new computer technology that was beginning to give many American workers the jitters. Although an economic boom was on the horizon, workers still smart-

CEOs Earn Far More Than Workers

The ratio of the average U.S. chief executive officer's salary to the average worker's pay was 185:1 in 2003, making the CEO's earnings 185 times the worker's salary. CEO pay reached its peak in the booming late 1990s and early 2000s, when it was 300 times the average work's pay. From 1992 to 2003, the median CEO received an 80.8 percent raise compared to an 8.7 percent hourly raise for the median worker. American CEOs make about three times as much as their counterparts abroad.

Ratio of CEO Pay to Average Worker's Pay

Source: Economic Policy Institute, "State of Working America, 2004-2005"

ing from the downsizing of the late 1980s tended to support raising the minimum wage. Republicans were leery of opposing them.

Meanwhile, a furious debate was under way within the economics and policy communities over a new way of looking at the effects of the minimum wage. Two economists, David Card of the University of California, Berkeley, and Princeton's Alan B. Krueger, set off the dispute when they sought to test the classical hypothesis that raising the minimum wage caused job loss.

Using data from a survey of fast-food restaurants in New Jersey and eastern Pennsylvania, and then government data from some 400 fast-food establishments in the same states, Card and Krueger concluded that a higher minimum wage did not cause employers to cut payrolls.

"It is always possible to find examples of employers who claim that they will go out of business if the minimum wage increases, or who state that they closed because of a minimum-wage increase," they wrote. "Our findings suggest that employment remains unchanged, or sometimes rises slightly, as a result of increases in the minimum wage." [38]

Card and Krueger viewed New Jersey and Pennsylvania as perfect test cases. New Jersey had raised its hourly minimum to $5.05, effective in 1992, giving it

the highest minimum wage in the country at the time. Pennsylvania's minimum remained at the federal level, then $4.25.

Other economists leaped to debunk the Card-Krueger study. Neumark, then at Michigan State University, and William Wascher, deputy associate director of the Federal Reserve Board, said Card and Krueger had used faulty data. Card and Krueger then used the government data to re-examine their hypothesis.

By 2000, side-by-side essays from both teams drew final conclusions. According to Card and Krueger, the increase in New Jersey's minimum wage "probably had no effect on total employment in New Jersey's fast-food industry, and possibly had a small positive effect." But, Neumark and Wascher concluded the minimum-wage increase "did not raise fast-food employment" in New Jersey. [39]

Significantly, however, Neumark and Wascher's findings did not support past business-sector claims that job loss would inevitably result from increasing the minimum wage, seemingly triggering newfound Republican hesitancy on the issue. In 1996, with Democrats determined to push passage of the first minimum-wage increase since 1991 and the first legislation on the issue since 1989, Congress raised the minimum to its current level, $5.15, over two years.

CURRENT SITUATION

Constitutional Right?

Advocates of raising the minimum wage are collecting signatures to place a $6.85-an-hour minimum wage proposal on the Ohio ballot in November 2006, led in part by the state AFL-CIO and ACORN.

Although the proposal is popular, it isn't bulletproof. Business lobbyists insist the proposal is fatally flawed because it requires an amendment to the state constitution. "It's going to be tough to sell people on amending the constitution," says John Mahaney, state president of the National

Federation of Independent Businesses. "Most people will feel it doesn't belong in the constitution. That's the Achilles' heel of the whole thing."

Katy Gall, state director of ACORN, says the constitutional route was chosen because it's simpler and faster than getting a law enacted by the legislature via a ballot initiative. An initiative requires first collecting signatures to submit the proposal to the legislature, then collecting signatures again if the measure doesn't pass. A state wage-raise proposal already failed this year, she noted. "And going to the legislature again gives them the opportunity to pass a smaller increase."

Wage-increase advocates in other states are also studying whether to take the constitutional-amendment route. Bob Schwartz, a Tucson lawyer who proposed that approach in Arizona, sees two advantages. "Once it passes, it's harder to change. And you need less language — ours says, 'This is a principle; the legislature should go ahead and do whatever is necessary to promote it.'"

The question of precisely how to increase the wage is especially pressing given the recent surprise defeat of a proposed increase to $7.50 an hour in Albuquerque. Opponents mounted a vigorous campaign aimed at a provision to give "any member of the public access to non-work areas" of a business to "inform employees of their rights under this ordinance and other laws." [40] The provision was aimed at allowing outsiders to come into a company to inform employees of their rights.

Carol Wight, CEO of the anti-raise New Mexico Restaurant Association, says the access issue "was definitely a crucial part of the win."

Some Layoffs Predicted in Pennsylvania

An estimated 3.1 percent of the 319,626 minimum-wage workers in Pennsylvania would lose their jobs if the hourly minimum wage were raised to $7.15, according to a study by the Commonwealth Foundation, which opposes minimum-wage increases. More than half of the layoffs would occur among employees under age 25, and 30 percent among employees with incomes under $25,000.

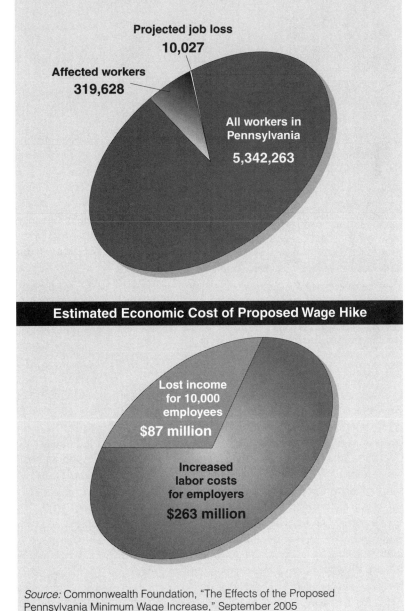

Source: Commonwealth Foundation, "The Effects of the Proposed Pennsylvania Minimum Wage Increase," September 2005

That prediction seems well-founded, especially given a pushback against living-wage city ordinances — which 11 states have now made illegal via so-called "preemption" laws. (*See sidebar, p. 154.*)

Action in New Mexico?

Republicans and businesses in New Mexico have already calculated the odds and the effects of increasing the state's minimum wage. "It's going to pass," says House Minority Leader Ted Hobbs, of Albuquerque, "and I think it will be a disaster across the state."

Gov. Bill Richardson, a Democrat, and House Speaker Ben Lujan, D-Santa Fe, say increasing the state minimum from the $5.15-an-hour federal level will be a top priority for the legislative session that begins in January 2006. Lujan says legislators are talking about possibly raising it to $7.50 an hour.

"It's unconscionable for anyone to offer a job to anyone at $5.15," Lujan says. "It's just not a wage that anybody can support their family on or even themselves." In any state, if federal and state minimum wages differ, the higher rate applies.

Given Democratic control of both legislative chambers, the Democrats are virtually certain to have their way on the matter, says Hobbs, a retired IBM executive. In addition, 75 percent of citizens polled by the *Albuquerque Journal* support raising the minimum wage, with 54 percent of respondents registering strong support. [41] Also, legislators will be meeting in Santa Fe, which has had a minimum wage of $8.50 an hour since 2004 for businesses employing at least 25 workers.

On Nov. 29, the New Mexico Court of Appeals rejected a challenge to the Santa Fe wage ordinance, after the local Chamber of Commerce and several businesses tried to have it declared invalid. [42]

Although Albuquerque — the state's biggest city — rejected a minimum-wage ordinance last October, New Mexico is clearly seen as friendly to increases in the minimum wage. "New Mexico has an image of being anti-business," says the restaurant association's Wight, also anticipating a wage raise. "And these kinds of laws certainly will not hurt that image."

Speaker Lujan notes that businesses didn't complain when the legislature in 2004 granted tax credits to businesses that pay salaries ranging from $28,000-$40,000 a year — more than double the minimum wage.

Getty Images/William Thomas Cain

Sen. Rick Santorum, R-Pa., chairman of the Senate Republican Conference, supports a hike in the minimum wage to $6.25 per hour. Last March he contrasted his approach to Sen. Edward M. Kennedy's proposed raise to $7.25. Santorum called his approach "surgical," saying Kennedy wanted to use a "blunt instrument."

Wage-raise advocates had been trying to ensure that all workers knew that the minimum had been boosted. But, asked whether omitting that section might have been a better idea, ACORN organizer Henderson acknowledges, "We didn't have to have it." But, his group was outfinanced. "Whether that provision was in the ordinance or not, the opposition was going to spend much more than we would and distort what we were saying."

The pro-raise side takes comfort in polls and other indicators showing strong public support. But business lobbyist Mahaney says public support may be broad, but it's not deep. "I haven't heard any great groundswell. Very few people make minimum wage."

All in all, Mahaney says, "This thing has more holes than Swiss cheese, and I assure you, sir, we will exploit each one."

Would raising the minimum wage harm the economy?

YES

Richard Berman
Executive Director, Employment Policies Institute

Written for *CQ Researcher*, December 2005

President Truman once quipped that he wanted a one-handed economist, since the economic advice he typically received took the unhelpful form of, "On the one hand . . . but on the other hand."

Since 1950, when Truman oversaw the biggest percentage increase in America's minimum wage, we have had a half-century of economic research that, unlike the Truman experience, has created a near-universal consensus among economists: From Federal Reserve Chairman Alan Greenspan on down, almost every expert in the field agrees that raising the minimum wage costs jobs. When it comes to the minimum wage, today's economists — with a few brave yet misguided exceptions — are all one-handed.

Here's the problem that isn't being addressed squarely in the minimum-wage debate: The government can tell an employer how much to pay someone, but it can't dictate who is hired. Increasing the cost of low-skilled labor encourages businesses to shed less productive employees. And while some job loss always occurs from a substantial wage hike, the displacement of low-skilled adults by literate high school kids is a more subtle and insidious effect. Unfortunately, a higher wage floor won't teach anyone to read, make change or show up for work on time.

While it's true that many minimum-wage earners already possess these skills, they quickly move up the wage ladder. Two-thirds earn a pay raise during the first year on the job. After improving skills, minimum-wage employees receive raises at a rate nearly six times higher than everyone else.

That leaves a small minority who lack the skills to justify a higher wage. "What happens to them when Congress passes a wage hike?" is the better question, not "What happens to the national economy?"

In fact, it's hard to believe that raising the minimum wage will have a real impact on the $12 trillion U.S. economy. It's the smaller universe of low-skilled adults who suffer the impact of employer rejection. These are the same people who can lose more in welfare than they gain after a small increase in taxable income. As President Bill Clinton suggested in 1992: "We can increase the Earned Income Tax Credit [EITC] by a couple of billion dollars a year and, far more efficiently than raising the minimum wage, lift the working poor out of poverty."

If you want to help alleviate poverty, don't look to the minimum wage. Think about increasing the EITC, which rewards work without killing learning opportunities.

NO

Jared Bernstein
Director, Living Standards Program, Economic Policy Institute

Written for *CQ Researcher*, December 2005

A moderate increase in the federal minimum wage would have little impact on the national economy. But it would help to close the gap between overall economic growth and low-wage working families' living standards.

The federal minimum wage has been raised 19 times since its inception in 1938. Eighteen states have minimum wages above the federal level. And more than 100 cities have living-wage laws, which require higher minimum salaries for workers at firms with city contracts or subsidies.

Thus, hundreds of "pseudo-experiments" — rare in empirical economics — have allowed us to test the impact of wage mandates. We can compare before and after, or, even better, compare nearby places that face similar economic conditions but have different minimum-wage laws. These studies have examined whether increases in the minimum wage lead to layoffs. Here's how Robert Solow, a Nobel laureate in economics, put it: "The evidence of job loss is weak. And the fact that the evidence is weak suggests that the impact on jobs is small."

A great example comes from the last federal minimum-wage increase, back in 1996-97. Massive job losses were predicted among those affected by the increase from $4.25 to the current level of $5.15. Instead, low-wage workers experienced the strongest job market in 30 years. Poverty fell to historic lows, particularly for the most disadvantaged workers — less-skilled minorities and single mothers.

Fast-forward to today, nearly 10 years later. The buying power of the minimum wage is down 17 percent. Only once since 1955 has the minimum been worth less, and that was in 1989, a year before it was raised.

According to those who oppose increasing the minimum, this erosion in the value of the minimum wage should be good for low-wage workers because as the minimum wage falls in real terms, minimum-wage workers are cheaper to employ, and thus employers should be hiring more of them. But the record during the current expansion shows just the opposite.

Wait, you're thinking, the latter 1990s was a boom, while the current period is bust-like, at least in terms of wage and income growth (and until recently, in terms of jobs, too). That's exactly my point. The minimum wage — raised in the mid-'90s and allowed to deteriorate in recent years — does not have a significant effect on the national economy. But it does help determine whether low-wage workers get a fair shake on payday.

At this point in the conflict, however, anti-wage-increase forces are moving past debating points to determine what to do after the almost-certain increases occur. "We want to be at the table talking about business incentives," Wight says.

The 1,100 restaurants she represents want protection against cities setting minimums higher than the state's, as well as a "training wage" for unskilled workers. The restaurants also would like the higher wages phased in gradually, so menu prices could go up slowly to reflect the higher labor costs.

Wight says, however, that when a city or state raises the minimum wage, it encourages lower-wage cities and

> **"It's unconscionable for anyone to offer a job to anyone at $5.15. It's just not a wage that anybody can support their family on or even themselves."**
>
> **— New Mexico Rep. Ben Lujan, D-Santa Fe**
> Speaker of the House

states to use their lower-wage status to "compete" for businesses and companies to relocate in the lower-wage communities or states. "When you make a minimum-wage island, you're pitting a New Mexico business against somebody in Texas. In Texas, they can pay lower wages, so why wouldn't a business go to Texas?" she asks.

Thus, the New Mexico restaurant industry says any increase in the minimum wage should be enacted by Congress, so it is effective nationwide. "Not that we believe that's a sound policy, economically, but if it's going to come from somewhere, it shouldn't be from state governments or localities," says Wight.

Wal-Mart Steps Up

The business giant that's usually the No. 1 target of unions and anti-corporate activists is now formally on their side — at least on one issue.

Wal-Mart Stores Inc. has added its voice to the generally liberal chorus calling for minimum-wage increases.

"The U.S. minimum wage . . . is out of date with the times," CEO H. Lee Scott told company directors and executives on Oct. 24. "We can see first-hand . . . how many of our customers are struggling to get by. We have seen an increase in spending on the 1st and 15th of each month and less spending at the end of the month, letting us know that our customers simply don't have the money to buy basic necessities between paychecks."

Scott spoke amid a rising tide of anti-Wal-Mart attacks and two weeks before the release of a documentary — "Wal-Mart: the High Cost of Low Price" — which accuses the company of taking advantage of its workers and crushing competitors. [43] "Wal-Mart is starting to feel some heat," says Robert L. Borosage, director of the Campaign for America's Future, a progressive research and advocacy organization. "Hopefully, that makes them more enlightened."

Whatever Wal-Mart's motives, does the country's biggest employer plan to push Congress to raise the minimum wage? "We've suggested for a lot of different reasons that Congress ought to take a look at a wage hike," says chief lobbyist Lee Culpepper, adding that Wal-Mart has yet to decide "if or how to be active on the issue."

Most of the company's critics haven't been expecting any action beyond Scott's speech. When asked at a Capitol Hill event promoting the documentary if Wal-Mart was serious about the minimum-wage issue, Sen. Kennedy smiled and said he didn't expect the company to be "enormously persuasive" on the matter, presumably because its motives would be questioned.

The company's own average wage is well above the minimum, at $9.68 an hour, which may have something to do with its position. [44] "My best reading is that they are by no means a low-wage employer, [but] their competition is," says economist Neumark of the Public Policy Foundation of California. "You want nothing more than to raise the wages of competitors."

Asked about the skepticism, lobbyist Culpepper says Scott's remarks were a "sincere sentiment being expressed by our CEO."

Whether or not Scott puts Wal-Mart's muscle behind a wage-raise bill, his remarks could give political cover to pro-business legislators who want to vote for a raise. However, Rob Green, vice president for federal relations at the National Restaurant Association says, "The jury is still out" on whether lobbying by Wal-Mart would affect the outcome.

OUTLOOK

The Price of Peace?

Kennedy and other advocates of raising the minimum wage are convinced that the wind is at their back. "We'll get this, I'm convinced, during the next year," says Kennedy.

Opponents are increasingly reluctant to speak out against the minimum wage, indicating that congressional sentiment is changing, says a Democratic Senate staffer. During the Oct. 19 floor debate on Kennedy's second and last attempt this year at inserting a minimum-wage-raise amendment into legislation, the staffer says, "We kept waiting and waiting for more people to come to the floor; they just don't want to speak against it."

Although there were enough votes to kill the measure — it failed 47-51 — only Senate Health, Education, Labor and Pensions Committee Chairman Enzi spoke out against it. While he backed a raise, he wanted more businesses exempt from paying a higher minimum and protection for small employers from what he said would be a major hike in payroll expenses.

"A 41 percent increase in labor costs forces a small-business person to face choices such as whether to increase prices, which often is not a choice, or face a potential loss of customers from lack of service or to reduce spending on health-insurance coverage or other benefits to employees or to terminate employees," Enzi said.

"If you look at recent votes in the Senate," says Green of the National Restaurant Association, "under the right circumstances, there would be passage." That's why Republicans insist on safeguarding smaller businesses, he explains.

In the House, the GOP leadership has better control of the agenda, making predictions about the future of the minimum-wage issue there much more speculative, Green says. In any case, given rising public interest in raising the minimum wage, there is every reason to expect the issue to surface in the 2006 congressional elections.

But advocates and opponents alike agree that deeper questions concerning the future of low-wage workers won't be resolved by relatively small increases in the hourly wage. Rather, they say, their future largely hinges on organized labor's fight for survival. In Ohio, Mahaney of the National Federation of Independent Business argues that minimum-wage advocates' real goal is to help unions in contract negotiations by raising the wage floor. "It's red meat for organized labor," he says.

In fact, three labor scholars argue, "A higher minimum wage would not only reduce the possibility that . . . firms will be undermined by competitors engaged in a race to the bottom but also reduce the incentives for sub-contracting and outsourcing to low-wage suppliers." [45]

The fundamental conclusion to be drawn after evaluating Americans' work lives is, "Choose your parents carefully," Boston University's Lang says sardonically. Serving as chair of the Brookline, Mass., school board has enabled Lang to examine the enormous role that socioeconomic background plays in determining indi-

> "It's going to pass, and I think it will be a disaster across the state."
>
> — **New Mexico Rep. Ted Hobbs, R-Albuquerque**
> House Minority Leader

vidual futures. "I'm upper-middle-class, so my kids have been told the rules of the game since they were *in utero*," Lang says. But African-American students have told him they had to pick up school and career advice from their friends. Class differences, school performance and job possibilities are inextricably linked to the minimum wage, Lang says, because most longtime low-wage workers invariably come from the bottom of the socioeconomic ladder.

Even some conservative commentators are starting to express concern that economic trends place low-wage workers at such risk that they could rebel. Christopher Caldwell, a senior editor at *The Weekly Standard*, a conservative news magazine, argues that raising the minimum wage shouldn't be seen anymore as a matter of economics. Referring to the strong tide on which the movement is riding, Caldwell writes, "It does not mean that, say, wrapping hamburgers is worth a dollar an hour more than we thought it was. But it may mean that social peace is." [46]

NOTES

1. Winthrop Quigley, "Voters Reject Minimum Wage Increase," *Albuquerque Journal*, Oct. 5, 2005, p. A1; "Unofficial Election Results for the City of Albuquerque," Bernalillo County Clerk, Oct. 4, 2005; www.bernco.gov/upload/images/clerk/city_05/complete Results.html.

2. The five were Connecticut, Hawaii, Minnesota, New Jersey and Wisconsin. For more information see "2005 Minimum Wage Bills," National Conference of State Legislatures, July 2005; www.ncsl.org/programs/employ/minimumwage 2005.htm; and "Minimum Wage Laws in the States — August 1, 2005," U.S. Department of Labor; www.dol.gov/esa/minwage/america.htm.

3. Department of Labor, *ibid.*

4. Forty-three percent of respondents categorized raising the minimum as a "top priority," and 39 percent classified it as an "important but lower priority." See "Bush Approval Lower Than for Other Two-Termers," Pew Research Center for the People & the Press, Jan. 13, 2005, p. 38; http://people-press.org/reports/pdf/235.pdf.

5. For background see Jane Tanner, "The Living Wage Movement," *CQ Researcher*, Sept. 27, 2002, pp. 771-790; for latest statistics, see, "Living Wage Successes," LivingWageResourceCenter, ACORN, updated May, 2005; www.livingwagecampaign.org/index.php?id=1958.

6. *Ibid.*

7. "Minimum Wage, Facts at a Glance," Economic Policy Institute, updated March 2005; www.epinet.org/content.cfm/issueguides_minwage_minwagefacts.

8. Richard V. Burkhauser and Joseph J. Sabia, "Raising the Minimum Wage: Another Empty Promise to the Working Poor," Employment Policies Institute, August 2005, p. 6; www.epionline.org/study_detail.cfm?sid=87&group=mw.

9. William J. Carrington and Bruce C. Fallick, "Do some workers have minimum wage careers?" *Monthly Labor Review*, May 2001, p. 17.

10. Kevin Lang, "Minimum Wage Laws and the Distribution of Employment," Employment Policies Institute, January 1995, p. 18; www.epionline.org/study_detail.cfm?sid=18.

11. "Economic Report of the President, 1999," pp. 111-112; www.gpoaccess.gov/eop/.

12. "Economic Report of the President, 2003," p. 120; www.gpoaccess.gov/eop/.

13. "State Minimum Wages and Employment in Small Businesses," Fiscal Policy Institute, April 20, 2004, pp. 6-10; www.fiscalpolicy.org.

14. Carrington and Fallick, *op. cit.*, pp. 17, 26.

15. Burkhauser and Sabia, *op. cit.*, pp. 28-29.

16. For 1995 percentages, see Jared Bernstein and John Schmitt, "Making Work Pay: The Impact of the 1996-97 Minimum Wage Increase," Economic Policy Institute, 1998, p. 6; www.epinet.org/content.cfm/studies_stmwp.

17. *Congress and the Nation*, Vol. IV, 1973-76, Congressional Quarterly, p. 415.

18. *Congress and the Nation*, Vol. X, 1997-2001, Congressional Quarterly, p. 798.

19. "Earned Income Tax Credits," National Conference of State Legislatures, undated (includes 2004 data); www.ncsl.org/statefed/WELFARE/eitc.htm#states.

20. Robert L. Greenstein, "The Earned Income Tax Credit: Boosting Employment, Aiding the Working Poor," Center on Budget and Policy Priorities, Aug. 27, 2005, cpbb.org; The Associated Press, "Earned Income Tax Program Unused by Many in Need," *Los Angeles Times*, April 12, 2004, p. C2.

21. "Poverty in the United States, Frequently Asked Questions," National Poverty Center, (undated); www.npc.umich.edu/poverty.

22. For background, see Christopher Conte, "Welfare, Work and the States," *CQ Researcher*, Dec. 6, 1996, pp. 1057-1080, and Sarah Glazer, "Welfare Reform," *CQ Researcher*, Aug. 3, 2001, pp. 601-632.

23. Carrington and Fallick, *op. cit.*, pp. 25-27.

24. Jared Bernstein, *et al.*, "The Minimum Wage Increase: A Working Woman's Issue," EPI Issue Brief, Economic Policy Institute, Sept. 16, 1999, p. 1; www.epinet.org/content.cfm/issuebriefs_ib133.

25. "Minimum Wage, Facts at a Glance," *op. cit.*

26. Aaron Bernstein, "Commentary: Minimum Wage: The States Get It," *BusinessWeek online*, Nov. 29, 2004; www.businessweek.com/print/magazine/content/04_48/b3910096_mz021.htm?chan=gl.

27. Ed Lazere, "New Findings From Oregon Suggest Minimum Wage Increases Can Boost Wages for Welfare Recipients Moving to Work," Center on Budget and Policy Priorities, May 29, 1998; www.cbpp.org/539ormw.htm.

28. For background, see Marcia Clemmitt, "Evaluating Head Start," *CQ Researcher*, Aug. 26, 2005, pp. 685, 708.

29. Unless otherwise indicated, this section is based on *Congress and the Nation*, Congressional Quarterly, Vols. I, 1945-1964; II, 1965-68; III, 1969-1972; IV, 1973-1976; V, 1977-1980; VI, 1981-1984; VII, 19885-1988; VIII, 1989-1992; IX, 1993-1996; X, 1997-2001; Jonathan Grossman, "Fair Labor Standards Act of 1938: Maximum Struggle for a Minimum Wage," Department of Labor; www.dol.gov/asp/programs/history/flsa1938.htm; James Mac Gregor Burns, *Roosevelt: The Lion and the Fox* (1956), pp. 143, 171, 180, 215-219, 342-344.

30. Text of the decision is at http://straylight.law.cornell.edu/supct/html/historics/USSC_CR_0295_0495_ZS.html.

31. Text of the decision is at http://straylight.law.cornell.edu/supct/html/historics/USSC_CR_0300_0379_ZO.html.

32. Grossman, *op. cit.*, p. 8.

33. Frank P. Huddle, "Minimum Wages," *Editorial Research Reports* [now *CQ Researcher*], Dec. 1, 1945, pp. 356-357.

34. *Ibid.*, p. 351.

35. *Ibid.*, p. 359.

36. Warren Brown and Martin Schram, "Reagan, Labor Chiefs Trade Peace Feelers," *The Washington Post*, Dec. 3, 1981, p. A1.

37. For background see Pamela Prah, "Labor Movement's Future," *CQ Researcher*, Sept. 2, 2005, pp. 709-732.

38. David Card and Alan B. Krueger, "Myth and Measurement: The New Economics of the Minimum Wage," 1995, p. 14.

39. David Neumark and William Wascher, "Minimum Wages and Employment: A Case Study of the Fast-food Industry in New Jersey and Pennsylvania: Comment"; David Card and Alan B. Krueger, "Reply," *American Economic Review*, Vol. 90, No. 5, December 2000, pp. 1362-1420; www.econ.jhu.edu/people/Barnow/neumarmw.pdf; www.irs.princeton.edu/krueger/90051397.pdf.

40. Quigley, *op. cit.*

41. *Ibid.*

42. Martin Salazar and Mark Oswald, "Santa Fe Living Wage Confirmed," *Albuquerque Journal*, Nov. 30, 2005, p. A1.

43. For background see Brian Hansen, "Big-Box Stores," *CQ Researcher*, Sept. 10, 2004, pp. 735-754.

44. Amy Joyce and Ben White, "Wal-Mart Pushes to Soften Its Image," *The Washington Post*, Oct. 29, 2005, p. D1.

45. Eileen Appelbaum, Annette Bernhardt and Richard J. Murnane, "Low-Wage America: An Overview," in Appelbaum, *et al.*, eds., *Low-Wage America: How Employers Re Reshaping Opportunity in the Workplace* (2003), p. 24.

46. Christopher Caldwell, "The social logic of a living wage," *Financial Times* (London), Oct. 22, 2005, p. 11.

BIBLIOGRAPHY

Books

Appelbaum, Eileen, Annette Bernhardt and Richard J. Murnane, eds., *Low-Wage America: How Employers Are Reshaping Opportunity in the Workplace*, Russell Sage Foundation, 2003.
The editors have compiled detailed, research-based essays on decreasing upward mobility in the low-wage sector of the economy. The overall perspective is in favor of a "living wage."

Card, David, and Alan B. Krueger, *Myth and Measurement: The New Economics of the Minimum Wage*, Princeton University, 1995.
Economists from the University of California, Berkeley (Card), and Princeton (Krueger) rejected the classic theory

that jobs become scarcer when the wage floor rises, igniting a still-ongoing debate over the effects of increasing the minimum wage on job availability. Their main critics, David Neumark and William Wascher, have written journal articles (see below), but no book.

Articles

Bernstein, Nina, "Family Needs Far Exceed the Official Poverty Line," *The New York Times*, Sept. 13, 2000, p. B1.
Economic realities have overtaken the methodology used for calculating who lives in poverty, and the minimum wage alone isn't enough to keep a family above the poverty line.

Caldwell, Christopher, "The social logic of a living wage," *Financial Times*, Oct. 22, 2005, p. 11.
A conservative writer for a London daily argues that raising wage minimums may provide insurance against social unrest.

Gosselin, Peter G., "If America is Richer, Why Are its Families So Much Less Secure?" *Los Angeles Times*, Oct. 10, 2004, p. A1.
Gosselin argues in a lengthy, anecdote-rich piece that the minimum wage's declining value relative to average pay is an indicator of how social safety nets are vanishing.

Henderson, Nell, "Skilled Labor in High Demand; Employers Lament Declining Ranks of Capable Workers," *The Washington Post*, Aug. 25, 2004, p. E1.
Jobs are going begging at the higher end of the pay scale, while skills — and wages — further down the ladder are stagnating.

Joyce, Amy, "Wal-Mart Chief Says Customers Need Increase in Minimum Wage," *The Washington Post*, Oct. 26, 2005, p. D2.
Wal-Mart Chief Executive H. Lee Scott Jr. asked Congress to raise the minimum wage, saying that his workers — who are also his customers — did not have enough money to buy basic necessities between paychecks.

Micklethwait, John, and Adrian Woolridge, "A Little Americanization Can Fix Europe's Economic Misery," *Los Angeles Times*, May 16, 2005, p. B11.

Two British journalists argue that Western Europe's labor laws — including high minimum wages in France and Germany — have contributed to poor productivity and competitiveness.

Weisman, Jonathan, "Measuring the Economy May Not Be as Simple as 1, 2, 3," *The Washington Post*, Aug. 29, 2005, p. A2.
Gauging the extent of poverty — which is important to the minimum-wage debate — is more complicated than most people have been led to believe, economists conclude.

Reports and Studies

Adams, Scott, and David Neumark, "A Decade of Living Wages: What Have We Learned?" *California Economic Policy* (quarterly journal of the Public Policy Institute of California), Vol., 1, No. 3, July 2005.
Leading critics of raising the minimum wage conclude that living-wage ordinances reduce poverty but shrink the job opportunities of low-skilled individuals.

Chapman, Jeff, "Employment and the Minimum Wage: Evidence from Recent State Labor Market Trends," *Briefing Paper*, Economic Policy Institute, May 11, 2004.
A staff economist at a liberal think tank examines employment data and concludes that minimum-wage increases do not result in major job losses.

Neumark, David, and William Wascher, "Minimum Wages and Employment: A Case Study of the Fast-Food Industry in New Jersey and Pennsylvania: Comment," *American Economic Review*, Vol. 90, No. 5, December 2000, pp. 1362-1396.
Two economists provide a detailed rebuttal of the Card-Krueger thesis that minimum-wage raises do not increase unemployment.

Yelowitz, Aaron S., "Santa Fe's Living Wage Ordinance and the Labor Market," *Employment Policies Institute*, Sept. 23, 2005.
A University of Kentucky economist concludes that Santa Fe's municipal minimum wage caused the unemployment rate in New Mexico's capital city to jump 3.2 percentage points.

For More Information

American Legislative Exchange Council, 1129 20th St., N.W., Suite 500, Washington, DC 20036; (202) 466-3800; www.alec.org. The bipartisan association for conservative state lawmakers supports state "preemption" legislation that outlaws municipal "living-wage" and minimum-wage ordinances.

Economic Policy Institute, 1333 H St., N.W., Suite 300 East Tower, Washington, DC 20005; (202) 775-8810; www.epi.org. A think tank with ties to organized labor that is a main source of research and analysis for advocates of raising the minimum wage.

Employment Policies Institute, 1775 Pennsylvania Ave., N.W., Suite 1200, Washington, DC 20006-4605; (202) 463-7650; www.epionline.org. A nonprofit think tank funded partially by businesses that serves as a main research center for opponents of raising the minimum wage.

Living Wage Resource Center, 88 3rd Ave., Brooklyn, NY 11217; (718) 246-7900, ext. 230; www.livingwagecampaign.org. The Association of Community Organizations for Reform Now (ACORN) set up the center as a hub for "living-wage" movements nationwide.

Raising the National Minimum Wage: Information, Opinion, Research, www.raiseminwage.org. The Web site posts documents from both sides of the minimum-wage debate.

U.S. Department of Labor, Employment Standards Administration, Wage and Hour Division, Frances Perkins Building, 200 Constitution Ave., N.W., Washington, DC 20210; 1-866-4-USAWAGE; www.dol.gov/esa/minwage/america.htm. Maintains the most up-to-date information on federal and state minimum wages.

8

Domestic Energy Development

Jennifer Weeks

A sign warns about health dangers associated with an oil drilling operation in the Los Padres National Forest, Calif. Public concerns about potential, negative health and environmental impacts from oil and gas exploration have helped block energy production on many public lands in the West — pitting the nation's energy needs against the need for environmental preservation.

WARNING

DETECTABLE AMOUNTS OF CHEMICALS KNOWN TO THE STATE OF CALIFORNIA TO CAUSE CANCER, BIRTH DEFECTS, OR OTHER REPRODUCTIVE HARM MAY BE FOUND IN AND AROUND THIS FACILITY.

(PROPOSITION 65, CALIFORNIA HEALTH AND SAFETY CODE SECTION 25249.5 et seq.)

Getty Images/David McNew

From *CQ Researcher*, September 30, 2005.

I n August, when Hurricane Katrina devastated thousands of acres in Louisiana, Alabama and Mississippi in one of the largest natural disasters in U.S. history, its impact was not limited to the Gulf Coast. Katrina's legacy will be felt nationwide for months to come because it destroyed or damaged dozens of offshore and onshore facilities that supply the nation with oil and natural gas.

The storm destroyed four offshore drilling rigs in the Gulf of Mexico, severely damaged nine others and set six rigs adrift. [1] Power outages and damage from Katrina's winds shut down four Gulf Coast oil refineries with a combined capacity of nearly 800,000 barrels per day — plants that are not expected to resume operation for several months. [2]

In addition, damage to transmission pipelines, import terminals and local electricity systems (which power many oil and gas facilities) shut down a quarter of the nation's domestic oil production and 16 percent of natural gas production. [3] Since oil and gas account for more than 60 percent of America's energy consumption, the impact has been rapid and far-reaching.

Even before Katrina blew ashore, growing world energy demand, unstable political situations in some producer countries and shortages of domestic refining and delivery capacity had already pumped up domestic oil and gas prices to record levels. World crude more than doubled from $22 per barrel in 2001 to $52 in mid-2005; the U.S. wellhead price for natural gas tripled — from $1.95 per thousand cubic feet in 1998 to $6.15 in June 2005. [4]

With production sharply cut back following Katrina, regular gasoline prices shot up by as much as 61 cents per gallon, peaking at $3.07 per gallon on average nationwide on Sept. 6. [5] A jump in

Offshore Drilling May Expand

Offshore leases account for nearly 30 percent of U.S. oil production and 20-25 percent of America's natural gas, with output expected to increase as technology improves. States have jurisdiction over energy development up to three miles from their coastlines; the federal government controls the Outer Continental Shelf (OCS) from the three-mile limit to 200 miles offshore. Current restrictions ban oil exploration in most national marine sanctuaries (NMS) and limit new oil and gas leases to some Alaskan coastal waters and the western Gulf of Mexico.

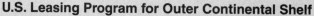

U.S. Leasing Program for Outer Continental Shelf

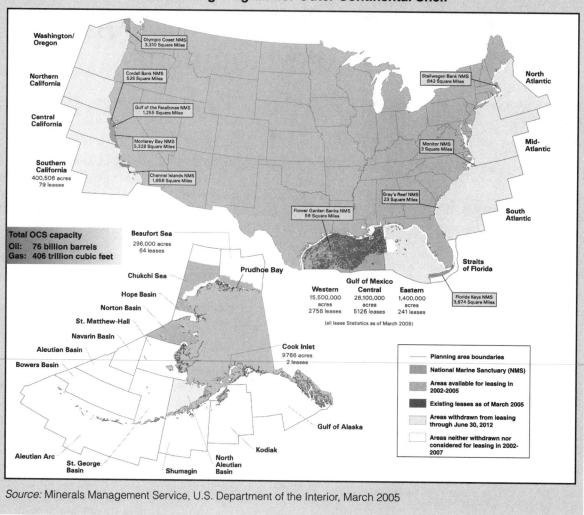

Source: Minerals Management Service, U.S. Department of the Interior, March 2005

jet fuel prices forced already ailing Northwest and Delta airlines over the edge into bankruptcy.

Three weeks later, Hurricane Rita dealt a second, less severe blow to Gulf energy facilities, shutting down about two dozen oil refineries in east Texas and western Louisiana along with several pipelines that deliver oil and gas to other regions. Many of the refineries restarted within several days after the storm passed, but because most Gulf coast energy facilities had shut down as Rita approached, temporary fuel shortages developed in parts of the South.

The Bush administration responded to the hurricanes by releasing oil from the U.S. Strategic Petroleum Reserve, waiving laws that required the use of special clean-burning gasoline blends in many U.S. cities. President Bush also called on Americans to conserve fuel by eliminating unnecessary driving.

"We can all pitch in by . . . being better conservers of energy," Bush said in a speech on Sept. 26, as he called for construction of more energy facilities to meet demand. "The storms have shown how fragile the balance is between supply and demand in America."

As winter approaches, Americans are due for another price shock — a dramatic rise in home heating bills. The Department of Energy projects that U.S. oil prices will increase by 34 percent and natural gas prices by 52 percent over last year's levels. Total U.S. energy spending in 2005 is expected to top $1 trillion — the highest share of national economic output since 1985. [6]

Aside from higher transportation and heating bills, rising energy costs are expected to trigger price hikes for travel, shipping and petrochemical by-products such as nylon, plastics and fertilizer. "The price of natural gas has had a significant negative impact on manufacturers that compete globally," says Paul Cicio, executive director of the Industrial Energy Consumers of America (IECA). For example, he says, about 80 percent of the cost of making plastics is the cost of ingredients, including natural gas.

Oil and Gas Reserves Concentrated in a Few Areas

Four regions contain more than three-quarters of the known U.S. crude oil reserves (top). Six areas hold nearly three-quarters of the proven natural gas reserves (bottom). Oil and gas developers, citing high fuel prices and technical advances in production, support opening more public lands and undersea areas to exploration. Conservationists counter that investing in energy efficiency and renewable fuels will do more to moderate energy prices and reduce U.S. dependence on foreign sources.

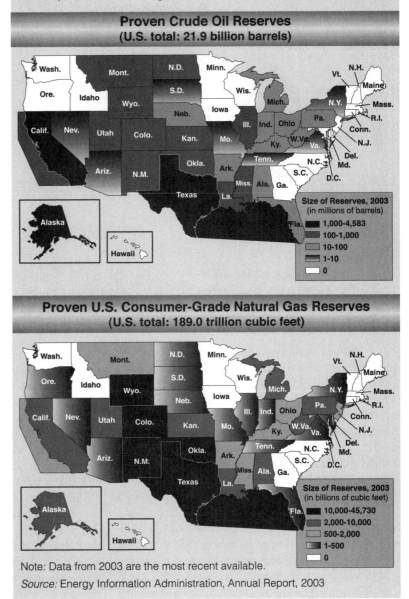

Note: Data from 2003 are the most recent available.

Source: Energy Information Administration, Annual Report, 2003

Katrina Disrupts Oil and Gas Supply

Petroleum and natural gas supply more than 60 percent of America's energy needs. Energy costs have risen dramatically in the wake of Hurricane Katrina, which damaged offshore oil platforms and other production facilities, cutting domestic oil production by 26 percent and natural gas production by 16 percent.

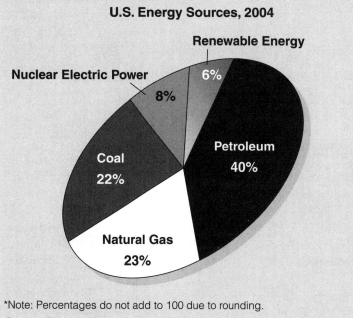

U.S. Energy Sources, 2004

Renewable Energy 6%

Nuclear Electric Power 8%

Petroleum 40%

Coal 22%

Natural Gas 23%

*Note: Percentages do not add to 100 due to rounding.

Source: "Monthly Energy Review," Energy Information Administration, August 2005

Low domestic gas prices have historically given U.S. manufacturers a competitive advantage over foreign companies. But Cicio says that advantage "has eroded in recent years, and we have lost thousands of manufacturing jobs." Today, natural gas is far more expensive in the United States than anywhere else in the world, because gas-rich countries like Russia and Algeria have larger deposits and the United States has only a few terminals for importing gas from overseas.

As for oil, the United States consumes more petroleum products (including heating oil, gasoline and other fuels) than any other country — 20 million barrels a day in 2004, or nearly a quarter of all oil produced worldwide. [7] Of that total, only 7.2 million barrels were produced domestically — a 50-year low. [8] To make matters worse, the United States is increasingly competing with emerging economies

like China and India for world oil supplies. Chinese oil consumption, for instance, has jumped from less than 5 million barrels a day in 2000 to 6.6 million barrels today. [9]

"We're talking about competition between the major consuming countries of today and the consuming countries of tomorrow," said Phil Flynn, an oil analyst and trader for Alaron Options and Futures in Chicago. "Just a few years ago China was exporting oil and . . . all of a sudden they're now the No. 2 importer in the world." [10]

Meanwhile, many oil producers are dealing with domestic and international political pressures. Authoritarian governments in Venezuela and Nigeria have been accused of failing to share national oil wealth with their citizens, and terrorists have targeted oil facilities in Bahrain, Iraq, Saudi Arabia and other Persian Gulf states.

In response to these pressures, President Bush has made boosting domestic oil and gas production the central pillar of his National Energy Policy, released in May 2001, specifically by calling for opening up public lands and offshore areas for exploration. [11]

"Our dependence on foreign energy is like a foreign tax on the American people," President Bush said in April 2005. "It's a tax our citizens pay every day in higher gasoline prices and higher costs to heat and cool their homes. It's a tax on jobs and it's a tax that is increasing every year." [12]

Among the areas Bush wants to open up for drilling is the pristine Arctic National Wildlife Refuge (ANWR), an area environmentalists have successfully lobbied to keep off-limits to oil development for decades. [13] This debate has come to embody the choice between energy production and environmental preservation, an issue on which the public remains deeply divided. (*See poll, p. 181.*)

"That's where the oil is. Historically, oil has come from onshore, but there aren't a lot of targets left in the Lower 48 — the traditional areas have been very intensively drilled," says Edward Porter, senior economist at the American Petroleum Institute (API). "That's forced us to go to new areas and to look to unconventional sources." (*See map, p. 169.*)

Environmentalists and renewable-energy advocates, on the other hand, say investing in greater energy efficiency and more use of renewable fuels will do more to moderate energy prices and reduce U.S. dependence on unstable foreign sources. "There is really nothing that can be done to change the fundamental geophysics of oil production in North America, and study after study has shown that we can clearly increase fuel economy by 30 to 50 percent, cost-effectively, within several decades without costing American jobs," says Bill Prindle, deputy director of the American Council for an Energy-Efficient Economy (ACEEE).

Environmentalists argued that Bush's energy plan was tilted towards production rather than conservation because of oil and gas industry influence on the administration. Both Bush and Vice President Dick Cheney are former oil executives. The administration's energy task force headed by Cheney, they pointed out, held numerous meetings with energy companies while developing an energy plan, but almost none with environmentalists or conservationists.

After the administration refused to disclose the names of those who met with the task force, several advocacy groups sued the administration, arguing that the names should be made public because the companies had effectively become members of a government task force. But in May the Supreme Court said the White House did not have to disclose the names of those it consulted on energy policy.

Although the names of task force participants are not public record, the energy industry's influence on politics is: It has donated at least $220 million to political campaigns since 1998, with three-fourths going to Republicans. [14]

Hunting and fishing enthusiasts also worry that expanded domestic oil and gas production may permanently damage public lands. "Open space and wild lands are diminishing throughout the West, and we're concerned that oil and gas development will accelerate that process," says Corey Fisher, Western field organizer for Trout Unlimited. "Science isn't keeping pace with energy development in the West. We need more thorough data collection and analysis of how oil and gas pro-

duction is affecting critical areas, so that we can quantify the impacts and take steps to reduce them."

New refineries, plants, pipelines and terminals are needed to meet rising domestic demand, but states and communities often are concerned about the impact on safety, the environment and property values. Balancing local priorities against the need for new energy facilities invariably stirs controversy.

Indeed, no new oil refineries have been built in the United States since 1976, mainly because the highly competitive refining industry works with small profit margins and has come under increasingly strict environmental restrictions in recent years. Although many existing refineries have been expanded to meet rising demand, they are already working at or near full capacity.

Suppliers of natural gas, meanwhile, say they need thousands of miles of new pipelines and additional liquefied natural gas (LNG) terminals to receive international shipments. LNG is natural gas that has been chilled to minus-260 degrees Fahrenheit to liquefy it for shipping. It accounts for only about 2 percent of U.S. gas use today, but is projected to represent 20 percent by 2020. [15] The United States currently has four operating LNG terminals, but more than 50 new facilities have been proposed at locations in North America, Mexico and the Caribbean. Many face stiff local opposition.

As the nation worries about energy supplies and prices in the wake of two devastating hurricanes, here are some of the issues being debated:

Will boosting domestic production help solve U.S. energy problems?

To increase America's energy independence and lower prices, many policymakers want to increase domestic oil and gas production, while others want to reduce consumption.

U.S. energy developers agree that conservation is important, but they also say increasing domestic production is essential — both to ease prices and to reduce America's vulnerability to volatile world energy markets. In their view, significant deposits of oil and gas remain untapped in the United States, particularly in the Rocky Mountains and Alaska and beneath deep coastal waters. But overly restrictive environmental limits on energy development, they argue, are widening the gap between energy supply and demand, putting America at the mercy of both skyrocketing prices and uncertain supplies.

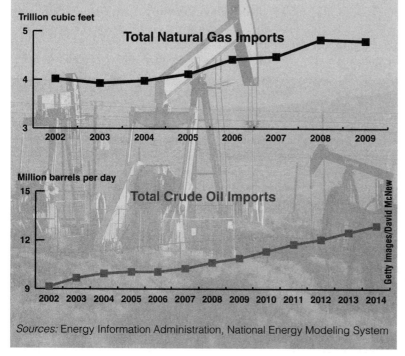

Energy Imports to Continue Rising

Despite recent efforts by the Bush administration to increase domestic energy production, U.S. imports of natural gas and oil will continue to increase.

Trillion cubic feet

Total Natural Gas Imports

5

4

3

2002   2003   2004   2005   2006   2007   2008   2009

Million barrels per day

Total Crude Oil Imports

15

12

9

2002 2003 2004 2005 2006 2007 2008 2009 2010 2011 2012 2013 2014

Sources: Energy Information Administration, National Energy Modeling System

Getty Images/David McNew

The federal Energy Information Administration (EIA) projects that increased U.S. oil and gas production would reduce energy prices over the short term — perhaps for the next five years — but after that prices will increase because remaining domestic deposits will be more remote and expensive to develop. [16] And even if production could be increased, say many analysts, it would do little to lower prices over the long term, particularly for oil, because oil prices are set in international markets.

"U.S. exposure to world oil price shocks is a function of the amount of oil it consumes and is not significantly affected by the ratio of domestic to imported product," said the bipartisan National Commission on Energy Policy. [17]

Industry representatives say obtaining more oil from domestic sources would reduce America's vulnerability to foreign governments that may manipulate prices (as Arab countries did in 1973 when they cut off exports to the United States). Increased domestic production "is not going to have a big impact on world oil prices, but it increases the diversity of supply, which is the key point about development," says API's Porter. "Not producing U.S. resources makes us more dependent on suppliers who are less reliable."

Environmentalists say conserving energy is a better way to reduce fuel costs and make America more energy-secure. For example, upgrading the quality of replacement automobile tires could save 7.3 billion barrels of oil over the next 50 years — one-third more oil than the amount available from the ANWR in the same time frame, according to the Natural Resources Defense Council (NRDC). And increasing automobile fuel efficiency to 40 miles per gallon by 2015 would save 60 billion barrels of oil over 50 years — more than 11 times the likely yield from ANWR, the group says. [18]

But Porter says ANWR's potential is too large to leave untapped. "If ANWR contains 10 billion barrels, it would be one of the biggest single discoveries in North America."

Increased domestic production would have a greater impact on natural gas prices, because gas is not yet traded in one unified international market, according to the IECA's Cicio. "Natural gas is priced regionally," so increased domestic development would lower U.S. natural gas prices, he says.

But environmentalists note that more than 80 percent of oil and gas reserves on public lands are already open to energy development, and the remaining areas — such as lands that are restricted seasonally to protect wildlife populations — have unique ecological and historical value that should be preserved. [19]

"A vast amount of federal acreage is under lease," says Dave Alberswerth, director of the Wilderness Society's program that monitors the Bureau of Land Management (BLM). "The BLM issued so many drilling permits in 2004 that the industry can't keep up with them. The West is experiencing an unprecedented boom in energy development, and the gas industry in particular is riding high."

Federal law requires that public lands be managed to promote multiple goals, including ecological, cultural and historic preservation as well as mineral extraction. But conservation advocates say the Bush administration is making oil and gas development a top priority at the expense of the other goals — for example, by leasing lands being considered for protection as wilderness areas. [20]

Sometimes those trade-offs are being made for little long-term gain, environmentalists say. For instance, if ANWR were opened to oil development, drilling would not begin until 2013 and peak about a decade later, according to the EIA. At that point, ANWR oil would only reduce the share of U.S. oil coming from imported sources from 70 percent to about 66 percent. And oil-producing countries could reduce output to offset the increased flow of U.S. oil, the EIA notes, preventing ANWR oil from significantly affecting world oil prices. [21]

Conservationists say energy efficiency measures could help reduce long-term energy prices and ease the stress on the nation's refineries and transmission lines, potentially eliminating the need to build expensive new facilities. As for natural gas, "Prices could be reduced by as much as 30 percent over a five-year time frame through cost-effective, energy-efficient technologies and practices that would reduce energy demand by about 1 percent annually," says Prindle, of the American Council for an Energy-Efficient Economy. "[That would] give you a huge price leverage."

Prindle says improved efficiency standards for appliances and programs to help electric power users reduce consumption "produce major natural gas savings, [because] when you save a unit of electricity, you save several units of gas at the power plant because some fuel is wasted in generation."

The Bush administration initially was skeptical about adopting energy-efficiency measures. Notably, Vice President Cheney commented in a 2001 speech that "Conservation may be a sign of personal virtue, but it is not a sufficient basis for a sound, comprehensive energy policy." More recently, however, President Bush has supported energy efficiency and renewable-energy measures as part of his efforts to press Congress for broad energy legislation.

But Bush has not suggested increasing automobile fuel efficiency, and it was not part of the just-enacted energy legislation. U.S. automakers have resisted increases in fuel-efficiency standards for passenger cars, which have not changed since 1985, claiming that

AP Photo/Pat Sullivan

Drilling in the Gulf of Mexico produces 29 percent of America's oil and 19 percent of its gas, most of it stored and processed in extensive onshore facilities, such as this complex near Houston. Although Hurricane Rita did not cause the widespread destruction of the energy infrastructure that many had feared, some experts wonder if it is wise to continue relying so heavily on oil and gas from the hurricane-prone region.

tougher regulations will make U.S. cars — particularly the highly profitable sport utility vehicles (SUVs) and pickup trucks — less competitive with foreign models, eventually costing America jobs.

Appliance standards, on the other hand, are "something that industry and advocates can agree on," says Prindle of ACEEE.

Should the United States allow new offshore drilling?

With onshore production in the Lower 48 states declining, energy companies want more coastal areas opened to oil and gas development, pointing out that advanced seismic exploration and drilling technologies greatly reduce the environmental impact of offshore production.

"When we began placing coastal areas off-limits to energy development in 1981, many of the technologies we use today were not available — and perhaps not even imagined," Charles Davidson, president of the Gulf Coast exploration company Noble Energy, told the Senate Energy Committee on April 19. "Today we have an important opportunity to focus on the future — and different policies that may allow careful consideration of offshore energy activity in select areas — building on exciting technology improvements." [22]

Currently, nearly 30 percent of U.S. oil and 20-25 percent of natural gas come from offshore wells. But those percentages are expected to rise, because the Outer Continental Shelf (OCS) holds an estimated 76 billion barrels of oil and 406 trillion cubic feet of natural gas recoverable with existing technology. [23] By comparison, the United States has proven oil reserves of only 22 billion barrels of oil and 189 trillion cubic feet of dry natural gas in land reserves and offshore deposits already open to leasing. [24]

Energy companies first drilled off the coast of California more than a century ago and later began exploring in the Gulf of Mexico. States oversee offshore energy development up to three miles from their coastlines, and the federal government controls the OCS — the area from the state three-mile limit to 200 miles offshore. After a major oil spill off the coast of Santa Barbara, Calif., in 1969, coastal states demanded more influence over offshore oil and gas leasing, which they feared would cause pollution and deflate property values. As a result, since 1981 the federal government has placed portions of the OCS off-limits to energy developers through 2012. Thus, new oil and gas leases are available today only in some Alaskan coastal waters and in the western Gulf of Mexico. (*See map, p. 168.*)

The Energy Policy Act of 2005, signed by President Bush in August, requires the Interior Department to conduct an inventory of offshore energy resources, using seismic testing (powerful air guns that locate undersea deposits using shock waves) in order to verify estimates of how much oil and gas may be available in areas not currently open to drilling. Environmental advocates fear that, especially in the wake of Katrina and Rita, Congress may consider going further and relaxing current moratoria to expand energy production into new areas less vulnerable to storm damage. "This 'inventory' is the first step towards opening our coast up to future oil drilling," Mark Massara, director of the Sierra Club's Coastal Campaign, wrote in early September. [25]

Energy companies cite their successes in the Gulf of Mexico as evidence that much more oil and gas can be produced offshore. "We have produced three times what we thought existed in 1974 — and we now estimate almost five times more remaining. The more we explore, the more we know," Noble's Davidson told the Senate Energy Committee. [26] A growing share of that offshore production comes from so-called deepwater deposits — those at least 1,312 feet deep — thanks in part to tax incentives Congress passed in 1995. Energy companies now work in depths up to 10,000 feet in the Gulf of Mexico, where operations require more sophisticated technologies and expertise than in shallower waters.

Despite increased levels of drilling, the rate and size of accidents related to offshore oil production has been declining since the 1970s, according to the National Research Council (NRC). In 2002 only 9 million barrels of petroleum products were being spilled or leaked into North American waters each year, down sharply from the 43 million barrels per year spilled in 1975. Offshore oil and gas development is responsible for only 2 percent of those spills. Natural seepage and municipal and industrial waste account for the bulk. Between 1971 and 2000, the median OCS spill was only three barrels, according to the Interior Department. [27]

The Interior Department says Hurricane Katrina did not produce any significant spills from offshore oil platforms, but 7.4 million gallons of oil spilled from onshore storage tanks and pipelines in coastal Louisiana, according to the Coast Guard. [28] At several refineries, tanks holding thousands of gallons of oil were lifted off their bases and ruptured, spilling oil into surrounding areas. Offshore producers are still assessing damage to thousands of undersea pipelines that carry oil from wells under the ocean floor to storage sites on land.

Initial reports indicated Hurricane Rita caused no additional large oil spills, possibly because the storm did not directly strike Houston with its heavy concentration of refineries and petrochemical plants.

Environmentalists say the damage and vulnerability the hurricanes exposed in the nation's energy underbelly further demonstrate the need to tighten up auto fuel-efficiency standards.

They also argue that spills are not the biggest problem with offshore drilling.

"Energy companies like to talk about how oil spills have become smaller and less frequent, but oil spills are probably the least of the impacts," says Lisa Speer, senior policy analyst with the Natural Resources Defense Council. "You only have to look at the Gulf Coast of Louisiana to see how onshore infrastructure, such as pipelines, transfer stations and roadways industrialize coastal areas. And the noise pollution from seismic exploration is harmful to marine mammals that use sound to communicate."

However, energy developers emphasize that new technologies such as directional drilling and improved navigation systems have made offshore oil and gas production much more environmentally friendly. The API says offshore oil platforms serve as resting sites for migrating birds and butterflies, and some decommissioned rigs have been converted to artificial reefs that are now centers for recreational fishing.

But Speer and other environmentalists contend that opening new offshore areas to leasing is unnecessary because, according to the Interior Department's Minerals Management Service, 80 percent of undiscovered offshore natural gas and 60 percent of offshore oil reserves that are economically recoverable are in areas already open to leasing. Especially in light of damage from Hurricane Katrina, they argue, opening new areas to drilling would simply increase environmental risks for little energy gain. "It's hard to imagine a more reckless response to a hurricane that generated major oil spills," says Speer.

Oil producers maintain that the correct response to hurricane damage is to diversify by developing resources in other regions. In a statement on Aug. 31, two days after Katrina made landfall, the American Petroleum Institute said, "Greater access to energy resources in this country is still needed to make our nation less vulnerable to the uncertainties of the worldwide marketplace."

Many coastal communities also oppose opening new areas to offshore drilling because of concerns about potential beach pollution and declines in property values. During debate on the energy bill in June 2005, 44 senators — including 27 from states with offshore drilling moratoriums — voted unsuccessfully to delete the provision calling for an inventory of offshore energy resources.

"Exploring off our coast would endanger North Carolina's booming tourism industry, a true economic engine of my state," said Sen. Elizabeth Dole (R-N.C.), in voting to strike the inventory.

But some cash-strapped states have become more receptive to offshore leasing, in light of potential revenues from energy production. Federal revenue from OCS leases and royalties totaled more than $36 billion between 1991 and 2000, of which states receive 27 percent to compensate for the impact of offshore development. [29]

Despite the potential windfall, the proposals are controversial. In March 2005, the Virginia General Assembly voted to urge the state's congressional delega-tion to support allowing offshore drilling off the state's coast, but Democratic Gov. Mark Warner vetoed the measure.

Does reliance on imported oil and gas threaten U.S. security?

Ever since President Richard M. Nixon launched Project Independence to end America's reliance on imported oil, U.S. leaders have repeatedly warned about the need for more energy self-sufficiency. In reality, however, just the opposite has occurred. Imported crude oil rose from 35.8 percent of U.S. consumption in 1975 to 56 percent in 2003, and the Department of Energy projects that this share will reach 68 percent by 2025. [30]

While the Bush energy plan seeks to increase domestic oil and gas production, it does not call for a significant reduction in oil imports, acknowledging instead that at least for the next several decades America will have to rely increasingly on imported energy.

Critics of the plan say Bush's proposal to expand domestic production misses a larger point: The United States uses too much oil and gas, making it vulnerable to price hikes and supply cutoffs by often politically unstable oil-exporting nations. Moreover, they complain, America's over-dependence on Middle East oil drives U.S foreign policy in that region, often forcing the United States to align itself with unpopular, authoritarian, oil-rich governments. The United States also feels compelled to maintain a large military presence in the region in order to ensure stable oil supplies and to intervene in regional conflicts, at considerable cost.

"At $20 billion a year in military expenditures to protect the flow of oil, the U.S. taxpayer is spending roughly an extra hidden $4 to $5 a barrel for the crude oil beyond its market price," writes Amy Myers Jaffe, an energy-studies fellow at Rice University's Baker Institute for Public Policy. [31]

And, as some critics of U.S. policy in the region point out, keeping U.S. troops in the Middle East threatens America's security by further inflaming anti-American hostility demonstrated so spectacularly in the Sept. 11, 2001, terrorist attacks on the World Trade Center and the Pentagon. Al Qaeda leader Osama bin Laden has repeatedly said that the United States was attacked on 9/11 — and will be attacked again — in part because of the presence of U.S. troops in Muslim holy lands in the Middle East.

CHRONOLOGY

1970s *Oil-supply crises stimulate efforts to reduce dependence on energy imports.*

1970 U.S. oil production begins to decline after peaking at 11.3 million barrels per day; imports account for a growing share of total consumption. In April, environmentalists hold the first Earth Day, partly in response to a major undersea oil-well leak near Santa Barbara, Calif.

Oct. 20, 1973 Arab members of the Organization of Petroleum Exporting Countries (OPEC) embargo oil exports to the United States, causing dramatic price hikes and triggering the nation's first energy crisis.

1975 Congress requires manufacturers to produce more fuel-efficient cars.

1977 President Jimmy Carter proposes energy conservation and efficiency standards to reduce dependence on oil imports. . . . Oil from Alaska's North Slope reaches markets.

1978-79 Iranian Revolution triggers a second "oil shock" on world markets. . . . Accident at Pennsylvania's Three Mile Island nuclear power plant raises fears about the safety of nuclear energy. A month later President Carter initiates oil-price deregulation.

1980s *OPEC's control over global oil prices weakens as new sources of oil are discovered. . . . U.S. research into alternative energy sources loses urgency as world oil prices drop.*

January 1981 Oil prices peak at $34 per barrel; inflation leads to a deep worldwide recession. . . . President Ronald Reagan accelerates oil-price decontrol.

March 1983 OPEC cuts prices for the first time.

April 26, 1986 An explosion at the Chernobyl nuclear power plant in Ukraine intensifies fears about nuclear power.

March 24, 1989 The tanker *Exxon Valdez* runs aground in Alaska's Prince William Sound, spilling 11 million gallons of oil. . . . Congress deregulates natural-gas prices.

1990s *Environmental concerns dominate energy policy debates and help boost demand for natural gas. . . . Falling oil prices promote increased consumption and reliance on imports. Americans switch to gas-guzzling sport-utility vehicles and minivans.*

1990 Iraq invades Kuwait on Aug. 2, interrupting Middle East oil exports and doubling oil prices. . . . Prices ease after an international coalition takes military action against Iraq in January 1991.

1992 Energy Policy Act increases U.S. investments in energy efficiency, renewable energy and alternative fuels.

1998 OPEC overproduction and an economic slowdown in Asia drives crude prices below $12 per barrel.

2000s *Election of a Republican administration with strong energy-industry ties spurs a shift from conservation to production.*

May 17, 2001 President Bush proposes increasing supplies of fossil and nuclear fuels, opening the Arctic National Wildlife Refuge (ANWR) to oil and gas exploration and reducing barriers to energy development on public lands. Opposition to ANWR drilling helps stall the measure in Congress for four years.

2004 Congress approves loan guarantees to build a natural-gas pipeline from Alaska's North Slope to the Lower 48 states.

December 2004 U.S. wellhead natural gas prices are more than triple their late-1990s levels.

2005 In March Senate votes 51-49 to open ANWR to oil development, but because the vote was on a non-binding budget measure, another vote is needed to provide legal authority for drilling. . . . Senate authorizes oil and gas exploration in ANWR. . . . In August President Bush signs the Energy Policy Act of 2005, which provides new incentives for oil and gas development but does not increase vehicle fuel efficiency. . . . Hurricanes Katrina and Rita damage refineries, pipelines and offshore drilling platforms in the Gulf of Mexico, driving energy prices higher. . . . President Bush responds by releasing oil from the Strategic Petroleum Reserve, waiving requirements for use of special clean-burning gasoline blends and urging Americans to conserve fuel by driving less.

Rice University's Jaffe further warns that as world oil markets continue to tighten, the United States will become even more reliant on countries like Saudi Arabia with their large reserves, even if the relationships are inconsistent with America's other goal of discouraging terrorism by promoting democracy in the Middle East. [32]

The Bush administration counters that it is working to promote democratic governments in the Middle East, but that reducing the U.S. military presence there in the near term would destabilize the region. "An immediate withdrawal of our troops in Iraq, or the broader Middle East, as some have called for, would only embolden the terrorists and create a staging ground to launch more attacks against America and free nations," President Bush said in a speech on Aug. 24, 2005.

Profligate U.S. energy consumption also makes America less safe because revenues from U.S. oil imports sometimes flow directly to governments that support or tolerate terrorist activities, particularly Saudi Arabia, says the Set America Free Coalition. The bipartisan alliance of national security experts recommended last September that the United States reduce its dependence on foreign oil by shifting the nation's transportation sector to new fuels and technologies.

"It is dangerous to be buying billions of dollars' worth of oil from nations that are sponsors of or are allied with radical Islamists who foment hatred against the United States," the group said in an open letter to the American people. "The petrodollars we provide such nations contribute materially to the terrorist threats we face." [33] The State Department acknowledges that the United States has concerns about human rights in Saudi Arabia, but calls the nation "an important partner in the campaign against terrorism." [34]

Greater use of non-oil domestic energy sources — such as wind and solar power and plentiful U.S. coal supplies — would reduce oil suppliers' leverage over the U.S. economy and help reduce the funding of groups hostile to American interests, say many analysts. [35] Increased production of domestic oil "does nothing" to reduce America's overdependence on oil and hence its vulnerability to oil price shocks, says Ian Parry, a senior fellow at Resources for the Future. Since two-thirds of America's oil is used for transportation, he says, the nation's long-term priority should be to develop new, high-efficiency vehicles and alternative fuels. [36]

Overreliance on imports also puts America at the mercy of international oil markets, where growing competition for oil and gas may threaten both traditional and potential new U.S. energy sources. Energy consumption is rising rapidly in India and China, which are experiencing robust economic growth. Both countries are investing in energy projects around the world that could lock up new sources of oil and gas. For instance, Venezuela — which now supplies the United States with about 1 million barrels of oil a day — is developing supply agreements with China, India and other developing countries.

Others fear that America's enormous energy infrastructure represents a huge security risk. Even before the 9/11 attacks, officials feared that energy storage, transportation and delivery systems could be targeted by terrorists. In addition to nuclear power plants, oil pipelines and refineries as well as LNG terminals are possible targets.

Oil refiners and petrochemical manufacturers have worked with state and federal officials to tighten plant security, especially after the 2001 attacks. However, watchdog groups say more can be done.

For instance, production processes could be changed to reduce the need to maintain large quantities of extremely dangerous chemicals on site. Two-thirds of America's 148 oil refineries have found substitutes for the highly toxic hydrofluoric acid, which can form a poisonous cloud on release. But 50 refineries in 20 states still store the acid on site, according to a report by U.S. Public Interest Research Group. [37]

BACKGROUND

Plentiful Energy

With large domestic deposits of oil, natural gas and coal, America has enjoyed a degree of energy independence and a quality of life envied by countries with fewer resources. In the 19th century coal fueled the country's industrial growth and heated homes. With the Texas oil boom at the turn of the 20th century, petroleum entered the mix. Then, during World War II the United States began developing natural gas — as both an energy source and an ingredient for chemical manufacturing.

By 1950 oil had surpassed coal as the primary U.S. energy source, driven by the postwar economic boom, rising demand for automobiles and the expansion of the nation's highway system. In response, energy companies began selling natural gas (a by-product of oil production)

Many Environmental Laws Regulate Oil and Gas Production

At least nine major laws regulate the impact of oil and gas production on the environment, but they generate their own controversies — and lawsuits. For instance:

- **The Clean Air Act** establishes emission limits for pollution sources like vehicles, factories and electric power plants. It also prescribes national air-quality levels, with special protections for the air quality in national parks and federal lands. In 2004 conservation groups sued the federal Bureau of Land Management (BLM) for allowing energy production activities in Wyoming's Powder River Basin, claiming that building and operating new wells and roads would create haze and smog that could threaten health and scenic vistas at nearby national parks and wilderness areas.

- **The Clean Water Act** regulates oil and gas pollution discharged into waterways. In January 2005, a federal judge said it was illegal under the law for coal-bed methane mine operators to dump millions of gallons of polluted wastewater into Wyoming's Powder River. The permit — issued under the Clean Water Act — failed to consider the impact of the discharges on local farms, ranches and undeveloped areas, the judge said.

- **The Coastal Zone Management Act** requires states to manage their coastlines according to a state coastal zone management plan and make sure that federal actions in coastal zones comply with the state plan.

- **The Federal Land Policy and Management Act** requires the BLM to ensure that resources on public lands are available for multiple uses and provide sustained yields for present and future generations. To achieve that goal, the BLM establishes conditions for use of public lands, including oil and gas leasing. But in April 2005 New Mexico sued the BLM, claiming it was allowing energy exploration on Otero Mesa — an environmentally sensitive high desert area — to proceed in a manner that would not adequately protect the region.

- **The National Environmental Policy Act (NEPA)** requires federal agencies to assess the environmental impacts of proposed actions, including oil and gas leasing, and evaluate alternatives. Yet, under the Energy Policy Act of 2005, NEPA reviews for oil and gas activities would be waived, including for new wells drilled in existing fields, seismic exploration (using sound waves to find underground deposits) and disposal of water from coal bed methane drilling.

- **The Natural Gas Act** gives the Federal Energy Regulatory Commission (FERC) authority to regulate construction and operation of facilities used in interstate natural gas commerce. In July 2004, the California Public Utilities Commission sued the federal government over FERC's approval of a proposed liquefied natural gas terminal in Long Beach. The commission argued that siting the terminal in a crowded urban area posed serious safety issues and opposed FERC's claim of exclusive authority over the proposal.

- **The Oil Pollution Act of 1990** improves the federal government's ability to respond to oil spills and establishes a trust fund — paid for with a tax on oil — to clean up spills when the responsible company cannot or will not pay. It also requires that all oil tankers over 5,000 tons entering U.S. waters after 2010 have double hulls.

- **The Outer Continental Shelf Lands Act** requires that any energy production on the Outer Continental Shelf be balanced with environmental protection. Although it puts the federal government in charge of offshore oil and gas development, it requires consultation with state and local governments.

- **The Safe Drinking Water Act**, which establishes standards for the quality of the nation's drinking water, regulates any activity — including energy production — that may contaminate groundwater. After scientific studies indicated that a popular method, hydraulic fracturing (pumping fluids into underground rock formations to crack them and release trapped oil and gas) threatens drinking water supplies, the 11th U.S. Circuit Court of Appeals ordered the Environmental Protection Agency in 1997 to regulate hydraulic fracturing under the law. But the EPA in 2004 concluded that hydraulic fracturing does not affect groundwater pollution. The agency's inspector general is investigating whether the agency ignored the earlier studies in making its 2004 determination. The Energy Policy Act of 2005 exempts hydraulic fracturing from regulation under the Safe Drinking Water Act.

and drilling for offshore oil in the Gulf of Mexico. America also started to import oil from abroad, mainly from Saudi Arabia. Some U.S. officials — worried about the risks of depending on foreign suppliers — supported research into making synthetic fuels from large domestic coal supplies. But when it became clear that this option would cost several times more than importing cheap foreign oil, the program folded. [38]

By the late 1950s, domestic oil production had peaked and annual yields were beginning to decline. So the United States built relationships with oil-exporting countries, and U.S. companies worked to expand the global oil industry. Oil prices fell as new reserves were developed worldwide, fueling unprecedented international economic growth. Because federal regulations held gas prices at artificially low levels, the United States invested less in developing its gas reserves.

As the impact of rapid industrial growth became clear, environmentalists began to call for a reduction in air and water pollution. The oil industry came under attack in 1969 when an undersea wellhead off the coast of Santa Barbara, Calif., suffered a blowout and leaked 200,000 gallons of oil, contaminating 35 miles of coastline. The Santa Barbara oil spill helped to catalyze the first Earth Day rally in 1970 and led to state and federal bans on new offshore drilling.

Supply Crises

America's era of cheap, plentiful oil ended on Oct. 20, 1973, when Arab members of the Organization of Petroleum Exporting Countries (OPEC) shut off oil exports to the United States. Prices rose sharply and panic buying ensued. The Nixon administration introduced an allocation system to distribute gasoline evenly across the United States. As a result, many Americans had to wait for hours in line at filling stations. The embargo and resulting flow of wealth from Western countries to Mideast oil exporters triggered a deep economic recession from 1973-75.

The 1973 oil shock spurred efforts to reduce U.S. dependence on imported oil. Construction began on a pipeline to bring Alaska's Prudhoe Bay crude oil to the Lower 48 states, ending three years of debate over the project's environmental impact. In 1975 Congress required automakers to increase the fuel efficiency of new cars to 27.5 miles per gallon on average (20.7 miles per gallon for light trucks) by 1987. It also established the Strategic Petroleum Reserve, a national stockpile of crude oil, to safeguard against future supply disruptions. Meanwhile, rising demand for natural gas caused shortages because price ceilings continued to discourage new production.

On taking office in 1977, President Jimmy Carter declared a national energy crisis and offered a plan to reduce U.S. dependence on foreign sources. Congress created the Department of Energy and approved new energy efficiency standards and tax incentives for investing in renewable energy sources. Carter also initiated phased deregulation of oil and gas prices in 1979, designed to encourage new exploration and allowing markets to set prices.

Before these measures could have much impact, however, the Iranian Revolution brought a militant fundamentalist Islamic regime to power in Tehran in 1979, shutting off Iranian oil exports and triggering the decade's second worldwide oil shock. Supplies were further disrupted with the outbreak of the Iran-Iraq War in 1980, which severely damaged both countries' oil industries. President Ronald Reagan responded by reorienting U.S. energy policy toward production of traditional fuels, accelerating energy deregulation, opening up more federal lands for oil exploration and reducing subsidies for renewable energy.

The second oil shock led to a worldwide recession in the early 1980s that sharply reduced demand for oil. Many industrialized countries turned to other fuels such as coal, natural gas and nuclear power. Non-OPEC exporters, such as Mexico and Britain — which discovered huge oil deposits in the North Sea in the 1960s — gained increasing shares of world oil sales.

In late 1985, OPEC countries abandoned production limits. The prices of West Texas intermediate crude oil, a benchmark product, fell from $27.99 per barrel in 1985 to $15.04 in 1986, and remained below $20 until 1990 when Iraq invaded Kuwait. [39] This third spike was less dramatic than the oil shocks of the 1970s, however, and prices were headed downward again by 1992.

Environmental Focus

As oil prices eased in the late 1980s, U.S. energy consumption once again started to climb, but environmental concerns soon led to policies with long-term implications for the oil and gas industry.

The first Bush administration advocated opening the Arctic National Wildlife Refuge to oil and gas exploration, but congressional support eroded after an Exxon oil tanker ran aground in Alaska's Prince William Sound in March 1989, leaving more than 1,000 miles of shoreline contaminated with crude oil.

In 1990 Congress mandated the use of cleaner-burning fuels in cities with severe air pollution, forcing U.S.

Oil workers search for oil in a corn field near Okawville, Ill. High oil prices help drive exploration in the farm belt, where an average well can produce 40-50 barrels a day.

refineries to produce a wider range of products. The law also limited smog- and ozone-forming emissions produced by electric power plants that burn fossil fuels. In response, electric power providers began to invest heavily in cleaner-burning gas-fired power plants.

In the 1990s President Bill Clinton opposed opening ANWR to oil and gas exploration and withdrew public lands in several states from energy development, further limiting domestic production. During his presidency nearly 10 million acres of federal lands were designated as wilderness and more than 58 million acres of national forests were put off-limits to energy production.

Although Clinton favored increased funding for energy efficiency and renewable fuels, strong economic growth and low oil prices drove U.S. energy consumption to new highs in the 1990s. Consumers shifted to larger, less-efficient automobiles — especially SUVs and passenger vans, which benefited from a loophole in fuel-efficiency standards that allowed them to have lower fuel economy than passenger cars.

New Disruptions

In the late 1990s, energy prices began to rise again. China and India were experiencing rapid growth and becoming major energy consumers, and OPEC cut production, despite the jump in demand. Political instability and corruption in key supplier countries — Venezuela, Nigeria and Russia — undercut production and investor confidence. In

the United States, a refinery shortage and environmental regulations made it difficult to produce enough specialty gasoline blends to meet demand.

Meanwhile, natural gas prices spiked, mainly in the United States. Unusually cold winters in 1999 and 2000 boosted demand for gas for home heating and electricity generation. By the end of the decade, demand exceeded dwindling domestic supplies, even as Canada, the main source of U.S. gas imports, was reaching maximum production levels. Many other gas-producing countries had abundant supplies to export, but the United States had only two LNG terminals at which it could process the imports.

Shortly after taking office in 2001, President Bush released a national energy policy focusing on increasing domestic supplies of oil, gas, coal and nuclear power. The administration moved to reduce barriers to domestic oil and gas production on public lands, lobbied vigorously for energy development in ANWR and called for building a new generation of nuclear power reactors. Bush's energy plan reduced spending on energy efficiency and renewables, although it included a Hydrogen Initiative, aimed at developing hydrogen power for vehicles and electricity by 2020. The plan also called for speeding up siting and construction of oil refineries, LNG terminals and gas pipelines.

Congressional Democrats and environmental advocates attacked the president's plan for emphasizing production over conservation. Congress considered several broad energy bills during Bush's first term, but could not agree on divisive issues such as drilling in ANWR and tightening fuel-efficiency standards for automobiles.

However, as oil and gas prices continued to climb, concerns about the economic impact of high energy prices grew. In the wake of Hurricane Katrina, the average world crude price reached $57 per barrel by mid-September 2005. [40]

CURRENT SITUATION

Energy Politics

Congress approved the Energy Policy Act of 2005 in late July, and President Bush signed it on Aug. 8.

"By harnessing the power of American innovation and technological development," a White House statement said, "the energy bill will help us transform the way that we use and produce energy — resulting in greater energy security, a growing economy and a healthier environment for generations of Americans to come."

Environmentalists, consumer advocates and conservative analysts said the law primarily provided tax breaks and subsidies for energy producers and will not reduce either prices or U.S. dependence on imports.

"If we could roll the clock back to 1905, this would be a very good bill. It would be about oil, gas and coal," said Rep. Edward J. Markey, D-Mass. "It is 2005, however. We should be talking about the new technology agenda for our country. This bill is a political and a moral and a technological failure."

The legislation did include new support for alternative fuels, including a requirement that by 2012 the United States use 7.5 billion gallons of renewable transportation fuels each year and a $2.75 billion tax credit for companies generating electricity using renewable fuels. But several provisions designed to reduce reliance on fossil fuels were omitted, including a requirement for electricity producers to generate 10 percent of their power from renewable fuels and higher fuel-efficiency standards for passenger cars.

Instead, the bill provided incentives for domestic oil and gas development, including streamlined procedures for approving drilling permits on public lands and reduced royalty payments. It provided $2.6 billion in tax credits for oil and gas production and refining and $500 million for research on deep-water drilling.

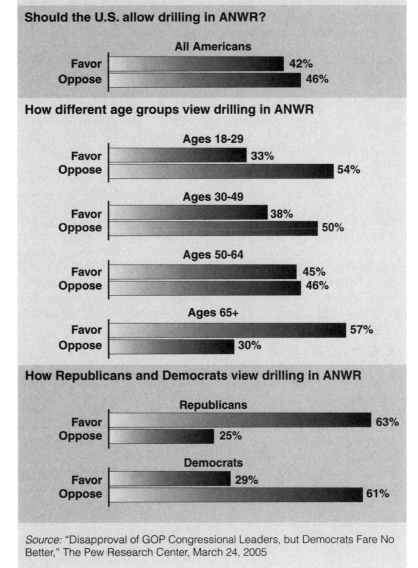

Drilling in Arctic Divides Old and Young

More than half of Americans ages 18-29 oppose oil and gas development in the Arctic National Wildlife Refuge (ANWR), while almost 60 percent of the public 65 and over favor drilling. Almost two-thirds of Republican voters favor drilling compared with only 29 percent of Democrats.

Should the U.S. allow drilling in ANWR?

All Americans
Favor 42%
Oppose 46%

How different age groups view drilling in ANWR

Ages 18-29
Favor 33%
Oppose 54%

Ages 30-49
Favor 38%
Oppose 50%

Ages 50-64
Favor 45%
Oppose 46%

Ages 65+
Favor 57%
Oppose 30%

How Republicans and Democrats view drilling in ANWR

Republicans
Favor 63%
Oppose 25%

Democrats
Favor 29%
Oppose 61%

Source: "Disapproval of GOP Congressional Leaders, but Democrats Fare No Better," The Pew Research Center, March 24, 2005

Critics say such provisions were unnecessary. "What [additional] incentive does the energy industry need to produce, when oil prices are already flirting with $60 a barrel and natural gas prices are triple what they were only a few years ago?" asked Jerry Taylor, director of natural resource studies at the libertarian Cato Institute. [41]

Turning Coal Into Clean-burning Gas

High natural-gas prices are triggering intense interest in gasification — turning coal and other carbon-based materials into synthetic gas or "syngas," a pollution-free mixture that can be used in many of the same applications as natural gas.

Besides allowing impurities to be removed, gasifying coal or other fuels allows carbon dioxide — the main greenhouse gas thought to cause climate change — to be removed during production and stored or sold for industrial applications. Thus, gasification could allow electricity to be produced from coal without contributing to global warming. [1]

In addition, power plants fueled with syngas are more efficient than conventional power plants, producing larger quantities of electricity from a smaller quantity of fuel. Gasification also can be used to produce chemicals and generate hydrogen for fuel and other uses.

William Rosenberg, professor of engineering and public policy at Carnegie Mellon University and a former senior official at the Environmental Protection Agency, argues that gasification has new relevance today as a solution to America's natural-gas supply crisis and to help wean America off its dependence on either dirtier coal or oil from unstable Middle Eastern countries.

"Most U.S. hydrocarbons are contained in coal, which produces a lot of pollution when it's burned. When you gasify coal, you . . . get a clean fuel," says Rosenberg. "We can get our primary energy from the Middle East, or we can have it from domestic sources."

The prices of oil and gas are high enough now to make coal gasification more cost-effective, he says, if the government were to provide some "reasonable federal incentives for the first plants."

Syngas is produced when a carbon-based fuel (such as coal, plant material or municipal solid waste) is heated under pressure in a gasifier, breaking the fuel down into synthetic gas and solid residues. The gas can be cleaned to remove pollution-causing impurities such as sulfur and particulate matter before it is used, making it a cleaner and more efficient fuel for power plants than coal or oil. [2]

To create electricity using synthetic gas, the gasifier is connected to a power plant that generates power in two cycles. First, the plant burns syngas to run a combustion turbine, producing waste heat that is then used to boil water and create steam to run a second turbine. Such a system is called an "integrated gasification combined-cycle" (IGCC).

Although gasification technology is widely used in industry, it has not yet been commercialized for producing electric power. Coal gasification plants cost about 20 percent more than traditional coal-burning power plants, so private companies are unlikely to build them without government support. And if the carbon dioxide in syngas is released to the atmosphere rather than captured for storage or use, coal gasification still contributes to climate change.

The Department of Energy has been researching coal gasification for many years and has financed commercial-scale gasification plants in Indiana and Florida. In 2003 President Bush announced a $1 billion, 10-year project called FutureGen, in which the Energy Department would help industry design and build a coal IGCC plant that would capture and store carbon emissions and produce hydrogen fuel.

But Congress provided only a fraction of the funding requested by the administration in 2004. Many experts argue that FutureGen is an isolated demonstration project and that a larger commitment is needed to bring IGCC technology into commercial use.

The bipartisan National Commission on Energy Policy recommended in December 2004 that the federal government provide up to $7 billion to build IGCC plants and demonstrate ways of capturing and storing carbon underground. The Energy Policy Act of 2005 includes $1.8 billion over nine years to develop clean-coal technologies, of which 70 percent must be used for gasification or related technologies, and allows the Department of Energy to provide loan guarantees for IGCC projects. It also provides a 20 percent investment tax credit for gasification projects that produce fuel and chemicals.

---

[1] For background, see Mary H. Cooper, "Global Warming Treaty," *CQ Researcher*, Jan. 26, 2001, pp. 41-64.

[2] Unless otherwise stated, this summary is based on U.S. Department of Energy, Office of Fossil Energy, "How Coal Gasification Works," Oct. 13, 2004.

Oil and gas developers say subsidies and tax benefits reduce the financial risk associated with exploration. "Tax incentives to increase domestic development have a history of success [and have] . . . increased development of natural gas sources that would not have otherwise occurred," Lee Fuller, vice president of the Independent

Is the administration balancing energy development with environmental protection?

YES
Rebecca W. Watson
Assistant Secretary of the Interior

From a letter to *Trout Unlimited*, Feb. 24, 2005

The Department of the Interior's energy program reflects the administration's belief that environmentally sound energy development is important to our national security and economic well-being. It also directly supports the Bureau of Land Management's (BLM) mandate to manage resources to "best meet the present and future needs of the American people." . . .

Out of 261 million acres managed by BLM, fewer than 325,000 are directly affected by oil and gas production activities. That is one-tenth of 1 percent. In the five basins found to have exceptionally high volumes of oil and gas reserves, more than a third (36 percent) of the surface area is closed to leasing by congressional acts, executive orders or identification of unique values in land use plans. . . .

Impacts of energy development are analyzed in National Environmental Policy Act documents at several decision-making stages. . . . In addition, impacts to cultural resources, threatened and endangered species, air and water are analyzed in separate permitting processes under state and federal law. We encourage collaboration and participation from the scientific community in this public process. . . .

Our leasing activities are more conservative than the previous administration's record. There has been a 2.2 percent decrease in the total number of acres leased during the years 2001-2004 when compared to 1997-2001 and a 27 percent decrease in total number of leases issued during the same time periods. However, under this administration there has been a marked increase in the development of existing leases. This responds to increased demand for natural gas as well as congressional direction to BLM to reduce backlogs of permits. These permits are issued with some of the strictest requirements for environmental protection on record. . . .

BLM also is initiating innovative ways to reduce environmental impacts of energy development. The recent decision regarding Otero Mesa in New Mexico, for example, allows long-term surface disturbance on only 860 acres out of a 2-million-acre planning area — four-hundredths of 1 percent — and developers must adhere to strict stipulations, such as ensuring native grasses and forbs are re-established and self sustaining during reclamation. . . .

The Department of the Interior is committed to working with our partners and the scientific community at local levels on site-specific concerns, using new information as it becomes available, to offer the best protection possible to wildlife while meeting the nation's growing energy needs.

NO
David Stalling
Western Field Coordinator, Trout Unlimited

From "Gas and Oil Development on Western Public Lands," *Trout Unlimited*, 2005

Ongoing efforts to expedite energy development on public lands have turned traditional multiple-use management on its head by elevating oil and gas exploration to a dominant position. As a result, gas and oil development is occurring at an unprecedented rate throughout the Rocky Mountain West, affecting tens of millions of acres, in some of the wildest places — with some of the best hunting and fishing — in the United States. . . .

The ecological effects of traditional gas and oil and coal-bed methane (CBM) development on public lands are extensive. Although the actual "footprint" of a well or pad may be relatively small, production requires pervasive infrastructure and development such as roads, pipelines and transmission corridors that can contaminate ground- and surface-water supplies, reduce water quantity, degrade fish habitat and fragment wildlife corridors, calving grounds and nesting areas. Since very little research has been conducted, there is more that we don't know than know.

For example, how will discharges of CBM water, high in dissolved solids and sodium, affect streams, tributaries and wetlands? What impacts will altered soil conditions have on streamside and riparian vegetation? With each CBM well dewatering coal seams at an average of 15,000 gallons per day, how will stream flows be affected? How will roads and increased noise and activity affect movements and use of habitat by elk, deer, pronghorn and sage grouse? What will the impacts be on winter range, migratory corridors and calving and fawning habitat? Will increased access to previously roadless lands increase hunting pressure, reduce habitat security, increase big-game vulnerability and therefore, eventually, reduce hunting opportunities?

According to the U.S. Energy Information Administration, streamlining environmental reviews and increasing access to federal natural gas on public lands would increase supplies by less than 1 percent and save the average U.S. household $5 per year through 2020. . . .

Currently, 32 million acres of public land are under lease for gas and oil development. There are more than 110,000 permitted natural gas wells on public lands, and the BLM has approved more than 10,000 new wells in the past three years. It will take an estimated 10-15 years to get to all the natural gas that geologists believe is available on our public lands — enough to supply our nation's needs for about two years.

Are the potentially devastating impacts to fish, wildlife and America's hunting and angling heritage worth it?

Getty Images/David McNew

An oil tanker docks at the Valdez Terminal, at the end of the 800-mile-long Trans-Alaskan pipeline, near the place where 16 years ago another tanker, the *Exxon Valdez*, ran aground and spilled 11 million gallons of crude oil. The accident contaminated more than 1,000 miles of Alaskan shores and killed thousands of seabirds, marine mammals and salmon. It also prompted Congress to block efforts by then-President George H.W. Bush to open the Arctic National Wildlife Refuge to oil exploration, but today's Congress appears poised to approve drilling at the refuge, at the request of Bush's son President George W. Bush.

Petroleum Association of America, told the House Energy Committee in February. [42]

To expand processing and transmission systems, the law will expedite federal judicial review for permitting natural gas pipelines and LNG facilities, and gives the Federal Energy Regulatory Commission (FERC) "exclusive authority" to approve the construction, expansion or operation of LNG facilities.

Opening Public Lands

The Bush administration has worked to speed up permitting for energy production on public lands, particularly in the Rocky Mountains. The Interior Department's Bureau of Land Management (BLM) has more than tripled the number of drilling permits approved annually — from 1,803 in fiscal 1999 to 6,399 in fiscal 2004.

According to a recent Government Accountability Office (GAO) report, the focus on permitting has hampered the BLM's ability to monitor the environmental impact of oil and gas production, triggering a growing number of challenges to agency decisions. The challenges are expected to increase as permitting decisions increasingly affect residential areas and environmentally sensitive zones. [43]

Environmentalists, citizens' groups and some state officials are alarmed at the scope of Western energy development under the Bush administration's policies, and some groups have challenged certain federal oil and gas policies in court.

In June 2004, Wyoming Democratic Gov. Dave Freudenthal said selling new oil and gas leases in his state's Pinedale region before a resource management plan for the area has been completed was "contrary to the goal of deliberate and responsible development" — particularly since 92 percent of the region was already leased for energy development. [44]

New Mexico's Democratic Gov. Bill Richardson sued the Interior Department over its proposed conditions for oil and gas drilling on Otero Mesa in the southern part of the state. "I recognize the need for oil and gas," Richardson says, "but the Interior Department should respect local concerns and its own rules and stay out of precious places in the West, from Montana and Wyoming down to New Mexico. The no-holds-barred, drill-drill-drill approach to the American West won't resolve the nation's energy problems, and it will destroy special places like Otero Mesa in the process." Bush administration officials contend that energy leases on public lands minimize the effects of drilling and provide reasonable protections for wildlife nearby. (*See "At Issue," p. 183.*)

Administration officials say oil and gas development are important national interests. BLM Director Kathleen Clarke called Gov. Richardson's proposed alternative plan for development of Otero Mesa "unbalanced." [45] Assistant Interior Secretary Rebecca Watson called Richardson's proposal "a no-drill plan." [46]

More heated debate over energy vs. environmental tradeoffs is expected in late 2005, when Congress may decide whether to approve oil and gas drilling in the ANWR — part of a budget reconciliation package. The House has voted several times to open ANWR, but the Senate has yet to pass binding legislation that would authorize drilling. Reconciliation measures are not subject to Senate filibusters, so ANWR drilling proponents will only need 50 votes to pass the bill rather than the 60 required to override a filibuster.

Environmentalists have promised an intense fight, but after five years of lobbying for drilling in ANWR, Bush could win passage. However, flood relief issues may push a reconciliation bill into 2006, delaying an ANWR showdown.

New Facilities

The new energy law will not eliminate bottlenecks in America's energy system. For example, only one new refinery is now under construction in the United States — the first since 1976.

"Permitting is only one problem," explains Sarah Emerson, managing director of Energy Security Analysis Inc., a Boston consulting firm. "Refining has traditionally been a low-profit business. You have to be very bullish on the price of petroleum products relative to crude oil to even consider building a brand new refinery. It's cheaper to build them offshore in the Caribbean — where permitting is easier — and import the products."

Refineries not only face difficult financial hurdles but also must overcome stringent environmental regulations and strong NIMBY ("not in my backyard") sentiment from potential neighbors.

Siting new LNG terminals could lower U.S. gas prices, bringing some relief to industrial and residential consumers. But several urban communities — including Long Beach, Calif., and Fall River, Mass. — are contesting proposals for new LNG terminals in their midst, arguing that the facilities pose serious security risks to developed industrial areas. Other regions are more receptive: FERC has approved several new LNG terminals in Louisiana and Texas without significant controversy and is considering about 40 more proposals.

But experts predict that only a fraction of the 40 plants will be built. [47] Damage to oil and gas facilities caused by Katrina and Rita could persuade FERC to give extra weight to proposals outside of the storm-vulnerable Gulf region, but the plants are not popular in California, New England and the Pacific Northwest.

Meanwhile, although U.S. energy demand is still trending upward, high fuel prices may be influencing energy consumption. Sales of large SUVs fell by 25 percent in May (compared to May 2004), while fuel-efficient hybrid vehicle sales more than doubled in the same period. [48] As of December 2004, 18 states and the District of Columbia had required power providers to produce a portion of their electricity from renewable fuels.

Polls show Americans are deeply concerned about high energy prices, particularly for transportation, home heating and cooling. Several surveys in the spring of 2005 found that 50 to 70 percent of respondents had reduced their driving in response to high gasoline prices, and 50 to 60 percent did not agree with President Bush's energy policy.

But Americans are quick to blame high energy prices on external factors, such as price manipulation by OPEC and energy companies, rather than on their own personal choices — such as driving gas-guzzling cars. Yet, majorities tend to support environmental protection and conservation over increased energy development. [49] (*See poll, page 181.*)

OUTLOOK

No Relief

Americans' best hope for lower energy prices may be the weather. A mild winter could reduce demand for heating oil and gas. However, the EIA has predicted "a potentially expensive winter heating season." [50] Even supporters of the energy bill agree it will not ease fuel prices or reduce U.S. dependence on foreign oil in the short term. But it will put policies in place that will improve the situation in the coming decade, they say.

"Five years from now, [the] energy bill will have stabilized energy prices, created hundreds of thousands of jobs, boosted our economy and protected our environment," said Senate Energy and Natural Resources Committee Chairman Pete Domenici, R-N.M.

Delivering on that promise could affect economic growth and the competitiveness of U.S. businesses. "Many of our manufacturers won't be here unless we see relief in the next four or five years," says Cicio of the Industrial Energy Consumers of America.

Increased domestic production will have some impact, but the effect will not be immediate. The EIA predicts that natural gas production from the Rocky Mountain states will increase through 2025 — although this could be slowed by environmental lawsuits — and a proposed Alaska natural gas pipeline will not start transporting gas to the Lower 48 states until 2016.

Building new LNG terminals will also take time, so increased LNG imports probably won't provide relief until 2008 or 2009. [51]

Energy analysts disagree about future oil price trends, but many expect instability in producer countries and rising demand from Asia to keep prices high for the foreseeable future: Chinese demand for natural gas is projected to double by 2010, and its demand for oil will more than double by 2025. [52]

With world energy supplies tightening and most Americans unwilling to trade off environmental protection for oil and gas production, the transportation sector — which accounts for the majority of U.S. oil imports — is increasingly targeted by both environmentalists and energy security hawks. Groups like the Set America Free Coalition are pushing development of non-petroleum transportation fuels, claiming the Bush administration's Hydrogen Initiative won't deliver energy benefits soon enough.

Meanwhile, high energy prices could force U.S. carmakers to increase fuel efficiency or risk losing market share and credibility. Bringing clean cars and renewable transportation fuels into the mainstream by 2010 represents the next frontier for U.S. energy policy.

Energy analyst Daniel Yergin, president of Cambridge Energy Research Associates, is optimistic that recent developments — from terrorist threats to storm damage in the Gulf states — will make America focus more closely on energy risks and energy security.

"Disruption on the scale of Katrina was never anticipated, neither for the Gulf's energy complex nor for the larger tragedy that unfolded," Yergin writes. "From now on, a hit of this scale will not be unexpected.

"But what else is out there? That is a question for the world's entire energy supply system. For surely, somewhere, the unexpected is brooding, and waiting to happen." [53]

NOTES

1. Minerals Management Service, www.mms.gov/ooc/Assets/Katrina091605/damage.pdf.

2. "Hurricane Katrina Situation Report #40," Office of Electricity Delivery and Energy Reliability, U.S. Department of Energy, Sept. 21, 2005.

3. "Hurricane Katrina's Effect on Gasoline Supply and Prices," American Petroleum Institute, http://api-ec.api.org/filelibrary/KatrinaSlides.pdf.

4. Energy Information Administration, www.tonto.eia.doe.gov.

5. "Short-Term Energy Outlook," Energy Information Administration, September 2005, p. 4.

6. *Ibid.*, p. 7.

7. *Ibid.*, Table 3.

8. "Annual Energy Review 2004," Energy Information Administration, p. 127.

9. Quoted on "CBS Sunday Morning," Sept. 11, 2005.

10. *Ibid.*

11. For background, see Mary H. Cooper, "Energy Policy," *CQ Researcher*, May 25, 2001, pp. 441-464.

12. "President Discusses Energy at National Small Business Conference," White House press release, April 27, 2005.

13. For background, see Mary H. Cooper, "Energy Security," *CQ Researcher*, Feb. 1, 2002, pp. 77-78.

14. Center for Responsive Politics, www.opensecrets.org/industries/indus.asp?Ind=E.

15. Annual Energy Outlook 2005, Energy Information Administration, pp. 95-96.

16. *Ibid.*, pp. 97-100.

17. "Ending the Energy Stalemate," National Commission on Energy Policy, December 2004, p. 3.

18. "A Responsible Energy Plan for America," Natural Resources Defense Council, April 2005, p. 4.

19. "Oil and Gas Development on Public Lands — Myths and Facts," *The Wilderness Society*, Sept. 19, 2005.

20. "Abuse of Trust," *The Wilderness Society*, 2004.

21. "Analysis of Oil and Gas Production in the Arctic National Wildlife Refuge," Energy Information Administration, March 2004.

22. Testimony of Charles Davidson before the Senate Energy and Natural Resources Committee, April 19, 2005.

23. "Assessment of Undiscovered Technically Recoverable Oil and Gas Resources of the Nation's Outer Continental Shelf, 2003 Update," Minerals Management Service, Department of the Interior, December 2004.

24. "U.S. Crude Oil, Natural Gas, and Natural Gas Liquids Reserves 2003 Annual Report," Energy Information Administration, November 2004, pp. 23 and 31.

25. www.sierraclub.org/ca/coasts/drilling_alert.asp.

26. From Davidson testimony, *op. cit.*

27. "Oil Spill Facts," Minerals Management Service, Department of the Interior, September 2002.

28. U.S. Coast Guard press release, Sept. 19, 2005.

29. Minerals Management Service, Department of the Interior, www.mrm.mms.gov/stats/pdfdocs/coll_off. pdf. By contrast, states receive half of the revenues from mineral leasing in public lands within their onshore boundaries, leading many states to feel they are entitled to a larger share of offshore leasing revenues.

30. David L. Greene, "Energy Prophets: U.S. Oil Dependence," *Oak Ridge National Laboratory Review*, Vol. 38, No. 1, 2005, p. 6; Annual Energy Outlook 2005, *op. cit.*, p. 101.

31. Amy Myers Jaffe, "United States and the Middle East: Policies and Dilemmas," paper for the National Commission on Energy Policy, p. 5, www.energycommission.org/research/.

32. For background, see Jonathan Broder, "Balancing Fuel and Freedom," *CQ Weekly*, Sept. 12, 2005, pp. 2384-2393.

33. Set America Free Coalition, www.setamericafree.org.

34. "Background Note: Saudi Arabia," www.state.gov/r/pa/ei/bgn/3584.htm#relations.

35. For background, see Mary H. Cooper, "Alternative Fuels," *CQ Researcher*, Feb. 25, 2005, pp. 173-196.

36. Ian Parry, "Petroleum: Energy Independence is Unrealistic," *Resources*, winter 2005, pp. 14-15.

37. "Needless Risk: Oil Refineries and Hazard Reduction," U.S. PIRG Education Fund, August 2004, p. 5.

38. Daniel Yergin, *The Prize: The Epic Quest for Oil, Money & Power* (1991), pp. 428-29.

39. BP Statistical Review of World Energy, *British Petroleum*, June 2004, p. 14.

40. Energy Information Administration, www.tonto.eia. doe.gov.

41. "Burning Money Produces Scant Energy," June 30, 2005, www.cato.org.

42. Testimony before the House Committee on Energy and Commerce Subcommittee on Air Quality, Feb. 16, 2005, pp. 20, 25.

43. "Oil and Gas Development: Increased Permitting Activity Has Lessened BLM's Ability to Meet Its Environmental Protection Responsibilities," Government Accountability Office, GAO-05-418, June 2005, pp. 17-26, 35-37.

44. Press release, Office of the Governor, June 8, 2004.

45. *Federal Register*, Jan. 25, 2005, p. 3557.

46. Quoted in "Interior Official Knocks Gov.'s Otero Proposal," *Albuquerque Journal*, April 2, 2004.

47. For more information see www.ferc.gov/industries/lng.asp.

48. U.S. Green Car Congress, www.greencarcongress. com.

49. Gallup Poll on production, conservation, March 7-10, 2005, www.pollingreport.com/enviro.htm.

50. "Short-Term Energy Outlook," *op. cit.*, p. 6.

51. Daniel Yergin testimony to the Joint Economic Committee, Oct. 7, 2004.

52. "China Country Analysis Brief," Energy Information Administration, updated August 2005, www.eia.gov/emeu/cabs/china.html.

53. Daniel Yergin, "The Katrina Crisis," *The Wall Street Journal*, Sept. 2, 2005.

BIBLIOGRAPHY

Books

Deffeyes, Kenneth S., *Beyond Oil: The View from Hubbert's Peak,* **Hill and Wang, 2005.**
A Princeton University geologist predicts that world oil production will peak in 2005 and assesses what alternative fuels can be used to meet global energy demand.

Klare, Michael T., *Blood and Oil: The Dangers and Consequences of America's Growing Petroleum Dependency,* **Metropolitan Books, 2004.**
An Amherst University professor of Peace and World Security Studies contends that dependence on oil imports undercuts U.S. security by drawing the nation into conflicts in unstable areas. He argues instead for energy conservation, greater use of renewable fuels and fewer alliances with corrupt oil-exporting governments.

Vaitheeswaran, Vijay V., *Power to the People: How the Coming Energy Revolution Will Transform an Industry, Change Our Lives, and Maybe Even Save the Planet*, Farrar, Straus and Giroux, 2003.

The Economist's energy and environment reporter predicts that the rise of market forces, greater concern about environmental impacts and technical innovations will lead to a clean energy future.

Articles

Arndt, Michael, "No Longer the Lab of the World," *Business Week*, May 2, 2005.

High natural-gas prices are driving U.S. chemical manufacturers to close domestic plants and invest in factories overseas.

Mouawad, Jad, "No New Refineries in 29 Years, but Project Tries to Find a Way," *The New York Times*, May 9, 2005, p. A1.

A proposal to build the first new U.S. oil refinery since 1976 would provide needed capacity but faces legal, political and economic hurdles.

Romero, Simon, "Demand for Natural Gas Brings Big Import Plans, and Objections," *The New York Times*, June 15, 2005, p. A1.

Liquefied natural gas (LNG) imports will become a key U.S. energy source over the next several decades, but only if enough facilities can be built to handle it. Some states think LNG terminals pose safety hazards and oppose federal siting plans.

Williams, Ted, "The Mad Gas Rush," *Audubon*, March 2004.

Environmentalists charge that rather than managing public lands for multiple uses, the Bush administration is giving priority to oil and gas development, which many say is polluting air, land and drinking water and threatening wildlife.

Reports and Studies

Baker Institute for Public Policy, "The Geopolitics of Natural Gas," March 2005.

Researchers at Stanford and Rice universities predict that an integrated world gas market will develop in the next 30 years, and exporters will try to control supplies to keep prices high. However, gas consumers will have other options, such as shifting to alternate suppliers and fuels.

Environmental Working Group, "Who Owns the West? Oil & Gas Leases," August 2004.

The energy industry has broad access to oil- and gas-drilling opportunities in a dozen Western states, where energy development has caused significant environmental damage but has not reduced U.S. dependence on imported oil.

Lovins, Amory B., *et al.*, "Winning the Oil Endgame: Investments for Profits, Jobs, and Security," Rocky Mountain Institute, 2005.

In a study co-funded by the Defense Department, a panel of energy experts offers a strategy for ending U.S. oil dependence that will provide net economic benefits. Key steps include doubling the efficiency of oil use, speeding deployment of super-efficient vehicles, building a biofuels industry and substituting natural gas for some oil uses.

National Research Council, "Cumulative Environmental Effects of Oil and Gas Activities on Alaska's North Slope," 2003.

The scientific group says 30 years of oil and gas development have had negative impacts on the tundra, on animals such as whales and caribou and on the health and cultures of native peoples. New technologies are reducing damage from oil exploration, but little has been done to restore contaminated sites.

U.S. Commission on Ocean Policy, "Managing Offshore Energy and Other Mineral Resources," in *An Ocean Blueprint for the 21st Century*, September 2004.

A section of a comprehensive review of U.S. ocean policy describes the existing framework for developing offshore resources such as oil and gas deposits and proposes steps to achieve a better balance between resource development and environmental protection.

For More Information

American Council for an Energy-Efficient Economy, 1001 Connecticut Avenue, N.W., Suite 801, Washington, DC 20036; (202) 429-8873; www.aceee.org. A nonprofit research and advocacy organization that supports energy efficiency measures to promote economic prosperity and environmental protection.

American Petroleum Institute, 1220 L Street, N.W., Washington, DC 20005-4070; (202) 682-8000; www.api.org. The trade association for the U.S. oil and natural gas industry.

Energy Information Administration, E130, 1000 Independence Avenue, S.W., Washington, DC 20585; (202) 586-8959; www.eia.doe.gov. The official source for U.S. energy information, including prices, consumption, production and forecasts.

Industrial Energy Consumers of America, 1155 15th St., N.W., Suite 500, Washington, DC 20005; (202) 223-1661; www.ieca-us.com. An advocacy organization for manufacturers that are large-scale energy consumers.

National Commission on Energy Policy, 1616 H Street, N.W., 6th floor, Washington, DC 20006; (202) 637-0400; www.energycommission.org. A bipartisan expert commission established to propose workable solutions to current energy challenges.

Natural Resources Defense Council, 40 West 20th Street, New York, NY 10011; (212) 727-2700; www.nrdc.org. An environmental advocacy organization involved in energy policy, clean air and water and protection of public lands.

Oil & Gas Accountability Project, P.O. Box 1102, 8631/2 Main Avenue, Durango, CO, 81302; (970) 259-3353; www.ogap.org. An alliance formed to reduce the social, economic and environmental impacts of oil and gas development.

Resources for the Future, 1616 P Street, N.W., Washington, DC 20036; (202) 328-5000; www.rff.org. An independent, nonpartisan think tank dedicated to improving environmental and natural resource policymaking through objective social science research; recently released a six-part briefing series exploring strategies for addressing global energy needs through 2050.

Set America Free Coalition, www.setamericafree.org. A bipartisan coalition of conservative and liberal think tanks, advocacy groups and individuals with expertise in national security, energy and environmental policy; created in 2004 by the Institute for the Analysis of Global Security to build public support for reducing U.S. dependence on imported oil.

9

Climate Change

Marcia Clemmitt

A heat wave throughout Europe last summer sends French bathers to the beach at Fos-sur-Mer, near Marseilles. Climate experts blame human-caused global warming for lethal summer temperatures in 2003 that killed 25,000 Europeans, including 15,000 in France.

From *CQ Researcher*, January 27, 2006.

I'm sitting up in Alaska where I can see that we are experiencing climate change," Sen. Lisa Murkowski, R-Alaska, told a Senate hearing last July. [1]

Indeed, said whale hunter Percy Nusunginya, ocean ice "used to be 20 to 30 feet thick, but now it is more like 10 feet." Like many of Murkowski's constituents, Nusunginya believes climate changes caused by global warming could be dangerous to his way of life. He fishes through pack-ice air holes 300 miles inside the Arctic Circle. "We are definitely warming up; the polar pack ice has all but gone." [2]

"Alaska is melting," agrees Richard A. Muller, a physics professor at the University of California at Berkeley, noting, "Even a small rise in average temperature is a looming catastrophe." [3] He recalls seeing "drunken trees" along the roadside — their shallow roots loosened in the softening soil — crazily leaning houses and meadows sunken three feet lower than the surrounding forest because the permafrost had melted. [4]

Across the globe, evidence of global warming is piling up:

- The number of glaciers in Montana's Glacier National Park has dropped from 150 — when the park was created in 1910 — to fewer than 30 today, all greatly shrunken.
- The legendary snows of Tanzania's Mount Kilimanjaro have melted about 80 percent since 1912 and could be gone by 2020. [5]
- Rising sea levels are killing Bermuda's coastal mangrove forests.
- World ocean temperatures have risen by a net 0.11 degrees Fahrenheit over the past four decades.

191

Impact of Climate Change Around the World

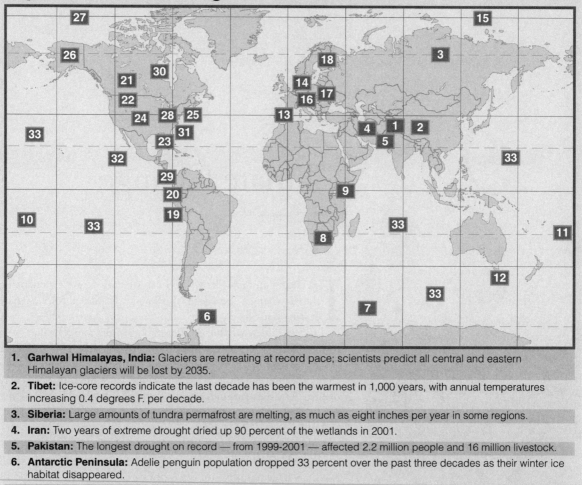

1. **Garhwal Himalayas, India:** Glaciers are retreating at record pace; scientists predict all central and eastern Himalayan glaciers will be lost by 2035.

2. **Tibet:** Ice-core records indicate the last decade has been the warmest in 1,000 years, with annual temperatures increasing 0.4 degrees F. per decade.

3. **Siberia:** Large amounts of tundra permafrost are melting, as much as eight inches per year in some regions.

4. **Iran:** Two years of extreme drought dried up 90 percent of the wetlands in 2001.

5. **Pakistan:** The longest drought on record — from 1999-2001 — affected 2.2 million people and 16 million livestock.

6. **Antarctic Peninsula:** Adelie penguin population dropped 33 percent over the past three decades as their winter ice habitat disappeared.

7. **Southern Ocean:** Waters around Antarctica rose 0.3 degrees F. between 1950-1980.

Source: Union of Concerned Scientists; www.climatehotmap.org

The evidence shows that human-caused warming is causing rapid, hard-to-predict and potentially dangerous change, James Hurrell, director of the Climate and Global Dynamics Division at the National Center for Atmospheric Research, told the Senate Energy and Natural Resources Committee in July. Global temperatures today are more than 1 degree Fahrenheit warmer than at the beginning of the 20th century, he said, and the rates of increase were greatest in recent decades: Nine of the last 10 years are among the warmest since 1860. As ocean temperatures warmed, global sea levels rose about 4-6 inches during the 20th century, he added.

"The climate is changing, and the rate of change as projected exceeds anything seen in nature in the past 10,000 years," Hurrell said. And while specific changes in some regions "might be benign . . . global warming will be disruptive in many, many ways," potentially causing "drought, heat waves, wildland fires and flooding" in some local areas. [6]

Now, a year after the first international treaty on climate change — the Kyoto Protocol — took effect, the ground is shifting in the debate over global warming. Today, only a few skeptics say warming is not occurring

8. **Southern Africa:** The warmest and driest decade was recorded in 1985-1995.

9. **Mount Kilimanjaro, Tanzania:** Eighty-two percent of the ice has disappeared since 1912; scientists predict all will be gone by 2020.

10. **Fiji:** The average shoreline has been receding half a foot per year for the past 90 years.

11. **American and Western Samoa:** Both are experiencing land loss as ocean waters rise, with Western Samoa's shoreline receding 1.5 feet per year for the past 90 years.

12. **Heard Island (Australia):** Air temperature has risen while the glaciers have decreased in size.

13. **Spain:** Half of all glaciers present in 1980 are gone.

14. **Denmark and Germany:** October 2001 was the warmest October on record, with temperatures in Germany up to 7 degrees F. above average.

15. **Arctic Ocean:** Ice volume decreased by 40 percent compared to 20-40 years ago.

16. **Europe:** Many butterfly species shifted their ranges northward by 22-150 miles.

17. **Europe:** Spring events, such as flowering, have advanced by six days, and autumn events, such as leaf coloring, have been delayed by about five days.

18. **Turku, Finland:** The growing season has lengthened by 10 days over the last century.

19. **Andes Mountains, Peru:** The Qori Kalis glacier's retreat rate accelerated sevenfold between 1963-1995.

20. **Chiclayo, Peru:** Average minimum temperatures increased substantially throughout the country.

21. **Edmonton, Alberta, Canada:** Warmest summer on record occurred in 1998.

22. **Glasgow, Montana:** For the first time, temperatures remained above 0 degrees F in December (1997).

23. **Florida:** During a June heat wave in 1998, temperatures remained above 95 degrees F for 24 days in Melbourne.

24. **USA:** An autumn heat wave from mid-November to early December in 1998 broke or tied more than 700 daily-high temperature records.

25. **Chesapeake Bay:** Marsh and island losses are occurring as the sea level is rising at three times the historical rate.

26. **Interior Alaska:** Permafrost thawing is causing the ground to subside 16-33 feet in places.

27. **Arctic Ocean:** The area covered by sea ice decreased by 6 percent from 1978-1995.

28. **Washington, D.C.:** Cherry trees are blossoming earlier.

29. **Monteverde Cloud Forest, Costa Rica:** Warmer Pacific Ocean temperatures have caused a reduction in dry-season mists, causing the disappearances of 20 species of frogs and toads.

30. **Western Hudson Bay, Canada:** The early spring breakup of sea ice has disrupted polar bear hunting patterns, causing decreased weight among adults and a decline in birthrate since the early 1980s.

31. **Bermuda:** Rising sea level is causing salt water to inundate and kill coastal mangrove forests.

32. **Pacific Ocean, Mexico:** Coral reefs are under severe stress due to higher temperatures and other factors.

33. **World Oceans:** Temperatures have risen by a net 0.11 degrees F. over the past four decades.

— mostly due to increased atmospheric concentration of so-called greenhouse gases * (GHGs) like carbon dioxide, which is emitted during the burning of fossil fuels, and methane gas, from animals and other sources. [7]

"Greenhouse gas concentrations in the atmosphere are now higher than at any time in the last 750,000 years," Hurrell said.

But the climate change debate is far from over. Arguments now center not on whether human-induced global warming is occurring but whether it is enough of a threat to warrant spending money to stop it. The Bush administration and most Republican members of Congress say no. Even lawmakers like Murkowski say action isn't warranted unless scientists can prove beyond doubt that dangerous levels of warming — caused by human activity — will occur.

Meanwhile, like Alaska, many states eye global warming as potentially devastating. New Hampshire officials

---

* The concentration in the atmosphere of some gases, such as CO_2, water vapor and ozone, increases the atmosphere's tendency to trap heat, much like the glass in a greenhouse.

Climate Change May Affect Public Health

The environment has long been known to play a big role in human health — from waterborne diseases like cholera to allergies caused by ragweed pollen. Now some researchers are blaming human-induced climate warming for killer European heat waves and even for increased incidence of malaria.

In response, many experts argue that public-health systems must prepare for new challenges. Planetary warming may stress already overburdened public-health systems, especially in developing countries. (*See graph, p. 195.*)

In some cities, air quality is particularly susceptible to warming, as evidenced by that fact that summer ozone pollution and stagnant air masses make it harder for people with asthma or cardiovascular disease to breathe, according to Harvard Medical School's Center for Health and the Global Environment. [1] The more severe drought and flood conditions predicted by some climate scientists could also mean widespread death and injury from worsened malnutrition, floods and landslides.

The range and severity of infectious diseases also may shift as climate alters.

The Harvard researchers say the range of malaria, one of the most disabling and widespread infectious diseases, already may be shifting and expanding due to climate change. Before the 1970s, for example, malaria did not afflict Africa's highlands. With warming, however, mountain glaciers have melted, and malaria-carrying mosquitoes have expanded their range into the mountains.

Conservative analysts, however, dispute the idea that malaria has only recently spread to non-tropical regions. Global-warming enthusiasts "made this up," says Myron Ebell, director of global warming and international environmental policy at the big-business-funded Competitive Enterprise Institute. "Even in the Little Ice Age, we had malaria and dengue fever [another mosquito-borne disease] in Washington, D.C., and Oslo [Norway]."

But that criticism misses the point, according to Jonathan Patz, an associate professor of environmental studies and population health at the University of Wisconsin-Madison. The malaria parasite does show up in temperate regions, Patz says, but it's not a problem because the disease's ability to spread is restricted in moderate climates.

Patz says the danger comes if malaria spreads into a region that has become warmer, which some scientists say may be already happening in Africa. In warm climates, malarial parasites can thrive, and the disease spreads easily, becoming difficult for medicine to halt.

"You can't just do one thing and make it go away," Patz says, so the spread into additional, warming regions would be a serious health threat.

"The lesson for the future is that we need to take a multi-pronged approach to the health effects of climate change," he continues. "Number one, we need a strong public-health infrastructure. There also must be an awareness that these long-time environmental pressures can make disease prevention even harder."

For example, if extreme weather events occur more often, as most climate-change models predict, floods that may have contaminated public water systems every 20 or 30 years in the past may become much more frequent. Then "there's a need to build that into public-health planning," says Patz. "This is where environmental policy becomes the same as public-health policy."

Putting environmental considerations back into the forefront of public health is in some ways a return to the past, Patz says. Before antibiotics and pesticides, "we used to be very environmentally oriented" in medicine, concerned with sanitation and the spread of disease. "Medical schools used to have strong departments of vector ecology" — the study of organisms like mosquitoes that don't cause disease but carry disease-causing pathogens — "but these were dismantled."

That focus needs to come back, Patz says.

---

[1] "Climate Change Futures: Health, Ecological and Economic Dimensions," Center for Health and Global Environment, Harvard Medical School, www.climatechangefutures.org/pdf/CCF_Report_Final_10.27.pdf.

warn that climate change threatens the twin foundations of the state's lucrative tourist industry. A ski season shortened by 20 percent, for instance, could cost $84 million a year in lost tourism revenue. [8] And warmer temperatures also could decimate the maple-dominated forests that attract admirers of colorful fall foliage to the Northeast. [9]

Outside the United States there is widespread support for action, probably because the consequences of human-induced climate change seem more apparent. In Europe, for example, an extreme heat wave in 2003 killed more than 25,000 people — nearly 15,000 of them in France. In May 2002, southeastern India suffered that country's highest-ever one-week death toll from heat; temperatures rose to 120 degrees Fahrenheit, and more than 1,200 people died.

"We are . . . conducting a vast experiment in the composition of the Earth's atmosphere" by allowing emissions to rise, said British environmentalist George Marshall of the activist group Rising Tide. "We have no right . . . to argue to future generations . . . that we were waiting to achieve a full scientific understanding" before acting. [10]

But Stephen Milloy, an adjunct scholar at the libertarian Cato Institute in Washington, warns that the precautionary principle leading Europeans to try to avert climate change now could result in "regulation based on irrational fears." [11]

Such regulation could seriously damage the economy, say many GOP congressional leaders, arguing that the known risks do not justify the potential costs of requiring businesses to limit energy use.

"The United States Senate is standing on firmer ground than ever against mandatory reduction of carbon dioxide, which could effectively throw our nation into an economic depression," said Sen. James Inhofe, R-Okla., chairman of the Senate Environment and Public Works Committee. [12]

But as more scientists and citizens express concern about dangerous environmental changes, some Republican lawmakers have begun to waver. "I have come to accept that something is happening with the Earth's climate," Senate Energy Committee Chairman Pete Domenici, R-N.M., said last July. And while he wasn't sure yet what should be done, he promised to hold more hearings. [13]

Even among those who urge action, however, there's little agreement on how best to reduce GHGs. Some economists recommend imposing "carbon taxes" to discourage excessive use of carbon-based fuels. Last May, New Zealand became the first country to impose such a tax, which is expected to add about 6 percent to household energy costs and 9 percent to business energy costs. [14] Also

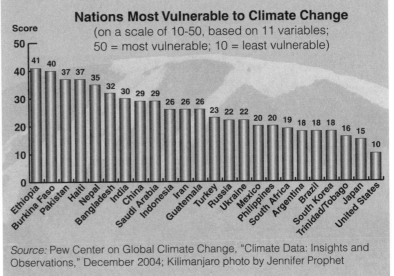

Ethiopia Is Most "Vulnerable" Nation

Ethiopia is considered as the country most vulnerable to the effects of global climate change. Vulnerable nations tend to be the least developed and characterized by weak governance systems, high poverty, poor access to water and sanitation and recent armed conflict. Ironically, such nations contribute least to climate change.

Nations Most Vulnerable to Climate Change
(on a scale of 10-50, based on 11 variables; 50 = most vulnerable; 10 = least vulnerable)

Score

Ethiopia 41, Burkina Faso 40, Pakistan 37, Haiti 37, Nepal 35, Bangladesh 32, India 30, China 29, Saudi Arabia 29, Indonesia 26, Iran 26, Guatemala 26, Turkey 23, Russia 22, Ukraine 22, Mexico 20, Philippines 20, South Africa 19, Argentina 18, Brazil 18, South Korea 18, Trinidad/Tobago 16, Japan 15, United States 10

Source: Pew Center on Global Climate Change, "Climate Data: Insights and Observations," December 2004; Kilimanjaro photo by Jennifer Prophet

last spring Paul Anderson — CEO of Duke Energy, a Charlotte, N.C., power company — surprised many by vowing to lobby Congress for a similar tax.

Unlike some other incentives, a tax could reach all energy-consuming sectors, including motorists, Anderson said. It also would encourage everyone to conserve fuel, to make "low-carbon fuel choices" and encourage development of low-carbon technology, he said. [15]

However, conservatives and many business leaders adamantly oppose a carbon tax. It "makes people poorer and gives government too much revenue," says Marlo Lewis, a senior fellow at the pro-market Competitive Enterprise Institute (CEI).

Congress has not yet contemplated a carbon tax, but some lawmakers from both parties support capping GHGs. Since 2003, Sens. John McCain, R-Ariz., and Joseph I. Lieberman, D-Conn., have sought an emissions cap as well as establishment of a permit system allowing low emitters to sell their permits to high emitters. Last year, Sen. Jeff Bingaman, D-N.M., proposed another cap-and-trade plan that would limit the cost of extra permits,

Top Greenhouse Gas Emitters

The United States, China and the 25-member European Union emit half of the world's CO_2 and other greenhouse gases (GHGs). Wealthier countries tend to have higher rates of consumption and more energy-intensive lifestyles, thus generating more emissions. Australia, the United States and Canada have some of the highest per-capita emissions. By contrast, the four largest developing countries — China, India, Indonesia and Brazil — account for 44 percent of Earth's population but only 24 percent of global emissions.

Country	Percent of world GHGs	Tons of carbon emissions per capita
United States	20.6%	6.6
China	14.8	1.1
European Union	14.0	2.8
Russia	5.7	3.6
India	5.5	0.5
Japan	4.0	2.9
Germany	2.9	3.2
Brazil	2.5	1.3
Canada	2.1	6.3
United Kingdom	2.0	3.1
Italy	1.6	2.5
South Korea	1.6	3.1
Ukraine	1.6	2.9
Mexico	1.5	1.4
France	1.5	2.3
Indonesia	1.5	0.7
Australia	1.4	6.8
Iran	1.3	1.9
South Africa	1.2	2.6
Spain	1.1	2.6

Source: Pew Center on Global Climate Change, "Climate Data: Insights and Observations," December 2004

below 1990 levels. The European Union (EU) implemented a regional cap-and-trade system to make it easier for high-emitting EU countries to comply.

But critics point out that even if all participating nations meet their initial Kyoto targets, global emissions will drop only minimally, not nearly enough to affect planetary temperature. The first round of cuts "doesn't even begin to address the problem," says Berkeley's Muller.

"Only a couple of nations" will meet their targets, says Patrick Michaels, a senior fellow at the Cato Institute.

Furthermore, the three nations considered key to substantial long-term reduction — China, India and the United States — are not part of Kyoto's first round. The United States, which emits an estimated 20 percent of all GHGs, has not ratified the protocol. Cutting U.S. emissions below 1990 levels on the required timetable would have been impossible, says Raymond Kopp, a senior fellow at Resources for the Future, a nonpartisan environmental research group. [16]

The U.S. economy and energy use have skyrocketed since 1990, so to reach the 1990 baseline the United States would have had to cut emissions 30 percent, Kopp says, adding, "There is no possible way the U.S. could agree to that target."

In summer 2005, the Bush administration — which acknowledges that human-caused global warming is occurring but opposes taxes and mandatory emissions limits — launched its own initiative, the Asia-Pacific Partnership on Clean Development and Climate. The group, which includes the United States, China, India, Japan, South Korea and Australia, will promote private-sector development and the distribution of clean-energy technologies. [17]

potentially making it less objectionable to business. Similar proposals in the House have not advanced.

In the absence of federal legislation, seven Mid-Atlantic and Northeastern states tentatively agreed to launch a regional cap-and-trade system for greenhouse gas emissions in 2009.

Meanwhile, by 2012, under the Kyoto Protocol, worldwide GHG emissions would be lowered to 5 percent

Meanwhile, rapidly developing nations like China and India specifically were exempted from the first round of Kyoto cuts. Yet the two huge countries are expected to add most to global emissions over the next century, as cars and electricity come to more of their 2-billion-plus populations. [18]

Despite deficiencies in Kyoto and the current cap-and-trade systems, they represent important first steps, Kyoto supporters say. Everybody understands that the emissions reductions that will be achieved under Kyoto's first round "are but a fraction of what we need," says Elliot Diringer, director of international strategies at the Pew Center on Global Climate Change. Nevertheless, the treaty establishes a legal framework for more significant future reductions, he says, and for "the countries that have accepted targets, it's driving them down the road" toward emissions cutbacks.

As economists, scientists and lawmakers weigh the risk of serious climate change against the cost of strategies that might avert it, here are some questions that are being debated:

Is the world at risk for dangerous climate change?

Climate-change skeptics once argued that the globe was not warming and that, even if it were, there was no proof that human activity had triggered the change. Now few hold such views. Instead, debate centers on whether the changes are likely to be dangerous to humans and the planet.

"The global mean temperature has been going up at a moderate pace from the 1970s, and we know that human activity is likely to contribute," says Myron Ebell, director of the climate change and international environment program at the Competitive Enterprise Institute. The pro-business group once argued strenuously that human activity was not causing warming.

Indeed, the planet's biodiversity has already been affected by the human-induced warming that has occurred to date, some scientists argue, pointing out that some stressed species have had to migrate closer to Earth's poles or further up mountains where it is cooler. Large-scale extinctions of such species are likely in the modern world where human development limits the ability of animals and plants to migrate.

Over the long term, failing to limit human contributions to global warming risks potentially catastrophic consequences for most countries, scientists told the

High tides breach a seawall on Tuvalu, in the South Pacific, in 2004. Islands and developing nations generally are most vulnerable to the effects of global climate change.

Getty Images/Torsten Blackwood

Senate Energy and Natural Resources Committee last July. While modest warming will have "both positive and negative impacts," said Mario Molina, a professor of earth, atmosphere and planetary sciences at the Massachusetts Institute of Technology (MIT), above a certain threshold "the impacts turn strongly negative for most nations, people and biological systems."

Molina warned of "devastating impacts" on ecosystems and biodiversity, severe flooding in urban centers and island nations, "significantly more destructive and frequent" droughts and floods, seriously affected agricultural productivity, exacerbated disease and dislocated populations. [19]

But Lewis, at CEI, says, "There is really no scientific cause for alarm. Yes, there will be change, and, yes, it will have costs and benefits, but to describe it as a catastrophe in the making? No."

Computer climate models only predict extreme changes when they're fed "unrealistic data," Ebell says. For example, modelers often exaggerate how much GHG emissions will rise because they overestimate the future wealth and energy usage of developing nations, he says. "If you put totally implausible numbers into models, you get these scary results."

Richard Lindzen, a professor of meteorology at MIT, agrees that climate models that produce scary scenarios are clearly inaccurate. Currently, planetary temperatures have risen by only "one-third to one-sixth" as high as the models project, he writes, "So either the models are greatly overestimating the sensitivity of the climate to manmade GHG or the models are correct but some unknown process is canceling the warming." Thus, in arguing for climate alarmism, "we are choosing the second possibility" and assuming that whatever is canceling the warming "will soon cease." [20]

But Stephen Schneider, co-director of Stanford University's Center for Environmental Science and Policy, says Lindzen's argument confuses the planet's temperature in its early stages of responding to GHG-induced warming with the final temperature it will register once a new equilibrium is reached. For example, he says, if a small steel ball at 50 degrees Fahrenheit is dropped into a large bucket of 70-degree water, the ball and water eventually will reach an equilibrium temperature near 70 degrees. But if you measure the ball's temperature after only an hour, it might have warmed up to only 55 degrees. Expecting to observe the full warming effect of past emissions today "would be like expecting the ball to hit 70 degrees in the first second," Schneider argues.

Evidence suggesting that dangerous warming is a real possibility — though not a certainty — has piled up in recent years as computer models have improved and satellite data have become available, Schneider says. "I got into this in 1970, and there were 10 papers worth reading. Now there are 1,000," he says.

His conclusion: Climate-change effects "may be either negligible or catastrophic," he says. But, he cautions, those who dispute that climate change could reach dangerous levels "totally rule out catastrophic" as a possibility, even though that's not justified by scientific findings.

Should the United States cap greenhouse gas (GHG) emissions?

Supporters of mandatory limits say slowing GHG emissions is like buying life insurance: It's a reasonable precaution that's worth the cost if a dire possibility turns out to be real.

Among academic economists, for example, "there is a 95 percent consensus" that, given the magnitude of the threat and the risk, "there should be action," says Professor Robert Stavins, of Harvard's John Fahrenheit Kennedy School of Government.

But opponents argue that government regulation is an expensive burden that would cripple business' ability to develop new technology. "I don't see any plausible justification for turning the global economy upside down," says CEI's Lewis. "Kyoto-like policies are simply all cost for no benefit." Even if Kyoto countries meet their initial commitments, he says, the amount of warming that will occur by 2050 will be only slightly lower than it would have been otherwise.

Capping U.S. energy use in line with protocol requirements would cost between $67 billion and $400 billion, he says. "Is it worth spending that" to accomplish a "reduction that is probably too small for anybody to reliably detect?" he asks. Environmentalists "say that you shouldn't gamble with the only environment you have. But we shouldn't gamble with the only economy we have, either."

Many advocates of emissions limits say that the warming slowdown projected by 2050 under the Kyoto cuts is an important first step in a long-term process. And the costs over several years only amount to 0.5 to 3.5 percent of the nation's annual gross domestic product (GDP). [21]

Worldwide, the total cost of stabilizing atmospheric concentrations of carbon dioxide could run as high as $18 trillion, according to Schneider and environmental economist Christian Azar, of Sweden's Chalmers University of Technology. But that is only 3 to 5 percent of annual global GDP, they argue, which the global economy can absorb fairly easily. Since global income is likely to grow by 2 to 3 percent annually, they say, the total cost of stemming climate change "would be overtaken after a few years of income growth." [22]

Moreover, limiting emissions to avert warming is just like taking precautions to mitigate other potential problems, which most people do in their everyday lives, says Peter Wilcoxen, an economist who directs the Center for Environmental Policy and Administration at Syracuse University's Maxwell School. "I compare it to driving on a slippery, icy road," he says. "We don't know if we'll have a bad accident, a minor fender-bender or get down the road with no problem." But, usually, "if we don't have to drive, we don't. And if we do have to drive, we slow down. By analogy, that means we should reduce emissions" where it's relatively painless, such as using more insulation.

Fear that government will impose costly anti-pollution regulations and later discover that the threat was non-existent are overblown, says economist Frank Ackerman, director of research and policy programs at Tufts University's Global Development and Environment

Institute. Europe has operated on the better-safe-than-sorry principle to impose environmental restrictions for decades, he says, and the United States did the same in the 1970s and '80s, with the Clean Air and Clean Water acts.

Since then, there has been almost no evidence that the regulation slowed growth or harmed businesses, says Ackerman, while most of the once-suspected threats — such as asbestos and lead — have turned out to be even more damaging than originally thought.

"Where are the big, expensive, false positives?" he asks. "Where did we spend ourselves into poverty mitigating a problem?"

Harvard's Stavins points out that the United States has significant experience with cap-and-trade policies, starting with local air-pollution permits in the '70s. Emissions limits had their biggest success in the 1980s, he says, when industry successfully removed lead from gasoline using tradable permits among refineries.

In fact, Stavins says, the cap-and-trade program used for lead is a good model for a GHG cap. That's because, as with lead, he explains, it's relatively easy to enforce CO_2 limits at the plants where fuel is produced, but next to impossible to monitor emissions from the millions of individual cars, businesses and homes that burn fossil fuels.

Should Congress enact a carbon tax?

Ask an economist, and you're likely to hear that a carbon tax is an ideal way to slow GHG emissions because it would discourage the use of carbon-intensive fuels. Taxes are simple, effective and multifunctional, they say. Conservative analysts and many business people, however, argue that a tax would only drain private-sector dollars from projects that could help humanity cope with global warming.

A carbon tax would encourage a shift from carbon-intensive fuels like coal while spreading its effects across several industries, says economist Gilbert Metcalf, of Tufts University, raising prices no more than about 4 percent. Meanwhile, he adds, it could produce "really significant revenue" at a time when the federal treasury is experiencing rising deficits. Metcalf estimates a carbon tax of about 10 cents extra on a gallon of gasoline could raise $40 billion a year in revenues.

No one knows exactly how much cutting GHG emissions would cost industry. In such a case, says Harvard's Stavins, economists usually prefer a tax to tradable permits because a company's costs are more predictable.

"With cap and trade, you can be surprised in a bad way," says Metcalf, noting that a limit imposed by lawmakers could turn out to be extremely expensive for industry.

Nevertheless, says Stavins, "politically, a tax is worse." Spurred by the tax, businesses would spend money to cut emissions but also pay taxes on what they failed to cut — a double whammy. Many economists argue that a carbon tax would encourage businesses to develop less carbon-intense technologies, but conservatives generally reject that argument.

"There's no evidence that by making energy more costly you can midwife the technological leap," says the CEI's Lewis. In Europe, where gasoline prices run as high as $7 a gallon — of which taxes make up an average 60 percent — "where is the great leap forward into the new future?" Europeans drive smaller cars and more diesels, but have not developed low-carbon technology, he says.

Instead, "if you want a technology revolution, you really need prosperity, capital," while a carbon tax would drain capital from the private sector, he says.

Kopp of Resources for the Future counters that, in fact, raising fuel prices has spurred market demand in Europe for hybrid cars, which run on a combination of gasoline and electric battery power. "As gas prices go up, the demand for hybrids is quite high," he says.

But Lewis says recent U.S. history hasn't backed up that idea. The gasoline price hikes of late 2005, haven't caused Americans to drive less, for example, he says.

In fact, retort advocates of emission controls, many Americans *are* buying hybrids.

Syracuse's Wilcoxen says people change their behaviors only if they believe a price change will last. For example, technological change did happen during the oil-price hikes of the 1970s, he points out. "U.S. energy consumption leveled off. We stabilized fossil-fuel consumption," he says. "People thought the price change was going to be permanent, so they started buying smaller cars and insulating their homes."

With both taxes and limits on GHG emissions having their drawbacks and detractors, a growing number of economists propose a "hybrid," or "safety-valve," system that incorporates elements from both.

To effectively control emissions, any "policy will have to be in effect longer than any other policy in the history of the world," says Wilcoxen. That's nearly impossible

CHRONOLOGY

1800s-1910s *In the first stage of the Industrial Revolution, coal burning increases greenhouse gases (GHGs) like carbon dioxide in the atmosphere. Some scientists theorize GHGs are warming the planet.*

1827 French scientist Jean-Baptiste Fourier hypothesizes that the atmosphere acts like a "greenhouse," keeping Earth warmer than it would be otherwise.

1896 Swedish scientist Svante Arrhenius speculates that carbon-dioxide buildup may warm the atmosphere.

1920s-1950s *The opening of oil fields in Texas and the Middle East in the 1920s accelerates fossil-fuel use. Scientists first report that the globe has been warming.*

1931 Severe drought begins turning the Plains States into a Dust Bowl that lasts nearly a decade. Some scientists blame the greenhouse effect.

1957 U.S. scientist David Keeling begins continuous monitoring of atmospheric carbon-dioxide levels and finds them rising year after year.

1960s-1980s *Scientific conferences and Department of Energy researchers focus attention in the 1960s on climate change. Improved computer modeling and satellite data collection speed climate-science development.*

1979 First World Climate Conference calls on governments to prevent potential human-caused changes to climate.

1985 Scientific conference in Villach, Austria, predicts that GHGs will cause the largest planetary temperature rise in human history during the first half of the 21st century, possibly raising sea levels by a meter.

1988 United Nations sets up Intergovernmental Panel on Climate Change to analyze new scientific findings.

1990s *The hottest years in recorded climate history occur; many nations push for international agreements to slow climate change.*

1992 U.N. Framework Convention on Climate Change is signed in Rio de Janeiro, pledging nations to voluntarily reduce GHG emissions.

1994 Fearful of flooding, the Alliance of Small Island States asks for a 20 percent cut in global GHG emissions by 2005.

1996 At a meeting of Framework Convention members, U.S. delegates agree to press for legally binding emissions cuts.

1997 The resulting Kyoto Protocol calls for legally binding emissions cuts in industrialized countries, averaging 5.4 percent by 2010. U.S. Senate declares the United States will not ratify a treaty that doesn't require "meaningful" emissions cuts by developing nations.

2000s *Kyoto Protocol is ratified, committing countries to binding cuts in GHG emissions. . . . Industrialization accelerates in India and China, with the potential to push global GHG emissions higher.*

2001 Reneging on a campaign pledge, President George W. Bush withdraws the United States from Kyoto Protocol talks.

August 2003 Severe heat wave kills thousands in Europe.

2004 One of the world's largest insurance companies, Swiss Re, estimates that within a few years climate-change damage will cost $150 billion annually. . . . Australian scientists develop a vaccine to reduce methane — a GHG — emitted by animals.

2005 Kyoto Protocol takes effect, following ratification by Russia in 2004. . . . New Zealand becomes first country to enact a carbon tax. . . . Seven Northeastern states form the Regional Greenhouse Gas Initiative to limit GHG emissions.

Jan. 11, 2006 First meeting of President Bush's Asia-Pacific Partnership on Clean Development and Climate is held.

with either a pure tax or a pure cap-and-trade system, he says. "A huge constituency" would lobby to abolish the cap-and-trade policy every year because of its unpredictable costs, and political opposition to taxes is a given.

A hybrid plan would allow the government to impose caps, and then issue free permits to each company for the level of emissions it was allowed. But if cutting emissions to that level became too difficult, a company could buy a one-year permit from the government at a set, relatively low price, says Wilcoxen. Knowing the price of the extra permit in advance would make the system of caps as predictable as a tax and also bring in some revenue for the government, he says.

BACKGROUND

An Uncertain World

Making climate-change policy would be much easier if scientists could predict the timing — and precise causes — of Earth's future temperature changes. But the climate system is exquisitely complicated, and the most science can provide is a broad consensus on a range of possibilities.

As early as the 1890s scientists — including Svante Arrhenius of Sweden and P.C. Chamberlain of the United States — theorized that CO_2 buildup in the atmosphere might cause climate change. But climate science, which depends on complex computer models and hard-to-gather present and past data on temperature variation, is a developing science.

Among scientists, there is a general — though not a unanimous — consensus that global warming is real, says Berkeley's Muller. "The evidence that the Earth has been warming over the past 100 years is pretty solid."

But consensus on that last point has changed in recent years. A decade ago, most scientists believed global warming began around the early 1900s and was caused by a jump in carbon dioxide emissions due to human activities like cutting forests and burning fuels. Today, most scientists believe that human activity has only caused the warming that has occurred since 1960, Muller says.

For the European Union, that consensus has been enough for governments to justify imposing limits. In the United States, however, many lawmakers in Congress fear that government regulation will harm free markets. That fear — combined with growing worry that climate change also could damage the economy — spurs politicians to demand quantifiable answers from scientists before imposing mandates on businesses.

"We're looking for a little more certainty" before committing to a climate-change policy, Alaska's Sen. Murkowski said at the Senate Energy hearing in July.

For many lawmakers, government action is not justifiable unless the risks of harm definitively outweigh economic losses that might result from emissions limits, which, one way or another, would force Americans to consume less fossil energy. Only data definitively quantifying the impact of human-induced climate change could establish that. But climate models can't provide that certainty.

Top Models

A scientific model in climatology is a set of ideas — expressed as mathematical equations — about how climate responds to changing conditions, such as varying amounts of energy from the sun and changing proportions of atmospheric gases. Fed with data about past and current conditions and projected future events, such as changing levels of CO_2 emissions, a computer model predicts future climate scenarios.

Scientists cannot state such scenarios as definitive, however, because of what Stanford's Schneider describes as "a cascade of uncertainties" in developing both models and data.

Climate models are based on ideas about how the atmosphere works, derived in part from historical data about the way the climate has shifted through the ages. But, "there are problems aplenty," even in figuring out today's temperatures around the world, let alone comparing them to the past or attributing change to specific causes, Muller wrote. "An accurate thermometer didn't exist until the 1900s."

To determine temperatures in earlier times, scientists examine the widths of tree rings, the ratio of oxygen isotopes in glacial ice, variations in species of microscopic animals found in sediment and historical records of occurrences, such as harbor closures. But, such proxy measurements are also affected by elements of the weather, Muller adds, such as rainfall, cloud cover and storm patterns. "Most proxies are sensitive to local conditions, and extrapolating to global climate can be hazardous." [23]

Setting a Value on the Future

As concern about climate change grows, policymakers increasingly find themselves at odds over how to balance current priorities against future threats.

Frank Ackerman, an environmental economist at Tufts University, in Boston, says traditional economic analysis is the wrong approach. A traditional economic analysis might conclude that initiatives to limit future climate changes impose unacceptable costs and sacrifices on the current generation, says Ackerman. For example, cutting carbon emissions means people must drive their cars less now.

Traditionally, however, dollars spent to purchase future benefits are discounted by economists by a few percentage points for each year the benefit will be deferred, reducing their "present-value" worth, Ackerman explains. Such "discounting" makes sense when we're figuring out how much money we can afford each month, for example, on a mortgage. "But is the fate of the Earth something that should be treated the same way?" Ackerman asks.

He argues that instead of looking to economists for answers, legislators should come to grips with the fact that setting environmental policy "will be a political process, even though we don't want to admit it."

Making political value judgments about the future requires a brand of ethical analysis that differs from what most people are used to, says Stephen Gardiner, an assistant professor of philosophy at the University of Washington.

In ethical terms, the traditional economic method of "discounting" future benefits amounts to "taking advantage" of our position in time, says Gardiner. In other words, we enjoy the pleasures of our energy-intense technology, even though it may impose substantial costs — even "catastrophic costs" — on people who have the misfortune to live after us.

Crafting policy to protect future generations "is not completely new," says Gardiner. But for climate change, "the issue is on a bigger scale, and the lag time is very pronounced," so the actions we take today may not be evident for hundreds of years. That being the case, Gardiner doubts lawmakers will be willing to act aggressively.

Until that happens, he says, they will naturally find it "politically convenient not to deal with" climate change.

Conservative analysts have a different view of our responsibility toward the future, however. Taking government action today is likely to only cripple the future and rob private citizens of money they could use to adapt to climate change, says Myron Ebell, director of global warming and international environmental policy at the industry-funded Competitive Enterprise Institute.

Instead of draining off money to pay taxes or meet government-imposed energy regulations, lawmakers should take a hands-off approach that will allow wealth to develop. Wealth and technological knowledge and sophistication help people deal with environmental challenges, he says. "A wealthy Bangladesh could deal with a typhoon."

Meanwhile, support for more attention to climate change as an ethical and moral problem has been building in an unusual constituency. Some evangelical Christians, traditionally identified with conservative, anti-environmentalist views, are developing a policy on global warming that may call for curbing greenhouse gas (GHG) emissions. [1]

The Evangelical Environmental Network (EEN) says that "nearly 500 Christian leaders" have signed its Evangelical Declaration on the Care of Creation.

"Urgency is required" to address warming because "we're making long-term decisions now" that will affect GHG emissions for decades, the group says. [2] "Addressing global warming is a new way to love our neighbors. Poor children will be hurt the most, and it is their stories we must remember when thinking and praying about global warming."

The EEN urges leaders to be "good stewards of natural resources" and support "government policies to do the same." It applauds a non-binding Senate resolution passed in June 2005 that dubs the Bush administration's approach on climate change as "insufficient." [3]

---

[1] Mark Bixler, "Leaders Direct Clout at Global Warming," *Atlanta Journal-Constitution*, Dec. 27, 2005.

[2] Evangelical Environmental Network, "Global Warming Briefing for Evangelical Leaders," www.creationcare.org/responses/faq.php.

[3] *Ibid.*

Like the data, the models being used are also works in progress, Muller says. Climate science is developing "fairly rapidly," he says, but not as rapidly as the science of storm prediction, for example, which now gives meteorologists much more certainty about the projected paths of hurricanes. In climatology, "we're still groping for the simple principles that we can use to predict things," he says.

Gauging the probability of future scenarios requires accurate descriptions of physical processes, such as how clouds reflect heat, as well as other factors, like future population growth, economic development and energy technologies. The multitude of factors and the degree of uncertainty means that different climate analyses "will arrive at very different estimates of the probability of dangerous climate change in 2100," explains Schneider. [24]

"How should you look at emerging data? Well, you don't get all excited about a block of ice melting off Antarctica and think that we will all drown," says Schneider. But, he adds, neither should one dismiss the corroborating evidence that is emerging, mostly in the form of "fingerprints" — specific examples of climate change that one would expect if the planet were warming substantially and if human activity was driving the change.

For example, over the past several decades the stratosphere — between nine and 31 miles above Earth's surface — has cooled, while surface temperatures have warmed. This suggests that GHG emissions and not increased sunshine are responsible for the trend, says Schneider. But could it be an accident, or from some other cause? he asks. "No single, new study will prove or disprove warming," he says.

For more certainty, scientists have sought many such "fingerprints," and observations from many fields now tend to confirm human-caused warming, which might rise high enough to be dangerous, says Schneider.

For example, scientists have tallied how many bird species return north from the tropics earlier each spring and how many plants sprout earlier each growing season. Recent data show about 80 percent of bird and plant cycles are occurring earlier.

Taken individually, no study allows a clear conclusion about climate change. "But when you get a lot of data like this, it tells you that, in fact, the dice are loaded in favor of warming," says Schneider.

Still, much remains a mystery. Controversy rages, for example, over the role of South America's huge Amazon rainforest in climate change. In the past, the Amazon was able to soak up large amounts of carbon dioxide from the atmosphere, providing a brake on atmospheric GHG buildup. Today, however, some scientists argue that widespread deforestation has actually made the Amazon rainforest a net contributor to GHG emissions, as trees are burned and debris rots.

Modeling and assembling data "take a long time" and don't yield clear-cut answers, Schneider acknowledges. "I know that's very frustrating for politicians and the media."

According to Muller, those frustrations are hindering development of climatology by substituting political battles for unbiased, unhurried study. Currently, climatology is "so primitive in its achievement, yet so important, that the combination is disastrous," he says.

Traditionally, science has advanced when rigorous, self-critical thinkers follow facts where they lead. But, because of its potential environmental and economic impact, climate science has attracted some honorable but agenda-driven scientists — on both sides of the issue, Muller says. "I see many well-meaning scientists dropping their scientific training because they're trying to be helpful" by producing the definitive answers policymakers crave, he says.

In the long run, climate science will be better served if researchers "present results with caution, and insist on equivocating," according to Muller. "Leave it to the president and his advisers to make decisions based on uncertain conclusions." [25]

But some climate-change critics are more cynical about their scientific opponents' motives. Cato's Michaels, for example, contends some scientists tout scary climate dangers just to keep federal research funds flowing. "They perceive they aren't going to get any attention if they don't overstate the case," he says. They're afraid if they express uncertainties, "the $2.5 billion gravy train will grind to a halt."

The Odds

Many climate researchers find a strong probability that increasing GHG emissions will push average global temperatures up 3.6 to 5.4 degrees Fahrenheit * in the 21st century — and possibly even 9 degrees Fahrenheit or more.

For example, according to Thomas Wigley, a senior scientist at the U.S. National Center for Atmospheric Research, and Sarah Raper, of the United Kingdom's University of East Anglia, there's a 90 percent probability that Earth's surface temperature will rise between 3 and 8.8 degrees Fahrenheit by 2100. [26]

Similarly, researchers at the University of North Carolina and Massachusetts Institute of Technology say current models predict a 50 percent chance of mean surface temperatures rising by more than 4.3 degrees Fahrenheit by 2100, and a 97.5 percent chance that the increase will be less than 8.8 degrees. [27]

---

* Or 2 to 3 degrees Celsius. Most scientific studies use Celsius.

Temperature changes in those ranges would "very likely" cause more hot days and more heat waves on all continents, leading to increased heat-related deaths and serious illness among the elderly and the urban poor, according to a majority of the U.N.'s International Panel on Climate Change (IPCC).

Increased heat also could have a devastating impact on tourism in poor, tropical countries, making them too hot to visit. There is also a 90-percent-plus probability that many regions would see more intense precipitation, increasing floods, mudslides and avalanches. [28]

Worsening regional drought conditions are only slightly less likely, with a 67-90 percent probability that many continents will have drier summers. That could reduce crop yields — potentially triggering famine — and shrink drinking-water resources, Schneider notes. [29]

Many scientists agree on the IPCC's probability assessments. But even if the whole world agreed, policy decisions would still not be easy, observed a National Academy of Sciences panel in 2000. "The word 'safe' . . . depends on both viewpoint and value judgment" and "changes dramatically" if you live in a country "with sufficient resources for adaptation" or in a poor country or small island nation whose residents have few relocation options. [30]

Further complicating things, climate change is a more all-encompassing issue — both in space and time — than any that humanity has dealt with before. For one thing, GHG emissions anywhere affect climate-related events everywhere. "When you think of air pollution — that's many times simpler," says Kopp of Resources for the Future. Greenhouse gas emissions come from so many sources "that it's off the charts. It may look like problems that we've had in the past, but it's exquisitely [more] complicated."

Moreover, in addition to long lag times between changes in emissions levels and climate alteration, a turn from carbon-intensive to low-carbon technologies can't be done on a dime. "You have automobile fleets all over the world, and they have about a 10-to-15-year lifespan," Kopp says.

Voluntary vs. Mandatory

The 1992 U.N. Framework Convention on Climate Change (UNFCCC) was launched to stabilize GHG emissions at 1990 levels by 2000, mainly through voluntary GHG reductions by industrialized countries.

By March 1994, 50 nations had ratified the treaty, bringing it into full effect. The United States, which had ratified it in 1992, was among 189 countries that signed the agreement. Soon after the UNFCCC took effect, however, several countries began to doubt that emissions reductions could be accomplished voluntarily. In response, UNFCCC participants in December 1997 negotiated an amendment to the treaty, the Kyoto Protocol, calling for legally binding emissions cuts.

Kyoto was not the quick sell the UNFCCC had been. It did not go into effect until February 2005 — after enough countries (those producing at least 55 percent of total emissions) ratified the agreement.

Although the United States was heavily involved in the long negotiation that produced the Kyoto accord in 1997, it has not ratified — and probably won't ratify — the agreement.

Meanwhile, many Kyoto signatories recognize a host of as-yet-unsolved problems with the treaty. These include continuing questions about how to get the private sector to alter the way it uses energy, how to involve developing nations without crippling their growing economies and whether affordable technologies can be developed to replace carbon-based fuels.

Europeans initially proposed a tax on GHG emissions — in order to persuade the private sector to change its ways. But U.S. businesses and many lawmakers adamantly opposed new taxes, and Europeans settled on a system that U.S. negotiators preferred — setting up a timetable for meeting national emissions targets. In recent years, however, U.S. lawmakers and the Bush administration have remained hostile to that approach as well.

In 1997, in response to the Clinton administration's participation in the Kyoto talks, the U.S. Senate rejected mandatory cuts when it approved, 95-0, the so-called Byrd-Hagel resolution. The non-binding resolution called on the United States to refuse mandatory cuts unless developing countries also were required to limit emissions, and backers demonstrated the limits would not harm the U.S. economy. [31]

Today, most Kyoto backers and critics agree the protocol is flawed, but supporters nonetheless praise it as an essential first step. "A sound international agreement" is vital on climate change because the issue has a serious "free-rider problem," says Harvard's Stavins. That is, if some countries cut emissions severely to avert warming — and incur the costs of doing so — other countries can benefit just as much, even if they keep emitting. Such problems require treaties and other legal means to push countries to participate against what may seem to be their own self-interest.

But Kyoto is "not a good structure, even if the U.S. were on board," Stavins argues. The treaty imposes targets that are "too little, too fast," mandating quite large cuts over the next five years but setting no long-term goals for the ensuing years. That's left too many countries worried that they won't meet initial targets, which has set off a new scramble to establish a long-term structure.

Despite problems, the protocol is an important milestone, given the transborder nature of warming and other environmental matters, says Ackerman of Tufts. "Warts and all, it's the beginning of a process where the world tries to negotiate its way toward something."

New Technology

In the 18th and 19th centuries, the Industrial Revolution opened the way to human-triggered climate change. Mushrooming industries in Europe and North America burnt coal and, later, oil and gasoline, emitting GHGs into the atmosphere. Meanwhile, logging worldwide felled forests that had once soaked up carbon dioxide from the air. [32]

And if technology got us into the global-warming dilemma, technology will have to get us out, many climate experts say. "We are not going to solve the problem without new technologies," many of which already exist but aren't being used, says Pew's Diringer. Heavy use of fossil fuels, especially coal, is the problem, he says. Potential solutions include fossil-fuel alternatives, cleaner ways to burn fossil fuels and more efficient machines. [33]

But no technology will be adequate on its own, and all have costs and drawbacks, says Alan Nogee, director of the clean energy program at the Union of Concerned Scientists, which advocates strong steps to avert global warming. "There's no silver bullet."

A top priority is to develop cleaner ways to burn coal. Despite its high carbon content, many developed nations — including the United States and Australia — depend heavily on domestic coal deposits for electricity, as do China and many other developing nations. [34] The Energy Information Administration (EIA) estimates that by 2025 energy demand by developing nations — primarily China and India — will be more than twice the level in 2002. In fact, by 2025 demand for energy in the developing world will be 9 percent higher than in existing industrialized countries, and climbing, according to the EIA.

Two technologies that show promise are coal gasification — which breaks coal down into its component parts and separates out the carbon — and coal sequestration — which stores the separated carbon long-term in the ground or underwater. But much more research and investment are needed before either technology is adaptable and affordable. Other alternative energy sources, from windmills to nuclear plants, also have roles to play, but they are controversial: Conservative analysts and industry tout nuclear power while environmentalists want a larger role for renewables. [35]

> ## "The evidence that the Earth has been warming over the past 100 years is pretty solid."
>
> — **Richard A. Muller**
> Physics professor at the University of California at Berkeley

"Clearly, renewables are not going to be an immediate solution," says University of Michigan Professor of political science Barry Rabe. "Solar costs are still pretty high." But there has been considerable progress incorporating variable power sources like wind — which are produced in small, non-centralized facilities — into electric-transmission grids, Rabe says.

Conservatives in the United States, however, counter that renewables like wind have little future. "The wealthy, connected, liberal people of Nantucket will say, 'You're not putting a windmill in the middle of my [ocean] view,' " says Cato's Michaels.

But Rabe says states like Nebraska and Texas that have abundant, cheap land are already generating wind power.

Europe, Japan and even China and India are also embracing renewables, says Nogee. "We invented the technologies in their modern form," he says. "But the failure of the U.S. government to provide consistent support means most of the markets have shifted abroad, including the manufacturing capability and the jobs."

Did "Warming" Cause Recent Hurricanes?

The ferocity of Hurricane Katrina and the record-high number of hurricanes spawned in the North Atlantic in the last two hurricane seasons have dramatically focused public attention on the question of whether global warming — and the resulting warmer ocean temperatures — might be causing more and stronger hurricanes.

The debate stems from the belief that warmer ocean temperatures "fuel" hurricanes — both in frequency and intensity. However, as with all controversies related to climate change, bitter debate rages, even as the science slowly develops.

"Katrina has nothing to do with global warming. Nothing," financial analyst and American Enterprise Institute fellow James K. Glassman confidently declared online in *Capitalism Magazine*. "Giant hurricanes are rare, but they are not new." [1]

Hurricane analysts who "have been around a long time . . . don't think this is human-induced global warming," meteorologist and hurricane-science pioneer William Gray of Colorado State University's Tropical Meteorology Project told Glassman. "The people that say that it is are usually those that know very little about hurricanes." [2]

But hurricane scientists like Gray "don't know a lot about global climate," shot back Judith Curry, chair of Georgia Institute of Technology's School of Earth and Atmospheric Science. "Their conclusions are based on their investigation of North Atlantic hurricanes" only — which represent only about 10 percent of hurricanes, worldwide — and "the North Atlantic does not have anything to do with what goes on globally." [3]

However, scientists aren't sure whether ocean temperatures actually cause hurricanes to intensify or even whether there is a correlation between warmer ocean temperatures and hurricane strength. Many other factors, such as the El Niño global weather phenomenon, can cause more frequent hurricanes, say weather and climate scientists.

Scientists agree on a few points, however, including the fact that global warming isn't needed to account for recent storms. Before Katrina, three other storms of similar magnitude occurred before the 1970s — two in 1935 and one in 1969 — the period of most of the human-induced global warming that has occurred so far. [4]

Moreover, more than one known climate cycle affects the number and severity of hurricanes in the region, causing hurricane-heavy periods to alternate with periods of fewer severe storms. One heavy-storm cycle, driven by so-called El Niño Oscillations, began in 1995, and "every year since . . . has seen above-average hurricane activity, with one exception." [5]

But as scientists seek telltale "fingerprints" of climate change in weather cycles, some are turning up evidence of a correlation between recent storms and the slow planetary warming that's occurred over the past 33 years, says the Pew Center on Global CLimate Change.

For example, as surface temperatures of tropical seas have risen in hurricane basins around the world since 1970, the frequency of very intense hurricanes has almost doubled, according to Curry and a colleague. [6]

Sea-surface temperatures are rising globally at the same time that atmospheric water vapor is increasing. That means that "the environment in which . . . hurricanes form is changing . . . in ways that provide more fuel for them," said Kevin Trenberth, head of climate analysis at the National Center for Atmospheric Research. A March 2004 hurricane in the South Atlantic off Brazil "was the first of its kind, and it's clear evidence that things are changing," Trenberth said. [7]

Are these correlations real? Do they indicate a long-term trend associated with global warming? No one knows for certain quite yet. However, "evidence . . . is starting to emerge of a human fingerprint in hurricane trends," concluded a recent cover story in the British magazine *New Scientist*. "It is not yet proof, but neither can it be ignored." [8]

[1] James K. Glassman, "Hurricane Katrina and Global Warming," *Capitalism Magazine*, Sept. 3, 2005, http://capmag.com.

[2] Quoted in James K. Glassman, "Hurricanes and Global Warming: Interview with Meteorologist Dr. William Gray," *Capitalism Magazine*, Sept. 12, 2005, http://capmag.com.

[3] Quoted in "The Evidence Linking Hurricanes and Climate Change: An Interview With Judith Curry," *Environmental Science & Technology Online News*, American Chemical Society, Oct. 20, 2005, http://pubs.acs.org.

[4] "Was Katrina's Power a Product of Global Warming?" Pew Center on Global Climate Change, www.pewclimate.org/.

[5] *Ibid.*

[6] Peter Webster *et al.*, "Changes in Tropical Cyclone Number, Duration, and Intensity in a Warming Environment," *Science*, Sept. 16, 2005, pp. 1844-1846.

[7] Quoted in "Hurricanes and Global Warming News Conference," Center for Health and Global Environment, Harvard Medical School, Oct. 21, 2004.

[8] Fred Pearce, "The Gathering Storm," *New Scientist*, Dec. 3, 2005, p. 36.

Should the U.S. join an international treaty on climate change?

YES Sen. James Jeffords, I-Vt.
Ranking minority member, Senate Committee on Environment and Public Works

From statement posted on Sen. Jeffords' Web site, December 2005

One of the most important issues facing mankind is the problem of human-induced climate change. The broad consensus within the scientific community is that global warming has begun, is largely the result of human activity and is accelerating.

Global warming will result in more extreme weather, increased flooding and drought, disruption of agricultural and water systems, threats to human health and loss of sensitive species and ecosystems. We must take action now to minimize these effects, for our children, our grandchildren and future generations.

[In December 2005], 189 countries met in Montreal to discuss global climate change. . . . Members of my staff traveled to Montreal and met with representatives and negotiators from other countries. They witnessed firsthand how the Bush administration worked very hard to dissuade other countries from agreeing to even discuss further commitments. This is not the position that our nation should be taking. We should be leading the way on climate change, not burying our head in the sand. . . .

The overwhelming majority of Americans support taking some form of action on climate change. A recent poll found 73 percent of Americans believe the U.S. should participate in the Kyoto Treaty. . . . The study found that 83 percent of Americans favor "legislation requiring large companies to reduce greenhouse-gas emissions to 2000 levels by 2010 and to 1990 levels by 2020." The current administration is completely out of step with the American public on this issue.

I am both discouraged and heartened by the outcome of the talks in Montreal. Those of us who care about stopping climate change did everything we could to help aid these talks, and despite the Bush administration resistance, the international dialogue on climate change will continue.

But dialogue is not nearly enough, and the consequences of additional delay are dire. The U.S. has been and remains the largest emitter of greenhouse gases. It has a responsibility to its own people and to the people of the world to be a leader on this issue. Thus far, it has been anything but a leader, and these talks highlighted that fact.

I look forward to the day when I can once again be proud of the United States' role in these talks, when we can enter these negotiations having done our part. I believe that is what we agreed to in 1992, when the Senate ratified the climate treaty, and it is high time we live up to our obligation.

NO Sen. James Inhofe, R-Okla.
Chairman, Senate Committee on Environment and Public Works

From statement delivered in Senate, Jan. 4, 2005

As I said on the Senate floor on July 28, 2003, "much of the debate over global warming is predicated on fear, rather than science." I called the threat of catastrophic global warming the "greatest hoax ever perpetrated on the American people," a statement that, to put it mildly, was not viewed kindly by environmental extremists and their elitist organizations. I also pointed out, in a lengthy committee report, that those same environmental extremists exploit the issue for fundraising purposes, raking in millions of dollars.

Since my detailed climate change speech in 2003, the so-called skeptics continued to speak out. What they are saying, and what they are showing, is devastating to the alarmists. They have amassed additional scientific evidence convincingly refuting the alarmists' most cherished assumptions.

Let's ask some simple questions. Is global warming causing more extreme weather events of greater intensity, and is it causing sea levels to rise? The answer to both is an emphatic "No." The number of such disasters in Asia, and the deaths attributed to them, [have been] declining fairly sharply over the last 30 years.

Or let's take hurricanes. A team led by the National Oceanic and Atmospheric Administration's Dr. Christopher Landsea concluded that the relationship of global temperatures to the number of intense land-falling hurricanes is either non-existent or very weak.

What about sea-level rise? In a study published in *Global and Planetary Change*, Dr. Nils-Axel Morner of Sweden found "there is no fear of massive future flooding as claimed in most global warming scenarios."

What I have outlined today won't appear in *The New York Times*. Instead you'll read much about "consensus" and Kyoto and hand wringing by its editorial writers that unrestricted carbon-dioxide emissions from the United States are harming the planet. You'll read nothing, of course, about how Kyoto-like policies harm Americans, especially the poor and minorities, causing higher energy prices, reduced economic growth and fewer jobs.

After all, that is the real purpose behind Kyoto, as Margot Wallstrom, the European Union's environmental minister, said in a revealing moment of candor. To her, Kyoto is about "leveling the playing field" for businesses worldwide. In other words, we can't compete, so let's use a feel-good treaty, based on shoddy science, fear and alarmism — and which will have no perceptible impact on the environment — to restrict America's economic growth and prosperity. Unfortunately for Ms. Wallstrom and Kyoto's staunchest advocates, America was wise to her scheme, and it has rejected Kyoto and similar policies convincingly.

Europe has a high target for renewable energy in its electric supply — 21 percent by 2010. However, as of May 2005, the European Environment Agency notes that Europeans have made only slow progress toward that goal and in fact went backwards in one recent year — 2002. The EU will need "significant further growth" to meet the ambitious goal. Most EU countries still depend on hydropower to meet the renewables quota, and there is little further capacity for dam building. Denmark and Finland, which have strong government policies to promote renewable development, are ahead of the pack. [36]

Despite Europe's difficulties, however, most analysts still say that the EU is well ahead of the United States on renewable energy.

China also enacted "ambitious" renewable-energy requirements for power generation that went into effect in January 2006, according to the environmental group Worldwatch Institute. And India now has the world's fourth-largest wind power industry.

Nevertheless, renewable sources can't meet all of the world's energy needs, and nuclear power "obviously" must also be considered, despite worries over terrorism, Alexander Downer, Australia's minister of foreign affairs, told the six-nation Asia-Pacific Partnership on Clean Development and Climate on Jan. 11. Australia, which does not use nuclear, hopes to export nuclear fuel to China. [37] U.S. Energy Secretary Samuel Bodman warned that nuclear materials exports were vulnerable to theft by terrorists and called on China to agree to anti-terror safeguards so the plan could proceed. [38]

Some industry leaders in the United States would like to see more nuclear plants, says Rabe, but they make many states nervous. Even in Illinois, where nuclear already generates more than 40 percent of electrical power, "ask them which Chicago suburb wants" the next nuclear plant, Rabe quips.

Increasing energy efficiency is also expected to play a role in reducing greenhouse gases, but the private sector will undoubtedly need a push — such as tougher efficiency standards — says Duke Energy's Anderson.

"The only way to reduce emissions is to consume less fuel," said Anderson. "Yet U.S. government fuel-efficiency standards for cars haven't changed since 1990. And the average fuel efficiency for new cars and trucks fell from 22.1 miles per gallon in 1988 to 20.4 miles per gallon in 2001. We're heading in the wrong direction." [39]

CURRENT SITUATION

Kyoto Crash?

Following a December global warming summit in Montreal, countries participating in the Kyoto Protocol are assessing how to reach targets for reducing GHGs without cooperation from three of the world's biggest current and potential emitters: China, India and the United States.

After acknowledging that most countries won't be able to meet their initial Kyoto targets, "signatories started talking about post-2012 commitments," says Resources for the Future's Kopp. But he says ratifying nations feel pressured to commit themselves to completely unrealistic cuts in order to maintain the appearance of movement toward Kyoto's goals without cutbacks by the United States, the world's biggest CO_2 emitter.

The EU is talking about "draconian" cuts that would compensate — on paper anyway — for non-participation by the United States, he says. "But when it came to talking about what they really want to do, it didn't happen."

The meeting had been called to assess progress and plot future action. As in the negotiations leading to Kyoto, especially tense discussions centered on how the United States and China will participate in future agreements.

The U.S. delegation initially avoided participating in substantive conversations, says Kopp, but in the closing hours, "China signaled a willingness to get involved." That put pressure on the United States to offer at least minimal future involvement, but it promised only to participate in informal talks.

Nevertheless, says Kopp, "If the [EU] can move China, it may be able to move the U.S." However, China is an easier sell right now, he says, because it is investing in energy resources for rapid, anticipated growth.

Syracuse's Wilcoxen says the news that most signatories probably won't meet their initial Kyoto targets was not a big surprise. "A lot of countries signed and ratified [the treaty] knowing that it was lies," he says. "Japan had known for five years they couldn't meet the targets."

Committing to the Kyoto targets-and-timetables approach was "a well-intentioned mistake," Wilcoxen adds. He says other mechanisms — such as carbon taxes and fixed-price annual emissions permits for high emitters — would work better than the emissions caps set out by the treaty. He calls the Kyoto process "a horrible waste of time" that "set the whole process back 10 or 12 years because there's been all this arguing over what is fundamentally flawed anyway."

Meanwhile, Europe's emissions-trading mechanism for Kyoto may be damaging European trade while failing to hold down emissions, Kopp says. The EU has not found a way to cap transportation emissions, which "are out of control," he says. That puts most of the burden on industries important to international trade, such as the power and manufacturing sectors. EU politicians say they would be willing to accept that outcome, if they were protected from losing out on trade to non-participating countries like China and the United States.

"You can imagine the difficult position this puts the EU in," says Kopp.

Washington Wavers

Although the federal government is still largely on the climate-change sidelines, the Bush administration proposed an initiative in 2005, and interest is growing in the Senate. The House remains aloof, however.

"Congress is currently shifting," says the Pew Center's Diringer. Senators have twice rejected the McCain-Lieberman cap-and-trade proposal to slow GHG emissions. But in June 2005, a Senate majority expressed interest in considering — if not acting on — the problem. Fifty-three senators voted for the Senate Climate Change Resolution — a non-binding resolution "finding" that there is a scientific consensus that human-caused climate change is occurring, and that "mandatory steps will be required to slow" GHG emissions.

The vote was "a bellwether that would have been hard to conceive of a year earlier," Diringer says.

The Senate also has a new climate-change proposal to consider, alongside McCain-Lieberman. New Mexico Sen. Bingaman's proposal to cap GHG emissions for U.S. industries would ease the cost of additional emissions permits for companies that couldn't initially meet their mandatory cuts.

While some climate-change proposals have seen debates, votes and some hearings in the Senate over the past few years, similar proposals introduced in the House have languished, and House leaders with jurisdiction over energy and environment issues have expressed extreme skepticism about global warming. Last year, for example, Chairman Joe Barton, R-Texas, of the House Committee on Energy and Commerce, caused an outcry among scientists when he launched an inquiry into the work of several climate scientists whose data has been cited by the IPCC, suggesting that the international panel was unjustly biased toward belief in global warming.

For his part, President Bush's new Asia-Pacific Partnership will share ideas and promote private-sector development of clean energy technologies. [40]

It's not clear what initiatives the partnership will pursue because "there's no budget for it yet," says the CEI's Lewis. But, like other conservative analysts, Lewis says the organization has promise and will give the world "a place to go after Kyoto, which contains the seeds of its own destruction."

For the new group, says Lewis, the administration wanted to start with a handful of countries that are large emitters, because "when you are dealing with a small number of people, you can do something serious."

But skeptics like Diringer note that, unlike Kyoto, the partnership "doesn't commit anybody to anything," so legislators won't feel an obligation to fund the initiative. "They will only be given the funding level that you can squeeze out of Congress in a given year."

Four partnership members — China, India, Japan and South Korea — have ratified Kyoto, although only Japan is required to make significant emissions cuts under that treaty. Partners Australia and the United States are not Kyoto members.

Action in States

While Congress may be moving at glacial speed to mitigate global warming, states are moving "at the speed of light," says the University of Michigan's Rabe.

In 1999, when he first began speaking on state climate-change initiatives, an environmental economist told Rabe that, "No state acting rationally would ever do this," he recalls. "Now, I can't keep up with what is happening."

Worries about energy availability and the rising cost of natural gas are spurring states to conserve energy and utilize alternative fuel sources — moves that will also cut GHG emissions. For example, 21 states now have mandated "renewable portfolio standards" (RPS) — requiring a portion of electrical power to be generated from renewable sources. "A year ago it was 17," says Rabe.

States with renewable standards represent over half the U.S. population, and standards have been enacted on a bipartisan basis, Rabe says. In fact, 16 of the 21 governors who have approved renewable standards have been Republicans.

Some states perceive threats in climate change, while others see opportunities. Sparsely populated New Mexico and Nebraska, for example, see economic opportunities in developing wind and solar power on their vast, open spaces.

Even states with strong oil and coal industries, such as Pennsylvania and Illinois, are on the renewables bandwagon, says Rabe. And in oil-rich Texas, Republican Gov. Rick Perry in summer 2005 raised the state's renewable standard — first enacted under then-Gov. George W. Bush — to require that about 5 percent of power be generated from renewables by 2009 — and double that by 2025.

Several states are also establishing multi-state partnerships to cap and trade GHG emissions. In December 2005, seven Mid-Atlantic and Northeastern states tentatively agreed to launch the Regional Greenhouse Gas Initiative, allowing emitters in the region to buy and sell emissions permits after caps are put into effect in 2009.

OUTLOOK

Momentum Gathers

Both supporters and critics of the Kyoto Protocol are searching for better ways to cut emissions and involve developing countries. And, as debate shifts from whether human activity is causing climate change to how likely it is to be dangerous, the United States may be edging closer to action.

The Senate is still far from endorsing government action to stem climate change, and the Bush administration and the House remain adamantly opposed. "We're a long way from passing anything in Congress," says Ebell of the Competitive Enterprise Institute.

But some analysts see movement in the Senate. Sen. Bingaman's proposal to cap emissions while limiting the cost to industry "could have a vote in the Senate" in a year or two, says Kopp, of Resources for the Future. "And it could pass there, though it won't in the House."

For actual federal enactment of a global-warming plan, "we probably need a change of administration," says Kopp.

And Congress is highly unlikely to ratify Kyoto or any other international agreement on climate change anytime soon, says economist Wilcoxen of Syracuse University.

"But it is within the realm of political possibility in the next five years," he says.

On the international scene, "a lot will happen in the next 24 months," Kopp says, particularly since China signaled interest at the Montreal meeting in getting involved.

Pew's Diringer hopes to see multiple, overlapping new protocols and organizations develop involving both Kyoto signatories and non-Kyoto countries working together to stem emissions, he says. For example, "you could have Kyoto and non-Kyoto countries" working together to disperse new technology, he suggests.

At present, though, the administration's Asia-Pacific Partnership remains a threat to new post-Kyoto international agreements, "because the administration's aim in part is to take the conversation outside the [U.N. framework]," Diringer says.

Unless more binding agreements happen, however, current Kyoto members will hesitate to commit to longer-term goals, Diringer warns.

"From a competitive [economic] standpoint, nobody can get involved [in Kyoto] without losing out," especially if others, such as the United States and China, don't go in, he says. Given the EU's current struggles, "it's very hard to imagine there'll be the political will to go further."

For that reason, says Kopp, future international climate talks will be a much bigger deal, with nations sending trade, transportation, energy and finance officials as well as environment ministers. Countries now realize "that you've got to have the other ministers in it too, because the environment ministers don't think of all the consequences."

Such a change might actually open up new possibilities, Kopp suggests. "That kind of multi-sector talk also gives you more policies to put on the table, so it might make it easier to make deals."

NOTES

1. Quoted in "Senate Energy and Natural Resources Committee Holds Hearing on Climate Change," transcript, Congressional Quarterly, July 21, 2005, www.cq.com.

2. Quoted in Kate Bissell, "Alaskan People Tell of Climate Change," Aug. 8, 2005, www.newsvote, bbc,co.uk.

3. Richard A. Muller, "Alaska is Melting: Can Kyoto Save It?" *Technology Review On Line*, April 16, 2004.

4. *Ibid.*

5. "Fast Facts on Global Warming," *National Geographic*, http://news.nationalgeographic.com.

6. Quoted in Senate Energy and Natural Resources Committee, *op. cit.*

7. For background, see Mary H. Cooper, "Global Warming Treaty," *CQ Researcher*, Jan. 26, 2001, pp. 41-64.

8. "Potential Climate Change Impacts in New Hampshire," Office of Planning, City of Keene, www.ci.keene.nh.us.

9. Climate Change and New Hampshire, Office of Policy, Planning and Evaluation, U.S. Environmental Protection Agency.

10. Quote in "Truth Will Out; Global Warming Is Caused By Human Activity," British Broadcasting Corporation, www.open2.net.

11. Stephen Milloy, "U.S. Should Not Import European Laws," *Junk Science*, Nov. 12, 2005, www.foxnews.com.

12. Quoted in David Mildenberg, "Duke CEO Not Finding Favor on His Call for a Carbon Tax," *Charlotte* [North Carolina] *Business Journal*, May 9, 2005.

13. Quoted in Senate Energy and Natural Resources Committee, *ibid.*

14. John Vidal, "New Zealand First To Levy Carbon Tax," *The Guardian*, May 5, 2005.

15. Quoted in "Paul Anderson, CEO of Duke Energy," *Sunday Sunrise Transcript*, March 13, 2005, http://seven.com.au/sundaysunrise/transcripts/19440.

16. For background on China, see Peter Katel, "Emerging China," *CQ Researcher*, Nov. 11, 2005, pp. 957-980.

17. Fact Sheet: President Bush and the Asia-Pacific Partnership on Clean Development, The White House, July 27, 2005, www.state.gov/g/oes/rls/fs/50314.htm.

18. For background, see Peter Katel, "Emerging China," *CQ Researcher*, Nov. 11, 2005, pp. 957-980, and David Masci, "Emerging Inda," *CQ Researcher*, April 19, 2002, pp. 329-360.

19. Quoted in Senate Energy and Natural Resources Committee, *op. cit.*

20. Richard Lindzen, "Is There a Basis for Global Warming Alarm?" presentation at the Yale Center for the Study of Globalization, Oct. 21, 2005.

21. *World Factbook*, "U.S. Central Intelligence Agency," www.cia.gov/cia/publications/factbook/geos/us.hrml.

22. Christian Azar and Stephen Schneider, "Are the Economic Costs of Stabilizing the Atmosphere Prohibitive?" *Ecological Economics*, February 2002.

23. Richard A. Muller, "Medieval Global Warming: The Peril of Letting Politics Shape the Scientific Debate," *Technology Review*, Dec. 17, 2003.

24. Stephen Schneider, *Climate Change*, http://stephen-schneider.stanford.edu/Climate/ClimateFrameset.html.

25. Muller, *op. cit.*

26. Quoted in "Communicating Uncertainty in the Science of Climate Change," International Center for Technology Assessment, www.icta.org/doc/Uncertainty%20in%20science-9-04.pdf.

27. *Ibid.*

28. Schneider, *op. cit.* For the original source, see "Climate Change 2001: Impacts, Adaptation, and Vulnerability," Intergovernmental Panel on Climate Change, 2001, www.grida.no/climate/ipcc_tar/wg2/009.htm#tabspm1.

29. *Ibid.*

30. *Climate Change Science: An Analysis of Some Key Questions*, National Academy of Sciences, 2000, p. 18.

31. www.nationalcenter.org/KyotoSenate.html.

32. For background, see Spencer Weart, *The Discovery of Global Warming*, June 2005, www.aip.org/history/climate/; and Mary H. Cooper, "Global Warming," *CQ Researcher*, Nov. 1, 1996, pp. 961-984.

33. For background, see Mary H. Cooper, "Alternative Fuels," *CQ Researcher*, Feb. 25, 2005, pp. 173-196.

34. Katel, *op. cit.*

35. For background, see Jennifer Weeks, "Domestic Energy Development," *CQ Researcher*, Sept. 30, 2005, pp. 809-832.

36. "Renewable Energy Consumption: May 2005 Assessment," European Environment Agency, themes.eea.eu.int/IMS/ISpecs/ISpecification200410071322 01/IAssessment1116504213343/view_content.

37. Stephanie Peating, "Nuclear Question Looms Large at Climate Change Talks," *Sydney* [Australia] *Morning Herald*, Jan. 12, 2006.

38. *Ibid.*

39. Paul Anderson, "Taking Responsibility," address delivered at a *Charlotte Business Journal* industry breakfast, April 7, 2005.

40. Fact sheet, "President Bush and the Asia-Pacific Partnership on Clean Development," The White House, July 27, 2005, www.state.gov/g/oes/rls/fs/50314.htm.

BIBLIOGRAPHY

Books

Cox, John D., *Climate Crash: Abrupt Climate Change and What it Means for Our Future,* **Joseph Henry Press, 2005.**
A science journalist explains how scientists discovered that very abrupt and extreme climate changes have occurred throughout Earth's history. He describes the uncertainties that surround the fundamental question: Could human greenhouse gas emissions help trigger an abrupt, catastrophic climate event?

Houghton, John, *Global Warming: The Complete Briefing,* **Cambridge University Press, 2004.**
A co-chair of the Scientific Assessment Working Group of the U.N.'s Intergovernmental Panel on Climate Change gives a full account of the scientific and ethical dimensions of global warming. The book provides references to the original scientific sources and pays special attention to how energy use relates to climate change.

Maslin, Mark, *Global Warming: A Very Short Introduction,* **Oxford University Press, 2005.**
One of a series of general introductions to current topics, the book summarizes the current debate over warming, focusing mainly on findings of the Intergovernmental Panel on Climate Change. Maslin is an associate professor at the University of London's Environmental Change Research Center.

Michaels, Patrick J., *Meltdown: The Predictable Distortion of Global Warming by Scientists, Poli-* *ticians, and the Media,* **Cato Institute, 2004.**
A climatologist at the University of Virginia and senior fellow at the libertarian Cato Institute argues that global warming has been hyped by scientists, advocates and journalists with vested interests in overstating research findings and the need for policy responses.

Tennesen, Michael, *Complete Idiot's Guide to Global Warming,* **Alpha Books, 2004.**
A science journalist provides a primer on the basic scientific and policy concepts in the climate-change debate.

Victor, David G., *Climate Change: Debating America's Policy Options,* **Council on Foreign Relations Press, 2004.**
An associate professor of political science at Stanford University lays out arguments for three possible U.S. policy options on climate change — relying on wealthy nations' ability to adapt to change; reinvigorating the Kyoto Protocol; and establishing a worldwide market for low-carbon technologies.

Weart, Spencer, *The Discovery of Global Warming,* **Harvard University Press, 2004.**
A historian of science recounts the long process through which scientists discovered and explored human-induced climate change, beginning in the late 19th century. Written for the general reader, the book describes the enabling technologies, blind alleys, uncertainties and disagreements found along the way. Weart updates and augments the book with much more detail on his Web site: www.aip.org/history/climate/.

Articles

Gardiner, Stephen M., "The Global Warming Tragedy and the Dangerous Illusion of the Kyoto Protocol," **Ethics and International Affairs, 2004.**
An assistant professor of philosophy at the University of Washington outlines ethics issues involved in setting policy on global warming.

Pearce, Fred, "The Gathering Storm," *New Scientist,* **Dec. 3, 2005, p. 36.**
A science journalist explains and updates the scientific controversy over global warming and hurricanes.

Reports and Studies

The Center for Health and the Global Environment, "Climate Change Futures: Health, Ecological and Economic Dimensions," Harvard Medical School, November 2005.
Public-health analysts who believe that climate change may be dangerous describe its potential health-related consequences.

International Climate Change Taskforce, "Meeting the Climate Challenge," January 2005; www.tai.org. au/Publications_Files/Papers&Sub_Files/Meeting%2 0the%20Climate%20Challenge%20FV.pdf.

Policy experts assembled by think tanks in the United States, United Kingdom and Australia make recommendations for government actions to reduce human-caused greenhouse gas emissions.

National Research Council Ocean Studies Board, "Abrupt Climate Change: Inevitable Surprises," *National Academies Press*, June 2002.
An expert panel of scientists describes the growing evidence for episodes of very abrupt climate changes throughout Earth's history. The report discusses the possibility that such abrupt change will occur in the future, triggered by human-induced global warming or possibly by other factors.

For More Information

Center for Health and the Global Environment, Harvard Medical School. 401 Park Dr., 2nd Floor, Boston, MA 02215; (617) 384-8530; http://chge.med.harvard.edu/. Researches the health implications of climate change.

Climate Change, http://stephenschneider.stanford.edu/. The Web site of Stanford climatologist Stephen Schneider, a believer in human-induced warming.

The Discovery of Global Warming, www.aip.org/history/climate/. A detailed history of climate-change science.

Energy Information Administration, 1000 Independence Ave., S.W., Washington, DC 20585; (202) 586-8800; www.eia.doe.gov/. Official government source for statistics on energy use.

Intergovernmental Panel on Climate Change, www.ipcc.ch/about/about.htm. Organization formed by the United Nations and the World Meteorological Organization.

National Climatic Data Center, 151 Patton Ave., Asheville, NC 28801-5001; (828) 271-4800; www.ncdc.noaa.gov/oa/about/ncdccontacts.html. Government agency that collects historical and current climate data.

Pew Center on Climate Change, 2101 Wilson Blvd., Suite 550, Arlington, VA 22201; (703) 516-4146; www.pewclimate.org. Nonprofit organization that issues information and promotes discussion by policymakers on the science, economics and policy of climate change.

RealClimate.org. www.realclimate.org. Climate scientists provide responses to emerging data and opinion regarding global warming.

Resources for the Future, 1616 P St., N.W., Washington, DC 20036; (202) 328-5000; www.rff.org. A nonpartisan think tank that conducts research on global warming and other environmental issues.

Still Waiting for Greenhouse, www.john-daly.com/. Web site founded by the late Australian global-warming skeptic John Daly.

World Climate Report, www.worldclimatereport.com. Analysis of new data and opinion on climate change, from the point of view of global-warming skeptics.

10

Death Penalty Controversies

Kenneth Jost

Former death row inmate Aaron Patterson is one of 17 wrongfully convicted men freed in Illinois, the only state with a death penalty moratorium. The American Bar Association has called for a nationwide moratorium on executions, citing documented problems in capital trials and sentencing such as racial discrimination, inadequate legal representation and other constitutional violations.

From *CQ Researcher*,
September 23, 2005.

R obin Lovitt says he didn't do it. He says Clayton Dicks was already lying mortally wounded on the floor of the Arlington, Va., pool hall when he came out of the restroom in the early morning hours of Nov. 18, 1998.

The jury in Lovitt's capital murder trial in September 1999 decided instead to believe a witness who testified he was "80 percent" certain he saw Lovitt stab Dicks and a jailhouse informant who said Lovitt later confessed to the crime while in custody.

Lovitt was sentenced to death, and his conviction and sentence upheld on appeal in the state courts. But court-appointed lawyers handling his federal habeas corpus case now say the state has made it impossible for Lovitt to prove his innocence by throwing away the physical evidence introduced at trial.

The evidence that a deputy court clerk discarded — ostensibly to save space in a crowded storage room — included a bloody pair of scissors that prosecutors depicted as the murder weapon. Lovitt's legal team, headed on a pro bono basis by former Whitewater special prosecutor Kenneth Starr, says the clerk's action prevents them from arranging for sophisticated DNA testing that could refute the prosecution's effort to link the scissors to Lovitt.

"The DNA along with the other evidence has been destroyed and destroyed in a very intentional way," says Starr, now dean at Pepperdine University School of Law in Malibu, Calif. Starr remains affiliated with the Washington office of Kirkland & Ellis, which is representing Lovitt, along with Rob Lee of the Virginia Capital Representation Resource Center in Charlottesville.

Lawyers for the state say discarding the evidence was an honest mistake that doesn't matter because the other evidence against

U.S. Executions Declined in Recent Years

The number of executions in the United States in the past three decades peaked at 98 in 1999 and then fell to 59 in 2004. Capital punishment opponents say the innocence issue contributed to the decline.

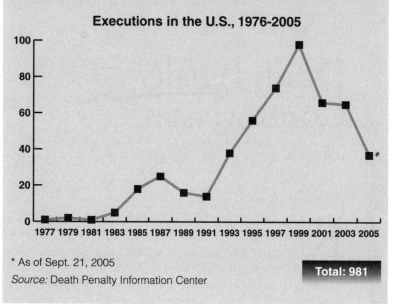

Executions in the U.S., 1976-2005

* As of Sept. 21, 2005

Source: Death Penalty Information Center

Total: 981

University's Cardozo School of Law to investigate such cases on an ongoing basis and is also president of the National Association of Criminal Defense Lawyers.

More broadly, the Death Penalty Information Center, which opposes capital punishment, claims that 119 people have been "released from death rows with evidence of their innocence" since 1973. The center calls these releases "exonerations" and counts 36 such cases just since 2000.

Death penalty supporters acknowledge the importance of DNA testing as a forensic technique for both the prosecution and the defense. But they dispute the broad characterization of the death row releases as exonerations and depict "actual innocence" — as opposed to exoneration through a technicality issue — as only a minor aspect of the protracted death penalty litigation in state and federal courts.

"The intense scrutiny that capital cases receive in the present system is finding and correcting the few cases of wrongful convictions," says Kent Scheidegger, legal director for the pro-law enforcement Criminal Justice Legal Foundation in Sacramento. "Our criminal justice system should be paying more attention to actual guilt and innocence and spending less resources litigating issues that have nothing to do with guilt."

Law enforcement groups emphasize in particular that anti-death penalty groups have yet to document a case in the modern era of someone who was executed and later proven conclusively to have been innocent of the crime.

"They're looking for the innocent defendant who was executed," says Joshua Marquis, district attorney in Clatsop County (Astoria), Ore., and chairman of the National District Attorneys Association's capital litigation committee. "They haven't found one yet. I don't think they're going to find one."

Nevertheless, death penalty opponents credit the innocence issue with contributing to a decline in the number of death sentences and the number of executions in the United States in the past few years. After peaking

Lovitt was so strong. "This case is not a DNA case," says Emily Lucier, a spokeswoman for the Virginia attorney general's office. [1] But the U.S. Supreme Court saw Lovitt's plea as strong enough to order a stay of execution on the evening of July 11, only four-and-a-half hours before Lovitt was scheduled to die by lethal injection.

Lovitt's case awaits further action by the justices at a time when the death penalty debate is focusing more than ever on the risk of convicting and executing an innocent defendant. [2] The advent of DNA testing — which has been credited with "exonerating" more than 160 prison inmates over the last 15 years, including 14 men on various states' death rows — has focused attention on using new technology to prevent executions of innocent defendants. [3]

"These DNA exonerations have proven to everybody that there are far more innocent persons in our criminal justice system than anyone had imagined," says Barry Scheck, the New York defense lawyer who pioneered the use of DNA evidence to support innocence claims. He helped found the Innocence Project at Yeshiva

Texas Leads States in Executions

Prisons in California, Texas and Florida alone hold 42 percent of the nation's 3,415 death row inmates. Since 1976 there have been 981 executions in the United States, including 37 so far this year. Texas has executed 348 people since 1976, far more than any other state.

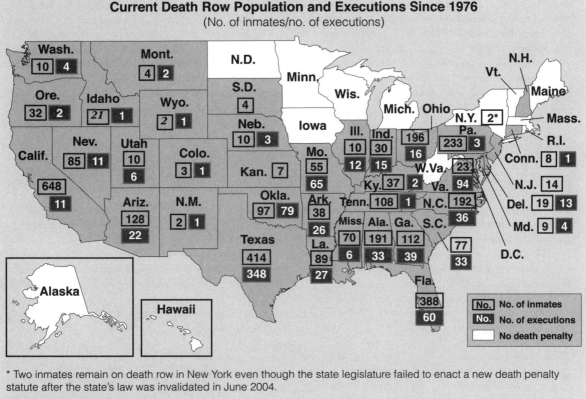

Current Death Row Population and Executions Since 1976
(No. of inmates/no. of executions)

Wash. 10 / 4	Mont. 4 / 2	N.D.			N.H. / Vt.
Ore. 32 / 2	Idaho 21 / 1	S.D. 4	Minn. Wis.	Mich. Ohio	Maine
	Wyo. 2 / 1	Neb. 10 / 3	Iowa	Ind. 30	N.Y. 2* / Pa.
Nev. 85 / 11	Utah 10 / 6	Colo. 3 / 1	Mo. 55 / 65	Ill. 10 / 12	Ind. 30 / 15	196 / 16	233 / 3	Mass. R.I.
Calif. 648 / 11		Kan. 7			W.Va. 23	Conn. 8 / 1
Ariz. 128 / 22	N.M. 2 / 1	Okla. 97 / 79	Ark. 38 / 26	Ky. 37 / 2	Va. 94	N.J. 14
		Texas 414 / 348	La. 89 / 27	Tenn. 108 / 1	N.C. 192 / 36	Del. 19 / 13
			Miss. 70 / 6	Ala. 191 / 33	Ga. 112 / 39	S.C. 77 / 33	Md. 9 / 4
Alaska	Hawaii			Fla. 388 / 60		D.C.

No. — No. of inmates
No. — No. of executions
☐ — No death penalty

* Two inmates remain on death row in New York even though the state legislature failed to enact a new death penalty statute after the state's law was invalidated in June 2004.

Source: Death Penalty Information Center

at 98 in 1999, the number of executions fell to 59 in 2004, according to the death penalty center, and appears likely to end somewhat below that number for 2005. (*See chart, p. 216.*)

"A large part of that is due to revelations about problems with the death penalty — in particular because innocent people were convicted and sentenced to death and in some cases came close to being executed," says Richard Dieter, the center's executive director. "That kept pushing the problem of the death penalty into the public eye."

Prosecutor Marquis acknowledges that the innocence issue has been useful for death penalty opponents.

"They succeeded in driving the debate away from the legal or moral issue, which they were losing," he says. But, he notes, polls show a substantial majority of Americans still support capital punishment. (*See chart, p. 220.*)

Public ambivalence about the death penalty is reflected in the seemingly conflicting mix of pending federal and state cases and proposals in Congress and state legislatures. The Supreme Court — which barred execution of juvenile offenders in a landmark ruling on March 1 — is being urged in the new term that begins Oct. 3 to make it easier for death row inmates to get federal court hearings on innocence claims. Congress, on the other

Is the Defendant Mentally Retarded?

Daryl Atkins won a landmark ruling from the U.S. Supreme Court in 2002 barring the execution of mentally retarded offenders. When Atkins' case returned to Virginia courts, however, a jury found that he is not mentally retarded and left him on death row for a 1996 robbery-murder.

The jury in Yorktown, Va., heard seven days of testimony and deliberated for 13 hours before deciding on Aug. 5 that Atkins is not mentally retarded under Virginia law. Jurors apparently credited testimony offered by prosecution witnesses that the 27-year-old Atkins manages to perform daily life functions over evidence introduced by the defense, including IQ scores below the threshold of 70 set by Virginia law to define mental retardation. [1]

Atkins' lawyers say they will appeal the panel's decision. For now, however, the result is one sign that the Supreme Court's decision in the case that bears his name will not produce the benefits that advocates for the mentally retarded had hoped or expected.

"The promise of *Atkins* has not been realized," says Robin Maher, director of the American Bar Association's death penalty representation project.

States faced no such difficult implementation decisions in applying the Supreme Court's March 2005 decision barring execution of juvenile offenders. The ruling in *Roper v. Simmons* means that anyone convicted of an offense committed under the age of 18 is ineligible for the death penalty. But in banning the death penalty for mentally retarded defendants in *Atkins v. Virginia*, the high court left it to the states to establish their own definitions of retardation.

Since the *Atkins* case, Virginia and seven other states — California, Delaware, Idaho, Illinois, Louisiana, Nevada and Utah — have changed their statutes to comply with the ruling, according to a compilation by the Death Penalty Information Center. In seven of the states, the judge determines if the defendant is mentally retarded; only in Virginia does the jury decide. [2]

The eight states consider offenders as mentally retarded if their IQ falls below a certain level, generally between 70 and 75, and if they demonstrate deficits in adaptive behavior before the age of 18.

Richard Dieter, executive director of the anti-death penalty group, calls the Virginia procedure "unusual" because mental retardation is determined in other states before the trial begins. Virginia's procedure calls for a trial on guilt or innocence with a hearing on mental retardation afterward before the same jury.

The procedure "colors the decision-making process," Dieter says, because it is hard for jurors to make an objective decision "once you tell the jury they're letting somebody off for the worst punishment."

Atkins was convicted of capital murder for abducting a U.S. airman outside a store, forcing him to withdraw $200 from an automated teller machine, and then shooting him eight times. A co-defendant who pleaded guilty in exchange for reduced charges claimed — but Atkins denied — that it was Atkins who did the shooting.

hand, is considering restricting state inmates' use of the centuries-old legal procedure called habeas corpus to challenge their convictions or sentences. *

Some state supreme courts are showing increased receptivity to death penalty challenges, and death penalty opponents are urging states to follow the lead of two Illinois governors in imposing a moratorium on executions. The only other statewide moratorium — imposed by a Democratic governor in Maryland — was rescinded by a Republican governor elected later the same year. After New York's highest court ruled that state's death penalty statute invalid, however, lawmakers decided not to enact a new version.

Meanwhile, the perennial issue of deterrence is drawing renewed attention with efforts by some researchers to show that abolishing or suspending the death penalty leads to an increase in murders. Other academics sharply dispute the studies. (*See sidebar, p. 226.*)

As the various death penalty debates continue in Washington and around the country, here are some of the other specific questions at issue:

---

* *Habeas corpus* — Latin for "you have the body" — is a procedure dating from England's *Magna Carta* (1215) that ensures the right of a defendant to petition a judge to determine the legality of his or her incarceration or detention by the government.

The ABA's Maher says procedures in other states are also unfair to mentally retarded offenders. "Almost all the statutes inappropriately place the burden of persuasion on the mentally retarded prisoner or require proof that does not comport with professional standards," Maher says. In addition, Maher says that several states with relatively large numbers of death penalty cases — including Texas, Alabama, Mississippi and Oklahoma — have refused to enact laws to protect the mentally retarded from executions.

A leading prosecutor, however, blames the Supreme Court for problems in implementing the decision. "States are lurching along trying to come up with statutes that comply with *Atkins*, but they're having problems because the court didn't really say what they needed to do," says Joshua Marquis, district attorney in Clatsop County, Ore., and chair of the National District Attorneys Association's capital litigation committee.

Courts in Texas, the state with the highest number of executions, have upheld death sentences in several cases involving mental retardation issues following guidelines set by the Texas Court of Criminal Appeals. In a ruling in February 2004, the

Darryl R. Atkins

Virginia Dept. of Corrections

Texas court rejected a mental retardation plea in upholding the death sentence imposed on Jose Briseno for the 1991 slaying of a local sheriff. The court reasoned that Briseno was not mentally retarded because he was able to devise plans and adjust to his surroundings. [3]

Prosecutors in Atkins' case made a similar argument about his problem-solving ability by offering testimony that while in prison, Atkins had been observed placing his soup bowl in a sink containing hot water to keep it warm. A defense expert, however, reached a different conclusion from the incident, saying that Atkins apparently failed to appreciate that the water would soon cool.

— *Melissa J. Hipolit*

[1] See Maria Glod, "Virginia Killer Isn't Retarded, Jury Says," *The Washington Post*, Aug. 6, 2005, p. A1; Donna St. George, "A Question of Culpability: Mental Capacity of Convicted Virginia Man Is a Murky Legal Issue," *The Washington Post*, July 23, 2005, p. A1.

[2] Death Penalty Information Center, www.deathpenaltyinfo.org/article.php? scid=28&did=668.

[3] Martha Deller and Max B. Baker, "Texas Courts Try to Set Rules for Executing Mentally Retarded Inmates," *Fort Worth Star-Telegram*, July 13, 2005.

Should the Supreme Court ease the rules for death row inmates to raise innocence claims?

A jury in rural East Tennessee convicted Paul House of murder in 1986 in the beating death of a neighbor, Carolyn Muncey. Prosecutors argued that House, a paroled sex offender from Utah, killed Muncey after an attempted rape. As evidence, the prosecutors showed that semen found on Muncey's body matched House's blood type.

More than a decade later, however, DNA testing — unavailable at the time of trial — conclusively established that the semen came not from House, but from Muncey's husband, Herbert. Lawyers working on

House's federal habeas corpus petition also uncovered other evidence casting doubt on the verdict, including testimony by two neighbors that Herbert Muncey had confessed to killing his wife long after the event.

Despite the evidence, the federal appeals court for Tennessee refused, by an 8-7 vote, to give House a chance to have his newly substantiated claim of innocence heard in federal court. Now, the U.S. Supreme Court is poised to consider House's case in order to decide how to balance the states' interest in maintaining the finality of criminal convictions against what death penalty critics contend is the real possibility of executing an innocent person.

Most Americans Support the Death Penalty

Nearly three out of four Americans support the death penalty, but only 61 percent believe it is applied fairly in this country. Most Americans believe that innocent people have been executed within the past five years, but the percentage who feel that way declined between 2003 and 2005.

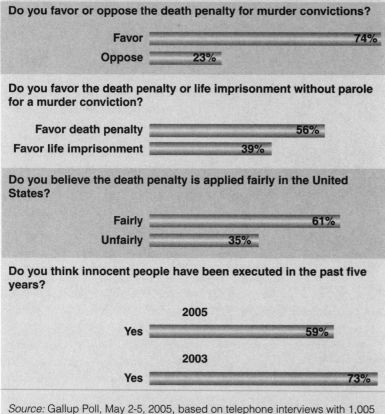

Do you favor or oppose the death penalty for murder convictions?

Favor 74%
Oppose 23%

Do you favor the death penalty or life imprisonment without parole for a murder conviction?

Favor death penalty 56%
Favor life imprisonment 39%

Do you believe the death penalty is applied fairly in the United States?

Fairly 61%
Unfairly 35%

Do you think innocent people have been executed in the past five years?

2005
Yes 59%

2003
Yes 73%

Source: Gallup Poll, May 2-5, 2005, based on telephone interviews with 1,005 randomly selected adults ages 18 and over

Together, the two cases created a narrow window for lower federal courts to use an inmate's actual innocence claim — if sufficiently strong — as a "gateway" to belatedly raising a federal constitutional issue. They left open the question whether a freestanding innocence claim — apart from any constitutional violation — could be the basis for a successful request for federal habeas corpus relief.

Death penalty critics emphasize that the first of the decisions was handed down the same year the first death row inmate was released for DNA-related reasons. The number of DNA exonerations since then demonstrates the need for the court to re-examine the decisions, they say.

"They set some very strict standards for actual innocence claims independent of any other constitutional claim," says Dieter of the Death Penalty Information Center. "In light of what we now know, it is time for the court to reflect on the revelations of science and what's happened in the death penalty world and give the lower courts some guidelines."

Prosecutors and law enforcement supporters, however, say the high court should maintain strict standards for state prisoners to meet before asking federal judges in effect to give them a second trial. "If you're going to retry every capital case, you're going to have an even more inefficient system than you have now," says Barry Latzer, a professor at City University of New York's John Jay College of Criminal Justice.

"It's natural for the system to have a very high hurdle for retrial of innocence claims," Latzer says. "The place for that is in the original trial, not on appeal."

But Scheck says there is "no evidence" that states with liberal rules on the use of newly discovered evidence are having significant problems.

The high court dealt with the issue in two decisions in the 1990s: *Herrera v. Collins* (1993) and *Schlup v. Delo* (1995). [4] In the first case, the court rejected a Texas death row inmate's effort to reopen his murder case based on late evidence blaming the offense on his brother, who had since died. In the second ruling, however, the court allowed a Missouri death row inmate a hearing to determine whether his innocence claim was strong enough to justify a second chance to challenge his conviction on constitutional grounds.

In House's case, lawyers with the Federal Defenders Service in Knoxville contend that the Sixth U.S. Circuit Court of Appeals rejected his petition based on a stricter rule than required by the Supreme Court. "The *Schlup* case does not require the elimination of all evidence of guilt," says attorney Stephen Kissinger. "The real test is what [the jury] would have done given all this evidence. The truth of the matter is that no jury has passed on the vast majority of the new evidence in this case."

Lawyers for the state, however, say the appeals court majority correctly followed the rule established in *Schlup*. Under that decision, they argue, House had to show that "in light of the new evidence, no juror, acting reasonably, would have voted to find him guilty beyond a reasonable doubt." They contend that the new DNA evidence does not contradict the prosecution's case against House and that the appeals court properly discounted other evidence, including Muncey's purported confession.

For his part, Scheidegger says new claims of actual innocence should normally be considered in executive clemency proceedings with federal court review available only as "a last-ditch backup."

"Any time a new avenue for review of capital cases is opened up, the possibility of abuse exists," he says.

But Dieter says governors rarely grant clemency, deferring instead to the courts. "It seems to be a passing of the buck on this issue," he says. In any event, he adds, "Clemency is for the extraordinary case where mercy or reduction of sentence is appropriate. Guilt or innocence is for the courts."

Should Congress pass legislation to limit federal habeas corpus claims?

In an attempt to deal with a growing flood of death row appeals, Congress passed a major overhaul of federal habeas corpus law in 1996 aimed at cutting back death row inmates' use of the procedure to challenge their convictions or sentences. The Antiterrorism and Effective Death Penalty Act — known as AEDPA — gives state inmates a one-year deadline to file a federal habeas corpus petition after all state proceedings are finished. It also generally bars the filing of a second federal petition and requires federal judges to defer to state rulings unless clearly mistaken or unreasonable.

In a steady stream of densely technical cases over the past nine years, the U.S. Supreme Court has been rela-

Illinois Gov. Rod R. Blagojevich signs the final piece of the state's death penalty reform package on Jan. 20, 2004, as state legislators observe. The most comprehensive death penalty reform package in that state's history was prompted by newspaper investigations showing that at least 13 innocent people had been convicted and sentenced to death in Illinois due to bias, errors and incompetence.

tively strict in interpreting the act's major provisions. But supporters of the law say some federal appeals courts — especially the Ninth Circuit, which covers California and eight other Western states — have liberally interpreted the act to allow inmates opportunities for hearings that it was intended to preclude.

To fix the supposed problem, two Republican lawmakers — Sen. Jon Kyl of Arizona and Rep. Dan Lungren of California — introduced a bill, the Streamlined Procedures Act, aimed at tightening the deadlines and standards for obtaining federal habeas relief. But an array of opponents — including death penalty critics, the American Bar Association and state and federal judicial bodies — say the bill would do little to speed death penalty challenges while cutting off access to federal courts for legitimate legal challenges and risking execution of innocent persons. [5]

Some supporters of the bill question the need for federal habeas review at all. "It's by and large unnecessary because the cases have already been thoroughly reviewed at the state level," says Latzer. "But if you must have it, it should be more efficient." Others do not go quite that far, but say the bill is needed because of what Scheidegger calls "the evasions" of AEDPA's restrictive provisions by some federal courts.

In introducing the bill, Kyl cited statistics showing that the number of habeas cases pending in federal courts increased from 13,359 in fiscal year 1994 to 23,218 in fiscal year 2003. But opponents of the measure say the figures do not show that AEDPA has failed to make it harder for inmates to actually get hearings in federal court or to win their cases. "You're never going to stop prisoners from filing petitions," says Virginia Sloan, president of the bipartisan Constitution Project, who is coordinating a campaign against the bill.

Among its many provisions, the bill would narrow grounds for habeas petitions and limit inmates' ability to amend claims. It would bar federal courts from considering any claim not properly raised in state courts unless an inmate had a "clear and convincing" claim of actual innocence. And it would require federal appeal courts to rule on habeas claims within 300 days of the filing of the inmate's legal brief.

The bill's provisions are "carefully crafted, common sense responses to some of the worst abuses we face," Tom Dologenes, head of the habeas corpus unit in the Philadelphia district attorney's office, told the Senate Judiciary Committee in July.

But opponents argue the bill goes in the wrong direction. "With all the exonerations we've seen in recent years, we should be expanding instead of cutting back on review," says Sloan.

Scheck particularly criticizes the provision that raises the standards for actual innocence claims. "This bill makes everything worse in terms of innocence litigation," he says.

Both the U.S. Judicial Conference and the National Conference of State Chief Justices and Court Administrators oppose the bill. In a letter to Senate Judiciary Committee Chairman Arlen Specter, R-Pa., the federal judges said the bill could "complicate" habeas cases and "lead to more, rather than less, litigation." For their part, the state judges adopted a resolution in August warning that the provisions restricting federal habeas relief would have "unknown consequences for the state courts and the administration of justice."

Supporters of the bill, however, say state courts do not need the additional oversight entailed in federal habeas cases. "The issue is whether there is confidence in the state courts, whether they can protect the rights of criminal defendants and death penalty defendants in particular," says Latzer. "I have confidence in them, and that diminishes the need for federal review in my mind."

Should states impose moratoriums on executions?

Illinois Gov. George Ryan, a conservative Republican, had supported the death penalty throughout his 20-plus years in politics. But investigations by Northwestern University journalism students and *Chicago Tribune* reporters during Ryan's first year as governor in 1999 convinced him that the state's system for sending people to death row was "fraught with error."

So in January 2000 Ryan took the then-unprecedented step of imposing an official moratorium on executions in the state. "Until I can be sure that everyone sentenced to death in Illinois is truly guilty, until I can be sure with moral certainty that no innocent man or woman is facing a lethal injection, no one will meet that fate," Ryan said. Three years later, just as he was about to leave office, Ryan went further: He pardoned four death row inmates and commuted the death sentences of 164 others to life imprisonment. [6]

Ryan's initial step drew wide praise, even from State's Attorney Dick Devine, the chief prosecutor in Cook County (Chicago). But Devine sharply criticized Ryan's later clemency action as "outrageous and unconscionable." [7]

Ryan followed up the moratorium by appointing a commission to make recommendations for improving the handling of death penalty cases, including providing better legal representation for defendants. Ryan's successor as governor, Democrat Rod R. Blagojevich, has kept the moratorium in effect pending an evaluation of some of the reforms adopted in November 2003. As of September 2005, however, only one other governor — Maryland's Parris Glendening — had followed Ryan's lead; and the move by Democrat Glendening was revoked in 2003 by his Republican successor, Robert Ehrlich.

Moratorium supporters include the American Bar Association, which called for the step in February 1997. Ron Tabak, a lawyer with a prestigious New York firm who works with the ABA committee created to push the proposal, says moratoriums are needed because of the variety of documented problems in capital trials and sentencing, including racial discrimination, inadequate legal representation and other constitutional violations.

"Every jurisdiction should have a moratorium, study the issues carefully, and try to see if they can fix the problems or decide on some other course of action," Tabak says.

Death penalty supporters, however, question the need for further studies and sharply criticize Ryan's actions in

Illinois or other proposals for suspending capital punishment. "I don't see any new problems that would call for studies," says Latzer. "This has been studied to death. I don't see any new problem except the problem of delays in carrying out executions."

"That's an abuse of the clemency power," says Scheidegger. "That's not why the governor has a clemency power: to issue a de facto repeal of the capital punishment statute."

"A moratorium is a moral dodge," says prosecutor Marquis. "We [already] have one in this country," he adds. "It's the 12 to 15 to 20 years it takes to get these cases through the courts."

Death penalty critics and opponents, however, echo the ABA's position that flaws in the system — and specifically the risk of executing an innocent person — demand careful study and a suspension of executions in the meantime.

"State moratoriums are an excellent idea," says Stephen Saloom, policy director of the Innocence Project. "They will allow states to stop and take a look at all the factors to be considered in assessing the accuracy of those death verdicts that have been handed down and even more so the potential for error in various parts of their system."

"We don't yet have a system that's totally reliable," says Dieter. "It would be a healthy process for the country to decide how much error we're going to allow, how to get that error down to an absolute minimum, and — knowing these changes are going to cost something — to decide whether it's worth it."

Scheidegger counters by citing a study by University of Houston economist Dale Cloninger that purportedly shows the Illinois moratorium resulted in an increase in murders as a result of reduced deterrence. Instead of adopting a moratorium to guard against a wrongful execution, Scheidegger says, the better step is "a more careful review of the cases to make sure they have the right guy."

For his part, Latzer warns that officials who favor moratoriums risk political retaliation. "If people in the state support the death penalty and the governor circumvents it, he has to face the consequences in the next election," Latzer says. *

---

* Ryan decided not to seek re-election in 2002 in the midst of a federal investigation of corruption in his administration. He was later indicted on 22 counts of racketeering, mail and tax fraud and other charges; he pleaded not guilty, and jury selection began on Sept. 19, 2005.

In Illinois, however, initial polls indicated public approval of Ryan's moratorium. And Tabak says public support for the idea has increased over time. "There's been a lot more public education and public understanding since then," he says. "As these efforts get more pronounced, there will be further results along these lines."

BACKGROUND

Running Debates

The death penalty has enjoyed popular approval and acceptance throughout U.S. history, but opposition on various moral and practical grounds dates from the nation's founding. Anti-death penalty sentiment rose to a near majority during the 1950s and '60s, and the number of executions declined. But support increased after the controversial 1972 Supreme Court decision to outlaw capital punishment as then administered and has remained generally strong since the court four years later upheld re-enacted death penalty laws. [8]

Capital punishment procedures were significantly changed during the 19th and 20th centuries, sometimes in evident response to public opinion. Abolitionist opponents helped bring about the division of murder into two degrees with the death penalty reserved only for the more serious, first-degree offense. The power to sentence defendants to death was also transferred from judges to juries in the 19th century. Death penalty opponents successfully campaigned against public executions and in favor of replacing the gallows with the supposedly more humane electric chair.

The first scientific poll on the subject, conducted in the mid-1930s, found that Americans supported the death penalty for murder by a substantial margin: 61 percent to 39 percent. [9] Subsequent annual Gallup Polls showed that support peaked at 68 percent in 1953, but fell over the next decade to a low of 42 percent in 1966. A Harris survey that year found near-majority disapproval: 47 percent. The decline coincided with civil rights and criminal-justice reform movements that focused public attention on racial discrimination and procedural injustices in capital trials and sentencing.

Increasing public disquiet about the death penalty also can be inferred from the decline in the number of executions during the same period. From a peak of around 190 a year in the late 1930s, the number of

CHRONOLOGY

1950s-1960s *Support for death penalty falls, along with number of executions.*

1953 Gallup Poll finds 68 percent support for capital punishment; executions average around 100 per year in early 1950s.

1966 Support for death penalty falls to 42 percent; two executions in a year are the last for more than a decade.

1970s-1980s *Supreme Court first abolishes, then reinstates capital punishment; begins to cut back on use of federal habeas corpus to challenge death sentences.*

1972 Supreme Court, in 5-4 ruling, invalidates all existing death sentences; public backlash boosts support for death penalty, while states move to revise capital punishment statutes.

1976 Supreme Court upholds capital punishment under "guided discretion" statutes, but bars mandatory death sentences.

1987 Supreme Court rejects effort to invalidate death penalty because it is most often imposed in murder cases where victim is white.

1989 Supreme Court limits use of new constitutional rulings in federal habeas corpus cases; upholds execution of mentally retarded offenders, older teens (16- or 17-year-olds).

1990s *Supreme Court, Congress tighten rules on habeas corpus; death penalty critics warn against risk of executing innocent persons.*

1991 Supreme Court says state inmates cannot raise constitutional claims in federal habeas corpus action if they miss deadlines for raising issue in state courts.

1992 Innocence Project founded to use DNA testing of post-conviction claims. . . . Supreme Court limits federal courts' duty to hold hearing in habeas corpus cases unless inmate raises factual innocence claim.

1993 Supreme Court sidesteps question whether stand-alone "actual innocence" claim can be grounds for habeas corpus review in federal court. . . . First wrongly convicted defendant is released based on DNA test results.

1994 Support for death penalty peaks at 80 percent.

1995 Supreme Court slightly eases test for death row inmate to use "actual innocence" claim to revive constitutional challenge to conviction or sentence.

1996 Congress passes Anti-terrorism and Effective Death Penalty Act (AEDPA) limiting and setting one-year deadline for federal habeas corpus petitions.

1997 American Bar Association calls for national moratorium on executions.

1998 Number of executions peaks at 98.

2000-Present *Death penalty critics use "innocence" cases to attack flaws in system; supporters say court reviews catch most errors.*

2000 Illinois Gov. George Ryan imposes moratorium on executions in state, citing risk of executing innocent person; as he leaves office three years later, commutes 164 death sentences to life imprisonment.

2002 Supreme Court bars death penalty for mentally retarded offenders; three years later, the defendant in the case, Daryl Atkins, is kept on death row after a Virginia jury rules he is not mentally retarded.

2004 New York court rules state death penalty law unconstitutional in June; nine months later, state legislative committee rejects bill to reinstate capital punishment, reducing number of death penalty states to 37. . . . Congress passes law to guarantee inmates right to post-conviction DNA testing.

2005 Supreme Court bars death penalty for juvenile offenders, throws out death sentences in four individual cases. . . . Justice John Paul Stevens says death penalty procedures entail "risks of unfairness." . . . High court due to open term on Oct. 3 with new chief justice, "actual innocence" cases on docket.

executions dropped to slightly more than 100 per year in the early 1950s and then fell by the mid-1960s to only one in 1965, two in 1966, and none during the decade starting in 1967.

As early as the 1930s some notorious death penalty cases had drawn the Supreme Court into overseeing state criminal justice systems. Most notably, the court in the so-called *Scottsboro* cases twice intervened to overturn the convictions and death sentences of nine young black men tried in a racially charged atmosphere in Alabama for allegedly raping two white women. By the 1960s, death penalty opponents — including the NAACP Legal Defense Fund — were mounting broader attacks that claimed the death penalty was unconstitutional under either the 14th Amendment's Equal Protection Clause or the Eighth Amendment's prohibition against cruel and unusual punishment.

The campaign climaxed on June 29, 1972, with the Supreme Court's decision in *Furman v. Georgia*, which invalidated all existing death sentences and death penalty statutes. The five justices in the majority each wrote separately: Two found the death penalty unconstitutional as "cruel and unusual punishment" under all circumstances, while three others objected to its arbitrary use. The four dissenters argued that the issue was for state legislatures, not the courts. [10]

However, public support for the death penalty was already growing by the late 1960s, and the Supreme Court's decision created a backlash that accelerated the shift. Gallup Polls conducted in 1972 before and after the *Furman* decision recorded an increase in pro-death penalty responses from 50 percent in March to 57 percent in November. For their part, state legislatures responded to the decision by adopting new laws aimed at curing the defects identified by the high court. Some states passed mandatory death penalty statutes, while others adopted so-called guided-discretion laws that gave juries aggravating and mitigating factors to consider in capital sentencing hearings. In 1976 the Supreme Court ruled the mandatory death penalty laws unconstitutional, but the justices upheld the guided-discretion statutes by a 7-2 vote. [11]

The ruling allowed the resumption of executions, which came slowly at first but gradually reached a peak of 98 in 1999. Public support for the death penalty also continued to rise, peaking at 80 percent in 1994. For its part, the Supreme Court rejected broad challenges to the death penalty, though it somewhat narrowed application of capital punishment and also established complex procedural rules for capital sentencing hearings. In one significant line of decisions, the court generally held that juries must be given broad discretion to consider any mitigating factors put forward by the defendant in an effort to avoid a death sentence, such as personal character, social background or minimal responsibility for the offense. [12]

Conflicting Goals?

With the constitutionality of capital punishment settled, supporters and critics of the death penalty pursued seemingly conflicting goals during the 1990s. Supporters, frustrated by the growing number of death row inmates awaiting execution, lobbied Congress successfully for restrictive procedural requirements on the use of federal habeas corpus to challenge state convictions or sentences. Meanwhile, critics and opponents of the death penalty called for more rigorous review of capital cases because of what they depicted as a large number of death row "exonerations" — cases in which condemned inmates had won reversals of their convictions or sentences. [13]

In the 1960s the Supreme Court had opened the door for state inmates to make greater use of federal habeas corpus petitions to try to overturn their convictions or sentences on federal constitutional grounds. By the 1980s, however, a more conservative high court under Chief Justice William H. Rehnquist was moving to limit habeas corpus. In one significant decision, the Rehnquist Court in 1989 generally blocked the use of new constitutional rulings as a basis for overturning convictions or sentences in habeas corpus proceedings. In two others, the court in the early 1990s barred inmates from filing federal habeas corpus petitions if they failed to abide by state procedural rules and made it harder for inmates to have federal courts rule on factual issues unless they raised a claim of actual innocence. [14]

Congress imposed further restrictions in the major overhaul of federal habeas corpus passed in 1996 as part of an anti-terrorism bill. The Antiterrorism and Effective Death Penalty Act generally required state inmates to file federal habeas corpus petitions within a year of exhausting state appeals and post-conviction proceedings. The law also barred a second or successive petition except in narrow circumstances as determined by a federal appeals court. And — in a major jurisdictional change — the act

Do Executions Deter Killings?

A dozen statistical studies have been published over the past decade claiming to show that capital punishment deters capital crimes. But some researchers say the studies are conceptually and technically flawed. In any case, say death penalty opponents, the question of deterrence has little influence today on public attitudes toward capital punishment. [1]

The effectiveness of executions as a deterrent has been argued at least since 18th-century England when, reportedly, pickpocketing — itself a capital crime — spiked at public hangings. More recently, *The New York Times* published a much-noticed report in 2000 showing that states with the death penalty had higher murder rates than states without capital punishment. [2]

Statistical work on the issue by U.S. economists dates back to the 1970s. Dale Cloninger, one of the earlier researchers in the field and now a professor at the University of Houston's School of Business in Clear Lake, says those early studies showed a deterrent effect. But Joanna Shepherd, an assistant professor at Emory University School of Law in Atlanta and a recent entrant in the field, describes the early studies as inconclusive and unsophisticated by present-day standards.

With more advanced techniques, however, Shepherd says new statistical studies — published in peer-reviewed economics journals — show a deterrent effect from executions. "We controlled for every conceivable factor that we thought might influence murder rates," Shepherd says of the work, including her studies.

Cloninger continues to write on the issue, including two studies linked to death penalty moratoriums: an unofficial, court-imposed lull in executions in Texas in the mid-1990s and Illinois' more recent official moratorium. In each instance, Cloninger says, the state's homicide rate increased during the moratorium; and killings in Texas fell after executions resumed. [3]

In her newest study, however, Shepherd says the effect of executions appears to vary from state to state. She finds a deterrent effect in only six states with comparatively more executions, no effect in others and a so-called "brutalization effect" in some other states — where executions appear to be associated with higher homicide rates. [4] While calling for additional studies, Shepherd suggests that the data show that a state needs to reach a certain threshold number of executions for the "deterrence effect" to outweigh the "brutalization effect."

---

required federal courts to defer to state court rulings unless the decision was "contrary to, or involved an unreasonable application of, clearly established Federal law, as determined by the Supreme Court of the United States." [15]

Meanwhile, critics and opponents of capital punishment were mounting a documented attack on the reliability of judicial proceedings that led to the growing number of death sentences. A combination of events brought the innocence issue to the forefront of public debate. [16] Most important was the new technology of DNA testing, which defense lawyers initially resisted but eventually recognized as potentially valuable to support claims of innocence by convicted defendants, including some on death row.

Two of the defense lawyers who pioneered the use of DNA testing — Scheck and Peter Neufeld — founded the Innocence Project as a nonprofit legal clinic to use post-conviction DNA testing to support innocence claims. By 1999, they claimed in a book that the project

had provided "stone-cold proof" that 67 people had been sent to prison for crimes they did not commit, including 11 sentenced to death. [17] Today, the project counts 162 "exonerations," including 14 in death penalty cases.

In addition, in-depth investigations have uncovered evidence of seriously flawed capital cases in Illinois and Oklahoma. In Illinois, students in a journalism course at Northwestern University helped uncover 13 cases of innocent defendants on death row, who were later exonerated. *The Chicago Tribune* put a dramatic headline on its own later, staff-written story: "Death Row Justice Denied: Bias, Errors and Incompetence Have Turned Illinois' Harshest Punishment Into Its Least Credible." [18]

Two years later, a March 2001 FBI report questioned testimony in eight cases by an Oklahoma City police laboratory scientist, Joyce Gilchrist, leading to an extensive re-examination of her role in some 23 capital cases, including 12 in which defendants had actually been exe-

Richard Berk, a professor of statistics and sociology at the University of California, Los Angeles, and Jeffrey Fagan, a professor of law and public health at Columbia University in New York City, are two veteran academics who sharply dispute the claims of deterrence. In a new analysis of the data, Berk says the claimed deterrent effect exists in only one state — Texas — and is not large there. "If you throw Texas out of the mix," he says, "there's nothing going on." [5]

Fagan, who is studying the issue under a grant from the Soros Foundation-funded U.S. Justice Fund told a legislative committee in Massachusetts in July that the deterrence studies are "fraught with technical and conceptual errors." He says other research also shows that better detection and apprehension would be more effective deterrents.

Cloninger says the deterrence studies show what most economists would expect: that the risk of punishment affects criminal behavior. "To an economist, it's sensible that murderers are sensitive to risk," he says. "Other people are." But Berk and Fagan both say would-be killers are unlikely to know the execution rate in a specific state or, in any event, to think about it before a crime. "This information is not available even if your criminal is a calculating machine," Berk says.

Death penalty supporters say the evidence of deterrence strengthens their position in countering fears of executing an innocent person. "If that were the only consideration as far as tradeoffs are concerned, it would be a very weighty one,"

says Kent Scheidegger, legal director of the pro-law enforcement Criminal Justice Legal Foundation in Sacramento, Calif. "But you have on the opposite side the very weighty consideration that you might be costing innocent lives" by not enforcing the death penalty.

Death penalty opponents, however, call the academic argument a standoff that does not matter to the overall public debate. "The death penalty is more about punishment and retribution and just deserts," says Richard Dieter, executive director of the Death Penalty Information Center. "Deterrence is not going to be the decisive factor as to whether we keep the death penalty or get rid of it."

[1] The pro-death penalty Criminal Justice Legal Foundation has listed the studies on its Web site: www.cjlf.org.

[2] Raymond Bonner and Ford Fessenden, "Absence of Executions: States With No Death Penalty Share Lower Homicide Rates," *The New York Times*, Sept. 22, 2000, p. A1.

[3] See Dale O. Cloninger and Roberto Marchesini, "Execution Moratorium, Commutations, and Deterrence: The Case of Illinois," working paper, August 2005 (http://econwpa.wustl.edu/eprints/le/papers/0507/0507002.abs); "Execution and Deterrence: A Quasi-Controlled Group Experiment," *Applied Economics*, Vol. 33 (2001), pp. 569-576.

[4] Joanna M. Shepherd, "Deterrence versus Brutalization: Capital Punishment's Differing Impacts Among States," *Michigan Law Review*, Vol. 4, Issue 2 (forthcoming November 2005).

[5] Richard A. Berk, "New Claims about Executions and General Deterrence: Déjà Vu All Over Again?" *Journal of Empirical Legal Studies*, Vol. 2, No. 2 (July 2005), pp. 303-330.

cuted. But state authorities who reviewed the capital cases expressed confidence that all of the defendants had been properly convicted without regard to Gilchrist's evidence in the cases. The investigation also resulted in May in the release of a defendant serving a sentence for rape. Gilchrist was fired in September because of "flawed casework testimony." [19]

The Supreme Court's two mid-decade rulings in "actual innocence" cases reflected a tentative approach. In the first — *Herrera v. Collins* — Chief Justice Rehnquist's opinion for the 6-3 majority in 1993 held that federal courts had no authority in habeas corpus cases to consider actual innocence claims apart from some independent constitutional violation. But he qualified the holding by saying that even if a "truly persuasive demonstration of 'actual innocence' after trial would render an execution unconstitutional," the inmate's evidence in the case fell "far short of any such threshold."

Two years later, though, a liberal majority held in *Schlup v. Delo* that a death row inmate was entitled to a hearing on a second federal habeas petition if he or she could show that a constitutional violation "probably resulted" in the conviction of an innocent person. Rehnquist led the dissenters in the 5-4 ruling.

After the decade's end, the pivotal justice in the two cases — Sandra Day O'Connor — acknowledged her own concerns about the issue. Speaking to a meeting of women lawyers in Minneapolis in July 2001, O'Connor said, "If statistics are any indication, the system may well be allowing some innocent defendants to be executed." After noting that Minnesota had no death penalty, O'Connor added, "You must breathe a sigh of relief every day." [20]

Changing Views?

Support for capital punishment sagged somewhat in the early years of the 21st century, seemingly in response to the work of death penalty critics and opponents. In the most dramatic event, Illinois Gov. Ryan specifically cited the risk of executing innocent persons in declaring his death penalty moratorium in January 2000 and then, as he left office in January 2003, commuting death sentences for the state's 164 condemned inmates. Meanwhile, the Supreme Court became somewhat more receptive to death row inmates' pleas by barring capital punishment for mentally retarded and juvenile offenders and setting aside death sentences in some individual cases because of racial discrimination, trial errors or inadequate legal representation.

During the Illinois moratorium, the commission Ryan created to study the state's flawed capital trials and sentencing procedures recommended a broad reform package, adopted in November 2003 after Ryan had left office. [21] The law gave defense lawyers access to all police notes, tightened police lineup procedures and mandated pretrial hearings on reliability of testimony from jailhouse informants. It also provided funding for pretrial or post-conviction DNA testing and removed the time limit on actual innocence claims in state courts.

Death penalty critics described the package as "historic," though it fell short of some recommended changes — including statewide oversight of death penalty cases. For his part, Gov. Blagojevich said he would keep the death penalty moratorium in place while the changes were put into effect.

In Maryland, Democrat Glendening followed a different sequence from Ryan's in first commissioning a study of racial bias in capital sentencing in 2001 and then imposing a death penalty moratorium in May 2002 while awaiting the results. The study found evidence that the death penalty was more likely to be sought in cases with white victims than in cases with black victims. But it was released in January 2003 — after Glendening had been defeated for re-election by the conservative Republican Ehrlich, who had vowed during his campaign to lift the moratorium. [22] The state has carried out one execution during Ehrlich's tenure: the lethal injection of convicted triple murderer Steven Oken on June 17, 2004. [23]

In Washington, death penalty critics were using the innocence issue to lobby for legislation to help inmates have access to post-conviction DNA testing. The five-year legislative fight culminated in October 2004 with passage of the Innocence Protection Act, which guarantees federal inmates the right to DNA testing within specified time limits or with court approval. The act also uses federal grants to encourage states to make DNA testing available to state inmates as well. [24]

Meanwhile, the Supreme Court was moving to narrow application of the death penalty and to exercise more critical oversight of state courts' handling of capital cases. In two landmark decisions, the court in 2002 and 2005 ruled that the Eighth Amendment's prohibition on cruel and unusual punishment barred the death penalty for mentally retarded or juvenile offenders. [25] In another case with broad application, the court in 2002 ruled that only juries, not judges, could make factual determinations needed to make defendants eligible for the death penalty. [26]

Equally significant, the court set aside death sentences in several individual cases. Many of the reversals appeared to rebuke two of the most conservative federal appeals courts that handled cases from states with large numbers of executions: the New Orleans-based Fifth Circuit with jurisdiction over Texas and the Richmond-based Fourth Circuit with jurisdiction over Virginia. In two Virginia cases, for example, the court upheld death row inmates' pleas — rejected by the Fourth Circuit — that their lawyers had provided constitutionally inadequate representation by failing to investigate social histories potentially useful as mitigating evidence to avoid the death penalty. In two Texas cases, the court ordered new hearings — refused by the Fifth Circuit — for condemned inmates' claims of racial discrimination in jury selection and improper withholding of damaging information about a key prosecution witness. [27]

The high court's critical scrutiny of capital cases peaked during the 2004-05 term. In addition to the ruling on juvenile offenders, the justices in four other cases set aside death sentences that had been upheld through appeals or post-conviction proceedings in federal and state courts:

- In a Pennsylvania case, the court somewhat strengthened the requirement that defense lawyers investigate defendants' background for potential mitigating evidence.
- In a Missouri case, the court ruled that the defendant was improperly shackled during the sentencing hearing.
- In a Texas case, the court summarily threw out a death sentence because the trial judge's instructions did not allow jurors to consider the defendant's mental retardation as a mitigating factor.

Group Says Innocent Man Was Executed

Larry Griffin maintained his innocence until the day he was executed in 1995 for a drug-related, drive-by shooting 15 years earlier. Now the St. Louis prosecutor's office is re-examining the case after a year-long investigation by a civil rights advocacy group concluded Griffin was innocent. [1]

The law professor who supervised the NAACP Legal Defense Fund (LDF) investigation says Griffin's case is an actual instance of a wrongful execution. If true, Griffin would be the first man in modern times proven to have been executed for a crime he did not commit. But the original prosecutor defends Griffin's 1981 verdict, and says the LDF just wants to use Griffin as "the poster child for the proposition that an innocent man was executed." [2]

Griffin was convicted of the June 26, 1980, shooting death of Quintin Moss, shot 13 times by men firing from a slow-moving car as Moss was selling drugs to another man, Wallace Conners, in a neighborhood used as an open-air drug market.

The case against Griffin consisted chiefly of identification by an eyewitness, Robert Fitzgerald, and evidence of motive: Moss was suspected of having murdered Griffin's older brother. Conners never identified Griffin, however, and moved away.

Moss' family, which had always doubted the case against Griffin, sought the LDF's help. Fund investigators found Conners in Los Angeles, where he told them Griffin was not among the shooters and that eyewitness Fitzgerald was not at the scene.

"He's innocent, and we've got very strong proof of it," says University of Michigan law professor Samuel Gross. If the case were brought to trial now, he added, "We'd win hands down."

But Gordon Ankney, the prosecutor in the case and now a private attorney in St. Louis, still believes in the verdict. "The truth . . . was presented in the courtroom under oath," he said recently.

After the LDF's report was released in June, St. Louis Circuit Attorney Jennifer Joyce assigned two lawyers to re-investigate the case. The investigation is expected to take several months.

---

[1] The 11-page report — a June 10, 2005, memorandum to attorneys representing the family of the homicide victim — can be found on the Web site of the *St. Louis Post-Dispatch* (www.stltoday.com) or on sites maintained by anti-death penalty groups, including Truth in Justice (www.truthinjustice.org). Account drawn from Terry Ganey, "Case Is Reopened 10 Years After Execution," *St. Louis Post-Dispatch*, July 12, 2005, p. A1.

[2] See Ganey, *op. cit.*; Gordon Ankney, "Judge Him on Evidence, Not on Opinion," *St. Louis Post-Dispatch*, July 25, 2005, p. B7.

- And in a follow-up to the earlier Texas racial discrimination case, the court sharply set aside the Fifth Circuit's decision to uphold the death sentence in the face of the high court's earlier ruling. [28]

Death penalty critics took heart from the high court's rulings as well as a decline in the number of executions and a dip in approval of the death penalty. Executions fell from a high of 98 in 1999 to 59 in 2004, according to the Death Penalty Information Center. Meanwhile, support for the death penalty in Gallup Polls fell to 66 percent in 2002 before climbing back to 74 percent in 2003 and 2005. And a majority of respondents — 73 percent in 2003, 59 percent in 2004 — said they believed an innocent person had been executed in recent years.

Supporters of capital punishment, however, emphasized the poll results showing that most Americans continue to support the death penalty. "They are concerned about executing an innocent person," says Latzer of the John Jay College of Criminal Justice. "But notwithstanding their concerns, they still overwhelmingly favor the death penalty."

CURRENT SITUATION

State Issues

Death penalty supporters appear to be somewhat on the defensive in state capitals around the country, but they continue to have the strength to block proposals to impose moratoriums on executions or abolish capital punishment. [29]

In one battleground state, for example, death penalty supporters and critics in North Carolina squared off all summer after a Senate-backed moratorium proposal won narrow approval in the House Judiciary Committee on May 31.

House Speaker Jim Black, a Democrat who supported the measure, put the bill on the chamber's calendar the next day. Fearing a defeat, however, Black never scheduled a vote before the legislature adjourned in early September. Instead, Black said he would create a special committee to study the death penalty, focusing on procedures for considering innocence claims by death row inmates. In announcing the plan, Black repeated his view that innocent people are now serving time in the state's prisons. "That is a horrendous thing for the state of North Carolina," he said. [30]

In one of the year's most important legislative fights, death penalty critics claimed victory when Texas Gov. Rick Perry, a Republican, signed a law on June 17 allowing a life sentence without possibility of parole as an alternative to the death penalty in capital murder cases. Some prosecutors and victims' rights groups had opposed the measure, fearing it would make death sentences harder to obtain. The law took effect on Sept. 1. [31]

Texas leads the country in executions with 349 since the Supreme Court allowed reinstitution of capital punishment in 1976. With an average of nearly 12 executions per year, Texas outpaces the average for the second-ranking state — Virginia — by a factor of nearly 4-to-1.

Earlier, New York's legislature left the state without a death penalty after the State Court of Appeals invalidated the state's capital punishment statute. After a round of sometimes-emotional hearings over the winter, the New York Assembly's Codes Committee on April 12 rejected, 11-7, a bill to adjust the death penalty law to comply with the appeals court's ruling. [32]

Eleven Democrats voted against the bill, while three Democrats and the committee's four Republicans voted to send it to the Assembly floor. The state Senate had previously approved a virtually identical bill. New York had gone without a death penalty law until 1995, when the state's newly elected Republican governor, George E. Pataki, fulfilled a campaign pledge by signing a capital punishment statute into effect. Six defendants had been sentenced to death under the law, but none had been executed before the Court of Appeals decision.

Bills to abolish the death penalty have been introduced in at least 16 other states in the past two years, according to the National Conference on State Legislatures, though none has passed. [33] In Connecticut, the state House of Representatives rejected an abolition

bill on March 30 by a vote of 89-60, with Democrats providing all but four of the votes in support of the measure. On May 13 the state carried out its first execution since 1960, when Michael Ross was put to death by lethal injection for killing eight young women in the early 1980s. Ross had waived further appeals.

Similarly, moratorium bills were introduced in at least seven states in 2005 in addition to North Carolina, but none passed. A group of Democratic lawmakers in California announced a plan in June to introduce a moratorium bill in 2006. With 648 inmates on death row, California has the largest death row population of any state; it has carried out 11 executions since 1976.

In North Carolina, moratorium supporters relied on claims that six innocent persons had been sent to death row in recent years, sometimes on documented instances of prosecutorial misconduct — chiefly, withholding of evidence. "We've had innocent people end up on death row, and there's no accounting for why that happened," says David Neal, a Durham defense lawyer who heads the North Carolina Committee for a Moratorium.

The state's district attorneys conference opposed the measure, describing it as a ploy to abolish the death penalty and disputing the likelihood of executing an innocent person. "We feel the processes are in place to check, double-check and double-double-check," says Peg Dorer, director of the North Carolina Conference of District Attorneys. She notes that a new law requires prosecutors to turn over all information to defense lawyers before trial.

Death penalty opponents say the legislative efforts — even if unsuccessful — contrast sharply with the moves in previous years to speed up appeals. "There's a realization that mistakes were made in the past, and we have to do better in the future," says Dieter.

But prosecutor Marquis says states for the most part are leaving death penalty laws alone. "You have states like New Mexico and North Carolina, where significant moves were made against the death penalty, and states like Iowa, Minnesota and Wisconsin, where significant moves were made to reinstate it," Marquis says. "None of the proposals passed."

High Court Cases

As the Supreme Court prepares to open its new term, presumably with a new chief justice and a vacancy to be filled, it has four death penalty cases already slated for review.

Should states adopt moratoriums on executions?

YES
Barry Scheck
Co-founder/Co-director, The Innocence Project, www.innocenceproject.org

Written for *CQ Researcher*, September 2005

Post-conviction DNA testing has exonerated 162 inmates (and counting), identified numerous real assailants and proved the innocence of 14 men sentenced to death. These exonerations have not just demonstrated the real risk of executing an innocent person but also exposed serious weaknesses in the state criminal-justice systems, indicating that moratoria are needed on executions.

DNA testing is not a panacea; it will not make any state's death penalty fair, accurate or just. It does not offer probative evidence in the vast majority of criminal cases.

Indeed, DNA exonerations have created a learning moment, an opportunity to deal with the causes of wrongful conviction that victimize the innocent and allow the real criminals to go free: Mistaken eyewitness identification, false confessions, incompetent defense lawyers, poor forensic science and law enforcement misconduct. These issues can and must be addressed to prevent execution of the innocent.

This is the heart of the death penalty moratorium debate. Reasonable people can differ about the morality of capital punishment. But it is not reasonable to excuse inequities in the administration of capital punishment. As the president has acknowledged, capital lawyers are not adequately trained or properly funded. Until the American Bar Association's Guidelines for the Administration of Capital Punishment are implemented, no citizen can be confident about the guilt of all death row inmates.

Consider as well scientific advances that come too late. Texas executed Cameron Willingham in 2004 despite exhortations from a leading expert that the arson evidence underlying Willingham's murder conviction was proven false by new scientific data. Soon afterward, Texas exonerated Ernest Willis from his arson murder death sentence when prosecutors agreed with the same expert and science offered in Willingham's case. Nothing could be done for Willingham — likely an innocent man — because the state had already killed him.

Are fair-minded supporters of capital punishment willing to make the system fair and accurate? Should Louisiana, whose indigent-defense system was already in fiscal crisis, spend millions now to pursue executions? Why not invest in better crime labs, decent defense counsel and eyewitness and police reforms? How can states fail to enact these good law enforcement measures that protect against wrongful executions and help apprehend real murderers?

Until states address these known systemic failures, they must impose moratoria on executions.

NO
Kent Scheidegger
Legal Director, Criminal Justice Legal Foundation, www.cjlf.org

Written for *CQ Researcher*, September 2005

Should the execution of Danny Rolling stay on hold when his current, and hopefully last, appeal is decided? That is what the moratorium backers propose. They want to hold every execution in America, regardless of how clear the murderer's guilt or how clearly deserved his sentence. They have yet to come up with a single convincing reason for such a drastic step.

There is no doubt whatever of Rolling's guilt. It was proven by both DNA and his confession. In a spree of rape, mutilation and murder he killed five college students in Gainesville, Fla., in 1990. Eleven years have passed since his sentence, while multiple courts have repeatedly considered and rejected arguments that have nothing to do with guilt or innocence.

This is not unusual. Only a handful of capital cases involve genuine questions of innocence. By all means, we should put those few on hold as long as it takes to resolve the questions, and the governor should commute the sentence if a genuine doubt remains. At the same time, we should proceed with the justly deserved punishment in the many cases with no such questions, and considerably faster than we do now.

The other arguments against the death penalty have failed. The claim of discrimination against minority defendants is refuted by the opponents' own studies. So, too, is the claim of bias on the race of the victim, when the data are properly analyzed.

It has also been shown that lawyers appointed to represent the indigent get the same results on average as retained counsel. For example, Scott Peterson, with the lawyer to the stars, sits on death row, while the public defender got a life sentence for the penniless Unabomber. The mitigating circumstance of Theodore Kaczynski's mental illness made the difference, not the lawyers.

On the other hand, a powerful reason for the death penalty becomes clearer every year. Study after study confirms that the death penalty does deter murder and does save innocent lives when it is actually enforced.

Conversely, delay in execution and the needless overturning of valid sentences sap the deterrent effect and kill innocent people.

To minimize the loss of innocent life, the path is clear. Take as long as we need in the few cases where guilt is in genuine question and proceed to execution in a reasonable time in a great bulk of cases where it is not.

The successors to the late Chief Justice Rehnquist and Associate Justice O'Connor could leave the court as closely divided as before on death penalty issues or might tip the scales slightly in favor of upholding challenged convictions or sentences in capital cases.

Federal Judge John G. Roberts Jr., President Bush's nominee for chief justice, appears on the verge of Senate confirmation following hearings before the Judiciary Committee that began on Sept. 12. Bush had originally named Roberts to succeed the retiring O'Connor but nominated him to be chief justice instead following Rehnquist's Sept. 3 death from thyroid cancer.

O'Connor apparently plans to be on the bench at the opening of the new term on Oct. 3 while awaiting action by Bush and the Senate on filling her post. In announcing her retirement on July 1, she said she would remain in office until her successor was nominated and confirmed.

Rehnquist had been a fairly consistent vote for upholding death sentences throughout his 33 years on the court, while O'Connor sometimes broke from the conservative majority to vote to overturn death sentences or narrow death penalty laws.

In confirmation hearings, Roberts gave only general hints of his likely views in death penalty cases — which he has not had to face in his two years on the federal court in Washington. Questioned about a memo written as a Reagan administration lawyer in the 1980s criticizing habeas corpus review, Roberts noted that reforms by the Supreme Court and Congress have eliminated the frequent practice of "repetitive" petitions.

Roberts said the current system of state and federal review of death was aimed at minimizing the risk of executing an innocent person, but he added that some risk is inevitable. "There is always a risk in any enterprise that is a human enterprise," Roberts said. The most effective way to reduce the risk of error in capital cases, he noted, was to make sure defendants have "competent counsel at every stage of the proceeding."

The Judiciary Committee was due to vote on Roberts' nomination on Sept. 22, with a vote in the full Senate expected to follow the next week — in time for Roberts to preside at the opening session Oct. 3.

The four cases that the justices have already agreed to hear during the new term include the actual innocence plea by Tennessee inmate House and appeals by three states — California, Kansas and Oregon — seeking to reinstate challenged death penalty laws or procedures.

The justices are also due to consider the plea by Virginia death row inmate Lovitt in their private conference on Sept. 26 and could add the case to the list for the term later that week.

In their filings, lawyers for House asked the high court to hear the case to resolve "inconsistency and confusion" among lower federal courts about the rules for considering post-conviction claims of actual innocence. They claimed that "powerful" new evidence, including DNA evidence, showed that House had been "wrongly convicted" of the murder of his former neighbor.

Lawyers for the state countered that the district court judge and the Sixth Circuit appeals court had correctly applied the Supreme Court's decision requiring a very strong showing of actual innocence to belatedly raise a constitutional claim. House's evidence did not meet that threshold but was "countered and undermined in virtually every respect," wrote Jennifer Smith, associate deputy Tennessee attorney general.

In the most significant of the other three cases, lawyers for the state of Kansas are seeking to reinstate a death penalty law struck down by the state's high court in December 2004. [34] In a 4-3 decision, the Kansas Supreme Court ruled the law unconstitutional because it required a death sentence if the jury determined that aggravating circumstances were "not outweighed" by mitigating circumstances. "Fundamental fairness requires that 'a tie goes to the defendant' when life or death is at issue," the majority wrote, quoting an earlier Kansas decision.

The case stems from the capital murder conviction and death sentence of Michael Marsh for the 1996 killing of a woman and her infant daughter. They were killed in their home during an extortion plot aimed at her husband that went awry when she unexpectedly arrived at the house instead of him. Lawyers for the Kansas attorney general's office contend that the state justices misinterpreted the governing Supreme Court precedent on weighing aggravating and mitigating circumstances.

In a second case, lawyers for the Oregon attorney general's office are asking the justices to reverse a state high court decision that death penalty defendants have a constitutional right to offer evidence of innocence during the sentencing phase after a guilty verdict. They argue that a capital defendant is entitled only to present evidence of "moral culpability" during the sentencing phase and not to "reargue his legal culpability or guilt." [35]

The final case is an appeal by lawyers for the state of California trying to reinstate a death sentence struck down because of what the Ninth Circuit appeals court ruled was a prejudicial jury instruction. [36] The California Supreme Court had ruled the error did not affect the sentence, but the federal appellate judges disagreed.

Arguments in the California case are set for Oct. 11, while the Oregon and Kansas cases are to be heard on Dec. 7. Arguments in the House case are scheduled for early 2006. Decisions in all four cases are due by the start of the court's recess at the end of June.

OUTLOOK

"Risks of Unfairness"?

Justice John Paul Stevens has become the latest member of the Supreme Court to voice strong concerns off the bench about the way that death penalty cases are handled in the United States. In a speech to the American Bar Association on Aug. 6, Stevens noted the "substantial number" of erroneously imposed death sentences and then suggested the need to re-examine jury-selection and sentencing procedures to eliminate what he called "special risks of unfairness" in death penalty cases. [37]

Stevens had gone even further three months earlier. In a speech in May to lawyers and judges at the Seventh Circuit Bar Association, the 85-year-old leader of the court's liberal bloc said, "This country would be much better off if we did not have capital punishment." [38]

At least three other justices have publicly criticized death penalty procedures in past speeches: O'Connor in 2001 and President Clinton's two appointees, Ruth Bader Ginsburg and Stephen G. Breyer, earlier. No one expects the current high court to abolish capital punishment, but death penalty critics and opponents are encouraged by what they see as a re-examination of the issue by the justices that parallels a similar reconsideration by the public at large.

"The court is part of the whole changing of focus on the death penalty," says Dieter of the Death Penalty Information Center. "It's stimulated because of the cases of innocence that everybody knows about."

Death penalty supporters minimize the significance of the court's recent decisions barring execution of juveniles and mentally retarded offenders and invalidating individual sentences in other cases. "That's not a veering

away from the death penalty for moral or constitutional grounds but a recognition that it should be reserved for the most serious crimes," says prosecutor Marquis. As for Stevens' speech, Marquis says it reflects "the justice's personal abhorrence for capital punishment."

Marquis predicts that Roberts' anticipated confirmation as chief justice and the nomination of a successor to O'Connor will shift the court, if at all, slightly more toward law enforcement positions in death cases. He speculates that Roberts will vote much as Rehnquist did in capital cases, while Bush's choice of a successor for O'Connor is likely to be "more supportive" of prosecutors than she was on death penalty issues.

The ABA's Tabak, however, tentatively forecasts continued critical scrutiny of death cases from the high court. "If they do not backtrack with changes in membership, they will continue to be somewhat more vigilant, as they have been in recent years," he says.

The decisions by the Kansas and Oregon supreme courts illustrate that some state tribunals are critically examining death penalty laws in their jurisdictions, though the Supreme Court's decisions to hear the states' appeals could signal that the justices think the state courts are going further than necessary to protect defendants' rights.

In state legislatures, meanwhile, lawmakers are tinkering with death penalty procedures while stopping short of endorsing moratoriums on executions. "Legislatures in states that have a death penalty are attentive to making it fair and workable," says Donna Lyons, criminal justice program director for the National Conference of State Legislatures.

In Washington, Congress is working on legislation that would increase federal aid to the states for DNA and other forensic testing. In his 2005 State of the Union address, President Bush unveiled plans to ask for $1 billion over five years to expand DNA testing capacity in order to guard against the risk of wrongful convictions. [39] State crime labs, supported by anti-death penalty groups, urged that the initiative be expanded to include other forensic techniques. By mid-September, both the House and the Senate had included forensics funding in Justice Department appropriations bills, with the final amount to be determined in a joint conference committee.

In his final year on the Supreme Court in 1994, Justice Harry A. Blackmun became convinced that it was impossible to administer the death penalty fairly. "From this day forward, I no longer shall tinker with the death penalty," Blackmun wrote in an impassioned, 7,000-word dissent from the court's refusal to take up a plea from a Texas death row inmate. [40]

Justice Antonin Scalia responded by accusing Blackmun of trying to "thrust a minority's view on the people." Since then, more than 750 defendants have been executed in the United States and the nation's death row population has increased by nearly one-fifth to its current level of slightly over 3,400.

NOTES

1. Quoted in Donna St. George, "Va. Man Nears Execution in Test of Destroyed DNA," *The Washington Post*, July 12, 2005, p. A1.

2. For previous coverage, see these *CQ Researcher* reports: Kenneth Jost, "Rethinking the Death Penalty," Nov. 16, 2001, pp. 945-968; Mary Cooper, "Death Penalty Update," Jan. 8, 1999, pp. 1-24.

3. For background, see Kenneth Jost, "DNA Databases," *CQ Researcher*, May 28, 1999, pp. 449-472.

4. *Herrera v. Collins*, 506 U.S. 390 (1993), and *Schlup v. Delo*, 513 U.S. 298 (1995).

5. The bill numbers are S 1088 and HR 3035.

6. For coverage, see Ken Armstrong and Steve Mills, "Ryan: 'Until I Can Be Sure.' Illinois Is First State to Suspend Death Penalty," *The Chicago Tribune*, Feb. 1, 2000, p. 1; Maurice Possley and Steve Mills, "Clemency for All: Ryan Commutes 164 Death Sentences to Life in Prison Without Parole," *The Chicago Tribune*, Jan. 12, 2003, p. 1. The *Tribune's* five-part investigative series was published in November 1999 under the title "The Failure of the Death Penalty in Illinois."

7. Quoted in Bill Kurtis, *The Death Penalty on Trial: Crisis in American Justice* (2004), p. 9.

8. For a concise history by a confirmed opponent, see Hugo Adam Bedau, "An Abolitionist's Survey of the Death Penalty in America Today," in Hugo Adam Bedau and Paul G. Cassell, *Debating the Death Penalty: Should America Have Capital Punishment?* (2004), pp. 15-24.

9. Public opinion data taken from Robert M. Bohm, "American Death Penalty Opinion: Past, Present, and Future," in James R. Acker, Robert M. Bohm, and Charles S. Lanier (eds.), *America's Experiment with Capital Punishment* (2d ed.), 2003, pp. 27-54. For current polling data, see the Web site of the Death Penalty Information Center (www.deathpenaltyinfo.org).

10. The citation is 408 U.S. 238 (1972). For background on this and subsequent Supreme Court decisions, see David G. Savage, *Guide to the U.S. Supreme Court* (4th ed.), 2004, pp. 655-662.

11. The citation is 428 U.S. 153 (1976). The 5-4 ruling to bar mandatory death penalty laws is *Woodson v. North Carolina*, 428 U.S. 280 (1976).

12. See, e.g., *Lockett v. Ohio*, 438 U.S. 586 (1978).

13. Some background drawn from Franklin E. Zimring, *The Contradictions of American Capital Punishment* (2003). Zimring, a professor at the University of California's Boalt Hall School of Law in Berkeley, is a strong opponent of the death penalty.

14. The decisions are *Teague v. Lane*, 489 U.S. 288 (1989); *Coleman v. Thompson*, 501 U.S. 722 (1991); and *Keeney v. Tamayo-Reyes*, 504 U.S. 1 (1992). For more background, see Savage, *op. cit.*, pp. 295-300.

15. See *1996 CQ Almanac*, p. 5-18.

16. See Zimring, *op. cit.*, pp. 157-162.

17. Barry Scheck, Peter Neufeld and Jim Dwyer, *Actual Innocence: Five Days to Execution and Other Dispatches from the Wrongly Convicted* (1999).

18. Ken Armstrong and Steve Mills, "Death Row Justice Denied: Bias, Errors and Incompetence in Capital Cases Have Turned Illinois' Harshest Punishment into Its Least Credible," *The Chicago Tribune*, Nov. 14, 1999, p. 1.

19. See Jim Yardley, "Oklahoma Retraces Big Step in Capital Case," *The New York Times*, Sept. 2, 2001, p. 12.

20. "O'Connor Questions Death Penalty," The Associated Press, July 3, 2001.

21. For coverage, see John Chase and Ray Long, "Death Penalty Reform Passes," *The Chicago Tribune*, Nov. 20, 2003, p. 1. For more complete information, see the Center for Wrongful Convictions' Web site, www.law.northwestern.edu/wrongfulconvictions.

22. For coverage, see Lori Montgomery, "Maryland Suspends Death Penalty," *The Washington Post*, May 10, 2002, p. A1; Susan Levine and Lori Montgomery,

"Large Racial Disparity Found by Study of Md. Death Penalty," *The Washington Post*, Jan. 8, 2003, p. A1.

23. See Susan Levine, "Maryland Executes Oken," *The Washington Post*, June 18, 2004, p. A1.

24. Jennifer A. Dlouhy, "Add-Ons End Years of Wrangling, Clear Path for DNA Testing Bill," *CQ Weekly*, Oct. 16, 2004, p. 2442.

25. The decisions are *Atkins v. Virginia*, 536 U.S. 304 (June 20, 2002); and *Roper v. Simmons*, — U.S. — (March 1, 2005).

26. The case is *Ring v. Arizona*, 536 U.S. 584 (June 24, 2002).

27. The cases are, respectively, *Terry Williams v. Taylor*, 529 U.S. 362 (April 18, 2000); *Wiggins v. Smith*, 539 U.S. 510 (June 26, 2003); *Miller-El v. Cockrell*, 537 U.S. 322 (Feb. 25, 2003); and *Banks v. Dretke*, 540 U.S. 668 (Feb. 24, 2004).

28. The cases are, respectively, *Rompilla v. Beard* (June 20, 2005); *Deck v. Missouri* (May 23, 2005); *Smith v. Texas* (Nov. 15, 2004); and *Miller-El v. Dretke* (June 13, 2005). Citations to U.S. Reports not yet available.

29. Information on legislative proposals can be found on Web sites of opposing advocacy groups: Justice for All (www.prodeathpenalty.com) and the Death Penalty Information Center (www.deathpenaltyinfo.org).

30. Quoted in Lynn Bonner, "House, Senate Finish Session," *The* [Raleigh, N.C.] *News & Observer*, Sept. 3, 2005, p. B3. For earlier action, see Mark Johnson, "N.C. Takes Step Toward Halting Death Penalty," *The Charlotte Observer*, June 1, 2005, p. 1A.

31. Mike Ward, "Life Without Parole Among 600 Laws Signed by Governor," *Austin American-Statesman*, June 18, 2005, p. A15.

32. Patrick D. Healy, "Death Penalty Bill Is Blocked by Democrats," *The New York Times*, April 13, 2005, p. B1. The decision is *People v. LaValle*, June 24, 2004. The court ruled the law unconstitutionally coerced jurors because it allowed a judge to impose a life sentence with parole eligibility if jurors were deadlocked between the two more severe alternatives: death and life without parole.

33. Sarah Brown Hammond, "Questioning Capital Punishment," *State Legislatures*, September 2005, pp. 32-33.

34. The case is *Kansas v. Marsh*, 04-1170.

35. The case is *Oregon v. Guzek*, 04-928.

36. The case is *Brown v. Sanders*, 04-980.

37. Gina Holland, "Stevens Focuses on Death Penalty Flaws," The Associated Press, Aug. 7, 2005. The text of Stevens' speech can be found on the Supreme Court's Web site: www.supremecourtus.gov.

38. Quoted in Monica Thomas, "O'Connor Exit 'Wrenching,' Stevens Tells Lawyers Here," *Chicago Sun-Times*, Aug. 7, 2005.

39. See Peter Baker, "Behind Bush's Bid to Save the Innocent: State of the Union Remarks Were the Culmination of Complicated Maneuvering," *The Washington Post*, Feb. 4, 2005, p. A9.

40. The case is *Callins v. Collins*, 510 U.S. 1141 (1994). See Linda Greenhouse, "Death Penalty Is Renounced by Blackmun," *The New York Times*, Feb. 23, 1994, p. A1.

BIBLIOGRAPHY

Books

Acker, James R., Robert M. Bohm and Charles S. Lanier (eds.), *America's Experiment with Capital Punishment: Reflections on the Past, Present, and Future of the Ultimate Penal Sanction* (2d ed.), Carolina Academic Press, 2003.
More than 30 contributors provide comprehensive coverage of death penalty issues being debated in the United States. Includes notes and references for each chapter, tabular materials. Acker is a professor at the University of Albany, Bohm at the University of Central Florida; Lanier is co-director of the Capital Punishment Research Initiative at the University of Albany.

Bedau, Hugo Adam, and Paul G. Cassell (eds.), *Debating the Death Penalty: Should America Have Capital Punishment?* Oxford University Press, 2004.
Eight contributors, evenly split between supporters and critics of the death penalty, examine various aspects of the capital punishment debate. Bedau is professor emeritus of philosophy, Tufts University, and a confirmed opponent of the death penalty; Cassell, a former law professor at the University of Utah and now a federal district court judge, supports capital punishment.

Kurtis, Bill, *The Death Penalty on Trial: Crisis in American Justice,* **Public Affairs, 2004.**
The veteran television correspondent provides a journalistic account of two exoneration cases originally used in a program for A&E Television Network.

Scheck, Barry, Peter Neufeld and Jim Dwyer, *Actual Innocence: Five Days to Execution and Other Dispatches from the Wrongly Convicted,* **Doubleday, 2000.**
Defense lawyers Scheck and Neufeld — founders of the Innocence Project — and Pulitzer Prize-winning columnist Dwyer recount stories of helping 10 men, including some death row inmates, prove their innocence after wrongful convictions.

Zimring, Franklin E., *The Contradictions of American Capital Punishment,* **Oxford University Press, 2003.**
The longtime death penalty opponent and University of California at Berkeley law professor examines what he calls the contradictions of public support for speeding death penalty cases while trying to minimize the risk of wrongful executions.

Articles

Armstrong, Ken, and Steve Mills, "Death Row Justice Denied: Bias, Errors and Incompetence in Capital Cases Have Turned Illinois' Harshest Punishment into Its Least Credible," *The Chicago Tribune,* **Nov. 14, 1999, p. 1.**
This is the first of five articles describing the newspaper's investigation of all 285 Illinois death penalty cases since the state reinstated capital punishment 22 years ago; the paper found serious flaws in the state's criminal justice system.

Dlouhy, Jennifer A., "Add-Ons End Years of Wrangling, Clear Path for DNA Testing Bill," *CQ Weekly,* **Oct. 16, 2004, p. 2442.**
Congress completed work on a DNA testing bill, which would give federal inmates access to genetic testing and seek to ensure defendants in capital cases have sufficient legal representation.

Ganey, Terry, "Was the Wrong Man Executed?" *St. Louis Post-Dispatch,* **July 11, 2005.**
St. Louis Circuit Attorney Jennifer Joyce reopened an investigation into the case of Larry Griffin, who was sentenced to death for a drive-by murder 25 years ago.

Levine, Susan, and Lori Montgomery, "Large Racial Disparity Found by Study of Md. Death Penalty," *The Washington Post,* **Jan. 8, 2003, p. A1.**
Maryland Gov. Parris Glendening commissioned a study to investigate racial bias in the state's capital sentencing in 2001, which found the death penalty was more likely to be sought in cases involving white victims than in cases with black victims.

Reports & Studies

Berk, Richard A., "New Claims About Executions and General Deterrence: Déjà Vu All Over Again?" *Journal of Empirical Legal Studies,* **Vol. 2, No. 2 (July 2005), pp. 303-330.**
This analysis claims the deterrent effect exists in only one state — Texas — and is not particularly influential there.

Shepherd, Joanna, "Deterrence versus Brutalization: Capital Punishment's Differing Impacts Among States," *Michigan Law Review,* **Vol. 4, Issue 2 (November 2005).**
The effects of capital punishment vary from state to state, the researcher finds.

Zimerman, Paul R., "State Executions, Deterrence and the Incidence of Murder," *Journal of Applied Economics,* **Vol. 7, No. 1 (May 2004), pp. 163-193.**
This study by the Criminal Justice Legal Foundation finds that the announcement of capital punishment creates a deterrence rather than the death penalty itself. Other studies showing that executions deter capital crimes can be found on the group's Web site, www.cjlf.org.

For More Information

American Association on Mental Retardation, 444 N. Capitol St., N.W., Suite 846, Washington, DC 20001-1512; (202) 387-1968; www.aamr.org. The largest and oldest organization devoted to mental retardation and related disabilities.

Criminal Justice Legal Foundation, 2131 L St., Sacramento, CA 95816; (916) 446-0345; www.cjlf.org. A pro-death penalty public-interest law organization working to ensure that the courts respect the rights of crime victims and law-abiding society.

Death Penalty Information Center, 1101 Vermont Ave., N.W., Suite 701, Washington, DC 20005; (202) 289-2275; www.deathpenaltyinfo.org. An anti-death penalty organization furnishing analysis and information on issues concerning capital punishment.

Innocence Project, 100 5th Ave., 3rd floor, New York, NY 10011; (212) 364-5340; www.innocenceproject.org. Seeks to exonerate the wrongfully convicted through DNA testing and to effect reforms to prevent wrongful convictions.

National Association of Criminal Defense Lawyers, 1150 18th St., N.W., Suite 950; Washington, DC 20036; (202) 872-8600; www.criminaljustice.org. Works to ensure justice and due process to persons accused of crimes.

National Conference of State Legislatures, 7700 East First Pl., Denver, CO 80230; (303) 364-7700; www.ncsl.org. A bipartisan organization that provides a forum for state legislators and their staffs to discuss state issues.

National District Attorneys Association, 99 Canal Center Plaza, Suite 510, Alexandria, VA 22314; (703) 549-9222; www.ndaa.org. Helps prosecutors by providing training, research and legislative advocacy.

11

Identity Theft

Peter Katel

Brett Kominitsky, 33, of Hartselle, Ala., spent three days in jail in 2004 for crimes committed by a thief who had stolen his identity. Identify theft victimizes nearly 10 million Americans each year and costs businesses and individuals $53 billion.

From *CQ Researcher*, June 10, 2005.

John Harrison had recently retired from the Army and was set-tling into a second career as a corrugated-box salesman in Connecticut when he received a call that changed his life. A policeman in Beaumont, Texas, wanted to know if Harrison had bought a Harley-Davidson motorcycle in Beaumont. No, Harrison replied.

The policeman told Harrison, now 44, that a 21-year-old man had bought the Harley and ridden it from Texas to North Carolina, where he was arrested during a domestic dispute with his girlfriend.

As the policeman had suspected, the young biker had stolen Harrison's identity and bought the motorcycle using Harrison's name and Social Security number.

But the Harley was only the beginning of the identity thief's shopping spree in late 2001. Using a counterfeit military ID with Harrison's name and Social Security number, the thief went on to spend more than $250,000 using some 60 credit cards and store and car-dealer accounts.

The thief was convicted and served a three-year prison term. But Harrison didn't get off so easily. The stress caused by months of trying to recover his identity and once-excellent credit rating sent him into therapy and then cost him his job.

Although he has since gotten a better position, Harrison still receives calls from bill collectors, and his credit rating hasn't fully recovered, forcing him to pay exorbitant interest rates on his credit card debt.

Criminologist Judith Collins was hit by an identity theft ring in 1999, but she was more fortunate than Harrison. "I was able to straighten everything out immediately," says Collins, who went on

Security Breaches Hit Facilities Nationwide

Personal data on more than 6 million U.S. consumers has been lost or stolen since the start of the new year. Institutions affected ranged from data brokers and banks to universities and federal agencies. Here is a representative sample of the breaches reported:

Date	Name	Type of breach	Number of people affected
June 6, 2005	CitiFinancial	Lost backup tapes	3,900,000
May 28, 2005	Merlin Data Services	Bogus accounts set up	9,000
May 4, 2005	Colorado Health Department	Stolen laptop	1,600 (families)
May 2, 2005	Time Warner	Lost backup tapes	600,000
April 28, 2005	Georgia Southern University	Hacking	"tens of thousands"
April 28, 2005	Wachovia, Bank of America, PNC Financial Services Group	Dishonest insiders	676,000
April 21, 2005	Carnegie Mellon University	Hacking	19,000
April 20, 2005	Ameritrade	Lost backup tape	200,000
April 18, 2005	DSW/Retail Ventures	Hacking	1,300,000
April 14, 2005	Polo Ralph Lauren/HSBC	Hacking	180,000
April 12, 2005	LexisNexis	Passwords compromised	Additional 280,000

Source: Privacy Rights Clearinghouse

to found the Identity Theft Crime and Research Laboratory at Michigan State University.

But no one has been able to protect the universe of personal information in cyberspace that identity thieves see as a vast digital gold mine.

In the first five months of 2005, information on nearly 10 million people held by financial institutions, stores, data companies and universities fell into unauthorized hands. The data was lost to hackers, fake businesses set up to obtain the information or thieves with stolen laptops. (*See chart, p. 240.*) In February, 1.2 million names in Bank of America files were exposed when backup tapes were lost. [1] In April, the Omaha, Neb.-based investment firm Ameritrade lost a computer backup tape containing account information on some 200,000 clients. [2] In May, a contractor for Time Warner lost tapes containing personal details on 600,000 present and former employees. [3]

And in early June, a Citigroup subsidiary reported the largest data loss yet: Backup tapes with data on 3.9 million customers were missing.

Two years ago, the Federal Trade Commission (FTC) estimated that 3.2 million consumers had become victims of identity theft during the previous year — targeted by thieves who opened new accounts, obtained new identification documents or took other steps to impersonate the victims. Another 6.6 million were victims of credit fraud, in which thieves who gained access to account numbers raided credit card or bank accounts. [4]

The FTC report also estimated that identity theft costs businesses and individuals about $53 billion a year. As a result, concern about identity theft has been building since the mid-1990s, when news of the crime began surfacing.

Moreover, FTC Chairwoman Deborah Majoras told the Senate Judiciary Committee on April 13, "victims spent almost 300 million hours correcting their records and reclaiming their good names. That is a substantial toll, and we take seriously the need to reduce it."

But some private-sector experts claim that government is far behind the curve when it comes to criminal technological innovations and that there is a boom in long-distance fraud by identity thieves who commit all their crimes online. "We don't know the half of it yet," says Avivah Litan, research director and computer security specialist for Gartner Inc., a consulting firm in Greenwich, Conn.

The credit-rating industry points out that while consumers may be upset about technology-assisted crime and loss of privacy, they like the convenience of merchants and banks being able to run instant credit checks at the point of purchase — using the same kind of online credit information used by the thieves. Such convenience comes with hazards, says Stuart Pratt, president and CEO of the Consumer Data Industry Association, which represents credit-reporting agencies. "We have to balance that against having nationwide lending systems wanting to reach out to tell me I can have a better rate, or that I can re-finance my house."

Even so, politicians feeling heat from constituents acknowledge that privacy-protection efforts under way since the 1970s and anti-identity-theft measures dating back to 1998 are ineffective. Litan estimates that identity-theft conviction rates range from 1 in 700 to only 1 in 1,000. [5]

On May 10, 2005, Senate Commerce Committee Chairman Ted Stevens, R-Alaska, announced to a packed hearing on the sale of personal information: "Over the recess, my staff attempted to steal my identity, and I regret to say they were successful. For $65, they were told they could get my Social Security number."

Ironically, while personal data crucial to identity thieves — names, addresses, Social Security numbers, jobs, mothers' maiden names — are legally and publicly available to anyone, definitive information on the magnitude of identity theft itself is virtually non-existent. [6] FTC researchers arrived at their estimates of the number of victims on the basis of a random telephone survey of 4,057 adults.

"No single hotline or database captures the universe of identity theft victims," the General Accounting Office (GAO) reported in 2002. "Some individuals do not even know that they have been victimized until months after the fact, and some known victims may choose not to report to the police, credit bureaus or established hotlines." [7]

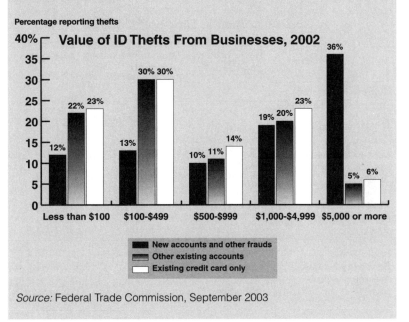

Average Loss Was $10,200 in Serious Cases

Businesses suffered the greatest losses when ID thefts involved people who had new accounts opened in their names or their information was used to commit other types of fraud. The average loss from such thefts was $10,200.

Percentage reporting thefts

Value of ID Thefts From Businesses, 2002

Legend:
- New accounts and other frauds
- Other existing accounts
- Existing credit card only

	Less than $100	$100-$499	$500-$999	$1,000-$4,999	$5,000 or more
New accounts and other frauds	12%	13%	10%	19%	36%
Other existing accounts	22%	30%	11%	20%	5%
Existing credit card only	23%	30%	14%	23%	6%

Source: Federal Trade Commission, September 2003

Thus, while anecdotal reports indicate widespread identity fraud, only 246,570 people registered identity-theft complaints in 2004 with the FTC — fewer than the 388,603 who reported other kinds of fraud, including those involving online shopping, advance-fee loans and other scams. [8]

"I am not sure that the average American is even aware of the FTC as the place to file identity-fraud reports," says Chris Jay Hoofnagle, West Coast director of the Washington-based Electronic Privacy Information Center (EPIC).

But some financial-services industry officials suggest identity theft isn't as prevalent as privacy/consumer advocates say it is. "The primary source of data is the FTC, where people are self-identifying as victims of identity theft," says Anne Wallace, executive director of the Identity Theft Assistance Center, a new service financed by 48 big lending institutions. "There are all kinds of issues with the accuracy of that — What is in that consumer's mind? What is their perception of

ID Fraud Costs $53 Billion and 297 Million Hours

Nearly 10 million Americans were victims of identity theft in 2002, costing businesses $47.6 billion. Individual victims paid another $5 billion out of their own pockets and spent 297 million hours trying to re-establish their credit identities.

Cost of ID Theft in Time and Money

	New Accounts/ Other Frauds	Misuse of Existing Accounts	All ID Fraud
Number of Victims:			
Percent of population	1.5%	Credit Card: 2.4% Non-Credit Card: 0.7%	4.6%
Number of persons*	3.23 million	6.68 million	9.91 million
Loss to Businesses:			
Average per victim	$10,200	$2,100	$4,800
Total**	$32.9 billion	$14.0 billion	$47.6 billion
Loss to Victims:			
Average per victim	$1,180	$160	$500
Total**	$3.8 billion	$1.1 billion	$5.0 billion
Hours Spent Resolving Problems:			
Average per victim	60	15	30
Total**	194 million	100 million	297 million

* Based on U.S. population age 18 and over of 215.47 million as of July 1, 2002.

** Totals are not exact due to rounding.

Source: Federal Trade Commission, "Identity Theft Survey Report," September 2003

However, Joanne McNabb, director of California's Office of Privacy Protection, contends that criminals more often steal data from within a company, or "skim" numbers with hand-held remote card-readers in restaurants and elsewhere. Other methods include "dumpster diving" for discarded receipts, legal documents and the like; computer hacking and "inside jobs" in which employees steal personal data to which they have access.

Thus, a careful, law-abiding citizen may shred his sensitive documents but still lose his identity data to a thief. Even those potentially affected by any of this year's major security breaches should not assume they have escaped unscathed just because they have not yet noticed any thefts from their accounts. "Thieves could sit on the information for a year," says Robert Douglas of Steamboat Springs, Colo., a former private investigator and author of an identity-theft training manual for the American Bankers Association. "It's like robbing a bank — you don't go out and spend the $100 bills right away."

identity theft? Are they talking about a forged check, an unauthorized transaction on a credit card?"

In fact, the FTC does distinguish between identity theft and credit card fraud, or the theft of a card number but not an entire identity. The distinction matters because financial-services companies, according to some consumer advocates, prefer to highlight credit card fraud on the grounds that much of it can be traced to careless clients.

A January 2005 report commissioned by Visa USA, Wells Fargo Bank and CheckFree Services Corp., a payment service for online purchases, concluded that lost or stolen wallets, checkbooks or credit cards account for 28.8 percent of the identity theft cases — the biggest single cause — in which victims know how their data was obtained. [9] (*See graph, p. 246.*)

As the fight against identity theft continues, here are some of the questions being debated:

Would tougher penalties or new security technologies halt identity theft?

Identity theft is ancient. The Identity Theft Assistance Center's Wallace points to the *Old Testament* tale of twin brothers Esau and Jacob as the first recorded case. *Genesis* tells of Jacob, the second-born son, tricking his blind father Isaac into giving him a blessing meant for Esau, by posing as hairy Esau — stealing Esau's identity.

"It's been going on a long time," Wallace says.

The ancient roots of identity fraud suggest that its disappearance is unlikely anytime soon. But a variety of strategies have been proposed to combat it.

The most obvious solution — increasing the criminal penalties — is rarely suggested. That is hardly surprising since increasing the penalties for identity fraud has not shown big results so far, experts say. First imposed in 1998, federal penalties for identity theft were set at a maximum of 20 years and then increased by up to five years in 2004. Yet identity theft increased during that six-year period.

Stiffer penalties don't work, says Dan Clements, founder of CardCops, an identity-fraud monitoring firm in Los Angeles, because the thieves usually do not live in the United States and/or they operate on the Internet. "The perpetrators are outside our jurisdiction," often in Eastern Europe, he says. "It's extremely hard for the Secret Service or anyone in our government to go after them." (*See sidebar, p. 250.*)

Larry Johnson, head of the Criminal Investigative Division of the Secret Service, told the Senate Judiciary Committee on April 13, 2005, that the "Eurasia-based computer underground" has been a factor in all high-tech crime since the early 1990s.

"Criminal groups involved in these types of crime routinely operate in a multi-jurisdictional environment," Johnson said, echoing identity-theft victims who describe being bounced from one police organization to another in state after state. "This has created problems for local law-enforcement agencies that generally act as first responders to criminal activities."

To cope with the jurisdiction problem in the United States, the Secret Service forms task forces that can reach across state lines, Johnson said.

To catch identity thieves based overseas, the Justice Department works with its foreign counterparts abroad, said Lawrence Brown, first assistant U.S. attorney for the Eastern District of California. "While not perfect, it is certainly preferable to no prosecution whatsoever." [10]

Hoofnagle of the Electronic Privacy Information Center points to a fundamental problem in curbing identity theft. "The more aggressive anti-fraud measures become, the more difficulties authorized people have using the system," he says. For example, a data-protection system that uses fingerprints will shut out a legitimate user whose finger is dirty.

Nevertheless, Hoofnagle concedes, most systems probably are weighted too heavily in favor of easy access to information.

Martin Abrams, executive director of the Center for Information Policy Leadership — an industry think tank

Data company executives and consumer advocates prepare to testify on identity theft before the Senate Judiciary Committee, on April 13, 2005. Lawmakers held several hearings on the problem this spring after personal data on millions of Americans was lost or stolen. From left, Kurt P. Sanford, LexisNexis; Doug C. Curling, ChoicePoint; Jennifer Barrett, Acxiom Corp.; Robert Douglas, PrivacyToday.com, and James Dempsey, Center for Democracy and Technology (back row).

— puts more faith in technological solutions. "We will have a revolution in identification management over time," Abrams says, citing Microsoft Corp., where employees have personalized cards to access their online work as well as the building where they work.

But other experts say technology will never solve the security problem. "Internet systems are continuously susceptible to vulnerabilities that require perpetual patching," argues Collins of Michigan State, author of the 2005 book *Preventing Identity Theft in Your Business.* "And even if the systems were 100 percent secure, at the end of the day computers do not steal identities — people do." Collins urges employers to focus more on limiting employees' access to sensitive information than on creating secure software and hardware.

Bruce Schneier, founder and chief technical officer of Counterpane Internet Security, in Mountain View, Calif., agrees, arguing that trying to protect identity data is a no-win proposition. The key is verifying transactions, he says. For instance, banks could use their data systems to check on whether an application to open a new bank account is based on legitimate information or whether the same applicant has just opened other new accounts in nearby cities.

"Tactics don't matter," Schneier says. "The goal is to stop fraud. If you defend against tactic A, criminals go to tactic B."

ChoicePoint Envisions DNA Database

A newcomer to the identity-theft issue could be forgiven for thinking that it's all about one company — ChoicePoint. Actually, there are several big data brokers, including LexisNexis and Acxiom. But Atlanta-based ChoicePoint was the only company whose top officials have appeared at every one of the five hearings held recently by House and Senate committees looking into identity fraud and threats to financial privacy.

ChoicePoint appeared repeatedly because it had the highest profile in the information business — even before news broke in February that the firm had unwittingly sold personal data to criminals.

The company had been expanding at breakneck speed. Since 1997, when it spun off from the Equifax credit-reporting agency, ChoicePoint has bought 41 firms in the drug-testing, employment-screening, direct-marketing and related fields. [1] In addition, its data-release problems go back several years. In 2000, the Pennsylvania Department of Transportation ended a contract with ChoicePoint because it was transmitting information about motorists over the Internet, where the information fell into the hands of a smaller, unauthorized data broker. [2]

But ChoicePoint someday may provide its clients with more than just names, addresses and Social Security numbers. "ChoicePoint officials envision a day when their databases of DNA — something they consider 'IDNA' or "the ultimate identifier" — or fingerprints or other biometrics will be employed routinely to identify everyone, dead and alive, innocent and criminal alike," *Washington Post* reporter Robert O'Harrow Jr. writes in a new book. [3]

So, to consumer activists and politicians looking to show that identity theft and overall privacy loss are linked, ChoicePoint is Exhibit A. The company declined to comment for this report, but at a May 10, 2005, hearing of the Senate Commerce Committee, Doug C. Curling, ChoicePoint's president and chief operating officer, said, "Data is expensive to acquire and time-consuming to analyze. What we want to give [customers] is just the right information at the right time."

The Electronic Privacy Information Center (EPIC) has asked the Federal Trade Commission to investigate the company on the grounds that it has been systematically evading the Fair Credit Reporting Act of 1970 (FCRA), which limits the sale of credit-report data to credit, insurance and employment purposes.

"Americans face a return to the pre-FCRA era if companies like ChoicePoint can amass dossiers on Americans without compliance with any regime of fair information practices," Chris Jay Hoofnagle, EPIC's West Coast director, wrote — along with Prof. Daniel Solove of The George Washington University Law School — in asking for the probe. [4] An investigation is under way, an FTC official says, adding that the agency's rules prohibit disclosing the precise subject matter.

Hoofnagle and Solove also cited what they called ChoicePoint's role in the controversial 2000 presidential

But, like others in the field, Schneier says the business goal of providing instant credit runs at cross-purposes with the slower pace needed for tighter security at the point of purchase. "Consumers love conveniences," he says, "I would love the convenience of walking into my house without a key."

In other words, there's a tradeoff: More security equals less convenience.

Should consumers be able to "freeze" their credit histories?

Some consumer advocates say giving consumers exclusive power to control access to their credit reports could reduce identity theft and, in some cases, stop identity thieves in their tracks.

Acquiring stolen goods requires credit, and each credit application generates a request for a credit report. If consumers could "freeze" access to their credit reports, then at the moment of purchase the store doing the credit check would first have to obtain permission from the consumer whose credit history is being checked. Such verification would discourage ID theft, say advocates of the credit-freeze approach.

The point of purchase is "the key moment," says Evan Hendricks, publisher of *Privacy Times* newsletter and a specialist on the credit-reporting business.

But critics warn that freezing credit reports will inconvenience individuals and slow down the pace of commerce.

To begin with, says the Consumer Data Industry Association's Pratt, consumers will not be able to unfreeze

election in Florida, where a company that ChoicePoint bought was hired to review the state's voter registration rolls for voters who were dead, registered in more than one county or had felony convictions. As a result of data errors in the review, up to 7,000 voters may have been erroneously removed from voter-eligibility lists; a disproportionate number of them were African-American. [5]

ChoicePoint officials have testified repeatedly in this year's round of hearings that the voter-rolls survey was done by Database Technologies, a firm ChoicePoint didn't purchase until after the Florida project was finished. And Florida authorities were supposed to have verified the information that the company turned up, ChoicePoint says on its Web site. [6]

As for the remainder of the EPIC arguments, Curling told the organization that its letter was "inaccurate, misdirected and misleading." ChoicePoint complies with the credit-reporting act where required, he said. Where that law does not apply, ChoicePoint follows state privacy laws and industry standards, Curling wrote. [7]

ChoicePoint executives also told Congress that the company responded to the latest data theft with internal reforms designed to prevent such security breaches. ChoicePoint says it now sells personal data only when it's needed for a "consumer-driven" purpose, such as buying insurance, renting an apartment or undergoing a background check for a job; being used as part of authentication or fraud-prevention operations for an existing corporate client or when a law-enforcement agency wants the data. The aim is to prevent sales to small firms — the kind that the data thieves pretended to be.

But EPIC wasn't satisfied. The center argued that the new policy would still allow data sales to small businesses as long as the Social Security number is provided in only partial form. A client still might be able to figure out the rest of the code, EPIC argued. And it said that ChoicePoint had not committed itself to fix a problem of correct information being attached to the wrong person's name. Finally, EPIC said, "Nothing binds ChoicePoint to its promise to maintain its reformed policies." [8]

Some members of Congress also were not satisfied with the voluntary reforms. "His company is, in fact, effectively the chief lobbyist to block any effective privacy laws from being passed," said Rep. Edward J. Markey, D-Mass., after questioning ChoicePoint Chairman Derek Smith. "And we're not going to get the answers we need for the public at this hearing."

---

[1] Electronic Privacy Information Center, "ChoicePoint," undated, www.epic.org/privacy/choicepoint.

[2] John M. R. Bull, "PennDot Fires Firm That Sold License Data Over Internet," *Pittsburgh Post-Gazette*, Jan. 7, 2000, p. B1.

[3] Robert O'Harrow Jr., *No Place to Hide* (2005), p. 133.

[4] www.epic.org/privacy/choicepoint/fcraltr12.16.04.html.

[5] Robert E. Pierre, "Botched Name Purge Denied Some the Right to Vote," *The Washington Post*, May 31, 2001, p. A1.

[6] "The Truth About ChoicePoint, DBT and the 2000 Elections in Florida," June 6, 2004, www.choicepoint.com/news/2000election.html.

[7] "ChoicePoint Corrects EPIC Errors, Calls for Privacy Group to Join Discussion," Dec. 29, 2004, www.choicepoint.com/news/statement_122904.html.

[8] "ChoicePoint's Response to the Sale of Information to Criminals is Inadequate," Electronic Privacy Information Center, March 28, 2005, www.epic.org/privacy/choicepoint.

---

their credit reports quickly. "It will not be an automatic toggle system to turn it on or off," Pratt says. "A file freeze is intended to be inconvenient. We assume the consumer has taken a serious step to have made this choice, so there won't be a toll-free number. Whether through a live person or an automated system, we're going to move the person through a series of protocols" to establish his identity.

In California, where legislators in 2003 enacted a law allowing residents to freeze their credit reports, consumers first send certified letters to each of the three national credit-reporting agencies asking them to block access to their records. The agencies then give the consumers a PIN with which the account can be unfrozen — to allow a car dealer to run a credit report, for instance. Using the PIN, a consumer can authorize each

agency's report with a phone call, but the thawing process can take up to three days.

Barbarba Haviluk, a resident of Carlsbad, Calif., froze her credit reports in 2004 after learning from a Discover Card fraud analyst that someone had stolen all her personal information. "It's really very convenient for me because I'm not opening credit cards or buying a car or a house," she says. "I don't even call it an inconvenience, but I'm not a person that opens an account everywhere I go."

Even some freeze supporters acknowledge that unfreezing credit histories could slow down the pace of commerce. And it's far from certain that consumers would want to go to the trouble of unfreezing their credit reports before driving out in a new car or taking home a big-screen TV.

Traditional Methods Dominate Identity Theft

The most common way to steal personal information, by far, is the time-honored method: obtaining a lost or stolen wallet, checkbook or credit card. Fewer than 2 percent of the crimes involved e-mails sent by criminals posing as businessmen.

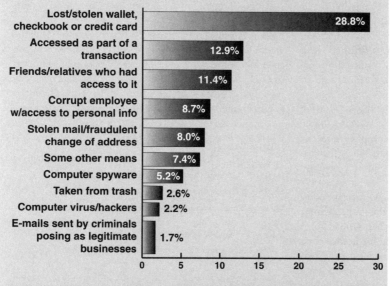

Methods Used to Steal Identities

Method	Percentage
Lost/stolen wallet, checkbook or credit card	28.8%
Accessed as part of a transaction	12.9%
Friends/relatives who had access to it	11.4%
Corrupt employee w/access to personal info	8.7%
Stolen mail/fraudulent change of address	8.0%
Some other means	7.4%
Computer spyware	5.2%
Taken from trash	2.6%
Computer virus/hackers	2.2%
E-mails sent by criminals posing as legitimate businesses	1.7%

Sources: "2005 Identity Fraud Survey Report," Javelin Strategy & Research, January 2005. The update of the Federal Trade Commission's 2003 "Identity Theft Survey Report" is based on a telephone survey of 4,000 consumers and was supported by CheckFree, Visa USA and Wells Fargo Bank. The Better Business Bureau and FTC acted as general advisers.

off the spigot," says Andrew Barbour, vice president of government relations for the Financial Services Roundtable, a trade association for banks and other lenders. "I would assume that unfreezing is not an instantáneous deal where you've got a 1-800 number you can call 24/7, and you're at the side of the road at 1 a.m. and you've got one credit card and it's maxed out and you need to pay the tow-truck driver."

"It probably will slow down commerce, but why shouldn't consumers have that choice?" asks anti-fraud consultant Douglas. "Why should they not have the ability to control that information?"

But Hendricks is skeptical of the motives of companies that sell credit reports, arguing they don't really want to give consumers control over their credit histories because they make money only when they sell reports. In addition, he says, identity thieves' requests for credit reports generate business just as legitimate requests do.

"Hogwash," responds Abrams of the Center for Information Policy Leadership and a former executive of Experian, one of the Big Three credit reporting agencies. Identity theft, he says, creates "an incredible demand for consumer assistance, which is incredibly expensive, and there's no way of recouping the cost."

Should data companies ask permission before selling a consumer's information?

Some consumer advocates say identity theft could be reduced if data-collection companies had to obtain consumers' permission before selling their personal information. The question — like much of the identity theft-prevention debate — centers on the inevitable conflict between having rapid, ultra-convenient business transactions or having slower-paced transactions with more security checking.

Because of the inconvenience, computer-security expert Schneier questions the practicality of freezes, even though he favors them. "I worry about measures that require the user to do something," Schneier says. "He's not going to."

Freeze supporters say slowing down commerce might not be such a bad thing. "People can decide — 'Do I want to have new credit on a three-day waiting time or instantly?' " says McNabb of the California privacy office. "Frankly, buying a car is something you might want to spend more than a day on."

Yet others say closing off access to a consumer's credit report could involve a more serious inconvenience than having to wait before taking delivery of a new TV.

"Suppose you have a car and a house and one credit card and are willing to take the consequences of turning

In addition to the companies that compile and sell credit reports, information-services companies, or data brokers, acquire data that is available — often for free — from various public records and then sort, analyze and sell it. ChoicePoint and LexisNexis — both of which were penetrated this year by data thieves — are the largest and best-known data brokers.

Information selling is big business. ChoicePoint alone has 5,000 employees, does business with 7,000 federal, state and local law-enforcement agencies, more than 700 insurance firms and many *Fortune* 500 companies and lending institutions. [11]

"None of us here, except maybe the data brokers, have control over anything in those files," Mari Frank, an Orange County, Calif., lawyer specializing in identity theft, told the Senate Commerce Committee on May 10.

Kurt Sanford, president and CEO of LexisNexis' corporate and federal-government markets, testified that consumers could see the data collected on them by his firm. If the company has made an error, it will make a correction unless the error comes from public records that the company scooped up at a county courthouse. "We can't have a database [that] is different than what's available in the public record," Sanford said. ChoicePoint President Doug C. Curling said much the same thing.

However, beyond the problem of access and fixing mistakes, privacy advocates question the whole idea of selling personal information, at least for business purposes.

Curling told the committee that under a new policy put in place by ChoicePoint after a security breach that was reported in February, "You wouldn't be able to set up an account to gain access to any products that contain sensitive, personally identifiable information." But ChoicePoint has about a dozen major competitors, he said, and "many, many" Internet-based data brokers are not affected by ChoicePoint's new policies.

Thus, he questions whether controls should exist on sales of personal information for some companies and not for others — especially those based in countries not subject to U.S. law.

Abrams, of the Center for Information Policy Leadership, suggests requiring consumer approval to sell certain kinds of extra-sensitive data, such as health information.

But Abrams agrees with others in the business community who say that regulating the information business should be limited and requiring consumers to OK sales of their information would restrict the credit market. Credit-card companies, for instance, find potential customers by having data companies assemble packages of prospective clients in certain demographic ranges of age, income and assets.

"There is a role for information in creating a more competitive marketplace by letting new parties enter the market," Abrams argues. "I believe the opportunity created there counterbalances the privacy gain" of allowing consumers to opt out of the credit market.

But those favoring preauthorization of sales of personal data, like computer-security guru Schneier, are not optimistic that Congress will enact such rules. "It's a phenomenally good idea," Schneier says, adding, "it's so pro-person and anti-business that we're never going to see it."

In fact, he and others point out, Europeans have far greater protection of their personal data than Americans, using an information-policy model put forth by the European Union.

"The Europeans require companies to provide consumers with notice, the ability to opt out with respect to non-sensitive commercial marketing of personal information, opt in with respect to sensitive personal information, the right of access to personal information collected, [and] reasonable security protections for the information," Sen. Byron Dorgan, D-N.D., noted at the Commerce Committee hearing.

"Should we consider doing something that is much more restrictive, much more protective?" Dorgan then asked the ChoicePoint and LexisNexis executives.

"If the restriction goes too far," Sanford of LexisNexis responded, "we will, in fact, enable the bad guys to do even more than they're doing now" because it might restrict law-enforcement access to data needed to hunt down fraudsters.

In any case, anti-fraud consultant Douglas told the Senate Judiciary Committee earlier this year, it may be too late to control identity theft through regulation because of the plethora of Internet-based information brokers.

"Even if all legitimate information brokers were secure, the flow of information would continue," he said.

CHRONOLOGY

1970s *In the early stages of the technological revolution, companies and government agencies vastly expand their data-collection activities while politicians, citizen activists and industry lobbyists try to set rules for managing the use of citizens' information.*

1970 Congress passes the Fair Credit Reporting Act, intended to protect consumer rights but changed during the legislative process to shield credit-reporting agencies from liability.

1971 University of Michigan law Professor Arthur R. Miller publishes one of the earliest predictions of the dangers of the information-technology boom — *The Assault on Privacy: Computers, Data Banks, and Dossiers* — noting that data has become an "economically desirable commodity and a source of power."

1974 Congress passes the Privacy Act to protect against government intrusion into citizens' lives, but it does not regulate use of personal data by private business.

1980s-1990s *Technological advances accelerate, allowing businesses to build markets using demographic characteristics, spurring the growth of identity theft.*

1988 Responding to growing fears about privacy erosion, Congress passes the Computer Matching and Privacy Protection Act, which regulates government use of multiple databases to find welfare cheaters, tax evaders or other criminals.

1992 Identity theft surfaces as an issue when Trans Union LLC, a national credit-evaluation agency, gets 35,235 identity-fraud complaints.

1996 Arizona legislature passes the nation's first anti-identity-theft law, classifying it as a felony.

1998 General Accounting Office (GAO) concludes identity theft is a growing threat but that no federal law targets the crime and no federal law-enforcement agency is responsible for fighting it. . . . Congress passes the first federal law against identity theft, establishing penalties of up to 20 years in prison.

1999 President Bill Clinton signs the Gramm-Leach-Blilely Act, which requires financial institutions to guard against unauthorized release of personal data.

2000-2004 *Identity theft becomes a familiar topic, but efforts to curb the crime show few results.*

December 2001 Federal Trade Commission (FTC) consumer hotline receives 3,000 reports a week of suspected identity thefts.

2002 Identity-theft reports to the FTC reach 161,896 — a 46 percent increase over the previous year.

2003 California enacts the nation's first law allowing consumers to "freeze" their credit reports. . . . FTC estimates 3.2 million people fell victim to identity theft during the preceding 12 months.

2004 President Bush signs a law that ratchets up penalties for identity-theft convictions and increases prison time if identity theft is used to commit terrorism.

2005 *Politicians turn up the heat on data companies after security breaches potentially expose millions of citizens to identity theft.*

Jan. 1-April 19 Legislators in 35 states introduce 124 bills aimed at curbing identity theft.

Feb. 17-May 20 Privacy Rights Clearinghouse of San Diego compiles reports on 32 breaches of data security at companies, universities and other institutions that potentially exposed data on some 5.4 million citizens.

April 13 The president of ChoicePoint Inc., one of the penetrated companies, admits to the Senate Judiciary Committee that the firm suffered a breach in 2001 that it didn't disclose to consumers at the time.

June 6, 2005 In the latest — and biggest — breach of security data in recent months, a subsidiary of Citigroup announces that a box of computer tapes containing personal financial information on 3.9 million customers was lost by United Parcel Service.

BACKGROUND

Digital Revolution

In hindsight, early types of identity theft look easy. As 1960s activist Abbie Hoffman wrote before going underground for seven years following a cocaine-trafficking sentence:

"If you use phony state and city papers such as birth certificate or driver's license, choose a state that is far away from the one in which you are located. . . . It might be advisable to get authentic papers using the phonies you have in your possession. In some states getting a license or a voting registration card is very easy. Almost all ID cards use one or another IBM Selectric to fill in the individual's papers." [12]

Hoffman published that advice in 1970. While he may have been prescient in anticipating the demand for false identities among the criminally inclined, his technical counseling was out of date within 20 years. An information revolution that was just beginning quickly transformed the way companies and individuals do business and handle information.

The change allowed vast amounts of data to be stored and instantly accessed from anywhere in the world. And software allowed that data to be cross-indexed in an infinite number of ways, giving businesses a far more complete picture of customers and their credit histories. [13]

Credit bureaus were among the first to grasp the possibilities of the new technology. Since the late 19th century, they had been collecting information on customers who didn't pay their debts. With computers, companies could broaden their scope to gather data on purchasing habits, earnings and assets. By the time the 21st century dawned, consumers could get their credit checked instantly in stores, allowing them to walk out with big-ticket items.

But even before consumers realized that computers one day would become standard office and home equipment, some observers saw a dark side to the new technology.

"The new information technologies have given birth to a new social virus — data-mania," University of Michigan law Professor Arthur R. Miller (now at Harvard Law School) wrote in his 1971 book *The Assault on Privacy: Computers, Data Banks, and Dossiers.* "We must begin to realize what it means to live in a society that treats information as an economically desirable commodity and a source of power." [14]

Privacy Battles

Miller's book reflected a growing public unease about the erosion of privacy. Sen. William Proxmire, a Wisconsin Democrat, sensed the mood and sponsored the Fair Credit Reporting Act of 1970, the first attempt to balance businesses' desire to know everything about prospective customers with consumers' rights to keep their personal information private. [15] The legislative battle over the bill marked the first time consumer/privacy advocates squared off against the business community. They have remained largely at odds ever since.

Despite Proxmire's best efforts, the law turned out to be "an industry bill," a lobbyist for the credit-bureau industry said. [16] It didn't give consumers access to their own credit reports and largely immunized companies from liability for prejudicial information contained in those reports. More important, the law allowed credit-reporting companies for the first time to sell marketers the so-called "credit header" sections of credit reports. Headers contain names, addresses, former addresses, phone and Social Security numbers, job information and birth dates.

Selling credit headers revolutionized American purchasing, Robert Hahn, director of the American Enterprise Institute-Brookings Joint Center, observed. "In 1970 . . . just one in six Americans possessed a [credit] card. Today, three in four carry cards," he wrote. And consumers, once at the mercy of a local mortgage banker, could now have their creditworthiness evaluated by prejudice-free computers so that "hundreds of lenders compete for [their] business on the basis of objective standards." [17]

But consumers had no control over what data those computers were given or who had access to the data, privacy scholar and George Washington University law Professor Daniel Solove pointed out. "The FCRA does little to equalize the unbalanced power relationship between individuals and credit-reporting companies," he concluded. [18]

As a result, citizen concern continued to grow. In 1974, Congress passed the Privacy Act, barring the federal government from collecting data about citizens for one purpose and using it for another. It also allowed citizens to view government records about them and to correct any mistakes. [19]

But the restriction on federal agencies' data sharing was not absolute. Agencies were permitted to share data

Tracking Down Identity Thieves Is Big Business

It's late at night, and the "ccpower" (credit-card power) chatroom is busy posting messages from around the world featuring names, addresses and strings of numbers. "I CAN WRITE ONLINE CHECK," says a message from somewhere in cyberspace. "HAVE NEW EBAY AND PAYPAL SCAM; HAVE NEW WU PAGE. HAVE ROYAL BANK LOGIN AND BOA ACCOUNT AND WELLS. PV ME FOR GOOD DEAL."

The "ccpower" site deals in stolen credit-card information. WU is Western Union, BOA is Bank of America, WELLS is Wells-Fargo Bank and PV means "private message."

This is the lawless territory patrolled by Dan Clements, founder and CEO of CardCops, a Los Angeles firm that monitors chatrooms that buy and sell credit-card numbers and personal IDs. "There's a tremendous amount of data flowing into cyberspace that is beyond the jurisdiction of the U.S.," Clements says. "So no law is going to have any teeth to help consumers."

Nonprofit groups also have joined the fight, including the Privacy Rights Clearinghouse and the Identity Theft Resource Center, both of San Diego, and the Identity Theft Crime and Research Laboratory at Michigan State University. In addition, the Federal Trade Commission and various state agencies advise identity-theft victims on what to do when they've been hit.

Clements is aiming at consumers who want a personal early-warning system. His 10,000 customers pay $14.95 a year to have his company troll through the nearly two-dozen "Internet relay chat" channels for fraudsters in the credit-card business and other scams. When the company's customers are located, they are immediately warned that their identities have been stolen. CardCops has alerted some 400 clients to date.

Clements says his firm is the only one that monitors chatrooms for identity-theft information, but he's expecting competition virtually any minute. While Clements and other Internet-security experts don't know the size of the anti-identity-fraud market, they're certain it's growing.

The traditional approach to stopping identity theft — used by the three big credit-rating agencies — is to monitor credit accounts for new purchases and newly opened accounts. Notified of transactions, users will know if they are legitimate or by a thief. The three agencies will also place free 90-day "alerts" on accounts to warn salesclerks to positively identify people trying to use them. [1]

collected for "compatible" purposes. In practice, the provision defeated the spirit of the law, privacy advocates say. In 1977, for example, federal payroll records were checked against welfare rolls to catch welfare cheaters.

Such data-sharing operations became so common that in 1988 Congress passed the Computer Matching Privacy Act, which required agencies wanting to use each other's data to specify the reason and what they expected to learn. And the government must verify any information that surfaces about individuals before taking adverse action against them. [20]

But the 1974 privacy law still only applied to the federal government, leaving the private sector largely unregulated. The loophole prompted government and law-enforcement agencies to contract out their information collecting and analyzing chores to private data brokers, such as ChoicePoint and LexisNexis. Although the government could not collect and cross-reference the kind of information the private sector was collecting, federal agencies were not prohibited from purchasing the information from private data brokers.

Most citizens were unaware of either how much of their personal information was being scooped up by the data brokers or how much of it was ending up in government hands. But privacy worries percolating since the 1960s and the secrecy with which credit reporting operated were both intensifying. Concerns about the accuracy of the information being collected was also increasing, since credit reports were used to determine whether consumers could buy cars, houses and other big-ticket items.

Indeed, the brokers often were better at collecting and selling information than at making sure it was correct. In 1991, Consumers Union examined 161 credit reports and found serious errors in 48 percent of them. [21]

In the next few years, 17 state attorneys general found the same pattern of inaccuracy. In the early 1990s, state governments negotiated settlements with the three big credit-reporting agencies, which led Congress in 1996 to

But business in the chatrooms moves so quickly that the conventional protective measures may be of limited value. The latest twist is identity thieves buying — perfectly legally — the birth certificates of people whose numbers they've stolen in order to capture the mother's maiden name, which is often necessary to open a bank account.

Just as the CardCops approach centers on monitoring online chatter as much as it does on electronically scanning data, beefing up data security at businesses also involves human as well as technical elements. Businesses of all kinds are a key link in the identity-theft chain, because thieves steal firms' customer data using every kind of trick imaginable.

Trace Security, a security firm in Baton Rouge, La., goes to unusual lengths to check its clients' security measures. In addition to sophisticated computer programs, it even has been known to use stepladders and fake pest-control-company uniforms. Clients hire Trace to try to penetrate their own security and get away with all the data it can. But penetration doesn't necessarily mean writing elaborate hacker codes. Instead, the operation might begin with setting up a fake Internet address that resembles the customer's domain as closely as possible. Address-doctoring makes the e-mail address from the phony home office look legitimate to anyone reading it quickly — an "o" in a real domain name, for instance, might be changed to a zero. Then, says Chief Technology Officer Jim Stickley,

"We can send an e-mail to branch managers on behalf of someone in the 'main office' about scheduling a pest-control visit. It works about 90 percent of the time. And we always have a woman call to schedule the appointment because people trust women more than men."

Once inside the office, the security consultants go to work. One trick is to block the doorway to the server room with an open ladder, preventing employees from walking in while data tapes and other valuables are being stuffed into satchels. "If it's not bolted down, we'll take it," Stickley says. "I've walked out with servers. People spend hundreds of thousands of dollars on a network, but they've forgotten about physical security."

Kevin D. Mitnick, a notorious hacker turned security consultant, agrees. [2] Mitnick did his hacking off-site, but as he writes in his new book, an inside job is always easier: "In most businesses, an attacker who can find a way of getting into the work areas of the facility can easily find a way to gain access to systems." [3]

---

[1] Rob Lieber, "Who's Helping Victims of Data Theft?," *The Wall Street Journal*, May 24, 2005, p. D1.

[2] See Brian Hansen, "A Tale of Two Hackers," in "Cyber-Crime," *CQ Researcher*, April 12, 2002, pp. 316-317.

[3] Kevin D. Mitnick, *The Art of Intrusion* (2005), p. 63.

---

pass the Consumer Credit Reporting Reform Act requiring credit agencies to accept consumer corrections. [22]

Consumers Union, which had been lobbying for the measure for years, celebrated the law's enactment as a victory while the Associated Credit Bureaus trade association insisted that companies had already voluntarily enacted the new provisions. [23]

Identity Theft

This year, *Washington Post* reporter Robert O'Harrow Jr. wrote in his book, *No Place to Hide*, that the storage devices of just one big data brokers, Axciom of Conway, Ark., could hold roughly the same amount of information as "a 50,000-mile-high stack of King James Bibles." Indeed, O'Harrow said Axciom's files already contained "billions of records about marital status, families and the ages of children . . . individuals' estimated incomes, the value of their homes, the make and price of their cars . . . unlisted phone numbers" —

information being used to produce "fine-grained portraits [of] roughly 200 million adults." [24]

Consumer advocates, politicians and the public may have been just waking up to the loss of privacy caused by the technology boom, but criminals were already cashing in on it. By 1992, when computers were still getting a foothold in offices and homes, Trans Union Corp., one of the big-three credit reporting agencies, received 35,235 consumer complaints about identity theft. That number increased 14-fold — to 522,922 — over the next five years. [25]

A growing number of news articles about identity theft stoked public concern, prompting a bipartisan congressional group to commission a study of the new crime trend by the General Accounting Office (now the Government Accountability Office. *

---

* Members were Sen. Charles Grassley, R-Iowa, chairman of the Senate Special Committee on Aging; Rep. Barbara B. Kennelly, D-Conn., and Rep. Gerald D. Kleczka, D-Wis.

GAO investigators found serious omissions:

- No federal agency had jurisdiction over identity-fraud cases;
- No law aimed specifically at identity thieves; and
- No law enforcement agencies were tracking identity fraud because they lacked a clear definition of the offense.

As the report noted, "The mere possession of another person's personal identifying information is not a crime in itself." [26]

The report helped Congress shape the nation's first anti-identity-theft law, passed in 1998. The Identity Theft and Assumption Deterrence Act for the first time made identity theft a specific crime, punishable by up to 20 years in prison. U.S. Sentencing Commission guidelines later set a minimum sentence of 10 months to 16 months — even if the victim lost no money and the thief had no previous criminal convictions. [27]

In 1999 Congress followed up with the Gramm-Leach-Bliley Act, which ordered banks, investment firms and insurance companies to prevent the unauthorized disclosure of financial information.

Nevertheless, the volume of identity-theft reports kept growing. Calls to an FTC consumer hotline went from 445 calls per week in November 1999 to 3,000 a week in December 2001. MasterCard and Visa reported that losses from identity theft and credit-card fraud jumped 43 percent, from $79.9 million in 1996 to $114.3 million in 2000. [28] By 2002, most of the states had responded, starting with Arizona, which in 1996 passed the first state anti-identity-theft law. California followed suit in 1997. By the end of 2002, 44 states had similar laws. [29] California's law authorizing consumers to freeze their credit reports took effect in 2003.

Meanwhile, in Washington, the FTC reported that identity-theft complaints rose to 161,896 in 2002 — a 46 percent increase over the previous year. The trend continued in 2003, when reports rose to 215,093, and in 2004, when complaints exceeded 246,000.

Prompted by the growing number of consumer complaints as well as industry concern over the growing patchwork of state requirements, Congress in 2003 amended the Fair Credit Reporting Act to require the three national credit bureaus to provide free credit reports to consumers who wanted to see if identity thieves had opened accounts using their names.

Consumer advocates called the bill weak, in part because it did not require law-enforcement agencies to thoroughly investigate stolen-identity cases. [30]

In California, the leading state in anti-identity-theft law, Congress' 2003 measure may supercede seven state statutes, including one allowing consumers to "opt out" of some information-sharing among financial institutions. Banks filed suit arguing that the federal law preempted the California provisions. The 9th U.S. Court of Appeals has not yet decided the case. Similar challenges are likely to arise in other states as well, though Hoofnagle of the Electronic Privacy Information Center argues that industry doesn't have a slam-dunk case. As a rule, says Hoofnagle, a lawyer, "courts don't want to preempt police power."

The following year, Congress added a mandatory two years of prison time to the penalties for identity thieves convicted of bank, wire or mail fraud and five additional years if the identity theft was used to commit a terrorist act.

In signing the bill on July 15, 2004, President Bush said, "When a person takes out an insurance policy or makes an online purchase or opens a savings account, he or she must have confidence that personal financial information will be protected and treated with care."

Reporter O'Harrow, who had been covering the issue for several years, took a more jaundiced view: "It remains to be seen whether identity thieves or terrorists even know about the penalties." [31]

CURRENT SITUATION

Security Breaches

During the first five months of 2005, the analysts and consultants who had been predicting an increase in identity theft saw their conclusions validated by reports of several shocking security breaches.

The first incident came to light on Feb. 17, when Nigerian national Olatunji Oluwatosin, 41, pleaded no contest to identity theft and was sentenced to 16 months in a California prison. He had formed at least 22 phony companies that contracted to buy personal information from ChoicePoint. Using that information, Oluwatosin bought merchandise in the names of people whose identities had been stolen.

By the time he was arrested for identity theft — after a ChoicePoint employee wondered why an established business would be sending faxes from a Kinko's store — ChoicePoint had already sold him records on at least 145,000 people. [32]

Then Bank of America revealed that it had lost the backup data tapes with information on 1.2 million credit-card holders; shoe store chain DSW said thieves had accessed information on 1.4 million customers; and LexisNexis acknowledged that hackers had obtained data on 310,000 people. [33] A series of smaller-scale breaches involved agencies and institutions ranging from retail chains to the University of California at Berkeley to the Nevada Department of Motor Vehicles.

ChoicePoint immediately announced it would no longer sell personal information to small businesses and would sell other personal information only in support of "consumer-initiated" transactions (such as car purchases), as anti-fraud tools for big corporate clients and in response to law-enforcement requests.

Even so, Congress focused most of its attention on the data collectors. Unlike stores or schools that gather information as a by-product of what they do, data collectors gather personal information for the sole purpose of selling it.

"This is an industry that's still in denial," Rep. Edward J. Markey, D-Mass, told a House Commerce Subcommittee hearing on March 15. "And it hopes to be able to ride out this scandal without Congress passing serious privacy legislation."

Notification Debate

The recent data-security breaches also revealed major weaknesses in state and federal laws governing the handling of personal information: California is the only state that requires companies to notify customers when their personal information stored in a company database has been compromised.

How to Protect Against Identity Theft

Because so much personal data lies outside individual Americans' control, individuals cannot eliminate identity theft on their own. But experts say several steps can be taken to minimize risk, including:

1. Check your credit reports yearly from all three big credit-reporting agencies.

2. Never give out your Social Security number unless there is a good reason.

3. Use a locked mailbox to send and receive all mail. Shred all bills and receipts before throwing them away.

4. Pay attention to when your bills arrive. If they don't come in, contact creditors. A missing bill could mean an identity thief has taken over your account and changed the mailing address.

5. Reduce the number of pre-approved credit card offers you receive. Call 888-5OPT OUT (you will be asked for your Social Security Number) to be included on a list of people who don't want these offers.

6. Sign up for the Federal Trade Commission's National Do Not Call Registry and the Direct Marketing Association's Telephone Preference Service.

7. Place passwords on your credit card, bank and phone accounts. In devising passwords, avoid using easily available information like your birth date.

8. Do not store financial information on laptops, which are easily stolen.

9. Before you dispose of a computer, eliminate all personal information stored on it — not simply by deleting files or reformatting the hard drive but by using a "wipe" utility program.

10. If you shop online, do not "park" your credit-card number on a vendor's site.

11. If you have a home broadband connection, make sure your anti-virus and anti-spyware programs are up to date and that you have a firewall.

12. In using your computer, do not open files sent by people you don't know.

Sources: Identity Theft Prevention Center, Privacy Rights Clearinghouse, Federal Trade Commission

---

"The reason you're hearing about all these breaches is 100 percent because of the California law," says Jim Stickley, chief technology officer of TraceSecurity, a Baton Rouge, La., firm that helps companies guard against data thieves. "If it hadn't have been for that, these companies wouldn't have said anything."

That was made clear during a Senate Judiciary Committee hearing on April 13, when Chairman Arlen Specter, R-Pa., asked, "Did ChoicePoint have a breach of security and fail to report it and notify the people whose information had been breached?"

"Yes, sir, it would appear in 2001 that happened," company President Curling replied.

Most Victims Do Not Call Police

Sixty percent of identity-theft victims did not call the police after learning they had been victimized in 2004. Only 38 percent of victims notified their local police departments, and police took a report in only 30 percent of the cases.

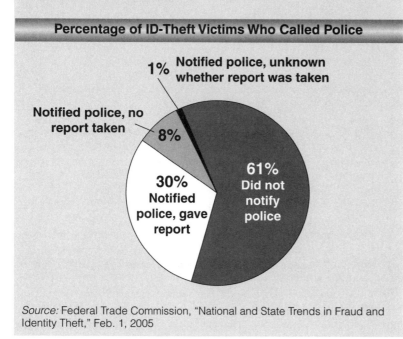

Percentage of ID-Theft Victims Who Called Police

1% Notified police, unknown whether report was taken

Notified police, no report taken 8%

30% Notified police, gave report

61% Did not notify police

Source: Federal Trade Commission, "National and State Trends in Fraud and Identity Theft," Feb. 1, 2005

After a few more exchanges, Specter bluntly told Curling and LexisNexis CEO Sanford: "We may very well face a necessity for some really tough legislation that will have you do your duty." Specter is the first high-ranking Senate Republican to join Democrats in endorsing federal legislation to regulate data brokers.

The two executives said they supported a federal notification law, but FTC Chairwoman Majoras told the committee that while she supported such a law she worried about "overnotification."

"What we have learned is that eventually consumers will become numb to notices if they're getting them consistently," she said. "If we define a breach very, very broadly, companies will have no choice but to be sending out constant notices to avoid liability, and we're worried that consumers will just think that it's a cry of wolf and stop worrying about it."

Her comment echoed the view of industry spokesman Pratt: "If there is a notification hair trigger, I think we

will have a 'cry-wolf' problem; with too many notices from too many companies overcomplying, consumers won't see that one *real* notice."

Pratt also notes that California exempts companies from notification if the missing personal information is encrypted — a provision he says would encourage companies to make personal data unreadable to unauthorized users.

Encryption aside, privacy advocates ridicule the notion that flooding consumers with breach notices could be counterproductive. "I think they realize people won't be numb — they'll be outraged," George Washington University's Solove says.

Phishing and Pharming

Besides notification, other approaches to fighting identity theft being debated include:

- Restricting or banning the sale of Social Security numbers, which have become the primary identity authenticator;
- Creating more oversight of companies that collect and sell personal information; and
- Attempting to fight both high-tech and low-tech approaches to stealing data.

On the low-tech front, Sen. Maria Cantwell, D-Wash., wants the Justice Department to investigate whether there is any connection between the boom in abuse of methamphetamine — an illegal stimulant — and identity fraud. A recent *New York Times* report revealed that some identity thieves employ meth addicts to comb through garbage dumps for discarded personal data like bill receipts and canceled checks. Meth addicts are especially attracted to projects requiring hours of repetitive tasks, the reporter found. [34]

Legislation aimed at high-tech identity theft includes bills aimed directly at "phishing" and "pharming" scams. Phishing involves sending out e-mails designed to lure victims to fake Web sites made to resemble sites for banks or other institutions; the victims are then per-

Should consumers be allowed to "freeze" their credit histories?

YES

Gail Hillebrand
Senior Staff Attorney
Susanna Montezemolo
Legislative Representative
Consumers Union's FinancialPrivacyNow.org
campaign

Written for *CQ Researcher*, June 2005

The recent rash of data-security breaches has prompted lawmakers to look for new ways to protect consumers from identity theft. The security freeze is a powerful new tool that would enable consumers to control who sees their credit file, thus preventing crooks from getting new credit in consumers' names. If access to the file is frozen, the identity thief is stopped cold.

Six states have enacted security-freeze laws, and other states are considering them. California, Colorado and Vermont have the best ones. They allow all consumers to freeze their credit histories. Texas and Louisiana permit freezes only by victims, while Washington allows freezes by victims and those notified of a security breach. Unfortunately, consumers elsewhere do not have the same right. State and federal lawmakers should work to make sure they get it.

Credit-reporting agencies are working to block security-freeze laws because they have a financial incentive to make it easy for creditors to get their hands on consumers' credit reports. In addition, they sell credit-monitoring services, which would become unnecessary if consumers control who sees their credit files.

These agencies claim that security freezes would interfere with quick credit for such things as car loans and mortgages. But few people make big financial purchases on the spur of the moment, and they could easily lift a security freeze temporarily when they need to do so.

The security freeze is stronger than existing tools available to consumers. Currently, identity-theft victims can put fraud alerts on their credit files and pay for credit-monitoring services to detect further abuse. But this won't erase the damage done by the time they discover their identity has been stolen.

Unfortunately, identity-theft victims often find out they have been targeted long after they've first been defrauded and end up spending, on average, $1,400 and 600 hours cleaning up their tarnished credit records. Meanwhile, they may have a tougher time obtaining a good interest rate on a car loan, home mortgage or credit card and may even be denied employment.

All consumers should be allowed to weigh the benefits of a security freeze against any potential inconvenience and decide whether they want this added protection. Credit-reporting agencies want to prevent consumers from making this choice. But shouldn't consumers have the right to freeze crooks out of their credit file?

NO

Stuart Pratt
President and CEO, Consumer Data Industry Association

Written for *CQ Researcher*, May 2005

What sounds like a good idea is, in reality, a failure to apply the practical to the way we all expect to live our lives. The fact is, we want to be able to apply for credit, refinance our homes, buy new cars, start small businesses and send our kids to college. In every one of these cases we want to take advantage of the best price when it is offered, and we don't want rigid rules to stop an application cold in its tracks.

Now, this isn't to say that speed is everything or is the only priority. Consumers expect and tolerate extra steps taken to verify identities, and they expect lenders to be careful about processing an application.

A new law that became effective Dec. 1, 2004, requires lenders to take additional steps to avoid identity theft and credit fraud. By having lenders verify identities, reconcile address variances and contact consumers where there are fraud alerts on file, these amendments to the Fair Credit Reporting Act created the accountability that consumers expect to be applied in every transaction. Consumers will benefit from these new rights and duties imposed on lenders and consumer-reporting agencies.

File freezing is not the answer, as has been shown in states that have such a law. We should all be dubious of legislation that will ostensibly protect us but really ends up penalizing us by imposing rigid rules.

Consumers will realize that they don't know which report to freeze or unfreeze, and they will experience how difficult it is to open up a file at just the right time for just the right transaction. Consumers also will experience the difficulty of maintaining multiple PIN numbers (and protecting them from ID theft), which cannot be used on the spot at a mortgage broker's or auto dealer's office to unfreeze their credit reports.

In short, consumers will see for themselves that a credit-file freeze is tantamount to freezing themselves out of the marketplace, and they will not be able to take advantage of the deals it offers to consumers.

Congress passed sweeping identity-theft legislation two years ago. We believe that the new federal provisions targeting ID theft should be given a chance to make an impact before passing additional legislation. The emphasis should be on enforcing existing laws, prosecuting criminals and educating consumers on how to prevent and spot credit-fraud risks, rather than creating additional legislation.

suaded to "update" their passwords and other information. Pharming also involves creating such sites but coding their Web addresses so bank customers trying to access legitimate sites end up on the fake ones. Sen. Patrick Leahy, D-Vt., and Rep. Darlene Hooley, D-Ore., are sponsoring bills aimed specifically at these methods of casting for victims. In Congress, action seemed likely this year on anti-phishing/pharming legislation, which no one opposes.

Imposing more oversight on the information-services industry is more complicated. Under questioning by Leahy during the April 13 Senate Judiciary Committee hearing, FTC Chairwoman Majoras said, "We are working hard to try to get a better handle on this industry. It's hard to know at this point whether we can even call it just an industry, because it seems to have many facets depending on how you define it."

But Majoras did not commit herself to supporting Leahy's idea of imposing "some kind of fair information practices" — a counterpart to the existing Fair Credit Reporting Act. The FTC boss said consumers may not be interested in some aspects of the data business, such as the collection of information on marketing practices. "That may be an area where consumers don't even want to be bothered," she said.

Banning the sale of Social Security numbers is a hotter topic, particularly for House Energy and Commerce Committee Chairman Joe Barton, R-Texas, whose ex-wife had her number stolen and used to obtain medical services at a Dallas hospital, which then billed her for emergency-room care she never received.

At a committee hearing on the ChoicePoint and LexisNexis security breaches, Barton grilled company officials about why the sale of Social Security numbers shouldn't be made illegal. Sanford of LexisNexis said his company protects the numbers by providing them only in shortened form to users without special authorization, such as law-enforcement agencies and bill collectors.

"I think that strikes the right balance in terms of making sure that we provide for lawful legitimate uses for this information but at the same time protecting the privacy of the consumers," he said.

ChoicePoint Chairman and CEO Derek Smith agreed that "publishing and making available for anybody to see your Social Security number is not an appropriate thing to do." But ChoicePoint needs the numbers to guard against mixing up data on people with the same

name. The United States has 23,000 people named William Smith, he noted.

Barton was not appeased. ChoicePoint and LexisNexis, he said, "don't make any real attempt" to ensure that buyers of Social Security numbers are going to use them for legitimate purposes. "But there's a very good chance we're going to put together a bill that will make it illegal to sell the Social Security number without the permission of the individual unless there's a legitimate law-enforcement purpose" or perhaps "one or two" other possible exceptions.

But would banning the sale of Social Security numbers make personal information more secure? Some experts argue that security has already deteriorated so far that a prohibition wouldn't make any difference.

An identification number or password that can be changed if data is compromised would work much better, says George Washington's Solove. "Look what happens when your credit card is stolen — you get a new card and number in an instant," he says.

State Regulations

While Congress debated, the recent string of data breaches shocked state politicians into action. California and a handful of other states had already been devising anti-identity-theft measures for some time, but the security breaches spurred legislative proposals in 42 states. As of June 3, 18 had passed or been enacted defining identity theft as a state crime, expanding its definition or toughening existing penalties. Other proposals in 26 states would authorize or strengthen credit-report freezes. [35]

Some of the legislation was included in comprehensive packages. In New York, Attorney General Eliot Spitzer proposed authorizing credit-report freezes, restricting the disclosure of Social Security numbers, requiring notification to consumers whose personal information has been disclosed and beefing up penalties against illegally downloading personal data.

"It has been said that the theft of one's identity and personal information is not a mater of 'if' but a matter of 'when,'" Spitzer said in a press release. "New York State must enact reforms to strengthen consumers' ability to control personal information and to facilitate the prosecution of identity-theft crimes."

Gov. Mitt Romney, R-Mass., also proposed a legislative package that would toughen penalties and require notification to consumers whose personal data may have fallen into the wrong hands. His proposals were among at least 12 measures pending in the legislature, where some form of anti-identity-theft legislation was considered likely to pass this year. [36]

"There was a time when identity theft was associated with petty crimes, perhaps underage people trying to buy beer," Romney said. 'Those days have been surpassed by individuals using identity theft as a means to obtain vast amounts of money and resources that belong to other people." [37]

The bill is pending, along with its rivals.

OUTLOOK

"Synthetic" Fraud

If all sides to the information theft-prevention debate agree on anything, it's that fraud schemes are evolving as rapidly as technology itself.

Even as lawmakers, justice officials, public-interest advocates and security experts debate ways to secure identification data, cutting-edge criminals may already have made much of that debate obsolete.

For instance, a federal grand jury in Newark, N.J., issued indictments recently against 19 people who allegedly ran an online business — complete with its own password-protected Web site — for trading in stolen credit-card and debit-card numbers. "Shadowcrew" was based in Arizona, but other, similarly ambitious schemes are headquartered abroad, law-enforcement officials say. [38]

In Miami, a businessman who sells printer ink and toner reported losing $90,000 from his online bank account to criminals who invaded his computer system with a "worm" that allowed them to order the money withdrawn and have it sent to them. But the thieves were not in a place where the Miami-Dade Police Department could pick them up. They apparently were in Latvia. [39]

Over the decades, countries have set up any number of cooperative agreements to jointly fight narcotics trafficking. Wouldn't a similar effort be possible against identity theft? Probably not, experts say. For one thing, identity theft is not as much of an issue elsewhere. "Other countries in general are not seeing the level of problems that we're seeing," says anti-fraud consultant Douglas. "There is protection of identity taking place in other countries that we're not seeing here." The bottom line, he says: "As long as [criminals] stay overseas, the likelihood of being caught, much less prosecuted, is very slim."

International Internet crime is not in itself a new phenomenon. The cutting edge of technology-assisted fraud is cutting far deeper than merely devising ways to steal long-distance. ID Analytics is a San Diego-based firm that sells anti-identity-theft software that analyzes transactions to spot anomalies that could indicate fraud — such as phony addresses and phone numbers whose area codes don't match addresses. The company claims that fraudsters have gone beyond stealing identities. Now they create new identities by obtaining a legitimate Social Security number assigned to someone, else and using it to create a completely fictitious identity, starting with secured credit accounts. These require collateral but not a credit check. Eventually, the criminal can build up enough documentation to establish a credit account, and then start looting.

A common pattern is to order online, have the goods shipped to a temporary address controlled by an accomplice — all online retailers allow different shipping and billing addresses — then rely on him to reship the goods.

Gartner's Litan agrees that "synthetic identity fraud" is not getting the attention it should, though she says its precise extent is virtually impossible to measure. "I take it very seriously."

"When you traditionally try to stop fraud, the greatest asset is the consumer — they'll check their credit report," says Thomas Oscherwitz, government affairs and privacy director of ID Analytics. "But this doesn't happen with synthetic fraud — they won't see it on their credit report."

The toughest form of identity fraud to fight, Oscherwitz said, would be a model in which criminals based abroad created synthetic identities that they were able to use for Internet-based looting. With that combination of fictitious identities and remote location, their chances of arrest would be minimal.

In creating identities, thieves take advantage of the vast quantity of information available to mix bits and pieces from various peoples' data biographies.

If that were not an ominous enough development, Abrams of the Institute for Information Policy Leadership suggests an even more disturbing possibility — a merger of fictitious identity and terrorism. The fact that identity thieves can rip off property in other peoples' names — or even in completely fictitious names — could one day seem trivial next to the formation of terrorist teams whose information-universe identities are completely made up. They could wreak havoc, and their real names might never surface.

"If terrorists are bad guys," Abrams asks, "why shouldn't we think that they are thinking about synthetic identities?"

NOTES

1. Privacy Rights Clearinghouse, "A Chronology of Data Breaches Reported Since the ChoicePoint Incident," April 20, 2005, www.privacyrights.org/ar/ChronDataBreaches.htm.

2. Todd R. Weiss, "Ameritrade warns 200,0000 clients about potential data breach," Computerworld, April 20, 2005, computerworld.com, and Privacy Rights Clearinghouse, *op. cit.*

3. Tom Zeller Jr., "Time Warner Says Data on Employees is Lost," *The New York Times*, May 3, 2005, p. C4.

4. "Identity Theft Survey Report," Federal Trade Commission, September 2003, pp. 7-9.

5. Stephen Mihm, "Dumpster-Diving for Your Identity," *The New York Times Magazine*, Dec. 21, 2003, p. 42.

6. Tom Zeller Jr., "Personal Data for the Taking," *The New York Times*, May 18, 2005, p. C1.

7. General Accounting Office [now, Government Accountability Office], "Identity Theft: Prevalence and Cost Appear to be Growing," March 2002, pp. 2-3.

8. "National and State Trends in Fraud & Identity Theft, January-December 2004," Federal Trade Commission, Feb. 1, 2005, p. 4; www.ftc.gov.

9. "2005 Identity Fraud Survey Report," Javelin Strategy & Research, January 2005, p. 4.

10. "Locking up the Evil Twin: A Summit on Identity Theft Solutions," California Office of Privacy Protection, March 1, 2005, Draft 4.4.05, p. 66.

11. Statement before Senate Judiciary Committee, April 13, 2005.

12. Abbie Hoffman, *Steal This Book* (1970 — republished 1996), pp. 224-225.

13. Unless otherwise indicated, the information in this background section comes from the following *CQ Researcher* reports: Brian Hansen, "Cyber-Crime,"

April 12, 2002, pp. 305-328; Patrick Marshall, "Cybersecurity," Sept. 26, 2003, pp. 797-820 and Patrick Marshall, "Privacy Under Attack," June 15, 2002, pp. 505-528; Evan Hendricks, *Credit Scores & Credit Reports: How the System Really Works, What You Can Do* (2004) and Robert O'Harrow Jr., *No Place to Hide* (2005).

14. Quoted in O'Harrow, *ibid.*, p. 41.

15. *CQ Almanac*, 1969-1972, pp. 668, 673.

16. Quoted in Hendricks, *op. cit.*, p. 161.

17. Robert Hahn, "Opposition to Credit Act May Prove Costly," *Los Angeles Times*, Nov. 16, 2003, p. M5.

18. Daniel J. Solove, *The Digital Person: Technology and Privacy in the Information Age* (2004), p. 67.

19. *CQ Almanac*, 1973-1976, pp. 585-586.

20. *CQ Almanac*, 1985-1988, p. 861.

21. Cited in Hendricks, *op. cit.*, p. 161.

22. *CQ Almanac*, 1993-1996, pp. 138-140.

23. Albert B. Crenshaw, "Consumers Get New Powers To Deal With Credit Woes," *The Washington Post*, Oct. 27, 1996.

24. O'Harrow, *op. cit.*, pp. 36-37.

25. General Accounting Office, "Identity Fraud: Information Prevalence, Cost, and Internet Impact is Limited," May 1998, pp. 3-4.

26. *Ibid.*, pp. 17-17, 20-23.

27. General Accounting Office, *op. cit.*, March 2002, p. 11.

28. *Ibid.*, pp. 4-7.

29. *Ibid.*, p. 11; and GAO, "Identity Theft: Greater Awareness and Use of Existing Data are Needed," June 2002.

30. Siobhan Hughes, "Senate Clears Credit Report Blocking Bill," *CQ Weekly*, Nov. 29, 2003, p. 2972.

31. "Remarks by the President at Signing of Identity Theft Penalty Enhancement Act," White House, July 15, 2004, www.whitehouse.gov/news/releases/2004/07; O'Harrow, *op. cit.*, p. 96.

32. Robert O'Harrow Jr., "ChoicePoint Data Cache Became a Powder Keg," *The Washington Post*, March 5, 2005, pl. A1.

33. Daniel Roth with Stephanie Mehta, "The Great Data Heist," *Fortune*, May 16, 2005, p. 66.

34. Mihm, *op. cit.*

35. "2005 Introduced Identity Theft Legislation," April 19, 2005, National Conference of State Legislatures, www.ncsl.org/programs/lis/privacy/idtheft.htm.

36. Bruce Mohl, "Romney weighs in on ID theft," *The Boston Globe*, May 19, 2005, p. C1.

37. Erik Davidson, "Romney measure targets ID theft," *Lowell* [Mass.] *Sun*, May 19, 2005.

38. Chassell Bryan-Low, "Identity Thieves Organize," *The Wall Street Journal*, April 7, 2005, p. B1.

39. Ian Katz, "Online Banking Victim Files Suit," *South Florida Sun-Sentinel*, Feb. 5, 2005, p. 1A.

BIBLIOGRAPHY

Books

Frank, Mari J., *Safeguard Your Identity: Protect Yourself With a Personal Privacy Audit*, **Porpoise Press, 2005.**
This guide to reducing the chances of becoming an identity-theft victim is written by a California lawyer who became a specialist on the topic after falling victim herself.

Hendricks, Evan, *Credit Scores & Credit Reports: How the System Really Works, What You Can Do*, **Privacy Times, 2004.**
A pioneering researcher and writer chronicles and dissects the credit-reporting system from a consumer perspective, offering advice to victims of identity theft and consumers who experienced credit-report errors.

Mitnick, Kevin D., *The Art of Intrusion: The Real Stories Behind the Exploits of Hackers, Intruders & Deceivers*, **Wiley Publishing, 2005.**
An ex-hacker who went to prison recounts tales from technology-assisted criminals and security experts.

O'Harrow, Robert Jr., *No Place to Hide*, **Free Press, 2005.**
A *Washington Post* reporter examines the rise of the information industry and its effect on individuals — including identity-theft victims — with special attention to the "data-brokers" that compile profiles on millions of Americans.

Solove, Daniel J., *The Digital Person: Technology and Privacy in the Information Age*, **New York University Press, 2004.**
A law professor at The George Washington University proposes giving individuals control over their personal information collected by companies and public agencies.

Sullivan, Bob, *Your Evil Twin: Behind the Identity Theft Epidemic*, **John Wiley & Sons, 2004.**
An MSNBC reporter and identity-theft specialist examines the lending industry, which in his view helps propel fraud.

Articles

Lieber, Ron, "Who's Helping Victims of Data Theft," *The Wall Street Journal*, **May 24, 2005, p. D1.**
A "cranky consumer" feature tests how companies caught up in this year's security breaches are helping — or not — those at risk.

Mihm, Stephen, "Dumpster-Diving for Your Identity," *The New York Times Magazine*, **Dec. 21, 2003, p. 42.**
Two identity thieves in the Pacific Northwest teamed up to pioneer the hiring of methamphetamine addicts to scour garbage dumps for personal files that could be exploited.

O'Harrow, Robert Jr., "ChoicePoint Data Cache Became Powder Keg," *The Washington Post*, **March 5, 2005, p. A1.**
The newspaper's identity-theft specialist examines how a major data company was penetrated by an identity-theft ring, whose scheme was eventually foiled by an alert employee.

Roth, Daniel, with Stephanie Mehta, "The Great Data Heist," *Fortune*, **May 16, 2005, p. 66.**
A string of data-security breaches this year has made identity theft an even hotter issue and shown that attempts to control it have fallen far short of the goal.

Weiser, Benjamin, and John Schwartz, "Identity-Theft Case Exposes Threat of Rogue Insiders," *The New York Times*, **Nov. 27, 2002, p. B1.**
An identity-theft scheme that victimized 30,000 consumers over three years began with an employee of New York-based Teledata Communications selling information to a fraud ring.

Reports

Federal Trade Commission, "Identity Theft Survey Report," September 2003.
This report was based on the first national survey exploring the prevalence of identity theft and the forms it took.

Federal Trade Commission, "National and State Trends in Fraud and Identity Theft," January-December 2004, Feb. 1, 2005.
The lead federal agency on the consumer-protection side of the issue reports the latest statistics showing that identity-theft reports continue to climb.

Gartner Inc., "Underreporting of Identity Theft Rewards the Thieves," July 2000.
A fraud specialist with a major consulting firm concludes that those who commit identity fraud enjoy favorable odds of getting away with it.

General Accounting Office, (now the Government Accountability Office), "Identity Fraud — Prevalence and Cost Appear to be Growing," March 2002.
Four years after Congress passed the first federal anti-identity-theft law, evidence indicates the crime is increasing.

Javelin Strategy & Research, "2005 Identity Fraud Survey Report," January 2005.
A California-based firm updated the 2003 FTC report with a new survey to chart the incidence, types and methods used in identity theft, concluding that most ID theft is committed offline. A 14-page summary is available free at www.javelinstrategy.com/reports.

For More Information

Consumer Data Industry Association, 1090 Vermont Ave., N.W., Suite 200, Washington, DC 20005-4905; (202) 371-0134; www.cdiaonline.org/. Lobbies on behalf of data companies and provides consumer information.

Electronic Privacy Information Center, 1718 Connecticut Ave., N.W., Suite 200, Washington, DC 20009; (202) 483 1140; www.epic.org. Advocates for more individual control of personal data and more oversight of data companies.

Federal Trade Commission, 600 Pennsylvania Ave., N.W., Washington, DC 20580; 1-877-FTC-HELP (382-4357); www.consumer.gov/idtheft/. The federal government's consumer-help agency in identity-theft cases; provides detailed information on where victims can address complaints and reports.

Identity Theft Resource Center, P.O. Box 26833, San Diego, CA 92196; (858) 693-7935; www.idtheftcenter.org/execletter.shtml. An information source aimed specifically at identity-theft victims, including templates for letters to companies and bill collectors.

Office of Privacy Protection, California Department of Consumer Affairs, 1625 N. Market Blvd., Suite N324, Sacramento, CA 95834; (866) 785-9663 [in California only] or (916) 445-1254; www.privacy.ca.gov. Represents the interests of Californians and provides links to helpful sources.

Privacy Rights Clearinghouse, 3100 5th Ave., Suite B, San Diego, CA 92103; (619) 298-3396; www.privacyrights.org/index.htm. Posts news and reports on identity-theft trends, including a running compilation of data-security breaches.

12

Pension Crisis

Alan Greenblatt

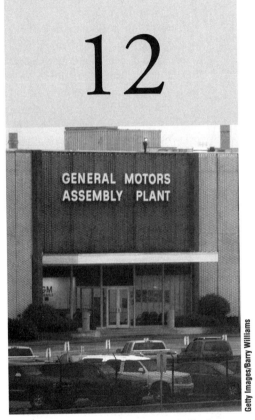

General Motors is closing nine plants in North America by 2008, including its facility in Doraville, Ga. Older companies like struggling GM must support multiple generations of retirees but have fewer active workers contributing to their pension funds. Hard times in the steel, airline and auto industries have caused huge deficits in corporate pension funds and the federal fund that guarantees private pensions.

Joe Necastro had no trouble finding work when he came home to Warren, Ohio, after serving on an aircraft carrier in Vietnam. Within a week, he landed a job in the test lab at Ajax Magnethermic Corp., a heavy-equipment maker.

Necastro had a good run with Ajax — 35 years. But as he neared retirement, the company struggled, was sold and began eliminating benefits — first severance pay, then health insurance.

Finally, the company shut down. But ownership had been dispersed among so many shell companies that none could be held legally responsible for the shortfall in the company's pension fund.

"Not sold, not bankrupt? How do I get pension?" Necastro wrote in a note to himself. [1]

Ajax's pension money had been set aside, but the value of its stock market holdings had declined, leaving only about half as much left as was needed to fulfill the company's pension promises. Luckily for Necastro and other older workers, the federal Pension Benefit Guaranty Corporation (PBGC) stepped in. Set up by Congress in 1974, PBGC promised to make good their pensions — but at a rate much reduced for some workers. *

However, the outcome could have been worse. At least Necastro and his buddies will receive a share of the pensions they were promised. Only 30,000 U.S. companies even offer guaranteed pensions today, down from a high of 112,000 companies in 1985. And the outlook for millions of workers, like Necastro, who counted on their employer-sponsored pensions, has become much cloudier.

From *CQ Researcher,*
February 17, 2006.

---

* The maximum annual payout is currently $47,659.08 per person. So retirees with pensions above that amount get penalized.

Ten Firms Had $11 Billion in Pension Shortfalls

The 10 largest pension defaults of the past 30 years were in the steel, aluminum or airline industries. Their $11 billion in pension debts represented about half of the claims turned over to the Pension Benefit Guaranty Corporation (PBGC) during that period.

Top 10 Firms Presenting Pension Claims to the PBGC
(1975-2004)

Firms	Claims (in $ billions)	No. of Participants	Average Annual Claim*
1. Bethlehem Steel	$3.754	97,015	$37,668
2. LTV Steel	$1.962	80,376	$24,418
3. National Steel	$1.146	35,404	$32,382
4. Pan American Air	$0.841	37,485	$22,438
5. US Airways Pilots	$0.726	7,168	$101,294
6. Weirton Steel	$0.688	9,196	$74,890
7. Trans World Airlines	$0.668	34,171	$19,560
8. Kaiser Aluminum	$0.565	17,591	$32,175
9. Eastern Air Lines	$0.552	51,187	$10,798
10. Wheeling-Pitt Steel	$0.495	22,144	$22,364
Top 10 total	**$11.397**	**391,737**	**$28,862**
All other total	**$9.303**	**1,009,097**	**$9,264**
TOTAL	**$20.700**	**1,400,834**	**$14,761**

* The maximum annual PBGC payout is $47,659 per person.

Source: Pension Benefit Guaranty Corporation (PBGC), "Pension Insurance Data Book, 2004"

In recent months, major companies such as United Airlines and auto-parts giant Delphi have turned to PBGC to relieve them of pension promises they can no longer keep. Verizon, IBM and Hewlett-Packard have all decided either to deny traditional pension plans to new hires or to suspend their existing pension programs altogether.

Meanwhile, company pension plans are underfunded by some $450 billion, while the PBGC is itself running a deficit of $22.8 billion.

But that deficit could quadruple over the next decade, according to a study released in September 2005 by the Congressional Budget Office. It estimated that PBGC shortfalls could reach nearly $87 billion over the next decade — and possibly $142 billion in 20 years.

"Based on this report, the choice is either for pensioners to lose over $100 billion in promised retirement benefits or for taxpayers to get slapped with a $100-billion bill for failed private pension plans. Neither is acceptable," said House Budget Committee Chairman Jim Nussle, R-Iowa. [2]

Three decades ago, pensions in both the government and private sectors were fixtures of the American workplace. Employers proudly touted retirement plans that provided set payments for life in order to recruit workers, and employees saw their pensions as an assurance that they would be provided for in their old age.

But today, huge funding deficits have put traditional pension plans under a severe strain. Newer companies refuse to offer them, while more established employers are doing everything they can to limit their pension liabilities.

As part of an emerging, historic change, many companies are shifting the responsibility of paying and planning for retirement onto individual workers. Other companies, meanwhile, have maintained pension programs they can't sustain — and are shifting their cost to the already underfunded PBGC, which is funded with pension-plan contributions from employers.

In recent years, the PBGC's finances have been severely strained by high-profile business failures, such as the LTV and Bethlehem steel companies. Several U.S. airlines, under intense pressure from new, low-cost airlines that do not offer traditional pension programs, have been particularly pinched by their burgeoning old-style pension obligations. Last year, United Airlines defaulted on its four pension plans, handing over $9.8 billion in pension shortfalls to PBGC. US Airways also reached a deal with PBGC last year, resolving $2.7 billion in pension obligations. Other bankrupt airlines, Delta and Northwest, are next in line and may add as much as $12 billion to PBGC's deficit.

But the airline industry isn't alone. In October the PBGC said it might have to assume responsibility for $4.1 billion of the $10.8 billion pension deficit faced by Delphi, which was spun off from General Motors. GM's own pension plan, meanwhile, is in serious jeopardy. [3]

Worried that taxpayers may be forced to make up the PBGC's short-fall, both the House and the Senate late last year passed bills designed to tighten up pension-funding rules. Lawmakers are expected to reconcile their competing proposals in the coming weeks (*see p. 274*).

"Not long ago, workers used to be pretty sure of a good pension plan. That's not the case anymore," said Charles E. Grassley, R-Iowa, chairman of the Senate Finance Committee, citing factors both within and outside lawmakers' purview. "We need to fix the problems within our control." [4]

Indeed, some experts lay the blame for underfunded pensions at Congress' doorstep, saying that federal pension rules make it too easy for corporations to wiggle out of their commitments — and then leave it to the PBGC to clean up their pension messes.

"Congress repeatedly has passed legislation that enables corporations to underfund their pensions, overstate their profits and postpone to another day any action that would lead them to keep their promises to employees," writes Martha Paskoff Welsh, an adviser on pension reform to the president of the liberal-leaning Century Foundation. [5]

When Congress passed the law governing private pensions 30 years ago, lawmakers never envisioned that entire industries — not just a few companies — would go bankrupt and struggle to meet their pension obligations. But that is exactly what has happened in many of the industrial sectors — including steel, auto and the airlines — that have traditionally provided the most generous retirement benefits. Now companies in these fields say they can't afford to expend their remaining assets on workers who are no longer active.

Others say pension funds should have been managed and funded separately from each company's main operations, with accounts that should be sacrosanct and dedicated to meeting old pension promises, even in companies that are far from robust. Regardless, all companies — and governments — are struggling with demographic changes as well.

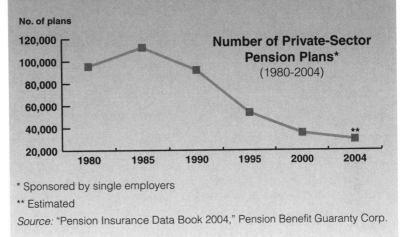

Number of Traditional Pension Plans Fell

American companies have been terminating their company-sponsored defined-benefit pension plans for years. Today, fewer than 30,000 companies offer employer-sponsored plans, down from an all-time high of 112,208 in 1985. Firms increasingly are sponsoring defined-contribution programs, such as 401(k) plans.

Number of Private-Sector Pension Plans*
(1980-2004)

* Sponsored by single employers

** Estimated

Source: "Pension Insurance Data Book 2004," Pension Benefit Guaranty Corp.

For one thing, pensions have become much more expensive than originally envisioned, primarily because life expectancy has grown. In 1950, the average life expectancy in the United States was 68.2 years. In 2002, it was up to 77.3 years. [6] The oldest baby boomers — the enormous generation born in the years following World War II — turn 60 this year, and it's been estimated that two-thirds of all the world's people who have ever reached age 65 are alive today.

The demographic changes mean relatively fewer people are working full time today — and paying into Social Security and other pension funds — compared to the number who are retired. "Back in the '30s, when Social Security started, there were 35 workers for every retiree," says David Wyss, chief economist for Standard & Poor's. Today, that ratio is fast approaching 2-to-1.

Similarly, older companies like struggling General Motors, which have fewer active workers contributing to their pension funds, must continue supporting multiple generations of retirees. Indeed, GM has been called "a pension budget fund and health-insurance business that happens to make cars." [7]

"The system really was designed in an era when everybody thought that the work force would continually

San Diego's "Bad Habit"

Numerous state and local governments face billion-dollar pension deficits, but San Diego's problem is particularly intense. Possibly because of what has been called a "corrupt conspiracy," the mayor recently resigned and several other officials were indicted. [1]

The trouble began a decade ago, when the city was tapped to host the 1996 Republican National Convention. To pay for refurbishing the convention center, officials dipped into the city's pension fund rather than raising taxes or issuing bonds.

It was the beginning of a bad habit.

As the economy began slowing, local officials continued using pension dollars for other purposes. "The key, Nobel Prize-winning breakthrough in economics was the discovery that the unfunded pension liability was a big hole where you could hide your debt," says City Attorney Michael Aguirre. In 2002, for example, unable to give raises to its employees, the city instead offered 25 percent pension increases — despite having just lowered the city's cash contributions into the fund.

"Under the corrupt scheme," editorialized *The San Diego Union-Tribune* last October, "the City Council agreed to increase pension benefits significantly if the retirement board, controlled by the labor unions and other city employees, approved a plan allowing the city to underfund the pension system." [2] Under the agreement, union officials were allowed to jack up their personal pensions in violation of tax rules.

The underfunding plan was approved despite the warnings of Diann Shipione, a pension board trustee, that over the long run it could bankrupt the city. [3] A private attorney for the board also warned it was probably illegal. [4]

Running for re-election in 2004, Mayor Dick Murphy denied that the city was in serious financial difficulty, even as its pension deficit was nearing the billion-dollar mark. He narrowly won but resigned a few months later, after *Time* named him one of the nation's three worst mayors. [5]

In December 2005, Aguirre reported that the city had already run up $10 million in legal bills. [6] The city was also spending heavily to try to make up its pension deficit, by then estimated at $1.4 billion. Last year it increased its annual contributions to the pension fund from about $80 million to $160 million and, according to Councilman Scott Peters, will soon raise them to more than $200 million — serious money in a city with a $2.5 billion budget.

On Jan. 6, 2006, the former pension system's director, staff attorney and five former trustees were indicted for conspiracy and fraud.

Although San Diego's problems are extreme, and the alleged conspiracy unusual, such financing decisions have become commonplace. Many governments that saw tax revenues start to dry up while their pension systems were still making money in the financial markets found it less painful to defer pension payments than to close police stations and libraries.

"Every single decision made in San Diego over the last 20 years was made in other cities as well," says former California Finance Director Steve Peace, also a former state senator from San Diego.

But San Diego's massive system failure has served as a warning to other governments. Just as emergency managers across the country are re-examining their plans in the wake of Hurricane Katrina, says Mark Funkhouser, city auditor in Kansas City, Mo., "most of us ran quick and looked at our pension systems to see if there was anything obviously out of line."

In San Diego, said newly elected Mayor Jerry Sanders, "one thing has become clear to me: San Diego's government systems are badly in need of repair." [7]

---

[1] "Corrupt Conspiracy; Internal memo details crooked pension scheme," *The San Diego Union-Tribune*, Oct. 6, 2005, p. B10.

[2] *Ibid.*

[3] Philip J. LaVelle, "Whistle-blower Was Right, But Feels No Vindication," *The San Diego Union-Tribune*, Jan. 7, 2006, p. A16.

[4] "City Attorney to Sue San Diego Union Leaders, Pension Panel Members," Copley News Service, Oct. 4, 2005.

[5] Terry McCarthy, "The Worst Mayors in America," *Time*, April 25, 2005, p. 22.

[6] Craig Gustafson, "S.D.'s Tab for Lawyers: $10 million," *The San Diego Union-Tribune*, Dec. 22, 2005, p. B1.

[7] "San Diego Mayor Wants Resignation Letters from City's Managers," The Associated Press, Jan. 3, 2006.

grow," says Carol A. Weiser, a benefits lawyer at Sutherland, Asbill & Brennan in Washington.

While American companies like GM and Ford struggle to pay their pension and health "legacy costs," rivals such as Toyota don't have nearly the same level of benefits eating into their bottom lines.

Over the last decade, virtually no company has created a traditional pension plan that offers workers "defined benefits" — guaranteed monthly payments after retirement. Instead, newer companies, such as Southwest Airlines and Microsoft, offer "defined-contribution" plans, such as tax-deferred 401(k) accounts. In defined-contribution plans, workers contribute a certain percentage of their salaries to their own retirement accounts, which their employer may fully or partly match. But the employer is not obliged to pay out any additional funds once the worker retires.

Defined-contribution plans actually slightly surpassed defined-benefit plans in total assets in 1997; both currently hold roughly $2 trillion in reserves.

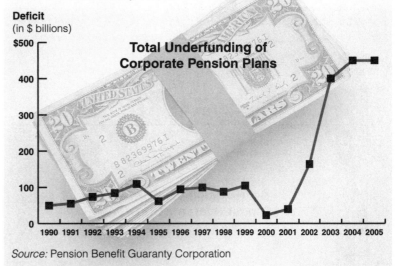

Corporate Pensions Are $450 Billion Short

Total underfunding of defined-benefit pension plans rose from $50 billion in 1990 to nearly a half-trillion dollars in 2004.

Deficit (in $ billions)

Total Underfunding of Corporate Pension Plans

Source: Pension Benefit Guaranty Corporation

Due to sluggish bond and stock markets in recent years, companies still offering traditional pensions — which rely on investment income — have not been able to accumulate assets fast enough to match their growing liabilities. To make up the difference, companies have had to contribute more cash out of their general operating budgets, causing further problems for companies that were struggling anyway. Some are even turning to investments in risky hedge funds (*see p. 279*).

But even healthy companies have been cutting back on their pension benefits. According to Watson Wyatt, a global consulting firm, 11 percent of the *Fortune* 1000 companies with defined-benefit plans froze or terminated them in 2004 — up from 7 percent the year before.

Some argue that such moves are necessary to compete in today's global marketplace. "The Cold War actually protected American workers, because there weren't that many places where you could get cheap labor," says John J. McFadden, a compensation expert at The American College in Bryn Mawr, Pa. But for today's employers, he says, "Any long-term obligation looks bad to them."

Companies that still run pension plans complain that they are highly regulated, answering to three separate federal agencies (the PBGC, the Internal Revenue Service and the Labor Department). Having to meet more stringent funding requirements, as Congress and the Bush administration want, could drive still more companies to drop their traditional pension plans, some argue.

"Some of the proposals are so draconian that they're going to be counterproductive and will drive some companies out of business or out of defined-benefit plans," says Alan Reuther, legislative director for the United Auto Workers (UAW). "The result will be more of the risk of retirement being shifted onto the backs of workers."

Reuther questions "the post-modern notion that blue-collar workers should be responsible for their own retirements because giant corporations can't handle it." [8] Many pension experts say companies that were able to offer pension benefits on the cheap when their funds' pension investments were profiting in the markets shouldn't complain now that those investments aren't earning as much — meaning the companies must contribute more.

"If the funding rules worked in insuring that companies had contributed sufficient assets to protect the liabilities, then we wouldn't be having this conversation," says Bradley D. Belt, executive director of the PBGC.

Whether the fault lies with increasing global competition, poor investment payoffs or complex accounting rules, the fact is that more and more companies are closing their traditional pension plans. Although these are

Pension Fund Has $23 Billion Deficit

The federal Pension Benefit Guaranty Corporation (PBGC) has a $23 billion deficit because of the growing number of failed companies and underfunded pension plans. But the Congressional Budget Office warns the shortfall could reach $142 billion in the next 20 years unless steps are taken to tighten pension-funding rules.

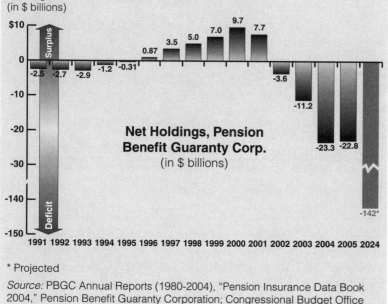

Holdings
(in $ billions)

Net Holdings, Pension
Benefit Guaranty Corp.
(in $ billions)

Surplus / Deficit values by year:
-2.5, -2.7, -2.9, -1.2, -0.31, 0.87, 3.5, 5.0, 7.0, 9.7, 7.7, -3.6, -11.2, -23.3, -22.8, -142*

1991 1992 1993 1994 1995 1996 1997 1998 1999 2000 2001 2002 2003 2004 2005 2024

* Projected

Source: PBGC Annual Reports (1980-2004), "Pension Insurance Data Book 2004," Pension Benefit Guaranty Corporation; Congressional Budget Office

— say, 1.5 percent of the worker's salary times the number of months at the firm.

But because Americans are living longer, companies must pay benefits much longer for each person than they had projected. As a result, troubled companies, such as United Airlines, have divested themselves of their defined-benefit pension plans, turning over their assets and liabilities to the Pension Benefit Guaranty Corporation (PBGC).

Meanwhile, newer companies like Microsoft and Southwest Airlines never offered employees the old-fashioned plans. Financial-services companies say it's been years since they've seen the launch of any new defined-benefit plans. At the same time, many healthy companies, such as Hewlett-Packard and Verizon, decided in 2005 that they wouldn't enroll new hires into their existing defined-benefit plans.

All of this leaves many observers wondering whether traditional pension plans are quickly becoming outmoded. "It's probably fair to say that a traditional defined-benefit plan has less relevance in today's world," says the PBGC's Belt.

often replaced with 401(k) or other individual retirement accounts (IRAs), defined-benefit plans provide the greatest security to retirees — a federally insured guarantee of payment until death.

It's becoming clear that individual Americans will have to finance more of their own retirements. And because Americans are poor savers, it's likely that many will struggle.

"The golden age of retirement as our fathers knew it won't be what it used to be," says James Morris, senior vice president for retirement at SEI Investments, in Oaks, Pa.

As the pension debate continues in Congress and elsewhere, here are some of the questions people are asking:

Are traditional pension plans becoming obsolete?

Private pension plans historically have offered "defined" benefits promising fixed monthly payments from retirement until death. The benefits were based on a formula

Clearly, traditional pension plans don't have the cachet they once did. But most *Fortune* 1000 companies still offer them, and no one thinks they will disappear anytime soon. Dallas Salisbury, president of the Employee Benefit Research Institute, says traditional pensions will remain in demand in industries where workers tend to stay put for a long period of time, such as government and utilities.

Traditional private pensions cover 21.6 million workers and continue to offer many advantages: They help to pool risk and cost less per person to administer than individual retirement accounts. [9] And the vast majority of them, despite the headline failures, are well-funded. "Many of these plans, even those that have been frozen and closed to new participants, will be around for up to 100 years," Salisbury predicts.

And these plans continue to serve the same purpose they always have — helping attract and retain skilled workers. "They are an important work-force management tool," says Bob Shepler, director of corporate finance and tax at the National Association of Manufacturers. "Employers want to reward their employees for staying with the company throughout their career."

At times, pension plans have also offered an even more tangible benefit to employers. During the 1990s, many companies were able to provide generous retirement benefits at no cost to themselves because their pension-plan investments were performing well in the booming stock market. Some did so well that companies were able to draw out funds and count them as pure profit.

"Nobody said anything about pension plans bankrupting companies during the 1990s, because the investment earnings of pension plans were fattening the bottom lines of all these companies," says McFadden, at The American College. "Ten percent of IBM's earnings in the '90s were due to pension funds. Now that's turned around, and companies are claiming pensions are pulling them down."

Shepler warns that the long-term viability of traditional pensions depends to a large extent on the final shape of legislation currently being negotiated in Congress. The bills being considered would shore up the PBGC, which is funded by premiums from companies offering traditional pension plans. But talk of tightening up pension-funding rules over a short timeframe frightens many companies.

"You want to breathe as much life into the defined-benefit plans that are left as you can without making demands that cannot be met," says North Carolina state Treasurer Richard H. Moore.

Olivia S. Mitchell, who directs the Pension Research Council at the University of Pennsylvania's Wharton School, doubts that Congress will be able to strike the right balance. She warns that lawmakers may shore up troubled plans at the expense of companies that have managed their pension liabilities well.

"If you raise premiums to clear up past mistakes [by other companies], you may drive out those companies that remain [in the PBGC system]," she says. "To try to charge higher premiums on companies still running defined-benefit plans, it seems to me, might cause a death spiral."

Getty Images/Tim Boyle

Newer companies like Southwest Airlines offer "defined-contribution" pension plans, such as tax-deferred 401(k) accounts, rather than traditional plans that offer workers "defined benefits," or guaranteed monthly payments after retirement. Under the newer plans, workers contribute a certain percentage of their salaries to their own retirement accounts, which their employer may match or partly match.

Others warn that no matter what Congress does, many companies will try to unload their pension plans as soon as they can. (Companies are penalized if they end pension plans with future liabilities that aren't 100 percent covered by current assets.) Many executives say it's simply too expensive to offer generous benefits into an unpredictable future when competitors aren't offering the same sort of packages.

"You're going to see less and less of the overall pension dollar go to defined-benefit plans every year," says Stephen W. Skonieczny, a New York-based partner in the employee-benefits group of Dechert LLP, an international law firm. "I don't know whether it will be 10 years or 15 years down the road, but the day will come when there aren't going to be any more defined-benefit plans."

Should employers fund their workers' retirements?

U.S. employers are under no obligation to offer their workers any sort of retirement income. Big firms began offering pensions over a century ago in hopes of retaining skilled workers. Pensions became commonplace following World War II, a staple of employment in heavy-manufacturing industries.

Even A. J. "Jim" Norby, who lobbies for pensioners as president of the National Retiree Legislative Network, says that pensions, like salaries and other benefits, "are a pure labor-relations issue." He adds: "There's no reason to pay an employee a pension, unless the employer decided that the employee was valuable enough to offer him one."

Moreover, even at their peak, traditional U.S. pension plans were hardly universal. At best, according to the Pension Research Council's Mitchell, less than half the American work force received retirement benefits. Now, as more and more companies are moving away from the old-fashioned fixed-income pension model, and fewer employees are spending their entire careers with one employer, companies are taking a fresh look at how much they are obligated to help pay for employees' retirement.

Not surprisingly, labor unions strongly favor pensions. "We think society has an obligation to ensure that people have adequate retirement income," says the UAW's Reuther. "The employer-based system has been a major element of providing that protection."

Many employers still want to offer retirement benefits, in hopes of attracting and retaining talented people. As fewer employers offer traditional defined-benefit pension plans, thousands of employers have set up 401(k) and other retirement accounts into which they may pour a certain percentage of workers' current salaries.

"Most companies feel an obligation to help their employees accumulate wealth for retirement," says Lynn D. Dudley, vice president of retirement policy at the American Benefits Council, which lobbies for big employers that sponsor pension plans. "The surveys I've seen on that point are very strong.'"

Shepler of the National Association of Manufacturers agrees but emphasizes that pensions are a voluntary management tool. "Employers cannot provide pensions at the expense of the business," he says. "There's a need to strike a balance."

Although offering a pension is voluntary, once a company promises to pay pensions it is legally obligated to pay out the full amount. Companies can alter their pension policies at any time, but once an individual retires, it's nearly impossible for the former employer to alter a worker's benefits package. "To renege on what they promised is virtually stealing from you, because you've already earned it," says C. William Jones, president of the Association of BellTel Retirees.

For that reason, many companies worried about being stuck with future liabilities are reducing current

workers' benefits. "Employers don't like to use their compensation money for people who don't work there any more," says McFadden, at The American College.

Still, retirement packages are generally considered a good idea. Federal tax policy gives breaks to companies and workers to encourage employer-based pensions. "The combination of the employer system and Social Security is really what made a good retirement for Americans," says Anna Rappaport, a benefits consultant in Chicago and former president of the Society of Actuaries.

Rappaport says there's nothing "magic" about employer-sponsored pensions, but notes that many people, and perhaps society as a whole, have come to rely on them. Moreover, the plans — which involve automatic contributions usually withheld from the employee's paycheck — tend to encourage better savings rates than individual retirement accounts. "People who have employer-sponsored plans are much more likely to save than those who don't," she says.

In fact, Americans are up to 20 times more likely to save if they're automatically enrolled in an employer-sponsored plan compared with those who are not enrolled, says Brian H. Graff, executive director of the American Society of Pension Professionals and Actuaries.

That creates a tension, he says. Some people believe the current system "is too paternalistic," Graff explains. "Our employer-based system forces savings upon people, and some might prefer to take the money and spend it. But as a practical matter, if we don't have this paternalism, people won't save."

The Bush administration, which puts a premium on individual responsibility, has recommended expanded tax breaks and incentives to get more individuals to save for retirement on their own.

But many people disagree, says Graff. "Lots of folks believe that, given the fact that Social Security isn't going to get any bigger, the only way we're going to get the vast majority of Americans to a comfortable retirement is through these employer-sponsored plans," he says, "So we should do everything we can to encourage them."

Morris, of SEI Investments, hopes policymakers address the question of legal liability for companies that want to help their employees better manage their retirement savings. Many companies are shy about offering detailed advice, he says, because they're afraid they'll be held responsible if investments don't pay off.

That kind of advice will be increasingly helpful as time goes on, suggests employee-benefits attorney Diane M. Morgenthaler, a partner at McDermott Will & Emery in Chicago. "We've begun a trend [in which] employees will have to take more and more responsibility for their own retirements," she says. "While there will be employer benefits, we'll see more and more individuals funding their own retirements."

Will today's working Americans be able to retire comfortably?

With many major employers backing away from their historic commitment to pension plans, some economists and other observers are concerned that Americans who are today in their 50s — or younger — won't be able to retire as comfortably as earlier generations.

"Unlike their parents and grandparents, they're unlikely to find an employer at the end of their working life who will replace a good deal of their income," says Graff. "Younger workers need to assume more responsibility for their future than ever before because of this trend of shifting expenses away from employer to employee."

Other trends are foreboding, as well. Social Security benefits may decline in the future. And Medicare, the federal health insurance program for seniors, is running a long-term deficit, leading some to worry that retirees will have to spend most of their limited income on health care. "Imagine accumulating your 401(k) money, and all of it has to be spent just to cover your health-insurance premiums," says Laurence J. Kotlikoff, an economist at Boston University.

But not everyone is pessimistic. Some experts point out that traditional pension plans are usually being replaced with 401(k) and other defined-contribution plans. While there's a danger that individuals can outlive their savings under such plans, they also offer the opportunity to save adequately for retirement.

Salisbury, the president of the Employee Benefit Research Institute, says many people in the newer pension plans have saved enough to create as much retirement income as workers who left the investment decision-making to their company under an old-fashioned plan. The average monthly retirement check from a defined-benefit plan is about $775 — about as much as one could earn from a modest 5 percent return on a $186,000 individual retirement account. And the average 401(k) balance, it turns out, for those between 60 and 65 years of age with 30 years of service is now $190,000, he says.

Other statistics also indicate that many older workers have managed to save that much in their retirement accounts. But younger workers are saving much less than they'll need for retirement, often in the belief that they will catch up later, say many economists.

Salisbury says with today's highly mobile work force many more Americans could fare better under newer plans like the 401(k) than with traditional pension plans. The federal government also has allowed other tax-free or deferred-tax plans designed to encourage retirement savings, such as Roth IRAs. The Bush administration has pushed expansion of such plans. The current pension bills under debate in Congress may make 401(k) enrollment automatic for many employees — giving many workers no choice but to save for retirement.

It would also help, Kotlikoff says, if the financial-services marketplace would do more to create and promote annuity plans, which would allow individuals to invest their retirement savings in a way that would pay out a set monthly amount. In too many cases, retirees withdraw their retirement money in a lump sum, leaving them vulnerable if they spend it down too quickly. "Employees need longevity protection," he says.

However, Kotlikoff and other economists are not sure that, as the retirement burden falls more and more on workers rather than companies, individuals will take adequate advantage of various savings plans. "Anybody who is age 40 — if you're not contributing at least 10 percent of your income, you should worry," says Larry Zimpleman, executive vice president of Prudential Financial Group, in Des Moines, Iowa.

The Wharton School's Mitchell hopes people will change their saving habits. "Just because there's some degree of financial illiteracy doesn't mean people can't learn and won't learn," she says. "That's good, because they're going to have to learn."

That is, such changes will have to occur if Americans are going to continue to enjoy the same levels of comfort in retirement as their immediate forebears. "People will live longer and work longer — and will have to invest more wisely, because I don't think that safety net is going to be there," says Morris, of SEI Investments. "The notion of retiring and playing golf every day, that's kind of an antiquated idea."

CHRONOLOGY

1940s-1960s *Pension plans become common in heavy industry during the postwar economic boom.*

1949 Ford Motor Co. capitulates to union demands for pensions, setting off a stampede of employer-funded plans. . . . Supreme Court supports National Labor Relation Board's contention that pensions are a proper issue for collective bargaining.

1960 Forty percent of private-sector workers are covered by employer-sponsored pension plans.

1963 Automaker Studebaker collapses, reneging on generous pension increases offered in recent years.

1970s-1990s *Pensions become more regulated and begin to lose favor among employers, who migrate toward newer retirement accounts.*

1974 Congress passes Employee Retirement Income Security Act (ERISA), setting standards for private-sector retirement accounts and creating the Pension Benefit Guaranty Corporation (PBGC).

1978 Congress allows creation of 401(k) accounts, enabling workers to defer tax liabilities on a percentage of their income until retirement.

1986 Tax Reform Act requires broader pension coverage of rank-and-file workers and faster vesting schedules, prompting some employers to drop their traditional pension plans.

1990 Congress updates ERISA, imposing an excise tax on money removed from pension funds by cash-strapped companies.

1991 Congress sets PBGC premiums at $19 a year per plan participant.

1997 Defined-contribution plans such as 401(k) accounts surpass traditional pensions in total cash reserves; Congress creates the Roth IRA, a retirement account funded with non-deductible contributions that are not taxed when used after retirement.

1999 IBM converts its traditional defined-benefit pension plan into a cash-balance plan, triggering an age-discrimination lawsuit. A 2003 ruling held the plan was discriminatory.

2000s *Pensions lose favor with employers; many plans fail in a bad investment climate.*

2001 President Bush's Commission to Strengthen Social Security recommends ways to overhaul the program that would introduce personal investment accounts; a tax bill increases contribution limits for 401(k) accounts and IRAs.

2002 PBGC posts losses of $11 billion; House passes Pension Security Act, limiting the amount of employee 401(k) contributions that can be invested in company stock and promoting worker education concerning retirement; bill dies in Senate.

May 10, 2005 United Airlines receives court permission to terminate its four employee pension plans — the largest pension default since passage of ERISA.

July 15, 2005 San Diego Mayor Dick Murphy resigns in disgrace over the city's $1.4 billion pension deficit; a new election is held in November.

Nov. 10, 2005 Federal Accounting Standards Board requires corporations to make pension liabilities more clear in their earnings statements and to count their liabilities against profits.

Nov. 15, 2005 PBGC reports a $22.8 billion deficit — a slight improvement on its $23.3 billion deficit in 2004.

Nov. 16, 2005 Senate votes 97-2 in favor of a measure to create more stringent pension-funding rules; House passes its version, 294-132, on Dec. 15.

Dec. 20, 2005 New York City transit workers worried about pensions and other benefits shut down the city's public transportation network for three days during the holidays.

Jan. 6, 2006 IBM freezes traditional defined-benefits pension plan and switches to a 401(k) plan, saying the move will save billions.

Feb. 1, 2006 Congress increases PBGC premiums from $19 to $30 per participant per year.

BACKGROUND

Railroad Ties

Veterans' pensions date back to the Revolutionary War, but private companies didn't provide pensions until after the Civil War. Older Americans were cared for by their families or, more often, continued working. In the 19th century, roughly 75 percent of all males over age 65 were still working. [10]

The antebellum economy had consisted largely of farms and small-scale handicraft-production firms. But during the latter half of the 19th century, the Industrial Revolution took hold, leading to a vast expansion in manufacturing. Between 1870 and 1910, the manufacturing work force quadrupled (from 3.5 million to 14.2 million workers). Family ties grew weaker as people sought factory work in large cities, away from their extended families.

Large corporations, led by the railroads, began offering pensions to help maintain a stable work force. Pensions kept workers attached to a company for long careers and also encouraged older, more expensive workers to leave the payroll. Simply putting older workers out on the street would have dispirited younger workers, who might grow concerned over their own fates.

"To keep worn-out, incapacitated workers on the payroll is an economic waste," writes law Professor James A. Wooten, of the State University of New York at Buffalo, summarizing the thinking of the day. "To turn such [people] adrift is not humane and exercises a depressing influence upon workers still in the prime of life." [11]

Industrial pensions first arose in the 1860s in Prussia, the heart of German industry. Workers who reached age 65 retired in exchange for limited pension payments for the rest of their lives. In 1875, American Express Co., then a transcontinental freight hauler, set up the first U.S. employer-sponsored pension plan, followed in 1880 by the Baltimore and Ohio Railroad. [12]

Railroads depended on pensions to develop experienced, permanent administrative staff to run their giant bureaucracies. Railroads sponsored most of the pension plans developed over the next several decades, but by the early 20th century several banks and utilities also provided pensions.

At first, pensions were discretionary — gratuities from a grateful employer for long and faithful service. But some began to frame pensions as a moral obligation to superannuated workers. In a 1912 book on old age, Lee Wielling Squier wrote, "From the standpoint of the whole system of social economy, no employer has a right to engage men in any occupation that exhausts the individuals' industrial life in 10, 20 or 40 years, and then leave the remnant floating on society at large as a derelict at sea." [13]

Congress, though, remained mostly sympathetic to the so-called personnel theory of private pensions, sharing the corporate view that they were primarily a means for managing work-force needs. The 1921 Revenue Act exempted income from pension and profit-sharing trusts — becoming the first tax incentive for employers to establish retirement-income benefits for workers.

But employees remained at risk. They received nothing if their employers went bankrupt, and only about 50 percent lived long enough — generally, to age 65 — to enjoy full benefits. Reformers viewed pensions as deferred wages and wanted companies to guarantee that more workers would actually receive pension payments. But corporations shunned the idea of creating special accounts that could be viewed as representing individual employees' assets.

Instead, pension plans became profit centers for companies during the roaring 1920s. Meanwhile, because of the way pension plans were set up, companies "demanded a sacrifice of liberty and mobility, what [Supreme Court Justice] Louis Brandeis called the 'new peonage,' in exchange for this shadowy benefit," writes historian Steven Sass. [14]

By 1935, when establishment of the Social Security System created a federal retirement plan for most Americans, only 3 to 4 million workers — less than 15 percent of the work force — were covered by private plans, mostly sponsored by a few older businesses that imposed strict age and years-of-service requirements. [15] That number would soon shrink. During the Great Depression, nearly 10 percent of companies that had provided pensions discontinued or suspended parts of their plans. Another 10 percent reduced benefits.

"Private pensions would henceforth be tied tightly to the need to reward key employees, and plan benefits would flow more swiftly to the higher-compensated employees," according to Sass. [16]

Social Security and other New Deal programs pushed federal income taxes higher — up to 70 percent on top earners. Pension plans became attractive shelters for highly

Pension Failures Take Human Toll

Ellen Saracini's husband, Vincent, had been the pilot of United Flight 175, one of the planes that terrorists crashed into the World Trade Center on Sept. 11, 2001.

But when the bankrupt United last year turned its underfunded pension fund over to the federal Pension Benefit Guaranty Corporation (PBGC), Saracini's widow's pension was cut in half — to $47,000 a year, the maximum payout allowed by the beleaguered agency, which is already running a $23 billion deficit.

"I can't help but ask myself at what point are companies allowed to take away so much from the lives of dedicated employees and their families," Saracini wrote in an "online hearing" organized by Rep. George Miller of California, ranking Democrat on the House Education and the Workforce Committee. "The PBGC's decision to allow United Airlines to end their pensions is just wrong." [1] More than 2,000 other unhappy United workers also responded.

Another United pilot, Gerald Innella, saw his pension of roughly $126,000 a year cut by nearly $80,000, forcing him and his wife to sell their retirement home and move in with younger relatives. [2]

As more and more companies suspend or end their traditional pension plans, many workers and their dependents are feeling similarly shortchanged. The prospect of workers reaching the end of their careers, only to find themselves financially strapped through no fault of their own, has been an important factor in the political debate on regulating pensions.

In California, Republican Gov. Arnold Schwarzenegger was forced to back down from his proposal last year to end the traditional defined-benefit pension for state and school employees after it became clear that the benefits of widows and orphans left behind by firefighters and police officers would have been cut.

"If someone were to get disabled on the job or lose their life, their families are not going to have the guaranteed security that this pension program provides for them right now," complained Heather McCormack, the widow of a fire captain who died on the job. [3]

Companies that offer defined-benefit plans cannot legally change the benefits of retirees, short of a failure such as United's. But it's perfectly legal to suspend, cancel or change plans for current workers. Many companies are refusing to enroll new workers into their pension plans. Others have suspended the benefits offered to current employees, meaning they will only receive the level of benefits they have already earned but will rack up nothing more in their retirement accounts.

Employers, after all, are under no obligation to provide retirement benefits; in fact, most don't. So a smaller check from PBGC is still more than most retired workers get.

But in industries where pensions have been a fact of life at least since World War II, the sudden threat to their well-being is causing anxiety. Personal bankruptcies have increased more than sixfold since 1980. Some economists blame the erosion of programs such as pensions and retiree health benefits for making the financial road so much bumpier for millions of Americans.

---

paid workers because the benefits were taxed more lightly than straight income. After years of fighting between Congress and Treasury officials over lost revenue, lawmakers passed the 1942 Revenue Act requiring broad employee participation in the plans, so top management couldn't create sheltering plans just for themselves.

Postwar Boom

As income taxes applied to more people during World War II, the tax relief afforded by pension plans became valuable to the general work force. Wartime wage-and-price controls also sparked a big increase in the number of companies offering pensions because companies were encouraged to offer non-inflationary compensation. Between September 1942 and December 1944, the IRS approved more than 4,000 plans. By 1945, 6.5 million employees were covered by private pensions — triple the number in 1938. [17]

Meanwhile, unions — which could not negotiate for wage increases because of wage controls — revised their long-held view of pensions as merely management tools and began to see them as desirable. After the war, the United Mine Workers began administering a multiemployer pension plan, to which several mining companies contributed. And Walter Reuther, head of the UAW, made pensions a priority.

"Business and government used to see it as their duty to provide safety nets against the worst economic threats we face," said Yale University political scientist Jacob S. Hacker, author of the book *The Great Risk Shift*. "But more and more, they're yanking them away." [4]

Because the United Auto Workers union agreed in November to allow General Motors (GM) to cut its retiree health-care liability by $15 billion, Gerald Roy, a retired GM employee, now pays monthly premiums and other medical expenses for the first time. Although that pinches, he worries more about his son, Jerry, who works for Delphi — the auto-parts maker spun off from GM in 1999. Delphi is operating under bankruptcy and threatening, like United, to hand its pension obligations over to the PBGC.

"What worries me most, or bothers me the most," said the senior Roy, "is him working for 28 years for GM, and he might lose his retirement." [5]

The younger Roy sounds more sanguine, telling *The New York Times*, "People survive somehow." Indeed, many workers are trying to find ways to change their financial positions, given the state of their employers and their pension funds. Hundreds of pilots have lobbied Congress to

Five United Airlines flight attendants, ages 55-64, created a provocative calendar to publicize concern about the airline's pension plan.

Courtesy www.stewsstripped.com/Bruce Baker

raise their mandatory retirement age from 60 to 65, giving them more time to recover money lost to pension cuts. [6]

Some flight attendants have tried measures that are both more creative and, perhaps, more desperate. At the top of the list are the five United flight attendants, ages 55 to 64, who posed provocatively in scanty costumes for a 2006 calendar called "Stewardesses Stripped (of Their Pension)." [7]

[1] Her testimony is available at http://edworkforce.house.gov/democrats/unitedsaracinitestimony.html.

[2] Dale Russakoff, "Human Toll of a Pension Default," *The Washington Post*, June 13, 2005, p. A1.

[3] Chuck Carroll and Rodney Foo, "Governor's Pension Proposal Denounced," *San Jose Mercury News*, March 26, 2005, p. 1B.

[4] Quoted in Peter S. Gosselin, "If America Is Richer, Why Are Its Families So Much Less Secure," *Los Angeles Times*, Oct. 10, 2004, p. A1.

[5] Danny Hakim, "For a G.M. Family, the American Dream Vanishes," *The New York Times*, Nov. 19, 2005, p. A1.

[6] Bloomberg News, "Pilots Ask Congress to Raise Retirement Age," *Los Angeles Times*, May 26, 2005, p. C3.

[7] Tim Gray, "Pension Roulette," *AARP Bulletin*, July-August 2005.

In 1947, Ford tentatively agreed to create the first pension plan in the automobile industry but backed out after passage of the Taft-Hartley Act. By limiting union activity, the law in effect gave the company greater concessions than it had been able to extract from the UAW during negotiations about pensions and other contract issues. (In 1949, the Supreme Court supported the National Labor Relation Board's contention that pensions were a proper issue for collective bargaining.)

The old "human-depreciation" idea, which held that companies had a responsibility to care for personnel in old age, just as they would pay to replace worn-out machinery, took root in 1949 with the report of a fact-finding board appointed by President Harry S Truman to rule on a labor dispute.

"The human machines, like the inanimate machines, have a definite rate of depreciation," the board concluded. "We think that all industry, in the absence of adequate government programs, owes an obligation to workers to provide for maintenance of the human body . . . and full depreciation in the form of old-age retirement." [18]

U.S. Steel balked at the obligation at first, but the report influenced the Ford-UAW negotiations (autoworkers tended to be younger than steel workers). Ford began offering pensions in 1949, followed by

Reps. George Miller, D-Calif., at left, and Jan Schakowsky, D-Ill., join members of the Association of Flight Attendants and the Machinists' union on May 10, 2005, to urge a Chicago bankruptcy court to reject a proposed pension agreement between United Airlines and the Pension Benefit Guaranty Corporation.

some unions abused their pension funds, notably the mob-influenced Teamsters under James R. Hoffa, who used the money in part to reward his allies.

UAW chief Reuther wanted workers' pensions to be more secure and seized on the collapse of Studebaker as a public relations opportunity to press his point. When Studebaker closed its South Bend, Ind., auto plant in 1963, its pension fund was $15 million short. After negotiations with the union local, some retirees received their full pensions, but vested employees under age 60 received only about 15 percent of the value of their pensions. Those who weren't vested, including employees under 40, got nothing. [20]

Four months later, a presidential commission said basic fairness and the substantial federal tax subsidy enjoyed by private pensions obligated pension funds to deliver promised benefits. The UAW pushed its case that pensions should be insured, but businesses scoffed. Sen. Jacob K. Javits, R-N.Y., who was sympathetic toward the idea of greater worker security, held hearings and helped plant human-interest stories that helped shift media coverage of the issue.

"Each year, thousands of Americans who think they are 'covered' fail to get the retirement benefits they've been counting on," reported *Reader's Digest* in 1971. "In the end, Congress will have to act if the pension rights of millions of Americans are to be protected." [21]

The effort moved some state legislatures to take up bills, leading business groups to lobby Congress for preemptive federal legislation. The landmark Employee Retirement Income Security Act of 1974 (ERISA) created "a far more complex institution, with the government joining employers and unions as an active and assertive participant," writes Sass. [22] In addition to creating the PBGC, it said companies offering pensions would have to adhere to federal funding and vesting rules. It also authorized the use of IRAs, setting the stage for later steps to encourage workers to save more for retirement. [23]

After ERISA

But passage of ERISA, in retrospect, marked the high-water mark for traditional, defined-benefit pension plans. Four years after its passage, Congress created a new retirement vehicle, known as a 401(k) after its location in the Revenue Act. As with many traditional pension plans, these accounts were initially created to give

General Motors the next year, triggering a pension gold rush; by 1960, 40 percent of private-sector workers were covered. [19]

The rise of collectively bargained pension rights — especially in sectors with union-administered, multi-employer plans such as construction, building trades and trucking — bred a sense of worker connection to their unions that began to replace the old model under which pensions were a tool to engender loyalty to a specific employer. There were investigations into allegations that

corporate executives the chance to shelter parts of their income (the top individual tax rate was then 70 percent). But within a few years, companies made them available more broadly to workers, and by 1985 assets in 401(k) accounts totaled $91 billion. [24] By 1997, defined-contribution plans such as 401(k)s held bigger reserves than traditional pensions, which currently cover just about 20 percent of all U.S. workers.

Employers argued that 401(k) accounts were better for workers than traditional pensions because they were fully portable — vested workers lost nothing if they changed jobs. But 401(k)s were also cheaper for employers, who put a set amount — say, 3 percent of the worker's salary — into the accounts and then their obligation was finished. Unlike traditional plans, they had no obligation after the worker retired.

In any event, traditional pension funds much bigger than Studebaker have failed in recent years. Some blame generous benefits, such as the "30 and out" early-retirement plans negotiated in the early 1970s by the UAW, which allowed retirement after 30 years of service. Others say even if companies struggle, their pension funds should still be healthy at the time of bankruptcy if they were being managed properly. Pension accounting, based on fluctuating rates of return on investments and largely maintained in secrecy, adds to the confusion.

"Depending on whom you talk to," writes Roger Lowenstein in *The New York Times*, "General Motors' mammoth pension fund is either fully funded or, as the PBGC maintains, it is $31 billion in the hole." [25]

Recent history is full of examples of companies whose pensions were supposedly healthy but turned out to be billions short after the dust of bankruptcy settled. Pension plans in general have been struggling recently due to a confluence of factors. Aside from people living longer and forcing companies to pay out more benefits than they had anticipated, stock market performance has been sluggish since 2000, forcing pension sponsors to compensate for poor returns by putting more cash into their funds.

Many companies that went bankrupt or had underfunded pension plans have dumped their pension obligations onto the PBGC in recent years, including Kaiser Aluminum and Kemper Insurance. But the biggest pension problems have been in older, struggling industries — the airlines, auto manufacturing and steel. PBGC Executive Director Belt told the Senate Finance Committee in June that "United, US Airways, Bethlehem

Steel, LTV and National Steel would not have presented claims in excess of $1 billion each, and with funded ratios of less than 50 percent — if the [funding] rules worked."

The biggest pension failure in U.S. history occurred last spring, when United Airlines declared bankruptcy and turned its pension obligations, including a $10 billion deficit, over to the PBGC. Like many other companies, United failed to change its habits when the boom years of the 1990s came to a close. Between 2000 and 2002 the company did not put any contributions into its four pension plans. Yet in 2002, even as the struggling company was lobbying for federal bailouts in the wake of the Sept. 11, 2001, terrorist attacks, it granted a 40 percent pension increase to its ground employees. [26]

If Belt blames the funding rules, the Wharton School's Mitchell blames ERISA itself. "ERISA [depended on] risk pooling. That concept doesn't work when entire industries go under, and that's what we're seeing. They never really had thought that entire industries would go down the tubes."

> **"Each year, thousands of Americans who think they are 'covered' fail to get the retirement benefits they've been counting on."**
>
> — Reader's Digest, 1971

CURRENT SITUATION

Congress Acts

From a purely economic perspective, "the last few years have not been kind to assets accumulating within pension systems," says Zimpleman, of the Prudential Financial Group. The worst-case scenario for traditional pensions, he says, is "low interest rates and poor equity markets — just what has been the scenario for the past five or six years."

But current pension problems appear to stem from more than just a cyclical downturn. Corporate America

Congress' Pension Plan Considered Generous

As members of Congress consider strengthening the private pension system, they do so in the knowledge that their own pension plan is more generous than most.

Just how much money lawmakers receive upon retirement depends on their length of service and other factors. They generally get between $40,000 and $55,000 a year. Members can receive their full pension by age 60 if they have served for 10 years or more. In some cases they can begin collecting at an even younger age. [1] In addition, lawmakers' pensions include automatic cost-of-living increases that most private-sector workers don't get.

Congressional pensions have been the source of a good deal of populist anger, much of it vented on the Internet. David Keating, senior counselor for the National Taxpayers Union, once said they were "yet another example of Congress run amok. The end results of this system are huge costs for taxpayers and incentives for members to stay longer and longer." [2]

Congressional pensions are not only generous but also more secure than private-sector plans. It would take an act of Congress to change them, after all. And even felons such as former Rep. Randy "Duke" Cunningham, R-Calif. — who pleaded guilty to taking $2 million in bribes — can continue to collect their payments while in prison. (Two Democratic senators recently introduced a bill to cancel pensions in such instances.) [3]

But it's not true, as many Web sites claim, that congressmen pay no Social Security taxes. Between Social Security and their pension plan, members of Congress contribute about 8 percent of their salaries to their own retirement coverage — a higher percentage than most federal employees.

[1] Patrick J. Purcell, "Retirement Benefits for Members of Congress," Congressional Research Service, Jan. 21, 2005.

[2] Jennifer S. Thomas, "Congress Taking Look at Its Pensions," *The St. Petersburg Times*, Jan. 28, 1995, p. A1.

[3] George E. Condon Jr., "Cunningham Has Become a Symbol of Corruption," Copley News Service, Feb. 9, 2006.

has experienced an unprecedented rash of failures, with too many companies making pension promises they couldn't keep. Their failures, in turn, have put pressure on healthier companies, which have had to both take up the slack in funding the federal pension-guarantee system and compete against businesses that have sloughed part of their labor costs onto the government.

The Bush administration has grown concerned that the string of billion-dollar bankruptcies could lead to a taxpayer bailout of the private pension system. PBGC is funded by contributions from corporate pension sponsors, who currently pay $30 a year per plan participant. But the fund now owes $22.8 billion more than it has in reserves.

The administration has supported tightening funding requirements and wants to see pension accounting become both clearer and more transparent to workers and auditors. It also wants to restrict companies from making unrealistic pension promises.

"The maze that has been created by the current funding rules is virtually incomprehensible," Labor Secretary Elaine Chao said in a recent speech outlining the administration's proposals. "If the government is going to ensure that companies can prudently plan for their workers' retirement, employers shouldn't need a rocket scientist to do so." [27]

Members of Congress have had to walk a tightrope as they work to turn the administration's ideas into legislation. Most agree pensions should be better funded, but there's little desire to ask taxpayers to assume responsibility for bailing out troubled funds — especially when most taxpayers don't have traditional pensions themselves. There's also concern that if funding rules become too stringent, more and more companies will get out of defined-benefit pensions.

"The key to all this is trying to strike a balance between improving the financial condition of both the PBGC and employer plans, yet recognize that this is a voluntary system," says Larry Sher director of retirement policy at Buck Consultants, in New York. "The last thing you want to do is push more and more companies out of the system and end up with very few defined-benefit plans left — and those that are left poorly funded."

Should Congress give airlines more time to pay down their pension debt?

YES Duane Woerth
President, Air Line Pilots Association International (ALPA)

From testimony before House Subcommittee on Aviation, June 22, 2005

Our industry has lost over $30 billion in the last four years and is projected to lose at least $5 billion this year. . . . When we add to this grim financial condition the factors of historically low interest rates and poor stock-market returns, we have a "perfect storm" for the pension woes we currently face. As a result of this witches' brew, we are on guard for even more pension-plan terminations. . . .

But ALPA believes these drastic results can be avoided with creativity and foresight — and appropriate legislative reforms.

Logically, since a pension plan is a long-term proposition, it should be funded over the long term. This would require reasonably predictable, level, periodic contributions, similar to the way homeowners pay their mortgage.

But when a deficit-reduction contribution is required . . . extraordinarily large contributions [are] required over very brief periods of time. This is like asking homeowners to pay off their 30-year house mortgage as if it were a car loan — over only three to five years — far too short a time to meet far too large an obligation.

But the devastating consequences of more pension-plan terminations in the airline industry can be avoided if appropriate legislation is enacted now. We believe the current pension-funding crisis is only temporary.

Given sufficient time, we believe that interest rates will rise, stock-market performance will improve and airline profitability will return. Sound retirement policy should not allow an employer to break its pension promise to employees just because of negative economic and financial conditions expected to last only a few short years. This is especially so when such negative conditions are viewed in the context of a pension plan, the duration of which is measured in decades.

Under current law, the only way an airline can avoid burdensome pension costs is by entering bankruptcy and terminating the plans. But if more and more airlines choose to shed their pension liabilities in bankruptcy, it sets up the potential for the "domino effect," in which all the other legacy carriers are incentivized, or even forced, to file bankruptcy in order to achieve the same cost savings and "level the playing field."

We believe that providing relief from the deficit-reduction contribution rules will go a long way toward removing the pension-plan termination incentive to enter bankruptcy, and will, as a result, help prevent further bankruptcies in the U.S. airline industry.

NO Bradley D. Belt
Executive Director, Pension Benefit Guaranty Corporation

From testimony before House Subcommittee on Aviation, June 22, 2005

Congress and the administration have been sympathetic to the plight of the airline industry. After Sept. 11, [2001] Congress created the Air Transportation Stabilization Board to administer up to $10 billion in loan guarantees to help [the] struggling industry.

Today, nearly four years later and with passenger traffic at record levels, the plea from certain carriers is for a different form of loan guarantee. That is what pension-funding rule changes represent — a loan from the pension plan to the company, co-signed by the PBGC [Pension Benefit Guaranty Corporation] and underwritten primarily by financially healthy companies whose premiums finance the insurance program.

Pension underfunding is neither an accident nor the result of forces beyond a company's control. On the contrary, it is a largely predictable and controllable byproduct of decisions made by corporate management. In the case of the airlines, a series of decisions allowed pensions to become significantly underfunded. Companies did not contribute as much cash as they could when times were good, and in certain cases contributed no cash at all when it was needed most. In some cases, they granted generous benefit increases that are proving difficult to afford.

These issues are not unique to the airline industry. We saw the same weaknesses lead to the same bad outcomes with the steel industry a few years ago. . . . Because the PBGC receives no federal tax dollars, and its obligations are not backed by the full faith and credit of the United States, losses suffered by the insurance fund must, under current law, be covered by higher premiums.

Not only will healthy companies be subsidizing weak companies with underfunded plans, they may also face the prospect of having to compete against a rival firm that has shifted a significant portion of its ongoing labor costs onto the government — clearly at issue in the airline industry.

Companies that sponsor pension plans have a responsibility to live up to the promises they have made to their workers and retirees. Yet under current law, financially troubled companies have shortchanged their pension promises by nearly $100 billion, putting workers, responsible companies and taxpayers at risk.

It is difficult to imagine that healthy companies would want to continue in a retirement system . . . in which the sponsor-financed insurance fund is running a substantial deficit. By eliminating unfair exemptions from risk-based premiums and restoring the PBGC to financial health, the administration's proposal will revitalize the defined-benefit system.

Steelworkers at the United Steelworkers local in River Rouge, Mich., listen to a discussion of their battered industry in March 2002. Steel firms that have filed for bankruptcy in recent years have presented unfunded pension claims in excess of $1 billion each to the Pension Benefit Guaranty Corporation.

Congress recently raised annual PBGC premiums from $19 to $30 per participant per year. Because such a move raises revenue, it was included in the fiscal 2006 budget package, which cleared Congress on Feb. 1. "No one is doing cartwheels about that," says Aliya Wong, director of pension policy for the U.S. Chamber of Commerce, but she thinks employers can live with it.

The rest of the pension-reform package still must be hashed out in a Senate-House conference.

The bill passed by the Senate on Nov. 16 would require companies to fund 100 percent of their pension obligations, giving underfunded companies seven years to make up the difference. If their plans are less than 80 percent funded at the end of seven years, companies would be barred from promising any additional benefit increases. [28] The bill also would require regulatory agencies to consider a company's credit rating, assuming that those with "junk-bond" status would be more likely to default. Fearing the measure will hurt automakers, Michigan's two Democratic senators cast the only votes against it.

Many companies complain that they are penalized, through excise taxes, if they contribute extra to their plans in good years. "Right now, there are rules that prevent companies from putting in extra money during market upticks, or when the business cycle is in their favor," says Shepler, of the National Association of Manufacturers. On the premise that such contributions are helpful in the long run, the House bill, passed Dec. 15, would allow employers to make additional deductible contributions to plans funded up to 150 percent of their current liability. (The Senate bill would allow contributions up to 180 percent.)

As with the Senate bill, the House measure also freezes benefits when plans are less than 80 percent funded. But the Senate measure gives airlines 20 years to make up any underfunding — a provision not included in the House bill. And the Bush administration has threatened to veto any bill that gives preference to a single industry. Supporters of the amendment, however, oppose burdening struggling airlines with more pension contributions than they can afford.

Cash-Balance Plans

Business leaders also are watching the regulation of so-called hybrid, or cash-balance plans, which combine features of traditional pensions and defined-contribution plans. Under a cash-balance plan, an employer sets up an account for each employee and funds it much like a traditional pension plan, with the employer paying the whole cost. Once the employee retires, the employer pays out the balance but is not responsible for making additional payments. The plans can be portable, so the employees can carry balances along to their next job.

"Cash-balance plans are the future," says Graff, of the American Society of Pension Professionals and Actuaries. "There's a whole world of companies that don't have defined-benefit plans at all, and a lot are thinking about the cash-balance design."

Cash-balance plans are widely used in Japan and have been fairly popular in the United States. Their growth was hampered, though, when a judge ruled in 2003 that IBM's cash-balance plan discriminated against older workers, who stood to lose money during the conversion from their traditional pension plan. Other courts have looked favorably on the plans, but businesses say Congress needs to clarify that the plans pass legal muster. Both of the pending pension-reform measures attempt to do that.

"Clearly, there needs to be greater legal certainty attached to being able to offer cash-balance plans," says the PBGC's Belt.

Regardless of the final state of the legislation, tougher accounting rules are inevitable. In November, the Financial Accounting Standards Board (FASB) announced that by the end of 2006 it would put forward new rules that "would take the effect of pension obligations out of the footnotes and [put them] directly onto corporate balance sheets," according to the Center on Federal Financial Institutions. [29] Moreover, by 2009, FASB will recommend comprehensive changes to all aspects of pension accounting.

Although the coming new standards promise greater clarity and less underfunding, they could have the unintended effect of pushing more companies out of traditional pensions. More companies are expected to be tempted to move their pension investments away from stocks and into bonds, which pay a fixed rate of return. That would reduce the volatility of their plan's assets but would cost companies more up front because they would have to put more into the plan initially.

Boston University economist Kotlikoff favors more investments in the safer but generally lower-performing bond market. "There's no reason that a firm that makes a commitment to pay somebody a pension, which is really a bond-like liability, should then be allowed to take money and gamble in the stock market, and if it does poorly make taxpayers pay for it," he says. Most pension managers today split their investments, putting about 60 percent in stocks and 40 percent in bonds.

Some pension managers, however, have steeply increased their investments in risky hedge funds: Pension investments in hedge funds are expected to reach $300 billion by 2008, up from $5 billion a decade ago. [30]

Despite the risk, pension managers have been lining up to invest. "We are trying to meet our 8 percent [rate of return], so our board decided to look at other investment options," said Roselyn Spencer, executive director of the City of Baltimore Employees' Retirement System,

which has put about $55 million, or 5 percent of its assets, in hedge funds. [31]

If rule changes force pension managers to invest more conservatively, effectively forcing businesses to increase their cash contributions, more companies probably would freeze their defined-benefit plans, refuse to cover new workers or even terminate their pensions altogether.

"If they get too tough and demand too much reality, it will throw everybody out of this business," says North Carolina Treasurer Moore, who oversees one of the few traditional state pension plans that is 100 percent funded as well as the nation's largest public 401(k) plan.

Public Pensions

Pension plans for government workers don't have to be fully funded, and most aren't. They operate under a different set of rules than private companies. Governments only need to keep enough cash on hand to pay out that year's benefits. But many are struggling to do even that.

According to Wilshire Associates Inc., Illinois ranks worst among the 50 states in its per capita unfunded pension liability, averaging $3,406 for each state resident, or a 2004 funding level of just 42.6 percent (meaning there were assets to cover less than half the amount the state would expect to pay out). Chicago's Civic Federation reports that Illinois has not funded its full pension bill in 35 years, and its five major funds are $35 billion in the red — more than 80 percent of the state's annual budget of $43 billion. At least 16 other states are in worse shape: Their pension deficits exceed their total annual budgets. [32]

The situation is the same in many localities. "It was always easy to pay off the retirees by promising money in the future, but knowing that appropriating the money was the next council's job, the next governor's job," says Wyss of Standard & Poor's.

Many legislatures and localities will have to invest large sums in their pension systems this year or make them less generous. That may be tough politically, as Gov. Schwarzenegger found last year when he attempted to shift state employees into a 401(k)-style retirement plan. Firefighters and public-safety officers balked, and the fallout damaged Schwarzenegger's entire "reform" agenda. Alaska, however, succeeded in shifting its employees to a defined-contribution system last year, and Michigan has closed its defined-benefit pension plan to some new employees. Other legislatures — including Colorado,

New Jersey and New Mexico — are looking at less drastic changes, such as having employees contribute more to their pensions or paying out benefits at a later age.

Several states have started defined-contribution plans and are offering their employees the choice between enrolling in them or a traditional pension plan. "This compromise does not really change much," writes Lowenstein, the financial writer. "Most employees who are given the choice opt, quite naturally, to keep their pensions." [33]

OUTLOOK

Continuing Pressure

Despite the current challenges, it's too early to write off traditional defined-benefit plans, most of which are well-funded. Many observers believe Congress can breathe new life into the pension system by straightening out the rules on cash-balance plans, which are generous to employees but eliminate employers' fear of unknown liabilities. Clarifying funding rules for traditional pension plans in ways that are acceptable to the business community will also relieve a lot of pressure.

"With appropriate changes in law, I think we will be able to meet the challenges down the road," says Belt of the Pension Benefit Guaranty Corporation.

Salisbury, of the Employee Benefit Research Institute (EBRI), is more skeptical. To make plans more secure, he says, companies will have to put more money in them, which will prove a bitter pill.

"At this point, the Senate bill, the House bill and the administration proposal all are likely to hasten the decline of defined-benefit plans and in the long term harm the PBGC, even though in the short term they will strengthen PBGC's cash flow," Salisbury adds. If such provisions pass, "A very large number of plan sponsors say it will cause them to consider freezing or terminating plans."

If most individuals determine that traditional, defined-benefit pension plans offer more security, but fewer employers believe they can afford to provide them, what is the likely outcome as the baby boomers reach retirement age? Most observers believe individual workers will face increased responsibility for their own retirements — and that many of them will fall short financially.

"There has to be some sort of replacement for the assets that defined-benefit plans pay people — there are

over \$2 trillion in defined-benefit plans," says Shepler, of the National Association of Manufacturers. "I'm not saying defined-contribution plans are bad, but the trends show that people are just not amassing the large amounts of wealth that people figured they would when they put these plans in."

States such as Texas are stepping up their financial-education efforts and, as word gets out that individuals will have to take more responsibility for their own retirements, more Americans may do a better job saving. EBRI has found that about two-thirds of Americans say they are behind on their personal savings, but almost all of them believe they can catch up. They may get some help from Congress, which is considering making employee enrollment in 401(k) plans automatic in most cases. Investment broker Merrill Lynch has run magazine advertisements recently comparing the retirement portfolios of older parents and their middle-aged children, suggesting that younger people face "more potential pitfalls."

Veteran pension consultant Rappaport warns that the fashionable, current idea — of making people work longer so they can save more for retirement and put fewer years of strain on their pension plans — may fall short. "It's great for people to plan to work later," she says, "but one of the things we've been finding in our research is that almost four out of 10 people retire earlier than they had planned to, due to health or losing a job."

Thus, today's workers will not only have to change their savings habits but will also have to worry about future cuts to Social Security and government retiree health coverage, which appear to be unsustainable at current levels.

"It all adds up to a probable declining standard of living for retirees, compared with what we have expected to see," says The American College's McFadden.

NOTES

1. Adam Geller, "When a Pension's Not There," *The Philadelphia Inquirer*, Dec. 31, 2005, p. D1.

2. The Associated Press, "Pension Deficit Is Expected to Surge," *Los Angeles Times*, Sept. 16, 2005, p. C3.

3. Eduardo Porter and Mary Williams Walsh, "Benefits Go the Way of Pensions," *The New York Times*, Feb. 9, 2006, p. C1.

4. Quoted in Adriel Bettelheim, "Moving to Close the Pension Gap," *CQ Weekly*, Oct. 1, 2005, p. 2624; for background, see Mary H. Cooper, "Employee Benefits," *CQ Researcher*, Feb. 4, 2000, pp. 65-88.

5. Martha Paskoff Welsh, "The Role of Congress in Pension Defaults," The Century Foundation, June 15, 2005; www.tcf.org/list.asp?type=NC&pubid=1034.

6. National Center for Health Statistics, "National Vital Statistics Reports," Sept. 18, 2003; www.cdc.gov/nchs.

7. "Now for the Reckoning", *The Economist*, Oct. 15, 2005, Special Report (2).

8. Roger Lowenstein, "The End of Pensions?" *The New York Times Magazine*, Oct. 30, 2005.

9. "Employee Benefits in Private Industry," National Compensation Survey, Bureau of Labor Statistics, March 2005.

10. Steven A. Sass, *The Promise of Private Pensions* (1997), p. 4.

11. James A. Wooten, *The Employee Retirement Security Act of 1974* (2004), p. 20.

12. For background, see Mary H. Cooper, "Retirement Security," *CQ Researcher*, May 31, 2002, pp. 481-504.

13. Quoted in Dan M. McGill, *Fundamentals of Private Pensions* (4th ed.), 1979, p. 17.

14. Sass, *op. cit.*, p. 61.

15. James H. Schulz, *The Economics of Aging* (6th ed.), 1995, p. 227.

16. Sass, *op. cit.*, p. 101.

17. *Ibid.*, p. 118.

18. McGill, *op. cit.*, p. 18.

19. Lowenstein, *op. cit.*, p. 56.

20. Wooten, *op. cit.*, p. 76.

21. Quoted in *ibid.*, p. 169.

22. Sass, *op. cit.*, p. 225.

23. For background, *Congress and the Nation, Vol. IV: 1973-1976* (1977), p. 690.

24. Donald L. Bartlett and James B. Steele, "The Broken Promise," *Time*, Oct. 31, 2005, p. 47.

25. Lowenstein, *op. cit.*, p. 56.

26. *Ibid.*

27. Quoted in "Elaine Chao Delivers Remarks at the National Press Club on Retirement Security," *CQ Transcriptions*, Jan. 10, 2005.

28. See Michael R. Crittenden, "Senate Solidly Backs Pension Rewrite," *CQ Weekly*, Nov. 18, 2005, p. 3138.

29. Douglas J. Elliott, "PBGC: Effects of Proposed Accounting Changes," Center on Federal Financial Institutions, Nov. 14, 2005.

30. Riva D. Atlas and Mary Williams Walsh, "Pension Officers Putting Billions Into Hedge Funds," *The New York Times*, Nov. 27, 2005, p. A1.

31. Ben White, "As Hedge Funds Go Mainstream, Risk Is Magnified," *The Washington Post*, Aug. 11, 2005, p. D1.

32. Peter Harkness, "Shortfalls in the Long Haul," *CQ Weekly*, Oct. 28, 2005, p. 2898.

33. Lowenstein, *op. cit.*, p. 56.

BIBLIOGRAPHY

Books

Sass, Steven A., *The Promise of Private Pensions: The First 100 Years*, Harvard University Press, 1997.
The associate director of the Center for Retirement Research at Boston College concludes that traditional pensions have faltered in recent years because of the decline of labor unions and the old-line corporations that supported them.

Wooten, James. A., *The Employee Retirement Security Act of 1974: A Political History*, University of California Press, 2004.
A law professor at the State University of New York at Buffalo shows how Congress overcame strong opposition from business to make pension funding a policy matter of national importance.

Articles

Atlas, Riva D., and Mary Williams Walsh, "Pension Officers Putting Billions Into Hedge Funds," *The New York Times*, Nov. 27, 2005, p. A1.
Pension plans and other large institutions are expected to put $300 billion into lightly regulated hedge-fund investments.

Bartlett, Donald L., and James B. Steele, "The Broken Promise," *Time*, Oct. 31, 2005, p. 32.
Veteran reporters conclude that congressional rules have made it easy for unscrupulous corporations to mismanage their pension funds and rip off retirees.

Bettelheim, Adriel, "Moving to Close the Pension Gap," *CQ Weekly*, Oct. 1, 2005, p. 2624.
The writer puts the current congressional debate over pension policy into historical context.

"Corrupt Conspiracy: Internal Memo Details Crooked Pension Scheme," *The San Diego Union-Tribune*, Oct. 6, 2005, p. B10.
A newspaper editorial outlines how alleged collusion between San Diego officials and the pension board led to the city underfunding its pension plan by $1.4 billion.

Greenhouse, Steven, "Transit Strike Reflects Nationwide Pension Woes," *The New York Times*, Dec. 24, 2005, p. A1.
A holiday transit strike in New York City over pensions and other benefits was emblematic of public-finance problems across the country.

Hakin, Danny, "For a G.M. Family, the American Dream Vanishes," *The New York Times*, Nov. 19, 2005, p. A1.
Four generations of the Roy family have relied on General Motors for employment, but they sense its good jobs and retirement plans have drawn to an end.

Harkness, Peter, "Shortfalls in the Long Haul," *CQ Weekly*, Oct. 28, 2005, p. 2898.
The publisher of *Governing* magazine examines the reasons why pensions have become a major thorn irritating the skins of state and local government officials.

Hinden, Stan, "Ready, Set . . . Retire?" *The Washington Post*, Dec. 25, 2005, p. B1.
A former retirement columnist warns that problems with private pensions, Social Security and health-insurance programs will cause a troubled old age for baby boomers.

Lowenstein, Roger, "The End of Pensions?" *The New York Times Magazine*, Oct. 30, 2005, p. 56.
A business writer suggests that government rules allowing corporations to underfund their pension systems caused the current woes. He argues that defined-contribution plans, such as 401(k) accounts, should be more carefully regulated because so many more people now depend on them.

Peterson, Jonathan, "Airline Execs Seek Revised Pension Rules," *Los Angeles Times*, June 8, 2005, p. C1.
The chief executives of Delta and Northwest airlines told the Senate they would need more time to properly fund their pension plans or they would be forced into bankruptcy. (Both airlines went bankrupt in September.)

Russakoff, Dale, "Human Toll of a Pension Default," *The Washington Post*, June 13, 2005, p. A1.
The failure of United Airlines' pension plan has put a strain on thousands of workers.

Walsh, Mary Williams, "Pensions: Big Holes in the Net," *The New York Times*, April 12, 2005, p. G1.
Despite regulations, it's almost impossible for plan participants to determine the financial health or underlying rules governing their pensions.

Reports and Studies

"Information on Cash Balance Plans," Government Accountability Office, October 2005.
Most workers receive bigger benefits under defined-benefit plans, but many companies provide additional money during transitions to cash-balance plans.

Passantino, George, and Adam B. Summers, "The Gathering Pension Storm," Reason Foundation, 2005.
The authors conclude that governments have been slower than the private sector in shifting from traditional pension plans and now promise "extravagant" retirement benefits to workers that are hurting taxpayers.

For More Information

American Society of Pension Professionals & Actuaries, 4245 North Fairfax Dr., Suite 750, Arlington, VA 22203; (703) 516-9300; www.asppa.org. A national organization for career retirement-plan professionals.

Center on Federal Financial Institutions, 1717 K St., N.W., Suite 600, Washington, DC 20036; (202) 347-5770; www.coffi.org. A nonprofit organization focused on the federal government's lending and insurance programs.

Center for Retirement Research, Boston College, Fulton Hall 550, 140 Commonwealth Ave., Chestnut Hill, MA 02467-3808; (617) 552-1762; www.bc.edu/centers/crr/index.shtml. A center devoted to research of retirement issues that fosters communication between academics and policymakers.

Employee Benefit Research Institute, 2121 K St., N.W., Suite 600, Washington, DC 20037-1896; (202) 659-0670; www.ebri.org. A research organization that studies employee-benefit programs and public policy affecting them.

Employee Benefits Security Administration, U.S. Department of Labor, 200 Constitution Ave., N.W., Washington, DC 20210; (866) 444-3272; www.dol.gov /ebsa. Federal agency responsible for the regulation of pension and welfare benefit plans.

Pension Benefit Guaranty Corporation, 1200 K St., N.W., Suite 120, Washington, DC 20005-4026; (202) 326-4000; www.pbgc.gov. A federal corporation that insures private pension plans.

Pension Research Council, Wharton School of the University of Pennsylvania, 3620 Locust Walk, 3000 Steinberg Hall-Dietrich Hall, Philadelphia, PA 19104; (215) 898-7620; prc.wharton.upenn.edu/ prc/prc.html. An academic center that sponsors research on private pensions, Social Security and related benefit plans.

Pension Rights Center, 1350 Connecticut Ave., N.W., Suite 206, Washington, DC 20036; (202) 296-3776; www.pensionrights.org. An advocacy group dedicated to protecting pension recipients.

U.S. Chamber of Commerce, 1615 H St., N.W., Washington, DC 20062-2000; (202) 659-6000; www. uschamber.com. A federation representing 3 million businesses as well as trade associations and state and local chambers.

13

Rebuilding New Orleans

Peter Katel

The working-class Lower Ninth Ward was among the hardest-hit New Orleans neighborhoods. A rebuilding plan proposed by the Bring New Orleans Back Commission in early January would give residents a role in deciding whether heavily flooded neighborhoods would be resettled. An earlier plan by the Urban Land Institute sparked controversy among African-Americans when it proposed abandoning unsafe areas, including parts of the Lower Ninth.

From *CQ Researcher,*
February 3, 2006.

Hurricane Katrina's floodwaters surged through tens of thousands of houses in New Orleans, including Dennis and Linda Scott's tidy, two-story brick home on Farwood Drive. The first floor has since been gutted, the ruined furnishings and appliances discarded.

Five months after floodwaters breached the city's levees and drainage canals, every other house for miles around is in the same deplorable shape. [1]

Like the Scotts, most of the residents who evacuated the sprawling New Orleans East area cannot decide whether to return, uncertain if their solidly middle class, mostly African-American neighborhoods will ever come back to life.

The disaster that began when Katrina's Category 3 winds hit New Orleans on Aug. 29, 2005, grinds on. [2] Yet the Scotts and their neighbors feel lucky to be alive.

"I'm one of the fortunate ones," says Scott, 47, who fled to Houston with his wife before the storm hit.

Linda's teaching job was swept away when the floods closed down the schools, so she's staying in Texas while Dennis works on the house and goes to his job as a communications specialist at Louis Armstrong International Airport. Their next-door neighbors, an elderly couple who stayed home, were drowned. Some three-quarters of Louisiana's 1,070 Katrina deaths occurred in New Orleans, where about 70 percent of the victims were age 60 and older. [3]

But "the east" is not alone. Similar devastation also afflicts some older neighborhoods, where lush gardens and sprawling villas reflect the city's French and Spanish heritage. [4]

Flooding Affected Most of Greater New Orleans

Flood water up to 20 feet deep covered more than three-quarters of New Orleans when storm surges pushed by Hurricane Katrina breached levees in 34 places. The Lower Ninth Ward and the New Orleans East district were among the hardest-hit areas.

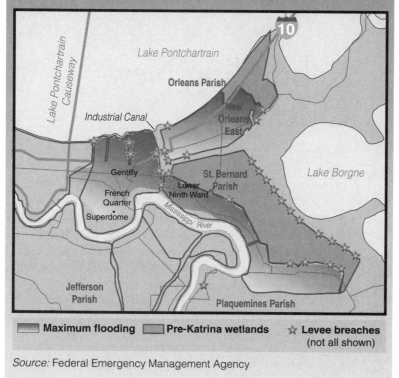

Legend: Maximum flooding   Pre-Katrina wetlands   ☆ Levee breaches (not all shown)

Source: Federal Emergency Management Agency

Losses in destroyed and damaged property, added to losses resulting from the shrinkage of the city's economy, amount roughly to $35 billion, estimates Stan Fulcher, research director of the Louisiana Recovery Authority in Baton Rouge.

Most residents are still gone, largely because most jobs — except those that involve either tearing down houses or fixing them up — have disappeared. Plans are only starting to be made to rebuild the city, and no one knows how much reconstruction money will be available.

Does Scott have a future in New Orleans? "I'm on hold," he replies.

That response comes up a lot among the city's residents and evacuees, often accompanied by a sense that the rest of the country has moved on — or views the French-founded, majority-African-American city as somehow foreign or not worth rebuilding.

"This is America you're talking about," lawyer Walter I. Willard says in frustration.

So American, in fact, that jazz was born there — amid a culture formed by the peculiarities of the city's slavery and segregation traditions. [9] "The West Africans [slaves] were allowed to play their music in Congo Square on Sundays. That happened nowhere else in the United States," famed New Orleans-born trumpeter Wynton Marsalis says. [10]

Slavery's legacy of racial and class divide has been part of the Katrina story from the beginning. New Orleans is two-thirds African-American, and the thousands of impoverished residents who were without cars to flee the approaching hurricane were overwhelmingly black. [11] "As all of us saw on television," President Bush acknowledged, "there's . . . some deep, persistent poverty in this region. That poverty has roots in a history of racial discrimination, which cut off generations from the opportunity of America." [12]

The continuing devastation mocks President Bush's stirring promise two weeks after the storm to mount "one of the largest reconstruction efforts the world has ever seen." [5]

Indeed, when the Senate Homeland Security and Governmental Affairs Committee toured the city four months later, members were "stunned" to see that "so much hasn't been done," said Chairwoman Susan Collins, R-Maine. [6]

Floodwaters up to 20 feet deep covered about 80 percent of the city and didn't recede until late September. [7] Fully half the city's homes — 108,731 dwellings — suffered flooding at least four feet deep, according to the Bring New Orleans Back Commission (BNOBC) formed by Mayor Ray Nagin. In some neighborhoods, Hurricane Rita, which struck later in September, brought additional flooding. [8]

Bush also conceded that the federal response to Katrina amounted to less than what its victims were entitled to — a point reinforced in early 2006, when Sen. Collins' committee released a strikingly accurate prediction of Katrina's likely effects, prepared for the White House two days *before* Katrina hit. [13]

But in a sense, New Orleans was crumbling from within even before the floods washed over the city. "The city had a lot of economic and social problems before — economics, race, poverty, crime, drugs," says musician and Xavier University Prof. Michael White. "Our failure to deal with harsh realities has sometimes been the problem."

In 2004, for example, the city's homicide rate hit 59 per 100,000 — the nation's highest. [14]

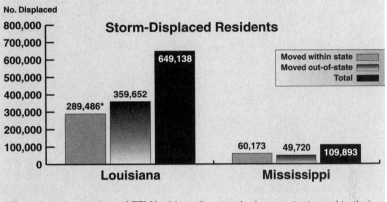

More Than 400,000 Residents Left Home States

Six times more Louisiana residents are still displaced from their homes than Mississippians. Of the more than 750,000 residents from both states displaced by Katrina, more than half are still living outside their home states.

Storm-Displaced Residents

* Based on the number of FEMA aid applicants who have not returned to their pre-Katrina addresses.

Source: Louisiana Recovery Authority

In that post-Katrina climate — fed by bitter memories of institutional racism — the African-American community is concerned that developers are planning to reduce the black portion of the city's population. U.S. Housing and Urban Development Secretary Alphonso Jackson, who is African-American, intensified those fears when he said, "New Orleans is not going to be as black as it was for a long time, if ever again." [15]

The concern remained an issue into early 2006, when Mayor Nagin, also African-American, declared on Jan. 16 that the city "should be a chocolate New Orleans . . . a majority-African-American city. It's the way God wants it to be." [16] The following day, after furious reactions from both the white and black communities, Nagin apologized. [17]

Nagin's provocative language aside, fears of a demographic shift seem well-founded. In late January, sociologist John R. Logan of Brown University said he had conducted a study that showed about 80 percent of New Orleans' black residents were unlikely to come back, in part because their neighborhoods wouldn't be rebuilt. [18]

The BNOBC sparked the most recent chapter of the race and redevelopment debate. The commission's rebuilding plan, unveiled in early January, would give

residents of the most heavily flooded neighborhoods four months to help figure out if their districts could be resettled. Homeowners in neighborhoods that can't be revived could sell their houses to a government-financed corporation for 100 percent of the pre-Katrina values, minus insurance payouts and mortgage obligations. The overall plan would cost more than $18 billion. [19] Federal, state and city approval is needed. [20]

Nowhere did the commission say that the poorest and most heavily damaged African-American neighborhoods should be abandoned. But the Washington-based Urban Land Institute (ULI), flatly recommended against extensive rebuilding in the most flood-prone areas, by implication including much of the working-class, largely African-American Lower Ninth Ward. [21]

Under the Jim Crow segregation system that lasted into the 1960s, residents point out, the Lower Ninth was the only place where African-Americans could buy property. "These people struggled to buy a little bit of land they could call home," says contractor Algy Irvin, 60, standing in the wrecked living room of his mother's house on Egania Street.

Irvin recalls earning $35 a week mopping hospital floors and paying $18 a week for his own $1,200 lot on

Can New Orleans' Musical Culture Be Saved?

Sunpie and the Louisiana Sunspots have the crowd at the House of Blues rocking as the group pounds out "Iko-Iko," a New Orleans standard with Creole lyrics and an irresistible beat.

The first night of Carnival is under way in the French Quarter, and the club is filling up for a long evening of music, with three more acts to follow. In the less touristy Marigny neighborhood, jazz pianist Ellis Marsalis is starting a slightly more sedate set at popular Snug Harbor.

Four months after Katrina hit, New Orleans is making music again. "So far, it's gone better than I would have thought, given the total lack of tourism," says Barry Smith, proprietor of the Louisiana Music Factory, where CDs and vinyl records of New Orleans artists account for some three-quarters of the stock of jazz, blues and gospel artists — both world-renowned and known only to locals. "I've definitely experienced a big increase in the number of local customers coming to the store, and a lot of the people who came here to work — from construction workers to Red Cross volunteers."

Few if any places in the United States come even close to New Orleans as an incubator of musical style and talent. As far back as 1819, a visitor wrote about the African music being played at Congo Square. And by the early 20th century, a musical tradition had formed in which Louis Armstrong — arguably the century's most influential musician — came of age. [1]

"All American music in the 20th century was profoundly shaped and influenced by New Orleans music," Tom Piazza writes in *Why New Orleans Matters.* [2]

The career of famed musician/producer Allen Toussaint illustrates the city's musical power. Toussaint wrote such 1960s hits as "Mother in Law" and produced and arranged the 1973 hit "Right Place, Wrong Time" for fellow New Orleans resident "Dr. John," as well as the disco standard "Lady Marmelade."

"He helped invent things we take as everyday in music — certain beats, certain arrangements," his partner in a record label said recently. [3]

Toussaint fled New Orleans after Katrina and has spoken optimistically of the city's future prospects. [4] But away from the club scene and music stores, the future looks less bright.

That's because the city's music springs from the very streets that Katrina emptied — the fabled "social aid and pleasure clubs," fraternal organizations that sponsor the Mardi Gras "Indian tribes," as well as the brass-band funeral processions that nourished jazz. All these influential institutions are maintained by people who mostly live paycheck to paycheck, says Michael White, a clarinetist and music scholar who holds an endowed chair in arts and humanities at New Orleans' Xavier University. [5]

nearby Tupelo Street — now also a ruin. "You can see why people don't want a fat-cat developer coming in, making millions," he says, giving voice to a common suspicion that declaring the neighborhood unsafe is merely a cheap means of clearing out its present inhabitants to make way for lucrative development. But Irvin adds, "If people are compensated, that's another story."

Post-Katrina television coverage also gave the impression that New Orleans' African-American population was uniformly poor. In fact, the city had a substantial black middle class. "I had no clue that people couldn't get out of here," says Anne LaBranche, an African-American from New Orleans East, who returned to the city in January after staying with friends in Birmingham, Ala. "I do not know a person who doesn't own a car."

The LaBranches are moving into a house owned by her father-in-law. Her physician husband Emile, whose family practice was destroyed by Katrina along with all the patients' records, has been looking for work. But other medical offices say they aren't hiring until they know how many people are coming back.

Across town, Cory Matthews, 30, a medical-technology salesman, also wonders whether he still has a place in the city. He is rebuilding the flood-damaged Uptown house he shares with his girlfriend, but as he puts up new Sheetrock and rewires, he worries that his physician customer base has shrunk. "I'm hoping we're making the right move," he says.

Certainly, nobody is expecting redevelopment to bring speedy population growth. An estimated 135,000 people remain in New Orleans — less than a third of the 462,000 pre-Katrina population. Nagin's commission

The New Orleans establishment recognizes the problem. "Financial losses for social aid and pleasure clubs, Mardi Gras Indian tribes and [brass band] second-line companies are conservatively estimated at over $3 million," the Bring New Orleans Back Commission reports. [6]

"These were poor people, but people who spent a lot of money on these events," says White, a New Orleans native who comes from a long line of musicians. "The thing of money is serious. If people don't have jobs, they're not going to be able to participate."

White himself suffered another kind of loss — his vast collection of vintage instruments and memorabilia that included a trumpet mouthpiece from jazz saint Sidney Bechet; 4,000 rare CDs and even rarer vinyl recordings; photographs of New Orleans musical legends and notes and tapes of interviews with musicians who have since died. All were stored at his house — and it's all gone.

Is resurrecting an entire popular culture any more possible than restoring White's collection? "It's not like there's

Courtesy www.ellismarsalis.com

Legendary jazz pianist Ellis Marsalis is a popular performer in Old New Orleans, which was largely spared by the flooding.

a central entity that can be rebuilt," says Piazza. "What steps can be taken to repatriate as many members of the African-American community and other communities — people who don't have the same kinds of resources as others to come back and rebuild, or who lived in areas where logistical challenges to rebuilding are all but insurmountable? That is the most difficult question about cultural renewal."

[1] For background, see Geoffrey C. Ward and Ken Burns, *Jazz: A History of America's Music* (2000), pp. 7-16; 40-46.

[2] Tom Piazza, *Why New Orleans Matters* (2005), p. 37.

[3] Quoted in Deborah Sontag, "Heat, and Piano, Back in New Orleans," *The New York Times*, Sept. 20, 2005, p. E1; for additional background see, "Inductees: Allen Toussaint," Rock+Roll Hall of Fame and Museum, undated, http://rockhall.com/hof/inductee.asp?id=200.

[4] *Ibid.*

[5] Ward and Burns, *op. cit.*, pp. 7-16.

[6] "Report of the Cultural Committee, Mayor's Bring New Orleans Back Commission," Jan. 17, 2006, pp. 8-9, www.bringneworleansback.org.

projects 247,000 residents by September 2008, while a more optimistic consultant projects 252,000 by early 2007. [22] The totals, however, don't specify whether the residents will be laboring at construction sites or behind desks.

Jay LaPeyre, president of the Business Council of New Orleans and the River Region, says laborers are desperately needed "for every type of manual labor — from skilled electricians and plumbers to low-skilled apprentices and trainees to service jobs at Burger King."

That kind of talk makes white-collar New Orleanians nervous. Tulane University, one of the city's major high-end employers, laid off 230 of its 2,500 professors. [23] Nearly all 7,500 public school employees were laid off as well, though some were rehired by the handful of charter schools that have sprung up. [24]

"It's become a blue-collar market," says Daniel Perez, who lost his night-manager job at the swanky Royal Sonesta Hotel after business dropped off. Perez applied in vain for dozens of professional or managerial jobs. He had almost decided to leave New Orleans before finally landing a position as a sales manager for *USA Today*.

For now, at least, even the service-industry job market is thinning, though the profusion of help-wanted signs in the functioning parts of the city convey a different impression. A planned Feb. 17 reopening of Harrah's Casino, for example, will take place with only half the pre-Katrina payroll of 2,500, says Carla Major, vice president for human resources.

On his Jan. 11 visit, President Bush touted New Orleans as still "a great place to visit." But his motorcade

Katrina Costs Dwarf Previous Disasters

Hurricane Katrina cost the Federal Emergency Management Agency $25 billion in the Gulf Coast — nearly three times more than the 2001 terrorist attacks on the World Trade Center and eight times more than Hurricane Rita, which followed on the heels of Katrina. The money pays for such services as temporary housing, unemployment assistance, crisis counseling and legal aid.

Disaster	FEMA Cost Estimate* ($ in billions)
Hurricane Katrina (2005)	$24.6
World Trade Center (2001)	$8.8
Hurricane Rita (2005)	$3.4
Hurricane Ivan (2004)	$2.6
Hurricane Wilma (2005)	$2.5
Hurricane Georges (1998)	$2.3
Hurricane Andrew (1992)	$1.8
Hurricane Hugo (1989)	$1.3
Loma Prieta Earthquake (1989)	$0.87
Hurricane Alberto (2000)	$0.6

* Flood-insurance reimbursements not included

Source: FEMA, December 2005

had skirted most of the devastation, going nowhere near, for instance, the Scotts' deserted neighborhood. [25]

"We can't move forward until we have positive information on what's happening," Scott says. "There are no banks, no schools, no electricity. We just want to be home."

As officials plan the city's future, here are some of the questions being debated:

Should some neighborhoods not be rebuilt?

The buzzword summing up the single toughest question about New Orleans' future is "footprint." That's urban-planner jargon for a city's shape and the amount of space it occupies. In New Orleans, the term has become code for the idea that flood-prone districts are best turned back into open-space "sponges" to absorb nature's future onslaughts.

But would that help? New Orleans and the entire Gulf Coast are sinking. New Orleans was built on sandy soil to begin with, but oil and gas extraction and upriver levee construction — which reduces the delta area's natural landfill process, called silting — have exacerbated the problem. And sea levels are rising due to global warming. [26] As a result, writes Virginia R. Burkett of the U.S. Geological Survey's National Wetlands Research Center in Louisiana, by 2100 parts of New Orleans "could lie [about 23 feet] below water level during a Category 3 hurricane." [27]

Even so, the extensive levee system was designed to defend the entire metropolitan area from floods. So the Katrina disaster didn't grow out of the development of flood-prone lands that never should have been urbanized, say opponents of shrinking the footprint. Instead, they argue, the catastrophe grew out of human failure in engineering, construction or maintenance — or in all three.

"If we can build levees in Iraq, we can build levees on the Gulf Coast," says Sen. Mary Landrieu, D-La. "And if we can build hospitals in Baghdad and Fallujah, we can most certainly rebuild our hospitals in this metropolitan area." [28]

But congressional power brokers aren't in the mood to redevelop flood-prone areas. "We are committed to helping the people of Louisiana rebuild," said House Appropriations Committee member Rep. Ray LaHood, R-Ill. But, "we are not going to rebuild homes that are going to be destroyed in two years by another flood. We are not just going to throw money at it." [29]

Some who call the flood a man-made failure don't oppose redesigning the city in a more environmentally sensible way — even if it means abandoning their own neighborhoods. "It's not what I want, but I could live with it," says LaBranche, who with her husband owns a home, an office building and rental properties in New Orleans East. "I don't want to go through this again."

But who should decide? "The idea that everybody gets to have what they want" is not practical, says business leader LaPeyre. He wants the government to use its power of eminent domain — the right to condemn private property and compensate the owner — to prevent redevelopment of areas unsuitable for residential and business use. [30]

Private companies, such as utility and insurance companies — will also influence decisions about where development will occur. "The market will do better than most people claim," he says. "If you're not going to have good services, most people will say, 'I don't want to live there.' "

Others argue that a neighborhood's residents should have a big voice. The Bring New Orleans Back Commission proposed letting residents of heavily damaged neighborhoods work with urban and financial planners to determine if their districts could be revived. The "neighborhood planning teams" would have until May to decide. The procedure grew out of opposition to the Urban Land Institute's recommendation against rebuilding in flood-prone areas.

"In an arbitrary and capricious manner to say that these areas — which were populated by black people because they were directed there — should now be turned into green space deepens the wound," says Councilwoman Cynthia Willard-Lewis, who represents several of the city's eastern neighborhoods. Many of the houses can be repaired and the communities brought back, she says, adding that she suspects the plan "was not based on what was safe but on whom they wanted to return."

William Hudnut, a former mayor of Indianapolis who holds the Urban Land Institute's public policy chair, says city leaders do not have the courage to tell residents what they don't want to hear. "The footprint has to be smaller and development more compact," he says. "An honest, tough-minded approach to rebuilding is part of what leadership is all about. It may be that some people would lose their political base or lose their jobs. But if a thing is worth doing, it's worth doing well and worth standing up for."

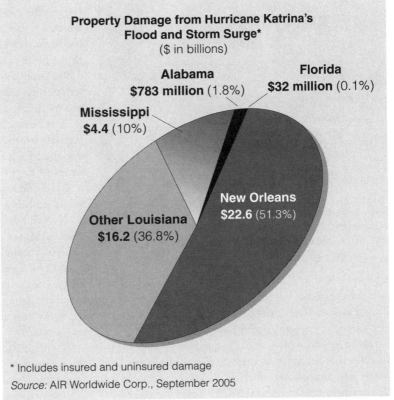

Katrina Saved Worst for New Orleans

Nearly 90 percent of Katrina's flood and storm damage occurred in Louisiana — more than half of it in New Orleans. The other three states affected by Katrina suffered only 12 percent of the damages.

Property Damage from Hurricane Katrina's Flood and Storm Surge*
($ in billions)

Alabama $783 million (1.8%)
Florida $32 million (0.1%)
Mississippi $4.4 (10%)
Other Louisiana $16.2 (36.8%)
New Orleans $22.6 (51.3%)

* Includes insured and uninsured damage

Source: AIR Worldwide Corp., September 2005

Ari Kelman, an environmental historian at the University of California at Davis, concedes that some neighborhoods should be abandoned. At the same time, he says, low-income African-American residents have well-founded fears that any planning and decision system will be stacked against them.

"People who don't have money also don't have power," says Kelman, author of a 2003 book on the interplay between human design and nature in New Orleans. "When politics get cooking in New Orleans, it's likely that the poor are going to get screwed."

Should the levee system be upgraded to guard against a Category 5 storm?

The levee system surrounding New Orleans was designed to withstand a Category 3 hurricane. Katrina

Getting Images/Robyn Beck

Skip LaGrange takes a break from cleaning out his flooded home in the Mid-City section of New Orleans, on Oct. 5, 2005. An estimated 135,000 people are now living in New Orleans — less than a third of the 462,000 pre-Katrina population.

had weakened to Category 3 by the time it made landfall, but the wall of water it sent ashore — the hurricane's "surge" — was born when the storm was still offshore and raging at Category 4 and 5 strength. [31]

So far, official attention has focused on possible errors in design, construction or maintenance of the levees. But many are also asking whether the system should be upgraded to protect against a Category 5 hurricane — the most powerful. Among Louisianans in general and New Orleanians in particular, support for a Category 5 system seems nearly universal.

"I would like to see the levees brought to Category 5 for my safety and that of my family and properties," says LaBranche, the displaced New Orleans homeowner.

But some government experts say a Category 5 levee system is a pipe dream. They point out Category 5 is open-ended, taking in all hurricanes whose winds exceed 155 mph and create storm surges greater than 18 feet. "What's the top end for a Cat 5 hurricane?" asked Dan Hitchings, director of Hurricane Katrina recovery for the Corps of Engineers. "There isn't one." [32]

That argument carries little weight in Louisiana. Some Louisiana lawmakers say that if the below-sea-level Netherlands can protect itself from floods, New Orleans shouldn't settle for less. "They built once-in-1,000-years

flood protection," Sen. Landrieu told a rally of some 75 displaced New Orleanians outside the White House last December. "We don't even have once-in-100-years [protection]."

No hurricanes strike in the North Sea, which surrounds the Netherlands. But the tiny country, some of which lies more than 20 feet below sea level, is vulnerable to powerful storms with winds that can reach 60 mph. Following a 1953 storm that killed more than 1,800 people, the country redesigned its protective system in ways that many New Orleanians say should serve as a model. [33]

The Netherlands system was designed to withstand a once-in-10,000-years storm. New Orleans' levees were designed for a once-in-200-300-years storm, says the Corps of Engineers. [34]

In addition, say Louisiana officials, a Category 5 system would probably cost about $32 billion. [35]

"It will probably be a pretty staggering price tag," acknowledges Craig E. Colten, a geography professor at Louisiana State University in Baton Rouge and author of a recent book on New Orleans' flood-protection history. But the long-term value of property protection would make an upgraded system a wise investment, he added, citing the prosperous Netherlands, an international shipping center.

But Rep. Richard Baker, R-La., cautions that debating a Category 5 upgrade now could distract from the immediate and urgent tasks facing New Orleans. "Construction toward a Category 5 standard would be a decade-long project," he says. "The statistical probabilities of a Category 5 hitting New Orleans are fairly small, especially since we just got hit. I think we have time."

No one denies the need for fixing the existing flood-protection system. The Bush administration has proposed $1.6 billion to restore the system to a Category 3 level of protection, and another $1.5 billion for further improvements. [36] Thus far, however, it has stayed out of the Category 5 argument. At a White House briefing on the new flood-protection plan, Donald E. Powell, the administration's coordinator of post-hurricane recovery projects, would only say that after the proposed improvements, "The levee system will be better, much better, and stronger than it ever has been in the history of New Orleans." [37]

The White House plan also includes a study, backed by Mayor Nagin, of whether a substantial upgrade to the system is needed. A preliminary report is due in May.

However, city officials argue that a system capable of protecting against a Category 5 storm is well within the range of engineering possibilities and would be good for both the city's and the country's economy. "We need to build toward Category 5 to provide . . . assurance to [potential] investors," says Gary P. LaGrange, director of the Port of New Orleans, and to protect the port, an essential part of the nation's trade system.

Should the nation pay for New Orleans to be rebuilt?

So far, Congress has committed $98.9 billion for post-hurricane recovery and rebuilding programs throughout the Gulf Coast, the Senate Budget Committee calculated. The funding came in two emergency appropriations in September totaling $62.3 billion, followed by several smaller spending authorizations. In December, expanding on a request by Bush, Congress redirected $23.4 billion in funds previously appropriated. [38]

It's uncertain, however, how much will go to New Orleans.

In any event, money appropriated so far includes $6.2 billion in Community Development Block Grants intended for Louisiana, and $22 billion for reimbursements to Gulf Coast homeowners from the federal flood-insurance program. But even with the emergency injections of cash, the flood-insurance program is "bankrupt," Senate Banking Committee Chairman Richard Shelby, R-Ala., said on Jan. 25. The acting director of the Federal Emergency Management Agency (FEMA) insurance division said the agency has paid out $13.5 billion in claims arising from the 2005 hurricane season — nearly as much as the agency has paid out in its 37-year existence. And 30 percent of the 239,000 claims have yet to be resolved. [39]

Federal hurricane-recovery coordinator Powell has been advocating directing much of the block grant money to the estimated 20,000 New Orleans homeowners who didn't have flood insurance because their neighborhoods weren't designated as flood plains. [40]

Given the huge costs involved and all the unknowns, lawmakers from other parts of the country are not exactly champing at the bit to pay for rebuilding New Orleans. The city's tenuous hydrological situation and the likelihood that it will be flooded again by other hurricanes lead some Americans to question whether the rest of the country should have to pay to rebuild the city in such a precarious location.

"There is a lot of — I suppose you can call it 'Katrina fatigue' — that people are dealing with out in the heartland," Rep. Henry Bonilla, R-Texas, told Louisiana Gov. Kathleen Babineaux Blanco, a Democrat, at a House Select Katrina Response Investigation Committee hearing last Dec. 14.

The situation has rekindled a long-simmering debate about whether Americans in the heartland should pay to constantly bail out people — usually those living on the coasts — who choose to live in areas prone to floods, hurricanes, landslides and earthquakes. "Is it fair to make people living in Pennsylvania or Ohio pay billions for massive engineering projects so that some of the people of New Orleans can go back to the way things were and avoid the hard choices that nature presents them?" asks economist Adrian Moore of the libertarian Reason Foundation of Los Angeles. [41]

Some lawmakers agree, although only a few have spoken out. "It looks like a lot of that place could be bulldozed," House Speaker Dennis Hastert, R-Ill. said shortly after the hurricane, raising hackles. He later explained he only meant that danger zones shouldn't be resettled. [42]

New Orleanians respond that other disaster-prone areas, including hurricane-exposed Florida coastal cities, get rebuilt with few questions asked about viability. "People build on mountainsides in California that fall in the ocean," notes Perez, the newspaper sales manager. "We're not the only vulnerable area in the country."

In addition, points out Republican Louisiana Sen. David Vitter, 25 percent of the nation's energy and most of the Midwest's grain exports are shipped through the port of New Orleans. "If people don't think there's a national stake in rebuilding New Orleans, that's fine. But they should get used to much higher gasoline prices," he said. "And people can forget about getting crops to foreign markets. You need a major city as the hub of all that activity."

But if federal funds are forthcoming to rebuild the city, they should have some serious accountability strings attached, given the city's long history of corruption and dysfunction, some argue. "A lot of . . . our constituents now are telling us that they [don't] want us to support funding for the Gulf region at this point without strong plans of accountability," Bonilla said.

Recognizing those sentiments — as well as the reality that the country is at war and its debt and deficits are rising — Louisiana politicians have proposed two major

CHRONOLOGY

1700s-1800s *From the time of its founding, New Orleans' vulnerability to nature is seen as the price of its incomparably strategic location.*

1718 New Orleans is founded on a natural levee along a bend in the Mississippi River.

1892 Adolph Plessy of New Orleans is arrested after testing segregation laws by riding in a "white" train car. U.S. Supreme Court later upholds his conviction in landmark *Plessy v. Ferguson* decision.

1900-1947 *A catastrophic flood reminds the city of its dangerous location.*

1927 Massive Mississippi floods see many African-Americans forced into levee-reinforcement work; two rural parishes are deliberately flooded to save New Orleans.

1929 The U.S. Army Corps of Engineers begins building a spillway on the Mississippi to channel floodwater away from New Orleans.

1930s *Expansion of city drainage systems allows urban expansion, but new neighborhoods are strictly segregated.*

Sept. 17-19, 1947 A Category 4 hurricane overwhelms levees, causing flooding over nine square miles of the city.

1950s-1970s *The city expands into drained wetlands, increasing its vulnerability to floods.*

1950 Land drained for suburban expansion reaches 49,000 acres.

Sept. 7, 1965 Hurricane Betsy slams the city with Category 3 winds, pushing a 10-foot storm surge through some levees.

Oct. 27, 1965 President Lyndon B. Johnson signs the Flood Control Act, which includes funding for a hurricane-protection system in New Orleans.

Aug. 17, 1969 Category 5 Hurricane Camille devastates Mississippi and Alabama, but reinforced protective systems keep most of New Orleans safe.

May 3, 1978 Heavy rainstorm flooding damages more than 70,000 homes.

1980s-1990s *Attempts by the city to guard against rainstorm floods prove inadequate, as fears of vulnerability to hurricanes begin to grow.*

April 1982 Rainstorm-caused floods damage 1,400 homes and other buildings.

1983 City expands pumping and drainage systems.

May 8-10, 1995 Flooding damages thousands of homes, causes six deaths.

2000-Present *Fears of hurricane vulnerability grow, as journalists and government officials warn about the weakness of the city's defenses.*

June 23-June 26, 2002 *Times-Picayune* warns of New Orleans' hurricane vulnerability.

Sept. 26, 2002 Hurricane Isidore hits Louisiana after weakening to a tropical storm, but still causes major flooding.

July 2004 FEMA officials conduct a drill featuring Category 3 "Hurricane Pam" hitting New Orleans and predict serious flooding, massive evacuation.

Aug. 29, 2005 Hurricane Katrina makes landfall east of New Orleans.

Sept. 15, 2005 President Bush visits New Orleans and pledges a massive disaster-recovery effort.

Jan. 11, 2006 Bring New Orleans Back Commission releases an "Action Plan" for re-creating the city.

Jan 17, 2006 Senators of both parties visit New Orleans and criticize slow progress on recovery.

Jan. 26, 2006 President Bush explains why he refused to support the creation of a public corporation to buy flood-damaged homes.

June 1 Hurricane season begins; repairs and improvements to levee system due for completion.

plans that they say would lower the federal spending burden for rebuilding New Orleans and the rest of the state.

But the White House has already refused to back one of these plans. Its author, Rep. Baker, proposed establishing a public corporation to buy or finance repairs on storm-damaged property. Homeowners who sold their houses to the corporation would get 60 percent of the pre-Katrina value of their holdings. The corporation would then resell the homes, if possible, and turn the proceeds back to the Treasury. Nagin's BNOBC adopted the idea, which some of its members called crucial to reviving the city.

"We were concerned about creating additional federal bureaucracies, which might make it harder to get money to the people," Bush said, explaining his rejection of Baker's idea. [43]

On Feb. 1, according to Baker's office, three former Republican governors of Louisiana — Murphy J. "Mike" Foster, Charles E. "Buddy" Roemer III, and David Treen — urged Bush to change his mind concerning Baker's bill, which they called the only practical method of disposing of thousands of ruined residential and business properties.

The congressman has been vowing to press ahead with his proposal, sponsored in the Senate by Sen. Landrieu. Bush's negative response would "constrict the opportunities for rapid redevelopment, and that's tough," said Reed Kroloff, architecture dean at Tulane University and a BNOBC member. [44]

But developer Joseph Canizaro, who helped put together the commission's plan, said block grant money and other unspecified funds could be found for a property buyback. [45]

The other plan to lower direct federal spending is a longstanding proposal to boost the state's share of money that the federal government earns from petroleum leases on the Outer Continental Shelf in the Gulf of Mexico off Louisiana's coast. One-quarter of U.S. crude oil production comes from Louisiana's offshore waters. [46]

The cost of repairing the state's hurricane-protection system "can be paid for simply by giving Louisiana our fair share of oil and gas revenues from the Outer Continental Shelf," Gov. Blanco told Bonilla at the House Select Committee hearing.

Coastal states like Louisiana receive 27 percent of the revenues from oil and gas leases from waters within their three-mile jurisdictions (federal waters extend another 197 miles). By contrast, states with oil and gas production on public lands receive 50 percent of the federal revenues, leading coastal states to feel they are entitled to a larger share of offshore revenues. [47]

Sen. Landrieu last year pushed a bill to grant coastal states 50 percent of the take from oil and gas leases in the areas off their shores. The bill died at year's end, but she is planning to revive it this year (see p. 300).

Rather than creating a new revenue source, however, the proposal would merely divert money to the state before the funds reach federal coffers, which bothered Bonilla. "It is wise when states and local governments come before us to show what they are doing to help themselves in terms of raising whatever revenue dollars you can," Bonilla told Blanco. "People would want to know . . . what is Louisiana doing in terms of everything you possibly can do to help yourself and not just look at the federal government and say, 'We need you to help us pay for these things.' "

But, he added, Americans would not "turn their back on those who want to help themselves."

BACKGROUND

Island City

New Orleans has been battling with nature ever since explorer Jean-Baptiste Le Moyne de Bienville founded the city in 1718. Its original name, in fact, reflected the city's relationship to the four bodies of water surrounding it — the Mississippi River, Lake Pontchartrain, Lake Borgne and the Gulf of Mexico. He called it *L'Isle de la Nouvelle Orléans* — the Island of New Orleans. [48]

"His enthusiasm for the river's commercial benefits blinded him to many of the challenges of building a city in the delta," environmental historian Kelman writes. These included: epidemics; "terrible to nonexistent" drainage; dampness; and "the threat of catastrophic flooding."

Still, Bienville's insight into the river's economic importance was on the money. The Mississippi was unrivalled as a highway deep into the North American continent, and remains so today. Some 500 million tons of goods — including about 60 percent of U.S. grain exports — are shipped downriver to the southern Louisiana port complex, which includes New Orleans. [49]

Experts Blame Levees, Not Storm

The newspaper headlines blamed "Killer Storm Katrina" for devastating New Orleans. But engineers largely blame the levees designed and built by the U.S. Army Corps of Engineers.

A team of experts who examined the protective system found no fewer than 34 storm-induced levee breaches, indicating that the engineering failures were far wider than initial reports indicated. [1]

"The performance of many of the levees and floodwalls could have been significantly improved, and some of the failures likely prevented, with relatively inexpensive modification," the team concluded. The simple addition of concrete "splash slabs," for instance, might have prevented soil levee tops from eroding.

In fact, even a task force assembled by the Corps of Engineers itself concluded "integral parts of the . . . hurricane-protection system failed." [2]

With the June 1 start of the 2006 hurricane season approaching, the Corps is trying to patch the immediate problems. Engineers and lawmakers, meanwhile, are evaluating the system's performance. So far, a lethal combination of design, construction and maintenance errors appears to underlie the disaster.

Blame extends from state-appointed "levee boards" responsible for inspection and maintenance to the Corps of Engineers, Sen. George Voinovich, R-Ohio, told the Senate Homeland Security and Governmental Affairs Committee on Dec. 14. And Congress deserved blame too, he said: "We have been penny-wise and pound-foolish" on funding upkeep and completion of the New Orleans levee system.

The Lake Pontchartrain and Vicinity Hurricane Protection Project includes 125 miles of levees, floodwalls and other structures. The system was supposed to bar storm surges from Lake Pontchartrain and channel any flooding out of the city via a series of canals. [3]

Though Congress approved the project in 1965, it was unfinished when Katrina struck. In the city itself, construction was 90 percent complete, but the lack of completion has not been blamed for the system's failure. [4] Rather, the devastation was intensified by the environmental changes in southern Louisiana since the system was first designed, the *Times-Picayune* reported as early as 2002. [5]

As the oil and gas industry expanded, the Corps of Engineers built or approved the necessary navigation channels in southern Louisiana and the Gulf of Mexico. And the industry expansion swallowed one-third to one-half of the wetlands — which have been disappearing at a rate of at least 25 square miles a year. Experts now know wetlands play a critical role during hurricanes, slowing storms as they make landfall. [6]

The first of New Orleans' protective barriers — called levees from the French verb "to lift" — were natural. In fact, New Orleans exists in the first place because the Mississippi's waters helped create a high section of riverbank along the section of the river that forms a crescent embracing old New Orleans — known today as the French Quarter. The sloping, natural levee was only 12 feet above sea level.

Settlers soon began adding to nature's work. Throughout the 18th and early 19th centuries — during the first period of French rule, the Spanish colonial period that followed in 1768-1801 and the French restoration in 1801-1803 — levees were built far upstream, and raised continually after flooding.

The levee work continued after the United States bought the city and vast swaths of the new nation's interior in 1803 for $15 million, or about 3 cents an acre.

Nine years after the so-called Louisiana Purchase, Louisiana became a state.

From the beginning, many people realized that building ever-higher levees up and down the river prevented its energy from being dissipated naturally in periodic floods. By the time the Mississippi reached New Orleans, it would be dangerously high and flowing at maximum force.

"We are every year confining this immense river closer and closer to its own bed — forgetting that it is fed by over 1,500 streams — and regardless of a danger becoming every year more and more impending," State Engineer P. O. Herbert warned in 1846. He argued for flood outlets along the river, but landowners resisted, not wanting their plantations flooded. [50]

In 1849, the river broke through several upstream levees, one of them 17 miles above New Orleans. The

So when Katrina made landfall across the region's depleted wetlands, the poorly designed and built levees and floodwalls couldn't withstand the full force of the storm surge.

A section of floodwall along the London Avenue Canal was so weakened that it likely would have been breached by the floodwaters — if the barrier on the opposite side of the canal hadn't failed first, an engineer told the Senate Environment and Public Works Committee on Nov. 17. "Multiple, concurrent failure mechanisms" were present, said Larry Roth, deputy executive director of the American Society of Civil Engineers. "The wall was badly out of alignment and tilting landward; as a result of the tilt, there were gaps between the wall and the supporting soil."

Additional pressure on the flood barriers came from the Mississippi River Gulf Outlet (MRGO), a 76-mile long canal built to give ships a shortcut from the Gulf to the Port of New Orleans. Instead, it gave Katrina a straight shot into the city — a "hurricane alley" — said Sen. David Vitter, R-La., who has called, along with others, for the canal's closure. The Corps says it will not conduct its annual dredging of the waterway, and hurricane experts say it may become less dangerous as it becomes shallower. [7]

Meanwhile, engineers have suggested that some residential areas be abandoned — to provide a flood-absorbing floodplain — and building codes amended to require that houses be elevated.

But the levee system also must be dealt with, Roth said. "If we are to rebuild the city," he said, "we must also rebuild its protections." [8]

[1] The team was assembled by the National Science Foundation (NSF), the American Society of Civil Engineers (ASCE) and the University of California at Berkeley. See R. B. Seed, *et al.*, "Preliminary Report on the Performance of the New Orleans Levee Systems in Hurricane Katrina on Aug. 29, 2005," Nov. 2, 2005, Figure 1.4, p. 1-10, www.ce.berkeley.edu/~inkabi/KRTF/CCRM/levee-rpt.pdf.

[2] "Performance Evaluation Plan and Interim Status, Report 1 of a Series: Performance Evaluation of the New Orleans and Southeast Louisiana Hurricane Protection System," Interagency Performance Evaluation Task Force, Jan. 10, 2006, Appendix A, p. 2, https://ipet.wes.army.mil.

[3] *Ibid*, pp. 1.2-1.3; Seed, *et al.*, *op. cit.*, p. A-2.

[4] "Performance Evaluation Plan," *op. cit.*, Appendix A, p. 2.

[5] John McQuaid and Mark Schleifstein, "Evolving Danger; experts know we face a greater threat from hurricanes than previously suspected," *The Times-Picayune* (New Orleans), June 23, 2002, p. A1.

[6] John McQuaid and Mark Schleifstein, "Shifting Tides," *The Times-Picayune* (New Orleans), June 26, 2002, p. A1.

[7] John Schwartz, "New Orleans Wonders What to Do With Open Wounds, Its Canals," *The New York Times*, Dec. 231, 2005, p. A26; Seed, *et al.*, *op. cit.*, p. 3.1; Matthew Brown, "Corps suspends plans to dredge MRGO," *The Times-Picayune* (New Orleans), Breaking News Weblog, Nov. 21, 2005, www.nola.com/t-p/.

[8] For background, see Larry Roth statement to Senate Committee on Environment and Public Works, Nov. 17, 2005, http://epw.senate.gov/hearing_statements.cfm?id=249000.

resultant flooding in the lowest section of New Orleans forced 12,000 mostly poor residents to abandon their dwellings or try to coexist with the water.

Afterward, the city raised the levees higher still. But A. D. Wooldridge, the state engineer who succeeded Herbert, declared in 1850 that reliance on levees "will be destructive to those who come after us." By then, some rose 15 feet.

Dynamiting the Levee

The engineers' warnings came to pass in early 1927. A series of rainstorms, coupled with unusually heavy spring runoff, swelled the huge river and overwhelmed the levees. Floodwater inundated 28,545 square miles of the Mississippi Valley as far north as Illinois, killing 423 people. By mid-April, more than 50,000 people had fled their homes. [51]

In New Orleans, powerful pumps kept floodwaters at bay — until a bolt of lightning disabled the power plant that kept the pumps humming.

A group of city leaders, who had formed the Citizens Flood Relief Committee, began campaigning to stop the flooding of the city by blowing a hole in the levee some 12 miles downstream.

Residents of the two thinly populated wetland parishes downstream, St. Bernard and Plaquemines, largely made their living fishing and trapping muskrats for their fur. The New Orleans political class persuaded Louisiana Gov. Oramel Simpson that those rural activities were worth sacrificing to protect New Orleans. Simpson gave the "river parish" residents three days to clear out. Muskrat trapping took years to recover.

For the poor African-Americans living along the river's southern reaches, the 1927 flood left bitter memories of

Getty Images/Robyn Beck

Engineers inspect a Katrina-damaged section of the London Avenue Canal on Sept. 21, 2005, three days before Hurricane Rita hit and reopened some levees that had been partially repaired. The city's flood-control system may not be completely repaired by June 1, the start of the 2006 hurricane season.

racial oppression and death. Especially in Mississippi, thousands of black men were conscripted into labor gangs that shored up the levee, often working at gunpoint. Some drowned as they worked, and a community leader who refused a summons because he'd been working all night was shot on the spot.

The race-hatred exacerbated by the flood triggered a vast expansion of the "great migration" of African-Americans from South to North. [52] For the black community, 1927 established a connection between natural disaster, racism and black exodus — a chain of events that many would later see repeating itself with Katrina.

New Expansion

The 1927 disaster led to improved federal flood-control systems and also launched a continuing debate over whether all Americans should have to pay to protect people living in disaster-prone places. [53]

In New Orleans, the 1927 flood also undermined the total dependence on levees for protection. Two years later, the Corps of Engineers began building a spillway at Bonnet Carré that could release river water into Lake Pontchartrain if the Mississippi rose to 20 feet in New Orleans. The spillway was completed in 1936.

By then, New Orleans residents had other reasons to feel safer. Electric and gasoline-powered motors had relieved major drainage problems. In a city sitting below sea level in a swampy area, difficulties in disposing of human and other waste had long endangered health and lowered the quality of life. Mosquito-borne yellow fever alone killed about 41,000 people between 1817 and 1905.

Draining surrounding swampland also allowed the opening up of new lands for settlement. From the 1930s to the post-World War II years, acreage to the north, east and west of the original city were transformed from wetlands into tract-housing territory. The suburbanization expanded into Jefferson Parish, just outside of the city.

Within New Orleans itself, the amount of land that had been drained for settlement expanded from 12,349 acres in 1895 to more than 90,000 by 1983.

On a dry day, the newly drained territory appeared suitable for housing. But after Katrina, the local paper, the *Times-Picayune*, published an 1878 map showing that nearly every part of the city that flooded in 2005 had been uninhabited in the years before the land was drained. Early residents understood exactly where not to live, the paper concluded. [54]

Hurricanes and Floods

Since the city's founding, the protective levee system had aimed mainly at holding back Mississippi flooding. But beginning in the mid-20th century, a series of powerful hurricanes changed the perception of where danger lay.

In 1947, a 112-mile-an-hour hurricane (they didn't have names yet) brought two-foot floods in a nine-square-mile area. Hurricanes Flossy (1956) and Hilda (1964) caused some damage but were dwarfed by the 160-mile-an-hour winds of Hurricane Betsy in 1965. Floodwaters reached eight feet in parts of the city; 75 people died, and 7,000 homes suffered damage.

In response, Congress passed the Flood Control Act of 1965, which funded expansion of the levee and canal system in and around New Orleans to protect against what today would be classified as a Category 3 hurricane. [55]

In 1969, just as construction of the expanded system began, Hurricane Camille slammed the Gulf Coast. Mississippi was hit hardest, but a section of the New Orleans levee complex also failed, flooding part of the city.

In succeeding years, even rainstorms became problematic. Nine inches of rain during a 1978 storm caused flooding of up to 3.5 feet in low-lying sections, damaging 71,500 homes. A series of heavy rainstorms between 1979 and 1995 also caused widespread damage, and in 1998, Hurricane Georges, a Category 2 storm that barely touched New Orleans, brought a water surge to within a foot of topping the levees. [56]

Waiting for the Big One

The steady growth in the number and intensity of hurricanes during the 1990s fed unease in New Orleans and prompted the *Times-Picayune* to publish — at the beginning of the 2002 hurricane season — a series of articles unflinchingly examining the risks New Orleans faced. "Officials at the local, state and national level are convinced the risk is genuine and are devising plans for alleviating the aftermath of a disaster that could leave the city uninhabitable for six months or more," the authors presciently wrote. [57]

In January 2005, Ivor van Heerden, deputy director of the Louisiana State University (LSU) Hurricane Center, told a conference on "coastal challenges" that a Category 3 or above storm striking New Orleans or any other coastal Louisiana city would be a "disaster of cataclysmic proportion." [58]

By then, the city's new-and-improved flood-protection system consisted of about 125 miles of levees, floodwalls and flood-proofed bridges and other barriers. In Orleans Parish, the renovation work was 90 percent complete. [59]

On Aug. 28, as Hurricane Katrina was rolling through the Gulf and heading for New Orleans, the National Weather Service called it "a most powerful hurricane with unprecedented strength." After landfall, "Most of the area will be uninhabitable for weeks, perhaps longer." [60]

Mayor Nagin, a newcomer to politics, had ordered the city evacuated. But buses for the tens of thousands of elderly and poor residents who didn't own cars were never dispatched.

Even before Katrina touched down near New Orleans on the morning of Aug. 29, a storm surge breached the levees along the Inner Harbor Navigation Canal (the "Industrial Canal"). At about the same time, an 18-foot surge from Lake Borgne pushed through a wall along the Mississippi River Gulf Outlet east of St. Bernard Parish and the Lower Ninth Ward. The resulting flooding soon reached the Lower Ninth. [61]

Over the next few hours, additional surges over the Industrial Canal sent even more floodwater into the Lower Ninth. Then, with Katrina moving westward near Lake Pontchartrain, another section of levee along the Industrial Canal gave way, followed by a breach of the 17th Street Canal floodwall, flooding the western end of the parish. [62]

In the days following the storm, New Orleans became an international symbol of government dysfunction. Tens of thousands of residents unable to evacuate clung to rooftops or flocked to the New Orleans Superdome, which was unequipped to receive them. By Sept. 12, FEMA Director Michael Brown had resigned under pressure — only days after being congratulated by President Bush. Belatedly, federal officials organized bus convoys and flights out of the city. [63]

Then, on Sept. 24, Hurricane Rita, a Category 3 storm, hit the Gulf Coast. New Orleans didn't lie directly in the storm's path, but the hurricane reopened some partly repaired levee breaches. As a result, the Lower Ninth Ward and the Gentilly neighborhood flooded again. Elsewhere in Louisiana and East Texas, the damage was far worse, with tens of thousands left homeless. [64]

By early December, only 10 percent of the city's businesses were up and running, and 135,000 residents, at most, had stayed or returned. They had a name for the only fully functioning part of the city — a strip of high ground that includes the French Quarter and other sections of old New Orleans: Like explorer Bienville, they called it "the island." [65]

CURRENT SITUATION

Redevelopment Plans

On Jan. 11, the Bring New Orleans Back Commission released its "Action Plan" for rebuilding the city, but action doesn't seem to be on the near horizon.

The plan recommended the formation of 13 neighborhood-planning committees, with work on recommendations to start on Feb. 20, finish by May 20 and be submitted to the city for approval by June 20. Reconstruction would begin by Aug. 20. [66]

Within days of the plan's release, however, a FEMA official said updated floodplain maps of the city wouldn't be available until the summer, depriving crucial information to homeowners considering rebuilding.

"If I were putting my lifetime savings in the single, biggest investment I'll ever make, I'd want to make sure I had minimized every possible risk," said Tulane's Kroloff, chairman of the commission's urban-design subcommittee. [67]

The delay in obtaining the updated flood-zone information would slow the reconstruction timetable, Kroloff said, but wouldn't prevent the neighborhood committees from canvassing past and present residents. "There are some people who are going to return no matter what, and some who aren't," he said. [68]

Other obstacles could further slow the plan's execution. Congress may not approve Rep. Baker's proposal to create a public corporation to buy and sell distressed properties, although BNOB Commissioner Canizaro hopes funds can be rounded up from FEMA and elsewhere. [69] The Louisiana legislature would have to create the nonprofit entity, provisionally entitled the Crescent City Recovery Corp., and New Orleans voters would have to OK changes to the city charter to authorize it. [70]

That vote could come as soon as April. But it remains to be seen how receptive voters will be to measures recommended by Nagin and the commission, especially in light of the criticism that greeted the plan when it was unveiled. Some property owners attacked the proposal as a land grab.

"If you come to take our property, you'd better come ready," homeowner Rodney Craft of the Lower Ninth Ward told the commissioners. [71]

"I hear the politicians talk, and nothing is being said — nothing," says Gail Miller, a retired New Orleans police officer who has returned to her home in New Orleans East, living upstairs but cooking in a motor home she and her husband park in the driveway. "The political situation worries me — the levees don't worry me a bit."

Another widespread worry is education. Since the state took over 102 of the city's 117 schools by designating them as a "recovery district," only about 8,000 of 60,000 pre-Katrina students are attending the handful of public and parochial schools that are operating. [72]

"One of the barriers to families returning is that the state took over the schools and is not opening them," says Councilwoman Willard-Lewis.

Many residents say, however, that reopening the schools as they were wouldn't be much help. The Urban Land Institute reported that before Katrina the public school system had an "educational quotient" ranking of 1 out of 100 — the nation's lowest. [73]

"Everybody knew that public education was broken before the storm," says Heather Thompson, a New Orleans native and Harvard Business School student. A graduate of the public schools' only secondary-level crown jewel, Benjamin Franklin High School, Thompson helped organize a consulting project by four dozen of her fellow business students to recommend recovery ideas for schools and other elements of civic life. [74]

Meanwhile, the shortage of school space seems likely to continue. "I want to get the very best leaders and the very best teachers for every child in Orleans Parish," said State Education Superintendent Cecil Picard, adding that he expects 15,000 public-school students when classes reopen in August. [75]

Port Bounces Back

Giant cranes are swinging containers off and on ships, warehouses are filled with bundles of rubber and coils of steel, and trucks headed inland are filling up with coffee beans. The Port of New Orleans is back up and running, though only months ago a quick comeback seemed improbable.

"On Aug. 30, somebody told me it would be six months before we got the first ship back," port Director LaGrange says. "I said our goal was to be at 70 percent of pre-Katrina activity by March 1 — the six-month anniversary [of Katrina]. We're pushing 65 percent now."

Immediately after Katrina struck, while Americans watched thousands of human tragedies unfolding in real time on television, shippers and merchants focused on the southern Louisiana port complex — the country's fourth-largest. [76] "The longer the ports remained closed, the greater the risk that we'd all be paying higher prices for coffee, cocoa, lumber, steel, zinc, aluminum and any number of other things," said Mark M. Zandi, chief executive of the Economy.com research firm. [77]

In a seeming paradox, Katrina largely spared the riverfront port area. Like the old French Quarter, most of the port sits atop the natural levee on which Bienville

Should New Orleans be completely rebuilt on its old footprint?

YES Sen. Mary Landrieu, D-La.
Member, Senate Appropriations Committee

Written for *CQ Researcher*, January 2006

More than five months ago, Hurricane Katrina and the subsequent breaks in numerous flood-control levees decimated one of our nation's greatest cities, my hometown, New Orleans.

Some have since questioned whether or not we should rebuild New Orleans, saying that we should abandon a city that has contributed so much to our great nation.

New Orleans is the capitol of our nation's energy coast. It was put there for a reason. We did not go there to sunbathe. We went there to set up the Mississippi River, to tame that river, to create channels for this country to grow and prosper. New Orleans was established so the cities and communities along the Mississippi River would have a port to trade with the world.

The indispensible Higgins boats that saved us during World War II were built in New Orleans. Forty-three thousand people built those boats and headed them out to Normandy. We're going to rebuild our shipping industry. We're going to rebuild our maritime industry, we will maintain our great port and we will continue to provide the energy that keeps our lights on across the nation.

Just because parts of New Orleans are below sea level is no reason to allow this great city to die. The Netherlands is a nation that is 21 feet below sea level at its economic heart, yet they still operate Europe's largest port — just as we operate America's largest port system.

The Dutch have proved that you can live below sea level and still keep your feet dry. They believe in an integrated system of water management. After a flood destroyed their nation in 1953, the Dutch said "Never again," and today they have created the world's most advanced storm-protection and flood-control system. If a nation half the size of Louisiana can do it, then surely the United States of America can.

We can and should rebuild every neighborhood — but maybe not exactly the way we did it the first time. This time we can build better, smarter, stronger neighborhoods.

One fact is certain: Every, single American citizen who calls New Orleans home has a right to come back and rebuild their neighborhoods, and the federal government should generously support that right.

New Orleans helped build America, and now America must help rebuild New Orleans, because America needs that great city — right where it is.

NO William Hudnut
Joseph C. Canizaro Chair in Public Policy, Urban Land Institute

Written for *CQ Researcher*, January 2006

There are those who understandably feel that New Orleans should be rebuilt in its entirety, and that blocks and neighborhoods throughout the pre-Katrina city should be rebuilt house by house as resources permit.

The emotional tug of going back to one's "roots" is strong. One cannot blame the City Council and others for demanding that all areas of the city, especially East New Orleans and the Lower Ninth, as well as Lakeview and Gentilly, be rebuilt simultaneously. But we need to ask: Is such a plan realistic? Does it make sense?

The city will not have the resources to take care of a widely dispersed population, and not all the evacuees will be returning. Critics of a smaller city dismiss such plans and ideas as "arrogant," "elitist" and "racist," because the low-lying areas are where mostly black and low-income residents lived before Katrina. But the questions persist.

I can think of two compelling reasons to envision a smaller New Orleans in the future. It will have a smaller population, and it will be safer.

As is often said, "Demography is destiny." If New Orleans once had 465,000 people, that was once and no more. The city was losing population before Katrina and has shrunk to a little over 100,000 today, with prospects of that number climbing to perhaps 250,000 by the time Katrina's third anniversary rolls around.

Is it prudent to think that this smaller number of people should occupy all the territory that almost twice that number did before August 2005, especially when the city will not have the financial resources, police, fire and EMS services and the like to care for such a scattered population? Two keys to a successful, vibrant city are diversity and density, which a sprawled-out land base does not provide.

Katrina has given New Orleans a chance to reinvent itself as a more compact, connected city on a smaller footprint. The city's recovering economy built on restored building blocks — culture, food, music, art, entertainment, tourism, bioscience and medical research, the port, energy production — will attract people back into mixed-use, mixed-income, racially balanced, pedestrian-friendly neighborhoods carefully planned by citizens, with parks, open space, new wetlands and light-rail transit added to the mix. All of that can be accomplished on less space than the city occupied heretofore.

Who was it that said, "Small is beautiful?"

founded the city. However, a major container terminal and a new cold-storage warehouse in eastern New Orleans were both destroyed.

Louisiana politicians frequently cite the port's importance to the economy as an argument for rebuilding New Orleans to its pre-Katrina scale. When she heard that the port might be able to function at full strength with a city somewhat smaller than pre-Katrina New Orleans, Sen. Landrieu, responded: "Where are the workers going to come from? You can't have a port without New Orleans."

LaGrange takes a more nuanced view. "You've got to have the work force here," he says, and they will need "the support services that a city provides — transit, schools, places to worship, grocery stores, gasoline stations. But if the city, for some reason, is smaller, I don't think that would be a tremendous effect on the output of the port."

Politics and Legislation

New Orleans' future lies in many hands, but federal lawmakers may be the most important, because they control the biggest money source.

"We are at your mercy," Gov. Blanco told Senate Homeland Security Committee members as they toured the disaster zone on Jan. 17. "We are begging you to stay with us." [78]

Landrieu plans to revive her proposal to channel 50 percent of offshore petroleum-lease revenues to the state. The money would be earmarked for post-Katrina reconstruction, says her spokesman, Adam Sharp.

Besides the Landrieu and Baker proposals, Louisiana politicians will continue to push for $2.1 billion in supplemental Medicaid funds to help pay for health care for Katrina victims — many suddenly homeless and unemployed — who had to enter the federally subsidized medical insurance program for low-income people. Congress adjourned at year's end without passing the Medicaid bill, but Landrieu says she'll also continue to push for that.

The fact that none of these proposals passed while Katrina's devastation was fresh would seem to show that the state's politicians "have some work to do" to get Congress' attention, said one of Baker's aides. Blanco, meanwhile, is preparing to call a special 12-day legislative session, beginning on Feb. 6. She wants state lawmakers to make the "levee boards" that supervise maintenance more accountable. The boards were widely criticized — even ridiculed — for laxity, following Katrina. [79]

Getting the schools going again remains a priority, and Blanco must hammer together by May a plan to reorganize the city's school system, now largely under state control. The state Board of Elementary and Secondary Education would have to rule on the plan. The BNOBC in January proposed a leaner administrative office — one superintendent and four or five assistants — and expanded authority for principals, who would be able to hire and fire their own staffs. Differences between "have" and "have-not" schools would be eliminated under the plan, and early-education programs would be initiated. [80]

Meanwhile, the often-criticized Blanco tangled with the City Council over what she called its resistance to installing FEMA-supplied trailers for needy families. The council was responding, in part, to complaints from some residents who objected to trailer villages in their neighborhoods.

"Disagreements over housing must end — and must end now," she told the council on Jan. 5. Council members denied that they had obstructed trailer installation. After a subsequent meeting between the governor and council members, sites for a total of 40,000 trailers were identified. [81]

Even the demolition of unsafe houses stirred controversy. When it appeared the city was about to bulldoze some Lower Ninth Ward houses deemed unsafe, residents and some council members sought a court order to stop it. U.S. District Judge Martin L. C. Feldman then OK'd a deal between the Nagin administration and Lower Ninth Ward residents requiring at least seven-days' notice before demolition. [82]

The court-approved settlement apparently resolved the demolition issues, but political conflicts between Nagin and the council remain. The beleaguered mayor is among the candidates up for re-election on April 22.

OUTLOOK

Pessimism and Paralysis

Optimism is in short supply in New Orleans, notwithstanding the brave talk of Louisiana politicians. The failure of the flood-protection system, the tragedy and chaos of the early days of the disaster and the devastated conditions that remain in much of the city five months after Katrina have not provided grounds for much hope.

President Bush, in his State of the Union address on Jan. 31, devoted 162 of the speech's 5,432 words to New Orleans, proposing no specific, new remedies. "As we meet . . . immediate needs, we must also address deeper challenges that existed before the storm arrived," Bush said, citing a need for better schools and economic opportunity. Among Louisiana politicians, even the president's fellow Republicans felt left out. "I was very disappointed at how small a part those national challenges — and I think are national challenges — were given in the speech," Sen. Vitter told the *Times-Picayune*.

"There's no sense of urgency from the city government, the state government or the federal government," says Dennis Scott, looking out on his devastated New Orleans East neighborhood.

Indeed, as of late January, the U.S. Army Corps of Engineers had completed only 16 percent of the levee repairs scheduled for completion by June 1, when the 2006 hurricane season begins. [83]

An outsider draws essentially the same conclusion as Scott. "The lack of unity in the political establishment is the paralyzing factor," says the Urban Land Institute's Hudnut. "There's almost a political stand-off between the governor's office, the mayor's office, the City Council and the Bring New Orleans Back Commission; but this is also partially a Washington issue. I don't see a lot of leadership coming from the White House team."

Republican Hudnut is one of many politicians and ordinary citizens to question the high cost of the war in Iraq with the needs of New Orleans. The war's direct cash cost alone through November 2005 was calculated at $251 billion, according to a study released in January by two former Clinton administration officials. [84] Thompson, the Harvard Business School student working on redevelopment plans, observes that the government ought to be able to "make money appear" for New Orleans in the same way as deficit financing is arranged for the war.

If talking openly about race relations holds promise for making them better, the New Orleans disaster might have served some purpose. Some black New Orleanians wonder aloud, though, if the color of the majority of the city's residents hasn't also slowed down the pace of recovery. Anne LaBranche, the doctor's wife from New Orleans East, can't think of any other reason.

"This was a man-made problem," she says, referring to the failure of the flood-protection system. And yet, previous hurricane damage in Florida and other Gulf Coast states has been paid for without debate on whether people should be living in such potentially risky areas, she says. "President Bush says he resents it when people say 'racism,' so tell me what it is," she says quietly. "Why the different treatment?"

If New Orleans has one advantage concerning race, it may be that the city's geography tends to throw people of different colors together more than in other locales. Another point in the city's favor is New Orleanians' loyalty to their city. It remains to be seen whether that's enough to overcome the economic, political and environmental obstacles.

Piano technician David Doremus has lived in New Orleans most of the past 30 years. He and his wife live in the unflooded Algiers neighborhood on the Mississippi's west bank, and they are committed to remaining in town with their daughters.

While he's unsure about how much piano tuning and rebuilding work he'll have in the near future, he can't imagine anywhere else that offers the pace of life, the social graces and the fishing that he enjoys in New Orleans — as well as the musical variety. "I work for a recording studio, and one of the first sessions I worked on after the storm was with Allen Toussaint and Elvis Costello," he says.

So Doremus is ready to commute 40 miles to work at a friend's piano business in Covington, La., for a year, if he has to, or even work at Home Depot. "My family back in Virginia thinks I'm nuts," he adds. "And my wife's family in Pittsburgh thinks she's nuts."

If the Doremuses are crazy, New Orleans needs all the nuts it can muster.

NOTES

1. Gary Rivlin, "Anger Meets New Orleans Renewal Plan," *The New York Times*, Jan. 12, 2006, p. A18.

2. When Hurricane Katrina made landfall at Buras, La., 35 miles east of New Orleans at about 6 a.m., it was originally rated at Category 4, the classification for storms with wind speeds of 131-155 mph. The National Hurricane Center later revised that classification down to Category 3, with winds of 111-130 mph. Some 24 hours before reaching Louisiana, Katrina varied between categories 4 and 5. For further detail, see Peter Whoriskey and Joby Warrick,

"Report Revises Katrina's Force," *The Washington Post*, Dec. 22, 2005, p. A3; Richard D. Knabb, *et al.*, "Tropical Cyclone Report: Hurricane Katrina, 22-30 August, 2005," National Hurricane Center, Dec. 20, 2005, p. 3, www.nhc.noaa.gov/pdf/TCR-AL1 22005_Katrina. pdf; and National Aeronautics and Space Administration, "Hurricane Season 2005: Katrina," www.nasa.gov/vision/earth/lookingatearth/h2005_katrina.html.

3. Nicholas Riccardi, "Most of Louisiana's Identified Storm Victims Over 60," *Los Angeles Times*, Nov. 5, 2005, p. A11; Nicholas Riccardi, Doug Smith and David Zucchino, "Katrina Killed Along Class Lines," *Los Angeles Times*, Dec. 18, 2005, p. A1.

4. While Katrina had weakened to Category 3 upon reaching Louisiana, the surges it created began when the storm was at categories 4 and 5 strength. For further detail, see "Tropical Cyclone Report," *op. cit.*, p. 9.

5. "President Discusses Hurricane Relief in Address to the Nation," White House, Sept. 15, 2005, www.whitehouse.gov/news/releases/2005/09/print/20050 915-8.html.

6. Bill Walsh, "Senators say recovery moving at snail's pace," *The Times-Picayune* (New Orleans), Jan. 18, 2006, p. A1.

7. Ralph Vartabedian, "New Orleans Should be Dry by End of Week," *Los Angeles Times*, Sept. 19, 2005, p. A8; "Performance Evaluation Plan and Interim Status, Report 1 of a Series: Performance Evaluation of the New Orleans and Southeast Louisiana Hurricane Protection System," Interagency Performance Evaluation Task Force, Jan. 10, 2006, p. 1, https://ipet.wes.army.mil.

8. "Action Plan for New Orleans: The New American City," Bring New Orleans Back Commission, Urban Planning Committee, Jan. 11, 2006, Introduction, www.bringneworleansback.org.

9. "It was not unusual for slaves to gather on street corners at night, for example, where they challenged whites to attempt to pass. . . ," historian Joseph G. Tregle is quoted in Eugene D. Genovese, *Roll, Jordan, Roll: The World the Slaves Made* (1972), pp. 412-413.

10. Quoted in Reed Johnson, "New Orleans: Before and After," *Los Angeles Times*, Sept. 5, 2005, p. E1. For more background on Congo Square, see Craig E.

Colten, *An Unnatural Metropolis: Wresting New Orleans From Nature* (2005), p. 72; and Gerald Early, "Slavery," on Web site for "Jazz," PBS documentary, www.pbs.org/jazz/time/time_slavery.htm.

11. "A Strategy for Rebuilding New Orleans, Louisiana," Urban Land Institute, Nov. 12-18, 2005, p. 17, www.uli.org/Content/NavigationMenu/ProgramsSer vices/AdvisoryServices/KatrinaPanel/ULI_Draft_New _Orleans%20Report.pdf.

12. "President Discusses Hurricane Relief," *op. cit.*

13. Joby Warrick, "White House Got Early Warning on Katrina," *The Washington Post*, Jan. 24, 2005, p. A2.

14. Steve Ritea and Tara Young, "Cycle of Death: Violence Thrives on Lack of Jobs, Wealth of Drugs," *The Times-Picayune* (New Orleans), p. A1; Adam Nossiter, "New Orleans Crime Swept Away, With Most of the People," *The New York Times*, Nov. 10, 2005, p. A1. Dan Baum, "Deluged, When Katrina hit, where were the police?" *The New Yorker*, Jan. 9, 2006, p. 59.

15. Quoted in, Joel Havemann, "New Orleans' Racial Future Hotly Argued," *Los Angeles Times*, Oct. 1, 2005, p. A14.

16. Brett Martel, The Associated Press, "Storms Payback From God, Nagin Says," *The Washington Post*, Jan. 17, 2006, p. A4.

17. Manuel Rog-Franzia, "New Orleans Mayor Apologizes for Remarks About God's Wrath," *The Washington Post*, Jan. 18, 2006, p. A2.

18. James Dao, "Study Says 80% of New Orleans Blacks May Not Return," *The New York Times*, Jan. 27, 2006, p. A16.

19. *Ibid.*; see also "Action Plan," (pages unnumbered); Frank Donze and Gordon Russell, "Rebuilding proposal gets mixed reception," *The Times-Picayune* (New Orleans), Jan. 12, 2006, p. A1.

20. Donze and Russell, *ibid.*; Rivlin, *op. cit.*

21. "A Strategy for Rebuilding," *op. cit.*; Frank Donze, "Don't write us off, residents warn," *The Times-Picayune* (New Orleans), Nov. 29, 2005, p. A1.

22. "Action Plan," Introduction, *op. cit.*; Gordon Russell, "Comeback in Progress," *The Times-Picayune* (New Orleans), Jan. 1, 2006, p. A1.

23. "Battered by Katrina, Tulane University forced into layoffs, cutbacks," The Associated Press, Dec. 9, 2005.

24. Susan Saulny, "Students Return to Big Changes in New Orleans," *The New York Times*, Jan. 4, 2006, p. 13; Steven Ritea, "School board considers limited role," *The Times-Picayune* (New Orleans), Dec. 7, 2005, p. A1.

25. Elizabeth Bumiller, "In New Orleans, Bush Speaks With Optimism But Sees Little of Ruin," *The New York Times*, Jan. 13, 2006, p. A12.

26. For background, see Marcia Clemmitt, "Climate Change," *CQ Researcher*, Jan. 27, 2006, pp. 73-96.

27. Virginia R. Burkett, "Potential Impacts of Climate Change and Variability on Transportation in the Gulf Coast/Mississippi Delta Region," Center for Climate Change and Environmental Forecasting, Oct. 1-2, 2002, p. 7, http://climate.volpe.dot.gov/workshop 1002/burkett.pdf. Burkett is chief of the Forest Ecology Branch of the U.S. Geological Survey's National Wetlands Research Center, in Lafayette, La.

28. In 2006, the Bush administration does not plan to seek new funds for reconstruction in Iraq. See, Ellen Knickmeyer, "U.S. Has End in Sight on Iraq Rebuilding," *The Washington Post*, Jan. 2, 2006, p. A1.

29. Michael Oneal, "GOP Cools to Katrina Aid," *Chicago Tribune*, Nov. 12, 2005, p. A7.

30. For background, see Kenneth Jost, "Property Rights," *CQ Researcher*, March 4, 2005, pp. 197-220.

31. R. B. Seed, *et al.*, "Preliminary Report on the Performance of the New Orleans Levee Systems on August. 29, 2005," University of California at Berkeley, American Society of Civil Engineers, Nov. 2, 2005, pp. 1.2-1.4.

32. Schwartz, *op. cit.*

33. For details, see John McQuaid, "The Dutch Swore It Would Never Happen Again," "Dutch Defense, Dutch Masters," "Bigger, Better, Bolder," *The Times-Picayune* (New Orleans), Nov. 13-14, 2005, p. A1.

34. "Performance Evaluation Plan," *op. cit.*, appendix A-2. John Schwartz, "Category 5: Levees are Piece of $32 Billion Pie," *The New York Times*, Nov. 29, 2005, p. A1.

35. *Ibid.*

36. Richard W. Stevenson and James Dao, "White House to Double Spending on New Orleans Flood Protection," *The New York Times*, Dec. 16, 2005, p. A1.

37. *Ibid.*

38. President Bush said on Jan. 26 the congressional appropriations amounted to $85 billion. For background and detail, see Joseph J. Schatz, "End-of-Session Gift for the Gulf Coast," *CQ Weekly*, Dec. 26, 2005, p. 3401; "Cost of Katrina Nearing $100 Billion, Senate Budget Says," *CQ Budget Tracker News*, Jan. 18, 2006; "Senate Budget Committee Releases Current Tally of Hurricane-Related Spending," Budget Committee, Jan. 18, 2006, http://budget.senate.gov/republican. "Press Conference of the President," [transcript] Jan. 26, 2006, www.whitehouse.gov/news/releases/2006/01/20060126.htm.

39. Quoted in Jacob Freedman, "Additional Flood Funds Needed to Cover Extensive Gulf Coast Damage," *CQ Today*, Jan. 25, 2006; Statement of David I. Maurstad, Acting Director/Federal Insurance Administrator, Mitigation Division, Federal Emergency Management Agency, Committee on Senate Banking Housing and Urban Affairs, Jan. 25, 2006, http://banking.senate.gov/_files/ACF43 B7.pdf.

40. Frank Donze, Gordon Russell and Lauri Maggi, "Buyouts torpedoed, not sunk," *The Times-Picayune* (New Orleans), Jan. 26, 2006, p. A1.

41. Adrian Moore, "Rebuild New Orleans Smarter, Not Harder," Reason Foundation, Jan. 11, 2006, /www.reason.org/commentaries/moore_20060111.shtml.

42. David Greising, *et al.*, "How Do They Rebuild a City?" *Chicago Tribune*, Sept. 4, 2005, p. A1.

43. "Press Conference of the President," *op. cit.*

44. Donze, Russell and Maggi, *op. cit.*

45. *Ibid.*

46. Robert L. Bamberger and Lawrence Kumins, "Oil and Gas: Supply Issues After Katrina," Congressional Research Service, updated Sept. 6, 2005, p. 1, www.fas.org/sgp/crs/misc/RS22233.pdf. For background on offshore leases, see Jennifer Weeks, "Domestic Energy Development," *CQ Researcher*, Sept. 30, 2005, pp. 809-832.

47. Marc Humphries, "Outer Continental Shelf: Debate Over Oil and Gas Leasing and Revenue Sharing," Congressional Research Service, Uupdated Oct. 27, 2005, pp. 1-4. http://fpc.state.gov/documents/organization/56096.pdf.

48. Unless otherwise indicated, all material in this section comes from Colten, *op. cit.*; and Ari Kelman, *A River and Its City: The Nature of Landscape in New Orleans* (2003).

49. Caroline E. Mayer and Amy Joyce, "Troubles Travel Upstream," *The Washington Post*, Sept. 5, 2005, p. A23.

50. Colten, *op. cit.*, pp. 25-26.

51. For background, see C. Perkins, "Mississippi River Flood Relief and Control," *Editorial Research Reports, 1927*, Vol. 2; and M. Packman, "Disaster Insurance," *Editorial Research Reports 1956*, Vol. I.

52. John M. Barry, *Rising Tide: The Great Mississippi Flood of 1927 and How it Changed America* (1998), pp. 311-317; p. 332

53. For background, see "Economic Effects of the Mississippi Flood," *Editorial Research Reports, 1928*, Vol. I.

54. Gordon Russell, "An 1878 Map Reveals that Maybe Our Ancestors Were Right to Build on Higher Ground," *The Times-Picayune* (New Orleans), Nov. 3, 2005, p. A1.

55. "Performance Evaluation Plan," *op. cit.*, Appendix A, p. 1; Willie Drye, " 'Category Five': How a Hurricane Yardstick Came To Be," *National Geographic News*, Dec. 20, 2005, http://news.nationalgeographic.com/news/2005/12/1220_051220_saffirsimpson.html.

56. John McQuaid and Mark Schleifstein, "The Big One," *The Times-Picayune* (New Orleans), June 24, 2002, p. A1.

57. *Ibid.*

58. Ivor van Heerden, "Using Technology to Illustrate the Realities of Hurricane Vulnerability," Jan. 25, 2005, www.laseagrant.org/forum/01-25-2005.htm.

59. "Performance Evaluation Plan," *op. cit.*, Appendix A, pp. 2-3.

60. "Urgent Warning Proved Prescient," *The New York Times*, Sept. 7, 2005, p. A21.

61. "How New Orleans Flooded," in "The Storm That Drowned a City," NOVA, WGBH-TV, October 2005, www.pbs.org/wgbh/nova/orleans/how-nf.html.

62. *Ibid.*

63. See Pamela Prah, "Disaster Preparedness," *CQ Researcher*, Nov. 18, 2005, pp. 981-1004.

64. "Rita's Aftermath," *Los Angeles Times*, Sept. 28, 2005, p. A1; Shaila Dewan and Jere Longman, "Hurricane Slams Into Gulf Coast; Flooding Spreads," *The New York Times*, Sept. 25, 2005, p. A1.

65. Anne Rochell Konigsmark, "Amid ruins, 'island' of normalcy in the Big Easy," *USA Today*, Dec. 19, 2005, p. A1; Gordon Russell, "Comeback in Progress," *The Times-Picayune* (New Orleans), Jan. 1, 2006, p. A1.

66. "Action Plan," *op. cit.*, Sec. 4, (pages unnumbered).

67. Gordon Russell and James Varney, "New flood maps will likely steer rebuilding," *The Times-Picayune* (New Orleans), Jan. 15, 2006, p. A1.

68. *Ibid.*

69. *Ibid.*

70. *Ibid.*

71. Russell and Donze, *op. cit.*, Jan. 12, 2006.

72. Ritea and Saulny, *op. cit.*

73. "A Strategy for Rebuilding New Orleans," *op. cit.*, p. 19.

74. For background, see, George Anders, "How a Principal in New Orleans Saved Her School," *The Wall Street Journal*, Jan. 13, 2006, p. A1.

75. Steve Ritea, "La. won't run N.O. schools by itself," *The Times-Picayune* (New Orleans), Jan. 3, 2006, p. B1.

76. Vanessa Cieslak, "Ports in Louisiana: New Orleans, South Louisiana, and Baton Rouge," Congressional Research Service, Oct. 14, 2005, p. 1, http://fpc.state.gov/documents/organization/57872.pdf.

77. Keith L. Alexander and Neil Irwin, "Port Comes Back Early, Surprisingly," *The Washington Post*, Sept. 14, 2005, p. D1.

78. Bill Walsh, "Senators say recovery moving at a snail's pace," *The Times-Picayune* (New Orleans), Jan. 18, 2006, p. A1.

79. Ed Anderson, "Special session set to begin Feb. 6," *The Times-Picayune* (New Orleans), Jan. 12, 2006, p. A2.

80. Steve Ritea, "Nagin's schools panel issues reforms," *The Times-Picayune* (New Orleans), Jan. 18, 2006, p. A1; "Rebuilding and Transforming: A Plan for World-Class Public Education in New Orleans," Bring New Orleans Back Commission, Jan. 17, 2006, pp. 10, 48.

81. Ed Anderson, "N.O. needs 7,000 more trailer sites, Blanco says," *The Times-Picayune* (New Orleans), Jan. 9, p. A1.

82. Adam Nossiter, "New Orleans Agrees to Give Notice on Home Demolitions," *The New York Times*, Jan. 18, 2006, p. A10.

83. Spencer S. Hsu, "Bush's Post-Katrina Pledges," *The Washington Post*, Jan. 28, 2006, p. A12.

84. Linda Bilmes and Joseph Stiglitz, "The Economic Costs of the Iraq War: An Appraisal Three Years After the Beginning of the Conflict," http://ksghome.harvard.edu/~lbilmes/paper/iraqnew.pdf. Former Deputy Assistant Commerce Secretary Bilmes is now at the Kennedy School of Government at Harvard; Stiglitz, a Nobel laureate economist, teaches at Columbia University.

BIBLIOGRAPHY

Books

Colten, Craig E., *An Unnatural Metropolis: Wresting New Orleans from Nature*, **Louisiana State University Press, 2005.**
A Louisiana State University, Baton Rouge, geographer chronicles the city's ongoing efforts to tame its watery environment.

Dyson, Michael Eric, *Come Hell or High Water: Hurricane Katrina and the Color of Disaster*, **Basic Civitas Books, 2006.**
A professor of humanities at the University of Pennsylvania — and a prolific author and commentator on issues of race and culture — dissects what he views as structural racism, government incompetence and class warfare against the poor in the Katrina disaster.

Kelman, Ari, *A River and its City: The Nature of Landscape in New Orleans*, **University of California Press, 2003.**
Using New Orleans' long and complicated relationship with the Mississippi River as a framework, an environmental historian at the University of California, Davis, examines why New Orleans developed as it did.

Piazza, Tom, *Why New Orleans Matters*, **Harper Collins, 2005.**
A jazz historian, novelist and New Orleans resident who evacuated the city during Katrina argues that American culture will be poorer if the working people who keep the city's traditions alive are permanently uprooted from the city.

Ward, Geoffrey C., and Ken Burns, *Jazz: A History of America's Music*, **Alfred A. Knopf, 2000.**
An author of popular history (Ward) and a renowned documentary filmmaker provide — with contributions by jazz scholars — a one-volume history of America's major cultural creation, with much attention to New Orleans' role.

Articles

Baum, Dan, "Deluged: When Katrina hit, where were the police?" *The New Yorker*, Jan. 9, 2006, p. 50.
A writer recounts how police and city government coped — or failed to — in the post-hurricane disaster.

Cooper, Christopher, "Old-Line Families Escape Worst of Flood and Plot the Future," *The Wall Street Journal*, Sept. 8. 2005, p. A1.
A profile of one of New Orleans' aristocrats brings the city's social inequalities to light in dispassionate fashion.

McQuaid, John, and Mark Schleifstein, "In Harm's Way," "Evolving Danger," "Left Behind," "The Big One," "Exposure's Cost," "Building Better," "Model Solutions," "Tempting Fate," "Shifting Tides," [series] *The Times-Picayune*, June 23-June 26, 2002.
Three years before Katrina, two reporters spell out the city's growing vulnerability to a massive hurricane, virtually telling the Katrina story.

Sontag, Deborah, "Delrey Street," *The New York Times*, Oct. 12, 2005, p. A1; Oct. 24, 2005, p. A1; Nov. 12, 2005, p. A9; Nov. 14, 2005 p. A1; Dec. 2, 2005, p. A20; Jan. 9, 2006, p. A1.
In a series of detailed profiles, a *New York Times* reporter examines how the lives of families from New Orleans' Lower Ninth Ward have been upended by Katrina.

Tizon, Alex Tomas, and Doug Smith, "Evacuees of Hurricane Katrina Resettle Along a Racial Divide," *Los Angeles Times*, Dec. 12, 2005, p. A1.
Two reporters analyzed change-of-address data to draw early conclusions on the racial effects of the disaster.

Reports and studies

"Action Plan for New Orleans: The New American City," Bring New Orleans Back Commission, Urban Planning Committee, Jan. 11, 2006, www.bringnew orleansback.org.
Civic leaders and officials provided the first detailed plan for redevelopment of New Orleans.

"An Unnatural Disaster: The Aftermath of Hurricane Katrina," Scholars for Progressive Reform, Sept. 2005, www.progressivereform.org/Unnatural_Disaster_512. pdf.
A liberal organization analyzes the disaster as a failure of unrestrained energy development and inadequate government regulation.

Katz, Bruce, *et al.*, "Katrina Index: Tracking Variables of Post-Katrina Reconstruction," updated Dec. 6, 2005, The Brookings Institution, www. brookings.edu/metro/pubs/200512_katrinaindex.htm.
To be updated periodically, this report compiles and organizes statistics in order to show economic and social trends as New Orleans recovers.

Seed, R. B., *et al.*, "Preliminary Report on the Performance of the New Orleans Levee Systems in Hurricane Katrina on August 29, 2005," University of California at Berkeley, American Society of Civil Engineers, National Science Foundation, Nov. 2, 2005, www.berkeley.edu/news/media/releases/2005/11/levee report_prelim.pdf.
Engineering experts provide an early look at the failures of the levee system that led to disaster.

For More Information

Bring New Orleans Back Commission, www.bringnew orleansback.org. The commission has been issuing detailed redevelopment plans.

The Brookings Institution, Katrina Issues and the Aftermath Project, Metropolitan Policy Program, 1775 Massachusetts Ave., N.W., Washington, DC 20036; (202) 797-6139; www.brookings.edu/metro/katrina.htm. The think tank provides policy proposals, commentary and statistics.

Center for the Study of Public Health Impacts of Hurricanes, CEBA Building, Suite 3221, Louisiana State University, Baton Rouge, LA 70803; (225) 578-4813; www.publichealth.hurricane.lsu.edu. A research center focusing on disaster prevention and mitigation.

Federal Emergency Management Agency, 500 C St., S.W., Washington, DC 20472; (800) 621-3362; www. fema.gov. The lead federal agency on disaster recovery; provides information on relief program requirements and application deadlines.

Greater New Orleans Community Data Center, www.gnocdc.org. A virtual organization that provides links

to the city's most recent social, economic and demographic statistics.

Louisiana Recovery Authority, 525 Florida St., 2nd Floor, Baton Rouge, LA 70801; (225) 382-5502; http:// lra.louisiana.gov. The state government's post-disaster reconstruction agency; provides information on the aid flowing to New Orleans.

New Orleans Area Habitat for Humanity, P.O. Box 15052, New Orleans, LA 70175-1732; (504) 861-2077, www.habitat-nola.org. A self-help housing organization building new homes in the city and nearby suburbs.

Savenolamusic, www.savenolamusic.com/index.php. An exhaustive listing of performance bookings and other resources (including medical assistance) for New Orleans musicians, including those forced out of the city.

Urban Land Institute, 1025 Thomas Jefferson St., N.W., Suite 500 West, Washington, DC 20007; (202) 624-7000; www.uli.org. The nonprofit organization for land-use and development professionals is the New Orleans city government's disaster-recovery consultant.

14

Disaster Preparedness

Pamela M. Prah

Hundreds of shipping containers, recreational vehicles and motorboats litter a residential area of Gulfport, Miss., after Hurricane Katrina hit. The storm killed more than 1,300 people in Louisiana, Alabama and Mississippi and racked up $200 billion in property damage and relief expenses, making it the costliest storm in U.S. history.

From *CQ Researcher*, August 26, 2005.

Six days before Hurricane Katrina tore through the Gulf Coast, Wal-Mart swung into action. As the deadly storm barreled toward New Orleans, the world's biggest retailer dispatched a fleet of tractor-trailer trucks loaded with generators, dry ice, thousands of cases of bottled water and other vitally needed supplies to nearby staging areas. [1]

Federal, state and local authorities also saw Katrina coming — but their delayed and deeply flawed response became a national scandal.

President Bush declared a state of emergency for Louisiana on Aug. 27, two days before the storm struck, making it eligible for federal assistance. When Katrina made landfall on Aug. 29, Bush issued a federal "declaration of emergency," activating the country's disaster plan. The $64,000 question is why it took so long for federal authorities to act.

Michael Brown, director of the Federal Emergency Management Agency (FEMA), was deemed so inept he was called back to Washington mid-disaster. Local officials were overwhelmed by the scope of the devastation and unsure who was in charge. More than 1,300 people died, and at one point more than 300,000 evacuees were housed in shelters in 40 states. [2] And politicians at all levels bickered openly about who was to blame for the horrific catastrophe that was unfolding on live TV for the world to see.

Critics charged that little thought had been given to helping people without the means to evacuate on their own — the elderly, disabled and poor.

As a result, residents who had banked on government help were left to fend for themselves. In New Orleans, levees broke, and as floodwaters rose thousands of residents huddled on rooftops. The

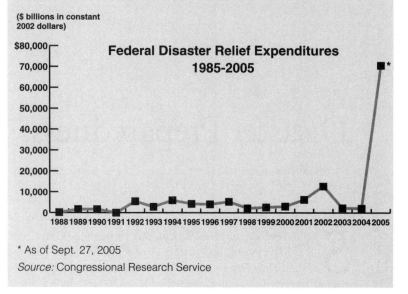

Disaster Relief Soared in 2005

The busy 2004 and 2005 hurricane seasons caused record spending on federal disaster relief this year. Expenditures in 2002 ranked second due to the Sept. 11, 2001 terrorist attacks.

($ billions in constant 2002 dollars)

Federal Disaster Relief Expenditures 1985-2005

* As of Sept. 27, 2005

Source: Congressional Research Service

20,000 people who took refuge in the Superdome found inadequate food and water, scant medical help and toilets that quickly were overwhelmed. Outside the disaster zone, government doctors stood by hundreds of empty cots, watching for patients who never arrived. Paltry resources were predeployed, or arrived late. Experts fear that sick and injured victims died for lack of timely care.

"If the federal government would have responded as quickly as Wal-Mart, we could have saved more lives," said Jefferson Parish Sheriff Harry Lee. [3]

Hurricane Katrina ranks as the most destructive storm in U.S. history. It destroyed some 200,000 homes in New Orleans alone and cost as much as $200 billion. Katrina directly affected more than a half-million people in Louisiana, Mississippi and Alabama. More than that, Katrina revealed what was widely seen as a shocking lack of readiness for another major catastrophe.

"The government's response to Katrina ranks as perhaps the biggest failure of public administration in the nation's history," wrote Donald F. Kettl, director of the Fels Institute of Government at the University of Pennsylvania." [4]

The fabled Big Easy suffered such extensive damage that some officials questioned the wisdom of rebuilding. (*See sidebar, p. 320.*)

Disaster experts blame much of the flawed response to Katrina on inadequate communications technology. Emergency-phone systems in different jurisdictions were "interoperable." Nearly forty 911 centers were knocked out, leaving citizens no way to call for help. New Orleans Mayor Ray Nagin was stuck in a hotel without a phone for two days while Louisiana Gov. Kathleen Blanco, a Democrat, reportedly couldn't get through to President Bush for two crucial days.

While looting was extensive, wildly exaggerated reports of mayhem and murder added to the sense of an out-of-control city. Even the arrival of more than 50,000 National Guard and 20,000 active-duty troops turned controversial, because critics said they came too late or were ordered not to stop the looters.

When Hurricane Rita hit Texas and Louisiana three weeks later, the response was better. But the system again faltered in late October when Hurricane Wilma — as predicted — hit Key West and Fort Lauderdale, forcing thousands of Floridians to wait in lines for water, gas, ice and insurance help.

Emergency experts and administration critics were particularly concerned about the bungled 2005 storm responses because hurricanes come with plenty of advance warning, but terrorist attacks, tornadoes and earthquakes don't.

"If we can't get Katrina right, how on Earth are we going to get a dirty bomb right, a bioterrorist attack right, the avian flu right?" asks Kathleen Tierney, director of the Natural Hazards Center at the University of Colorado in Boulder.

And most homeland security experts say another terrorist attack on the United States is all but inevitable.

As for New Orleans, experts have long known the below-sea-level city was a catastrophe waiting to happen. The federal government in 2001 ranked the potential damage to New Orleans from a hurricane as among the three likeliest, most catastrophic disasters facing this country. [5] Engineers said the city's levees would not withstand the strongest of hurricane winds. Indeed, when FEMA and Louisiana authorities practiced responding to a severe mock hurricane in July 2004, they anticipated conditions eerily similar to those wrought by Katrina: the evacuation of a million people, overflowing levees and the destruction of up to 600,000 buildings. [6]

Critics say the country should have been better prepared, particularly after the Sept. 11, 2001, terrorists attacks revealed that communications systems used by emergency workers from different jurisdictions often did not work with one another. Yet three years after the attacks, emergency equipment used in more than 80 percent of America's cities was still not interoperable with federal agencies, and 60 percent of the cities did not have communication systems that meshed with state emergency centers. [7]

The White House and Congress are both investigating the government's botched response to Katrina, but they had better act fast. Experts at the National Hurricane Center warn that the country has entered a new weather cycle that will produce more frequent "super-hurricanes" for the next 20 years, threatening cities even as far north as New York. [8]

"Houston, Galveston, Tampa Bay, southwest Florida, the Florida Keys, southeast Florida, New York City, Long Island and, believe it or not, New England, are all especially vulnerable," Max Mayfield, director of the National Hurricane Center's Tropical Prediction Center, told a Senate panel on Sept. 20.

The picture isn't much brighter for earthquakes, which threaten 75 million Americans in 39 states. [9] Experts say the United States has been lucky that recent earthquakes have occurred relatively far from populated areas, but that a major quake eventually is going to hit a big city like San Francisco.

Katrina Was Costliest U.S. Disaster

By far the most expensive disaster in the nation's history, Katrina is expected to cost at least three times more than the second-costliest U.S. disaster, the 1988 heat wave and drought.

Ten Costliest U.S. Natural Disasters
(1980-2005)

Year	Cost ($ in billions)	Disaster	Location
2005	$200 (est.)	Hurricane Katrina	Gulf Coast
1988	$61.6	Heat wave, drought	Central, Eastern U.S.
1980	$48.4	Heat wave, drought	Central, Eastern U.S.
1992	$35.6	Hurricane Andrew	South Florida, Louisiana
1993	$26.7	Floods	Midwest
1994	$25	Earthquake	Northridge/San Francisco, Calif.
2004	$14	Hurricane Charley	Florida, S.C., N.C.
1989	$13.9	Hurricane Hugo	S.C., N.C.
2004	$12	Hurricane Ivan	Florida, Alabama
1989	$10	Earthquake	Loma Prieta, Calif.

Sources: National Climatic Data Center, National Oceanic and Atmospheric Administration; Insurance Information Institute

FEMA has long been criticized as a dumping ground for White House political appointees. A report on the agency's blunders in responding to Hurricane Andrew in 1992 noted, "Currently, FEMA is like a patient in triage. The president and Congress must decide whether to treat it or let it die." [10]

But even FEMA critics concede that part of the problem is that many Americans mistakenly see the agency as a national fire-and-rescue squad, equipped with its own fire trucks, personnel and advanced technology. FEMA actually is a tiny agency — only 2,500 employees — charged with coordinating all the federal help available to states and localities.

"The federal government is never going to be the nation's first-responder. We shouldn't be, we don't have the capability to be, and we won't be," said White House homeland security adviser Frances Fragos Townsend, who is spearheading a review of the federal government's response to Katrina. [11]

Some, including President Bush and the U.S. Conference of Mayors, ask whether the military should take the lead in disaster response. [12] Others still champion

Katrina flooded three-quarters of New Orleans and revealed gaping weaknesses in the nation's disaster-response system. Many experts question the government's ability to deal with future catastrophes.

FEMA but say that budget cuts and changes following 9/11 — and the country's preoccupation with terrorism — have jeopardized FEMA's effectiveness. For example, nearly three out of every four grant dollars that the Department of Homeland Security (DHS) handed out to first-responders in 2005 were for terrorism-related activities. [13]

"It's like we've adopted the philosophy that if you are prepared for a terrorist event, then you are prepared for any event that could possibly affect the people of the United States," says Albert Ashwood, director of Oklahoma's Department of Emergency Management.

As politicians debate the effectiveness of FEMA and lessons learned from Katrina, here are some questions being discussed:

Is the United States prepared for another major disaster?

Many emergency-management experts say the country is ready for the next "disaster," but not for another "catastrophe" like Katrina. Others say the country falls woefully short on both counts.

In disasters, not everyone in the affected area is a victim, explains John R. Harrald, director of the Institute for Crisis, Disaster and Risk Management at George Washington University, in Washington, D.C. Typically roads, communications and medical systems are still in good enough shape for first-responders to get in and help. For example, three blocks from the collapsed Twin Towers on Sept. 11, New Yorkers still had electricity and phones.

In a "catastrophic event" like Katrina, however, all systems fail. Entire swaths of the Gulf Coast had no communications; city halls and police stations were destroyed; power, water and sewer systems ceased functioning. New Orleans lost virtually its entire infrastructure — transportation, telecommunications, energy and medical systems.

Disaster experts say preparedness depends on the locale. California is prepared for earthquakes, Florida for hurricanes (notwithstanding recent problems after Wilma); and the Northeast and Midwest for major snowstorms, experts say. These areas are prepared because they have learned from experience. "If you do something a number times, you get good at it," says David Aylward, secretary of the ComCARE Alliance, an organization of safety groups, first-responders and medical professionals.

But Tierney of the Natural Hazards Center worries that the country is not only unprepared for catastrophes but also ill-equipped for "ordinary" disasters, largely because of the latest reorganization of the country's disaster management system.

After the 2001 terrorist attacks, the federal government realized its response plan for "extreme events" needed to be revamped to deal with the terrorism threat. But Tierney wonders if local officials fully understand the revised 426-page National Response Plan — released in December 2004 — or their roles in it. [14] "We don't know the extent to which states and local governments have absorbed the new response philosophies under the national response plan," she says. "If Hurricane Katrina is any indication, we're in deep trouble."

Critics say the new plan focuses almost exclusively on terrorism rather than natural disasters. For instance, of the 15 emergency scenarios that the plan recommends states and localities train and prepare for — 13 are terrorist events.

Likewise, terrorism prevention now receives the lion's share of federal emergency-preparedness dollars. In 2005 some $180 million was allocated nationwide for state and local governments to fund emergency management, but it was in the form of 50-50 matching grants, which require local governments to supply a dollar for every federal dollar received. At the same time, the federal government dispersed $2.3 billion for anti-terrorism measures, with no matching funds required, explains Ashwood.

But supporters of the new federal plan point out that even before Sept. 11, FEMA had provided funds for "all-hazards" emergency preparedness. The Government Accountability Office (GAO) concluded this year that while most funding today is targeted at preventing terrorist attacks, the all-hazards approach is generally working, training first-responders for skills needed for both kinds of disasters. [15]

However, says Aylward, the country spends far too little on emergency medicine — only $3.5 million in 2005 for states to build up medical-trauma capacity. A flu pandemic, for example, could send 2.3 million Americans to hospitals, many in need of respirators — but there are only 105,000 respirators available in U.S. hospitals, and most are already in constant use. [16]

"We've pumped billions of dollars into preparedness since 9/11, but virtually none of that has gone to the one place where we know 80 percent of patients go first," said Rick Blum, president of the American College of Emergency Physicians. [17]

Most agree that the country falls particularly short in emergency communications. Many communities do not have technology that allows first-responders, government officials and others to stay in contact with each other. And local, state and federal officials also do not have systems in place enabling them to communicate with one another during an emergency.

In the aftermath of Katrina, some rescuers finally got a radio system that let them talk to one another — only after FedEx technical adviser Mike Mitchell of Memphis realized while watching Katrina TV coverage that a broken FedEx radio antenna in New Orleans could be adapted with some spare parts, a generator and radios. He made his way to the city, and atop a 54-story building near the convention center he installed a new nine-foot FedEx radio antenna that an Army helicopter lowered to him. [18]

Hurricane Katrina's Unprecedented Impact

Katrina affected an area roughly the size of Great Britain and will cost an estimated $200 billion.

During the relief effort:

- **72,000 federal workers and 50,000 National Guard troops were deployed;**
- **33,000 people were rescued by the Coast Guard;**
- **300,000 evacuees were sheltered in more than 40 states;**
- **717,000 households received $1.5 billion in federal aid;**
- **27 million hot meals were served by the Red Cross; and**
- **93 Disaster Recovery Centers were operated.**

Source: Dept. of Homeland Security

The independent commission that investigated the 9/11 attacks recommended that more spectrum, or airwaves, be reserved for public-safety use, but Congress has yet to act. "We know, looking back at 9/11, that lives were lost because we didn't have interoperability and didn't have access to public radio spectrum," former Sen. Timothy J. Roemer, D-Ind., a 9/11 Commission member, told Congress. [19] "We know that lives were lost in New Orleans because we didn't have this capability."

The Homeland Security department's study on interoperability won't be finished until summer 2006, and a Federal Communications Commission (FCC) report on the need for additional spectrum is due in December. [20]

"If something knocks out phones, electricity, the Internet and radio towers, is there a backup so that responders can still communicate?" Aylward asks. "To my knowledge, no one has done that."

In addition to first-responders' radios, Katrina knocked out 40 call centers that provide 911 assistance, and more than 20 million telephone calls did not go

Are You Prepared?

Disasters can wipe out basic services — water, gas, electricity or telephones. Often emergency personnel cannot reach everyone right away. Experts stress the importance of individuals being prepared to take care of themselves for at least three days or until basic services are restored or help arrives.

Create a Family Disaster Plan

- Establish two places to meet in the event your home is damaged or roads are blocked — one near the home and one outside of the immediate area.
- Arrange a way to contact each other should you be separated during a disaster. Since local phone calls may be impossible, designate an out-of-state person as the "family contact."
- Plan for an urgent evacuation. Keep a backpack or duffle bag packed in advance with:
  - First aid kit, prescription drugs for three days and extra eyeglasses (copies of the drug and eyeglass prescriptions).
  - Flashlight, batteries, battery-powered radio, bottled water.
  - A change of clothes, a sleeping bag or bedroll and pillow for each household member.
  - Car keys (and keys to where you are going if it is a friend's or relative's house).
  - Checkbook, cash, credit cards, driver's license or personal identification, Social Security card, proof of residence (deed or lease), insurance policies, birth and marriage certificates, stocks, bonds and other negotiable certificates, wills, deeds and copies of recent tax returns.

"Sheltering in Place"

Have an Emergency Preparedness Kit (preferably stored in waterproof containers) prepared in advance with sufficient supplies for your family to survive in your home for at least three days without power or municipal services, including:

- The same supplies you would take with you when evacuating. (See above.)
- Water (a gallon per person per day).
- Foods that do not require refrigeration or cooking.
- Special items or medical equipment for infants and family members.
- Sanitation supplies: toilet paper, towelettes, soap, hand sanitizer, toothbrush, contact lens supplies, feminine supplies, garbage bags.
- Tool kit with matches in waterproof container, pliers, paper/pencil, map of the area.
- Non-electronic entertainment, games, books.

For more information, contact www.prepare.org or www.redcross.org. Fact sheets and a 204-page guide from FEMA are available at www.fema.gov/are youready/.

Sources: American Red Cross, FEMA

news and emergency information, and emergency workers and public safety officials had difficulty coordinating their efforts. The New Orleans Police Department, for example, was severely crippled for three days following the storm. [23]

FCC Chairman Kevin Martin told Congress that Katrina made the commission realize that when 911 call centers go down, "there's not even a standard protocol" for rerouting the calls. So when Hurricane Rita followed shortly after, federal authorities made sure 911 centers knew to contact telephone companies with backup plans.

Satellite-phone companies did not lose service during Katrina and were able to provide phone and video links to police, emergency personnel and news outlets. Ironically, when the storm hit, New Orleans was one of 25 cities taking part in an "integrated wireless network" program spearheaded by the departments of Justice, Homeland Security and Treasury designed to usher in the next generation of radio systems for federal law enforcement. [24]

Ashwood, of the National Emergency Management Association, says that while enabling responders to communicate with one another is extremely important, it pales in comparison to the need for first-responders to know each other and what each one does.

"If you want to talk about the big communications problem in this country, that's it," says Ashwood. "It has nothing to do with radios."

through the day after the hurricane struck. [21] The hurricane also knocked 80 percent of the radio stations and 70 percent of the TV stations off the air. [22] Hundreds of thousands of hurricane victims were unable to receive

Should the military play the lead role in disaster response?

President Bush has asked Congress to consider allowing the military to take the lead in certain disaster responses. "It is now clear that a challenge on this scale requires greater federal authority and a broader role for the armed forces — the institution of our government most capable of massive logistical operations on a moment's notice," Bush said in a Sept. 15 televised speech from New Orleans. [25]

Indeed, after Katrina, the public saw the military as the only government entity that seemed able to restore order swiftly. Bush tapped Coast Guard Vice Adm. Thad W. Allen to temporarily head the government's response to Katrina. And no-nonsense Lt. Gen. Russel Honore, the military's task force commander, epitomized why the military should take the lead. Mayor Nagin called him a "John Wayne dude" who can "get some stuff done." [26]

But many officials vehemently oppose tapping the military to lead the federal response to disasters. Governors in particular don't want to lose control of their National Guard troops, whom they call up for natural disasters, crowd control and quelling civil violence. Moreover, active-duty soldiers are prohibited from enforcing civilian laws or providing police services by the 1878 *Posse Comitatus* Act. *

Of 38 governors asked by *USA Today* about Bush's idea, only Republicans Mitt Romney of Massachusetts and Tim Pawlenty of Minnesota supported it. [27] Even the president's brother, Gov. Jeb Bush, R-Fla., opposes more federal involvement. "Federalizing emergency response to catastrophic events would be a disaster as bad as Hurricane Katrina," Gov. Bush told Congress in October. "Just as all politics are local, so too are disasters. The most effective response is one that starts at the local level and grows with the support of surrounding communities, the state and then the federal government." [28]

Typically, active-duty soldiers are called in only if local, state and other federal resources are overwhelmed and the lead federal agency — typically FEMA — requests help. Under the Stafford Act, the president can declare a federal emergency or disaster and deploy troops, but only to help deliver aid. [29] Lt. Gen. Honore reminded his soldiers that New Orleans wasn't Iraq and to keep their guns pointed down.

To seize control of the Katrina mission, President Bush would have had to invoke the Insurrection Act, which allows federal troops to suppress a rebellion and

Ousted FEMA Director Michael Brown answers lawmakers' questions about the agency's response to Hurricane Katrina. Brown defended his agency's performance, blaming many of the problems in Louisiana on state and local authorities.

enforce federal laws. Bush's father invoked the law in 1992 during riots in south-central Los Angeles following the acquittal of police officers charged in the beating of Rodney King.

Pentagon leaders are waiting for completion of a Defense Department review before making recommendations on whether to amend current laws prohibiting the military from policing local communities. The Pentagon reportedly is considering creating new "rapid response" units trained to respond to domestic catastrophes. The units would be used rarely and would quickly transfer responsibilities to civilian authorities. [30]

Defense Secretary Donald H. Rumsfeld stressed in September that the current system "works pretty well" for dealing with most natural disasters, but that Hurricane Katrina was "distinctly different" because "the

---

* *Posse Comitatus* ("power to the county" in Latin) was passed after the Civil War to end the use of federal troops in Southern states.

first-responders [were] victims themselves, and as such, somewhat overwhelmed by the catastrophic nature of Hurricane Katrina and the floods" that followed. [31]

The New Orleans Police Department was unable to account for 240 officers on its 1,450-member force following Hurricane Katrina and has since fired more than 50 officers for desertion. [32]

Actually, military officials began deploying ships and personnel before receiving specific requests from the DHS or FEMA. In fact, they began preparing responses a week before Katrina hit. [33]

A day after the hurricane struck, the DHS declared Katrina an "incident of national significance," which under the new National Response Plan should trigger a coordinated federal response. By the following day, the amphibious assault ship *USS Bataan* arrived with supplies off New Orleans, but not until Sept. 5 — a week after Katrina hit — did troops arrive. [34]

The governors of Louisiana and Mississippi had both declared states of emergency before Katrina made landfall, but many of their National Guard units were deployed overseas. Within 10 days of the hurricane hitting, National Guard personnel from all 50 states had joined in the relief operations, an unprecedented effort. [35]

Some wonder whether lives would have been saved in New Orleans if the military had been in charge from the beginning. "When you have a disaster that overwhelms state and local government and requires a federal response, the Department of Defense is the agency best positioned to do it," said Lawrence Korb, former assistant secretary of Defense for manpower and personnel during the Reagan administration. [36]

Sen. John W. Warner, R-Va., chairman of the Senate Armed Services Committee, supported an expanded military role in emergencies even before Katrina hit, calling for a change in the *Posse Comitatus* law. [37] "The current framework of law did not in any way render less effective the inner working of the [National] Guard and active forces in this Katrina situation," Warner said in September. "But who knows about the next one?" [38]

Mayors also would like the military to take a more active role in relief — at least in the first few days after a disaster — and want to get military help without needing the state's approval. [39] But the military is already stretched thin with deployments in Iraq and Afghanistan, and many question whether adding more domestic tasks would undermine military readiness. [40]

Plus, it would depart from the longstanding tradition of keeping the U.S. military out of civilian affairs.

"Putting full-time warriors into a civilian policing situation can result in serious collateral damage to American life and liberty," said Gene Healy, a defense expert at the libertarian Cato Institution. [41]

Expanding the military's role was also explored after Hurricane Andrew ripped through South Florida in 1992. At Congress' request, the National Academy of Public Administration studied the proposition and eventually opposed it. Essentially, the academy concluded the current structure allows the military to provide support to civilian authorities, such as logistics and humanitarian aid, but that ultimately civilians must maintain decision-making authority. [42]

States and localities should be able to turn to the military, but disaster response is "entirely a civilian function," says George Washington University's Harrald.

The key, according to state and local officials, is better coordination. "Hurricane Katrina, and to some extent Rita, revealed the need for improved intergovernmental response to catastrophic disasters," Audwin M. Samuel, mayor pro tem of Beaumont, Texas, told Congress. [43]

Robert W. Klein, director of the Center for Risk Management at Georgia State University, does not oppose a military-led response, but, he says, ideally a "properly staffed, properly charged and properly oriented" FEMA would take the lead role. But in either scenario, he says the military role should happen automatically. "The disaster czar or disaster general shouldn't be waiting for a phone call."

Does politics reduce FEMA's effectiveness?

Some experts say that structural changes were made at FEMA after Sept. 11 strictly for political reasons — and that the country's preparedness has suffered. Others contend that incompetence — not politics — is a bigger factor at FEMA.

Former FEMA Director Brown told the special House panel investigating Katrina he didn't want to make the problems surrounding the response partisan. But noting he didn't have problems evacuating Alabama and Mississippi, Brown added, "I can't help that Alabama and Mississippi are governed by Republican governors, and Louisiana is governed by a Democratic governor." [44]

Brown largely blamed post-Katrina missteps on strained relations between Gov. Blanco and Mayor Nagin — both Democrats. "I very strongly personally regret that I was unable to persuade [them] to sit down, deal with their differences and work together. I just couldn't pull that off," he said. [45]

For their part, neither Blanco nor Nagin had anything positive to say about FEMA or the White House. After the storm, Blanco reportedly was unable to reach either President Bush or his chief of staff and had to plead for help via a message left with a low-level adviser. [46] Nagin angrily complained on national television that federal officials "don't have a clue what's going on down here" and called on them to "get off your asses and do something." [47]

Some speculate that Bush was reluctant to step in and take control in a Southern state run by a Democrat, and a woman at that. "Can you imagine how it would have been perceived if a president of the United States of one party had pre-emptively taken from the female governor of another party the command and control of her forces?" a senior administration official told *The New York Times*. [48]

But in 17 years of emergency management, Ashwood says he has never seen politics enter into decisions. "It's after-the-fact finger-pointing," he says. "It's people saying, 'Well, I might have made mistakes, but I didn't make as many as that guy.'"

George Washington's Harrald agrees: "I don't think anyone intentionally, for political reasons, made bad decisions. Bad decisions and inaction were a matter of competence, not intent."

Some experts point out that in the mid-1990s — after its disastrous response to Hurricane Andrew — FEMA overcame its reputation for being slow and bureaucratic, but that post-9/11 changes have undermined the agency's ability to respond to natural disasters. "The system that exists today is nothing like the emergency-management system that had been built up over the last 30 years," says Tierney of the Natural Hazards Center in Colorado. "Those patterns were radically reversed after 9/11. All this talk about FEMA, FEMA, FEMA" misses the point. "We're operating under a homeland-security policy system now, not a comprehensive emergency-management system."

For example, when FEMA was incorporated into the new DHS after Sept. 11, it lost its status as an independent agency with direct access to the president. Instead, the agency and its 2,500 employees became one of 22 agencies folded into the 180,000-employee DHS.

"The driving force behind the creation of DHS was the need of elected officials to . . . be seen as responding to the attacks of Sept. 11, 2001," said Kettl at the University of Pennsylvania. [49] But in the process, he said, FEMA's role in disaster response was weakened.

Richard W. Krimm, a former senior FEMA official for several administrations, agreed. "It was a terrible mistake to take disaster response and recovery . . . and put them in Homeland Security," he said. [50]

Critics say it is now impossible for FEMA to implement the four steps that make up comprehensive emergency management. The first is mitigation, which is the ongoing effort to reduce the potential impact disasters can have on people and property, such as engineering bridges to withstand earthquakes and enforcing effective building codes to protect property from hurricanes. The other steps are preparedness, response and recovery.

"These four steps should be seamlessly integrated," says Tierney. But since Sept. 11, "The comprehensive emergency-management approach has been broken up."

Moreover, key FEMA posts were not filled by people experienced in emergency management. James Lee Witt, the Clinton administration FEMA director who was widely credited with turning FEMA around, previously had headed the Office of Emergency Services in Arkansas. Ousted FEMA Director Brown had little emergency-management experience, having joined the agency as legal counsel after several years at the International Arabian Horse Association.

"You get the impression that for higher-level appointments at FEMA, political connections weighed heavier than qualifications," says Klein of Georgia State University. Indeed, of the eight top officials at FEMA, only two had experience with fire and emergency services, and they were not used early on in the Katrina response, according to William Killen, president of the International Association of Fire Chiefs. "The coordination would have been a lot better if there had been more people with operational experience in emergency response in position," Killen told a House panel. [51]

Brown also lacked the same access to the president that Witt had enjoyed under Clinton. "That direct relationship to the White House is crucial," former Gov. Bob Wise, D-W.Va., told Congress. "All the other federal

CHRONOLOGY

1800-1950s *President Franklin D. Roosevelt increases federal government's role in disasters.*

1803 The first federal disaster relief law, the Congressional Act of 1803, provides assistance to Portsmouth, N.H., after an extensive fire.

May 31,1889 Johnstown, Pa., is devastated by the worst flood in the nation's history, killing more than 2,200 residents.

Sept. 8, 1900 Hurricane destroys Galveston, Texas, killing 6,000 residents.

Sept. 16, 1928 Hurricane kills 2,500 in South Florida.

1933-34 The Reconstruction Finance Corporation and Bureau of Public Roads are authorized to make disaster loans.

1936 Flood Control Act of 1936 gives Army Corps of Engineers greater authority to implement flood control projects.

1960s-1970s *Washington boosts federal role in disaster preparedness and response.*

1961 John F. Kennedy administration creates the Office of Emergency Preparedness inside the White House to deal with natural disasters.

1974 Disaster Relief Act permits president to declare "disaster areas," thus providing federal help to states.

Sept. 16, 1978 President Jimmy Carter creates Federal Emergency Management Agency (FEMA).

1980s-1992 *FEMA comes under fire.*

Aug. 7, 1978 Carter declares a federal emergency at Love Canal, the neighborhood near Niagara Falls, N.Y., contaminated by hazardous wastes.

1980 FEMA is accused of stretching its authority by responding to Cuban refugee crisis in Miami.

1985 FEMA director resigns amid charges of misusing government funds; the agency is lampooned in the comic strip "Doonesbury."

1989 FEMA's sluggish response to Hurricane Hugo prompts Sen. Ernest Hollings, D-S.C., to call the agency "the sorriest bunch of bureaucratic jackasses" he had ever seen.

1992 FEMA's response to Hurricane Andrew in Florida is bungled; Congress considers abolishing FEMA.

1993-2001 *FEMA is rehabilitated under Clinton.*

1992 President Bill Clinton picks James L. Witt, a 14-year veteran of Arkansas' emergency services, as FEMA director and makes him a Cabinet member.

1993-94 Witt streamlines disaster relief-and-recovery operations; FEMA wins praise for efforts in 1993 flooding in Midwest and the 1994 Northridge, Calif., earthquake.

1995 The Murrah Federal Building in Oklahoma City is bombed, killing 168 and raising questions about FEMA's role in responding to terrorist attacks.

Sept. 11, 2001 The World Trade Center and Pentagon are attacked; nearly 3,000 people are killed.

2001-Present *Budget cuts, reorganization and loss of experienced employees weaken FEMA's ability to respond to disasters.*

March 1, 2003 FEMA becomes part of the Department of Homeland Security, losing its independence and Cabinet status.

Aug.-Sept. 2004 Four hurricanes hit Florida, a pivotal state in the ongoing presidential campaign. President George W. Bush quickly declares the state a disaster area, making it eligible for federal assistance.

Aug.-Sept., 2005 Numerous hurricanes are spawned in the Atlantic, including Katrina, which strikes the Gulf Coast on Aug. 29, causing massive flooding and destruction. FEMA's poor response prompts Congress and the White House to review the nation's preparedness.

agencies must know that the FEMA director and the president communicate directly and that there isn't anyone between them." [52]

The reorganization of FEMA required Brown to send budget and policy requests to the DHS secretary, who would then pitch FEMA's issues to the president. After being fired as FEMA director, Brown complained bitterly to the House panel that his budget requests had never made it to the president and that his budget and staff were cut.

Experts outside the agency agree that many competent FEMA officials left the agency out of frustration or were contracted out after the reorganization, leaving key posts without expertise. In fact, many of the DHS employees assigned to the Gulf Coast after Katrina had to first spend two to three days studying federal emergency-management rules, including the types of aid available to hurricane victims. [53]

"The organization just wasn't there. We lost that and didn't really realize it," says Harrald. "There was not an awareness that the system was collapsing."

The new emphasis on terrorism also undercut FEMA. "After Sept. 11, they got so focused on terrorism they effectively marginalized the capability of FEMA," said George D. Haddow, a former Clinton administration FEMA official. [54]

BACKGROUND

FEMA's Roots

The federal government hasn't always taken an active role in natural disasters.

The Congressional Act of 1803, considered the first piece of disaster legislation, provided federal assistance to Portsmouth, N.H., following a huge fire.

Over the next century, Congress passed more than 100 measures in response to hurricanes, earthquakes, floods and other natural disasters, but those actions were ad hoc, often overlapping and disjointed. [55] Local communities, on the whole, were expected to handle disaster relief.

Even the 1900 hurricane that killed 6,000 people in Galveston, Texas — the most deadly U.S. natural disaster — triggered only a limited federal response. The Army Corps of Engineers helped build a new sea wall, but it was up to the locals to help survivors and rebuild the flattened city. [56]

The efforts of future President Herbert Hoover in Florida following two deadly hurricanes in the late 1920s probably helped the then-secretary of Commerce win the presidency in 1928. [57] In 1926, a hurricane hit South Florida, killing about 240 people. Two years later, less than two months before the election, another hurricane hit Lake Okeechobee, killing 2,500. Hoover visited the area following both storms and was instrumental in the push for new channels and levees. Since then, presidents have found that their own responses to natural disasters can affect the outcome of an election, with some historians dubbing the phenomenon as "The Photo-op Presidency." [58]

During the Depression, President Franklin D. Roosevelt initiated a more active federal role in disaster response. For instance, he authorized the Reconstruction Finance Corporation, established by Hoover in 1932 to bolster the banking industry, to make reconstruction loans for public facilities damaged by earthquakes, and later, other disasters. In 1934 the Bureau of Public Roads was given authority to provide funding for highways and bridges damaged by natural disasters. The Flood Control Act of 1936, which gave the Army Corps of Engineers greater authority to implement flood control projects, also became law during FDR's era.

This piecemeal approach lasted until the 1960s and early '70s, when a series of hurricanes and earthquakes spurred the federal government to become more involved. In 1961, the Kennedy administration created the Office of Emergency Preparedness inside the White House to deal with natural disasters. Then in 1968, Congress created the National Flood Insurance Program (NFIP), which offered new flood protection to homeowners. The insurance was available only to those in communities that adopted and enforced a federally approved-plan to reduce flood risks.

The Disaster Relief Act of 1974 laid out the formal process that permits a president to declare "disaster areas," which are eligible for federal assistance, including money for state and local governments to make repairs, clear debris and provide temporary housing and unemployment and cash assistance for individuals. The law was amended in 1988 and renamed the Robert T. Stafford Disaster Relief and Emergency Act, after its chief sponsor, a Republican senator from Vermont. It remains the main federal disaster law.

In the late 1970s, hazards associated with nuclear power plants and the transportation of hazardous substances were

Should New Orleans Be Rebuilt?

President Bush has vowed to rebuild New Orleans, and Congress has already started doling out reconstruction funds. But is that a good idea? Hurricane Katrina put 80 percent of the city under water, destroying some 200,000 homes.

House Speaker J. Dennis Hastert, R-Ill., came under withering criticism, particularly from Democratic lawmakers who represent New Orleans, when he said rebuilding "doesn't make sense," adding, it "looks like a lot of that place could be bulldozed." Hastert later said he was not "advocating that the city be abandoned or relocated." [1]

But some experts argue that rebuilding a city below sea level, on land that is sinking, near a large lake and in a hurricane-prone area is simply another disaster waiting to happen — and taxpayers shouldn't have to keep picking up the tab.

"Should we rebuild New Orleans . . . just so it can be wiped out again?" asked Klaus Jacob, a geophysicist and adjunct professor at Columbia University's School of International and Public Affairs. Even strengthening the levee system isn't the answer, Jacob said. "The higher the defenses, the deeper the floods that will inevitably follow," he wrote. [2]

"It is time to face up to some geological realities and start a carefully planned deconstruction of New Orleans," Jacob continued, "assessing what can or needs to be preserved, or vertically raised and, if affordable, by how much."

The city is nestled in a so-called bowl, sandwiched between levees holding back Lake Pontchartrain to the north and the Mississippi River to the south. Some places are up to 10 feet below sea level; areas nearer the river generally are higher in elevation.

Traditional homeowner insurance policies do not cover losses from floods, so homeowners, renters and businesses that want insurance must turn to the National Flood Insurance Program (NFIP) for coverage. Nationwide, about half of eligible properties are covered by flood insurance. [3]

Many people wrongly believe that the U.S. government will take care of their financial needs if they suffer damage due to flooding. In fact, federal disaster assistance is only available if the president formally declares a disaster, which he did for Katrina. But often, federal disaster-assistance loans must be repaid. That is on top of any mortgage loans that people may still owe on the damaged property.

Katrina was the largest and costliest flood disaster in U.S. history. FEMA estimates flood insurance payouts for 225,000 claims from hurricanes Katrina and Rita could hit $23 billion, far exceeding the $15 billion that has been paid out since the NFIP program began in 1968. [4]

While FEMA collects the premiums, it lacks reserves and must borrow from the U.S. Treasury to meet the payouts. Congress in September temporarily increased the amount FEMA could borrow to $3.5 billion from $1.5 bil-

added to the list of potential disasters. Eventually, more than 100 federal agencies were authorized to deal with disasters, hazardous incidents and emergencies. Similar programs and policies existed at the state and local level, further complicating disaster-relief efforts.

Frustrated with the overlapping programs and confusing bureaucracy, the nation's governors urged President Jimmy Carter to centralize federal emergency functions. Carter responded with a 1979 executive order that merged some 100 separate disaster-related responsibilities into a new agency — FEMA. [59]

For the first time, Carter said, "key emergency-management and assistance functions would be unified and made directly accountable to the president and Congress." [60] As the federal government's lead disaster agency, FEMA established official relationships with organizations such as

Catholic Charities, the United Way, the Council of Jewish Federations and the American Red Cross.

The Red Cross is the only relief organization chartered by Congress "to maintain a system of domestic and international disaster relief." In fact, the National Response Plan specifically calls on the Red Cross to provide local relief. During Katrina, the Red Cross provided hurricane survivors with nearly 3.42 million overnight stays in more than 1,000 shelters. And, in coordination with the Southern Baptist Convention, it served nearly 27 million hot meals to victims.

Political Storms

In addition to natural disasters, FEMA handled the 1970s cleanup of Love Canal, near Niagara Falls, N.Y., contaminated by buried toxic wastes; the 1979 accident at the Three

lion and is considering upping that to $8.5 billion under a measure pending in Congress. [5]

Private insurers are expected to pay about $40 billion in Katrina damage, according to Robert P. Hartwig, chief economist at the Insurance Information Institute. [6] The institute said the percentage of homes with flood insurance affected by Hurricane Katrina varied in Louisiana from nearly 58 percent in some areas down to 7 percent. In many areas, homeowners and business owners were not required, or even encouraged, by their banks or their insurance companies to purchase flood insurance, partly because outdated floodplain maps were used.

Critics say taxpayers are too often left holding the bag for those who continually build in flood-prone or other risky areas. "Are we going to continue to bail out people who will continue to build in very, very hazardous areas?" asked Sen. Richard Shelby, R-Ala., chairman of the Banking, Housing and Urban Affairs Committee, which examined the NFIP program in October. [7]

Congress in 2004 approved a pilot program that would impose higher insurance premiums for property owners at severe risk of suffering repeated flood damage.

Rather than allowing rebuilding in lowlying areas, some suggest more radical approaches: "Moving the city is clearly going to be an option," said John Copenhaver, a former FEMA Southeast regional director. "It would be an unbelievably expensive and difficult proposition, but it has to be on the table." [8]

And such a solution is not unprecedented. The government has helped move entire towns following disasters, including Soldiers Grove, Wis., after a 1979 flood. And businesses were moved in several communities — including Valmeyer, Ill., and Pattonsburg, Mo. — after floods in 1993. [9]

Hastert said undoubtedly New Orleans residents would rebuild, adding, however: "We ought to take a second look at it. But you know, we build Los Angeles and San Francisco on top of earthquake fissures, and they rebuild, too. Stubbornness." [10]

---

[1] The Associated Press, "Hastert: Rebuilding New Orleans 'doesn't make sense to me,'" Sept. 2, 2005.

[2] Klaus Jacob, "Time for a Tough Question: Why Rebuild?" *The Washington Post*, Sept. 6, 2005, p. A25.

[3] Testimony of William Jenkins, Government Accountability Office, before Senate Banking, Housing and Urban Affairs Committee on National Flood Insurance Program, Oct. 18, 2005.

[4] Testimony of David Maurstad, Acting Mitigation Division Director, FEMA, before U.S. Senate Banking Housing and Urban Affairs Committee on National Flood Insurance Program, Oct. 18, 2005.

[5] Liriel Higa, "FEMA Would Get Second Boost in Borrowing Authority Under House Bill," *CQ Weekly*, Oct. 31, 2005, p. 2925.

[6] Peter Whoriskey, "Risk Estimate Led to Few Flood Policies," *The Washington Post*, Oct. 17, 2005, p. A1.

[7] Transcript of hearing of Senate Banking, Housing and Urban Affairs Committee on National Flood Insurance Program, Oct. 18, 2005.

[8] Seth Borenstein and Pete Carey, "Experts debate rebuilding New Orleans," *The* [San Jose] *Mercury News*, Sept. 1, 2005.

[9] FEMA Region X press release, "New Planning Guide Helps Communities Become Disaster-Resistant," April 26, 1999.

[10] The Associated Press, *op. cit.*

Mile Island nuclear power plant, near Harrisburg, Pa., and the 1980 "Mariel boat lift" crisis, in which 125,000 Cuban refugees converged on South Florida. Carter declared all the affected regions disaster areas, although critics said the refugee crisis was not, technically, a disaster.

In the early and mid-1980s, FEMA also faced political and legal disasters. During the Reagan administration Congress, the Justice Department and a grand jury investigated senior FEMA political officials on a variety of charges, including misuse of government funds. FEMA Director Louis O. Guiffrida resigned in 1985, and the agency was repeatedly lampooned in the comic strip "Doonesbury." [61]

In its early years, FEMA was, like much of the federal government, preoccupied with protecting Americans from the threat of the Soviet Union. "When I entered this profession 17 years ago, FEMA and emergency man-agement in general were quasi-military, [trying to] figure out where a nuclear attack was going to take place and how to relocate the nation's citizens," Oklahoma's Ashwood recently told Congress. [62]

But just as the Cold War was ending in the late 1980s and early '90s, a pair of hurricanes and an earthquake put FEMA — then plagued by morale problems, poor leadership and conflicts with its state and local partners — in a negative national spotlight. [63]

FEMA was widely criticized for its slow response to Hugo, the 1989 hurricane that devastated Charleston, S.C. Sen. Ernest Hollings, D-S.C., described FEMA as "the sorriest bunch of bureaucratic jackasses" he had ever encountered in the federal government. [64] Hugo caused $7 billion in damage in the United States, making it the costliest hurricane in U.S. history at that time.

Less than a month later, San Francisco was hit by the Loma Prieta earthquake — the largest quake along the San Andreas Fault since the 1906 San Francisco earthquake. Although FEMA was unprepared for the quake — which caused nearly $6 billion in damage and 63 deaths — California was ready, thanks to "good mitigation practices in building codes and construction . . . and some good luck," wrote former FEMA official Haddow. [65]

When Hurricane Andrew struck in 1992, it further devastated FEMA's credibility along with parts of South Florida and Louisiana. The agency's response to the disaster, which caused $25 billion in damage and left thousands without shelter and water for weeks, was blasted as disorganized.

"Where in the hell is the cavalry on this one?" asked Miami-Dade County Emergency Management Director Kate Hale. [66] "They keep saying we're going to get supplies. For God's sake, where are they?"

President George H. W. Bush, who was running for re-election, then dispatched federal troops, mobile kitchens and tents. Within a week, nearly 20,000 troops were in South Florida. [67] Nonetheless, many analysts say FEMA's poor performance cost Bush votes in the 1992 election, in which he was defeated by Democrat Bill Clinton.

Some three weeks after Andrew, one of the most powerful hurricanes in Hawaiian history hit Kauai. This time, FEMA sent disaster teams to Hawaii even before Iniki struck.

After Andrew and Iniki, some critics proposed abolishing FEMA and giving the military a bigger disaster role. The National Academy of Public Administration, however, recommended establishing a White House Domestic Crisis Monitoring Unit to ensure "timely, effective and well coordinated" federal responses to catastrophes. [68]

Reforming FEMA

President Clinton gave the agency a shot in the arm when he nominated Witt as FEMA director — the first with experience as a state emergency manager. Clinton elevated the post to Cabinet level, and Witt urged governors to similarly elevate their state emergency-management directors. [69]

Witt is credited with streamlining disaster relief and recovery operations and focusing workers on "customer service." When floods ravaged the Midwest in 1993 and an earthquake shook Los Angeles the next year, FEMA crisis-management teams quickly delivered aid to the injured. After the floods, Witt persuaded the federal government to buy flood-prone properties in the Midwest and relocate businesses and residents, saving taxpayers millions of dollars when floods struck again in 1995. [70]

FEMA also won praise for its response to a 1994 earthquake in Northridge, Calif., a modern urban environment generally designed to withstand earthquakes. Although $20 billion in damages resulted, few lives were lost.

The Oklahoma City bombing on April 19, 1995, raised questions about FEMA's role in responding to terrorist attacks. Debates raged among officials at FEMA and the Justice and Defense departments over who should be the first-responder — fire, police, emergency management or emergency medical services? Terrorism was part of FEMA's "all-hazards" approach to emergency management, but it lacked the resources and technologies to address specific terrorism issues such as weapons of mass destruction. [71]

When George W. Bush became president, like Clinton he appointed a close friend to head FEMA, Joe Allbaugh, Bush's former chief of staff as governor of Texas and his campaign manager during the 2000 presidential race. Allbaugh's lack of emergency-management experience was not an issue during his confirmation hearings. [72]

In a speech the day before the 9/11 attacks, Allbaugh outlined firefighting, disaster mitigation and catastrophic preparedness as his top priorities. [73] Ironically, on Sept. 11 Allbaugh and other FEMA senior leaders were in Montana, attending the annual meeting of the National Emergency Management Association, whose members are state emergency officials. FEMA immediately activated the Federal Response Plan.

Some elements of the response to 9/11 — particularly the communication problems — revealed major weaknesses in the country's ability to respond to terrorism and raised questions about the capabilities and appropriate role of states and localities in managing a massive disaster. Less than a week later, President Bush announced the formation of a Homeland Security Office, and a year later, on Nov. 25, 2002, Congress approved the Homeland Security Act, consolidating 22 federal agencies, including FEMA, into the new Department of Homeland Security — the largest government reorganization in 50 years.

When FEMA was officially transferred to DHS on March 1, 2003, it lost its Cabinet-level status and its independence. It also lost some of its personnel and funding to another new agency, the Office of Domestic Preparedness. In addition, $80 million was transferred from FEMA's coffers to help pay for DHS's overhead, and in 2003 and 2004 FEMA lost $169 million to DHS for other purposes, including funds FEMA was supposed to have saved from being folded into DHS. [74]

Since then, up to a third of the staff has been cut from FEMA's five Mobile Emergency Response Support detachments — teams that deploy quickly to set up communications gear, power generators and life-support equipment to help federal, state and local officials coordinate disaster response. [75]

"Over the past three-and-a-half years, FEMA has gone from being a model agency to being one where . . . employee morale has fallen, and our nation's emergency management capability is being eroded," veteran FEMA staffer Pleasant Mann told Congress in 2004.

The Bush administration also cut Corps of Engineers' flood control funds. "For the first time in 37 years, federal budget cuts have all but stopped major work on the New Orleans area's east bank hurricane levees," the New Orleans *Times-Picayune* reported in June 2004. [76]

Meanwhile, the natural disasters continued. Nine tropical systems affected the United States in 2004, causing some $42 billion in damage. [77] President Bush issued 68 major disaster declarations — the most for a single year in nearly a decade. [78]

In 2004 — as Bush was running for re-election — an unprecedented four hurricanes (Charley, Frances, Ivan and Jeanne) slammed into Florida, which had been a pivotal state in Bush's race for the White House in 2000. Careful to avoid his father's delays after Hurricane Andrew in 1992, Bush quickly declared the state a federal disaster area, making it eligible for federal assistance. Less than two days later the president was touring hard-hit neighborhoods in southwest Florida. [79]

Bush handled the next storm, Frances, in a similar fashion, drawing partisan allegations that he was using the hurricane as a photo opportunity. The president was "touting a $2 billion aid package that has already been promised to Florida as a result of Hurricane Charley," complained Rep. Robert Wexler, a Democrat from West Palm Beach. [80] The aid package was not without controversy. At least 9,800 people from Miami-Dade County received more than $21 million in assistance even though Frances hit 100 miles away and inflicted little damage in the county.

Hurricane victims slog past a police officer standing guard in flooded downtown New Orleans. Water was up to 12 feet high in some areas. The storm forced more than 300,000 people to evacuate their homes, mainly in Louisiana and Mississippi.

Still, the 2004 hurricane destruction in Florida was unprecedented. An estimated one in five Florida homes was damaged, and 117 people died. [81]

Two months later, Bush won the state and the presidency.

CURRENT SITUATION

Katrina Aftershocks

In the wake of Hurricane Katrina, the DHS is "re-engineering" its disaster preparedness; Congress is trying to figure out what went wrong and how to pay for the damage; and states and localities are reviewing their emergency plans.

Katrina ignited weeks of contradictory testimony, finger-pointing and conflicting reports from federal, state and local officials. There's no argument, however, that all three levels of government were ill prepared for a deadly storm they all knew was coming.

"It turned out we were all wrong," said White House homeland security adviser Townsend. "We had not adequately anticipated." [82] The review of the disaster being spearheaded by Townsend is expected to make recommendations by the end of 2005.

Homeland Security Secretary Michael Chertoff also acknowledged to lawmakers that Katrina overwhelmed FEMA and promised to revamp the agency and hire

Thousands wait for food, water and medical aid outside the New Orleans Convention Center on Sept. 1, 2005 — three days after Hurricane Katrina struck New Orleans.

more experienced staff. [83] "Dealing with this kind of an ultra-catastrophe . . . requires a lot of work beforehand, months beforehand," Chertoff said in October. [84]

Several Democrats, including Sen. Hillary Rodham Clinton, N.Y., say Chertoff's proposed changes don't go far enough and that the administration's changes in the agency have gutted it. "The bureaucracy created by moving FEMA under the Department of Homeland Security is clearly not working," she said in introducing legislation restoring FEMA to Cabinet-level rank. [85]

The Democrats have boycotted Congress' probe into the Katrina relief efforts and called for an independent commission similar to the panel that investigated the 9/11 attacks. But Senate Majority Leader Bill Frist, R-Tenn, noted in a letter to Democratic Minority Leader Harry Reid of Nevada that it took longer than a year for Congress to form an outside commission to investigate the federal government's handling of the Sept. 11 attacks. Such a delay now, Frist wrote, "would put more people at risk for a longer time than is necessary." [86]

The administration is pressing ahead with its own reforms. Chertoff, for example, said FEMA needs to learn from the military and private companies that were able to keep communication lines open. DHS is setting up "emergency reconnaissance teams" that will be deployed to catastrophes to provide up-to-the-minute reports to federal planners, who can then send the appropriate resources. [87]

Meanwhile, FEMA continues to come under fire for spending $236 million to temporarily house Katrina vic-

tims and emergency workers on cruise ships. FEMA also was criticized for handing out $2,000 checks to hurricane victims. In three Louisiana parishes, for example, FEMA issued more checks than there are households, at a cost of at least $70 million. [88]

Katrina-related contracts have also stirred controversy, including a $500 million debris-removal contract awarded to AshBritt Environmental, which has ties to Mississippi Gov. Haley Barbour, a former Republican National Committee chairman. [89] And former FEMA Director Allbaugh and his wife founded a company that has received federal contracts for Gulf Coast cleanup. [90] Homeland Security Inspector General Richard Skinner said in October he is investigating "all the contracting activities that took place immediately following this disaster from day one." [91]

Contracting questions aside, many emergency-management experts worry most about communication problems between federal, state and local authorities. Chertoff said his department is reviewing emergency-operations plans for every major urban area to ensure they are clear, detailed and up-to-date. "That includes a hard, realistic look at evacuation planning ranging from earthquakes to subway bombings," he said.

Local Reviews

Every city in the country is looking at its evacuation plan" in the aftermath of Katrina, says Aylward of the ComCare Alliance.

States and localities aren't always finding what they expected. A week before Hurricane Wilma hit, Gov. Bush touted Florida's hurricane readiness before a House panel. "Local and state governments that fail to prepare are preparing to fail," he said. [92]

The next week, however, when Wilma struck, "We did not perform to where we want to be," Bush said, noting that many residents failed to prepare and ended up overwhelming local government water-and-ice distribution sites. "People had ample time to prepare. It isn't that hard to get 72 hours' worth of food and water," he said, repeating the advice officials gave days before the storm. [93]

But enabling all levels of government to communicate with one another has been harder. "Since 9/11, enormous investments of time, effort and taxpayer money have been made to craft a system in which all levels of government can communicate and coordinate for the most effective response possible, whether to a natural disaster or a terrorist attack.

Did race play a role in the government's slow response to Hurricane Katrina?

YES
The Rev. Jesse L. Jackson, Sr.
Founder and President, National Rainbow/PUSH Coalition

Written for *CQ Researcher*, November 2005

Race played a role in who was left behind. Race seems to be a factor in who will get back in. Class played a role in who was left behind. Class may play a role in who is let back in.

Incompetence and cronyism played a role, especially in the slowness of the response. No-bid contracts to out-of-state corporations suggest that role has not yet ended.

The hurricane hit the whole region, without concern for skin color or wealth — but Katrina's impact was multiplied if you were African-American or poor — and so many facing the worst flooding were both.

We can't forget that years of neglect and disinvestment in public goods and services — after years of politically motivated attacks on the role of government in our society — left the people of New Orleans defenseless. Some had the individual resources to escape; many did not. And race and class are heavily correlated with those who did not.

Then there is the war. Tax money spent on invading Iraq, rather than for needed goods and services at home, such as levees. National Guard troops stuck in Baghdad, not saving lives in Biloxi.

The whole world watched in horror as helpless people were stranded and neglected in the wealthiest, most powerful nation ever to exist. It must never happen again.

Let's rebuild New Orleans. Instead of experimenting on real people in trouble with an agenda based on right-wing economic ideology, we should rebuild, reinvest in and revitalize all of New Orleans.

The rescue is not over yet. People continue to need relief, shelter, food. They want jobs, living wages and the chance to come back home. Small businesses and contractors want to help do the rebuilding. New housing must be built in Louisiana, and affordable housing provided in the meantime, near people's jobs and neighborhoods. Families and communities must be reunified.

Reconstruction must be bottom-up, not top-down, and include everyone. Reconstruction should emphasize public investment to rebuild levees, construct mass transit and sewers, open up new schools and parks. I have suggested a Civilian Reconstruction Corps to provide former residents with work, training and a chance to be part of rebuilding their homes and their city.

Too many people were abandoned during Katrina. Surely we will not abandon them again, by not bringing them home and helping them participate in the rebirth of their own beloved New Orleans.

NO
John McWhorter
Senior Fellow, Manhattan Institute

Written for *CQ Researcher*, November 2005

The almost all-black crowds sweltering, starving and dying in the Convention Center after Hurricane Katrina showed us that in New Orleans, as in so many other places, by and large to be poor is to be black. This is the legacy of racism, although opinions will differ as to whether that racism is in the past or the present.

But to claim that racism is why the rescue effort was so slow is not a matter of debate. It is, in fact, absurd.

To say "George Bush doesn't care about black people" is to honestly believe that if it were the white poor of Louisiana who happened to live closest to the levees, then barely anyone would have even gotten wet, and 50,000 troops would have been standing at the ready as soon as Katrina popped up on meteorologists' radar screens. The National Guard would have magically lifted the long-entrenched bureaucratic restrictions that only allow states to assign troops when it is proven that they are needed. Suddenly, against all historical precedent, just for that week, the Federal Emergency Management Agency would have morphed into a well-organized and dependable outfit.

But what about the hurricane that Katrina displaced as the third strongest on record to hit America — Andrew in 1992 — which left 250,000 people homeless? Ground zero for this one was Homestead, Fla., where whites were a big majority. So help was pouring in as soon as the rain stopped, right?

Well, not exactly. "Where in the hell is the cavalry on this one?" asked Kate Hale, Miami-Dade County emergency-management director, on national television. People went without electricity or food and dealt with looters for five days, just like in New Orleans. FEMA was raked over the coals for the same bureaucratic incompetence that is making headlines now.

Is it so far-fetched to admit that the problem after Katrina as well was the general ineptness of America's defenses against unforeseen disasters? A little event called 9/11 comes to mind. Two presidential administrations neglected increasingly clear signs that Osama bin Laden was planning to attack us on our shores. In general, bureaucracies are notoriously bad at foresight and long-term planning, and FEMA has never exactly been a counter-example.

Of course, there will be those who will insist, no matter what the evidence, that racism slowed down the rescue effort. But this is essentially the way a certain kind of person affirms their sense of importance when they lack healthier ones.

Worst-Case Scenarios

Scientists and storm chasers always have their sights on the next disaster. Experts at the National Hurricane Center, for example, say Katrina won't be the last major hurricane to strike a big city, forecasting that even New York City is vulnerable. Other catastrophes that scientists think could occur include:

- Gulf Coast tsunami (generated by a fault line in the Caribbean)
- East Coast tsunami (caused by asteroid falling into the Atlantic Ocean)
- Heat waves (as the population ages, urban areas get hotter and electricity systems are strained)
- Midwest earthquake
- Colossal volcanic eruption at Yellowstone National Park could destroy life for hundreds of miles and bury half the country in ash up to 3 feet deep
- Los Angeles tsunami (generated by an earthquake fault off Southern California)
- Asteroid impact
- New York City hurricane
- Pacific Northwest megathrust earthquake (could cause a tsunami like the 2004 tsunami in South Asia)

Source: Live Science, http://livescience.com

That did not occur with Katrina," said Sen. Susan Collins, R-Maine, chairwoman of a Senate panel that examined FEMA's recovery efforts. [94]

Indeed, fire chiefs who responded to Katrina told Congress there was an "utter lack of structure and communication at any level of government in the first 10 days." [95] As for former FEMA Director Brown, he was in an area totally cut off from communications when the hurricane hit and "probably would have been better off staying in Washington," says Harrald of George Washington University.

Some relief may be on the way. The proposed budget savings package working through Congress would free up spectrum for emergency responders and provide between $500 million and $1 billion in grants to local government to buy "interoperable" communication equipment. [96]

Congress is considering creating a national alert office capable of disseminating warnings of natural disasters and terrorist attacks using a wide range of media, including cell phones, cable and satellite TV and radio and PDAs (personal digital assistants). A Senate panel on Oct. 20 approved a measure sponsored by Sen. Jim DeMint, R-S.C., chairman of the Commerce Subcommittee on Disaster Prevention and Prediction. "Without a proper way to alert those in danger, even the most accurate disaster prediction is useless," he said. [97] The House does not have a companion bill.

Congress has approved more than $62 billion in emergency aid following Katrina, but more than $40 billion remained unspent as of late October. The White House wants to shift $17 billion of the unspent portion to levee reconstruction, road repairs and other basic infrastructure work in the region. [98]

Lawmakers already have shifted $750 million from FEMA to a program that lends money to local governments to maintain essential services such as police and fire protection. The measure was signed shortly after New Orleans Mayor Nagin announced plans to lay off 3,000 city employees because of funding shortfalls.

Cleaning up after Katrina is expected to dwarf clean-up expenses of past disasters. For example, about 150 million cubic yards of debris will have to be removed from four Gulf Coast states — 10 times more than Hurricane Andrew left behind in Florida in 1992, which was several times greater than the amount hauled away (at a cost of $1.7 billion) after the World Trade Center Twin Towers collapsed. [99]

While Congress is debating how to pay this year's hurricane bill, some argue that now is the time to develop a more coherent disaster policy. "The response to the disaster has been to open up the wallet and dump it out," said U.S. Rep. Dennis Cardoza, D-Calif. [100]

David Moss, a Harvard Business School economist who studies disaster financing, agrees. "Right now we cover major disaster losses mainly on an ad hoc basis," he says. "We wait until the disaster strikes, and then we spend whatever seems necessary to relieve the victims."

Natural disasters also batter the insurance industry. It estimates Katrina alone is likely to cost at least $34.4 billion in insured property losses. [101]

Florida Insurance Commissioner Kevin McCarty has asked government officials nationwide to support a "national catastrophe fund." One of its supporters is Rep. Mark Foley, R-Fla., who has sponsored a bill to amend the federal tax code to allow insurance companies to voluntarily set aside, on a tax-deferred basis, reserves to pay for future catastrophic losses. And Sen. Kay Bailey Hutchinson, R-Texas, proposes setting up an emergency reserve fund for domestic disasters and emergencies.

Moss says insurers could also include a "catastrophe rider" on every insurance policy covering losses stemming from terrorism and natural disasters, and the federal government could also offer some sort of "backstop" covering losses above a certain level, such as $100 billion.

Homeowners' insurance policies do not cover flood damage caused by the storm surges that accompany hurricanes. Experts estimate that Katrina caused $44 billion in flood damage. Flood insurance is available through the National Flood Insurance Program, but it is expensive, and many homeowners do not buy it. In addition, the New Orleans maps used to determine if a home is in a floodplain were apparently out of date, and many homeowners whose homes flooded had been told that they were not in danger of being flooded.

OUTLOOK

Just Talk?

While there is a lot of talk about improving disaster preparedness and response, few experts expect radical changes any time soon.

"The investigations are focusing on individual blame, rather than system failures," says George Washington University's Harrald. "The hubris in Washington is that we can solve everything by passing a law or reorganizing something inside the Beltway. It's a little more complicated."

Ashwood, director of emergency management in Oklahoma, agrees. "All we are doing right now is just talking. Nobody is doing anything else." He adds that while it's all good that people in Washington want answers, some of the scrutiny is misdirected. He notes that 90 auditors have

been sent to monitor the 72 full-time FEMA employees who work on disaster recovery. "Ninety auditors covering 72 people," he says. "That's ridiculous."

Meanwhile, on Capitol Hill, many lawmakers — particularly Democrats -feel the Katrina investigations are losing steam. "In the case of 9/11, it took a while to develop, and only after intense political pressure from the families," said former Rep. Lee Hamilton, D-Ill., who co-chaired the 9/11 Commission. "I don't see anything comparable" happening for the Katrina disaster. [102]

The fact that FEMA reacted quicker to hurricanes Rita and Wilma also may dampen the urgency for action, experts say. Others worry that the attention on Katrina may give short shrift to future floods, earthquakes and other disasters. "That is part of the human experience. We react to the last disaster," Harrald says.

While homeland security adviser Townsend admits that a "failure of communication" within the federal government and with state and local officials was the "single most important" contributor to the Katrina breakdown, some disaster experts aren't optimistic that even that situation will change. [103]

"The federal government needs to take a leadership role to pull the agencies together," said Priscilla Nelson, a former National Science Foundation executive. "That really hasn't happened yet . . . [and] I don't have a reasonable expectation it will. People are organized in a way that doesn't promote integration or accountability or authority." [104]

The University of Pennsylvania's Kettl says the federal government's "lack of imagination" — cited by the 9/11 Commission as a reason for the government's failure in 2001 — contributed to its poor performance after Katrina. The United States has failed to "build the capacity to deal with costly, wicked problems that leave little time to react," he wrote, and instead is "trying to solve the most important challenges of the 21st century by retreating back to models from the past." [105]

Aylward of ComCare says the discussions sparked by Hurricane Katrina miss a key point. "There's a real mistaken idea that disasters are somehow different from day-to-day events. But these are the same firemen, the same police, all the same people on the ground using the same radios, same computers," he says. "We ought to be focusing on improving the day-to-day response of emergency agencies."

For her part, the University of Colorado's Tierney hopes individual citizens will become more prepared.

"The ultimate first-responders in any disaster are members of the public," she says. "If we want to be prepared for the future terrorist attack, for the future disasters in this country, we have to build within neighborhoods and through local community organizations to help people to be self-sufficient, to help others when disaster strikes. Katrina certainly taught us that."

NOTES

1. Devin Leonard, "The Only Lifeline Was the Wal-Mart," *Fortune*, Oct. 3, 2005, p. 74.

2. Testimony of David Paulison, acting under secretary for emergency preparedness, before Senate Homeland Security and Governmental Affairs Committee, Oct. 6, 2005.

3. Leonard, *op. cit.*

4. Donald F. Kettl, "The Worst is Yet to Come: Lessons from September 11 and Hurricane Katrina," University of Pennsylvania, Fels Institute of Government, September 2005.

5. Eric Berger, "The foretelling of a deadly disaster in New Orleans," *The Houston Chronicle*, Dec. 1, 2001. See also Dean E. Murphy, "Storm Puts Focus on Other Disasters in Waiting," *The New York Times*, Nov. 13, 2005, p. A1.

6. FEMA press release, "Hurricane Pam Exercise Concludes," July 23, 2004. See also Joel K. Bourne, Jr. "Gone with the Water," *National Geographic*, October 2004.

7. U.S. Conference of Mayors, "Report on Interoperability," June 28, 2004.

8. Prepared testimony of Max Mayfield, director, National Hurricane Center, before Senate Commerce Committee's Disaster Prediction and Prevention Subcommittee, Sept. 20, 2005.

9. Fact sheet, U.S. Geological Survey, Earthquake Hazards Program.

10. National Academy of Public Administration, "Coping With Catastrophe: Building an Emergency Management System to Meet People's Needs in Natural and Manmade Disaster," February 1993.

11. White House transcript, "Press Briefing by Homeland Security and Counterterrorism Adviser Frances Fragos Townsend," Oct. 21, 2005.

12. White House transcript, "President's Remarks During Hurricane Rita Briefing in Texas," Sept. 25, 2005.

13. U.S. Government Accountability Office, "Homeland Security: DHS' Efforts to Enhance First Responders' All Hazards Capabilities Continue to Evolve," July 2005.

14. The National Response Plan is available at www.dhs.gov/interweb/assetlibrary/NRP_FullText.pdf.

15. *Ibid.*

16. Jerry Adler, "The Fight Against the Flu," *Newsweek*, Oct. 31, 2005, p. 39.

17. *Ibid.*

18. Ellen Florian Kratz, "For FedEx, It Was Time To Deliver," *Fortune*, Oct. 3, 2005, p. 83.

19. Testimony before House Energy and Commerce Subcommittee on Telecommunications and the Internet, Sept. 29, 2005.

20. Testimony of David Boyd, director of SAFECOM Program, Department of Homeland Security, before House Energy and Commerce Subcommittee on Telecommunications and the Internet, Sept. 29, 2005.

21. Testimony of Kevin Martin, chairman, Federal Communications Commission, before House Subcommittee on Telecommunications and the Internet, Sept. 29, 2005.

22. *Ibid.*

23. Testimony of Chuck Canterbury, National President, Fraternal Order of Police, before House Homeland Security Subcommittee on Emergency Preparedness, Science and Technology, Sept. 29, 2005.

24. Transcript of House Energy and Commerce Subcommittee on Telecommunications and the Internet, Sept. 29, 2005.

25. White House transcript, "President Discusses Hurricane Relief in Address to the Nation," Sept. 15, 2005.

26. CNN, "Lt. Gen. Honore a 'John Wayne dude,' " Sept. 3, 2005.

27. Bill Nichols and Richard Benedetto, "Govs to Bush: Relief our job," *USA Today*, Oct. 3, 2005.

28. Prepared testimony of Gov. Jeb Bush before U.S. House Committee on Homeland Security, Oct. 19, 2005.

29. Congressional Research Service, "Hurricane Katrina: DOD Disaster Response," Sept. 19, 2005.

30. Barbara Starr, "Military ponders disaster response unit," CNN, Oct. 11, 2005 and Ann Scott Tyson, "Pentagon Plans to Beef Up Domestic Rapid-Response Forces," *The Washington Post*, Oct. 13, 2004, p. A4.

31. The Associated Press, "NOPD Fires 51 for Desertion," CBS News, Oct. 28, 2005.

32. Department of Defense news briefing, Sept. 27, 2005.

33. Congressional Research Service, *op. cit.*

34. *Ibid.*

35. *Ibid.*

36. "NewsHour with Jim Lehrer," "Using the Military at Home," Sept. 27, 2005.

37. Congressional Research Service, "The Posse Comitatus Act and Related Matters: A Sketch," June 6, 2005.

38. Anne Plummer, "Change in 'Posse' Law Unwise, Say Critics," *CQ Weekly*, Sept. 26, 2005, pp. 2550-2551.

39. U.S. Conference of Mayors, "The U.S. Conference of Mayors Hold Special Meeting on Emergency Response and Homeland Security," Oct. 24, 2005.

40. For background see Pamela M. Prah, "War in Iraq," *CQ Researcher*, Oct. 21, 2005, pp. 881-908, and Pamela Prah, "Draft Debates," *CQ Researcher*, Aug. 19, 2005, pp. 661-684.

41. Gene Healy, "What of 'Posse Comitatus'?" *Akron Beacon Journal*, Oct. 7, 2005, reprinted on Cato Institute Web site, www.cato.org/pub_display.php?pub_id=5115.

42. National Academy of Public Administration," *op. cit.*

43. Testimony before U.S. House Committee on Homeland Security, Oct. 19, 2005.

44. Transcript of House Select Katrina Response Investigation Committee, Sept. 27, 2005.

45. *Ibid.*

46. *Time*, "4 places Where the System Broke Down," Sept. 18, 2005, p. 38.

47. CNN, "Mayor to Feds: Get Off Your Asses," Sept. 2, 2005, www.cnn.com/2005/US/09/02/nagin.transcript/.

48. Eric Lipton, Eric Schmitt and Thom Shanker, "Political Issues Snarled Plans for Troop Aid," *The New York Times*, Sept. 9, 2005, p. A1.

49. Kettl, *op. cit.*

50. Peter G. Gosselin and Alan C. Miler, "Why FEMA was Missing in Action," *Los Angeles Times*, Sept. 5, 2005.

51. Testimony before Homeland Security Subcommittee on Emergency Preparedness, Science and Technology, Sept. 29, 2005.

52. Transcript, House Transportation and Infrastructure Subcommittee on Development, Public Buildings and Emergency Management, Oct. 6, 2005.

53. Rebecca Adams, "FEMA Failure a Perfect Storm of Bureaucracy, *CQ Weekly*, Sept. 12, 2005, p. 2378.

54. Frank James and Andrew Martin, "Slow response bewilders former FEMA officials," *Chicago Tribune*, Sept. 3, 2005, p. A1.

55. "FEMA History," www.fema.gov/about/history.shtm.

56. James O'Toole, "U.S. help for disaster victims goes from nothing to billions," *Pittsburgh Post-Gazette*, Oct. 2, 2005.

57. Ken Rudin, National Public Radio, "The Hurricane and the President (Hoover, That Is)," Oct. 5, 2005.

58. Aaron Schroeder and Gary Wamsley Robert Ward, "The Evolution of Emergency Management in America: From a Painful Past to a Promising but Uncertain Future," in *Handbook of Crisis and Emergency Management* (2001), p. 364.

59. "FEMA History," *op. cit.*

60. White House statement, June 19, 1978.

61. George D. Haddow and Jane A. Bullock, *Introduction to Emergency Management* (2003), p. 8.

62. Testimony before House Transportation and Infrastructure Subcommittee on Economic Development, Public Buildings and Emergency Management, Oct. 6, 2005.

63. Haddow and Bullock, *op. cit.*

64. *Ibid.*

65. http://seismo.berkeley.edu/faq/1989_0.html.

66. *CQ Historic Documents 1993*, "President George Bush on Disaster Relief for Florida and Louisiana After Hurricane Andrew," Aug. 24, 1992.

67. Ali Farazmand, *Handbook of Crisis and Emergency Management* (2001), p. 379.

68. National Academy of Public Administration," *op. cit.*

69. Haddow and Bullock, *op. cit.*

70. Adams, *op. cit.*

71. Haddow and Bullock, *op. cit.*, p. 12.

72. Haddow and Bullock, *op. cit.*, p. 12.

73. *Ibid*, p. 13.

74. Justin Rood, "FEMA's decline: an agency's slow slide from grace," www.govexec.com, Sept. 28, 2005.

75. *Ibid.*

76. Dick Polman, "A possible sea change on federal spending," *The Philadelphia Inquirer*, Sept. 7, 2005.

77. www.ncdc.noaa.gov/oa/climate/research/2004/hurricanes04.html.

78. www.fema.gov/news/newsrelease_print.fema?id=15967.

79. Charles Mahtesian, "How FEMA delivered Florida for Bush," Govexec.com, *National Journal*, Nov. 3, 2004.

80. Adam C. Smith, "Hurricanes roil the political waters," *St. Petersburg Times*, Sept. 8, 2004.

81. www.ncdc.noaa.gov/oa/climate/research/2004/hurricanes04.html.

82. White House transcript, "Press Briefing by Homeland Security and Counterterrorism Advisor Fran Townsend," Oct. 21, 2005

83. Transcript, House Select Katrina Response Investigation Committee, Oct. 19, 2005.

84. *Ibid.*

85. Statement, Sept. 6, 2005 http://clinton.senate.gov/news/statements/details.cfm?id=24526&&.

86. Susan Ferrechio and Martin Kady II, "Little Headway on Compromise for Select Panel to Examine Katrina Response," *CQ Today*, Sept. 20, 2005.

87. *Ibid.*, transcript, Oct. 19, 2005.

88. Sally Kestin, Megan O'Matz and John Maines, "FEMA's waste continues as millions in extra payments given out for Katrina," *Sun-Sentinel*, Oct. 20, 2005.

89. Eamon Javers, "Anatomy of a Katrina Cleanup Contract," *Business Week*, Oct. 27, 2005.

90. Leslie Wayne and Glen Justice, "FEMA Director Under Clinton Profits From Experience," *The New York Times*, Oct. 10, 2005 and Jonathan E. Kaplan, "Former FEMA chief Albaugh in the middle," *The Hill*, Sept. 30, 2005. See also "Profiting from Katrina: The contracts," Center for Public Integrity, www.publicintegrity.org/katrina.

91. Transcript, House Transportation and Infrastructure Subcommittee on Economic Development, Public Buildings and Emergency Management Hearing on FEMA After Katrina, Oct. 6, 2005.

92. Testimony before House Committee on Homeland Security, Oct. 19, 2005.

93. The Associated Press, "Gov. Bush Criticizes State's Storm Effort," Oct. 27, 2005.

94. Transcript of Senate Homeland Security and Governmental Affairs Committee Hearing on Status Report on FEMA Recovery Efforts, Oct. 6, 2005.

95. Killen, *op. cit.*

96. Amol Sharma, "Senate Panel Approves Bill That Would Create A National Alert Office, *CQ Weekly*, Oct. 20, 2005.

97. Tim Starks, "Unpromising Prospects for First Responders," *CQ Weekly*, Nov. 14, 2005, p. 3034.

98. Liriel Higa and Stephen J. Norton, "Louisiana Senators Remain Disappointed with Bush's Rebuilding plan," *CQ Today*, Oct. 28, 2005.

99. Spencer S. Hsu and Ceci Connolly, "La. Wants FEMA to Pay for Majority of Damage to State Property," *The Washington Post*, Oct. 28, 2005, p. A14.

100. Edmund L. Andrews, "Emergency Spending as a Way of Life," *The New York Times*, Oct. 2, 2005, p. A4.

101. Insurance Information Institute, "Catastrophes: Insurance Issues," November 2005.

102. Tim Starks, "Critics Expecting Little from Hurricane Probes," *CQ Today*, Oct. 18, 2005.

103. White House transcript, Townsend briefing, Oct. 21, 2005.

104. Brain Friel and Paul Singer, "Gaps remain in government strategy for handling natural disasters," *National Journal*, Govexec.com, Oct. 28, 2005.

105. Kettl, *op. cit.*

BIBLIOGRAPHY

Books

Bea, Keith, *Federal Disaster Polices After Terrorists Strike*, Nova Science Publishers, 2003.
Prepared at the request of members of Congress, this book is primarily about terrorism, but it provides a good introduction to the Robert T. Stafford Disaster Relief and Emergency Assistance Act, the country's main federal disaster-assistance law.

Farazmand, Ali, (ed.), *Handbook of Crisis and Emergency Management*, Marcel Dekker, 2001.
A professor of public administration at Florida Atlantic University has compiled essays and case studies of crisis and emergency management, as well as a good primer on Federal Emergency Management Agency history.

Haddow, George D., and Jane A. Bullock, *Introduction to Emergency Management*, Butterworth-Heinemann, 2003.
Two former FEMA officials provide background on the history of disaster response and preparedness and strategies for improving planning and mitigation.

Articles

"FEMA: A Legacy of Waste," *South Florida Sun-Sentinel*, Sept. 18, 2005, p. A1.
A team of *Sun-Sentinel* reporters examined 20 disasters nationwide and found a pattern of mismanagement and fraud at FEMA.

"4 Places Where the System Broke Down," *Time*, Sept. 19, 2005, pp. 28-42.
A team of *Time* reporters shows how confusion, incompetence and fear of making mistakes hobbled the government at all levels in the New Orleans relief efforts, laying blame on the mayor, governor, FEMA director and secretary of Homeland Security.

Adams, Rebecca, "FEMA Failure a Perfect Storm of Bureaucracy," *CQ Weekly*, Sept. 12, 2005.
The reporter provides an overview of FEMA's challenges and pending proposals in Congress in the wake of the agency's sluggish response to Hurricane Katrina.

O'Toole, James, "U.S. help for disaster victims goes from nothing to billions," *Pittsburgh Post-Gazette*, Oct. 2, 2005.
The federal government has been assuming an increasing role in trying to make individuals, businesses and local governments whole after natural disasters, but there is no plan to budget for natural disasters.

Rood, Justin, "FEMA's decline: an agency's slow slide from grace," www.govexec.com, Sept. 28, 2005.
This article from a magazine for government executives discusses the budget and staffing cuts that FEMA has experienced in recent years and concludes that FEMA "was not the agency it once was" when Katrina struck.

Sappenfield, Mark, "Military wary of disaster role," *The Christian Science Monitor*, Sept. 29, 2005.
In some respects, the greatest opponent of giving the military more authority in U.S. disaster relief is the military itself.

Reports

Government Accountability Office, "Hurricane Katrina: Providing Oversight of the Nation's Preparedness, Response and Recovery Activities," Sept. 28, 2005.
This report to Congress includes a 10-page list of past GAO studies related to hurricanes and other natural disasters, including preparedness, the military's role and insurance.

Insurance Information Institute, "Catastrophes: Insurance Issues," November 2005.
A leading insurance industry group explains in simple language how catastrophes affect the insurance industry and how Katrina is prompting a re-examination of how the country pays for natural disasters.

Kettl, Donald, "The Worst is Yet to Come: Lesson from September 11 and Hurricane Katrina," University of Pennsylvania Fels Institute of Government, September 2005.
A professor of public policy specializing in state issues and homeland security concludes that policymakers need to pull FEMA out of the Department of Homeland Security and establish better communications systems.

National Academy of Public Administration, "Coping with Catastrophe: Building an Emergency Management System to Meet People's Needs in Natural and Manmade Disasters," February 1993.
A panel of experts that convened in the wake of the slow federal response to Hurricane Andrew in 1992 recommends that the military not take the lead in disaster responses.

National Academy of Public Administration, "Review of Actions Taken to Strengthen the Nation's Emergency Management System," March 1994.
This follow-up report, requested by FEMA Director James L. Witt, concluded that progress was being made but that FEMA needed fewer political appointees in leadership positions and that the president should establish a Domestic Crisis Monitoring Unit.

For More Information

American Red Cross, 2025 E St., N.W., Washington, DC 20006; (202) 303-4498; www.redcross.org. The congressionally chartered nonprofit provides disaster relief nationwide. Its Web site tells how to prepare for disasters.

Centers for Disease Control and Prevention, 1600 Clifton Road, Atlanta, GA 30333; (404) 639-3311; www.bt.cdc.gov. Provides information on emergency preparedness for bioterrorism, chemical and radiation emergencies, natural disasters and contagious diseases.

Department of Homeland Security, Washington, DC 20528; (202) 282-8000; www.dhs.gov. The principal agency charged with preventing terrorist attacks within the United States and minimizing the damage from attacks and natural disasters.

Federal Emergency Management Agency, 500 C St., S.W., Washington, DC 20472; (800) 621-3362; www.fema.gov. Provides information on preparedness, emergency response, the National Flood Insurance Program, how to apply for disaster relief, latest details on Katrina and a copy of the National Response Plan. A list of all 50 state emergency-management offices is at www.fema.gov/fema/statedr.shtm.

National Emergency Management Association, P.O. Box 11910, Lexington, KY 40578; (859) 244-8000; www.nemaweb.org. Represents state emergency-management directors.

National Hurricane Center, Tropical Prediction Center, 11691 S.W. 17th St., Miami, FL 33165-2149; (305) 229-4470; www.nhc.noaa.gov. Tracks and forecasts hurricanes.

Insurance Information Institute, 110 William St., New York, NY 10038; (212) 346-5500; www.iii.org. Represents the insurance industry and tracks the impact of catastrophes, floods and terrorist acts on the industry.

International Association of Emergency Managers, 201 Park Washington Court, Falls Church, Va. 22046-4527; (703) 538-1795; www.iaem.com. Represents local emergency managers and tracks federal homeland security grants and policies that affect local emergency officials.

U.S. Geological Survey's Earthquake Hazards Program, 12201 Sunrise Valley Dr., MS 905, Reston, VA 20192; 1-888-275-8747; http://earthquake.usgs.gov/. Provides information on worldwide earthquake activity and hazard-reduction. Web site lists the largest U.S. earthquakes.

15

Mexican immigrants in Homestead, Fla., negotiate with a man seeking four workers on May 7, 2004. Illegal immigrants make up only about 5 percent of the U.S. work force, but critics say they are taking many Americans' jobs by offering to work for low wages and no benefits. Immigration advocates counter that immigrants do the jobs Americans don't want and bolster the economy.

From *CQ Researcher*,
May 6, 2005. (Updated May 2006).

Illegal Immigration

Peter Katel and Patrick Marshall

The only future awaiting María and Juan Gomez in their tiny village in Mexico was working the fields from sunup to sundown, living mostly on tortillas and beans. So 11 years ago, when they were both 17, they crossed into the United States illegally, near San Diego. Now ensconced in the large Latino community outside Washington, D.C., they are working hard at building a life for themselves and their young son.

Juan and María (not their real names) follow a simple strategy — staying out of trouble and undercutting competitors. Juan does landscaping, charging about $600 for major yard work — about $400 less than the typical legal contractor. María cleans houses for $70; house-cleaning services normally charge $85 or more.

They aren't complaining, but María and Juan know they offer bargain-basement prices. "You walk down the street, and every house being built, Hispanics are building it," María says in Spanish. "This country is getting more work for less money."

Indeed, some sectors of the economy might have a hard time functioning without illegal workers. Brendan Flanagan, director of legislative affairs for the National Restaurant Association, insists, "Restaurants, hotels, nursing homes, agriculture — a very broad group of industries — are looking for a supply of workers to remain productive," he says, because in many parts of the country, native workers aren't available at any price. Moreover, lobbyists for employers insist that their members can't tell false papers from the real ones that employees present to prove they're here legally.

But Harvard economist George Borjas counters that when an American employer claims he cannot find a legal or native-born worker willing to do a certain job, "He is leaving out a very key part

Most Illegal Immigrants Live in Four States

More than half of the nation's more than 10 million illegal immigrants live in four states — California, Texas, Florida and New York.

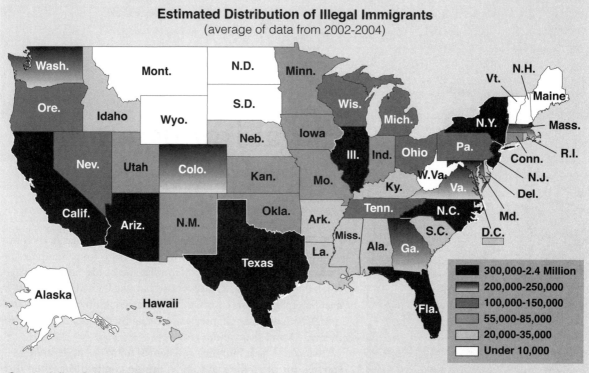

Estimated Distribution of Illegal Immigrants
(average of data from 2002-2004)

Legend:
- 300,000-2.4 Million
- 200,000-250,000
- 100,000-150,000
- 55,000-85,000
- 20,000-35,000
- Under 10,000

Source: Jeffrey S. Passel, "Estimates of the Size and Characteristics of the Undocumented Population," Pew Hispanic Center, March 21, 2005, based on data from the March 2004 "Current Population Survey" by the Census Bureau and Department of Labor

of that phrase. He should add 'at the wage I'm going to pay.' " [1]

Many Americans blame illegal immigrants like María and Juan not only for depressing wages but also for a host of problems, including undermining U.S. security.

But the U.S. government refuses to tighten up the border, they say.

"The reason we do not have secure borders is because of an insatiable demand for cheap labor," says Rep. Tom Tancredo, R-Colo., a leading immigration-control advocate in Congress. "We have the ability to secure the border; we choose not to. The Democratic Party sees massive immigration — legal and illegal — as a massive source of voters. The Republican Party looks at the issue and says, 'Wow, that's a lot of cheap labor coming across that border.' "

Some other politicians are following Tancredo's lead. In April 2005, California Gov. Arnold Schwarzenegger ratcheted up his anti-illegal immigration rhetoric. Praising anti-immigration activists monitoring the Mexican border in Arizona, he said, "Our federal government is not doing their job. It's a shame that the private citizen has to go in there and start patrolling our borders."

There are more than 10 million immigrants living illegally in the United States, compared with 3.5 million only 15 years ago, according to the non-profit Pew Hispanic Center. [2] And since 2000 the illegal population has been growing by a half-million illegal immigrants a year — nearly 1,400 people a day, according to the Census Bureau and other sources. [3]

While illegal immigrants make up only about 5 percent of the U.S. work force, they are rapidly making their presence known in non-traditional areas such as the Midwest and South. Willing to work for low wages, undocumented workers are creating a political backlash among some residents in the new states, which have seen a nearly tenfold increase in illegal immigration since 1990.

"Immigration is now a national phenomenon in a way that was less true a decade ago," Mark Krikorian, executive director of the nonpartisan Center for Immigration Studies said. "In places like Georgia and Alabama, which had little experience with immigration before, people are experiencing it firsthand. Immigrants are working in chicken plants, carpet mills and construction. It's right in front of people's faces now." [4]

The debate has taken on populist undertones, says Dan Stein, president of the Federation for American Immigration Reform (FAIR), because some in the public perceive a wide gap between policymakers' positions and popular sentiment in affected regions. "The issue is about elites, major financial interests and global economic forces arrayed against the average American voter," said Stein, whose group favors strict immigration policies. "The depth of anger should not be underestimated." [5]

Grass-roots organizations have formed in seven states to push for laws denying public services for illegal immigrants and Rep. Tancredo hints he may run for president to "build a fire" around the need for immigration reform. [6]

But reform means different things to different people.

To Rep. F. James Sensenbrenner Jr., R-Wis., chairman of the House Judiciary Committee, reform means imposing new restrictions on asylum seekers, blocking states from issuing driver's licenses to illegal immigrants and finishing a border fence near San Diego. "We will never have homeland security if we don't have border

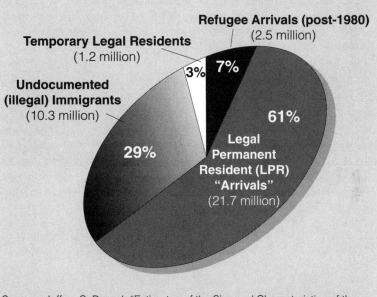

Majority of Immigrants in U.S. Are Legal

More than 21 million legal "permanent" immigrants live in the United States — more than twice the number of illegal immigrants.

Status of Immigrants in U.S.

Refugee Arrivals (post-1980) (2.5 million)

Temporary Legal Residents (1.2 million)

Undocumented (illegal) Immigrants (10.3 million)

3% 7%

29%

61%

Legal Permanent Resident (LPR) "Arrivals" (21.7 million)

Sources: Jeffrey S. Passel, "Estimates of the Size and Characteristics of the Undocumented Population," Pew Hispanic Center, March 21, 2005, based on data from the March 2004 "Current Population Survey" by the Census Bureau and Department of Labor

security," Sensenbrenner said in March 2005. [7] Sensenbrenner's tough, new Real ID bill, which requires proof of citizenship or legal status in the United States in order to get a driver's license, was signed into law in May 2005 and will take effect in May 2008.

To Sen. John McCain, R-Ariz., reform means enabling illegal immigrants to stay here legally because, he contends, the nation's economy depends on them. "As long as there are jobs to be had . . . that won't be done by Americans [illegal immigrants] are going to come and fill those jobs," he said in April 2005. [8]

Echoing McCain, President Bush has endorsed the creation of a "guest worker" program that would grant temporary legal status to illegal workers. "If there is a job opening which an American won't do . . . and there's a willing worker and a willing employer, that job ought to be filled on a legal basis, no matter where the person

Immigration Debate Moves Behind the Wheel

The tension was high in suburban Atlanta in October 2005 when protesters confronted hundreds of illegal immigrants who were marching to demand the right to obtain driver's licenses.

The peaceful, sign-waving march soon turned ugly, as angry epithets were hurled back and forth across busy Buford Highway. "This is my country! You are criminals! You cannot have my country!" shouted D.A. King, a former insurance salesman and self-styled anti-immigrant vigilante. Boos and hisses erupted from the mostly Hispanic immigrants across the street. [1]

The heated exchange, caught by a CNN television crew, captured the intensifying debate over driver's licenses for illegal immigrants. Eleven states now issue such licenses, and several others are considering permitting similar laws, but a growing grass-roots movement opposes the licenses, including groups like the American Resistance Foundation, founded by King.

The immigrants' supporters say illegal workers are the backbone of the nation's economic success and that being able to drive legally would allow them to open bank accounts and do other tasks requiring an official identification card. It would also make America's roads safer, the proponents say, by holding immigrants to the same driving and insurance requirements as U.S. citizens. Unlicensed drivers are nearly five times more likely to be in a fatal crash than licensed drivers, and uninsured drivers cause 14 percent of all accidents, according to the AAA Foundation for Traffic Safety. [2]

But King and others say uncontrolled immigration depresses wages, increases crime and causes neighborhood blight, and that granting undocumented workers driver's licenses would only legalize illegal behavior.

Until now the debate over immigrant driver's licenses has been restricted to a few traditional border states, like California, where a new law permitting undocumented workers to get licenses helped defeat Democratic Gov. Gray Davis during the 2003 gubernatorial recall election. Lawmakers repealed the law shortly after Arnold Schwarzenegger was inaugurated as governor, and Schwarzenegger has since vetoed related bills. He wants the licenses of undocumented workers to bear a unique mark.

Now the debate has moved to states throughout the country. In Utah and Tennessee, state laws now give illegal workers so-called "driving privilege cards," which warn in bold, red letters they cannot be used as legal identification. [3] New York State's motor-vehicles commissioner in April 2005 denied license renewals and suspended the licenses of illegal immigrants without a Social Security card or acceptable visa. [4] The state's Supreme Court, which made a preliminary ruling rejecting the commissioner's action, is currently hearing the issue.

Now some in Congress want to jump into the fray — even though issuing driver's licenses has long been the domain of the states. In January 2005, Wisconsin Republican Rep. F. James Sensenbrenner Jr. proposed the Real ID Act, which would establish national driver's license standards, toughen asylum requirements and speedy completion of a fence on the U.S.-Mexico border near San Diego. But the driver's license provision has caused the most debate.

"My bill's goal is straightforward: It seeks to prevent another 9/11-type attack by disrupting terrorist travel," Sensenbrenner said. The bill would require states to verify that driver's-license applicants reside legally in the United States before issuing a license that could be used for federal identification purposes, such as boarding an airplane. [5]

The bill, which Sensenbrenner attached to a "must-pass" emergency military-spending bill, was approved by Congress and signed into law on May 11, 2005, and is scheduled to go into effect in May 2008.

The bill's supporters say providing secure driver's licenses to illegal immigrants will improve national security, because licenses are now the de facto form of identification in the United States. The 9/11 Commission, which investigated the Sept. 11, 2001, terrorist attacks, found that the attackers used driver's licenses rather than passports to avoid creating suspicion. [6]

"At many entry points to vulnerable facilities, including gates for boarding aircraft," the commission's 2004 report noted, "sources of identification are the last opportunity to ensure that people are who they say they are and to check whether they are terrorists." [7]

comes from," Bush said after a meeting at his Texas ranch on March 23, 2005, with Mexican President Vicente Fox and Canadian Prime Minister Paul Martin. [9]

The issue of immigration has, in fact, set the Republican Party against itself, with the more conservative elements of the party arguing for strict enforcement

During House debate, Sensenbrenner said that the Real ID bill might have prevented the Sept. 11 attacks because it requires that any license or ID card issued to visitors expire on the same date the person's visa expires.

"Mohamed Atta, ringleader of the 9/11 murderers, entered the United States on a six-month visa [which] expired on July 9, 2001. He got a [six-month] driver's license from the state of Florida on May 5, 2001," Sensenbrenner said. "Had this bill been in effect at the time, that driver's license would have expired on July 9, and he would not have been able to use that driver's license to get on a plane." [8]

Immigrants and community leaders in New York City protest on April 13, 2004, against a state policy that denies driver's licenses to hundreds of thousands of immigrants. The protest followed a crackdown on individuals without Social Security numbers.

Getty Images/Stephen Chernin

instant verification of birth certificates, without providing the time or resources needed," says the National Conference of State Legislatures. [10]

Moreover, says Joan Friedland, a policy attorney with the National Immigration Law Center, the law is just "smoke and mirrors" because it is "an inadequate and meaningless substitute for real, comprehensive reform and doesn't resolve the problem of national security."

But Martin says a national law that coordinates driver's-license policies across the nation is vital to security. "Right now, there is virtually a different approach in every state," he says. "People who wish to take advantage of the system can easily target whichever state has the most lax requirements."

— **Kate Templin**

Jack Martin, special projects director for the Federation for American Immigration Reform (FAIR), which seeks to halt illegal immigration, says the difficulty of distinguishing between "illegal aliens merely looking for jobs and potential terrorists looking to carry out attacks" argues against granting licenses to non-citizens. "People who have entered the country illegally — regardless of their motives — should not be able to receive a driver's license," he says.

But critics of the law say denying driver's licenses to illegal immigrants would pose a greater threat to U.S. safety. "Allowing a driver the possibility to apply for a license to drive to work means that person's photograph, address and proof of insurance will be on file at the local DMV," a recent *Los Angeles Times* editorial argued. "And that is something to make us all feel safer." [9]

The Real ID Act "threatens to handcuff state officials with impossible, untested mandates, such as requiring

[1] Quoted from "CNN Presents: Immigrant Nation: Divided Country," Oct. 17, 2004.

[2] www.aaafoundation.org/pdf/UnlicensedToKill2.pdf.

[3] T. R. Reid and Darryl Fears, "Driver's License Curtailed as Identification," *The Washington Post,* April 17, 2003, p. A3.

[4] Nina Bernstein, "Fight Over Immigrants' Driving Licenses Is Back in Court," *The New York Times,* April 7, 2005, p. B6.

[5] www.house.gov/sensenbrenner/newsletterapril2005.pdf.

[6] For background, see Kenneth Jost, "Re-examining 9/11," *CQ Researcher,* June 4, 2004, pp. 493-516.

[7] National Commission on Terrorist Attacks Upon the United States, p. 390.

[8] Frank James, "Immigrant ID Rules Debated," *Chicago Tribune,* March 12, 2005, News Section, p. 1.

[9] "Real ID, Unreal Expectations," *Los Angeles Times,* April 6, 2005.

[10] National Conference of State Legislatures, www.ncsl.org.

of the borders and expulsion of illegal aliens. The Republican-controlled House passed HR4437 in December 2005, a measure that contains procedures for

securing the borders, harsher penalties for those assisting illegal entry into the country and provisions for deporting illegal aliens. The legislation does not provide for a

Illegal Migrants Leaving Traditional States

Eighty-eight percent of the nation's illegal immigrants lived in the six traditional settlement states for immigrants in 1990, but the same states had only 61 percent of the total in 2004. In other words, an estimated 3.9 million undocumented migrants lived in other states — nearly a tenfold increase.

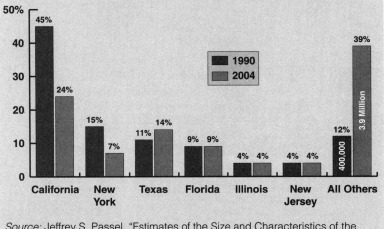

Changes in Immigrant Settlement Patterns, 1990-2004

Source: Jeffrey S. Passel, "Estimates of the Size and Characteristics of the Undocumented Population," Pew Hispanic Center, March 21, 2005, based on data from the March 2004 "Current Population Survey" by the Census Bureau and Department of Labor

At the state level, controversy over illegal immigration has helped build and destroy political careers. In California, for example, Schwarzenegger's promise to repeal legislation allowing illegal immigrants to obtain driver's licenses helped him topple Democrat Gray Davis in the 2003 recall election for governor. Tensions are still running high outside the political arena.

Some activists go so far as to call immigration a product of organized crime. "The same people responsible for drug shipments from the south are also dealing in sex slaves and illegal labor and weapons," claims William Gheen, president of Americans for Legal Immigration, in Raleigh, N.C. "Our businesses should not be working with these people or encouraging these people. Some companies want more Third World labor on the territory of 'we the people' of the USA."

But Juan Hernandez, former director of the Center for U.S.-Mexico Studies at the University of Texas at Dallas, says immigration opponents are simply appealing to primitive fears. "There are many jobs that would not be performed if undocumented people were not here. Why can't we come up with ways in which individuals who want to come from Mexico to the United States can get a quick permit, come up, do a job and go back?"

Immigration control has long been a hot-button issue, but the concern in previous years was largely about jobs and wages. In post-9/11 America, many observers view illegal immigration as a national security matter.

"The borders are out of control," says T.J. Bonner, president of the National Border Patrol Council, the union representing some 10,000 border officers. He claims the patrol catches no more than a third of illegal border crossers. "We have a situation where business is controlling our immigration policy rather than sound decisions that take into account all the factors, including homeland security.

guest worker program or any type of amnesty for illegal aliens.

At the same time, the Republican-controlled Senate has proposed more liberal legislation. Bipartisan backing for an immigration bill that would allow illegal immigrants already here to apply for legal residence after six years of temporary legal status nearly resulted in Senate passage in April 2006. S2612, sponsored by Republican senators Chuck Hagel of Nebraska and Mel Martinez of Florida, and cosponsored by Sen. Edward M. Kennedy (D-Mass.), fell victim to a controversial attempt by some Republican senators to insert amendments into the compromise legislation. Senate leaders, however, promised to grapple with the issue again immediately after Congress' spring recess.

Despite vociferous debate within the Republican Party, S2612 attracted the tepid support of President Bush. "Massive deportation of the people here is unrealistic," Bush said in a speech on April 24, 2006. "It's just not going to work." [10]

While some may dismiss Bonner's concerns as overly alarmist, others point out that stepped-up border-security spending is not stopping the growing illegal immigration.

Over the past 13 years, billions of dollars have been spent on border-control measures, including walls and fences in urban areas, electronic sensors and more personnel. From 1993 to 2004, the federal government quintupled border enforcement spending to $3.8 billion and tripled the Border Patrol to more than 11,000 officers, according to Wayne Cornelius, director of the Center for Comparative Immigration Studies at the University of California, San Diego. [11]

Customs and Border Protection Commissioner Robert Bonner (no relation to T.J. Bonner) told lawmakers in March that a reorganization that combined the Border Patrol, Immigration and Naturalization Service and the Customs Service into one agency under the Department of Homeland Security had improved deterrence. "This consolidation has significantly increased our ability to execute our anti-terrorism and traditional missions at our nation's borders more effectively than ever before," he said." [12]

Then why have illegal border crossings been increasing?

For one thing, the government has nearly stopped enforcing 1986 sanctions on employers who hire illegal immigrants. According to Mary Dougherty, an immigration statistician at the Homeland Security Department, in 2003 the agency levied only $9,300 in fines against employers. Dougherty cautioned that her data might be incomplete, but *Time* reported in 2004 that the number of fines imposed on employers dropped 99 percent during the 1990s from 1,063 in 1992 to 13 in 2002. [13]

Demetrios Papademetriou, director of the Migration Policy Institute, a Washington think tank, says that illegal immigration "maintains a standard of living for everyone in America that is, in a sense, beyond what we can really afford. When you continue to have low-wage workers streaming in, all products and services become cheaper. It has actually become a subsidy to every person in America. We have all become hooked."

For instance, at least 50 percent of the nation's farmworkers are poorly paid illegal immigrants. Americans spend less on food than the citizens of any other industrialized country, the Agriculture Department's Economic Research Service found. [14]

In the final analysis, the lack of enforcement benefits employers and hurts workers, says Ana Avendaño

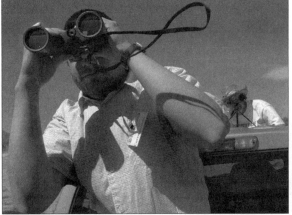

Members of the Minutemen activist group search for illegal immigrants crossing into the United States along a stretch of the Mexican border near Douglas, Ariz., on April 4, 2005. Members of the controversial group said they wanted to aid the understaffed U.S. Border Patrol.

Denier, director of the AFL-CIO Immigrant Worker Program. "Employers have a very vulnerable population to whom they can pay lower wages, and because of business control over public policy, it is OK to have this class of workers that is fully exploitable."

But problems here are unlikely to force illegal immigrants like Juan and María to return home.

"If it were just about us, yes," she says. "But for the sake of our son, no. Here he has a chance to go to college. In Mexico, no matter how hard we work we don't have the possibility of paying for him to go to college. What we want is that he not suffer the humiliations we have had to suffer."

As Congress, the states and citizens' groups debate the effects of illegal immigration, here are some of the key questions being asked:

Does illegal immigration hurt American workers?

Virtually every immigrant comes to the United States for one reason: to work.

About 96 percent of the 4.5 million illegal immigrant men now in the country are working, concludes Jeffrey Passel, a former U.S. Census Bureau demographer who is now senior research associate at the Pew Hispanic Center. All told, some 6 million immigrants — about 5 percent of the labor force — are in the country illegally.

A group of 130 Mexicans who entered the United States illegally board a charter flight in Tucson, Ariz., to Mexico City on July 12, 2004. The flight is part of a "voluntary repatriation" program run jointly by the U.S. and Mexican governments.

Is the illegal work force large enough to hurt the job security of U.S. citizens?

Quite the contrary, argues John Gay, co-chairman of the Essential Worker Immigration Coalition, a lobbying group of 34 employers — including hotels, restaurants and building firms — that depend on immigrants. "I think back to the 1990s, a decade of economic growth," he says. "We ended with 30-year lows in unemployment and a decade of record-setting immigration, legal and illegal. That tells me immigrants didn't displace millions of Americans; they helped employ Americans."

Gay says low-paid workers help businesses thrive, allowing them to hire the native-born and legal immigrants for higher-paying jobs. In addition, immigrants are consumers themselves, so they boost the national economy.

But what helps business doesn't necessarily help Americans who share the lowest rungs of the socioeconomic ladder with illegal immigrants, according to Jared Bernstein, director of the Economic Policy Institute's Living Standards Program, which has strong ties to organized labor. "There is solid evidence that a large presence of low-wage immigrants lowers wages of domestic workers in low-wage sectors," Bernstein says. "Most economists should bristle at the notion that immigrants are filling jobs that native workers won't take. Maybe they won't take them because of low compensation and poor working conditions. In the absence of immigrants, the quality of some of those jobs probably would improve, and American workers probably would take them."

Bernstein favors controlling the flow of immigrant workers, rather than trying to bar them altogether.

But Michael McGarry, a maintenance worker in Aspen, Colo., and spokesman for the controversial Minuteman Project, says illegals hurt the economy and that they all should be kept out. The group deployed more than 100 volunteers — some of them armed — to spot and report illegal immigrants along a stretch of the Mexican border in April 2005. "People keep forgetting there is something called the law of supply and demand," says McGarry, who represented the group in April 2005 when it recruited citizens to report illegal immigrants along the Mexican border in Arizona. "If you flood the country with workers, that is going to compete down wages and benefits and conditions."

Harvard economist Borjas, whom many consider the leading expert on the economic effects of immigration, calculated that in the late 1990s immigration added a modest $10 billion to the economy — not a lot in a country with a national income in 1998 of about $8 trillion, Borjas wrote. [15]

The key, he argues, is not the overall gain but who won and who lost because of illegal immigration. [16] "Some businesses gain quite a bit and are not willing to give up the privilege — agriculture, the service industry and upper-middle-class Californians who hire nannies and gardeners. People who gain, gain an incredible amount."

Borjas calculated that immigrants' work in 1998 helped those businesses gain roughly $160 billion, including the savings from the lower wages they were paying, plus their overall economic growth. [17] The figures don't distinguish between illegal and legal immigrants, but among low-skilled entrants to the United States, illegal immigrants are in the majority.

Economist Philip Martin, an expert on U.S.-Mexico relations at the University of California, Davis, generally agrees with Borjas on the supply/demand side of the situation. "The economy would not come screeching to a halt," Martin says, without illegal immigrants. At the same time, he acknowledges, they are "important to particular industries."

A detailed 2002 study of illegal Latino immigrants in Chicago — where they made up 5 percent of the work force — supports Martin's analysis. Two-thirds of the workers held low-wage jobs, including cleaning, packaging, child care, restaurant labor, grounds keeping and maintenance. Wages were depressed by an average of 22 percent for men and 36 percent for women. (Wages of undocumented Eastern European men and women were depressed by 20 percent.) "Attaining additional levels of education, having English proficiency and accumulating additional years of U.S. residency *do not neutralize the negative wage effect of working without legal status*," the report said (emphasis in original). [18]

The AFL-CIO's Avendaño acknowledges that undocumented workers push wages down. "Mexican workers are walking into a situation where an employer, with a wink and a nod, will say, 'I'll pay you less than the minimum wage.' It is very important for the AFL-CIO to not be put in a position where we're choosing domestic workers over foreign workers. To us, the answer is a reasonable immigration system."

Stein, of the Federation for American Immigration Reform (FAIR) argues that "earned legalization" proposals that include guest worker provisions, such as the legislation currently being debated in the Senate, amount to schemes to provide employers with a ready supply of low-wage workers. Once immigrants get legal permanent residence, they can't be exploited as readily as illegal immigrants, Stein says, so the six-year legalization process keeps employers supplied with cheap labor.

"These are replacement workers for a very large swath of the American work force," he says. "I say, stop trying to shift the costs for cheap labor onto the backs of hard-working families. They try to sell us all on the idea that low-cost, illegal labor cuts consumer costs, but there are enormous, incalculable costs imposed on society at large [by illegal immigrants] — public education, emergency medical care, housing assistance, housing itself and criminal justice costs."

Are tougher immigration controls needed to protect national security?

"We have some people who are coming in to kill you and your children and your grandchildren," says Rep. Tancredo, who has made immigration control his political mission. "Anyone seeking to come into this country without getting a lot of attention drawn to him would naturally choose the borders and come in under the radar screen along with thousands and thousands and thousands of others."

Tancredo worries about men like Mohamed and Mahmud Abouhalima, who were convicted for their roles in the 1993 bombing of the World Trade Center. The two Middle Eastern terrorists illegally took advantage of one of two immigration-reform programs to acquire "green cards" (which signify legal permanent resident status) under the 1986 Special Agricultural Workers Program for farmworkers.

The brothers obtained the green cards through flaws in the Immigration and Naturalization Service (INS) inspection system, according to the National Commission on Terrorist Attacks Upon the United States (the 9/11 Commission). The agency's "inability to adjudicate applications quickly or with adequate security checks made it easier for terrorists to wrongfully enter and remain in the United States throughout the 1990s." [19]

In a sense, that failure followed logically from Justice Department policy. The report continues, "Attorney General [Janet] Reno and her deputies, along with Congress, made their highest priorities shoring up the Southwest border to prevent the migration of illegal aliens and selectively upgrading technology systems," the 9/11 commission staff concluded. [20] (The INS was then part of the Justice Department.)

Unlike immigrants trekking across the desert, the 19 9/11 terrorist attackers, including 15 Saudis and a citizen of the United Arab Emirates (UAE), flew into the United States on airliners, their passports stamped with legally obtained student or tourist visas. [21]

To be sure, one airport immigration inspector stopped a member of the 9/11 attack team from entering the United States. Mohammed al Kahtani of Saudi Arabia was turned around at Orlando International Airport because he had a one-way ticket, little money, couldn't speak much English and couldn't explain the reason he was visiting. "The inspector relied on intuitive experience . . . more than he relied on any objective fac-

CHRONOLOGY

1800s *After waves of European immigrants are welcomed, anti-immigrant resentment builds.*

1882 Chinese Exclusion Act specifically bars additional Chinese immigrants.

1920s *Public concern about the nation's changing ethnic makeup and hard economic times prompt Congress to limit immigration and set quotas intended to preserve the nation's ethnic makeup.*

1921-1929 Congress establishes a national-origins quota system, effectively excluding Asians and Southern Europeans.

1924 U.S. Border Patrol is created to stem the flow of illegal immigrants, primarily across the Mexican border.

1940s-1950s *Labor shortages and expansion of U.S. economy during World War II attract Mexican laborers. U.S. accepts war survivors, welcomes refugees from communist countries and overhauls immigration laws.*

1942 U.S. creates Bracero guest worker program, allowing immigrant Mexican farmworkers to work temporarily on American farms.

1948 Congress authorizes extra 200,000 visas for concentration camp survivors, later raised to more than 400,000.

1952 Congress passes landmark Immigration and Nationality Act, codifying existing quota system favoring immigrants from northern Europe but exempting Mexican farmworkers in Texas.

1953 U.S. exempts refugees fleeing communist countries from quota system.

1960s-1970s *Amid growing Civil Rights Movement, U.S. scraps the biased quota system and admits more Asians and Latin Americans.*

1965 Major overhaul of immigration law scraps national quotas, giving preference to relatives of immigrants.

1966 Congress orders those fleeing Fidel Castro's Cuba to be admitted automatically if they reach U.S. shores.

1980s *Tide of illegal immigrants rises dramatically, prompting policy makers to act.*

1986 Number of illegal immigrants apprehended on U.S.-Mexican border reaches a peak of 1.7 million. Congress again overhauls immigration law, legalizing undocumented workers and for the first time imposing sanctions on employers of illegal immigrants.

1990s-2000s *Immigration laws fail to deter illegal immigrants, creating backlash that prompts another overhaul of immigration laws; national-security concerns cloud immigration debate after two terrorist attacks on U.S. soil by Middle Eastern visitors.*

1993 World Trade Center is bombed by Middle Eastern terrorists, two of whom had green cards; mastermind had applied for political asylum.

1996 Number of illegal immigrants in U.S. reaches 5 million; Congress passes major immigration-reform law beefing up border security and restricting political asylum.

1997 Most of California's anti-illegal immigrant statute is declared unconstitutional.

Sept. 11, 2001 Terrorists with visas attack World Trade Center and Pentagon; anti-immigrant backlash ensues.

2004 The 9/11 Commission points to "systemic weaknesses" in border-control and immigration systems.

Jan. 20, 2005 President Bush calls for a "temporary worker" program that would not include "amnesty" for illegal immigrants.

May 2005 Sen. F. James Sensenbrenner's Real ID bill, which would block states from issuing driver's licenses to illegal immigrants, is signed into law.

April 9, 2006 Hundreds of thousands of demonstrators march in the streets of cities across the United States, calling for legal status for illegal immigrants.

April 20, 2006 Homeland Security Secretary Michael Chertoff announces a federal crackdown on employers who hire illegal aliens.

May 1, 2006 Hundreds of thousands of immigrants again took to the streets in cities across the country to call for legal status. Many of the participants left work and schools in an effort to demonstrate the economic importance of illegal immigrants.

tor that could be detected by 'scores' or a machine," the commission observed.

As a result, the commission said: "We advocate a system for screening, not categorical profiling. A screening system looks for particular, identifiable suspects or indicators of risk." [22]

Sensenbrenner says the driver's-license prohibition in his Real ID bill will complicate life for terrorists who do manage to slip in. "If you read the 9/11 report, they highlight how al Qaeda studied document fraud and other vulnerabilities in the system," said Jeff Lungren, a spokesman for the House Judiciary Committee. "They undertook the risk and effort to get valid U.S. driver's licenses and state I.D. cards . . . because they allow you to fit in." [23]

Immigrant-rights advocates argue, however, that Sensenbrenner's driver's-license provisions will complicate the lives of citizens and legal residents without damaging terrorists' capabilities.

Timothy Sparapani, legislative counsel for the American Civil Liberties Union (ACLU), says the law "is not going to do anything to deter people coming to this country." Instead, he argues, "the provisions . . . will make it much more complicated and burdensome for every American to get their first driver's licenses or renewals. They will not only have to prove they are citizens of a particular state, they will have to provide certified birth certificates; you'll have to go to a state birth certification agency. Some states don't have them."

Although terrorists have a track record for finding holes in the border-control system, border enforcement isn't actually targeting terrorists, says Jennifer Allen, director of the Border Action Network, a Tucson-based immigrant-defense organization. "A border wall is not going to deter terrorists," she argues. What stepped-up enforcement is achieving, she says, is "ongoing harassment" of people on the U.S. side of the border — particularly those whose Latin features identify them as possible foreigners.

Border Patrol union President Bonner acknowledges that most illegal immigrants are only looking for jobs. But he suggests that concentrating patrol forces on the 2,000-mile Southwest border is leaving the 3,145-mile Canadian border relatively unprotected. Some 9,000 officers are assigned to the Mexican border, he says, compared with only about 1,000 on the Canadian line. "We'll get a call from the Royal Canadian Mounted

Police, and they'll say — 'Sixty Koreans landed here, and they're heading your way.' Sometimes we see them and sometimes we don't."

The Mexican and Canadian borders are indeed vulnerable, Papademetriou of the Migration Policy Institute acknowledges. But a 2003 institute report concludes that immigration policy is not an effective anti-terrorism tool. A report he co-authored concluded: "The government's major successes in apprehending terrorists have not come from post-Sept. 11 immigration initiatives but from other efforts, such as international intelligence activities, law enforcement cooperation and information provided by arrests made abroad." [24]

Should illegal immigrants in the United States be allowed to acquire legal status?

Legalization is one of the major dividing lines between illegal-immigration-control forces and employers and other immigrants'-rights advocates.

The guest worker proposal currently being considered in the Senate would allow foreigners to take jobs in the United States for a specified period, perhaps three years. Foreigners already here illegally also would be able to join the program and then apply for permanent residence after six years. Although President Bush generally supports the temporary worker portion of the proposal, he has not said whether he favors legalization.

Backers of the plan reject the term "amnesty," which implies a mass pardon for those covered by the proposal. "For security reasons, for human-rights reasons and for labor reasons, there is a vested interest in legalizing or regularizing the status of individuals," says a member of Sen. John McCain's staff. "Sen. McCain doesn't believe it's possible to round up everyone and send them home. [But] it can't be an amnesty. With high fines, background checks [for criminal violations] and through the temporary-worker program, people will be proving their reliability."

Critics of the Senate legislation argue that guest worker programs amount to amnesty, even if the term itself is not used. "The whole supposed guest worker program is really an amnesty," says McGarry, of the Minuteman Project. "This would be a disaster. An amnesty, by definition, is something the government forgives. Breaking into the country is a crime."

Supporters of legalization say that the main argument in favor of their position is that it is the only effective way to deal with the fact that undocumented immigrants are

Mexico's Call for Reform Still Unheard

To some Americans, undocumented Mexicans are job-stealing, non-English-speaking threats to American culture, economic well-being and national security.

"I'm afraid that America could become a Third World country," Atlanta-area realtor Jimmy Herchek told CNN. "We're importing poverty by millions every year." [1]

To other observers, Mexicans and other illegal workers are crucial to the economy. "There are major benefits to both employers and consumers — in other words, all of us. [T]his supply of labor makes it possible to produce your goods and services more cheaply," said Wayne Cornelius, director of the Center for Comparative Immigration Studies at the University of California at San Diego. "So there are literally hundreds of thousands of employers in this country that have a major stake in continued access to this kind of labor."

And in Mexico, the 6 million illegal migrantes in the United States are viewed as heroes, often braving death in desert crossings to take tough construction and service jobs in the United States to support families back home. More than 3,000 Mexicans died trying to cross the border between 1996 and 2004, but those who arrive safely and find work in the United States sent home $16 billion last year — Mexico's third-largest source of revenue. [2]

However, the immigrants' courage and dedication to their families — not to mention the benefit to the U.S. economy from their low-wage labor — haven't earned them the right to work legally in the United States. Far from it, says Mexico's ambassador to the United States, Carlos de Icaza, who supports a program to allow migrantes to live and work legally in the United States.

"Migrants are very vulnerable," he says in an interview at his office near the White House. "The difficult situation of these hard-working people makes them subject to abuse."

Many are mistreated once they arrive in the United States — either by anti-immigrant activists, abusive border guards or unscrupulous employers, who know illegal workers are reluctant to report salary and other abuses to author-

ities. Indeed, stories about U.S. mistreatment of migrants are daily fare in Mexico. El Universal, one of Mexico City's most influential newspapers, reported in April that 4,400 Mexicans were injured or mistreated by anti-immigrant civilians or Border Patrol agents in 2004. [3]

Icaza says that setting up a legal way for Mexicans to work in the United States would direct them to communities where their labor is needed and wanted, helping to dissipate the tensions that arise now when lots of Mexicans arrive suddenly in communities offering seasonal jobs.

Illegal immigrants have traditionally settled in California, Florida, New York and a few other states, but in recent years enclaves have sprung up in North Carolina, Georgia, Tennessee and other states unaccustomed to the phenomenon. [4]

Often, local residents complain the new immigrants cost taxpayers money for health care, schools and social services and bring gang-related crime. "What I saw happen in California over 30 years is happening here in just a few years," James Burke, 57, a retired ironworker from Cullman, Ala., said as he signed up volunteers to push for immigration control. [5]

Burke is part of a grass-roots movement seeking tougher immigration rules and border patrols. "Our goal is to stop illegal immigration and get rid of the illegal immigrants who are here," he said. [6]

Those goals are clearly at odds with the Mexican government's campaign to forge an immigration accord with the United States that would allow Mexicans to work here legally. Drawing on his apparent friendship with George W. Bush, Mexican President Vicente Fox began his presidency five years ago promising to strike an immigration deal with the United States.

Shortly after taking office, Fox invited his newly elected American counterpart to his ranch. The two presidents assigned top officials to start negotiating a deal. "Geography has made us neighbors," Bush said, standing next to Fox, both men in cowboy boots. "Cooperation and respect will make us partners." [7]

already here. And having illegal immigrants in the work force allows employers to pay them less than they'd be able to earn as legal residents. Such exploitation makes legalization "so crucial," says the AFL-CIO's Avendaño.

She says a December 2004 decision by the Appellate Division of the New York State Supreme Court proves that an unfair, two-tiered labor system is acquiring legal status. The court ruled an illegal immigrant who was

In fact, the pre-9/11 climate was so immigration-friendly that Mexico's foreign minister confidently bragged that Mexico wouldn't settle for anything less than a deal legalizing Mexicans already in the United States. "It's the whole enchilada or nothing," Jorge G. Castañeda said. [8]

So far, it's been nada. Nothing. For Fox the politician, the lack of action is especially bad news for his legacy. Mexico's constitution allows only one six-year term, and Fox's term ends in July 2006. Yet, comprehensive immigration reform in the United States seems as distant as ever.

President Bush and Mexican President Vicente Fox discussed immigration at Bush's Texas ranch in March 2004. Bush supports a guest worker program for illegal immigrants in the U.S. but opposes legalization.

"Folks here could always go out and get a construction job for a decent wage," said Lee Bevang, in Covington, Ga. "But the contractors have totally taken advantage of illegal aliens, paying them wages no American can live on. My husband has been laid off. The concern about this is just huge." [10]

[1] Quoted on "Immigrant Nation: Divided Country," CNN Presents, Oct. 17, 2004.

[2] The desert death figure comes from Wayne Cornelius, "Controlling 'Unwanted' Immigraton: Lessons from the United States, 1993-2004," Center for Comparative Immigration Studies, University of California-San Diego, Working Paper No. 92, December, 2004, p. 14, www.ccis-ucsd.org/PUBLICATIONS/wrkg92.pdf. The remittances figure comes from "Las Remesas Familiares en Mexico," Banco de Mexico, noviembre, 2004,http://portal.sre.gob.mx/ime/pdf/Remesas_Familiares.pdf. In English, a study by the Inter-American Development Bank has slightly older statistics: "Sending Money Home: Remittance to Latin America and the Caribbean," May 2004, www.iadb.org/mif/v2/files/StudyPE2004 eng.pdf.

"Fox staked his presidency on getting a bilateral [immigration] agreement with the United States," says Manuel García y Griego, a specialist on U.S-Mexico relations at the University of Texas, Arlington. On the other hand, "Mr. Bush has spent his political capital very selectively, only on things that are close to his heart — making tax cuts permanent, Iraq. I don't see immigration in that category."

But Icaza insists the United States needs an accord as urgently as Mexico. For security reasons alone, he says, the United States must know who is living in the country illegally — and a legalization program would allow illegal residents to step forward with impunity.

Moreover, Icaza says, citing almost word-for-word the Council of Economic Advisers' latest annual report to the president: "The benefits to the U.S. economy are larger than the costs associated with Social Security, health and education." [9]

But the amnesty proposal may not go very far if Bush perceives the issue as alienating his political base in the Southern and Midwestern "red states" that are now attracting many migrantes.

[3] Jorge Herrera, "Impulsa Senado protecciÛn a connacionales," p. 17, www.eluniversal.com.mx/pls/impreso/version_himprimir?p_id=12435 3&p_seccion=2.

[4] Jeffrey S. Passel, "Estimates of the Size and Characteristics of the Undocumented Population," Pew Hispanic Center, March 21, 2005, www.pewhispanic.org.

[5] David Kelly, "Illegal Immigration Fears Have Spread; Populist calls for tougher enforcement are being heard beyond the border states," *Los Angeles Times*, April 25, 2005.

[6] *Ibid.*

[7] Mike Allen and Kevin Sullivan, "Meeting in Mexico, Presidents Agree to Form Immigration Panel," *The Washington Post*, Feb. 16, p. A1.

[8] Patrick J. O'Donnell, "Amnesty by Any Name is Hot Topic," *Los Angeles Times*, July 22, 2001, p. A1.

[9] "Economic Report of the President," February 2005, p. 115, http://www.ewic.org/documents/ERP2005-Immigration.pdf.

[10] Quoted in Kelly, *op. cit.*

injured while working on a construction site was entitled to lost wages — but valued only at what he would have earned in his home country. "It is our view that plaintiff, as an admitted undocumented alien, is not entitled to recover lost earnings damages based on the wages he might have earned illegally in the United States. . . . [W]e limited plaintiff's recovery for lost earnings to the wages he would have been able to earn in his home country." [25]

Illegal Immigrants Mostly From Latin America

More than 80 percent of the more than 10 million undocumented immigrants in the United States in March 2004 were from Latin America, including 57 percent from Mexico.

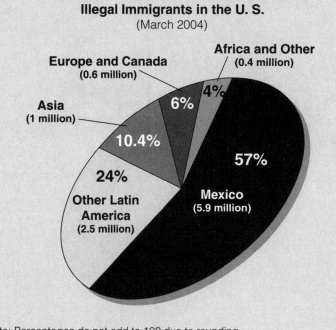

Illegal Immigrants in the U. S.
(March 2004)

Europe and Canada
(0.6 million)

Africa and Other
(0.4 million)

Asia
(1 million)

6%

4%

10.4%

57%

24%

Mexico
(5.9 million)

Other Latin
America
(2.5 million)

Note: Percentages do not add to 100 due to rounding.

Source: Jeffrey S. Passel, "Estimates of the Size and Characteristics of the Undocumented Population," Pew Hispanic Center, March 21, 2005, based on data from the March 2004 "Current Population Survey" by the Census Bureau and Department of Labor

illegals shouldn't be here. Employers should be held accountable for labor standards for all employees. The beauty part of erasing employer advantage is that it dampens the incentive for illegal flows."

BACKGROUND

Earlier Waves

The United States was created as a nation of immigrants who left Europe for political, religious and economic reasons. After independence, the new nation maintained an open-door immigration policy for 100 years. Two great waves of immigrants — in the mid-1800s and the late 19th and early 20th centuries — drove the nation's westward expansion and built its cities and its industrial base. [26]

But while the Statue of Liberty says America accepts the world's "tired . . . poor . . . huddled masses," Americans themselves vacillate between welcoming immigrants and resenting them — even those who arrive legally. For both legal and illegal immigrants, America's actions have been inconsistent and often racist.

In effect, Avendaño says, the ruling "legitimizes Third World labor conditions" in the United States.

Immigration-control advocates say the solution lies in keeping out the bulk of illegal immigrants trying to enter while cracking down on businesses that employ illegal workers. "If you enforce the law against employers," Rep. Tancredo says, "people who cannot get employment will return" to their home countries. "They will return by the millions."

That way, Tancredo says, a mass roundup would not be required.

Bernstein of the Economic Policy Institute favors a variant of the Tancredo approach that avoids its punitive aspects. Illegal immigrants "ought to have labor protection," he says. "That's not contradictory to the notion that

In the 19th century, thousands of Chinese laborers were brought here to build the railroads and then were excluded — via the Chinese Exclusion Act of 1882 — in a wave of anti-Chinese hysteria. Other Asian groups were restricted when legislation in 1917 created "barred zones" for Asian immigrants. [27]

The racist undertones of U.S. immigration policy were by no means reserved for Asians. Describing Italian and Irish immigrants as "wretched beings," *The New York Times* on May 15, 1880, editorialized: "There is a limit to our powers of assimilation, and when it is exceeded the country suffers from something very like indigestion."

Nevertheless, from 1880 to 1920, the country admitted more than 23 million immigrants — first from

Northern and then from Southern and Eastern Europe. In 1890, Census Bureau Director Francis Walker said the country was being overrun by "less desirable" newcomers from Southern and Eastern Europe, whom he called "beaten men from beaten races."

In the 1920s, public concern about the nation's changing ethnic makeup prompted Congress to establish a national-origins quota system. Laws in 1921, 1924 and 1929 capped overall immigration and limited influxes from certain areas based on the share of the U.S. population with similar ancestry, effectively excluding Asians and Southern Europeans.

But the quotas only swelled the ranks of illegal immigrants — particularly Mexicans, who only needed to wade across the Rio Grande. To stem the flow, the United States in 1924 created the U.S. Border Patrol, the enforcement arm of the INS, to guard the 6,000 miles of U.S. land bordering Canada and Mexico.

During the early 1940s the United States relaxed its immigration policies, largely for economic and political reasons. The Chinese exclusion laws were repealed in 1943, after China became a wartime ally against Japan in 1941. And in 1942 — partly to relieve wartime labor shortages and partly to legalize and control the flow of Mexican agricultural workers into the country — the United States began the Bracero (Spanish for "laborer") guest worker program, which allowed temporary workers from Mexico and the Caribbean to harvest crops in Western states.

After the war, Congress decided to codify the scores of immigration laws that had evolved over the years. The landmark Immigration and Nationality Act of 1952, retained a basic quota system that favored immigrants from Northern Europe — especially the skilled workers and relatives of U.S. citizens among them. At the same time, it exempted immigrants from the Western Hemisphere from the quota system — except for the black residents of European colonies in the Caribbean.

Mass Deportation

The 1952 law also attempted to address the newly acknowledged reality of Mexican workers who crossed the border illegally. Border Patrol agents were given more power to search for illegal immigrants and a bigger territory in which to operate.

"Before 1944, the illegal traffic on the Mexican border . . . was never overwhelming," the President's Commission on Migratory Labor noted in 1951, but in

An immigrant works on new homes being built in Homestead, Fla., on May 7, 2004. An estimated 337,000 undocumented immigrants live in Florida, according to the Department of Homeland Security.

the past seven years, "the wetback traffic has reached entirely new levels. . . . [I]t is virtually an invasion." [28]

In a desperate attempt to reverse the tide, the Border Patrol in 1954 launched "Operation Wetback," transferring nearly 500 INS officers from the Canadian perimeter and U.S. cities to join the 250 agents policing the U.S.-Mexican border and factories and farms. More than 1 million undocumented Mexican migrants were deported.

Although the action enjoyed popular support and bolstered the prestige — and budget — of the INS, it exposed an inherent contradiction in U.S. immigration policy. The 1952 law contained a gaping loophole — the Texas Proviso — a blatant concession to Texas agricultural interests that relied on cheap labor from Mexico.

"The Texas Proviso said companies or farms could knowingly hire illegal immigrants, but they couldn't harbor them," said Lawrence Fuchs, former executive director of the U.S. Select Commission on Immigration and Refugee Policy. "It was a duplicitous policy. We never really intended to prevent illegals from coming."

Immigration Reform

The foundation of today's immigration system dates back to 1965, when Congress overhauled the immigration rules. From the 1920s to the 1960s, immigration had been markedly reduced, thanks largely to the effects of the Great Depression, World War II and the quota system established in the 1920s.

From 1930 to 1950, for instance, fewer than 4 million newcomers arrived — more than a 50 percent drop from the high immigration rates of the early 20th century. The heated debates that had accompanied the earlier waves of immigration faded. "Immigration didn't even really exist as a big issue until 1965 because we just weren't letting that many people in," said Peter Brimelow, author of the 1995 bestseller *Alien Nation.*

That all changed in 1965, when Congress scrapped the national-origin quotas in favor of immigration limits for major regions of the world and gave preference to immigrants with close relatives living in the United States. The 1965 amendments to the 1952 Immigration and Nationality Act capped annual immigration at 290,000 — 170,000 from the Eastern Hemisphere and 120,000 from the Western Hemisphere. By giving priority to family reunification as a basis for admission, the amendments repaired "a deep and painful flaw in the fabric of American justice," President Lyndon B. Johnson declared at the time.

However, the law also dramatically changed the immigration landscape. Most newcomers now hailed from the developing world — about half from Latin America. While nearly 70 percent of immigrants had come from Europe or Canada in the 1950s, by the 1980s that figure had dropped to about 14 percent. Meanwhile, the percentage coming from Asia, Central America and the Caribbean jumped from about 30 percent in the 1950s to 75 percent during the '70s.

The government had terminated the Bracero program in December 1964, bowing to pressure from unions and exposés of the appalling conditions under which the braceros were living and working. But after having allowed millions of temporary Mexican laborers into the country legally for years, the government found that it was now impossible to turn off the spigot. Despite beefed-up Border Patrol efforts, the number of illegal migrants apprehended at the border jumped from fewer than 100,000 in 1965 to more than 1.2 million by 1985.

In 1978 the Select Commission on Immigration and Refugee Policy concluded that illegal immigration was the most pressing problem facing immigration authorities, a perception shared by the general public. [29] The number of border apprehensions peaked in 1986 at 1.7 million, driven in part by a deepening economic crisis in Mexico. Some felt the decade-long increase in illegal immigration was particularly unfair to the tens of thousands of legal petitioners waiting for years to obtain entry visas.

"The simple truth is that we've lost control of our own borders," declared President Ronald Reagan, "and no nation can do that and survive." [30]

In the mid-1980s, a movement emerged to fix the illegal immigration problem. Interestingly, the debate on Capitol Hill was marked by bipartisan alliances described by Sen. Alan K. Simpson, R-Wyo., as "the goofiest ideological-bedfellow activity I've ever seen." [31] Conservative anti-immigration think tanks teamed up with liberal labor unions and environmentalists favoring tighter restrictions on immigration. Pro-growth and business groups joined forces with longtime adversaries in the Hispanic and civil rights communities to oppose the legislation.

After several false starts, Congress passed the Immigration Reform and Control Act (IRCA) in October 1986 — the most sweeping revision of U.S. immigration policy in more than two decades. Using a carrot-and-stick approach, IRCA granted a general amnesty to all undocumented aliens who were in the United States before 1982 and imposed monetary sanctions — or even prison — against employers who knowingly hired undocumented workers for the first time. The law also included a commitment to beef up enforcement along the Mexican border.

IRCA allowed 3.1 million undocumented aliens to obtain legal status. Within two years, the number of would-be immigrants detained at the border each year fell from a peak of more than 1.7 million in 1986 to fewer than 900,000 in 1989.

"Once word spreads along the border that there are no jobs for illegals in the U.S., the magnet no longer exists," INS Commissioner Alan Nelson said in 1985. But that assessment was premature.

Political Asylum

Nowadays, illegal migrants come not only from neighboring countries but also from the world's far corners. Homeland Security Department officials have seized ships off the U.S. East and West coasts loaded with would-be illegal Chinese immigrants. Hundreds of others arrive on airplanes with temporary visas and simply stay past their visa-expiration dates.

As it is policing the borders, the department must also determine whether those immigrants seeking political asylum are truly escaping persecution or are merely seeking greener economic pastures. Historically, U.S. immi-

Are today's immigrants assimilating into U.S. society?

YES

Tamar Jacoby
Senior Fellow, Manhattan Institute; editor,
Reinventing the Melting Pot: The New
Immigrants and What it Means to be
American *(2004)*

From "Think Tank," Public Broadcasting Service, June 24, 2004

It's always been true that Americans have loved the immigrants of a generation or two ago and been frightened by the immigrants of their era. They think the past worked perfectly, and they look around and exaggerate how difficult it is in the present.

Your average American says, "Well, I hear all this Spanish spoken." But in the second generation, if you grow up here you may not learn [Spanish] in school; you may learn it on the street, but you become proficient in English. By the third generation, about two-thirds of Hispanics speak only English. You can be in Mexican-American neighborhoods in California and hear all the adults speaking to each other in Spanish, and the little siblings speak to each other in English.

The bulk of immigrants who are coming now are people who understand cultural fluidity, understand intermarriage [and] find that a natural, easy thing. They understand the mixing of cultures and find the binary nature of our views of race and our views of out and in very alien. And that bodes well for assimilation.

One statistic tells the story. In 1960, half of American men hadn't finished high school. Today, only 10 percent of American men have not finished high school. The people who used to drop out of high school in 1960 did a kind of job that Americans don't want to do anymore. Immigrants don't tend to displace American workers. They have some effect on wages — a small, temporary effect. But it's not a zero-sum game. They help grow the economy.

The key is [for immigrants to] buy into our political values and play by the rules. It's a balance between that sense of shared values and shared political ideals — and then [doing] whatever you want to do at home.

After 9/11, Americans were very frightened. Polls showed huge numbers — two-thirds or higher — thought that the borders should be closed or that we should have much lower [immigration] numbers. Some of those surface fears are ebbing, but I think people [remain] uneasy. [Yet] there's a kind of optimism and a faith in America and in America's power to absorb people that you could tap into. If you said we have control but we are absorbing them, I think you could get people to go for higher [immigration] numbers. And when you look at the big picture — are today's immigrants assimilating? The evidence is: Yes.

NO

Victor Davis Hanson
Fellow, Hoover Institution; author, Mexifornia: A
State of Becoming *(2003)*

From *World Magazine*, April 2, 2005

With perhaps as many as 20 million illegal aliens from Mexico, and the immigration laws in shreds, we are reaching a state of crisis. Criminals abound to prey on illegal aliens because they assume their victims are afraid to call the police, carry mostly cash, don't speak English, live as transients among mostly young males and are not legal participants in their communities.

If there were not a perennial supply of cheap labor, wages would rise and would draw back workers to now despised seasonal jobs; something is terribly wrong when central California counties experience 15 percent unemployment and yet insist that without thousands of illegal aliens from Oaxaca crops won't be picked and houses not built. At some point, some genius is going to make the connection that illegal immigration may actually explain high unemployment by ensuring employers cheap labor that will not organize, can be paid in cash and often requires little government deductions and expense.

Attitudes about legality need to revert back to the pre-1960s and 1970s, when immigration was synonymous with integration and assimilation. We need to dispense with the flawed idea of multiculturalism and return to the ideal of multiracialism under the aegis of a unifying Western civilization.

First-generation meritocratic Asians at places like University of California at Berkeley and the University of California at Los Angeles provide an example. What is the Asian community doing that its Mexican counterpart is not? Is it family emphasis on education, a sense of separation from the motherland, a tendency to stress achievement rather than victimization, preference for private enterprise rather than government entitlement? We need to discuss these taboo and politically incorrect paradoxes if we really wish to end something like four of 10 California Hispanic high-school students not graduating. Too many are profiteering and finding careers out of perpetuating the failure of others — others who will be the dominant population of the American Southwest in another decade.

In all public discourse and debate, when the racial chauvinist screams "racist" in lieu of logic, we all need to quit recoiling or apologizing, and instead rejoin with "Shame on you, shame, shame, shame for polluting legitimate discussion with race."

We need to return to what is known to work: measured and legal immigration, strict enforcement of our existing laws, stiff employer sanctions, an end to bilingual documents and interpreters — in other words, an end to the disastrous salad bowl and a return to the successful melting pot.

Unintended consequences)
lots of versions

gration law has been more receptive to political refugees if they come from communist countries.

"It used to be clear," said Doris Meissner, former INS commissioner. "Mexicans were economic, Cubans and Vietnamese were political. That changed when the Haitian boat people started coming in the 1970s. Their reasons for leaving were both political and economic." [32]

Unlike Cuban refugees arriving on boats — who are automatically admitted under the 1966 "Cuban Adjustment Act" — Haitian "boat people" in the 1970s were routinely imprisoned while their applications were being processed. In 1981, the U.S. government began intercepting Haitians' boats on the high seas and towing them back to Haiti. That practice continues. As for Cubans, the Clinton administration established a "wet foot/dry foot" policy — still in effect — that sends fleeing Cubans who don't actually touch U.S. soil back to Cuba; those who make a case for "credible fear of persecution" in Cuba are sent on to third countries.

Complicating the asylum picture, in the 1980s growing numbers of Central Americans began fleeing noncommunist regimes in war-torn countries like El Salvador and Guatemala. But their chances of obtaining political asylum were slim, so many came in illegally.

Human rights advocates argued that the inconsistencies in the treatment of Central American and Haitian refugees amounted to racial and political discrimination. From 1981 through 1986, the federal government deported nearly 18,000 Salvadorans while granting permanent-resident status to 598. [33] During the same period, half of the immigrants from Poland — then under communist rule — were granted asylum.

"Cubans and Poles were accepted without significant questioning," said Ernesto Rodriguez, an immigration expert at the University of Houston, "Central Americans were grilled and usually not accepted, despite the fact that lives were endangered. [Polish President] Lech Walesa would never have survived in Guatemala."

Responding to the unequal treatment, churches and some U.S. communities — Berkeley, Los Angeles, Chicago and others — began offering sanctuary to Central American refugees. By 1985, the sanctuary movement had spread to more than 200 parishes of all denominations. In 1985 several leaders of the movement were tried for being part of an "alien-smuggling conspiracy."

Four years later, the sanctuary movement was vindicated when the U.S. government (in settling a lawsuit filed by a coalition of religious and refugee organizations) agreed to reconsider the cases of tens of thousands of Central Americans previously rejected for political asylum. A 1990 immigration law created a new "temporary protected status" shielding from immediate deportation people whose countries were torn by war or environmental disaster. The provision was written with Central Americans in mind. Eventually, so many cases clogged the system that in 1997 Congress passed the Nicaraguan Adjustment and Central American Relief Act, which allowed thousands of Central Americans to bypass the backlogged asylum system and apply directly for permanent legal residence.

But the 1990 law also made broader changes. It increased the number of foreigners allowed to enter the United States each year from 500,000 to 700,000 (dropping to 675,000 in 1995). More important, it nearly tripled the annual quota for skilled professionals from 55,000 to 144,000. To alter the 1965 law's preference for Latin American and Asian immigrants, it set new quotas for countries seen as having been unfairly treated by the earlier law, with newcomers from Europe and skilled workers receiving a greater share of entry visas.

Changes in 1996

In the 1990s nearly 10 million newcomers arrived on U.S. shores, the largest influx ever — with most still coming from Latin America and Asia.

President Bill Clinton realized early in his presidency that the so-called "amnesty" program enacted in 1986 had not solved the illegal-immigration problem. And in the Border States, concern was growing that undocumented immigrants were costing U.S. taxpayers too much in social, health and educational services. On Nov. 8, 1994, California voters approved Proposition 187, denying illegal immigrants public education or non-essential public-health services. Immigrants'-rights organizations immediately challenged the law, which a court later ruled was mostly unconstitutional. But the proposition's passage had alerted politicians to the intensity of anti-illegal immigrant sentiment. [34]

House Republicans immediately included a proposal to bar welfare benefits for legal immigrants in its "Contract with America," and in 1995, after the GOP had won control of the House, Congress took another stab at reforming the rules for both legal and illegal immigration. But business groups blocked efforts to reduce legal immigration, so the new law primarily focused on curbing illegal immigration.

The final legislation, which cleared Congress on Sept. 30, 1995, nearly doubled the size of the Border Patrol and provided 600 new INS investigators. It appropriated $12 million for new border-control devices, including motion sensors, set tougher standards for applying for political asylum and made it easier to expel foreigners with fake documents or none at all. [35] The law also severely limited — and in many cases completely eliminated — non-citizens' ability to challenge INS decisions in court. [36]

But the new law did not force authorities to crack down on businesses that employed illegal immigrants even though there was wide agreement that such a crackdown was vital. As the Commission on Immigration Reform had said in 1994, the centerpiece of any effort to stop illegal entrants should be to "turn off the jobs magnet that attracts them."

By 1999, however, the INS had stopped raiding work sites to round up illegal immigrant workers and was focusing on foreign criminals, immigrant-smugglers and document fraud. As for cracking down on employers, an agency district director told *The Washington Post*, "We're out of that business." The idea that employers could be persuaded not to hire illegal workers "is a fairy tale." [37]

Terrorism and Immigrants

The debate over immigration heated up dramatically after the 9/11 terrorist attacks. Although none of the terrorists were immigrants, all were foreigners. And some had received help in obtaining housing and driver's licenses from members of Middle Eastern immigrant communities. [38]

There were no indications that Middle Eastern immigrants in general had anything to do with the attacks or with terrorism. But in the days and weeks following the attacks, federal agents rounded up more than 1,200 Middle Easterners on suspicion of breaking immigration laws, being material witnesses to terrorism or supporting the enemy. By August 2002, most had been released or deported. [39]

Nevertheless, a senior Justice Department official said the jailings had "incapacitated and disrupted some ongoing terrorist plans." [40]

Whatever the effects on terrorism, there is no question that 9/11 and the government response to the attacks put a dent in legal immigration. In fiscal 2002-

2003 — the latest period for which statistics are available — the number of people granted legal permanent residence (green cards) fell by 34 percent; 28,000 people were granted political asylum, 59 percent fewer than were granted asylum in fiscal 2000-2001. [41]

But the growth of illegal immigration under way before 9/11 continued afterward, with 57 percent of the illegal immigrants coming from Mexico. [42]

Due to the family-reunification provision in immigration law, Mexico is also the leading country of origin for legal immigrants — with 116,000 of the 705,827 legal immigrants in fiscal 2002-2003 coming from Mexico. [43] No Middle Eastern or predominantly Muslim countries have high numbers of legal immigrants, although Pakistan was 13th among the top 15 countries of origin for legal immigrants in 1998. [44]

CURRENT SITUATION

A Party Divided

Driven by concerns over national security, and with midterm congressional elections approaching, the intensity of the debate over immigration has increased markedly over the past year, both in Congress and in the streets.

In Congress — both houses of which are controlled by Republicans — the immigration issue has divided the Republican Party, with the conservative House favoring more restrictive controls on immigration and the Senate stalled by debate over somewhat more liberal legislation that includes guest worker provisions and a path to legalization for illegal immigrants.

In December 2005, the House passed HR 4437, which would amend the Immigration and Nationality Act to strengthen enforcement of immigration laws and enhance border security, by a vote of 239-182. Significantly, the bill included no provisions for a guest worker program, for amnesty or for a path to legalization for illegal immigrants.

Several immigration bills were introduced in the Senate in 2005 and early 2006 but each failed to attract enough support to proceed. Senate Majority Leader Bill Frist, R-Tenn., for example, sponsored S2454, a bill that would have provided for additional border controls but which did not address illegal immigrants already in the United States. Sen. John McCain, R-Ariz., sponsored S1033. Backed by business groups and by Sen., Edward

M. Kennedy, D-Mass., S1033 would have allowed illegal immigrants to remain in the country and, after six years, apply for legal staus after passing a background check and paying a $1,000 fine.

The one piece of legislation that came close to passage in early 2006 was S2612, sponsored by Republican senators Chuck Hagel of Nebraska and Mel Martinez of Florida, and cosponsored by Sen. Edward M. Kennedy (D-Mass.). The bill would strengthen border security, create a temporary guest worker program and provide a path to U.S. citizenship for most of the illegal immigrants already here. Bipartisan backing for the bill disappeared just prior to Congress' spring recess, however, over the issue of numerous amendments proposed by the Republican leadership.

Upon returning from recess, Republican and Democratic Senate leaders promised, on April 26, to work together to revive the sweeping immigration bill.

Even if Senate Republicans and Democrats are able to work out their differences, however, any resulting legislation is likely to face a tough battle in the House, which has already passed its much more conservative immigration bill.

Reacting to the proposed revival of S2612 by Senate leadership, Rep. John A. Boehner, R-Ohio, the House majority leader, said that any such legislation that would put a vast majority of illegal immigrants on a path to citizenship would face strong opposition. "I don't think that would be supported by the American people," Boehner told reporters. [45]

While the battle over pending legislation heats up in Congress, the prospect of implementing the Real ID law, signed into law in 2005, is generating increasing controversy among the states. The law, which requires states to verify the citizenship of those applying for or renewing driver's licenses, is scheduled to go into effect in May 2008. But many state officials are warning that two years is not enough time and the job is far too expensive for the states to shoulder the burden alone.

Indeed, at the end April 2006, the National Governors Association and the National Conference of State Legislators issued a report saying that the states had been given neither enough time nor enough money to comply with the law and that implementation would take at least eight years.

"It's absolutely absurd," Gov. Mike Huckabee of Arkansas, chairman of the National Governors Association, told reporters. "The time frame is unrealistic; the lack of funding is inexcusable." [46]

Public opinion is also growing more divided as midterm elections approach. In mid-April 2006, demonstrations in cities across the country drew hundreds of thousands of marchers. On May 1, hundreds of thousands more people participated in what some billed as "the Great American Boycott of 2006." The idea was for immigrants, legal and illegal, to demonstrate their economic contribution to the country by staying away from their jobs on May Day.

In terms of numbers alone, the demonstrations of April and May were impressive. But they may also have spurred a backlash among some sectors of the public. "The size and magnitude of the demonstrations had some kind of backfire effect," John McLaughlin, a Republican pollster, told reporters after the first round of marches. "The Republicans that are tough on immigration are doing well right now." [47]

Rep. Steve King, an Iowa Republican, agrees. He told reporters his office had received a number of calls from angry voters. "It is one thing to see an abstract number of 12 million illegal immigrants," King told reporters. "It is another thing to see more than a million marching through the streets demanding benefits as if it were a birthright. I think people resent that." [48]

Perhaps coincidentally, in mid-April the federal government also announced a crackdown against those who hire illegal immigrants. Announcing the arrest of more than 1,100 illegal immigrant employees at a pallet supply company in Houston on April 20, Homeland Security Secretary Michael Chertoff pledged to take stronger action against companies that do such illegal hiring.

"We target those organizations, we use intelligence to define the scope of the organization, and then we use all of the tools we have — whether it's criminal enforcement or the immigration laws — to make sure we come down as hard as possible and break the back of those organizations," Mr. Chertoff said at a news conference. [49]

State Debate

The hard-line approach is no less evident at the state level. In April 2005, for example, the Arkansas State Senate rejected legislation that would have made illegal immigrants eligible for in-state tuition. The state attorney general had ruled that the bill might have violated the 1996 immigration law. Similar bills are pending in North Carolina, Massachusetts, Oregon and Nebraska.

Arizona voters in 2004 approved Proposition 200, which requires proof of citizenship before voting. The new law also requires the state and local governments to check the immigration status of anyone applying for unspecified "public benefits" and to report any illegal immigrants who apply. [50]

Proponents said the law's "benefits" provision was designed to plug a loophole that enabled illegal immigrants to obtain welfare because of holes in the system. "Such benefits are an incentive for illegal aliens to settle in Arizona and hide from federal authorities," state Rep. Russell Pearce, R-Mesa, said. [51]

But the law didn't actually prohibit anything that wasn't already forbidden, opponents said. Ray Ybarra, who was observing the Minuteman Project for the American Civil Liberties Union, told a reporter that it simply restated existing prohibitions on illegal immigrants voting or getting welfare. He called the new law an outgrowth of "fear and misunderstanding." [52]

The law has led immigration-control forces to propose legislation that would bar illegal immigrants from state colleges, adult-education classes and utility and child-care assistance. The proposed legislation, which was under consideration in early May 2005, set off a new round of debate. Arizonans shouldn't have to subsidize services for people in the country illegally, argued state Rep. Tom Boone, R-Glendale, the bill's sponsor. Opponents countered that Hispanic citizens would have to suffer extra scrutiny simply because of their appearance. [53]

A Democratic opponent tried to add sanctions against employers who hire illegal immigrants. Republicans voted that down on the first attempt.

Perhaps because Arizona is on the border and its Proposition 200 passed by referendum, the legislation received more national attention than a similar measure enacted in Virginia this year.

As in Arizona, the Virginia law requires anyone applying for non-emergency public benefits — such as Medicaid and welfare — to be a legal U.S. resident. Democratic Gov. Mark Warner downplayed the measure's effects, even as he signed it into law, saying it restated federal prohibitions against illegal immigrants receiving some public benefits. [54]

Arizona's law is a model for immigration-control forces in other states. In Colorado, organizations that want to cut back illegal immigrants' access to state services are planning to follow the Arizona pattern by bringing the proposal before voters in a referendum, since the state legislature didn't act on the idea. But among voters at large, organizers of the referendum drive predict they'll have no trouble getting more than the 70,000 signatures needed to put the proposal on the 2006 election ballot. [55]

The legislation is "playing to the worst fears and instincts of people," said Democratic state Rep. Terrence Carroll, an opponent. "It has a very good chance of passing." [56]

In North Carolina, meanwhile, five proposals are designed to crack down on illegal immigration by denying driver's licenses to undocumented immigrants and forcing employers who hire them to cover some of their medical expenses. Immigration is a recent phenomenon in the state, and a big one. An estimated 300,000 illegal immigrants have settled in North Carolina — a 43 percent increase from 2000 to 2004 — driven by demand from farmers, the service industry and construction companies. [57]

And most recently, on April 17 of this year, Georgia enacted a tough new immigration law that requires those seeking many state benefits to prove they are in the United States legally. The law also provides sanctions for employers who knowingly hire illegal immigrants.

Assimilation Debate

In small communities experiencing unprecedented waves of new immigrants, many residents feel that the overwhelming numbers of Latinos showing up in their towns are changing American culture. They say that Mexican immigrants — perhaps because they need only walk across the border to return home — stick to themselves and refuse to learn English or to assimilate as readily as previous waves of immigrants.

"They didn't want to socialize with anybody," said D.A. King, describing the Mexicans who moved into a house across the street from his Marietta, Ga., home. "They filled their house full of people. At one time, there were 18 people living in this home." [58]

Harvard historian Samuel Huntington, in his controversial new book *Who Are We: The Challenges to America's National Identity*, worries that the sheer number of Latino immigrants has created a minority with little incentive to assimilate, potentially creating an America with a split identity.

"Continuation of this large immigration [without improved assimilation] could divide the United States into a country of two languages and two cultures," writes Huntington, who heads the Harvard Academy for

International and Area Studies. "Demographically, socially and culturally, the *reconquista* (reconquest) of the Southwestern United States by Mexican immigrants is well under way. Hispanic leaders are actively seeking to transform the United States into a bilingual society." [59]

But many reject Huntington's argument. "The same thing was said about African-Americans . . . about the Irish," a Georgia restaurant owner, who asked not to be identified, told CNN. "It's the same old song and over time it's proved to be a bunch of bologna. I believe these people are just like any other newcomers to this country. They can immigrate in and they're doing a great job here. And why should they be any different?" [60]

Those like Huntington and King say they are not against legal immigrants but oppose unchecked illegal immigration. King, in particular, is so furious with the government's refusal to enforce immigration laws against what he sees as the "invasion and the colonization of my country and my state and my city" that he founded the Marietta, Ga.-based American Resistance Foundation, which pushes for stricter enforcement of immigration laws.

Whenever he calls the INS to report seeing dozens of undocumented workers milling on local street corners waiting for employers seeking day laborers, he says, "I have never gotten through to a person, and I've never gotten a return phone call." [61]

"To whom does an American citizen turn when his government will not protect him from the Third World?" King asks. "What do we do now?"

Asa Hutchinson, former undersecretary of the Department of Homeland Security, which oversees the INS, had a mixed message in addressing King's frustration.

"I would certainly agree with him that we have to enforce our law, and it's an important part of my responsibilities," Hutchinson told CNN last October. "But whenever you look at the family that is being very productive and has a great family life contributing to American society, but in fact they came here illegally, I don't think you could excuse the illegal behavior. But you also recognize they're not terrorists. They're contributing to our society. We understand the humanitarian reasons that brought them here." [62]

Hutchinson said the dilemma for U.S. officials is particularly difficult when those illegal immigrants have had children born here, who are now U.S. citizens. "Do you jerk the parents up and send them back to their home country and leave the two children here that are U.S. citizens?

"Those are the problems that we're dealing with every day. Yes, we certainly want to enforce the law, but we have to recognize we also are a compassionate country that deals with a real human side as well."

Asylum

Political asylum accounts for few immigrants but plays an outsized role in the immigration debate. Most legal immigrants settle in the United States because the government decides to allow them in, and illegal immigrants come because they can. But asylum-seekers are granted refuge because the law requires it — not just federal law but international humanitarian law as well. The Convention Relating to the Status of Refugees of 1951, which was updated in 1967, says that no one fleeing political, racial or religious persecution can be returned involuntarily to a country where he or she is in danger. [63]

However, the United States and all other countries that grant asylum can determine who qualifies for that protection and who doesn't. "Irresponsible judges have made asylum laws vulnerable to fraud and abuse," Rep. Sensenbrenner said in promoting his Real ID bill, which would limit the right to asylum by raising the standard for granting asylum and allowing judges to take an applicant's demeanor into account.

"We will ensure that terrorists like Ramzi Yousef, the mastermind of the first World Trade Center attack in 1993, no longer receive a free pass to move around America's communities when they show up at our gates claiming asylum," Sensenbrenner said. [64]

Civil liberties advocates say terrorists today could not breeze through an immigration inspection by demanding asylum because the 1996 immigration overhaul tightened after Yousef and others abused it. Above all, the 1996 immigration act authorized immigration inspectors to refuse entry to foreigners without passports or with illegally obtained travel documents. [65]

In addition, says Erin Corcoran, a Washington-based lawyer in the asylum-rights program of Human Rights First (formerly, the Lawyers Committee for Human Rights), asylum seekers now get their fingerprints and photos checked at each stage in the process. "Real ID just heightens the burden of proof that a genuine applicant must meet," Corcoran says, arguing that terrorists are more than capable of adjusting to the new security environment. "A terrorist would have everything in order."

The 1996 law tightened up the process in other ways as well. If a foreigner asks for asylum when trying to enter the United States, he must get a so-called "credible fear interview." If an asylum officer concludes that a "significant possibility" exists for the foreigner to win asylum, a judge might rule that the foreigner shouldn't be deported. If the asylum officer decides that foreigners haven't met the "credible fear" standard, they are held and then deported. But those who do meet the standard may be released while they await hearings on their asylum claims. [66]

And even getting to the first step of the asylum process is difficult. In fiscal 1999 through 2003, asylum was requested by 812,324 foreigners, but only 35,566 were granted credible fear interviews. [67] Of the 36,799 asylum applicants whose cases were decided during the same period, 5,891 were granted asylum or allowed to remain in the United States under the international Convention Against Torture; 19,722 applicants were ordered deported, and 1,950 withdrew their applications. Another 2,528 were allowed to become legal permanent residents. [68]

OUTLOOK

Focus on Mexico

Immigration predictions have a way of turning out wrong. The 1986 Immigration Reform and Control Act didn't control illegal immigration. The 1994 North American Free Trade Agreement didn't create enough jobs in Mexico to keep Mexicans from migrating. The 1996 Immigration Enforcement Improvement Act didn't lessen the flow of illegal immigrants. Cracking down on illegal crossings in big cities like San Diego and El Paso only funneled migrants into the deadly desert of northern Mexico. And announced measures to step up border enforcement didn't stop illegals from coming in — both before or after 9/11 — although legal immigration did drop.

Faced with such a track record, many immigration experts say legislation and law enforcement may not be the best ways to change immigration patterns, especially where illegal immigration is concerned.

"The absence of consensus on alternatives locks in the current policy mix, under which unauthorized immigrants bear most of the costs and risks of 'control' while benefits flow impressively to employers and consumers,"

Cornelius of the University of California has concluded. "Promised future experiments with guest worker programs, highly secure ID cards for verifying employment eligibility and new technologies for electronic border control are unlikely to change this basic dynamic. [69]

"The back door to undocumented immigration to the United States is essentially wide open," he said. "And it is likely to remain wide open unless something systematic and serious is done to reduce the demand for the labor." [70]

Steven Camarota, research director of the Washington-based Center for Immigration Studies, which advocates tougher immigration controls, agrees. "There is a fundamental political stalemate," he says. "You have a divide in the country between public opinion and elite opinion. Elite opinion is strong enough to make sure that the law doesn't get enforced but is not strong enough to repeal the law. Public opinion is strong enough to ensure that the law doesn't get repealed but not strong enough to get the law enforced. For most politicians a continuation of the status quo doesn't have a huge political downside."

Nevertheless, Stein of FAIR argues that Beltway insiders are only slowly catching on to what's happening in the country at large. "The issue is building very rapidly in terms of public frustration," he says. "You talk to [congressional] representatives, they'll tell you that you go to a town meeting and talk about the budget or one of the issues that the party wants to talk about, and the discussion will last five minutes. Mention immigration and two hours later you're still on it. It's on fire out there."

Developments in Mexico may be as important to the future of U.S. immigration policy as anything that Washington politicians do, says Martin, at the University of California. If the populist mayor of Mexico City, Manuel López Obrador, wins the presidency of Mexico in 2006, he says, the mutual distrust between the international business community and left-leaning politicians who favor government intervention in the economy could play a key role in immigration to the United States: "That will slow down foreign investment," making it likely that illegal immigration would continue at a high level, he says.

Martin doubts there is much potential for political violence and destabilization in Mexico. Nevertheless, hundreds of thousands of people turned out in Mexico City in April to protest a move to prosecute López Obrador for a minor legal violation, raising the specter of serious political conflict. [71] If that happens, immigration could be seen as a political — as well an economic — safety valve.

"That may be the best rationale for letting illegal immigration be what it is," says Borjas of Harvard, who otherwise opposes that trend. "I could see the point to that."

With little likelihood of substantial change to the immigration picture, virtually all observers agree that there is one potential exception: a major terrorist act committed in the United States by an illegal border-crosser. In that event, Borjas says, "Who knows what the outcome would be?"

NOTES

1. Quoted in "CNN Presents: Immigrant Nation: Divided Country," Oct. 17, 2004.

2. Jeffrey S. Passel, "Estimates of the Size and Characteristics of the Undocumented Population," March 21, 2005, Pew Hispanic Center, www.pewhispanic.org.

3. Census Bureau, Statistical Abstract of the United States, 2004-2005, p. 8; www.census.gov/prod/2004pubs/04statab/pop.pdf; Office of Policy and Planning, U.S. Immigration and Naturalization Service, "Estimates of the Unauthorized Immigration Population Residing in The United States: 1990 to 2000," http://uscis.gov/graphics/shared/statistics/publications/Ill_Report_1211.pdf; Steven A. Camarota, "Economy Slowed, But Immigration Didn't: The Foreign-Born Population 2000-2004," Center for Immigration Studies, November 2004,www.cis.org/articles/2004/back1204.pdf.

4. Quoted in David Kelly, "Illegal Immigration Fears Have Spread; Populist calls for tougher enforcement are being heard beyond the border states," Los Angeles Times, April 25, 2005.

5. Ibid.

6. Ibid.

7. Seth Hettena, "Congressmen call on Senate to pass bill to fortify border fence," The Associated Press, March 29, 2005.

8. PR Newswire, "Senator John McCain Surprises U.S. Constitutional Development Class at Annapolis . . . ," April 21, 2005.

9. "President Meets with President Fox and Prime Minister Martin," White House, March 23, 2005, www.whitehouse.gov/news/releases/2005/03/print/20050323-5.html.

10. Elisabeth Bumiller, "In Immigration Remarks, Bush Hints He Favors Senate Plan," The New York Times, April 25, 2006, p. 22.

11. Wayne Cornelius, "Controlling 'Unwanted' Immigration: Lessons from the United States, 1993-2004," Center for Comparative Immigration Studies, University of California, San Diego, December 2004, p. 5, www.ccis-ucsd.org/PUBLICATIONS/wrkg92.pdf.

12. Statement, March 15, 2005; www.cbp.gov/xp/cgov/newsroom/commissioner/speeches_statements/mar17_05.xml.

13. Donald L. Bartlett and James B. Steele, "Who Left the Door Open," Time, Sept. 20, 2004, p. 51.

14. Birgit Meade, unpublished analysis, Economic Research Service, U.S. Dept. of Agriculture.

15. George J. Borjas, Heaven's Door: Immigration Policy and the American Economy (1999), pp. 87-104.

16. Ibid, pp. 103-104.

17. Ibid, pp. 90-91.

18. Chirag Mehta et al., "Chicago's Undocumented Immigrants: An Analysis of Wages, Working Conditions, and Economic Contributions," February 2002, www.uic.edu/cuppa/uicued/npublications/recent/undocimmigrants.htm.

19. "Immigration and Border Security Evolve, 1993 to 2001," Chapter 4 in "Staff Monograph on 9/11 and Terrorist Travel," National Commission on Terrorist Attacks Upon the United States, 2004, www.9-11commission.gov/staff_statements/911_TerrTrav_Ch4.pdf.

20. Ibid.

21. Ibid.

22. The 9/11 Commission Report (2004), pp. 248, 387.

23. T. R. Reid and Darryl Fears, "Driver's License Curtailed as Identification," The Washington Post, April 17, 2005, p. A3.

24. Muzaffar A. Chishti et al., "America's Challenge: Domestic Security, Civil Liberties, and National

Unity After September 11," Migration Policy Institute, 2003, p. 7.

25. Gorgonio Balbuena, *et al. v. IDR Realty LLC, et al*; 2004 N.Y. App. Div.

26. Unless otherwise noted, material in the background section comes from Rodman D. Griffin, "Illegal Immigration," *CQ Researcher*, April 24, 1992, pp. 361-384; Kenneth Jost, "Cracking Down on Immigration," *CQ Researcher*, Feb. 3, 1995, pp. 97-120; and David Masci, "Debate Over Immigration," *CQ Researcher*, July 14, 2000, pp. 569-592.

27. For background, see Richard L. Worsnop, "Asian Americans," *CQ Researcher*, Dec. 13, 1991, pp. 945-968.

28. Quoted in Ellis Cose, *A Nation of Strangers: Prejudice, Politics and the Populating of America* (1992), p. 191.

29. Cited in Michael Fix, ed., *The Paper Curtain: Employer Sanctions' Implementation, Impact, and Reform* (1991), p. 2.

30. Quoted in Tom Morganthau *et al.*, "Closing the Door," *Newsweek*, June 25, 1984.

31. Quoted in Dick Kirschten, "Come In! Keep Out!," *National Journal*, May 19, 1990, p. 1206.

32. For background, see Peter Katel, "Haiti's Dilemma," *CQ Researcher*, Feb. 18, 2005, pp. 149-172.

33. Cose, *op. cit.*, p. 192.

34. Ann Chih Lin, ed. *Immigration*, CQ Press (2002), pp. 60-61.

35. William Branigin, "Congress Finishes Major Legislation; Immigration; Focus is Borders, Not Benefits," *The Washington Post*, Oct. 1, 1996, p. A1.

36. David Johnston, "Government is Quickly Using Power of New Immigration Law," *The New York Times*, Oct. 22, 1996, p. A20.

37. William Branigin, "INS Shifts 'Interior' Strategy to Target Criminal Aliens," *The Washington Post*, March 15, 1999, p. A3.

38. *The 9/11 Commission, op. cit.*, pp. 215-223.

39. Adam Liptak, Neil A. Lewis and Benjamin Weiser, "After Sept. 11, a Legal Battle On the Limits of Civil Liberty," *The New York Times*, Aug. 4, 2002, p. A1. For background, see Patrick Marshall, "Policing the Borders," *CQ Researcher*, Feb. 22, 2002, pp. 145-168.

40. *Ibid.*

41. Deborah Meyers and Jennifer Yau, US Immigration Statistics in 2003, Migration Policy Institute, Nov. 1, 2004, www.migrationinformation.org/USfocus/display.cfm?id=263; and Homeland Security Department, "2003 Yearbook of Immigration Statistics," http://uscis.gov/graphics/shared/statistics/yearbook/index.htm.

42. Passel, *op. cit.*, p. 8.

43. Meyers and Yau, *op. cit.*

44. Lin, *op. cit.*, p. 20.

45. Jim Rutenberg and Rachel L. Swarns, "Senate Leaders Work to Resuscitate Immigration Bill," *The New York Times*, April 26, 2006, p. 16.

46. Pam Belluck, "Mandate for ID Meets Resistance From States," *The New York Times*, May 6, 2006.

47. David D. Kirkpatrick, "Demonstrations on Immigration are Hardening a Divide," *The New York Times*, April 17, 2006, p. 16.

48. *Ibid.*

49. Eric Lipton, "U.S. Crackdwon Set Over Hiring of Immigrants," *The New York Times*, April 21, 2006, p. 1.

50. "Proposition 200," Arizona Secretary of State, http://www.azsos.gov/election/2004/info/PubPamphlet/english/prop200.htm.

51. *Ibid.*

52. Jacques Billeaud, "Congressman: Prop 200's passage was key moment in effort to limit immigration," The Associated Press, April 2, 2005.

53. Jacques Billeaud, "Arizona lawmakers try to add restrictions for illegal immigrants," The Associated Press, March 24, 2005.

54. Chris L. Jenkins, "Warner Signs Limits on Immigrant Benefits," *The Washington Post*, March 30, 2005, p. B5.

55. David Kelly, "Colorado Activists Push Immigration Initiative," *Los Angeles Times*, March 13, 2005, p. A23.

56. *Ibid.*

57. Michael Easterbrook, "Anger rises toward illegal immigrants," *Raleigh* [N.C.] *News & Observer*, April 17, 2005, p. A1.

58. CNN, *op. cit.*

59. Samuel Huntington, "The Hispanic Challenge," *Foreign Policy*, March/April 2004.

60. CNN, *op. cit.*

61. King's quotes are from *ibid.*

62. Hutchinson's quotes are from *ibid.*

63. "The Wall Behind Which Refugees Can Shelter," U.N. High Commissioner for Refugees, 2001; www.unhcr.org.

64. Dan Robinson, "Congress — Immigration," Voice of America, Dec. 8, 2004, www.globalsecurity.org/security/library/news/2004/12/sec-041208-3c7be91f.htm.

65. "Asylum Seekers in Expedited Removal," United States Commission on International Religious Freedom, Executive Summary, pp. 1-2, Feb. 8, 2005, www.uscirf.gov/countries/global/asylum_refugees/2005/february/index.html.

66. *Ibid.*

67. *Ibid*, p. 295.

68. *Ibid.*

69. Cornelius, *op. cit.*, p. 24.

70. CNN, *op. cit.*

71. Ginger Thompson and James C. McKinley Jr., "Opposition Chief at Risk in Mexico," *The New York Times*, April 8, 2005, p. A1.

BIBLIOGRAPHY

Books

Borjas, George J., *Heaven's Door: Immigration Policy and the American Economy*, Princeton University Press, 2000.
A Harvard economist who is a leading figure in the debate over immigration and the economy argues for encouraging immigration by the highly skilled while discouraging the entry of low-skilled workers.

Dow, Mark, *American Gulag: Inside U.S. Immigration Prisons*, University of California Press, 2004.
A freelance journalist penetrates the secretive world of immigrant detention and finds widespread abuse of prisoners who are granted few, if any, legal rights.

Huntington, Samuel P., *Who Are We?: The Challenges to America's National Identity*, Simon & Schuster, 2004.
A Harvard professor argues that mass immigration, especially from Latin America, is flooding the United States with people who are not assimilating into mainstream society.

Jacoby, Tamar, ed., *Reinventing the Melting Pot: The New Immigrants and What It Means To Be An American*, Basic Books, 2004.
Authors representing strongly differing views and experiences on immigration contribute essays on how the present wave of immigrants is changing — and being changed by — the United States. Edited by a pro-immigration scholar at the moderately libertarian Manhattan Institute.

Lin, Ann Chih, ed., and Nicole W. Green, *Immigration*, CQ Press, Vital Issues Series, 2002.
This useful collection of information on recent immigration policy and law changes also includes steps that other countries have taken to deal with issues similar to those under debate in the United States.

Articles

Cooper, Marc, "Last Exit to Tombstone," *L.A. Weekly*, March 25, 2005, p. 24.
A reporter visits the Mexican desert border towns where immigrants prepare to cross illegally into the United States and finds them undaunted by the dangers ahead.

Jordan, Miriam, "As Border Tightens, Growers See Threat to 'Winter Salad Bowl,' " *The Wall Street Journal*, March 11, 2005, p. A1.
Lettuce farmers plead with immigration officials not to crack down on illegal immigration at the height of the harvest season in Arizona.

Kammer, Jerry, "Immigration plan's assumption on unskilled workers contested," *San Diego Union-Tribune*, March 31, 2005, p. A1.
Even immigrants who once lacked legal status themselves are worried about the continued influx of illegal immigrants, because they drive down wages.

Porter, Eduardo, "Illegal Immigrants are Bolstering Social Security With Billions," *The New York Times*, April 5, 2005, p. A1.
Government figures indicate that illegal immigrants are subsidizing Social Security by about $7 billion a year by paying taxes from which they will never benefit.

Seper, Jerry, "Rounding Up All Illegals 'Not Realistic,'" *Washington Times*, Sept. 10, 2004, p. A1.
The undersecretary of homeland security acknowledges that law enforcement officials are not hunting for all illegal immigrants, something he said would be neither possible nor desirable.

Reports and Studies

Lee, Joy, Jack Martin and Stan Fogel, "Immigrant Stock's Share of U.S. Population Growth, 1970-2004," Federation for American Immigration Reform, 2005.
The authors conclude that more than half of the country's population growth since 1970 stems from increased immigration, raising the danger of overpopulation and related ills.

Orozco, Manuel, "The Remittance Marketplace: Prices, Policy and Financial Institutions," Pew Hispanic Center, June 2004.
A leading scholar of remittances — money sent back home by immigrants — analyzes the growth of the trend and the regulatory environment in which it operates.

Stana, Richard M., "Immigration Enforcement: Challenges to Implementing the INS Interior Enforcement Strategy," General Accounting Office (now Government Accountability Office), testimony before House Judiciary Subcommittee on Immigration, June 19, 2002.
A top GAO official finds a multitude of reasons why immigration officials have not been able to deport criminal illegal immigrants, break up people-smuggling rings and crack down on employers of illegal immigrants.

"Refugees, Asylum Seekers and the Department of Homeland Security: One Year Anniversary — No Time for Celebration," *Human Rights First*, April 2004.
Some rights of asylum-seekers are being eroded as the number of people granted asylum drops, the advocacy organization concludes, urging changes in procedures.

For More Information

Center for Comparative Immigration Studies, University of California, San Diego, La Jolla, CA 92093-0548; (858) 822-4447; www.ccis-ucsd.org. Analyzes U.S. immigration trends and compares them with patterns in Europe and Asia.

Center for Immigration Studies, 1522 K St., N.W., Suite 820, Washington, DC 20005-1202, (202) 466-8185; www.cis.org. A think tank that advocates reduced immigration.

Civil Homeland Defense, P. O. Box 1579, Tombstone, AZ 85638; (520) 457-3008. An offshoot of the Minuteman Project that encourages citizens to patrol the Mexican border in Arizona against illegal immigrants.

Federation for American Immigration Reform, 1666 Connecticut Ave., N.W., Suite 400, Washington, DC 20009; (202) 328-7004; http://fairus.org. A leading advocate for cracking down on illegal immigration and reducing legal immigration.

Migration Dialogue, University of California, Davis, 1 Shields Ave., Davis, CA 95616; (530) 752-1011; http://migration.ucdavis.edu/index.php. An academic research center that focuses on immigration from rural Mexico and publishes two quarterly Web bulletins.

Migration Policy Institute, 1400 16th St., N.W., Suite 300, Washington, DC 20036; (202) 266-1940; www.migrationpolicy.org. Analyzes global immigration trends and advocates fairer, more humane conditions for immigrants.

National Immigration Law Center, 3435 Wilshire Blvd., Suite 2850, Los Angeles, CA 90010; (213) 639-3900; http://nilc.org. Advocacy organization aimed at defending the legal rights of low-income immigrants.

16

War in Iraq

Pamela M. Prah

A Navy chaplain at Camp Pendleton, Calif., leads a memorial service last May for American and British troops killed in Iraq while serving with the First Marine Division. Since a U.S.-led coalition invaded Iraq in March 2003, more than 1,900 U.S. troops have been killed and 15,000 wounded. The death toll also includes some 200 coalition forces, at least 24,400 Iraqi civilians and an estimated 50,000 insurgents killed or captured.

Getty Images/David McNew

From *CQ Researcher,*
October 21, 2005.

"A nd so it begins, another sunrise, another day in Iraq," Zachary Scott-Singley, 24, an Arabic linguist in the U.S. Army, writes in his daily blog from Tikrit, the hometown of ousted Iraqi dictator Saddam Hussein.

"The land of 1,000 lies. Where we tell each other things are getting better when really we have only gotten used to the smell of our own sh*t mixed with theirs," writes Scott-Singley who participated in the 2003 invasion and is on his second tour because the Army extended his stay.

Scott-Singley doesn't support the Iraq war and would rather be in Louisiana helping Hurricane Katrina survivors. "Perhaps if we were home we could have saved more lives," he muses.

But another 24-year-old soldier relishes patrolling Kirkuk with the new Iraqi army. "Iraq is a new place, believe me," writes blogger "Ma Deuce Gunner," who mans an M2 machine gun. "By fighting this war here, we are not only procuring freedom for a new country but we are taking the fight to our enemy." [1]

Both soldiers are on the frontlines of the war in Iraq, but their differing viewpoints reflect the same deep divide the war has opened among Americans back home. Nearly two-and-a-half years after a U.S.-led coalition launched Operation Iraqi Freedom and after some 2,000 U.S. soldiers and from 24,700-100,000 Iraqi civilians have been killed, many Americans are asking whether the war is making America safer from terrorism and how long U.S. troops should stay in Iraq.

Americans' views on Iraq were largely split throughout 2005, but approval tumbled in mid-September, when only 32 percent approved of the situation in Iraq, according to a *USA Today*/CNN

Iraq Lies in Volatile Region

Two-and-a-half years after the war in Iraq began, 138,000 U.S. troops still remain in Iraq — leading some Americans to question whether the Bush administration should prepare a withdrawal timetable. But others say it is unwise to even consider departing and leaving a now largely defenseless country subject to internal religious and ethnic strife and "naked to its enemies" in one of the world's most volatile, heavily armed regions.

Source: GlobalSecurity.org

poll by the Gallup organization, and a record high 59 percent said invading was a mistake. In September, only 38 percent approved of President Bush's handling of the war — an all-time low — according to a *Washington Post*/ABC News poll. [2]

Meanwhile, at the White House President Bush and Jalal Talabani, the first democratically elected president in Iraq, offered optimism and a united front as they stood side-by-side in the East Room in September and reaffirmed their commitment to building a free Iraq. But both refused to lay out a schedule for U.S. troop withdrawal.

"When the mission is complete, our troops will come home," said Bush. [3] "A timetable will help the terrorists, will encourage them that they could defeat a superpower of the world and the Iraqi people" said Talabani, a lawyer, journalist and member of the Kurdish minority. (*See graph, p. 362.*)

However, 61 percent of Americans favor bringing most troops home from Iraq within the next year, according to an August Harris poll. [4]

Concerns are growing as suicide bombings and violence continue to kill and maim hundreds each month, and the United States fails to capture a key mastermind of terrorism in Iraq: Abu Musab al-Zarqawi. The Jordanian, linked with Osama bin Laden and the al Qaeda terrorist network, is America's "most wanted" terrorist in Iraq. [5]

But many experts fear that if the U.S. military leaves too soon, civil war could erupt in Iraq. Sunni Arabs, who represent 20 percent of the population, stand to lose the power they enjoyed under Hussein to Shiite Arabs and Kurds.

Another worry is that the departure of U.S. troops before defeating the insurgents would turn Iraq into the new breeding ground for terrorists.

"We can leave the country to be preyed upon by murderers who want to turn the country into a Taliban-like nation, a haven for terrorist camps and a factory of hatred, or we can stand and fight by defending liberty and democracy in Iraq and demonstrating an alternative to the ways of terror and of Saddam Hussein," Sen. Mitch McConnell, R-Ky., said. [6]

But no one knows how long it will take for Iraqis to handle their own security. The Pentagon estimated in late September that there are 197,000 trained Iraqi police and military personnel. [7] The U.S. goal is 350,000, but the Pentagon says withdrawal is not tied to a specific number of security forces. [8] Talabani said he hoped Iraqi security forces would be prepared to take over within two years.

That's not soon enough for Cindy Sheehan, whose son Casey died in Iraq. She re-energized the anti-war movement in August with her vigil outside Bush's Crawford, Texas, ranch. Some members of Congress also are demanding specific withdrawal deadlines. (See "At Issue," p. 379.)

The United States needs "to define the mission of our military in Iraq and to issue a plan and timeframe for accomplishing that mission," said Sen. Russell D. Feingold, D-Wis.

Republican Sen. Chuck Hagel of Nebraska also complains the administration lacks a strategy to win the war. In fact, Hagel compares the situation in Iraq to Vietnam, a comparison rejected by his fellow senator and Vietnam veteran Sen. John McCain, R-Ariz. (See sidebar, p. 376)

War supporters say removing Hussein from power made the world — and the United States — safer. "Even if Saddam didn't have weapons of mass destruction, he certainly gave every appearance he was up to his old

Coalition Contributes 22,000 Troops

The 27 nations in the coalition assisting the United States in Iraq have contributed about 10 percent of the total number of troops fielded by the United States and Iraq.

Military Personnel in Iraq
(as of July 13, 2005)

Non-U.S. Coalition Countries	Number of troops
United Kingdom	8,000
South Korea	3,600
Italy	3,000
Poland	1,700
Ukraine	1,650
Australia	900-1,370
Georgia	850
Romania	800
Japan	550
Denmark	530
Bulgaria	400
Remaining 16 Coalition Countries	1,920
U.S. (September 2005)	138,000
Iraq (September 2005)	87,800

Source: The Brookings Institution, "Iraq Index: Tracking Variables of Reconstruction and Security in Post-Saddam Iraq," www.brookings.edu/iraqindex

tricks again," says John Pike, director and founder of GlobalSecurity.org, a Web site on military and homeland-security issues.

However, despite Vice President Dick Cheney's May assessment that the Iraq insurgency was in its "last throes," the violence hasn't ended. In September alone, more than 200 Iraqis were killed in dozens of suicide and car bombings orchestrated by al-Zarqawi in retaliation for an Iraqi-U.S. military operation in Tal Afar. Al-Zarqawi, a Sunni, is trying to instigate a religious and ethnic civil war in Iraq pitting Sunnis against Shiites.

The Iraqi interior ministry estimated in July that insurgents were killing more than 800 Iraqi civilians and police officers a month. (See box, p. 365.) [9] The Web site www.Iraqbodycount.org estimates that 24,700-28,000 civilians have died since the war began, while the British

A woman votes in Baghdad during a referendum on Iraq's new draft constitution on Oct. 15; passage was expected. Insurgents unsuccessfully tried to thwart that election as well as a referendum last January to select a 275-seat National Assembly — the first democratic election in 50 years. Elections for a permanent government are scheduled for December.

medical journal *Lancet* put the figure at 100,000. [10] At least 3,000 Iraqi military and police have been killed. [11]

The estimated 20,000 insurgents in Iraq appear determined to kill as many Americans as possible in hopes that a growing casualty count will prompt U.S. withdrawal. They also want to frighten Iraqis into refusing to cooperate with U.S. forces and ultimately to prevent a "legitimate, democratic Iraqi government" from being established, writes Andrew F. Krepinevich Jr., executive director of the Center for Strategic and Budgetary Assessments. [12]

Krepinevich and others argue that the United States is paying now for earlier mistakes, particularly the lack of pre-war planning of what to do after U.S. forces took over. "The Bush administration was never willing to commit anything like the forces necessary to ensure order in post-war Iraq," writes Larry Diamond, a senior fellow at Stanford University's Hoover Institution and former senior adviser to the Coalition Provisional Authority (CPA) in Baghdad. [13] Diamond argues that an additional 100,000 troops might have been enough to prevent the widespread looting and chaos that occurred.

And the war has left Iraqi citizens — now free from Hussein's murderous reign — struggling with difficult daily life. In addition to the violence, electricity, water and sewage services are sporadic, and unemployment has been estimated at up to 40 percent. [14]

In some ways, Iraqi women are no better off than before U.S. forces ousted Hussein, whose trial on murder and torture charges began on Oct. 19 (*see p. 382*). Many can no longer drive or walk in the streets at night as freely as they did in prewar Iraq, and many are too afraid to play a big political role for fear of being a target of extremists. There also have been reports of religious extremists intimidating women and girls into wearing veils. [15]

The U.S. invasion of Iraq "took down a criminal regime and left a nation without an operational state," said retired Gen. Barry McCaffrey, a professor of international security studies at the U.S. Military Academy. [16]

While electricity is sporadic, unemployment high and violence a concern, most Iraqis appear optimistic. Less than 40 percent of Iraqis think their lives were better before the war, and nearly half think the country is heading in the right direction, according to recent polls. [17]

More Iraqis now have access to telephones, the Internet and independent news — all which were restricted during Hussein's regime. The country now has nearly 200 independent TV stations and newspapers — up from zero — and 4.5 million have telephones, including cell phones, up from less than 1 million before 2003. [18]

But in the United States, some argue the war is threatening U.S. security by draining troops and money — nearly $5 billion a month. "The money that [is] being spent on the war should be spent at home on things like shoring up the levees of New Orleans," says Phyllis Bennis, a fellow with the liberal Institute for Policy Studies and Foreign Policy. "There is a very direct price being paid today for the cost of that war."

The Bush administration insists the war in Iraq is a vital part of the global war on terrorism and dismisses charges that the deployment of National Guard and reserve troops in Iraq hindered the federal government's response to Hurricane Katrina. "We can and will do both," said Defense Secretary Donald H. Rumsfeld. [19]

As the country debates the war in Iraq, here are some questions being asked:

Did the Bush administration devote enough resources to winning the war and securing the peace?

Even before U.S. forces landed in Iraq in March 2003, military experts debated whether the administration's war plan provided for enough troops.

Just weeks before the United States led more than 150,000 coalition forces into Iraq, former Army Chief of

Staff Eric Shinseki told a Senate panel the U.S. military would need "several hundred thousand soldiers" to conquer Iraq; some Army officers advocated 400,000 troops. [20] Even Ambassador L. Paul Bremer III, who governed Iraq after the invasion, later said the United States should have deployed more troops when it invaded. [21]

Experts say the Bush administration had banked on the Iraqi people welcoming U.S. troops as liberators. The administration argued that with Hussein out, Iraq's transition to democracy would resemble that of East Germany and Czechoslovakia in the late 1990s, which moved peacefully to new governments after the Soviet Union's dissolution.

Stanford University's Diamond said the Bush administration thought it could hand the country over to Iraqi expatriates such as Ahmed Chalabi, who would quickly create a new democratic state. [22] Instead, widespread looting, destruction and chaos reigned.

Some experts said the United States showed arrogance in the planning and early weeks of the war. "The arrogance phase was [thinking we could go] in undermanned, underresourced, skim off the top layer of leadership, take control of a functioning state and be out by six weeks — and get the oil funds to pay for it," a U.S. official told author George Packer, according to Packer's new book about the war, *The Assassins' Gate*. And then-Deputy Secretary of Defense Paul Wolfowitz had told a congressional panel, "The oil revenue of [Iraq] could bring between $50 billion and $100 billion dollars over the course of the next two or three years. We're dealing with a country that could really finance its own reconstruction." [23]

Four former CIA analysts who examined U.S. prewar intelligence concluded that policy-makers focused too much on Iraq's alleged weapons of mass destruction (WMD) and not enough on cultural and political issues after the invasion. [24] "The policy community was recep-

The Iraq War at a Glance

Fighting the War

U.S. troops wounded, as of Oct. 16, 2005	15,063
U.S. troops killed, as of Oct. 16, 2005	1,962
Iraqi military and police killed, as of Oct. 16, 2005	3,403
Iraqi civilians killed as a result of acts of war, as of Oct. 16, 2005	17,616
Foreign fighters detained or killed (May 2003-September 2005)	51,470
Estimated strength of insurgency, as of Sept. 2005	No more than 20,000
Estimated foreign fighters in insurgency, as of September 2005	700-2,000
Average number of daily insurgent attacks in 2005	47

Life in Iraq Today

Average hours of electricity available per day (October 2005)	15.0
Nationwide unemployment rate (September 2005)	27-40%
Commercial TV and radio stations and independent newspapers/magazines before war	0
Commercial TV stations (July 2005)	29
Independent newspapers/magazines (July 2005)	170
Average monthly teacher's salary before new government	$2
After new government	$100

Source: The Brookings Institution, "Iraq Index: Tracking Variables of Reconstruction and Security in Post-Saddam Iraq," www.brookings.edu/iraqindex

tive to technical intelligence on WMD, where the analysis was wrong, but paid little attention to analysis on post-Saddam Iraq, which was right," the analysts wrote in July 2004. [25] Nevertheless, despite pressure to find a link between Hussein and al Qaeda, "the intelligence community remained firm in its assessment that no operational or collaborative relationship existed."

Rumsfeld defended the war plan and said the looting was not as bad as some media reports portrayed. "I read eight headlines that talked about chaos, violence, unrest. And it just was Henny Penny — 'The sky is falling,' " the secretary said in an April 2003 news briefing. "Stuff happens. . . . Freedom is untidy." [26]

Bremer himself was widely criticized for his decision to dissolve the Iraqi army and fire all government leaders and workers who were members of Hussein's Baath Party, including teachers, doctors and other civil servants. The actions left U.S. authorities without either

Gunfire, Homemade Bombs Kill Most

Most U.S. casualties in Iraq have been caused by gunfire and homemade bombs, or improvised explosive devices (IEDs). Car bombs account for only 5 percent of deaths and rocket-propelled grenades for less than 4 percent.

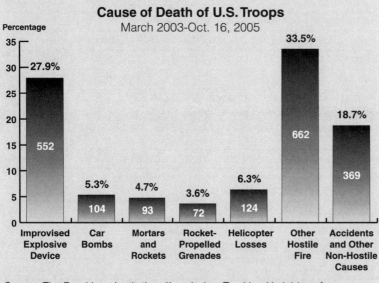

Cause of Death of U.S. Troops
March 2003-Oct. 16, 2005

Percentage

- Improvised Explosive Device: 27.9% (552)
- Car Bombs: 5.3% (104)
- Mortars and Rockets: 4.7% (93)
- Rocket-Propelled Grenades: 3.6% (72)
- Helicopter Losses: 6.3% (124)
- Other Hostile Fire: 33.5% (662)
- Accidents and Other Non-Hostile Causes: 18.7% (369)

Source: The Brookings Institution, "Iraq Index: Tracking Variables of Reconstruction and Security in Post-Saddam Iraq," www.brookings.edu/iraqindex

trained military personnel to form a new Iraqi military to help restore order or enough teachers for schools. Moreover, critics say, Bremer's actions pushed Iraqis into the arms of the insurgents. The actions "left tens of thousands of armed soldiers and officers cut out of the new order and prime candidates for recruitment by the insurgency," wrote Stanford's Diamond, the former adviser to the Coalition Provisional Authority in Baghdad. [27]

Michael E. O'Hanlon, a senior fellow in foreign policy studies at the Brookings Institution, disagrees with those who say the United States should have invaded with twice as many troops. But, he concedes that several key tasks — such as securing weapons caches, better protecting the borders and extending security — "weren't done in the aftermath of the invasion, some of which would have required more people."

Because the United States didn't have a plan, he says, troops were unable to maintain civil order. To do that, the United States should have had 50 percent more forces in the first six months after the invasion, O'Hanlon says, and then should have maintained 10,000 to 20,000 more thereafter.

Anthony H. Cordesman, a senior fellow at the Center for Strategic and International Studies (CSIS), said that while the United States was able to show that it could fight "a conventional regional war with remarkable efficiency at low cost and very quickly," the administration did not plan for what was "almost certain to follow." [28]

That failure to plan created "much of today's strain on our forces," said Cordesman, a military expert who previously worked for Sen. McCain and the departments of Defense and State.

Michael Swetnam, chairman of the Potomac Institute for Policy Studies, says the swiftness of the war shows the United States provided enough resources to win, but he notes that "securing the peace is another thing altogether."

"The federal government didn't have a very good idea how to do this in Iraq, and we are still learning how to do it in New Orleans," he says, noting that it took five days to restore order after Katrina hit.

Bennis, of the Institute for Policy Studies and Foreign Policy, says "there aren't enough troops in the world to do what [Bush administration officials] claimed they wanted to do, which is to overthrow a government, destroy an army, collapse all existing security agencies, declare a democracy and [put] something that looks like the U.S. government in power."

Earlier this summer, *USA Today* reported that a Marine regiment that took heavy casualties in Iraq, including 19 killed from a Reserve unit in Ohio, had repeatedly asked for 1,000 additional troops but was turned down. [29]

Rumsfeld has rejected any talk of a troop shortage. "The idea . . . that because someone wished they had more [troops] at a given moment suggests that the total number is wrong, I think is a non-sequitur." [30]

Many Americans — especially parents and families of soldiers in Iraq — have been concerned that troops were deployed without sufficient armor or equipment. When Rumsfeld visited Iraq-bound troops in Kuwait in December 2004, a soldier asked him why troops had to dig through local landfills for scrap metal to armor their vehicles. The question prompted cheers from some of the 2,300 soldiers assembled. "You have to go to war with the army you have, not the army you want," Rumsfeld famously responded. [31]

Initially, Pentagon planners thought only 800 heavily armored vehicles would be needed in Iraq, but later estimates called for up to 6,000. [32] The strategy had been to use lighter equipment, such as Humvee trucks and light-armored vehicles, to make the forces more agile, but planners hadn't expected such a long occupation or insurgents' extensive use of roadside bombs and rocket-propelled grenades (RPGs). Earlier this year, top Army officials told Congress soldiers in Iraq and Afghanistan now have more than 6,400 "up-armored" Humvees — vehicles refitted with heavier armor — compared to 250 in 2003. [33]

Some experts say the administration should have focused more on winning the hearts and minds of Iraqis, such as initiating "a big jobs effort," says O'Hanlon of Brookings.

Cordesman called the administration's aid package "incompetent and ineffective," aimed more at helping U.S. defense contractors than Iraqis. "Dollars are as important as bullets," he wrote. [34]

McCaffrey has urged the administration to put thousands of Iraqis to work rebuilding heavily bombed

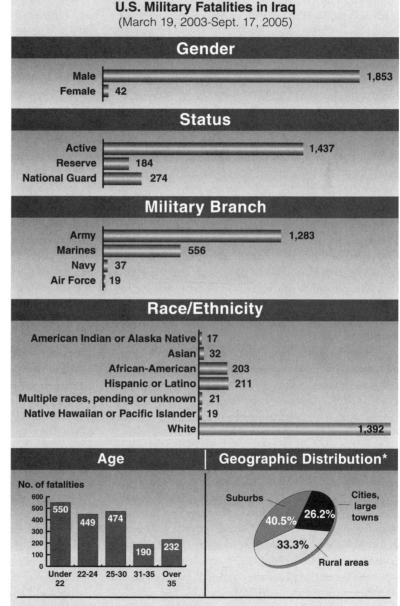

Most U.S. Fatalities Are Young, White

Most of the U.S. service members killed in Iraq have been suburban whites under age 22. The Army has lost more than twice as many soldiers as the Marines, and more than three times as many active-duty service members have been killed as reservists or guardsmen.

U.S. Military Fatalities in Iraq
(March 19, 2003-Sept. 17, 2005)

Gender
- Male: 1,853
- Female: 42

Status
- Active: 1,437
- Reserve: 184
- National Guard: 274

Military Branch
- Army: 1,283
- Marines: 556
- Navy: 37
- Air Force: 19

Race/Ethnicity
- American Indian or Alaska Native: 17
- Asian: 32
- African-American: 203
- Hispanic or Latino: 211
- Multiple races, pending or unknown: 21
- Native Hawaiian or Pacific Islander: 19
- White: 1,392

Age
No. of fatalities
- Under 22: 550
- 22-24: 449
- 25-30: 474
- 31-35: 190
- Over 35: 232

Geographic Distribution*
- Suburbs: 40.5%
- Cities, large towns: 26.2%
- Rural areas: 33.3%

* From March 19, 2003-March 20, 2005.

Source: The Brookings Institution, "Iraq Index," www.brookings.edu/iraqindex

Fallujah. "We need a Pierre l'Enfant of Fallujah," he told Congress, referring to the Frenchman who planned Washington, D.C.

Should the United States set a deadline for leaving Iraq?

As polls found in August, Americans' support for the war is dwindling, putting pressure on the administration to leave Iraq. [35] During their August 2005 break, lawmakers say they were peppered with questions from constituents about a pullout.

Even Republicans who ardently supported the war, like North Carolina's Rep. Walter B. Jones, want a withdrawal timetable. He joined a bipartisan House group asking the administration to announce a timetable by year's end. [36]

"No one is talking about 'cutting and running,'" Jones said, noting that with the political process going forward and the number of trained Iraqi security forces increasing daily, "it is perfectly reasonable for the American military presence in Iraq to, at some point, begin to decrease." [37]

Moreover, Sen. Feingold has argued, "Contrary to the conventional wisdom, the administration's refusal to [plan for a withdrawal] is actually an advantage for insurgents and terrorists. This large U.S. military presence smack in the middle of the Arab world is a major recruiting tool for international terrorist networks, and young men are coming to Iraq from around the world to get on-the-job training in attacking Americans."

But the president and key leaders in Iraq won't set a departure date for U.S. troops. "We will set no timetable for withdrawal," Talabani said last month during his first visit to the White House as president. [38]

"Setting an artificial timetable would send the wrong message to the Iraqis, who need to know that America will not leave before the job is done," Bush said in a televised, primetime address on June 28. [39] And Rumsfeld said a deadline would "throw a lifeline to terrorists." [40]

Top Pentagon officials say up to 30,000 troops could leave by next spring or summer, but that the criteria for withdrawing coalition forces are "conditions-based, not calendar-based." [41] Those criteria include adopting a permanent Iraqi constitutional government, a shrinking insurgency and Iraq's security and police forces taking over security responsibilities from the U.S. military.

Meanwhile, neither congressional proposal urging a timetable for withdrawal has garnered much support — even from Democrats. Both Senate Minority Leader Harry M. Reid of Nevada and Delaware Sen. Joseph Biden Jr., the ranking Democrat on the Foreign Relations Committee, reject timetables. [42] Setting a deadline for pulling out of Iraq would be a "mistake," Biden said, because it would "only encourage our enemies to wait us out." [43]

Instead of a deadline, Cordesman told a Senate panel last summer, the United States should "support Iraq until it is ready to take over the mission and the insurgents are largely defeated." [44]

Swetnam, of the Potomac Institute for Policy Studies, agrees. "The insurgency can just sit back and say, 'Well the day after they are gone, we'll step in and cause trouble.'" However, he thinks at least three or four years are needed to properly train Iraqi police and security officials. "We have quite a ways to go before they are really qualified or capable of protecting themselves."

Pike of GlobalSecurity.org says it is illogical to talk about a complete withdrawal from a now-unarmed country "in the world's most volatile region that is armed to the teeth." He asks: "For the next 15 years, is Iraq just going to be naked to its enemies?"

The United States should focus on the "reduction" rather than the "withdrawal" of forces, says Brookings' O'Hanlon. Withdrawal implies that U.S. forces are simply leaving Iraq and going home, he says, while reduction conveys the notion that the United States is transferring responsibility to the Iraqis while keeping some forces in-country as long as necessary.

O'Hanlon suggests the United States reduce its forces — 30,000 to 40,000 — by the end of next year and keep on hand "rapid reaction teams" and military advisers working with Iraqi forces. "That would strike the right balance between backing up the Iraqis and countering the image that we are still occupying the country," he says.

Krepinevich, of the Center for Strategic and Budgetary Assessments, suggests the United States shift the focus from killing insurgents to providing security and opportunity to Iraqis. His "oil-spot strategy," which has drawn considerable attention in Washington, calls for a major shift in U.S. military strategy. [45]

"Since the U.S. and Iraqi armies cannot guarantee security to all of Iraq simultaneously, they should start by focusing on certain key areas and then, over time, broadening the effort — hence the image of an expanding oil spot," Krepinevich wrote in *Foreign Affairs*.

Krepinevich, author of *The Army and Vietnam*, said his strategy is better than either setting an arbitrary timetable for withdrawal or the administration's "stay the course" approach, but he admitted it would take at least a decade of commitment, hundreds of billions of dollars and more U.S. casualties.

"But this is the price that the United States must pay . . . to achieve its goals in Iraq," he wrote. [46]

Is the Iraq war making America safer from terrorism?

President Bush says the war in Iraq is key to making America safe because it is an important component of the global "war on terror." But critics say the war and the U.S. presence in Iraq have made the country a magnet for terrorists.

"Our mission in Iraq is clear. We're hunting down the terrorists. We're helping Iraqis build a free nation that is an ally in the war on terror," the president said in June at Fort Bragg, N.C. "We are removing a source of violence and instability and laying the foundation of peace for our children and our grandchildren."

In October, Bush asked, "Would the United States and other free nations be more safe, or less safe, with Zarqawi and bin Laden in control of Iraq, its people and its resources?" [47]

The war in Iraq has contributed to the absence of terrorist attacks in the United States, says Pike of GlobalSecurity.org, because "Iraq has turned into fly paper for jihadists" who can now "embrace martyrdom easily" via suicide missions in Iraq rather than traveling to the United States.

But Swetnam of the Potomac Institute for Policy Studies sees the war as a double-edged sword. While it may be "keeping the terrorists from fighting us here," he says, it has also become "a rallying cry" for the recruitment of more terrorists.

A recent National Intelligence Council report seems to agree, claiming that Iraq has replaced Afghanistan as the training ground for the next generation of terrorists. "The al-Qa'ida membership that . . . trained in Afghanistan will gradually dissipate, to be replaced in part by the dispersion of the experienced survivors of the conflict in Iraq," the report said. [48]

But Rumsfeld rejects that notion. "People are being trained elsewhere and going into Iraq," he said. [49]

Sen. John Kerry, D-Mass., said Iraq "has become the new hotbed of terror . . . because the presence of American troops is a magnet for jihadists." [50]

Fewer and fewer Americans say the Iraq war has made the United States safer. The percentage who believe the invasion has helped to protect the United States from another terrorist attack dropped to 38 percent in August — from 46 percent in November 2004. [51]

Former President Bill Clinton has said Iraq takes U.S. troops away from the larger priority: al Qaeda. "We cannot relax our efforts to [undermine] al Qaeda, because that's still by far a bigger threat to our security," he said in mid-September. [52]

O'Hanlon of Brookings says the verdict is still out on whether the United States is safer. However, he rejects linking the Iraq war to the war on terror. While Hussein had links to terrorists in the Middle East, O'Hanlon says, there is no evidence he ever cooperated with al Qaeda.

"The invasion of Iraq was not [done] in the context of the war on terror," O'Hanlon says. "It was in the context of making sure the Persian Gulf did not have a nuclear-armed megalomaniac with a track record of invading his neighbors."

Other critics say the demands of the war — in troops and money — threaten U.S. security at home and abroad. The $4.9 billion a month being spent on the war could have been spent on schools, health care, roads, new military equipment or making the country's borders safer, critics argue. [53] Moreover, Bennis of the Institute for Policy Studies and Foreign Policy said much of the chaos after Hurricane Katrina could be blamed on the fact that a third of the state's National Guard was deployed in Iraq at the time.

"As we've seen with the impact of the hurricane, this war has made us far less safe," Bennis says, noting that 48,000 members of the National Guard and reserves are in Iraq, many of whom are full-time police officers, firefighters and emergency medical personnel. Nearly the same number of National Guard — 50,000 — were dispatched to Louisiana, Mississippi and other Gulf Coast areas devastated by the storm, according to the Defense Department.

Repeated deployments to Iraq and Afghanistan have stretched the U.S. Army so thin that many active-duty combat units are spending more than one out of every two years on foreign battlefields, leaving few brigades ready to respond to crises elsewhere, said a recent RAND Corporation report. [54]

"No matter how you feel about this war, it's hard to find anyone who will say the military isn't overextended," says Paul Rieckhoff, an Army Reserve officer

CHRONOLOGY

1990s-2002 *Persian Gulf War sets the stage for U.S. 2003 invasion of Iraq.*

Aug. 1990 Iraq occupies oil-rich Kuwait.

Jan.-Feb. 1991 President George H. W. Bush puts together U.S.-led international coalition that liberates Kuwait within 100 hours.

April 1991 U.N. Security Council requires Iraq to destroy all weapons of mass destruction (WMD) and long-range missiles and allow U.N. inspections.

Jan. 29, 2002 President George W. Bush calls Iraq part of an "axis of evil."

Sept. 14, 2002 Iraq agrees to admit weapons inspectors for the first time in almost four years. U.S. and Britain reject the offer as a ruse.

Oct. 10-16, 2002 House and Senate authorize U.S. action against Iraq.

2003 *Coalition forces invade Iraq and oust Saddam Hussein.*

Feb.-March 14 President Bush assembles small coalition of countries to support military action against Iraq, including Britain, Spain and Bulgaria; France, Germany and Russia want more time for inspections and diplomacy.

March 17 President Bush demands that Hussein leave Iraq within 48 hours.

March 19-20 Hussein refuses, and Bush orders air strikes against Baghdad, followed by a land invasion of more than 150,000 coalition troops.

April 9 Coalition forces gain control of most of Baghdad, symbolically ending Hussein's 24-year dictatorship. The next day, looters lay siege to Baghdad.

May 1 President Bush lands in a jet on the *USS Abraham Lincoln* and declares an end to major combat operations in Iraq. U.S. combat deaths stand at 115.

July 22 Coalition forces kill Hussein's sons, Uday and Qusay.

Dec. 12 Hussein is found hiding underground on a farm outside Tikrit.

2004 *Criticism of war mounts as WMD threat is debunked, Abu Ghraib prison scandal erupts.*

Jan. 28 David Kay, former head of U.S. weapons inspection teams in Iraq, says prewar intelligence was "almost all wrong" about Hussein's WMD arsenal.

April 28 Photos of U.S. soldiers abusing Iraqis at Abu Ghraib prison near Baghdad spark scandal.

May 8 U.S. contractor Nicholas Berg is beheaded by Iraqi militants in retaliation for the treatment of prisoners at Abu Ghraib. An Islamic Web site shows a video of the murder.

June 28 U.S. transfers sovereignty over Iraq from Coalition Provisional Authority to interim Iraqi government.

2005 *Amid continuing violence, Iraqis go to polls to elect National Assembly, approve new constitution.*

Jan. 12 White House announces official end to the unsuccessful search for WMDs, one of the main justifications for the war.

Jan. 14 National Intelligence Council says Iraq has replaced Afghanistan as training ground for terrorists.

Jan. 30 Some 8.5 million Iraqis (58 percent of registered voters) defy insurgents' threats and go to the polls to select 275-seat National Assembly.

June 23 Gen. John P. Abizaid, commander of U.S. forces in the Middle East, says insurgency is as strong as it was six months earlier.

July 14 Insurgents are killing more than 800 Iraqi civilians and police officers each month, Iraqi interior ministry says.

Oct. 15 Iraqi voters approve draft constitution. A total of 1,962 service members have been killed as of Oct. 16.

Dec. 2005 Election scheduled to elect new Iraqi government.

who founded Operation Truth in 2004 to "amplify the soldiers' voice in the American public dialogue."

But Rumsfeld rejects any suggestion that the war imperiled hurricane relief efforts. "We have the forces, the capabilities and the intention to fully prosecute the global war on terror while responding to this unprecedented humanitarian crisis here at home," the secretary said. [55]

BACKGROUND

Past Is Prologue

Understanding the 1991 Persian Gulf War is necessary to understand why the United States and its allies invaded Iraq in 2003 and why the political infighting persists today in Iraq.

U.S. relations with Iraq have been mostly tense for the past 50 years, but they hit a new low in August 1990, when Iraq invaded and conquered Kuwait, its small, oil-rich neighbor — and an important U.S. ally — claiming it was historically part of Iraq. [56]

When Hussein refused to comply with a United Nations deadline to leave Kuwait, 27 countries joined a U.S.-led coalition that launched Operation Desert Storm on Jan. 16, 1991. Kuwait was freed within 100 hours, but President George H. W. Bush — the current president's father — opted not to try to capture Baghdad or overthrow Hussein. Instead, he urged the country's long-persecuted groups — Kurds in the north and Shiites in the south — to rise up and overthrow Hussein, implying American support that never materialized. Iraqi forces brutally crushed a Kurdish rebellion, leaving tens of thousands of civilians dead.

After the Persian Gulf War, the U.N. Security Council in April 1991 required that Iraq scrap all weapons of mass destruction (WMDs) and long-range missiles and allow U.N. inspectors to verify that Iraq had eliminated all WMDs. But Hussein did not comply with repeated U.N. mandates and made it difficult for inspectors to do their job. In fact, he continued to provoke the United States and its allies, including allegedly plotting to assassinate former President Bush.

Nearly a decade later, when the younger Bush came into office in 2001, he was clearly fed up with Hussein's failure to comply with U.N. weapons requirements. [57] Planning for a post-Hussein regime change began as early as October 2001, according to documents released

An Iraqi mother holds photos of her sons during a memorial for victims of a suicide bomber in New Baghdad in July 2005. The two boys were among 32 children killed as U.S. soldiers handed out chocolate in the street near a recruiting center.

in August 2005 by the National Security Archive, an independent, non-governmental research institute and library located at The George Washington University in Washington, D.C. [58]

Since the war began, the president has offered three different explanations for the invasion of Iraq: (1) Hussein had WMDs and was prepared to use them; (2) Iraq had aligned itself with terrorist groups and was an important front on the war on terror; and (3) ending Hussein's reign would bring democracy to Iraq and to the Middle East.

Early on, the administration focused primarily on the first justification for war. Bush told the nation, for example, in an October 2002 televised speech from Cincinnati, Ohio, that Iraq "on any given day" could attack the United States or its allies with biological or chemical weapons. [59] He also made clear in a speech at West Point that the United States would not wait to be attacked but that, in some cases, it must "impose pre-emptive, unilateral, military force when and where it chooses" — a new defense doctrine that critics say violates the U.N. Charter's provisions on the use of military force. [60]

As a result, while the first President Bush had been able to persuade allies worldwide to support and participate in Operation Desert Storm, the younger Bush encountered reluctance or outright opposition to his campaign. France, Germany and Russia, for example, wanted to give more time to U.N. inspections, which resumed in late 2002 for the first time in nearly four years.

Fighting the War in Cyberspace

Unlike any other conflict in history, the Iraq war is being partly waged in cyberspace. The World Wide Web is awash with news and propaganda from the frontlines, including soldiers' blogs, updates from the fledgling Iraqi government and instructions from jihadists wanting to kill U.S. troops in Iraq. [1]

The blogs about combat run the gamut, with many revealing pride and patriotism, others showing frustration or homesickness. "We were in a bad neighborhood well past curfew in the car bomb capital of the world," writes Mark Partridge Miner, 22, a National Guard infantryman describing a night in Baghdad that ended with an Iraqi teenager losing an eye. In his last entry on "Boots in Baghdad: A Grunt's Life," Miner says he is heading home after a year in Iraq. "I can't even begin to describe to you what it feels like." (www.bootsinbaghdad.blogspot.com)

A Marine in Fallujah nicknamed Stingray says he knows his blog is being read by "you-know-who," so he focuses on showing pictures of everyday life in Iraq. He does, however, have a thing or two to say about the media. Sure, he writes, a reporter is technically correct saying that "only 60 percent of the homes in the southern part of Fallujah have power or water," but he adds bitterly, "prior to our arrival, ZERO PER-CENT . . . had power or water." (http://5thcag.blogspot.com)

U.S. and Iraqi officials typically use the Web to spin the news. The Iraqi Transitional Government has a flashy Web site (www.iraqigovernment.org) with photos and press releases in English and Arabic; so does the Iraqi Special Tribunal that is prosecuting former Iraqi President Saddam Hussein (www.iraq-ist.org).

The U.S. Embassy in Baghdad (http://baghdad.usembassy.gov/iraq/) provides updates on Iraq political activities and tips on doing business in Iraq, helping Iraqi women and donating to the rebuilding efforts. The U.S. State Department (http://usinfo.state.gov/) has an online Iraqi photo gallery that includes a shot of the handwritten note to President Bush from then-National Security Adviser Condoleezza Rice confirming the transfer of sovereignty to Iraq. Viewers can see that Bush wrote "Let Freedom Reign!" on the note. Both the Pentagon (www.mnf-iraq.com/) and White House (www.whitehouse.gov/infocus/iraq/) have pages devoted strictly to Iraq.

Even Shiite religious leader Grand Ayatollah Ali al-Sistani has his own Web site (www.sistani.org/html/eng/), which includes statements about Iraqi elections and the 75-year-old leader's health.

America's strongest ally was British Prime Minister Tony Blair. The lobbying by the United States and Britain to get other countries to support military intervention against Iraq included a dramatic Feb. 5, 2003, presentation from U.S. Secretary of State Colin Powell before the U.N. Security Council. Powell used an array of maps and satellite intelligence to convince Security Council members that Iraq had failed to disarm. But after a two-day debate that ended on March 12, most countries wanted to give inspections more time. [61]

However, Bush decided to proceed without the U.N. Britain, Australia and 17 other European countries supplied troops for Bush's "coalition of the willing." The United States was disappointed in its ally Turkey, Iraq's neighbor. The Pentagon had hoped to send some 60,000 troops through Turkish territory into Iraq, but Turkey's parliament balked. It did allow U.S. planes to use Turkish airspace for combat missions, but land shipments were restricted to food, fuel and non-military supplies.

Kuwait, the country that the United States helped free in Desert Storm, was the main staging area for the invasion, where contingents of U.S. and British armed forces converged in late 2002 to prepare for the invasion.

Toppling Hussein

No one really knows whether Hussein thought the United States was bluffing, but he did not heed Bush's March 17, 2003, demand — in a broadcast heard around the world — that Hussein and his two sons leave Iraq within 48 hours. Their refusal to do so, Bush said, would result in military conflict, "commenced at a time of our choosing."

Two days later, Bush ordered air strikes against Baghdad, followed by a land invasion. Americans were gripped by the striking up-to-the-minute reports and video from reporters "embedded" with frontline military units. Television audiences worldwide watched in expectation, for example, as missiles destroyed a house in southern Baghdad where Hussein was supposedly meet-

But just as political and religious leaders rely on the Web to publicize their views of the war, so do those fighting U.S. forces. Jihadist Web sites, for example, provide tips for making bombs and the infamous IEDs, or improvised explosive devices, that have killed more than more than 500 U.S. troops and 4,000 Iraqi civilians. [2]

Abu Musab al-Zarqawi, the Jordanian linked to al Qaeda, has used the Internet to broadcast videos of several beheadings of U.S. contractors. And photographs of U.S. soldiers abusing Iraqi prisoners at Abu Ghraib were distributed worldwide via the Internet. An Internet posting also let the world know that al-Zarqawi thought the devastation from Hurricane Katrina was an answer to the prayers of Iraqis and Afghans who suffered under U.S.

A U.S. Army poster being distributed in Iraq offers $5 million for the capture of terrorist leader Abu Musab al-Zarqawi.

AFP Photo/Getty Images/Marwan Naamani

occupation, according to a Sept. 11 notice, posted to coincide with the fourth anniversary of al Qaeda's terrorist attacks in the United States. [3]

"The enemy is empowered by modern communications, expertly using the virtual world for planning, recruiting, fundraising, indoctrination and exploiting the mass media," Army Gen. John P. Abizaid, commander of U.S. forces in the Middle East, said recently. "They know that propaganda and grabbing headlines are more important than military operations." [4]

[1] For background on blogs, see Kenneth Jost, "Free-Press Disputes," *CQ Researcher*, April 8, 2005, pp. 293-316.

[2] "Iraq Index," Brookings Institution, Sept. 26, 2005, pp. 5, 11.

[3] "Al-Zarqawi: Katrina an answer to prayers," CNN, Sept. 11, 2005.

[4] Transcript of U.S. Senate Armed Services hearing, Sept. 29, 2005.

ing with his sons. Although it provided spectacular footage, the Iraqi leader and his sons escaped.

In the first week, troops encountered strong resistance from Iraqi soldiers and paramilitary fighters along the way to Baghdad, particularly in Nasiriyah and Basrah. Worried Americans back home, however, were soon buoyed by dramatic footage of the April 1 rescue of Army Pvt. Jessica Lynch by Special Operations forces from a hospital in Nasiriyah. The 19-year-old West Virginian had been injured and captured by the Iraqis when her convoy was attacked. The Pentagon was later criticized for exaggerating Lynch's ordeal, including initial statements that she had emptied her rifle fighting off her attackers.

U.S. forces gained control of most of Baghdad on April 9. The toppling of a 30-foot-tall cast-iron statue of Hussein symbolically ended his 24 years as Iraq's dictatorial leader and remains one of the war's most enduring images. In July, coalition forces killed Hussein's sons, Uday and Qusay — infamous for their brutality — during a fierce

gun battle. Hussein himself was captured in December, hiding in a hole at a farmhouse in central Iraq.

President Bush's announcement that major fighting in Iraq had ended provided yet another memorable image, one that the White House no doubt would like to forget. On May 1, clad in a flight suit, the president climbed out of a jet fighter cockpit onto the *USS Abraham Lincoln*, stood before a huge banner that read "Mission Accomplished" and declared to a roaring crowd of sailors, "Major combat operations in Iraq have ended."

Up to then, 115 U.S. soldiers had been killed.

Euphoria to Insurgency

From a military standpoint, the administration's plan for invading Iraq with 150,000 U.S. and coalition troops and ousting Hussein largely succeeded. But the administration also banked on the Iraqi people greeting U.S. forces as liberators and Iraqis friendly to the United States taking over the government. Under that scenario, the United States figured it could reduce its troop levels to 30,000 by the fall of 2003, from about 150,000. That didn't happen.

While Iraqis were glad to be free of Hussein, they did not rush to help the United States maintain order, and Iraqi exiles sympathetic to the U.S. government failed to quickly establish a legitimate government. Instead, by mid-April, there was widespread looting and chaos while U.S. and allied forces — untrained in maintaining civil order among unarmed civilians — stood by and watched. Hospitals and government office buildings were stripped bare while looters ransacked the Iraqi national library of books and the museum of ancient treasures. Even worse, looters damaged the country's oil-production and power and water infrastructures, which were already in bad shape. As of May 2005, Iraq was producing less oil and electricity than before the United States invaded. [62]

Unemployment soared to as high as 60 percent in some areas, as 35,000 government workers who were members of Hussein's Baath Party were fired and Iraq's 400,000-strong army disbanded. [63]

A growing insurgency ensued, and nearly every major city saw some sort of political violence. Hardest hit were the cities in the central region of Iraq known as the "Sunni Triangle" and the capital city of Baghdad. The insurgency also meant that U.S. troops had to stay to maintain order, and with each passing day the insurgents appeared to grow stronger and more deadly in their attacks.

Kidnapping became a widely used tactic. Insurgents took nearly 200 hostages in 2004, mostly American and foreign contractors hired by the United States to provide services. While many were freed, at least 30 were killed; many were beheaded, their murders filmed and dispersed via the Internet. [64]

Militants said they beheaded Nicholas Berg, a Pennsylvania radio tower contractor, in retaliation for the treatment of Iraqi prisoners at Abu Ghraib prison in Baghdad. In spring 2004, photos of U.S. soldiers abusing and humiliating Iraqi prisoners triggered disgust worldwide. Congressional and military investigations ensued, and in January 2005 Army reservist Charles Graner, considered the ringleader, was sentenced to 10 years imprisonment for his role in Abu Ghraib.

Graner and another former guard were convicted at trial, while six other soldiers struck plea bargains. [65] Pfc. Lynndie England, who was photographed holding a naked prisoner on a leash, was sentenced in September to three years behind bars. No officers have been tried, though several received administrative punishments.

Two leaders have emerged from the various anti-American factions and insurgent groups in Iraq: al-Zarqawi, the jihadist Sunni linked with al Qaeda, and Moqtada al-Sadr, a radical Shiite cleric.

In 2004, four U.S. contractors in Fallujah were killed and mutilated, and the headless body of one was hung from a bridge. Believing that al-Zarqawi had established headquarters in Falluja, Marines laid siege to the city. In November, some 10,000 U.S. troops occupied Falluja after days of fighting destroyed much of the city.

Meanwhile, Sadr took over mosques in Kufa and Najaf in retaliation for the United States shutting down his virulently anti-American newspaper. In response, the United States issued a warrant for his arrest, but eventually Shiite cleric Ayatollah Ali al-Sistani brokered a truce.

Despite the violence, the United States transferred power back to the Iraqis two days ahead of schedule — on June 28, 2004. The ceremony was held in secret to prevent insurgent attacks. Insurgents unsuccessfully tried to thwart the historic nationwide elections in January 2005. Some 8.5 million Iraqis (about 58 percent of registered voters) selected a 275-seat National Assembly in the first democratic election in 50 years.

But continuing violence has stymied U.S. rebuilding efforts. [66] By late 2004, an estimated one-fifth of all reconstruction funds flowing into Iraq were being used to protect foreign contractors. [67]

Meanwhile, exhaustive searches revealed no weapons of mass destruction, and the Bush administration began playing down the WMD rationale for the war. David Kay, the former head of the U.S. weapons inspection teams in Iraq, told a U.S. Senate committee in early 2004 that no WMDs have been found in Iraq and that prewar intelligence about Hussein's arsenal had been "almost all wrong."

The final report by weapons experts, released in October 2004, said Iraq had destroyed its biological and chemical weapons after the 1991 Gulf War and had never seriously tried to restart its program to develop nuclear weapons. [68]

In January 2005 the White House announced the search for WMDs was officially over, and the president began saying the rationale for the war was to establish democracy in the Arab world. [69] He also tied Iraq to the administration's war on terrorism.

"After Sept. 11, I made a commitment to the American people: This nation will not wait to be attacked again. . . . We will take the fight to the enemy. Iraq is the latest battlefield in this war," the president said in June 2005. [70]

CURRENT SITUATION

Questioning the War

When Iraqis vote in December on a permanent government, U.S. officials hope it will take them another step closer to democracy and to providing their own security.

But the public as well as many lawmakers on Capitol Hill are questioning whether the Bush war strategy is working, given the continuing insurgency, the rising cost and the perception of a U.S. military stretched thin at home and abroad. "There is concern: When will it end? How will we know the troops are coming home?" asked Rep. Roscoe G. Bartlett, R-Md., a member of the House Armed Services Committee. [71]

Americans' support for the war has fallen to an all-time low. More than 8-in-10 Americans are "very" or "somewhat concerned" that the $5 billion being spent each month is draining away money needed at home, particularly with the cost of post-Hurricane Katrina repairs already running into the tens of billions. [72] And 55 percent of the public favor bringing soldiers home, while just 36 percent agree with Bush that current levels should be maintained to help secure peace and stability. [73] On Sept. 24, an estimated 100,000 protesters in Washington, D.C., demonstrated against U.S. involvement in Iraq.

Lawmakers, some of whom face stiff re-election races next year, worry about the growing angst. "Public support in my state has turned," Sen. Lindsey Graham, R-S.C., said last summer. "People are beginning to question. And I don't think it's a blip on the radar screen. We have a chronic problem on our hands." [74]

Meanwhile, top administration and Pentagon officials sometimes have painted divergent pictures of the war. A month after Vice President Cheney said the Iraqi insurgency was in its "last throes," Gen. John P. Abizaid, commander of U.S. forces in the Middle East, told Congress it remained as strong as it had been six months earlier. [75]

In the face of the waning support, President Bush has urged Americans to "stay the course" in Iraq. "Wars are not won without sacrifice, and this war will require more sacrifice, more time and more resolve," he said on Oct. 6. [76]

The president and first lady visit Staff Sgt. Dale Beatty, 26, and his family while he recuperates at Walter Reed Army Medical Center. The Army National Guardsman from Statesville, N.C., lost both legs when his armored Humvee hit an anti-tank mine in northern Iraq.

For his part, Rumsfeld last summer refused to set a withdrawal date, admonishing lawmakers, "Timing in war is never predictable — there are no guarantees." He added: "And any who say we have lost or are losing are flat wrong. We are not." [77]

Rumsfeld's comments were directed at those — including Republicans — who question the administration's steadfast optimism. "Things aren't getting better; they're getting worse," Sen. Hagel said in June. "It's like they're just making it up as they go along. The reality is that we're losing in Iraq." [78]

But administration supporters say the stakes are too high for the United States to bail out. "If we fail in Iraq, you will see factionalization and eventual Muslim extremism and terrorist breeding grounds" there, said Sen. McCain in late August.

During hearings and meetings with lawmakers in September, Rumsfeld and top U.S. generals defended the administration's strategy. Both Gen. George W. Casey Jr., who oversees U.S. forces in Iraq, and Gen. Abizaid told the Senate Armed Services Committee that Iraqi security forces are growing but still need more time before taking over. [79]

McCain maintains the United States needs more troops and faults military brass for being too optimistic. "I don't think this committee or the American public has ever heard me say that things are going very well in Iraq,"

Is Iraq Another Vietnam?

I raq is Arabic for Vietnam," proclaimed the signs carried by some of the 100,000 demonstrators who gathered in Washington on Sept. 24 to protest the U.S. war in Iraq.

With the war dragging on, many Americans are wondering if the United States is caught in another political and military quagmire. In 1973, with anti-war protests erupting at home, the U.S. pulled out of Vietnam after 58,000 American soldiers had been killed fighting to prevent South Vietnam from being taken over by communist North Vietnam. [1] Two years later, the North Vietnamese overran the South, and today the reunified country remains communist.

The Bush administration adamantly rejects any comparison between Iraq and Vietnam. "The analogy is false," the president said last year. [2]

But to some, Bush's steadfast optimism and refusal to alter U.S. strategy is reminiscent of President Lyndon B. Johnson, who repeatedly said things were going well in Vietnam. [3] Likewise, many question Bush's strategy linking U.S. departure from Iraq to turning the country over to newly trained Iraqi forces. They see it echoing Vietnamization — President Richard M. Nixon's plan to train the South Vietnamese to take over combat in the Vietnam War.

"The job [in Iraq] remains ill-defined, beyond slogans about freedom and democracy," Georgetown University Professor Anthony Lake, who served as national security adviser under President Bill Clinton, wrote in demanding a clear exit strategy for Iraq. "We owe it to our interests and our society — and especially to our military, who could some day be blamed, as they were so unfairly in Vietnam, for failing to achieve vague goals that were, in the end, unachievable." [4]

However, Defense Secretary Donald H. Rumsfeld dismisses Iraq-Vietnam comparisons. "Anyone knowledgeable about history will note a great many more dissimilarities than similarities between . . . the situation in Iraq and the situation in Vietnam," he said. "The differences are notable, many and marked." [5]

But Henry Kissinger, Nixon's secretary of State during Vietnam, told CNN he has "a very uneasy feeling" that some of the same factors that damaged support for the Vietnam conflict are re-emerging in Iraq. [6]

Sen. Chuck Hagel, R-Neb., a decorated Vietnam veteran, has said Iraq "is not dissimilar to where we were in Vietnam" and that the longer the United States remains there, the more the similarities will emerge. [7]

Sen. John McCain, R-Ariz., who spent more than five years in a North Vietnamese prison, strongly disagrees, however. "Iraq is not Vietnam," McCain said bluntly. "The whole situation . . . was very, very different. Vietnam never had a legitimate government in Saigon that the people believed in and trusted. And when we left Vietnam, there wasn't a fear that the Vietnamese would come after us. If we fail in Iraq, it will be cataclysmic" for the United States, he said, predicting that Iraq would become a breeding ground for Muslim terrorists who "would pose a direct threat to the security of the United States." [8]

The stakes in Iraq are even higher than they were in Vietnam in the 1960s and '70s, say the president, McCain and others. The Iraq war began just after Bush launched the "war on terrorism" in response to the Sept. 11, 2001, attacks. "The terrorists are testing our will and resolve in Iraq," the president said. "The only way [they] can win is if we lose our nerve and abandon the mission." [9]

responded Gen. Richard B. Myers, who retired as chairman of the Joint Chiefs of Staff shortly after the hearing. "This is a hard sell." [80]

When Rumsfeld went to Capitol Hill earlier in the summer, he faced tough questions about the war and sharp criticism about his leadership, including a challenge from Sen. Edward M. Kennedy, D-Mass. — a vocal war critic — to resign.

Rumsfeld eventually conceded that completely defeating the opponents of a democratic Iraq would take years. "Insurgencies tend to go on five, six, eight, 10, 12

years," he said. [81] In fact, he said, U.S. and coalition forces no longer are trying to eliminate the insurgency entirely: "We're going to create an environment [in which] the Iraqi people and the Iraqi security forces can win against that insurgency."

Some experts aren't sure that will happen as fast as the U.S. public might like. While U.S. forces have made progress in Baghdad and western parts of the country, it's unclear whether they have "really crippled any part of the insurgency," Cordesman of CSIS said. [82]

And it's not clear the United States can train enough

The enemy in Vietnam was different too, says McCain. The Soviet Union and China aided and supplied the North Vietnamese. The terrorists and insurgents in Iraq are foreigners and do not have the support of most Iraqis, Rumsfeld said. [10]

However, Sen. Edward M. Kennedy, D-Mass., sees many parallels between the two wars. "We thought in those early days in Vietnam that we were winning," Kennedy said. "We thought victory on the battlefield would lead to victory in war and peace and democracy for the people of Vietnam. In the name of a misguided cause, we continued in a war too long." [11]

Public opinion about the Iraq war, however, seems to have soured much quicker than it did about Vietnam. A majority of Americans began to call Iraq a "mistake" within about 15 months, while it took more than three years for a majority to call Vietnam a mistake, according to the Gallup Poll. [12]

"You've got to be careful about drawing analogies," said Stanley Karnow, author of the acclaimed *Vietnam: A History.* But, he added, "You are beginning to see the public turning off on Iraq. The same was true in Vietnam." [13]

Michael Rubin, a scholar at the conservative American Enterprise Institute, understands how images of a defeated U.S. military in Vietnam resonate with critics of the current war. After returning from Iraq last January, he wrote, "Watching

Former Alabama police officer Brian Rewolinski teaches new Iraqi police how to shoot an AK-47.

television on any Baghdad evening, I would see [news footage of] American diplomats fleeing Vietnam. To the Iraqi audience the message was clear: 'Bush may say America has staying power, but it is weak.' " [14]

[1] Department of Veterans Affairs, Fact Sheet, "America's Wars," November 2004.

[2] White House transcript, "President Addresses the Nation in Prime Time Press Conference," April 13, 2005.

[3] Robert G. Kaiser, "Iraq Isn't Vietnam But They Rhyme," *The Washington Post*, Dec. 28, 2003, p. B1.

[4] Anthony Lake, "Achievable goals in exiting Iraq," *The Boston Globe*, Jan. 24, 2005.

[5] Transcript of Department of Defense news briefing, Sept. 27, 2005.

[6] CNN, "Kissinger finds parallels to Vietnam in Iraq," Aug. 15, 2005, www.cnn.com/2005/POLITICS/08/15/us.iraq/.

[7] Hagel appeared on ABC's "This Week" on Aug. 21, 2005.

[8] McCain was speaking on CBS's "Face the Nation" on Aug. 28, 2005.

[9] White House transcript, Sept. 22, 2005.

[10] CNN, "Rumsfeld: Iraq not fated to civil war," Aug. 23, 2005; www.cnn.com/2005/US/08/23/rumsfeld.iraq/.

[11] Text of Kennedy speech to the Johns Hopkins School of Advanced International Studies, Jan. 27, 2005.

[12] Gallup Poll News Service, "Iraq Versus Vietnam: A Comparison of Public Opinion," Aug. 24, 2005.

[13] Todd S. Purdum, "Flashback to the '60s: A Sinking Sensation of Parallels Between Iraq and Vietnam," *The New York Times*, Jan. 29, 2005, p. A12.

[14] Michael Rubin, "Unilateral Withdrawal Is Irresponsible, Jan. 28, 2005; www.aei.org/publications/filter.all, pubID.21898/pub_detail.asp.

Iraqis quickly enough for them to take over their own country anytime soon. "Let's not kid ourselves when we hear reports of 172,000 'trained and equipped' Iraqis," Sen. Biden said this summer. [83] Very few of those forces can operate independently without U.S. support, he said.

Defending the War

The administration has admitted that the newly trained Iraqi security forces are in different levels of preparedness. Some are "green as grass" while others are "battle-hardened and very, very good," Rumsfeld said. [84] But as

of late September, top Pentagon officials told Congress only a single Iraqi battalion — down from three during the summer — is capable of fighting independently. [85]

Swetnam of the Potomac Institute for Policy Studies says the administration's policy — "As Iraqis stand up, Americans will stand down" — is simple and right, but the administration hasn't convinced the American people. "They really need to work on their communication skills because they have failed miserably at that," he says.

Meanwhile, administration officials and President Talabani continue to stress the positive. The terrorists

Student's Animated Map Shows War Deaths

For college student Tim Klimowicz, the daily barrage of news from the battlefront in Iraq was overwhelming and the growing tally of U.S. casualties numbing. So he used a homework assignment for a class at New York's School of Visual Art to show visually what thousands of words in newspaper and broadcast accounts could not reflect.

The 25-year-old designed an animated map of Iraq that marks the death of each soldier with a small dot where the soldier died, beginning on March 19, 2003 — the start of the war. (www.obleek.com/iraq/index.html) Together with an audible "click," each casualty first appears as a white flash, then a red dot that fades to black. Incidents in which several soldiers were killed have clusters of red spots and louder clicks. The flashes spike, for instance in April 2004 and again in November 2004, when U.S. Marines battled insurgents in Falluja. As the calendar counts down, the map is soon littered with dots.

"I did this project because the numbers didn't mean much," he said. The map runs for about two minutes and covers fatalities through Oct. 6, 2005. Klimowicz says he will update it regularly. "If it goes a decade, I'll keep at it." [1]

So far, the map flashes the deaths of more than 1,800 U.S. service members as well as more than 100 soldiers from Britain, Italy and 13 other coalition forces. Klimowicz had originally wanted to include Iraqi military and civilian deaths but quickly realized that was impossible. No one really knows how many Iraqis have died; estimates range from 24,700-28,000 to 100,000. [2]

Reactions to Klimowicz's map reflect Americans' conflicting emotions about the war. The liberal blog Daily Kos says it "helps you visualize the reality of the fallen soldiers in Iraq," while a pro-war Belmont Club blog says the map "shows why America won't be defeated. The tide of battle has moved into the depth of the Sunni area."

Klimowicz is not alone in using high-tech methods to provide perspective on the war. (*See sidebar, p. 372*.) But unlike most other blogs and Internet sites, Klimowicz wanted his map to be apolitical. "I just really wanted people to take it like it is," he told *The Wall Street Journal*. "I didn't really want to go over the top and try to assert my views on them." [3]

---

[1] Aaron Rutkoff, "Counting the Casualties in Iraq," *The Wall Street Journal*, Aug. 19, 2005.

[2] CNN, "Study puts Iraqi death toll at 100,000" Oct. 29, 2004.

[3] Rutkoff, *op. cit.*

---

failed to stop Iraqi elections in January or the drafting of a new constitution, Rumsfeld has pointed out.

On Oct. 15 Iraqi voters appeared to have approved the country's first constitution since Hussein was deposed, setting the stage for Iraqis to go to the polls again in December to elect a permanent National Assembly. The document, which lays out the country's basic laws, faced opposition from many Sunni Iraqis, who argued that several provisions favored Shiites and Kurds at their expense.

For example, Sunnis feared the new constitution would allow Kurds and Shiites to form oil-rich regional governments in the north and the south, respectively, with both groups keeping the oil earnings for themselves. Sunnis also objected to the banning of former members of Hussein's Baath Party from public office. Many Sunnis were Baathists — some with high-ranking positions — but many others joined the party because keeping their jobs required it. A last-minute compromise shortly before the Oct. 15 vote will allow a new commit-

tee to review the disputed provisions and present any changes to the new parliament that is elected on Dec. 15.

President Bush hailed the Iraqi voter turnout, noting that more Sunnis went to the polls in October than in January, when most Sunnis boycotted the vote for an interim government. That election formed the transitional government that drafted the constitution. "By all indications, the Sunnis participated in greater numbers in this election than last time," the president said on Oct. 16. "And that's good news. After all, the purpose of a democracy is to make sure everybody . . . participates in the process."

Many experts, however, say the new constitution could further split the country and fuel the insurgents if Sunnis feel they are shut out. "This is an enormous fiasco," Juan Cole, a University of Michigan historian and a specialist in Shiite Islam, told *The Washington Post*. He said the constitution appeared to fail in two Sunni provinces, which "really undermines its legitimacy, and this result guarantees the guerrilla war will go on." [86]

Should the United States set a deadline for withdrawing troops from Iraq?

YES

Sen. Russell D. Feingold, D-Wis.
Member, Senate Committee on Foreign Relations

From the Congressional Record, June 29, 2005

It has been over two years since the president launched the war in Iraq, but we still don't have a defined mission or time frame that would allow us to hold ourselves accountable for . . . achieving those goals. My resolution calls for a plan for the subsequent withdrawal of U.S. troops, so that we can provide some clarity with regard to our intentions and restore confidence at home and abroad that there is an end date in mind. . . .

After the shifting justifications for this war, after the premature declarations of "mission accomplished," after the exciting and inspiring elections, we still don't have any kind of finish line for our military engagement in Iraq. The American people and our troops deserve a sound plan that is linked to real time frames and real achievements. . . .

A real time frame will also help us achieve our security goals in Iraq. The most common argument against clarifying how long we plan to keep troops in Iraq goes something like this: If we reveal a timetable, insurgents and terrorists will simply lie in wait, emerging in force to achieve their goals once we are gone.

But any responsible timetable for U.S. withdrawal would be based just on the establishment of a competent Iraqi force. Americans won't leave until that force has the training it needs to succeed . . .

Contrary to the conventional wisdom, the administration's refusal to set a plan and timetable about just how long vast numbers of U.S. troops will remain in Iraq is actually an advantage for insurgents and terrorists. This large U.S. military presence smack in the middle of the Arab world is a major recruiting tool for international terrorist networks, and young men are coming to Iraq from around the world to get on-the-job training in attacking Americans. . . .

What's more, the indefinite presence of vast numbers of American troops could also undercut the legitimacy of the Iraqi government in the eyes of many — ironically, destabilizing Iraq despite our best intentions. Having a timetable for the transfer of sovereignty and having a timetable for Iraqi elections have resulted in real political and strategic advantages for the U.S. Having a timetable for the withdrawal of troops should be no different.

NO

Sen. Mitch McConnell, R-Ky.
Member, Senate Appropriations Subcommittee on Military Construction, Veterans' Affairs, and Related Agencies

From the Congressional Record, June 29, 2005

The president made it clear how high the stakes are in Iraq by demonstrating that Iraq is front and center in the global war on terror. Just listen to Osama bin Laden. Bin Laden is quoted as saying: "The whole world is watching this war" and that the Iraq war will result in either "victory and glory or misery and humiliation." Al Qaeda certainly recognizes how high the stakes are. So do our European allies.

Yet we continue to hear the refrain from some quarters that it is time to cut and run, that we should set an arbitrary deadline for withdrawal, to get out while we can. If Sept. 11 taught us anything, it is that retreating in the face of terrorism and hoping for the best is not the way to protect American lives. Quite the opposite: It is a display of weakness, and it is an invitation to America's enemies. As the president forcefully conveyed . . . we must take the fight to the enemies, or they will take the fight to us on our shores and on their terms. . . .

The president rightly noted the progress that is being made on the ground. The elite media in our country, however, [are] always focusing on bad news. They teach them in journalism school that only bad news is news. You would never know, for example, that more than 600 Iraqi schools have been renovated to date, or that construction is under way at 144 new primary health-care facilities across that country. You won't find that written about in the elite media.

Iraq has two ways it can go. We can leave the country to be preyed upon by murderers who want to turn the country into a Taliban-like nation, a haven for terrorist camps and a factory of hatred, or we can stand and fight by defending liberty and democracy in Iraq and demonstrating an alternative to the ways of terror and of Saddam Hussein. We can help Iraqis help themselves and, in the process, help the United States by making the Middle East a more democratic and peaceful region.

And when Iraq is strong enough to stand up on its own two feet, and Iraqi security forces can fully defend their own country, our troops will stand down and come home.

Getty Images/Taylor Jones

Getty Images/Joe Raedle

For and Against

Cindy Sheehan, whose son Casey died in Iraq, leads anti-war demonstrators to a rally in Austin, Texas, on Aug. 31, 2005 (top). Sheehan re-energized the anti-war movement with her vigil outside President Bush's Texas ranch. But many members of Congress and the public reject Sheehan's call for a withdrawal timetable, including Janet Griffin and Dean Oehler (bottom). They participate in a pro-Iraq war rally near Bush's ranch on Aug. 27.

While the day of the vote was largely peaceful, the next day, coalition forces launched air strikes in and around Ramadi, a Sunni Arab city west of Baghdad that strongly opposed the constitution, killing some 70 people. [87]

Rumsfeld also predicts that "the terrorists will fail again" if they try to disrupt the upcoming Dec. 15 election for a new Iraqi government. [88]

For his part, Talabani credits the U.S. military with preventing civil war. "Zarqawi has tried but failed to advocate civil war by mainly attacking Shiites to drive [them] to rebel," he said. [89]

The process of drafting the constitution exposed deep divisions between Iraq's Sunni and Shiite Muslims and ethnic Kurds, leading some experts to fear a civil war. Although Shiites make up 60-65 percent of Iraq's Muslim population, during Hussein's reign the Sunni-dominated Baath Party held most top political posts. [90] Sunnis, who today make up most of the insurgents, oppose provisions in the constitution that outlaw the party and allow the creation of federal regions that could split Iraq into factions. The Kurds, for example, want to maintain their autonomy and keep their own militia.

Foreign Minister Saud Faisal of Saudi Arabia recently warned that the ethnic and religious tensions in Iraq are moving that country "toward disintegration" that could turn into a civil war that draws neighboring countries into the conflict. [91]

CSIS' Cordesman said that, given the depth of religious and ethnic loyalties in Iraq, any decision about withdrawing U.S. troops should depend on Iraqis' ability to create a new Iraqi identity that all groups can embrace. The key, he wrote in a recent analysis, is to include Sunnis in the political process and "defuse the native Iraqi role in the insurgency." [92]

Al-Zarqawi has denounced democracy primarily because it separates religion and government. He believes the laws of Islam are the only true laws. Al-Zarqawi and his followers believe that Iraq is the land of "caliphs," or the spiritual heads of Islam, and that the country has to expel all those who help or support the "infidels" — namely Americans who al-Zarqawi says have dishonored Muslim men and violated Muslim women. Al-Zarqawi and his supporters hope to expel the Americans from Iraq and then take the fight to other Muslim lands. Some experts fear that a U.S. departure before democracy is in place could enable radical religious leaders to take control of Iraq.

On Oct. 11, U.S. intelligence authorities released what they said was a letter from al Qaeda's top strategist, Ayman al-Zawahiri, to al-Zarqawi that declared: "The victory of Islam will never take place until a Muslim state is established . . . in the heart of the Islamic world, specifically in the Levant, Egypt and the neighboring states of the [Arabian] Peninsula and Iraq. With his eye on that prize, al-Zawahiri added that regional conflicts in Chechnya, Afghanistan and elsewhere are "just the groundwork" for the full-scale confrontation in the Arab heartland.

President Talabani and Bush administration officials have complained that the media have focused too much on the violence and not accurately on Iraq's progress. "We hear only about the negative side in Iraq," Talabani said, and not enough about the new schools, hospitals and businesses under way. [93] U.S. reconstruction projects have renovated 3,200 Iraqi schools, built 140 new hospitals and trained 100,000 teachers, according to Gen. Myers. [94]

O'Hanlon of Brookings also sees "good news" in Iraq that is often knocked off the front pages by the violence, including progress on managing inflation, rewriting banking laws and adopting strict budgetary rules to prevent deficit spending. Telephone and Internet use continue to increase, and school enrollment is up 20 percent since 2000, he says.

But even supporters of the war admit there is still much to be done on the economic and social front. "I don't understand why they can't get the electricity on. I don't understand why they haven't gotten the water fixed. I don't understand why oil production has not

improved," says Pike of Globalsecurity.org. Crude-oil production and overall power generation were lower in 2005 than before the 2003 war began. [95]

Pentagon officials claim progress is being made, but slowly. "It's a long-term developmental challenge," Gen. Casey told Congress last summer. [96] He noted that insurgents are targeting the country's infrastructure in their attacks, particularly Iraq's oil facilities. Since the war began, there have been 277 attacks on oil pipelines, installations and personnel. [97]

Meanwhile, back in the United States, the war effort is putting particular strain on the part-time soldiers of the National Guard and reserves. "We're simply asking too much of the Guard in particular through multiple, repeated and lengthy deployments," said Sen. Susan Collins, R-Maine. [98]

The military has deployed more than 1 million troops to Iraq and Afghanistan since 2001, including nearly 490,000 Guard and reserve members. Some 60,000 have been mobilized more than once since 9/11, leading some to question whether the draft should be reinstated to spread the burden among a broader swath of the American population. [99]

In fact, troops in Iraq are stretched so thin that some commanders denied emergency leave for members of the Mississippi National Guard who lost their homes to Katrina and wanted to be with their families. [100]

To make matters worse, the Army and National Guard missed recruitment goals for the fiscal year. [101] To attract new soldiers, the Army in May began offering 15-month active-duty tours rather than the usual four-year enlistment, and soldiers already in Iraq are being offered $15,000 bonuses if they stay longer.

Reservist Rieckhoff, the founder of OperationTruth, says the Iraq war has "badly damaged" the volunteer army. Forcing soldiers to stay after their contracts expire and having the National Guard serve long tours of duty make this war "the most demanding time in the volunteer army's history," he says.

OUTLOOK

Unanswered Questions

No one knows whether Iraq will become the crown jewel of democracies in the Middle East, embroiled in a civil war or a fiercely anti-American Muslim state. President

Talabani is counting on U.S. forces leaving within two years as Iraqi security forces grow in size and capability. But others expect a longer time frame.

In fact, most experts predict that U.S. forces will remain in Iraq for years to come.

"It's reasonable to assume that some level of force will probably be in Iraq for a very, very long time," says Swetnam of the Potomac Institute for Policy Studies, noting the United States still has troops in Europe 60 years after World War II ended. It will take three to five years for the United States to draw down its current level of 140,000 troops to 15,000, which he calls a more "reasonable level."

Anti-war advocate Bennis of the Institute for Policy Studies and Foreign Policy, however, predicts that growing public doubts about the war will prod Washington to bring home the troops. "There's going to be an upsurge of demands on the administration to end the war and a demand on Congress to stop funding the war," she says.

Pike of Globalsecurity.org scoffs at that notion. While Bush's poll numbers are as low as former President Lyndon B. Johnson's during the Vietnam War, he says, the anti-war groups "haven't been able to organize their way out of a Glad bag."

For his part, President Bush paints the future of Iraq in broad and stark terms. "Either we defeat the terrorists and help the Iraqis build a working democracy or the terrorists will impose their dark ideology on the Iraqi people and make that country a source of terror and instability to come for decades," he told reporters after a Sept. 22 briefing at the Pentagon. [102]

But not everyone agrees that the new Iraqi government would be "democratic" — or even friendly to the United States. "It's hard to imagine that if people [in Iraq] really have the right to choose their own government they would choose anybody who is very chummy with the United States these days," Bennis says.

Swetnam expects Iraq to create its own version of democracy, one that "won't look like a Western-style democracy" that Americans would recognize. The new Iraqi government likely will resemble Turkey, he says, which has been democratic since the 1950s but has faced periods of instability and intermittent military coups. [103]

Krepinevich, the retired lieutenant colonel at the Center for Strategic and Budgetary Assessments, has a bleaker view. If the United States isn't willing to devote at least a decade and hundreds of billions of dollars to the effort, "Washington should accept . . . a more modest goal: leverage its waning influence to outmaneuver the Iranians and the Syrians in creating an ally out of Iraq's next despot." [104]

As for former dictator Hussein, his just-begun trial is viewed as an important test of Iraq's new political system. "People want justice for a man who directly caused three wars and killed thousands of people," said Iraqi Prime Minister Ibrahim Jafari, whose brother and four other relatives were killed during Hussein's rule. [105]

Some Iraqis, particularly Sunnis, who had power under Hussein, are questioning the legitimacy of the court trying Hussein while others ask why it has taken nearly two years to bring him to trial. "To provide a measure of truth and justice for hundreds of thousands of victims of gross human rights violations in Iraq, fair trials are essential," Richard Dicker, director of Human Rights Watch's International Justice Program, said in an Oct. 16 statement. "The proceedings must be fair and be seen to be fair, and that means ensuring that the accused can vigorously defend themselves."

Some fear the trial could lead to more violence from Hussein loyalists, but Iraqi officials say they are determined that the proceedings will be fair. "A lot of people are anxious for this to happen," said U.S. Ambassador to Iraq Zalmay Khalilzad. "And the eyes of Iraqis and the world will be focused on the trial. It will be one of the most important events of our time." [106]

John Kunich, an international law specialist at Appalachian College of Law in Grundy, Va., said that the impact of the trial could go beyond Iraq's borders. "This is really a first in the Arab world — a former leader being called to account for his crimes, in the dock like an ordinary criminal. There's no telling how potent that will be." [107]

NOTES

1. The two soldiers' blogs are at http://misoldier-thoughts.blogspot.com and http://madeucegun-ners.blogspot.com.

2. Michael A. Fletcher and Richard Morin, "Bush's Approval Rating Drops to New Low in Wake of Storm," *The Washington Post*, Sept. 13, 2005, p. A8.

3. White House Transcript, "President Welcomes President Talabani of Iraq to the White House," Sept. 13, 2005.

4. Press release, Harris Poll, "Pessimism about Iraq Continues to Increase, According to Latest Harris Poll," Aug. 25, 2005.

5. For background, see Peter Katel, "Global Jihad," *CQ Researcher*, Oct. 14, 2005, pp. 857-880.

6. *Congressional Record*, June 29, 2005, p. S7547.

7. Department of Defense News Transcript, Oct. 5, 2005.

8. *Ibid.*

9. Michael Howard, "Civilians bear brunt of Iraqi insurgency," *The Guardian*, July 15, 2005.

10. CNN, "Study puts Iraqi death toll at 100,000" Oct. 29, 2004.

11. "Iraq Index," Brookings Institution, Sept. 12, 2005, p. 9.

12. Andrew F. Krepinevich Jr., "How to Win in Iraq," *Foreign Affairs*, September/October 2005.

13. Larry Diamond, "What Went Wrong," *Foreign Affairs*, September/October 2004.

14. Brookings "Iraq Index," *op. cit.*, p. 26.

15. "Iraqi women forced to veil," BBC, June 13, 2003.

16. Memorandum for Senate Foreign Relations Committee from Gen. Barry R. McCaffrey, July 18, 2005.

17. Brookings, "Iraq Index," *op. cit.*, pp. 27, 32.

18. *Ibid.*

19. Transcript, news briefing, Secretary of Defense Donald Rumsfeld and Chairman of the Joint Chiefs Gen. Richard Myers, Sept. 6, 2005.

20. Eric Schmitt, "Army Chief Raises Estimate of G.I.s Needed in Postwar Iraq," *The New York Times*, Feb. 25, 2005, and transcript of PBS "Frontline," "The Invasion of Iraq," Feb. 26, 2004.

21. Robin Wright and Thomas E. Ricks, "Bremer Criticizes Troop Levels," *The Washington Post*, Oct. 5, 2004, p. A1.

22. Larry Diamond, *op. cit.*

23. Transcript, U.S. House Appropriations Committee hearing, March 27, 2003.

24. John Diamond, "CIA review faults prewar plans," *USA Today*, Oct. 12, 2005, p. 1A.

25. Richard Kerr, Thomas Wolfe, Rebecca Donegan and Aris Pappas, "Issues for the US Intelligence Community," Studies in Intelligence, Vol. 49, No. 3, October 2005, pp. 47-54.

26. Transcript of Pentagon press briefing, April 11, 2003, www.defenselink.mil/transcripts/2003/tr20030411-secdef0090.html.

27. Larry Diamond, *op. cit.*

28. Anthony H. Cordesman, Working Draft, "Resources versus Strategy and Force Transformation," Center for Strategic and International Studies, April 12, 2005, p. 3.

29. Kimberly Johnson, "Unit had asked for more Marines," *USA Today*, Aug. 8, 2005, p. 1A.

30. Transcript of U.S. Department of Defense news briefing, Aug. 9, 2005.

31. "Troops put thorny questions to Rumsfeld," CNN, Dec. 9, 2004.

32. *Ibid.*

33. "Posture of the United States Army, 2005," statement of Francis Harvey, secretary of the Army, and Peter Schoomakeer, Army Chief of Staff, to Congress, Feb. 6, 2005, p. 12.

34. Testimony of Anthony H. Cordesman, Center for Strategic and International Studies, before U.S. Senate Foreign Relations Committee, July 18, 2005.

35. *USA Today*/CNN Gallup Poll, op. cit. See also, The Gallup Organization, "Majority of Americans Maintain Negative Views on Iraq," Aug. 9, 2005.

36. John M. Donnelly, "Bipartisan House Resolution Brings Unease Over Iraq War Into Public View," *CQ Weekly*, June 20, 2005, p. 1657.

37. Press release, Rep. Walter Jones statement on Iraq Resolution, June 16, 2005.

38. White House transcript, "President Welcomes President Talabani of Iraq to the White House," Sept. 13, 2005.

39. Text of President Bush's June 28, 2005 speech, www.whitehouse.gov/news/releases/2005/06/2005 0628-7.html.

40. Transcript of hearing of U.S. Senate Armed Services Committee on military strategy and operations in Iraq, June 23, 2005.

41. Eric Schmitt, "Military plans gradual cuts in Iraq forces," *The New York Times*, Aug. 6, 2005, p. A1.

"Report to Congress, Measuring Stability and Security in Iraq," released July 21, 2005.

42. Peter Baker and Shailagh Murray "Democrats Split Over Position on Iraq War," *The Washington Post*, Aug. 22, 2005, p. A1.

43. Remarks to Brookings Institution, June 21, 2005.

44. Cordesman testimony, *op. cit.*

45. David Brooks, "Winning in Iraq," *The New York Times*, Aug. 28, 2005, Sect. 4, p. 11.

46. Krepinevich, *op. cit.*

47. White House transcript, "President Discusses War on Terror at National Endowment for Democracy," Oct. 6, 2005.

48. "Mapping the Global Future," National Intelligence Council, Jan. 13, 2005, p. 93.

49. Transcript of Department of Defense news briefing, Aug. 23, 2005.

50. Quoted on "Meet the Press," July 3, 2005.

51. Press Release, The Harris Poll, "Pessimism About Iraq Continues to Increase, According to Latest Harris Poll," Aug. 25, 2005.

52. Transcript of ABC News "This Week with George Stephanopolous," Sept. 18, 2005.

53. Anne Plummer, "Iraqi Insurgency: No Easy Options," *CQ Weekly*, Sept. 5, 2005, p. 2298.

54. "Stretched Thin: Army Forces for Sustained Operations," RAND Corp., July 13, 2005.

55. Rumsfeld/Myers new briefing, *op. cit.*

56. For background, see David Masci's "Confronting Iraq," *CQ Researcher*, Oct. 4, 2002, pp. 793-816.

57. CQ Press, Historic Documents 2003, "President Bush on the Prospect of War with Iraq," pp. 135-151 and 713-954.

58. National Security Archive, George Washington University, *Electronic Briefing Book No. 163*, available at www.gwu.edu/~nsarchiv/ NSAEBB/NSA EBB163/iraq-state-02.pdf, posted Aug. 17, 2005.

59. White House transcript, "President Bush Outlines Iraqi Threat," *Cincinnati Museum Center*, Oct. 7, 2002.

60. White House transcript, "President Bush Delivers Graduation Speech at West Point," West Point,

N.Y., June 2, 2002. For background, see Mary H. Cooper, "New Defense Priorities," *CQ Researcher*, Sept. 13, 2002, pp. 721-744.

61. Press release No. 7687, United Nations Security Council, March 12, 2003.

62. Government Accountability Office, "Rebuilding Iraq: Status of Funding and Reconstruction Efforts," July 2005, p. 3.

63. Freedom House Backgrounder, "Iraq Country Report 2005," p. 306.

64. CQ Press, *Historic Documents of 2004*, "Iraqi Prime Minister Allawi on Security Challenges," p. 874-882.

65. The Associated Press, CNN, "England gets 3 years for Abu Ghraib, Sept. 28, 2005; www.cnn.com/ 2005/LAW/09/27/prisoner.abuse.england.ap/.

66. Masci, *op. cit.*

67. Freedom House, *op. cit.*

68. U.S Central Intelligence Agency, "Comprehensive Report of the Special Adviser to the DCI on Iraq's WMD: Key Findings," Oct. 6, 2004.

69. For background, see Kenneth Jost and Benton Ives-Halperin, "Democracy in the Arab World." *CQ Researcher*, Jan. 30, 2004, pp. 73-100.

70. Text of President Bush's June 28, 2005 speech, www.whitehouse.gov/news/releases/2005/06/2005 0628-7.html.

71. John M. Donnelly, "Growing Anxiety and Falling Poll Numbers Raise Concerns About Iraq Policy," *CQ Today*, Sept. 2, 2005.

72. Raymond Hernandez and Megan Thee, "Iraq's Costs Worry Americans, Poll Indicates," *The New York Times*, Sept. 17, 2005.

73. John Harwood, "Katrina Erodes Support In U.S. for Iraq War," *The Wall Street Journal*, Sept. 15, 2005.

74. Transcript of U.S. Senate Armed Services Committee hearing, June 23, 2005.

75. *Ibid.*

76. White House transcript, "President Discusses War on Terror at National Endowment for Democracy," Oct. 6, 2005.

77. Transcript of hearing of U.S. Senate Armed Services Committee on military strategy and operations in Iraq, June 23, 2005.

78. Kevin Whitelaw, "Hit by friendly fire," *U.S. News & World Report*, June 27, 2005, www.usnews.com/usnews/news/articles/050627/27bush.htm.

79. Transcript of U.S. Senate Armed Services Committee hearing, Sept. 29, 2005.

80. *Ibid.*

81. "Iraqi PM: Security in Two Years," CNN, June 27, 2005, www.cnn.com/2005/WORLD/meast/06/27/iraq.main.intl/.

82. Ellen Knickmeyer, "U.S. Claims Success in Iraq Despite Onslaught," *The Washington Post*, Sept. 19, 2005, p. A1.

83. Statement by Sen. Joseph Biden (D-Del.), July 18, 2005.

84. Transcript of DoD news briefing, July 20, 2005.

85. Transcript of U.S. Senate Armed Services hearing, Sept. 29, 2005.

86. Glenn Kessler, "For U.S., a Hard Road is Still Ahead in Iraq," *The Washington Post*, Oct. 17, 2005, p. A10.

87. CNN, "Iraqi airstrikes kill dozens in Ramadi," Oct. 17, 2005.

88. Transcript of Department of Defense briefing, Sept. 9, 2005.

89. Nora Boustany, "Talabani Upbeat on Iraq's Challenges and its Neighbors," *The Washington Post*, Sept. 14, 2005, p. A28.

90. CIA *World Fact Book, 2005*, Iraq, www.cia.gov/cia/publications/factbook/geos/iz.html.

91. Robin Wright, "Iraq Faces Disintegration, Saudi Says," *The Washington Post*, Sept. 23, 2005.

92. Anne Plummer and John M. Donnelly, "Struggling to Build an Army of One Iraq," *CQ Weekly*, July 4, 2005, p. 1798.

93. DoD transcripts, Sept. 9, 2005.

94. DoD transcripts, Aug. 9, 2005.

95. Government Accountability Office, *op. cit.*

96. Transcript of U.S. House Armed Services Committee hearing on "Progress of Iraqi Security Forces," June 23, 2005.

97. www.iags.org/iraqpipelinewatch.htm.

98. Transcript of U.S. Senate Armed Services Committee hearing, June 23, 2005.

99. For background, see Pamela Prah, "Draft Debates," *CQ Researcher*, Aug. 19, 2005, pp. 661-684.

100. Ellen Knickmeyer, "Scores Denied Leave Time to Aid Displaced Families," *The Washington Post*, Sept. 11, 2005, p. A13.

101. U.S. Department of Defense press release, "DoD Announces Recruiting and Retention Numbers for September," Oct. 11, 2005.

102. White House transcript, "President Discusses War on Terror and Hurricane Preparation," Sept. 22, 2005.

103. CIA, *op. cit.*, www.cia.gov/cia/publications/factbook/geos/tu.html#Govt.

104. Krepinevich, *op. cit.*

105. Ellen Knickmeyer, "Iraqi's Premier Urges a Speedy Trial for Hussein," *The Washington Post*, Oct. 18, 2005, p. 20.

106. "Concerns that upcoming trial of Saddam Hussein in Iraq may provoke more violence," NBC News, Oct. 16, 2005.

107. Richard Willing and Steven Komarow, "Questions mount as Saddam's trial opens," *USA Today*, Oct. 18, 2005, p. 1A.

BIBLIOGRAPHY

Books

Diamond, Larry, *Squandered Victory: The American Occupation and the Bungled Effort to Bring Democracy to Iraq*, Times Books, 2005.
A former senior adviser to the Coalition Provisional Authority concludes the United States should have provided more troops to stop post-invasion looting and recognized sooner the importance of Shiite religious leaders.

Murray, Williamson, and Maj. Gen. Robert H. Scales Jr., *The Iraq War: A Military History*, Belknap Press of Harvard University Press, 2003.
Two military historians provide an account of the air and ground operations in Iraq and the origins of the war.

Packer, George, *The Assassins' Gate: America in Iraq*, Farrar Straus Giroux, 2005.
A staff writer at the *New Yorker* examines the political arguments leading up to the invasion and the chaos that unfolded after Hussein's fall.

Articles

Barry, John, Richard Wolffe and Evan Thomas, "War of Nerves," *Newsweek*, July 4, 2005, p. 20.
The article contrasts the optimistic views of the Bush administration with the insurgents' steady flow of violence.

Knickmeyer, Ellen, "U.S. Claims Success in Iraq Despite Onslaught," *The Washington Post*, Sept. 19, 2005, p. A1.
An overview reveals the difficulty U.S. and Iraqi forces face in crafting a national Iraqi army and a government that represents all ethnic and religious factions.

Krepinevich, Andrew, "How to Win in Iraq," *Foreign Affairs*, September/October 2005.
A retired lieutenant colonel and author of *The Army and Vietnam* says the United States should focus on protecting Iraqi civilians, not killing insurgents.

Plummer, Anne, and John M. Donnelly, "Struggling to Build an Army of One Iraq," *CQ Weekly*, July 4, 2005, p. 1798.
The authors discuss the challenges the United States faces in building an Iraqi force capable of securing its own country without U.S. help.

Sappenfield, Mark, "U.S. tempers its view of victory in Iraq," *The Christian Science Monitor*, Sept. 16, 2005.
Sappenfeld looks at whether the continuing toll of the insurgency is reshaping Pentagon expectations about victory.

Steinberg, James B., and Michael O'Hanlon, "The Iraq War: Departure Does Not Mean Defeat," *The Financial Times*, Feb. 23, 2005.
Two Brookings Institution experts recommend withdrawing most U.S. troops from Iraq over 18 months but continuing to keep 30,000 to 50,000 soldiers there after that.

War: Departure Does Not Mean Defeat," *The Financial Times*, Feb. 23, 2005.
Two Brookings Institution experts recommend withdrawing most U.S. troops from Iraq over 18 months but continuing to keep 30,000 to 50,000 soldiers there after that.

Ware, Michael, "Chasing the Ghosts," *Time*, Sept. 26, 2005, p. 32.

From the frontlines, Ware chronicles the struggle of U.S. forces to quell an "elusive and inexhaustible enemy."

Reports and Studies

"Comprehensive Report of the Special Advisor to the Director of Central Intelligence on Iraq's Weapons of Mass Destruction," Sept. 30, 2004.
The final report to the CIA concludes Iraq had destroyed its biological and chemical weapons after the 1991 Persian Gulf War.

Cordesman, Anthony H., "Iraq Briefing Book," Center for Strategic and International Studies, updated regularly; www.csis.org/features/iraq.cfm.
The author of the 2003 book *The Iraq War: Strategy, Tactics, and Military Lessons* provides reports, analyses and articles that examine postwar Iraq.

Gardiner, Nile, "The Case Against British Withdrawal from Iraq," Heritage Foundation, Oct. 4, 2005, www.heritage.org/Research/MiddleEast/wm871.cfm.
A fellow at the conservative group argues that a British pullout would damage the Anglo-U.S. alliance that has led the war on terror, threaten Iraq's future and hand a victory to al Qaeda and Iraq's insurgents.

"Iraq Index," Brookings Institution, updated every Monday and Thursday; www.brookings.edu/iraqindex.
Statistics are presented on a wide range of military and economic matters.

"The Iraq Quagmire: The Mounting Costs of War and the Case for Bringing Home the Troops," Institute for Policy Studies and Foreign Policy, Aug. 31, 2005; www.ips-dc.org/iraq/quagmire/index.htm.
The liberal think tank lays out the social, economic and political costs of the Iraq war and concludes the price is too steep.

"Rebuilding Iraq: Status of Funding and Reconstruction Efforts," Government Accountability Office, July 2005; www.gao.gov/new.items/d05876.pdf.
The watchdog arm of Congress concludes that Iraq's crude-oil production and overall power generation capabilities are more constrained in 2005 than before the 2003 U.S. invasion.

For More Information

American Enterprise Institute, 1150 17th St., N.W., Washington, DC 20036; (202) 862-5800; www.aei.org. A conservative think tank that has produced a series of articles about Iraq and a recent conference on "Remaking Iraq" that included insights from Islamic scholars and an Iraqi National Assembly member.

Brookings Institution, 1775 Massachusetts Ave., N.W., Washington, DC 20036; (202) 797-6462; www.brookings.edu. Publishes a regularly updated "Iraq Index" including economic, public opinion and security data.

Carnegie Endowment for International Peace, 1779 Massachusetts Ave., N.W., Washington, DC 20036-2103; (202) 483-7600; www.carnegieendowment.org. A think tank that publishes Foreign Policy magazine and has produced several policy briefs on Iraq and promoting democracy in the Middle East.

Cato Institute, 1000 Massachusetts Ave., N.W., Washington, DC 20001-5403; (202) 842-0200; www.cato.org. A libertarian research foundation that convened a special task force of scholars and policy experts to examine U.S. strategic interests in Iraq; produced a book in 2004, *Exiting Iraq: Why the U.S. Must End the Military Occupation and Renew the War Against Al Qaeda*.

Center for Strategic and Budgetary Assessments, 1730 Rhode Island Ave., N.W., Suite 912, Washington, DC 20036; (202) 331-7990; www.csbaonline.org. A think tank that focuses on defense planning, military readiness, weapons system and other defense issues. The Web site also includes a reprint of the center's Executive Director Andrew F. Krepinevich's "How to Win in Iraq" essay.

Center for Strategic and International Studies, 1800 K St., N.W., Suite 400, Washington, D.C. 20006; (202) 887-0200; www.csis.org. Studies a wide range of security issues; independently assessed the situation in Iraq for the Defense Department.

Council on Foreign Relations, 58 East 68th St., New York, NY 10021; (212) 434.9400; www.cfr.org. An independent think tank that publishes Foreign Affairs magazine and has produced a series of articles and background reports on issues important to Iraq.

Embassy of the United States, Baghdad, Iraq, APO AE 09316, Baghdad, Iraq; http://baghdad.usembassy.gov/iraq. Web site includes the latest embassy news and links to Iraqi election and governmental agencies.

Freedom House, 1301 Connecticut Ave., N.W., 6th Floor, Washington, DC 20036; (202) 296-5101; http//freedomhouse.org. A human rights group founded more than 60 years ago by Eleanor Roosevelt and other reformers that advocates for democracy and freedom around the world; Web site includes articles and research on Iraq.

GlobalSecurity.org, 300 N. Washington St., Suite B-100, Alexandria, VA 22314; (703) 548-2700; www.globalsecurity.org. An independent online service providing news, background and statistics on military preparedness, weapons of mass destruction, intelligence and homeland security.

Institute for Policy Studies, 1112 16th St., N.W., Suite 600, Washington, DC 20036; (202) 234-9382; www.ips-dc.org. Liberal think tank that has produced a series of reports on Iraq.

Iraq Daily; www.iraqdaily.com. This World News Network Web site provides the latest news, weather and photos from Iraq while Iraqi Transitional Government (www.iraqigovernment.org) includes political news, press releases, updates on reconstruction projects from the Iraqi government. Available both in Arabic and English.

Middle East Institute, 1761 N St., N.W., Washington, DC 20036-2882; (202) 785-1141; www.mideast.org; Conducts research on the Middle East.